AMERICAN WOMEN WRITERS, 1900–1945

AMERICAN WOMEN WRITERS, 1900–1945

A Bio-Bibliographical Critical Sourcebook

Edited by
Laurie Champion
Emmanuel S. Nelson, Advisory Editor

GREENWOOD PRESS
Westport, Connecticut • London

Library of Congress Cataloging-in-Publication Data

American women writers, 1900–1945 : a bio-bibliographical critical sourcebook / edited
by Laurie Champion.
    p. cm.
  Includes bibliographical references and index.
  ISBN 0–313–30943–4 (alk. paper)
    1. American literature—Women authors—Bio-bibliography—Dictionaries. 2. Women
and literature—United States—History—20th century—Dictionaries. 3. American
literature—20th century—Bio-bibliography—Dictionaries. 4. Authors, American—20th
century—Biography—Dictionaries. 5. Women authors,
American—Biography—Dictionaries. 6. American literature—Women
authors—Dictionaries. 7. American literature—20th century—Dictionaries. I. Champion,
Laurie.
PS151.A45 2000
810.9'9287'09041—dc21   00–022336

British Library Cataloguing in Publication Data is available.

Library of Congress Catalog Card Number: 00–022336
ISBN: 0–313–30943–4

First published in 2000

Greenwood Press, 88 Post Road West, Westport, CT 06881
An imprint of Greenwood Publishing Group, Inc.
www.greenwood.com

Printed in the United States of America

The paper used in this book complies with the
Permanent Paper Standard issued by the National
Information Standards Organization (Z39.48–1984).

10 9 8 7 6 5 4 3 2 1

CONTENTS

PREFACE

Women writers historically have been denied respectable literary voices through such means as unequal publishing opportunities and biased readings of the limited number of works published. Lack of opportunities for education, along with social expectations that required women to perform unpaid household labor, also has discouraged women artists and kept their voices unheard or unappreciated. Recently, women writers have begun to receive long overdue critical attention, especially since the 1970s during the second wave of American feminism.

This reference book adds to the continuing struggle to recognize women writers generally and to the ongoing celebration of American women writers specifically. It represents American women writers from the beginning of the twentieth century to the end of World War II, a period that, among other significant historical events, encompasses two of the most important literary movements in twentieth-century U.S. history: modernism and the Harlem Renaissance. It presents contributions American women writers made to these movements as well as illuminates the distinguished roles they played in shaping the more broadly defined American literary tradition.

As its title suggests, *American Women Writers, 1900–1945: A Bio-Bibliographical Critical Sourcebook* provides overviews of American women writers who wrote or published their most significant works between 1900 and 1945. (Some of these works were written during the first half of the century but remained unpublished for decades.) Each author entry consists of four sections: Biography, Major Works and Themes, Critical Reception, and Bibliography, which includes both primary and secondary sources. Each author entry offers biographical information about the author, an analysis of the author's major works, an overview of the critical reception of the author's works, and a bibliography that lists works by the author and introduces readers to works that have been written about the author and her works. The entries are organized alphabetically, according to the author's last name or to accepted convention, as in the case of Native American or Asian women writers—Mourning Dove, for example, is alphabetized according to "Mourning."

Writers who have received a considerable amount of critical attention in recent decades such as Willa Cather, H. D., Eudora Welty, and Zora Neale Hurston are included, as well as those who remain neglected such as Anita Scott Coleman and Jovita González de Mireles. The authors discussed also represent diversity in terms of ethnicity. Many of these authors have been ignored by critics not only because of gender bias but also because of racial bias. In spite of this twofold bias, women of color contributed significantly to U.S. literature during the first half of the twentieth century.

Adding to the growing body of women's works that are included in the literary canon, as well as to anthologies and scholary studies that recognize women's contributions to literature, this reference seeks to continue to challenge attitudes that implicate women writers as a mob of scribblers.

Working on this reference book has not only been professionally rewarding; it also has been personally fulfilling. I would like to thank all the scholars who contributed to this volume. Without their cooperative spirit, time, and effort this reference book could not have been completed. Special thanks to contributors Bruce A. Glasrud and Rhonda Austin, two colleagues who diligently worked with me in the final stages of preparing this volume. I also appreciate the encouragement and efforts of Emmanuel S. Nelson, the series editor, for wisdom expressed in his solicitation of manuscripts that recognize women and minority writers. Thanks also to George Butler of Greenwood Press for his instrumental role in overseeing the preparation of the manuscript.

INTRODUCTION

Laurie Champion

Despite formidable obstacles, including a long history of gender-biased oppression, difficulties seeking education and securing employment, and limited publishing opportunities, many American women succeeded as writers during the first half of the twentieth century. Although many of these authors were middle- or upper-class white women, those of color also contributed greatly to the literature produced during this time period. Perhaps their overall contribution is depicted best in the subtitle of Sylvia Ann Grider and Lou Halsell Rodenberger's *Texas Women Writers: A Tradition of Their Own* (1997). Indeed, the contributions made by American women authors of the first half of the twentieth century represent a unique tradition of American literature.

Women were able to establish their own tradition as well as contribute to modernism and the Harlem Renaissance, the two major artistic movements that occurred between 1900 and 1945. Modernism, the most influential literary movement in America during the twentieth century, is based both on rebellion against the ideas, morals, and society that influenced Victorian literature and on rejection of the styles and techniques used to portray Victorian attitudes. The industrial revolution created immense change in society and in the economy, and Freud's notions of the unconscious and the human psyche influenced the intellectual milieu. While modernism spread across America and Europe, the Harlem Renaissance was specifically an American movement. The Harlem Renaissance represents the first significant movement of African American artists, who gathered socially and professionally in New York City and produced some of the most distinguished African American literature. The Harlem Renaissance prompted new literary magazines and other venues for publication for blacks, who were traditionally denied access to white publishing markets. Women artists played significant roles during the Harlem Renaissance and modernism, not only as writers but also as artists in general, as mentors, and as advocates of gender equality.

Women writers helped to define modernism and the Harlem Renaissance, but they also departed from the themes and subjects of their male cohorts and developed unique artistic styles and techniques. In addition to establishing themselves as significant contributors to the movements, women authors frequently depicted characters, subjects, and themes that challenged sexism as well as made bold political statements that sought gender equality to develop their own tradition within the major artistic movements. They defied the attitudes of some of their male counterparts by focusing on issues such as family roles that frequently exploit women, gender and racially biased economic opportunities, and the importance of women working together to create more progressive social and political attitudes. Authors such as Ellen Glasgow, Willa Cather, and Zora Neale Hurston built upon ideas that began at the turn of the century and started a new tradition that defines early twentieth-century women. Producing significant American writings that span literary genres, these women continued ideas established by their predecessors while simultaneously breaking new ground for a new generation of American women writers.

The legacies left by American women writers of the first half of the twentieth century continue to inspire women, both professionally as writers and personally as individuals. Many of these earlier authors shared notorious friendships with other women artists, who served as mentors, as colleagues, and as friends. Frequently, women directly encouraged those who aspired to write by developing long-lasting personal relationships and indirectly inspired women by creating strong female characters who provided role models for women writers and readers alike. Djuna Barnes credited her grandmother, who managed a London salon visited by women such as Lady Wilde and Elizabeth Cady Stanton, as the most influential person of her childhood. Both personal and professional mentorships include Marianne Moore's encouragement of Elizabeth Bishop (Moore wrote the introduction to Bishop's first book publication) and Katherine Anne Porter's promotion of Eudora Welty's career (Porter wrote the introduction to Welty's first collection of short stories). Zona Gale, who shared an enduring friendship with Charlotte Perkins Gilman, helped launch Margery Latimer's career and became her longtime mentor and confidante. These types of relationships in which women writers supported, encouraged, and promoted other women writers were essential in the male-dominated literary world of early twentieth-century America.

Along with directly supporting other women writers, American women authors indirectly served as role models for other women by depicting female characters who help and support each other. This type of relationship among women is frequently portrayed through the use of framed narratives, in which a woman character tells a story to another woman. For example, in Alice Maude Ewell's short story "Wycham's Ordinary," an old woman describes her experiences as an inn housekeeper to two young girls. Beyond the plot of the framed tale, the point of the enveloping narrative celebrates women's storytelling as a means both to help women understand their lives and to shape their identities. Similarly, Janie, the protagonist of Zora Neale Hurston's *Their Eyes Were Watching God*, leaves her rural hometown, experiences events that help her achieve independence and cultural identity, and returns to her hometown to share her experiences with Pheoby. Not only does Janie's story inspire Pheoby, but because Pheoby will repeat the story, Janie's experiences will become a part of the town's oral history that will continue to influence future generations of women to seek independence and identity. These types of framed narratives demonstrate the importance of women inspiring other women by portraying women who do so and by allowing readers to "hear" the framed tale along with the characterized listener and thus vicariously gain insights revealed directly to the fictionalized listener.

Modern American women writers also contributed greatly to literature in their roles as hosts for social functions and as editors. One of the most influential women writers of the modern period, Gertrude Stein, who coined the term "lost generation," played an essential role in mentoring other writers by offering valuable artistic advice, providing, along with Alice B. Toklas, a gathering place for artists and, like many artists of the period, creating works that allude to and celebrate other artists. Similarly, Dorothy Parker founded the "round table" of the New York City Algonquin Hotel, the most notorious "literary salon" in America at the time.

Marianne Moore's role as editor of *Dial* is as important to her contributions to modernism as her status as poet. Moore's editorship of this international magazine, which published fiction, poetry, essays, and visual art by artists such as T. S. Eliot, Ezra Pound, William Carlos Williams, W. B. Yeats, Picasso, and Georgia O'Keefe, helped shape and define modernism. Likewise, promoting African American writers after the height of the Harlem Renaissance, Dorothy West founded and edited the literary magazine *Challenge*; when it folded, she began *New Challenge*, which she edited with Marian Minus and Richard Wright. Contributors of West's journals include notable authors such as Margaret Walker, Ralph Ellison, Frank Yerby, and Richard Wright. The various roles of these women, who also contributed significantly to American literature by producing original works, enabled them to inspire, promote, and shape the artistic direction of other artists.

While many modern American women writers wrote from international perspectives, the period is also representative of some of America's finest regional women writers. Many of these writers blend regional color with feminism to create strong female characters who exemplify specific regions of the country. The prairie women of Willa Cather's *O Pioneers!* and *My Ántonia* exemplify strong women who defy traditional women's roles and who are able to endure physical hardships and appreciate the land that represents their heritage. Similarly, Mary Austin's strong and courageous women characters find personal freedom and identity when they travel to the West and overcome hardships. Southern women writers such as Flannery O'Conner, Eudora Welty, and Carson McCullers are also significant regional writers of the modern period. They simultaneously capture traditional southern subjects such as religion and ties to the family and transcend southern themes and techniques by addressing universal notions such as the search for identity and exploring traditional techniques such as alluding to classic myths to delineate complex human conflicts.

Some of these women writers use specific settings to portray folklore and customs of rural populations. Trained as an anthropologist, Zora Neale Hurston illustrates rural Eatonville, Florida, and its population's local cultural practices, folklore, social customs, spiritual beliefs, and dialect. Amidst Hurston's celebration of African American folk heritage, she demonstrates women's triumphs in terms of their struggles for gender and cultural identity. Similarly, Jovita González de Mireles, Cleofas M. Jaramillo, Fabiola Cabeza de Baca Gilbert, and Josefina Niggli celebrate Mexican American folk customs such as traditional ways of cooking and conventional modes of storytelling. These women's artistic renditions of folklore illustrate Mexican American customs and document and preserve Mexican history and culture. Other women minorities who celebrate diverse cultures include Mourning Dove and Sui Sin Far, who use fictional devices to reveal true aspects of Native American and Chinese American culture, respectively. Illustrations of folklore and preservations of cultural history by modern American women writers also reveal features of diverse cultures relevant to women's experiences.

While some women writers focus on problems of the poverty-stricken to challenge class hierarchies, other women reveal middle-class or socially elite characters to show the problems of class hierarchies from the perspective of the "privileged." In their portrayals of the middle class or the socially elite, many women authors use urban settings. Much of Edith Wharton's fiction concerns New York aristocracy at the turn of the century and demonstrates the personal sacrifices individuals must make when trapped in oppressive social systems that demand conformity. Dorothy West's novels portray prestigious northeastern African American elites and often satirize blacks who conform to white upper-class values. West's contemporaries Nella Larsen and Jessie Redmon Fauset also present socially prestigious blacks who suffer from a lack of cultural identity.

Whether modern American women writers set their works regionally, nationally, or internationally, they all contributed to and influenced the literature of the first half of the twentieth century. Unfortunately, after initial success, many of these women writers fell into obscurity. It was not until the second wave of American feminism during the 1970s that many of their works were either discovered and published for the first time or rediscovered and brought back into print. During the 1970s, feminist scholars also began to reassess the roles their predecessors played in shaping American literature. These feminists have paved the way for future scholars to continue to offer American women writers their long overdue place in the American literary canon. It is my hope that this reference book will contribute to efforts to recognize and celebrate American women writers.

BESS STREETER ALDRICH
(1881–1954)

Denise D. Knight

BIOGRAPHY

Fiction writer Bess Streeter Aldrich was born on February 17, 1881, in Cedar Falls, Iowa, the youngest of eight children of James and Mary Streeter. As a child she enjoyed reading, berry picking, gardening with her mother, and listening to frontier stories about her pioneering ancestors. Aldrich attended public schools in Cedar Falls, graduating at the age of seventeen. During her teen years, she won two fiction-writing contests sponsored by newspapers and magazines. In 1898, she enrolled at the Iowa State Normal School, earning her teaching certificate in 1901. For the next five years, she taught primary school in Iowa and Utah and continued to write, publishing several children's stories.

In 1907, she married Charles S. Aldrich, a lawyer and banker who had served as a captain in the Spanish-American War. The newlyweds lived in Tipton, Iowa, before moving to Elmwood, Nebraska, with their baby daughter, Mary, in 1909. In Elmwood they moved into a stately home, "The Elms," where Aldrich spent afternoons writing while her baby napped. Aldrich's discipline paid off; in 1911, she was astounded to receive a check for $175 from *Ladies' Home Journal* for her short story "The Little House Next Door."

Between 1912 and 1920, the Aldrich family expanded, with the arrival of three sons, James, Charles, and Robert. Aldrich continued to write, placing her work in such venues as *McCall's, Harper's Weekly*, and *American Magazine*. The income from these magazines was modest, and she collected between $1 and $100 per story. By 1919, however, editors were clamoring for her contributions, and Aldrich was able to name, and generally to receive, her price.

In May 1925, Aldrich's happy life took a tragic turn when Charles suffered a cerebral hemorrhage and died at the age of fifty-two. Shortly thereafter, economic circumstances forced Aldrich to transform her part-time writing "hobby" into a full-time career. Aldrich rose to the occasion, publishing over forty stories and more than a dozen books between 1925 and 1954. Her most famous novel, *A Lantern in Her Hand*, was published in 1928 to rave reviews. Most notable among the novels that followed were *A White Bird Flying* (1931), *Miss Bishop* (1933), and *The Lieutenant's Lady* (1942).

In 1946, Aldrich sold her home in Elmwood and moved to Lincoln, Nebraska, to be close to her daughter. In her later years, her writing slowed, and she produced, on average, just one story a year. In 1952, Aldrich was diagnosed with cancer and succumbed to the disease on August 3, 1954, at the age of seventy-three. She is buried next to her husband in Elmwood, Nebraska.

MAJOR WORKS AND THEMES

Aldrich's writing career spanned more than half a century, beginning with a short story, "A Late Love," published in the *Baltimore News* in 1898, and ending with "The Outsider," another short piece that appeared in the *Christian Herald* in 1954. While her literature runs the gamut from children's tales to Christmas stories, the struggle of the frontier woman is at the heart of Aldrich's best fiction, including *The Rim of the Prairie* (1925), *A Lantern in Her Hand* (1928), and *Spring Came on Forever* (1935). It was *A Lantern in Her Hand*, however, that would win Aldrich international acclaim.

A Lantern in Her Hand explores the day-to-day struggles of Abbie Deal, a character whose invincible courage allows her to triumph over every adversity, including droughts, prairie fires, snake bites, blinding blizzards, and the death of her newborn infant. Aldrich deliberately capitalized on human drama as a significant and successful ingredient in her aesthetic formula. By placing ordinary human beings—housewives, farmers, pioneers, children—in situations that tested their courage, exposed their weaknesses, and revealed their strengths, she was able to invoke universal themes that readers could readily embrace.

A Lantern in Her Hand begins with Abbie Deal's adult children gathering in her home after her death; the remainder of the novel is a reconstruction of her life from the age of eight. One of the major thematic emphases embedded in the text is Abbie's fear of death, which stems from a traumatic episode in her early childhood. Death is never far from her thoughts; she seems, in fact, to spend a lifetime preparing for it, which both humanizes her and renders her sympathetic to the reader.

Aldrich irreverently states at the beginning of the novel (which takes place between the years 1854 and 1926), "This is the story of the old lady who died while the meat burned [on the stove] and the children played 'Run, Sheep, Run,' across her yard" (6). As her middle-aged children—a banker, a state legislator, a professional singer, a university professor, and a homemaker—convene in "the old parlor with its familiar objects" (6), they are consumed by grief and guilt that their mother died alone. Only Abbie's twelve-year-old granddaughter, Laura, possesses the wisdom that allows her to view the death without the sentiment that clouds the perceptions of Abbie's adult children. Laura's unconventional views help to illuminate an important subtext in the novel: the ability of Abbie to detach herself from emotional entanglements with others. Despite her obvious love for her children, for example, Abbie describes herself, in the language of painful self-sacrifice, as being "like an old mother partridge who had plucked all the feathers from her breast for the nest of her young" (298).

It is in the safety and privacy of a fantasy world that Abbie rejects the conventional roles of wife, daughter, and mother that dominate her life. We see Abbie's repudiation of those roles reinforced in both the interior monologues and the third-person narrative summaries that occur throughout the novel. On the surface, Abbie projects a cheerful persona, but her character harbors enormous resentment about opportunities she has lost.

One of her biggest regrets is that her greatest dreams go unfulfilled. While concealed from her family, Abbie's bitter disappointment is obvious to the reader. Aldrich writes, "Abbie Deal [lived] two lives; one within herself, wracked and tortured,—the other, an outward one which met all the old duties and trivial obligations with composure" (176). This duality between the "tortured" and "composed" selves, or the private and public personas, is seen throughout the novel. Her regret over the sacrifice of her own dreams for the benefit of others is a recurring theme. One by one, her children, and later her grandchildren, appropriate Abbie's dreams: to be a singer, artist, and writer. Shortly before her death, she cries bitter tears: "[I]t just came over me . . . in a sort of wave . . . all of the wonderful things I planned to do when I was young . . . and never did" ([Aldrich's ellipses] 293).

In the final analysis, *A Lantern in Her Hand* operates on several levels: The novel tells a story of strength and courage, of the beauty and devastation of nature, of a woman whose fear of intimacy leaves her strong but emotionally unfulfilled. Still, Aldrich never presents Abbie Deal as a pathetic figure; rather, she is a stoic woman who finds a way to survive.

Survival also informs Aldrich's 1931 novel, *A White Bird Flying*. A sequel to *A Lantern in Her Hand*, *A White Bird Flying* begins just two days after Abbie Deal's death and follows Laura Deal through the trials of young adulthood, early marriage, and motherhood. Like *A Lantern in Her Hand*, *A White Bird Flying* is largely didactic and emphasizes the importance of keeping one's perspective in the face of adversity. Similarly, *Miss Bishop*, published in 1933, follows the fifty-two-year career of an unmarried college professor who is forced to resign when a new college president is hired and vows to make changes. Initially bitter at being forced out, Miss Bishop undergoes a change of heart when she reviews her life achievements and realizes the value of her accomplishments.

Aldrich's final novel, *The Lieutenant's Lady*, published in 1942, marked a thematic departure for Aldrich, who used actual post–Civil War diaries to write a fictional account of a young woman who marries an army lieutenant and ends up leading a difficult life as an army wife.

CRITICAL RECEPTION

Despite the fact that she enjoyed a prominent literary career during her lifetime, few contemporary scholars of early twentieth-century American literature were familiar with Aldrich's work until the reissuance of *A Lantern in Her Hand* by the University of Nebraska Press in 1994. So popular was the novel when it was published in 1928, however, that within eighteen months of its original release *A Lantern in Her Hand* was in its twenty-first printing. It reached the best-seller lists in March of 1929, where it remained for several years.

Reviewers found much to praise in *A Lantern in Her Hand*. One newspaper reviewer characterized the novel as "a splendid tribute to the pioneer woman, whose part in the growth of our country cannot be measured." Another critic remarked, "One likes the Plains states better, and has more faith in the United States, for reading the book [which] is so true, so natural, and so American." Yet another critic described the novel as "a picture as thrilling and joyously fresh as the prairie sky. A most welcome addition to those . . . documents that recount the development of our national consciousness" (qtd. in Petersen 87).

In 1942, *A Lantern in Her Hand* was added to "other classics for classroom use in the Modern Literature Series," which also featured Crane's *The Red Badge of Courage* and Wharton's novel *The Age of Innocence* (Petersen 89). In 1950, it was named one of the top ten books in providing an accurate depiction of American life (Martin 41). By the time it was rereleased by the University of Nebraska Press in 1994, the novel had been translated into over twenty languages.

Aldrich's other novels also fared well with critics. *A White Bird Flying* (1931) reached the best-seller lists within two weeks of its publication. *Good Housekeeping* reported, "The secret of this popular writer's success in getting close to her readers' hearts lies in her ability to appeal to our deeper instincts" (qtd. in Petersen 111). Similarly, *Miss Bishop* (1933) made the best-seller lists within a month of publication and became one of the six best-selling novels of 1933. Later that year, Metro-Goldwyn-Mayer optioned the movie rights to *Miss Bishop*, eventually producing the film under the title *Cheers for Miss Bishop* in 1941.

Aldrich's writing was occasionally criticized for its sentimentalism, a charge that is being renewed today as a contemporary assessment of her work emerges. In addition to sentimentalism, other critics, including Martin, for example, cite Aldrich's "irritating tendency toward didacticism" and her insistence on "pointing [out] a moral . . . that readers are quite capable of finding for themselves" as deficiencies in Aldrich's writing (Martin 32).

BIBLIOGRAPHY

Works by Bess Streeter Aldrich

Mother Mason. New York: Appleton, 1924. (Short stories)
The Rim of the Prairie. New York: Appleton, 1925.
The Cutters. New York: Appleton, 1926. (Short stories)
A Lantern in Her Hand. New York: Appleton, 1928. Lincoln: University of Nebraska
     Press, 1994.

A White Bird Flying. New York: Appleton, 1931.
Miss Bishop. New York: Appleton, 1933.
Spring Came on Forever. New York: Appleton, 1935.
The Man Who Caught the Weather. New York: Appleton, 1936. (Short stories)
Song of Years. New York: Appleton, 1939.
The Drum Goes Dead. New York: Appleton, 1941.
The Lieutenant's Lady. New York: Appleton, 1942.
Journey into Christmas. New York: Appleton, 1949. (Short stories)
The Bess Streeter Aldrich Reader. New York: Appleton, 1950.
A Bess Streeter Aldrich Treasury. New York: Appleton, 1959.
Bess Streeter Aldrich: The Collected Short Works, 1907–1919. Ed. Carol Miles Petersen. Lincoln: University of Nebraska Press, 1995.

Studies of Bess Streeter Aldrich

Dalstrom, Harl A. "Bess Streeter Aldrich's Frontier Omaha, 1866–1868." *Heritage of the Great Plains* 28.2 (1995): 15–33.

Lambert, Lillian. "Bess Streeter Aldrich." *Midland Schools* [Des Moines, IA] 42.8 (1928), University of Northern Iowa Archives, 299.

Martin, Abigail Ann. *Bess Streeter Aldrich*. Boise, ID: Boise State University Press, 1992.

Meier, A. Mabel. "Bess Streeter Aldrich: A Literary Portrait." *Nebraska History* 50 (1969): 67–100.

Petersen, Carol Miles. *Bess Streeter Aldrich*. Lincoln: University of Nebraska Press, 1995.

Witt, Nancy L. "Bess Streeter Aldrich: Iowa Author." *Iowa Woman* 10.3 (1990): 11–15.

GERTRUDE ATHERTON
(1857–1948)

Catherine Cucinella

BIOGRAPHY

Gertrude Atherton, novelist, essayist, and short story writer, attempted throughout her sixty-year career to come to terms with both her hatred and her love for her birthplace, San Francisco, California. After her parents, Thomas Ludovich Horn and Gertrude Franklin, divorced in 1860, Atherton spent her early childhood on her grandfather Stephan Franklin's ranch near San Jose. Although well read, Atherton received an informal education, attending several schools. After a year at Sayre Institute in Lexington, Kentucky, Atherton returned to her grandfather's ranch to live with her now twice-divorced mother. In 1868 Gertrude eloped with George Henry Bowen Atherton, one of her mother's suitors.

Disillusioned with marriage, Gertrude established a life independent of her husband several years before his death in 1882. Her financial dependence on her husband throughout her marriage contributed to Atherton's desire to establish herself as a writer. In 1883, using the pseudonym "Asmodeus," she wrote "The Randolphs of Redwood," the first narrative in her career-long story chronicle of California. In order to situate herself in literary circles, Atherton left San Francisco in 1888, and for the next forty-three years, she alternated her residences between the United States and Europe. In 1931, she returned to live in California, where she died in 1948.

Atherton's oeuvre consists of novels, essay and short-story collections, a history of California, several books on San Francisco, historical novels set in Greece or Rome, a fictionalized biography of Alexander Hamilton, and an autobiography as well as articles on feminism, politics, and war published in newspapers and magazines. Atherton also worked in Hollywood as one of Goldwyn's Eminent Authors and received honorary degrees from Mills College in literature and from the University of California, Berkeley, in law. In 1940 she became the first to be named California's Most Distinguished Woman, and in 1943, the Library of Congress exhibited her manuscripts and memorabilia.

MAJOR WORKS AND THEMES

Several recurring themes circulate among Atherton's major works: the individual pursuit of happiness, the importance of place in this pursuit, women's struggles against a conventional society, the transformation of an ugly duckling into a beautiful swan, and the depiction of reality within an imaginative framework. Charlotte McClure writes that "the individual's questioning of or questing for a purpose in life within the boundary of social institutions serves as [Atherton's] major and basic fictional motif" (*Gertrude Atherton* 31). Inevitably, Atherton's novels address the influence of social constructions on the attainment of happiness.

In *Patience Sparhawk* (1897), two major themes emerge: Patience's quest for happiness, and her confrontation with social conventions. As Patience rises through the social classes, she finds the expectations of the elite just as limiting and confining as the poverty of her childhood. Within her upper-class marriage, Atherton's heroine discovers the alienation of women from mainstream America because of their relegation to the "woman's sphere." *Patience* exposes the ennui that exists for upper-class women, and although it portrays various types of marriages, none emerge as fulfilling options for women. Patience's decision to leave her upper-class marriage and to search for happiness outside of marriage reinforces Atherton's contention that happiness, especially for women, often entails the rejection of social conventions.

In her California novels, Atherton's heroines often embody the "spirit" of the state, and this embodiment frequently casts California as a character in the narrative. The California that emerges in Atherton's fictions demonstrates the same anxieties that confront her female protagonists: confusion regarding the split between fantasy and reality, pragmatism and idealism. The negotiation with this confusion generates a desire for a progressive American state and a nostalgia for the romance of a lost Arcadia, which "afforded comforting assurance of romance and caste" (Starr 356). *The Doomswoman* (1893) presents the conflict between the romance of Mexico and the reality of America through Deigo Estenega, who endeavors to make California a modern state while retaining its Mexican character. In *A Daughter of the Vine* (1899), Estenega returns to find the Mexicans marginalized by a firmly entrenched American aristocracy. In these novels and in her short-story collection *The Splendid Idle Forties, Stories of Old California* (1902), Atherton romanticizes Mexican California while rejecting a modern Mexican California.

Much of Atherton's fiction emerges as a hybrid of romance and realism that blends "reality" with invention. Atherton's fictional biography, *The Conqueror, Being the True and Romantic Story of Alexander Hamilton*, (1902) exemplifies this hybridity. Atherton romanticizes the reality of Hamilton's life and, according to McClure, "invented the biographical novel" (*Gertrude Atherton* 36). Emily Wortis Leider writes, "*The Conqueror* makes no attempt to be restrained or objective" (195). Atherton's paradigm prescribes that reality need not be presented with restraint or objectivity; instead, romance, imagination, and invention characterize her presentation of life.

This blend of romance, imagination, and invention underwrites the thematic concerns of Atherton's best-selling novel *Black Oxen* (1923). While exposing the illusions of romantic love, this novel examines the place of the aging woman in society. The novel concerns the rejuvenatation of a fifty-eight-year-old woman through radiation of the ovaries. *Black Oxen* does not argue for "growing old gracefully"; instead, it "is . . . a propaganda novel with a message directed at women no longer young: ladies go out and find yourself a doctor who will restore your youth via the Steinach Treatment" (Leider 296). *Black Oxen* explicitly locates a woman's power in youth and beauty. Although Countess Zattiany, the rejuvenated socialite, opts for power rather than romantic love, the novel makes clear that this option arises because the Countess has regained her youth and her beauty while retaining the knowledge gained through a lifetime. Thus, as Leider argues, although "*Black Oxen* has enormous vitality . . . its vision is a dark one" (303). Indeed, Atherton presents a bleak picture regarding the viability of an aging woman in American society in this novel that exposes societal expectations and urges women to circumvent those conventions.

CRITICAL RECEPTION

Charlotte McClure identifies a "critical ambivalence" regarding Atherton scholarship. This ambivalence centers on the decision to treat Atherton's "achievement in relation to her personality or to her literary intention" (*Gertrude Atherton* 138). Critics, however, seem intent on identifying the biographical impulses in Atherton's novels and short stories. Her themes regarding the individual pursuit of happiness and the importance of place and social milieu in identity construction frequently mimic the writer's own experiences, as does her inclusion of California in her novels. However, Atherton's oeuvre includes much that lies outside of California, and her nonfiction work suggests that much of her concern also lies outside of her own experience.

Although Starr asserts that Atherton "was a novelist because she wrote novels, not because she had any sense of art or craft or profession" (364), other critics recognize her direct challenge to existing literary movements and genres. Early critics labeled her work "literary anarchy" because of Atherton's "rebellious departure from the conventional and expected themes, characterizations, and methods of writing" (McClure, *Gertrude Atherton* 130). Furthermore, her fiction reacts to "the middle-class (bourgeois) conformity" of the realistic school of fiction, and Atherton "never missed an opportunity to revile Howells and the domestic realism of his novels, which she equated with tame gentility and boring convention" (Leider 74). Although many of Atherton's contemporary reviewers faulted the sensational content of her novels, most praised Atherton for her literary innovations and her ability "to tell a story, to create characters" and to hold the reader's interest (McClure, *Gertrude Atherton* 132–33).

Atherton's representation of women has and continues to garner critical attention. Leider's assertion that Atherton "had invested her career in the glorification of female independence of spirit and the denigration of maternity, subservience, and monotonous domestic routine" proves representative of this critical concern (248). Gail Thain Parker suggests that Atherton's rejection of Howells and American Realism points to Atherton's understanding of the antagonistic and adverse effects of that literature toward women (qtd. in McClure 139). Repeatedly, Atherton attacked Howell's "commonplace," which for Atherton meant the literary confinement of women to conventional roles. Atherton's heroines defy these conventions and often emerge as "Amazonian" or "superwomen." Although criticized for her heroines, Atherton "saw no need to apologize for choosing superwomen as heroines, since she continued to avow her contempt for everything 'commonplace' " (Leider 337). Despite Atherton's insistence on independent and adventurous heroines, anxiety arises regarding whether or not to declare Atherton a feminist or a feminist writer. Leider observes that "Atherton's New Woman heroines command a manipulative sexuality used to attract and control," much like Atherton herself, and that "Atherton was the kind of feminist who complains about how ugly most other feminists are" (5). Citing Atherton's "courage, capacity for work, and independent spirit" as well as her "narcissism, competitiveness, worship of power, and lack of compassion," Leider acknowledges that as a role model for the twentieth-century feminist Atherton both attracts and repels. Atherton did, however, emerge as a symbol of the New Woman, and this aspect of both her fiction and her life unsettled many of her reviewers.

Rather than identifying Atherton as a feminist, McClure calls her a social historian who offers "critical observations on a civilization that are based on her own assumptions of the relationship between human nature and culture" (*Gertrude Atherton* 142). These observations more often than not involved the relationships between men and women and between women and their society. According to McClure, Atherton perceived the socially and culturally constructed social roles as the cause of "the ennui of women, the tyranny of men, and the parental abuse of power over children" (*Gertrude Atherton* 140). These social constructions ultimately "separated individuals from their own internal rhythms and from nature's rhythms"; and according to McClure, Atherton "located the greatest possibility of expanding the human spirit, particularly of women, in the encouragement of individual talent at the expense of merely fulfilling traditional roles" (*Gertrude Atherton* 140–41).

BIBLIOGRAPHY

Works by Gertrude Atherton

What Dreams May Come. Chicago: Belford, 1888.
Hermia Suydam. New York: Current Literature, 1889.

Los Cerritos, a Romance of the Modern Times. 1890. Ridgewood, NJ: Gregg, 1968.

A Question of Time. New York: Lovell, 1891.

The Doomswoman. 1893. Upper Saddle River, NJ: Literature House, 1970.

Before the Gringo Came. New York: Tait, 1894. (Short stories)

A Whirl Asunder. New York: Stokers, 1895.

His Fortunate Grace. New York: Appleton, 1897.

Patience Sparhawk and Her Times. 1897. Upper Saddle River, NJ: Literature House, 1970.

American Wives and English Husbands. London: Service, 1898.

The Californians. 1898. Ridgewood, NJ: Gregg, 1968.

The Valiant Runaways. New York: Dodd, 1898.

A Daughter of the Vine. London: Lane, 1899.

Senator North. 1900. Ridgewood, NJ: Gregg, 1968.

The Aristocrats, Being the Impression of Lady Helen Pole during Her Sojourn in the Great North Woods as Spontaneously Recorded in Her Letters to Her Friend in North Britain, the Countess of Edge and Ross. 1901. Ridgewood, NJ: Gregg, 1968.

The Conqueror, Being the True and Romantic Story of Alexander Hamilton. New York: Macmillan, 1902.

The Splendid Idle Forties, Stories of Old California. 1902. Ridgewood, NJ: Gregg, 1968. (Short stories)

Mrs. Pendleton's Four-in-Hand. New York: Macmillan, 1903.

Rulers of Kings. New York: Harper, 1904.

The Bell in the Fog and Other Stories. 1905. New York: Garrett, 1968.

Ancestors. New York: Doubleday, 1907.

The Gorgeous Isle. New York: Doubleday, 1908.

Tower of Ivory. New York: Macmillan, 1910.

Julia France and Her Times. New York: Macmillan, 1912.

California, an Intimate History. 1914. Freeport, NY: Books for Libraries, 1971. (History)

Perch of the Devil. New York: Stokes, 1914.

Mrs. Balfame. New York: Stokes, 1916.

The White Morning. New York: Stokes, 1918.

The Avalanche, a Mystery Story. New York: Stokes, 1919.

Transplanted. New York: Dodd, 1919.

The Sisters-in-Law, a Novel of Our Time. New York: Stokes, 1921.

Sleeping Fires. New York: Stokes, 1922.

Black Oxen. New York: Boni, 1923.

The Crystal Cup. New York: Boni, 1925.

The Immortal Marriage. New York: Boni, 1927.

The Jealous Gods, a Processional Novel of the Fifth Century B.C. *(Concerning One Alcibiades)*. New York: Liveright, 1928.

Dido, Queen of Hearts. New York: Liveright, 1929.

The Sophisticates. New York: Liveright, 1931.

Adventures of a Novelist. New York: Liveright, 1932. (Autobiography)

The Foghorn. 1934. Freeport, ME: Books for Libraries, 1970.

Golden Peacock. Boston: Houghton, 1936.

The House of Lee. New York: Appleton, 1940.

The Horn of Life. New York: Appleton, 1942.
My San Francisco, a Wayward Biography. New York: Bobbs, 1946. (History)

Studies of Gertrude Atherton

Leider, Emily Wortis. *California's Daughter: Gertrude Atherton and Her Times*. Stanford: Stanford University Press, 1991.

McClure, Charlotte S. "A Checklist of the Writing of and about Gertrude Atherton." *American Literary Realism, 1870–1910* 9 (1976): 103–62.

———. *Gertrude Atherton*. Boise, ID: Boise State University Press, 1976.

———. *Gertrude Atherton*. New York: Twayne, 1979.

———. "Gertrude Atherton (1857–1948)." *American Literary Realism, 1870–1910* 9 (1976): 95–101.

Starr, Kevin. "Gertrude Atherton, Daughter of the Elite." *Americans and the California Dream, 1850–1915*. By Starr. New York: Oxford University Press, 1973. 345–64.

MARY HUNTER AUSTIN
(1868–1934)

Elizabeth Wright

BIOGRAPHY

Mary Hunter Austin was born on September 9, 1868, in Carlinville, Illinois, the second daughter of eight children born to George Hunter, a lawyer, and Susanna Savilla Graham Hunter, an aspiring teacher who abandoned her own career plans in order to become a wife and mother. As a young girl, Mary idolized her father, who encouraged the development of his daughter's skills as a writer until his death in 1878. George Hunter's death was a painful event for Austin because it meant an end to the relative comfort in which her family lived. Forced to move the family from their comfortable farm into town, Austin's mother struggled to support the family with a widow's pension. During this time, Mary and her mother grew apart despite their shared interest in feminist issues; their rift was mainly due to the death of Mary's younger sister Jennie, who also died in 1878 of diphtheria. Mary blamed herself for the death of her sister and felt it could have been prevented had her mother sent for a doctor sooner.

In 1884, Austin enrolled at Blackburn College in Illinois. Because of health problems, however, her family decided she should transfer to the State Normal School in Bloomington, Illinois. Austin was angered by this decision, which may have led to her breakdown in 1885. After recuperating at her mother's home, Austin returned to Blackburn College, from which she graduated in 1888 with a degree in Mathematics and Science.

After receiving her degree, Austin accompanied her mother and younger brother to California, where her older brother James had lived since 1887. The Austin family hoped that the change of scenery would benefit Mary's fragile mental and physical health. Indeed, the trip to California exceeded all expectations: Inspired by the beauty of the western landscape, Austin regained her strength. In 1889 Austin published her first nonfiction essay based upon her experiences in California, later reprinted as the book *One Hundred Miles on Horseback*. As Austin worked to establish herself as a writer, she taught school.

In 1891, Austin married Stafford Wallace Austin, an engineer. During the early years of their marriage, the Austins moved frequently as Wallace searched for a permanent and well-paying job. Austin continued to teach school in order to support herself and her husband, who briefly participated in a scheme to irrigate the Owens Valley. After this plan failed, Wallace reluctantly turned to school teaching. In 1892, the Austins' only child, Ruth, was born, and Mary published her first short story, "The Mother of Felipe." Ruth was born mentally handicapped, a condition that was tremendously distressing to Austin. Because Ruth required constant attention and care, Austin struggled to find the time to devote to her writing during this period. Additionally, Wallace's decreasing enthusiasm for Austin's writing led to constant tension for the couple, as Austin was determined to use her writing as a means of supporting Ruth.

During the late 1890s, Austin's marital problems intensified. In 1899, Austin moved with Ruth to Los Angeles, where she became friends with Charles Lummis, an ethnographer and archeologist who supported the literary careers of Austin and Charlotte Perkins Gilman. During this time Austin began to publish a series of works including *The Land of Little Rain* (1903) and *The Basket Woman* (1904). Austin was also forced to make a difficult decision about her daughter, deciding in 1905 to commit Ruth to the Institution for the Retarded in Santa Clara, where she remained until her death from influenza in 1918.

In 1906, Austin purchased land in Carmel, a move that seemed to signal her intention to settle permanent roots in the West, yet Austin left the burgeoning artist colony in 1907 to travel to New York and Europe, thus beginning several years of extensive travel. During this time, doctors diagnosed her with breast cancer. Believing that she had only months to live, Austin journeyed to Italy. After a spontaneous recovery that she attributed to her spirituality, Austin returned to the United States in 1910, where she lived in New York and worked for the woman's movement, a movement Austin sympathizes with in her novel *A Woman of Genius* (1912).

In 1914, Mary and Wallace Austin divorced. Austin continued to divide her time between New York and California until 1918, when she began spending time in Santa Fe. Austin established permanent residence in Santa Fe in 1925 when she built "Casa Querida," or "beloved house." While living in Santa Fe, Austin was a fervent supporter of Native American rights.

Mary Austin died in Santa Fe of a heart attack on August 13, 1934.

MAJOR WORKS AND THEMES

An avid traveler, Austin's fiction and nonfiction recreates the landscapes and cultures she encountered during her time spent in the Southwest. Austin's first book, *The Land of Little Rain* (1903), records many of the stories she gathered while living in southern California. Twenty-one years later, *The Land of Journeys Ending* (1924), with its focus on New Mexico landscape and culture, was intended to serve as a companion volume to *The Land of Little Rain*. In between, Austin published several other books based on her travels through California and New Mexico, including *California: Land of the Sun* (1914) and *One Smoke Stories* (1934). In addition to recording the landscape she viewed, Austin's writing calls for the preservation of wilderness. In the novel *The Ford* (1917), for instance, she creates a hero who launches an irrigation project that makes the land more productive, yet also conserves both land and water for future use.

Much of Austin's writing signals her interest in Native American culture: In *The Basket Woman* (1904), for example, Austin records the stories she learned from the Paiute Indians in California. The publication of *Outland* in 1910 suggests that Austin was not afraid to satirize herself, as she creates a heroine who is fascinated by Indian culture. Austin continues to discuss Native American culture in the play *The Arrow Maker* (1911), in which she attempts to incorporate the poetic rhythms of Indian language into a play focusing on a Paiute sorceress, and in *The American Rhythm* (1923), arguing that Native American rhythmic patterns affect American poetic tradition. Finally, in *Taos Pueblo* (1930) Austin's words describe what Ansel Adams captured on film while photographing the historic pueblo.

Even as Austin's writing reveals her intent to preserve Native cultures threatened by the arrival of European settlers, it alludes to the freedom awaiting women courageous enough to travel to the West. In her collection of short stories entitled *Lost Borders* (1909), Austin creates a series of women characters who have been disappointed by the lives society has chosen for them. Stories such as "The Walking Woman" suggest that the West provides enough physical and psychic space for women to walk off the various "illnesses" they suffer during their lives. Austin makes this very point in her autobiography, *Earth Horizon* (1932), as she credits the West for making her spiritually whole.

Perhaps because of her own failed marriage, Austin wrote at length about women and men struggling to find fulfilling relationships. Much of Austin's fiction focuses on intelligent women whose education has ill prepared them for the roles they will be expected to play as wives. In the early short story "Frustrate," for example, Austin portrays the agony experienced by an intelligent woman who realizes that her physical appearance may jeopardize her future chances for happiness. And in *Isidro* (1905), *Santa Lucia* (1908), and *The Lovely Lady* (1913), Austin suggests that while marriage should be based on both friendship and romance, gendered expectations often interfere with the development of fulfilling relationships.

Just as Austin was concerned by how marriage may stunt a woman's intellectual and emotional development, her fiction addresses how motherhood may be similarly debilitating. In *A Woman of Genius* (1912), for example, Olivia Lattimore wants to become an actress but must settle instead for marriage and early motherhood because she lives in a small town. The deaths of both her child and her husband free Olivia to develop her talents, yet the novel's argument is clear: While not all women are predisposed to parenting, society permits women to imagine little else for their lives.

Several Austin novels build upon her experiences in New York City, as well as her unsuccessful relationship with the social reformer Lincoln Steffens. The dishonest social reformer appears in *Love and the Soul Maker* (1914), in *No. 26 Jayne Street* (1920), and in the posthumously published novella *Cactus Thorn* (1988), in which Dulcie Adelaide murders her lover, a New York politician, after learning he is engaged to another woman. Although much of Austin's fiction depicts women trapped in unhappy relationships, Austin's final novel, *Starry Adventure* (1931), does present a model relationship as the main character learns to value a woman of sincerity over a woman who exudes false sophistication.

CRITICAL RECEPTION

Austin was acquainted with a wide and varied group of writers including Jack London, George Sterling, Lincoln Steffens, Willa Cather, Charlotte Perkins Gilman, and Mabel Dodge Luhan; yet despite her notoriety in literary circles, she struggled to find a broad audience for her published work. In a series of articles on this subject, Karen Langlois suggests that this may have been due to her publishers' failure to market her writing effectively. After her death, much of Austin's work fell out of print even as biographies written by T. M. Pearce pointed to Austin's significance. The publication in 1987 of two edited collections of Austin's short stories, Melody Graulich's *Western Trails: A Collection of Short Stories by Mary Austin* and Marjorie Pryse's *Stories from the Country of Lost Borders* made Austin's work accessible to a broader audience. This, combined with the 1989 publication of Esther Stineman's biography, *Mary Austin: Song of a Maverick*, has led to a cornucopia of critical work on the author.

Perhaps because Austin so enjoyed being in the company of other writers, a good bit of scholarship examines Austin's writing in the context of other American writers and major literary movements such as realism and modernism. In addition, critics note that Austin's writing plays an integral role in our understanding of the American West. Much of the work focusing on Austin as a western writer situates her writing within the context of other western authors, including Frank Norris and Edward Abbey. Much has also been said about Austin's treatment of Native Americans in her writing. Mark T. Hoyer, for example, examines how Austin integrates Native American culture into her writing, while Noreen G. Lape argues that Austin's treatment of Native Americans often verges on the edge of appropriation. Still others have examined Austin's writing in terms of what it can tell contemporary readers about women's experiences in the West. In her influential essay "Regeneration through Liberation: Mary Austin's 'The Walking Woman' and Western Narrative Formula," Faith Jaycox uses Austin's short story to examine how the West provided newfound freedom for women. Lois Rudnick notes Mary Austin's writing helps to unravel traditional masculine perceptions of the West. Cynthia Taylor makes a similar point when she argues that Austin feminizes western landscape in her fiction.

The emergence of a critical school known as Ecocriticism, with its study of humanity's relationship with the natural environment, has spurred an onslaught of essays placing Austin within the context of other nature writers as well as essays examining how Austin represents wilderness spaces in her writing. Still other critics examine Austin's work as an environmentalist: Vera Norwood, for example, suggests in "Heroines of Nature: Four Women Respond to the American Landscape" that Austin's writing dismantles stereotypes about women and their relationship to nature.

Even as critics use Austin's writing to understand the construction of terms such as "*nature*" and "*wilderness*," other scholars focus on the feminist slant of Austin's writing. As Melody Graulich suggests in the afterword to Austin's autobiography *Earth Horizon*, Austin has created a series of trails for feminists to follow. And as Janis Stout notes in "Mary Austin's Feminism: A Reassessment," Austin had "a vision of harmonious resolution of gender roles that relies on feminization of the male, as well as liberation of the female" (97). Perhaps because Austin was so interested in borders during her life, much of the criticism on Austin's work crosses borders of its own. Melody Graulich and Elizabeth Klimasmith's 1999 collection of essays *Exploring Lost Borders: Critical Essays on Mary Austin* continues this trend.

BIBLIOGRAPHY

Works by Mary Hunter Austin

One Hundred Miles on Horseback. 1889. Los Angeles: Dawson's Book Shop, 1963. (Nonfiction)

The Land of Little Rain. Boston: Houghton, 1903. (Short stories)

The Basket Woman. Boston: Houghton, 1904. (Short stories)

Isidro. Boston: Houghton, 1905. (Novel)

The Flock. Boston: Houghton, 1906. (Novel)

Santa Lucia. New York: Harper, 1908. (Novel)

Lost Borders. New York: Harper, 1909. (Short stories)

[Pseud. Gordon Stairs]. *Outland*. London: Murray, 1910. (Novel)

The Arrow Maker. New York: Duffield, 1911.

A Woman of Genius. New York: Doubleday, 1912. (Novel)

The Lovely Lady. New York: Doubleday, 1913. (Novel)

California: Land of the Sun. New York: Macmillan, 1914. (Short stories)

Love and the Soul Maker. New York: Appleton, 1914. (Novel)

The Ford. Boston: Houghton, 1917. (Novel)

The Trail Book. Boston: Houghton, 1918. (Short stories)

The Young Woman Citizen. New York: Woman's, 1918. (Novel)

No. 26 Jayne Street. Boston: Houghton, 1920. (Novel)

The American Rhythm. New York: Harcourt, 1923. (Nonfiction)

The Land of Journeys' Ending. New York: Century, 1924.

Everyman's Genius. Indianapolis: Bobbs, 1925. (Nonfiction)

Lands of the Sun. Boston: Houghton, 1927. (Short stories)

The Children Sing in the Far West. Boston: Houghton, 1928. (Short stories)
Taos Pueblo. Photographs Ansel Adams. San Francisco: Grabhorn, 1930.
Experiences Facing Death. Indianapolis: Bobbs, 1931. (Nonfiction)
Starry Adventure. Boston: Houghton, 1931. (Novel)
Earth Horizon: An Autobiography. Boston: Houghton, 1932.
Can Prayer Be Answered? New York: Farrar, 1934. (Nonfiction)
Indian Pottery of the Rio Grande. Pasadena, CA: Esto, 1934. (Nonfiction)
One Smoke Stories. Boston: Houghton, 1934. (Short stories)
The Mother of Felipe and Other Early Stories. Ed. Franklin Walker. Los Angeles: Book
    Club of California, 1950. (Short stories)
Stories from the Country of Lost Borders. Ed. Marjorie Pryse. New Brunswick, NJ:
    Rutgers University Press, 1987. (Short stories)
Western Trails: A Collection of Short Stories. Ed. Melody Graulich. Reno: University of
    Nevada Press, 1987.
Cactus Thorn. Fwd. Melody Graulich. Afterword Melody Graulich. Reno: University of
    Nevada Press, 1988. (Novella)
Beyond Borders: The Selected Essays of Mary Austin. Ed. J. Ellis Reuben. Carbondale:
    Southern Illinois University Press, 1996. (Nonfiction)
A Mary Austin Reader. Ed. Esther F. Lanigan. Tucson: University of Arizona Press,
    1996. (Anthology)

Studies of Mary Hunter Austin

Gelfant, Blanche H. " 'Lives' of Women Writers: Cather, Austin, Porter/and Willa, Mary,
    Katherine Anne." *Novel: A Forum on Fiction* 18 (1984): 64–80.
Graulich, Melody. Afterword. *Earth Horizon*. By Mary Austin. Albuquerque: University
    of New Mexico Press, 1991. 373–94.
———. " 'I Thought at First She Was Talking about Herself': Mary Austin on Charlotte
    Perkins Gilman." *Jack London Journal* 1 (1994): 148–58.
Graulich, Melody, and Elizabeth Klimasmith, eds. *Exploring Lost Borders: Critical Es-
    says on Mary Austin*. Reno: University of Nevada Press, 1999.
Harrison, Elizabeth. "Zora Neale Hurston and Mary Hunter Austin's Ethnographic Fiction:
    New Modernist Narratives." *Unmanning Modernism: Gendered Re-Readings*. Ed.
    Elizabeth Jane Harrison and Shirley Peterson. Knoxville: University of Tennessee
    Press, 1997. 44–58.
Hoyer, Mark T. *Dancing Ghosts: Native American and Christian Syncretism in Mary
    Austin's Work*. Reno: University of Nevada Press, 1998.
Jaycox, Faith. "Regeneration through Liberation: Mary Austin's 'The Walking Woman'
    and Western Narrative Formula." *Legacy: A Journal of American Women Writers*
    6 (1989): 5–12.
Karell, Linda K. " 'The Immanent Pattern': Recovering a Self in Mary Austin's *Earth
    Horizon*." *A/B: Auto/Biography Studies* 12 (1997): 261–75.
———. "Lost Borders and Blurred Boundaries: Mary Austin as Storyteller." *American
    Women Short Story Writers: A Collection of Critical Essays*. Ed. Julie Brown.
    New York: Garland, 1995. 153–66.
Langlois, Karen S. "A Fresh Voice from the West: Mary Austin, California, and Amer-
    ican Literary Magazines, 1892–1910." *California History* 69 (1990): 22–35.

————. "Marketing the American Indian: Mary Austin and the Business of Writing." *A Living of Words: American Women in Print Culture*. Ed. Susan Albertine. Knoxville: University of Tennessee Press, 1995. 151–68.

————. "Mary Austin and Houghton Mifflin Company: A Case Study in the Marketing of a Western Writer." *Western American Literature* 23 (1988): 31–42.

————. "Mary Austin and Lincoln Steffens." *Huntington Library Quarterly: A Journal for the History and Interpretation of English and American Civilization* 49 (1986): 327–53.

————. "Mary Austin and the New Theatre: The 1911 Production of *The Arrow Maker*." *Theatre History Studies* 8 (1988): 71–87.

————. "Mary Austin's *A Woman of Genius*: The Text, the Novel and the Problem of Male Publishers and Critics and Female Authors." *Journal of American Culture* 15.2 (1992): 79–86.

Lape, Noreen Groover. " 'There Was a Part for Her in the Indian Life': Mary Austin, Regionalism, and the Problems of Appropriation." *Breaking Boundaries: New Perspectives on Women's Regional Writing*. Ed. Sherrie A. Inness and Diana Royer. Iowa City: University of Iowa Press, 1997. 124–39.

McClure, Charlotte S. "From Impersonations to Persons: Breaking Patterns, Finding Voices." *Private Voices, Public Lives: Women Speak on the Literary Life*. Ed. Nancy Owen Nelson and Jane Tompkins. Denton: University of North Texas Press, 1995. 225–37.

Morrow, Nancy. "The Artist as Heroine and Anti-Heroine in Mary Austin's *A Woman of Genius* and Anne Douglas Sedgewick's *Tante*." *American Literary Realism* 22.2 (1990): 17–29.

Norwood, Vera L. "Heroines of Nature: Four Women Respond to the American Landscape." *The Ecocriticism Reader: Landmarks in Literary Ecology*. Ed. Cheryll Glotfelty and Harold Fromm. Athens: University of Georgia Press, 1996. 323–50.

O'Grady, John P. *Pilgrims to the Wild: Everett Ruess, Henry David Thoreau, John Muir, Clarence King, Mary Austin*. Salt Lake City: University of Utah Press, 1993.

Pearce, T. M. *The Beloved House*. Caldwell, ID: Caxton, 1940.

————, ed. *Literary America, 1903–1934: The Mary Austin Letters*. Westport, CT: Greenwood, 1979.

————. *Mary Hunter Austin*. New York: Twayne, 1956.

Rudnick, Lois. "Re-Naming the Land: Anglo-Expatriate Women in the Southwest." *The Desert Is No Lady: Southwestern Landscapes in Women's Writing and Art*. Ed. Vera Norwood and Janice Monk. New Haven, CT: Yale University Press, 1987. 10–26.

Ruppert, James. "Discovering America: Mary Austin and Imagism." *Studies in American Indian Literature: Critical Essays and Course Designs*. Ed. Paula Gunn Allen. New York: MLA, 1983. 243–58.

————. "Mary Austin's Landscape Line in Native American Literature." *Southwest Review* 68 (1983): 376–90.

Scheick, William J. "Mary Austin's Disfigurement of the Southwest in *The Land of Little Rain*." *Western American Literature* 27 (1992): 37–46.

Schlenz, Mark. "Rhetorics of Region in *Starry Adventure* and *Death Comes for the Archbishop*." *Regionalism Reconsidered: New Approaches to the Field*. Ed. David Jordan. New York: Garland, 1994. 65–85.

Stineman, Esther Lanigan. *Mary Austin: Song of a Maverick*. New Haven: Yale University Press, 1989.

Stout, Janis P. "Mary Austin's Feminism: A Reassessment." *Studies in the Novel* 30 (1998): 77–101.

———. "Willa Cather and Mary Austin: Intersections and Influence." *Southwestern American Literature* 21 (1996): 39–59.

Taylor, Cynthia. "Claiming Female Space: Mary Austin's Western Landscape." *The Big Empty: Essays on the Land as Narrative*. Ed. Leonard Engel. Albuquerque: University of New Mexico Press, 1994. 119–32.

Wild, Peter. "The Dangers of Mary Austin's *The Land of Little Rain*." *North Dakota Quarterly* 56.3 (1988): 119–27.

———. "Sentimentalism in the American Southwest: John C. Van Dyke, Mary Austin, and Edward Abbey." *Reading the West: New Essays on the Literature of the American West*. Ed. Michael Kowalewski. Cambridge: Cambridge University Press, 1996. 127–43.

Witschi, Nicholas. "Sinclair Lewis, the Voice of Satire, and Mary Austin's Revolt from the Village." *American Literary Realism* 30.1 (1997): 75–90.

Work, James C. "The Moral in Austin's *The Land of Little Rain*." *Women and Western American Literature*. Ed. Helen Winter Stauffer and Susan J. Rosowski. Troy, NY: Whitston, 1982. 297–310.

DJUNA BARNES (LYDIA STEPTOE) (1892–1982)

Carmine Esposito

BIOGRAPHY

Djuna Barnes was born on June 12, 1892, in Cornwall-on-Hudson, New York. Barnes was educated at home by her eccentric father Wald Barnes, her English mother Elizabeth Chappell, and her paternal grandmother Zadel Barnes Gustafson. Barnes identified Zadel (who participated in early temperance and feminist crusades, was a journalist and spiritualist, and had conducted a London salon that included Lady Wilde and Elizabeth Cady Stanton) as having the greatest influence on her early life.

In 1897, Fanny Faulkner, Wald's mistress, moved in with the Barnes family. When Barnes was eighteen, she "married" Percy Faulkner, a man thirty-four years her senior and the brother of her father's mistress. This "marriage" only lasted a couple of months, as Barnes returned to the Huntington Township, Long Island farm where her family now resided. In 1912, as the family's financial situation worsened due to Wald's refusal to work, Zadel forced Wald to choose between his two families. When Wald chose his family with Fanny, Barnes, her mother, and her four brothers moved to New York City.

In New York City, Barnes studied art at Pratt Institute and the Art Students League, and Guido Bruno exhibited a sampling of her Beardsleyan drawings in Greenwich Village. In 1913, Barnes launched her journalistic career when her articles began appearing in the *Brooklyn Eagle*. While in New York, Barnes contributed articles and interviews to various newspapers and magazines such as *New York Morning Telegraph, New York Herald, Vanity Fair*, and *Theatre Guild*. A collection of her interviews, along with twenty-three of her drawings, was published posthumously in *Interviews* (1985). Barnes also published several articles under the name Lydia Steptoe. Barnes began publishing poetry and short stories in 1911, and in 1915, Guido Bruno published a chapbook of her poetry, *The Book of Repulsive Women*. Barnes was awarded the O. Henry Prize in 1918 for her short story "A Night among the Horses." During this period, Barnes also began writing plays. Three of her one-act plays were staged by the Provincetown Players and gained her the respect of Eugene O'Neill.

Barnes was sent to Paris in 1921 as a correspondent for *McCall's*. There she joined a group that included Marsden Hartley, Berenice Abbott, Man Ray, and Robert McAlmon. Here she also began her tempestuous love affair with Thelma Wood, a silver point artist from St. Louis. Her relationship with Wood ended in 1931 and served as the basis for her most famous novel, *Nightwood* (1936). *A Book*, a collection of Barnes's short stories, poems, plays, and drawings, was published in 1923; and in 1928, Barnes published both *Ladies Almanack*, which was quickly banned by U.S. Customs, and her first novel, *Ryder*. Barnes spent the next several years traveling between Paris, London, and New York. During her time in Paris and London, Barnes became well acquainted with the writers James Joyce, Ezra Pound, Gertrude Stein, and T. S. Eliot (who would become her editor at Faber & Faber and who would write the introduction to *Nightwood*).

While in Paris, Barnes became friends with Natalie Clifford Barney and Peggy Guggenheim, both of whom helped financially support Barnes for the rest of her life. In 1940, Barnes settled at Patchin Place in Greenwich Village. She remained at Patchin Place as a near recluse until her death. In 1958, Barnes published her last major work, *The Antiphon*, a surrealist play in blank verse. On June 18, 1982, Djuna Barnes died at ninety years of age.

MAJOR WORKS AND THEMES

Barnes's early stories are characterized by ambiguity, violence, and the grotesque. Her characters are often isolated, either through expatriation, physical deformity, or sickness. This isolation often leads these characters to live lives filled with frustration, tension, and sexual complications. Two examples of these early stories are "The Rabbit" and "Spillway." In "The Rabbit," Rugo Amietiev, a simple Armenian farmer, finds himself in Manhattan when he inherits a tailor shop. Rugo falls in love with Addie, who instructs him that to prove his love for her he must perform a heroic act. Rugo kills a rabbit from a nearby butcher shop as proof of his love for Addie. At the story's end, we never know if Rugo has won Addie's love, but we do know that his deed has killed the innocence that he had at the story's start. In "Spillway," Julie Anspacher returns home after having spent five years in a sanatorium for tuberculosis. Returning with her is her illegitimate daughter, the child of a love affair with another patient. Confronted with his wife's infidelity, Julie's husband retires to his hunting loft. The story ends with a gunshot that signals to the reader either Pator's suicide or his commencement of target practice.

In *Ladies Almanack*, Barnes satirizes and celebrates Natalie Barney's famous lesbian literary salon. *Ladies Almanack* is written in twelve sections meant to correspond to the months of the year and is marked by humor, explicit sexuality, and verbal wit. *Ryder*, published the same year as *Ladies Almanack* and Barnes's first novel, has been described as a picaresque novel. *Ryder* tells the thinly disguised story of Barnes's own unconventional family. Wendell Ryder's absurd mission in life, much as Barnes's own father's, is to love women and procreate. Influenced by James Joyce's *Ulysses, Ryder* focuses on style rather than plot or character. *Ryder* parodies the prose styles of various authors and historical periods such as the Bible, Chaucer, and the epistolary novel. *Ladies Almanack* and *Ryder* satirize the hypocrisy present in middle-class sexual mores while pointing out the folly of indiscriminate promiscuity.

Nightwood tells the story of Robin Vote and the effect she has on the three people who fall in love with her. *Nightwood* exemplifies the techniques of modern literature while also serving as a precursor to post-modern concerns. *Nightwood* contains Barnes's most memorable character and one of the most intriguing characters in twentieth-century literature—the transvestite doctor Matthew O'Connor. O'Connor serves as the reader's guide through the descent into the novel's surrealistic world of night. O'Connor could be speaking for the novel itself when he says, "I have a narrative, but you will be hard put to find it" (141).

The Antiphon, a tragedy in blank verse, marked the last of Barnes's major works. *The Antiphon* tells the story of an alienated family and explores the conflict between a mother and daughter, who have been the victims of a cruel husband and father. In the end, the mother is unable to identify with her daughter or approve of the life her daughter leads, one she secretly envies. At the conclusion of the play, the mother murders her daughter by smashing her skull with a curfew bell. *The Antiphon*, like all of Barnes's works, presents life as being characterized by alienation and human relationships as being defined by estrangement.

CRITICAL RECEPTION

Early criticism of Barnes's work can best be described as uneven. One early review of *Ryder* calls it a piece of rubbish, and Leslie Fiedler suggests that *Nightwood* contains "dislocated lyricism, hallucinated vision and oddly skewed language" (467), whereas Edwin Muir states, "Miss Barnes' prose is the only prose by a living writer which can be compared with that of Joyce, and in one point it is superior to his: in its richness in exact and vivid imagery" (149). Shari Benstock has suggested that this early critical reaction is the result of Barnes's work not easily supporting the modern enterprise.

With the publication of *Silence and Power*, the critical dialogue surrounding Barnes's work has shifted. This collection of critical essays explores Barnes's work from various sociopolitical positions. This move from seeing Barnes as a modern artist to seeing her as both a feminist and a lesbian artist has led to the rediscovery of some of Barnes's most ignored works, specifically *The Book of Repulsive Women* and *Ladies Almanack*. This reevaluation has also led to a renewed interest in some of her more well-known work and a new way of approaching one of her most enigmatic works, *The Antiphon.*

The experimental nature and quality of Barnes's work, which make it difficult to both understand and categorize, will cause it to continue to be relatively ignored critically. Barnes's work and life seem to be just as resistant to feminist and lesbian concerns as they were to modern concerns. Barnes's greatest legacy may come from writers such as Isak Dinesen, Lawrence Durrell, Anaïs Nin, and John Hawkes, who have identified her as having influenced their work.

BIBLIOGRAPHY

Works by Djuna Barnes

The Book of Repulsive Women: Eight Rhythms and Five Drawings. New York: Bruno's Chapbooks II, 1915.
A Book. New York: Boni, 1923.
Ladies Almanack. (Written by a Lady of Fashion). Dijon, France: Darantiere, 1928.
Ryder. New York: Boni, 1928.
A Night among the Horses. New York: Boni, 1929. (A new addition of *A Book*, with three stories added)
Nightwood. London: Faber, 1936.
The Antiphon: A Play. London: Faber, 1958.
The Selected Works of Djuna Barnes. New York: Farrar, 1962.
Spillway. London: Faber, 1962.
Creatures in an Alphabet. New York: Dial, 1982.
Smoke and Other Early Stories. Ed. Douglas Messerli. College Park, MD: Sun & Moon, 1982.
Interviews. Ed. Alyce Barry. Washington, DC: Sun & Moon, 1985.
New York. Ed. Alyce Barry. Los Angeles: Sun & Moon, 1989.
At the Root of the Stars: The Short Plays. Ed. Douglas Messerli. Los Angeles: Sun & Moon, 1994.
Collected Stories of Djuna Barnes. Ed. Douglas Messerli. Los Angeles: Sun & Moon, 1996.
Poe's Mother: Selected Drawings. Ed. Douglas Messerli. Los Angeles: Sun & Moon, 1996.

Studies of Djuna Barnes

Benstock, Shari. *Women of the Left Bank: Paris 1900–1940.* Austin: University of Texas Press, 1986.
Broe, Mary Lynn, ed. *Silence and Power: A Reevaluation of Djuna Barnes.* Carbondale: Southern Illinois University Press, 1991.
Field, Andrew. *Djuna: The Life and Times of Djuna Barnes.* New York: Putnam, 1983. Rev. ed. (*Djuna: The Formidable Miss Barnes*). Austin: University of Texas Press, 1985.
Fiedler, Leslie. *Love and Death in the American Novel.* New York: Criterion, 1960.

Herring, Philip. *Djuna: The Life and Work of Djuna Barnes*. New York: Viking, 1995.
Muir, Edwin. *The Present Age from 1914*. London: Cresset, 1939.
Plumb, Cheryl J. *Fancy's Craft: Art and Identity in the Early Works of Djuna Barnes*.
        Selingsgrove, PA: Susquehanna University Press, 1986.
Scott, James B. *Djuna Barnes*. Boston: Twayne, 1976.

ELIZABETH BISHOP
(1911–1979)

Kirstin R. Hotelling Zona

BIOGRAPHY

Elizabeth Bishop was born in Worcester, Massachusetts, on February 8, 1911. Her father died eight months later from Bright's disease, and Bishop saw her mother for the last time in 1916 when she was permanently institutionalized in a mental hospital. Bishop spent her happiest childhood years in Nova Scotia among maternal family members, but in 1917, Bishop's wealthy paternal grandparents brought her to live with them in Worcester, Massachusetts, in an effort to expose their granddaughter to a more "refined" lifestyle. Bishop was miserable there and developed debilitating asthma that would plague her for the rest of her life. For the next several years, Bishop lived variously in Boston with an aunt, in Nova Scotia, at summer camp on Cape Cod, and at boarding school in Natick, Massachusetts. While in high school, Bishop wrote several poems and stories, publishing many of them in the school literary magazine, *The Blue Pencil*. She continued to write and publish as a student at Vassar College in upstate New York, during which time she and some friends launched a short-lived alternative literary journal, *Con Spirito*. She graduated with a degree in English in 1934.

A few months before she graduated from college, Bishop met Marianne Moore, with whom she would forge a lifelong friendship. Moore encouraged Bishop to write at a critical stage in her development, offered careful critiques of her work, and in 1935, wrote the introduction to Bishop's first book publication in the anthology *Trial Balances*. Twelve years later, Bishop was introduced to Robert Lowell, another very close friend and fellow poet. In many ways these two friendships are representative of the vital tensions that mark Bishop's poetry: cagey yet honest; reserved yet direct; observational yet interiorizing.

As the titles of Bishop's books suggest, such tensions often emerge as they concern notions of home and travel. From her first book of poems, *North & South* (1946), to her last, *Geography III* (1976), Bishop explored her thirst for travel in writing. After college she traveled throughout Europe, and in 1938 Bishop bought a house with a friend in Key West, Florida, where she lived for nine years. In 1946 Bishop won the Houghton Mifflin Literary fellowship for her first book of poetry, *North & South.* Over the next six years, Bishop won several prestigious awards and fellowships, and in 1951, she set off for a voyage to South America. En route she became ill in Rio de Janeiro, where an old friend, Lota de Macedo Soares, helped nurse her back to health. The two women fell in love, and Bishop stayed in Brazil for the next fifteen years, living with Lota in the mountains outside Rio. She often referred to these years as the happiest of her life, and though Bishop had other loves in her lifetime, Lota would be her primary companion. While in Brazil, Bishop published her next two books, *Poems* (including *North & South* and *A Cold Spring*) in 1955 and *Questions of Travel* in 1965. She continued to garner awards, such as the Pulitzer Prize for Poetry in 1956, as well as many fellowships that allowed her to continue her travels. During her later years in Brazil, Bishop's alcoholism and asthma became progressively worse, and her relationship with Lota began to deteriorate. In 1966 Bishop accepted her first teaching post, at the University of Washington in Seattle. Meanwhile, Lota became increasingly depressed and, in 1967, committed suicide.

During the next several years, Bishop lived between Cambridge, Massachusetts, where she taught at Harvard from time to time, and at her house in Brazil. She traveled to the Galapagos Islands, Peru, Ecuador, Sweden, Finland, and Norway. In her later years, she settled into a routine, teaching at Harvard during the school year and spending her summers on North Haven, an island off the coast of Maine. *Geography III*, the last book of poems published during Bishop's lifetime, appeared in 1976, winning the National Book Critics Circle Award the following year. It seems natural that the poems in this collection are concerned largely with memory, looking back at Bishop's early years in Nova Scotia and New England. After a lifetime of travel, Bishop, too, had returned to the place she'd begun. She died at home, in Boston, on October 6, 1979.

MAJOR WORKS AND THEMES

Elizabeth Bishop is perhaps the most unplaceable American poet of our time. A study of her work summons the categories with which we map American poetry only to reveal their limitations. While deeply influenced by major modernists such as T. S. Eliot and Marianne Moore, Bishop came of age as a poet in postdepression America, at a time when artistic enterprise was increasingly justified in sociopolitical terms. But unlike poets such as Adrienne Rich or Robert Lowell, Bishop was always skeptical of overtly political or confessional poetry. A woman of eclectic interests and convictions, Bishop's poetry explores the liminal spaces where demarcations are drawn—where self bleeds into other, the past blurs with the present, and desire skirts the edges of disdain.

Like her mentor Marianne Moore, Bishop identified herself as a fiction writer before becoming a full-time poet. Several of her short stories, such as "Then Came the Poor" and "Chimney Sweepers," remain uncollected in various Vassar College periodicals from the early 1930s. These stories are marked by a pervasive concern with trauma and a strangely direct yet surreal narrative voice that would eventually distinguish her first book of poems. Her finest and most overtly autobiographical short story, "In the Village," appeared in *New Yorker* in 1953. This and a handful of Bishop's other short stories can be found in *Elizabeth Bishop: The Collected Prose* (1984). Also included in this prose collection are several important essays, such as "Efforts of Affection," in which Bishop offers a provocative tribute to her friend Marianne Moore.

Bishop is best known, however, for her remarkable poems, the first collection of which appeared in 1946. The title of this book, *North & South*, announces a fascination with geography—both literal and figural—that permeates all of Bishop's work. From her earliest poems to her latest, Bishop is interested in questions of perspective, detailing the world around her with acute visual accuracy. But Bishop does not present her precise imagery as a conduit to truth; rather, her poems interrogate the authority of singular perspective just as they rely on the author's eye to give them life. This paradoxical approach to perspective especially is overt in Bishop's early poems. "The Map," the first poem in *North & South*, introduces this concern as the speaker ruminates about a map's cartography: Do the greens and blues that edge the land represent shadows or shallows? Does the land pull at the sea from under, or does the sea embrace the land? To Bishop's unorthodox eye, the map sparks questions that trouble the assumptions at the heart of the mapmaker's project: objective perspective and the authority of visual representation.

Importantly, the speaker in "The Map" interrogates her own authority as a means to query others'. This commitment to self-questioning is an integral aspect of Bishop's poetry, signaled in her early poems by skewed and surreal points of view, tenuous identities, and a blurring of the boundaries between waking and sleeping. Poems such as "Sleeping on the Ceiling" and "Sleeping Standing Up" find comfort in distorted perspectives as they explore the contingency between physical location and ways of interpreting. As their titles suggest, these poems are inspired by that hazy borderland between dreaming and consciousness and are rife with images of the moon and reflective surfaces.

This preoccupation with the porous border between the unconscious and conscious is at the heart of other early poems such as "Love Lies Sleeping" and "The Weed." "Love Lies Sleeping" summons the distinctions between inversion and distortion, asking us to consider the revelatory potentials of each. In this way the poem echoes another early piece called "The Gentleman of Shallot," in which the central character cannot distinguish between the half of himself that is reflected in a mirror and the half that lies outside it. This humorous poem charts the psychic dance of self-definition whereby otherness is internalized in order to reflect a sense of sameness, or self. As in "The Map," reflection (or representation) and reality are fused to delineate one's perspective.

This attention to the slippery space between self and other guides Bishop's blurring of the abject and ideal in her poems about race and class. While Bishop does not write overtly about contemporary politics, she reveals interest in the power dynamics that underpin social relations. This is evident in early poems such as "Cootchie," in which the suicide of a black female servant is introduced within a shifting field of oppositions: black versus white, servant versus master, life versus death, and freedom versus servitude. But the poem ends as the indifferent sweep of a lighthouse's beam blurs the sharp contrasts with which the poem began. Seducing the reader with familiar oppositions, Bishop asks that we question our own patterns of identification and the impulse to make sense of things in the absence of established resolve.

Bishop published her second book, *Poems* (including *North & South* and *A Cold Spring*), in 1955. While the poems in *A Cold Spring* are less surreal, more open, and ostensibly more personal than those in *North & South*, they continue to explore the themes that permeate the first collection. For instance, "Faustina, or Rock Roses" begins where "Cootchie" ends. Having proffered the laden opposition of black versus white in the first poem, Bishop rigorously deconstructs the alignment of whiteness and ideality in "Faustina." Like "Cootchie," this poem is named after a black female servant who tends an elderly white woman. But unlike "Cootchie," "Faustina" presents whiteness as the mark of vulnerability, tired illusions, and tenuous, decayed control.

In 1965 Bishop published her third book of poems, *Questions of Travel*, which is divided into two sections, "Brazil" and "Elsewhere." Most of the poems in this book were written when Bishop lived in Brazil with her lover Lota de Macedo Soares, to whom the collection is dedicated. Pointing to personal details, as well as to the prosy verse of these poems, many critics have suggested that Bishop's later works are more autobiographical than her earlier ones. Indeed, Bishop's later poems are full of scenes and characters from her life in Brazil as well as from her beloved childhood days in Nova Scotia. Nevertheless, it is important to note that Bishop's growing focus on her own life is paralleled by an increasingly intense examination of otherness, as the title of her third book suggests.

Like Bishop's earlier poems, those in *Questions of Travel* query the normative ideals that lie at the heart of our notions of difference. However, these later poems are distinct in the degree to which their speakers are implicated in the ways of seeing that the poems call into question. Take, for example, the first poem in the collection, "Arrival at Santos." The speaker is a tourist in South America, and she is both repulsed and enchanted by the foreignness she encounters. At moments, the poem depicts an embarrassing, unself-conscious xenophobia. At other times, though, the speaker drifts without warning into unguarded empathy. These shifts situate the speaker astride the gulf between native and tourist, self and other. In doing so, the poem illuminates the discomforting liaison between intrigue and abjection.

The next two poems in *Questions of Travel* build upon and respond to the tensions at the heart of "Arrival at Santos." "Brazil, January 1, 1502" immediately establishes a parallel between the speaker and the Spanish colonizers of Brazil as it interweaves the perspectives of both. At the same time, the speaker is identified with the natives of Brazil, in particular with the "maddening" indigenous women who were raped and pushed aside by the colonizers. In comparison to "Arrival at Santos," the stakes of exploration are much higher in this poem, while the opposing parties are even less clearly defined. "Brazil, January 1, 1502" is one of Bishop's few overtly feminist poems, but even so it rejects unhampered distinctions between victim and victimizer; all are implicated in the struggle toward ethical exchange. "Questions of Travel" is the third poem in Bishop's book of the same title, and it is here that she poses the question of whether we should have stayed home, "wherever that may be" (*Complete Poems* 94), a concern central to this collection. The speaker of this poem is distinct in her awareness of the liminal position she occupies; while romanticizing the other, she consistently makes us aware of the part she plays in constructing the other's exotic appeal. Other poems in this book such as "Munuelzhino" and "Squatter's Children" employ this same strategy as they explore issues of class and race more directly.

The central contingency between travel and home, or other and self, that runs through *Questions of Travel* prepares us well for *Geography III*, the last collection published while Bishop was alive. This book contains some of Bishop's most well-known pieces, such as "In the Waiting Room," "Crusoe in England," "The Moose," and the villanelle "One Art." All of the themes that emerge in her earlier works converge in this last collection of verse: explorations of selfhood and otherness, intersections of reality and illusion, and the trials of loving and coping with loss. In keeping with the general trend of Bishop's career, these poems are the most direct and overtly autobiographical of all her poems; indeed, "In the Waiting Room" is narrated by a six-year-old speaker named "Elizabeth." But *Geography III* is also a book written by a poet at the end of her life; it is a book about memory, a book that looks back and, in doing so, finds fresh intrigue in the process of recollection itself. It is not surprising, then, that Bishop's most autobiographical collection of poems challenges most successfully the illusion of coherent selfhood that the term "autobiography" often assumes.

The final version of Bishop's *Complete Poems* was published in 1983. In addition to the books mentioned thus far, this collection contains some uncollected poems, such as the wonderful triad "Rainy Season; Sub-Tropics," and several poems published after *Geography III*. The best of these include "Santarem," a beautiful poem that recalls the style and substance of Bishop's later two books. "Pink Dog" and "Exchanging Hats" are uncharacteristically explicit as they explore female empowerment and the mutability of gender roles, which is perhaps why they remained uncollected while Bishop was alive.

CRITICAL RECEPTION

Bishop studies have proliferated in the last ten years. This recent wave of criticism has remedied the reductive portrait of Bishop offered routinely in earlier readings: shy, reticent, observational, apolitical. Drawing heavily on archival materials, Brett Millier's critical biography *Elizabeth Bishop: Life, and the Memory of It*, depicts a complicated poet of immense passion and deep insecurities; a feminist lesbian who did not believe in separatism or identity politics; a restless, unsettled mind, wary of appearances and staid assumptions. Several published interviews fortify this understanding of Bishop, as does the collection of interviews and anecdotes *Remembering Elizabeth Bishop: An Oral Biography* by Peter Brazeau and Gary Fountain. *Elizabeth Bishop and Her Art*, edited by Lloyd Schwartz and Sybil Estes, contains a diverse selection of essays by several well-known poets and critics and is an excellent starting point for the newcomer to Bishop studies. Although it is somewhat dated, Candace MacMahon's *Elizabeth Bishop: A Bibliography, 1927–1979* offers a listing of primary and secondary sources that is also indispensable to any Bishop scholar.

Several readers have devoted book-length studies to Bishop's poetics of restraint. In *The Unbeliever: The Poetry of Elizabeth Bishop*, Robert Dale Parker argues that Bishop's poetry is skeptical and unsettling, especially in its "unlikely" treatment of motherhood (27). C. K. Doreski asserts that Bishop's disdain of the sentimental and picturesque led critics to conclude erroneously that her poetry is timid. Along these lines, Jerredith Merrin suggests in *An Enabling Humility: Marianne Moore, Elizabeth Bishop, and the Uses of Tradition* that Bishop's appropriations of seventeenth-century male influences demonstrate "commitment rather than self-serving collusion with patriarchal culture, female self-assurance rather than male-placating poetic insurance" (2).

Like Merrin, several critics have been drawn to the complex relationship between Bishop and her mentor Marianne Moore. Two essays, one by Bonnie Costello entitled "Marianne Moore and Elizabeth Bishop" and another by Lynn Keller, "Words Worth a Thousand Postcards: The Bishop/Moore Correspondence," offer helpful overviews of their letters and relations. David Kalstone's classic *Becoming a Poet: Elizabeth Bishop with Marianne Moore and Robert Lowell* provides an elegant if somewhat conventional analysis of Bishop's poetic as it developed in relationship to her two very different yet cherished friends. Betsy Erkkila emphasizes the difficulties as well as the devotion that linked Bishop and Moore in *The Wicked Sisters: Women Poets, Literary History, and Discord*. Joanne Feit Diehl takes a different approach to their relationship in *Elizabeth Bishop and Marianne Moore: The Psychodynamics of Creativity*, employing Melanie Klein's psychoanalytic theory of object-relations to chart a mother/daughter dynamic between Bishop and Moore underpinning their poetics.

Feminist readings of Bishop have blossomed in recent years, illuminating, among other characteristics, her poetics of love and embodiment as well as her struggles as a lesbian poet. *Elizabeth Bishop: The Geography of Gender*, edited by Marilyn May Lombardi, provides a fairly comprehensive sampling of critical approaches to gender in Bishop's poems. A number of the authors represented in this collection have developed their essays into book-length studies. For example, Lorrie Goldensohn, in *Elizabeth Bishop: The Biography of a Poetry*, laments the absence of "wholly original" and "daring" explorations of sexuality in Bishop's verse (72), while arguing that a continuum of discomfort with female embodiment exists throughout Bishop's poetry. In *The Body and the Song: Elizabeth Bishop's Poetics*, Lombardi extends her essay-length analysis of Bishop's physical hardships (such as her asthma and her alcoholism) to show how her poetic is inextricable from her often traumatic experience of embodiment. Victoria Harrison takes a somewhat different approach, utilizing a number of theorists (William James, Nancy Chodorow, Jaques Lacan, Gayatri Spivak, to name a few) to show how Bishop's poetics of intimacy express her antiessentialist feminist stance. This is, in part, how Harrison accounts for Bishop's notorious resistance to women-only anthologies.

While feminist readings of Bishop offer many different and even contrasting perspectives, a majority of them strive to establish an autobiographical emphasis at the heart of Bishop's poetic. Goldensohn expresses this effort well: "[T]he hiding . . . in Bishop's transparently descriptive style, makes it often difficult to see how in this most private, apparently least confessional of contemporary poets, her passion for accuracy and exactitude extends to a passion for autobiographical record" (53). Such readings are part of a tendency within Bishop criticism at large to map her career as progressively autobiographical. Thomas Travisano was one of the first to spark this trend; in *Elizabeth Bishop: Her Artistic Development*, Travisano asserts that Bishop's later work is less guarded and more personal, and therefore more courageous, than her earlier poems.

At the same time, a handful of critics have recently troubled (implicitly or explicitly) this autobiographical focus in their readings of Bishop. In particular, Langdon Hammer contends in his essay "The New Elizabeth Bishop" that Bishop's poetry challenges the "stereotypical subject of contemporary lyric autobiography . . . the expressive self prized in American poetry since mid-century" (148–49). In "Trompe L'Oeil: Elizabeth Bishop's Radical 'I,' " Louis Cuculla argues that Bishop rejects the notion of an autonomous self through an appropriation of conventional tropes, subverting "phallocratic structures" in the process (248). Lee Edelman also contests the notion of Bishop's autobiographical essence in "The Geography of Gender: Elizabeth Bishop's 'In the Waiting Room.' "

Building on this critical tradition, Bonnie Costello's book *Elizabeth Bishop: Questions of Mastery* provides the most sustained and subtle analysis of Bishop's poetics of self. Costello characterizes Bishop as an early postmodernist, based in part on her view that Bishop attempts to "loosen the relation between the eyes and an imperious, transcendental 'I' that would master or possess what it sees by ordering around a center" (6). Such an analysis sheds light on Bishop's fascination with otherness, for as James Longenbach implies in *Modern Poetry after Modernism*, Bishop's perspective on subjective truth underpins a lifelong interest in the mappings of social difference. Nevertheless, Bishop herself was wary of overtly political poetry, and critics have been slow to explore the ways in which her poems treat social conflict. One exception is Margaret Dickie, whose recent book *Stein, Bishop, and Rich: Lyrics of Love, War, and Peace* proffers Bishop's war poetry as a foundation for examining her prevalent interest in racial and class differences. Still, Bishop's complicated treatment of race and class in particular remains relatively underexplored; the time is ripe for fresh work in this field.

BIBLIOGRAPHY

Works by Elizabeth Bishop

North and South. Boston: Houghton, 1946.
Poems: North & South—A Cold Spring. Boston: Houghton, 1955.
The Diary of "Helena Morley." Trans. Elizabeth Bishop. New York: Farrar, 1957. (Prose)
Questions of Travel. New York: Farrar, 1965.
Selected Poems. London: Chatto, 1967.
The Collected Poems. New York: Farrar, 1969.
Geography III. New York: Farrar, 1976.
The Complete Poems 1927–1979. New York: Farrar, 1983.
Elizabeth Bishop: The Collected Prose. Ed. Robert Giroux. New York: Farrar, 1984.
One Art: Letters. Ed. Robert Giroux. New York: Farrar, 1994.

Studies of Elizabeth Bishop

Brazeau, Peter, and Gary Fountain. *Remembering Elizabeth Bishop: An Oral Biography*. Amherst: University of Massachusetts Press, 1994.
Brown, Ashley. "An Interview with Elizabeth Bishop." *Shenandoah* 17 (1966): 3–19.
Costello, Bonnie. *Elizabeth Bishop: Questions of Mastery*. Cambridge: Harvard University Press, 1991.
———. "Marianne Moore and Elizabeth Bishop: Friendship and Influence." *Twentieth Century Literature* 30 (1984): 130–49.
Cuculla, Louis. "Trompe L'Oeil: Elizabeth Bishop's Radical 'I.' " *Texas Studies in Literature and Language* 30.2 (1988): 246–71.
Dickie, Margaret. *Stein, Bishop, and Rich: Lyrics of Love, War, and Peace*. Chapel Hill: University of North Carolina Press, 1997.
Diehl, Joanne Feit. *Elizabeth Bishop and Marianne Moore: The Psychodynamics of Creativity*. Princeton, NJ: Princeton University Press, 1993.
Doreski, C. K. *Elizabeth Bishop: The Restraints of Language*. Oxford: Oxford University Press, 1993.
Edelman, Lee. "The Geography of Gender: Elizabeth Bishop's 'In the Waiting Room.' " *Contemporary Literature* 26 (1985): 179–86.

Erkkila, Betsy. *The Wicked Sisters: Women Poets, Literary History, and Discord.* New York: Oxford University Press, 1992.

Goldensohn, Lorrie. *Elizabeth Bishop: A Biography of a Poetry.* New York: Columbia University Press, 1992.

Hammer, Langdon. "The New Elizabeth Bishop." *Yale Review* 82 (1994): 135–49.

Harrison, Victoria. *Elizabeth Bishop's Poetics of Intimacy.* Cambridge: Cambridge University Press, 1993.

Kalstone, David. *Becoming a Poet: Elizabeth Bishop with Marianne Moore and Robert Lowell.* Ed. Robert Hemenway. New York: Farrar, 1989.

Keller, Lynn. "Words Worth a Thousand Postcards: The Bishop/Moore Correspondence." *American Literature* 55 (1983): 405–29.

Lombardi, Marilyn May. *The Body and the Song: Elizabeth Bishop's Poetics.* Carbondale: Southern Illinois University Press, 1995.

———, ed. *Elizabeth Bishop: The Geography of Gender.* Charlottesville: University Press of Virginia, 1993.

Longenbach, James. *Modern Poetry after Modernism.* New York: Oxford University Press, 1997.

MacMahon, Candace W. *Elizabeth Bishop: A Bibliography, 1927–1979.* Charlottesville: University Press of Virginia, 1980.

McCabe, Susan. *Elizabeth Bishop: Her Poetics of Loss.* University Park: Pennsylvania State University Press, 1994.

Merrin, Jerredith. *An Enabling Humility: Marianne Moore, Elizabeth Bishop, and the Uses of Tradition.* New Brunswick, NJ: Rutgers University Press, 1990.

Millier, Brett. *Elizabeth Bishop: Life, and the Memory of It.* Berkeley: University of California Press, 1993.

Parker, Robert Dale. *The Unbeliever: The Poetry of Elizabeth Bishop.* Urbana: University of Illinois Press, 1988.

Schwartz, Lloyd, and Sybil Estes, eds. *Elizabeth Bishop and Her Art.* Ann Arbor: University of Michigan Press, 1983.

Spires, Elizabeth. "An Afternoon with Elizabeth Bishop." *Vassar Quarterly* 55 (1979): 4–9.

———. "The Art of Poetry XXVII: Elizabeth Bishop." *Paris Review* 22 (1981): 57–83.

———. "Elizabeth Bishop." In *Poets at Work.* Ed. George Plimpton. New York: Viking, 1989. 365–86.

Starbuck, George. "The Work!: A Conversation with Elizabeth Bishop." *Ploughshares* 3 (1977): 11–29.

Travisano, Thomas J. *Elizabeth Bishop: Her Artistic Development.* Charlottesville: University Press of Virginia, 1988.

LOUISE BOGAN
(1897–1970)

Laurie Champion and
Richard J. Williamson

BIOGRAPHY

Louise Bogan was born on August 11, 1897, in Livermore Falls, Maine. She was one of three children born to Daniel Joseph Bogan and Mary Helen (Shields) Bogan, who were of Irish descent. Bogan cited her birth as occurring "ten years before Auden . . . and about two thousand years after Sappho" (Limmer, *Letters* 188). She attended a convent in New Hampshire and later the Girls' Latin School in Boston, where she began writing poetry. She later completed a year at Boston University.

Bogan declined a scholarship to Radcliffe and married Curt Alexander in 1916. They had one daughter, Mathilde, who was born in Panama. Alexander, a professional soldier, died in 1920, after he and Bogan had separated. Bogan moved to Manhattan to pursue a literary career in 1919 and, in 1925, married Raymond Holden, an affluent poet and novelist. They were divorced in 1937. Bogan's poems were first published in the *New Republic*. Later, her poetry appeared in distinguished magazines and journals such as *Nation, Poetry: A Magazine of Verse, Scribner's*, and *Atlantic Monthly*. Bogan's first book of poems, *Body of This Death*, appeared in 1923. This work was followed by the collection *Dark Summer* in 1929. Bogan won the John Reed Memorial Prize from *Poetry* magazine in 1930. In 1933 and 1937, Bogan worked abroad on a Guggenheim Fellowship.

In 1931, Bogan became a regular reviewer of poetry for *New Yorker*, eventually acquiring the position of poetry editor. While in this position, she was recognized for setting the standard for fair, objective criticism of poetry. Bogan's noted fastidiousness as a metrist and technician, evident in such poems as "Medusa," "Knowledge," and "Women," enhanced her insight and skills as a critic of poetry. It was also during this time that Bogan suffered a series of nervous breakdowns.

The Sleeping Fury, which reflects the influence of Yeats on Bogan's work, appeared in 1937, and the following year Bogan received *Poetry* magazine's

Helen Haire Levinson Prize. In the 1950s and 1960s, Bogan published a prose work, *Achievement in American Poetry: 1900–1950*, along with several critically acclaimed collections of poetry. She won the 1954 Bollingen Prize with Leonie Adams. An intensely private person, Bogan disliked publicity throughout her career. During her final years, Bogan experienced several bouts of clinical depression. She died from a coronary occlusion on February 4, 1970, in New York City.

MAJOR WORKS AND THEMES

In her early works, Bogan displays formalism, technical finesse, and a melancholic tone attributed to the influence of William Butler Yeats's poetry. In the early poems published in the *New Republic*, as well as the poems in the collection *Body of This Death* (1923), *Dark Summer* (1929), and *The Sleeping Fury* (1937), Bogan's intellectuality and technical fastidiousness are evident, along with what some critics perceive as remoteness and detachment. Bogan's use of traditional English forms and meter led Yvor Winters to place her among other members of what he termed the "reactionary generation" of modern poets, including Allen Tate, Hart Crane, and Winters himself.

Bogan's first collection of poetry, *Body of This Death* (1923), a collection of twenty-seven poems, presents strong images that represent Bogan's signature trait of tightly written verse. Throughout the collection, subjects emerge such as the difficulties of romantic relationships, sexual frustrations, and comparisons between art and life. The poems display sparseness, direct expression, and avoidance of excess adjectives and adverbs. Some of the poems concern feminist issues, such as the profound "Women," in which the poet achieves a brilliant ironic stance by creating a persona who appears to voice a lamentation for the limitations of women while unwittingly illustrating women's accomplishments and abilities. Writing in the tradition of specifically female lyricists, other poems such as "Betrothed," "Portrait," "My Voice Not Being Proud," "Medusa," "The Crows," "The Changed Woman," "Chanson un Peu Naïve," and "Fifteen Farewell" reflect women speakers and feminist subjects. The collection includes some of Bogan's most successful lyric poems, demonstrating her sparse, technical approach in which irony and the emotional horrors of modern life are enhanced by the straightforward, terse delivery. In future collections, Bogan often included poems from *Body of This Death*.

Among Bogan's most recognized poems are "Medusa," "The Sleeping Fury," "The Dream," "M., Singing," "The Mark," "Song for the Last Act," "Old Countryside," "Dark Summer," and "Hence-Forth, from the Mind." These and other poems reveal the tremendous depth and range of Bogan's poetic accomplishments. They represent the traditional subjects of lyric poetry such as love, time, nature, death, life, and art that Bogan often reveals in her poetry. Her use of traditional metrics, a technique frequently compared with that of English metaphysical poets, is also apparent throughout these and other poems. For example,

"The Dream," written in the framework of formalized poetry and consistent meter, presents frightening personal and nightmarish imagery, personal iconography, and eventual mitigation of anxieties. Similarly, "M., Singing," published in 1937, presents a focus on a psychological theme, metaphorically addressing the means by which deeply established fears and "beings without heart or name" are articulated. This poem reveals Bogan's interest in the emphasis in modern poetry on what she called "subconscious and irrational processes" (*Achievement* 10).

Bogan demonstrates her acute understanding of the beginnings and development of Modern poetry in the critical work *Achievement in American Poetry: 1900–1950*, which was published in 1951. The work presents an incisive examination of the impact of modernism on poets of the modern era. The book also served as a popular and informative introduction to modern poetry. Bogan's *Collected Poems*, published in 1954, presented the high point of her career. The poems in the collection display limpid diction, varied rhythms, dramatic structure, and themes such as physical decay, sexual love, and human relationships. In 1955, several of the critical reviews Bogan had written for *New Yorker* as poetry editor and reviewer appeared in *Selected Criticism, Prose, Poetry* (1955).

In 1968, two years before her death, Bogan published the acclaimed *The Blue Estuaries: Poems, 1923–1968*. The book captured the critical notice and broad acclaim that Bogan believed had eluded the earlier collections *Poems and New Poems* (1941) and *Collected Poems: 1923–1953* (1954). A mysterious poem from *The Blue Estuaries*, "The Meeting," concerns the speaker's dreamlike encounter with a vague, faceless male figure, "a symbol of loss," who ultimately fails to communicate with her or establish a meaningful rapport. The speaker concludes the poem by comparing this male figure to "a faithless brother," who grasps and then releases the speaker's hand.

Both Bogan's poetry and her critical works played important roles in the development of modern poetry. In *Achievement in American Poetry: 1900–1950* (1951), Bogan praises the efforts of modern poets to explore "fresh sources of moral, as well as of aesthetic, courage" (8). Her poems of sparse expression, incisive observation, and penetrating art contributed significantly to that exploration. As critic Malcolm Cowley said of Bogan in 1941: She has "done something that has been achieved by very few of her contemporaries: she has added a dozen or more to our small stock of memorable lyrics. She has added nothing whatever to our inexhaustible store of trash" (625). Thirty years since Bogan's death, Cowley's assessment of her contribution to modern poetry remains true today.

CRITICAL RECEPTION

Although such collections of her poetry as *Poems and New Poems* (1941) and *Collected Poems: 1923–1953* (1954) did not garner the critical praise and broad recognition Bogan wanted, many of her early works, as well as her later collection *The Blue Estuaries: Poems, 1923–1968* (1968), have received enthusiastic critical responses.

From the outset of her career, many of Bogan's noted contemporaries praised her work as representing a significant contribution to the modern movement. Yvor Winters lauded her technique and metrical patterning and placed her in the camp with poets such as Allen Tate, Hart Crane, and the great English lyricists. Marianne Moore compared Bogan with W. H. Auden, Gerard Manley Hopkins, Ezra Pound, William Butler Yeats, and William Carlos Williams and praised her ability to write terse, compact verse. Ford Madox Ford placed Bogan's poetic achievements alongside those of George Herbert and John Donne. Allen Tate referred to Bogan as the most accomplished woman poet of the period. Auden predicted that Bogan's poetry would become important to the American literary canon, whereas Theodore Roethke said that she "writes out of the severest lyrical tradition in English," reflecting techniques that demonstrate "the short poem at its best" (142).

While contemporary critics continue to admire the depth of experience, emotional impact, and brilliant craftsmanship evident in Bogan's verse, some have examined her poems from more recent schools of literary criticism such as feminism and examine Bogan's female speakers and feminist subjects. Contemporary critics continue the patterns established by earlier critics of Bogan's work, comparing her techniques with those of traditional English lyricists and confirming her reputation among critics as a powerful voice and lyricist of the modern period.

BIBLIOGRAPHY

Works by Louise Bogan

Body of This Death. New York: McBride, 1923.
Dark Summer. New York: Scribner's, 1929.
The Sleeping Fury. New York: Scribner's, 1937.
Poems and New Poems. New York: Scribner's, 1941.
Works in the Humanities in Great Britain 1939–1946. Comp. Louise Bogan. Washington, DC: Library of Congress, 1950.
Achievement in American Poetry: 1900–1950. Chicago: Regnery, 1951.
Collected Poems: 1923–1953. New York: Noonday, 1954.
Selected Criticism: Prose, Poetry. New York: Noonday, 1955.
The Golden Journey: Poems for Young People. Ed. Louise Bogan and William Jay Smith. New York: Reilly, 1965.
The Blue Estuaries: Poems, 1923–1968. New York: Farrar, 1968.
A Poet's Alphabet: Reflections on the Literary Art and Vocation. Ed. Robert Phelps and Ruth Limmer. New York: McGraw, 1970.
Journey around My Room: The Autobiography of Louise Bogan. Ed. Ruth Limmer. New York: Viking, 1980.

Studies of Louise Bogan

Auden, W. H. "The Rewards of Patience." Rev. of *Poems and New Poems*, by Louise Bogan. *Partisan Review* 9 (1942): 336–40.

Bowles, Gloria. *Louise Bogan's Aesthetic of Limitation*. Bloomington: Indiana University Press, 1987.

———. "Louise Bogan: To Be (or Not to Be?) Woman Poet." *Women's Studies* 5 (1977): 131–35.

Colasurdo, Christine. "The Dramatic Ambivalence of Self in the Poetry of Louise Bogan." *Tulsa Studies in Women's Literature* 13 (1994): 339–61.

Collins, Martha, ed. *Critical Essays on Louise Bogan*. Boston: G. K. Hall, 1984.

Cowley, Malcolm. "Three Poets." Rev. of *Poems and New Poems*, by Louise Bogan. *New Republic* 10 Nov. 1941: 625–26.

DeShazer, Mary. "My Scourge, My Sister: Louise Bogan's Muse." *Coming to Light: American Women Poets in the Twentieth Century*. Ed. Diane Wood Middlebrook and Marilyn Yalom. Ann Arbor: University of Michigan Press, 1985. 92–104.

Dodd, Elizabeth C. *The Veiled Mirror and the Woman Poet: H. D., Louise Bogan, Elizabeth Bishop, and Louise Glück*. Columbia: University of Missouri Press, 1992.

Elder, Olson. "Louise Bogan and Leonie Adams." *Chicago Review* 8 (1954): 70–87.

Ford, Ford Madox. "The Flame in Stone." Rev. of *The Sleeping Fury*, by Louise Bogan. *Poetry* 50 (1937): 158–61.

Frank, Elizabeth. *Louise Bogan: A Portrait*. New York: Knopf, 1985.

Kerr, Frances. " 'Nearer the Bone': Louise Bogan, Anorexia, and the Political Unconscious of Modernism." *Literature, Interpretation, Theory* 8 (1998): 305–30.

Kerrigan, William. "Louise Bogan: Marvell of Her Day." *Raritan* 18.2 (1998): 63–80.

Knox, Claire E. *Louise Bogan: A Reference Source*. Metuchen, NJ: Scarecrow, 1990.

Miller, Brett C. "Louise Bogan." *American Poets since World War II*. Vol. 169 of *Dictionary of Literary Biography*. Ed. Joseph Conte. Gale: Detroit, 1996. 54–62.

Moore, Marianne. "Compactness Compacted." Rev. of *Poems and New Poems*, by Louise Bogan. *Nation* 15 Nov. 1941: 486.

Novak, Michael Paul. "Love and Influence: Louise Bogan, Rolfe Humphries, and Theodore Roethke." *Kenyon Review* 7 (1985): 9–20.

Peterson, Douglas. "The Poetry of Louise Bogan." *Southern Review* 19 (1983): 73–87.

Ramsay, Paul. "Louise Bogan." *Iowa Review* 1.3 (1970): 116–24.

Ridgeway, Jacqueline. *Louise Bogan*. Boston: Twayne, 1984.

Roethke, Theodore. "The Poetry of Louise Bogan." *Critical Quarterly* 3 (1961): 142–50.

Smith, William Jay. "Louise Bogan: A Woman's Words." *The Streaks of the Tulip: Selected Criticism*. By Smith. New York: Lawrence-Delacorte, 1972. 31–56.

Tate, Allen. Rev. of *The Sleeping Fury*, by Louise Bogan. *Southern Review* 3.1 (1937): 190–92.

Winters, Yvor. "The Poetry of Louise Bogan." Rev. of *Dark Summer*, by Louise Bogan. *New Republic* 16 Oct. 1929: 247–48.

MARITA ODETTE BONNER
(1898–1971)

Allison Berg

BIOGRAPHY

Although among the most prolific African American women writers of the New Negro Renaissance, Marita Bonner has not yet received the critical attention she deserves. Born on June 16, 1898, Marita Odette Bonner grew up in Boston, attending primary and secondary schools in Brookline and graduating from Brookline High School in 1918. While her father, Joseph Bonner, was a native Bostonian, her mother, Mary A. Nowell, was from Petersburg, Virginia, the daughter of a free woman and a slave. Bonner's father attended the Boston Latin School for boys but did not finish high school; he worked as a machinist to support his wife and four children: Joseph, Jr., Bernice Annette, Marita, and Andrew, who died in infancy.

A gifted pianist who received advanced musical training in high school, Bonner chose to focus on English and comparative literature at Radcliffe College, where she enrolled in 1918. Her literary talent was recognized when she won admission into the much-sought-after writing seminar of Charles T. Copeland. Copeland's advice to Bonner—that she continue to write but avoid becoming "bitter" about race—must have struck Bonner as ironic, given Radcliffe's refusal to allow black students to live on campus. Although she was forced to live at home and commute to Radcliffe, Bonner was active on campus, winning the Radcliffe songwriting competition in 1918 and 1922 and founding a chapter of the black sorority Delta Sigma Theta.

After graduating from Radcliffe in 1922, Bonner taught high school for two years at the Bluefield Colored Institute in Bluefield, Virginia, before accepting a position at Armstrong High School in Washington, D.C., where she taught from 1924 to 1930. The premature deaths of her parents (her mother in 1924, her father in 1926) profoundly impacted Bonner, who saw herself as "left alone and struggling" (qtd. in Roses and Randolph "Marita" 167). Yet it was in the midst of this personal crisis that her first essay, and subsequently most oft-quoted work, "On Being Young—a Woman—and Colored," was published in the *Cri-*

sis. Between 1925 and 1929, Bonner published five short stories, three plays, two essays, and two book reviews in *Opportunity* and *Crisis* and was a member of Georgia Douglas Johnson's Washington, D.C., "S" Street Salon. Between 1933 and 1941, she published an additional ten stories. The brief hiatus between 1930 and 1933 coincides with her marriage to Brown University graduate William Occomy and their move to Chicago in 1930. Nonetheless, the birth of three children did not noticeably affect Bonner's literary output in the late 1930s; indeed, she was one of the three most prolific short story contributors to *Opportunity* during this time period (Musser 74).

However, Bonner published nothing between 1941, the year she and her husband joined the First Church of Christ, Scientist, and her death in 1971. It is unclear what influence, if any, her membership in the church had on the cessation of her writing career; another factor may have been Bonner's return to full-time teaching in 1944, when her youngest child reached school age. Between 1944 and her retirement in 1963, Bonner taught at Phillips High School and the Dolittle School in Chicago. While she did not publish after 1941, she evinced an interest in writing as late as 1968, when she indicated on a Radcliffe alumna questionnaire that she was enrolled in a correspondence course offered by the Famous Writers' School (Flynn, "Marita" 228).

Until 1987, when fifteen of Bonner's previously published stories, along with her plays, essays, and five unpublished stories, were collected in *Frye Street and Environs*, Bonner's place among the most important of early twentieth-century African American writers was unacknowledged. The belated scholarly attention given to her work links Bonner to Zora Neale Hurston, Nella Larsen, and Angelina Weld Grimké, other Harlem Renaissance writers whose literary careers halted abruptly.

MAJOR WORKS AND THEMES

Virtually all of Bonner's works deal with the converging influences of race, gender, and class on individual African Americans' pursuit of the American Dream. Because most of her stories provide an unromanticized view of urban environments (chiefly Chicago) and demonstrate a consistent attention to class differences, she is sometimes named as an influence on later black naturalist writers including Richard Wright. However, Bonner was more formally experimental than the term "naturalist" connotes. Moreover, her portraits of urban Chicago portray the city less as a site of dualistic black-white conflict than as a multiethnic microcosm of America in which Irish, Chinese, Jewish, Italian, and Danish immigrants compete with each other and with African Americans for economic and social advancement.

Bonner's 1925 essay "On Being Young—a Woman—and Colored" describes the ruthlessness of this competition, in which African Americans, "pinioned in the seaweed of a Black Ghetto . . . [mill] around like live fish in a basket. Those at the bottom crushed into a sort of stupid apathy by the weight of those on top. Those on top leaping, leaping; leaping to scale the sides; to get out" (*Frye Street* 3–4). This essay is typical of Bonner's impassioned prose style, as well as of her unstinting critique of racial, gender, and economic discrimination. Here she rails against the "warped and stunted" Anglo-Saxon, who can "see a colored woman only as a gross collection of desires, all uncontrolled" (5), and against the rich, who have acquired "Money to build with, money to destroy. Money to swim in. Money to drown in. Money" (6). The essay ends by advising black women to adopt a philosophical patience toward the repeated failure of male-dominated cultures to link "Truth" with "Understanding" (7):

> So—being a woman—you can wait.
> You must sit quietly without a chip. Not sodden—and weighted as if your feet were cast in the iron of your soul. Not wasting strength in everlasting gestures as if two hundred years of bonds and whips had really tricked you into nervous uncertainty.
> But quiet; quiet. Like Buddha—who brown like I am—sat entirely at ease, entirely sure of himself; motionless and knowing. . . .
> . . . "Perhaps Buddha is a woman." (7)

While many of Bonner's short stories focus on the particular difficulties faced by African American women, two of her finest stories, "One Boy's Story" and "Nothing New," offer sympathetic portrayals of young black men equally constrained by racial and gender ideologies. In "One Boy's Story," which interweaves the biblical story of David and Goliath and the classical myth of Oedipus, Bonner renders convincingly the first-person voice of a young, black boy who unknowingly kills his white father. In "Nothing New," the aspiring painter Denny is chastised by his father for displaying a "feminine" interest in art: "Why don't you run and wrestle and race with the other boys? You must be a girl. Boys play rough and fight!" (*Frye Street* 70). When he defies his father's wishes and enrolls in art school, Denny falls in love with a white female student, is attacked by a white male student who tells him to "Stay on your own side!" and, when he acts on his murderous rage toward this student, confirms whites' suspicions that "when a nigger got in school he got crazy" (76). Like many of Bonner's short stories, "Nothing New" combines an objective, almost sociological description of interracial conflict with an impressionistic motif, here involving a "lovely, dusky" purple flower whose "milky perfume" beckons to Denny from the "white kids' side" of Frye Street (72).

In *The Purple Flower*, the most ambitious of her three plays, Bonner uses this same image to symbolize the exclusivity of the American Dream. Variously described by critics as allegorical, surrealistic, and expressionistic, *The Purple Flower* describes the attempts of the "Us's" to gain access to a purple flower located on a hill controlled by "White Devils." The play identifies four possible routes to the Purple Flower—Work, Books, God, and Money—but concludes with the Us's issuing a revolutionary warning to the White Devils: "You have taken blood. You must give blood. . . . There can be no other way" (*Frye Street*

45–46). Departing from the conventions of the naturalistic folk and propaganda plays typical of the Harlem Renaissance, Bonner offers a deliberately nonrealistic setting and racially ambiguous protagonists. The play's ironic use of the term "Skin-of-Civilization" is typical of Bonner's attempts, in such stories as "Black Fronts" and "Drab Rambles," to reveal the constructed nature of racial categories.

CRITICAL RECEPTION

Bonner's writing was so well received at the time of its publication that she frequently won the annual literary prizes offered by *Opportunity* and *Crisis*. Her essay "On Being Young—a Woman—and Colored" and two of her plays received first prizes in *Crisis* competitions, whereas her three-part story "A Possible Triad on Black Notes" took first *and* second place in the 1933 *Opportunity* contest. But because Bonner's stories, essays, and plays were only recently collected into a single volume, there is a dearth of critical commentary on her work prior to 1987, when *Frye Street and Environs* appeared to extremely favorable reviews. *Writing for New York Times Book Review*, Doris Jean Austin reported that "these brilliant flashes of the Chicago ghetto of Bonner's imagination exist perfectly in cameo. Each is a hard, unrelenting jewel of a story, rendered with exquisite craftsmanship (15)," whereas Nellie McKay, writing for the *Women's Review of Books*, concluded that Bonner deserved a place among "major black artists of the 1920s and 1930s (28)."

Joyce Flynn's 1987 introduction to *Frye Street and Environs* and Lorraine Roses and Ruth Randolph's 1987 essay in *Black American Literature Forum* provide insightful, broad-based discussions of Bonner's life and short stories, whereas Judith Musser's 1997 essay in *Studies in Short Fiction* focuses more closely on the theme of education in Bonner's stories. Although short stories make up the bulk of Bonner's published writing, her dramatic works, particularly *The Purple Flower*, have received a disproportionate share of critical attention (see Abramson, Berg and Taylor, Harris, Hill, and McKay).

BIBLIOGRAPHY

Works by Marita Odette Bonner

All works are short stories unless otherwise indicated.
"The Hands—a Story." *Opportunity* 3 (1925): 235–37.
"On Being Young—a Woman—and Colored." *Crisis* 31 (1925): 63–65. (Essay)
"Nothing New." *Crisis* 33 (1926): 17–20.
"The Prison-Bound." *Crisis* 32 (1926): 225–26.
[Pseud. Joseph Maree Andrew]. "And I Passed By." *Ebony and Topaz*. Ed. Charles S. Johnson. New York: National Urban League, 1927. 158–60.
"Drab Rambles." *Crisis* 34 (1927): 335–36, 354–56.

[Pseud. Joseph Maree Andrew]. "One Boy's Story." *Crisis* 34 (1927): 297–99, 316–20.
The Pot Maker (A Play to Be Read). Opportunity 5 (1927): 43–46.
The Purple Flower. Crisis 35 (1928): 9–11, 28, 30. (Play)
Rev. of *Gritny People*, by Robert Emmett Kennedy. *Opportunity* 6 (1928): 130.
"The Young Blood Hungers." *Crisis* 35 (1928): 151, 172. (Essay)
Exit—An Illusion. Crisis 36 (1929): 335–36, 352. (Play)
Rev. of *Autumn Love-Cycle*, by Georgia Douglas Johnson. *Opportunity* 7 (1929): 130.
"A Possible Triad on Black Notes, Part One: There Were Three." *Opportunity* 11 (1933): 205–7.
"A Possible Triad on Black Notes, Part Two: Of Jimmie Harris." *Opportunity* 11 (1933): 242–44.
"A Possible Triad on Black Notes, Part Three: Three Tales of Living: Corner Store." *Opportunity* 11 (1933): 269–71.
"Tin Can." *Opportunity* 12 (1934): 202–5, 236–40.
"A Sealed Pod." *Opportunity* 14 (1936): 88–91.
"Black Fronts." *Opportunity* 16 (1938): 210–14.
[Pseud. Joyce N. Reed]. "Hate Is Nothing." *Crisis* 45 (1938): 388–90, 394, 403–4.
"Hongry Fire." *Crisis* 46 (1939): 360–62, 376–77.
"The Makin's." *Opportunity* 17 (1939): 18–21.
"The Whipping." *Crisis* 46 (1939): 172–74.
"Patch Quilt." *Crisis* 47 (1940): 71, 72, 92.
"One True Love." *Crisis* 48 (1941): 46–47, 58–59.
Frye Street and Environs: The Collected Works of Marita Bonner. Ed. Joyce Flynn and Joyce Occomy Stricklin. Boston: Beacon, 1987.

Studies of Marita Odette Bonner

Abramson, Doris. "Angelina Weld Grimké, Mary T. Burrill, Georgia Douglas Johnson, and Marita O. Bonner: An Analysis of Their Plays." *Black American Literature Forum* 21 (1985): 9–13.
Austin, Doris Jean. "The Voyeur in the Mirror." Rev. of *Frye Street and Environs*, by Marita Bonner. *New York Times Book Review* 13 March 1988: 14–15.
Berg, Allison, and Merideth Taylor. "Enacting Difference: Marita Bonner's *Purple Flower* and the Ambiguities of Race." *African American Review* 32 (1998): 469–80.
Chick, Nancy. "Marita Bonner's Revolutionary Purple Flowers: Challenging the Symbol of White Womanhood." *Langston Hughes Review* 13 (1994–1995): 21–32.
Flynn, Joyce. Introduction. *Frye Street and Environs: The Collected Works of Marita Bonner*. Ed. Joyce Flynn and Joyce Occomy Stricklin. Boston: Beacon, 1987. xi–xxvii.
———. "Marita Bonner Occomy." *Afro-American Writers from the Harlem Renaissance to 1940*. Vol. 51 of *Dictionary of Literary Biography*. Ed. Trudier Harris. Detroit: Gale, 1987. 222–28.
Harris, Will. "Early Black Women Playwrights and the Dual Liberation Motif." *African American Review* 28 (1994): 205–21.
Hill, Errol. "The Revolutionary Tradition in Black Drama." *Theatre Journal* 38 (1986): 408–26.

McKay, Nellie, "Renaissance Woman." Rev. of *Frye Street and Environs*, by Marita Bonner. *Woman's Review of Books* July 1988: 27–28.

———. " 'What Were They Saying?': Black Women Playwrights of the Harlem Renaissance." *The Harlem Renaissance Re-Examined*. Ed. Victor Kramer. New York: AMS, 1987. 129–48.

Musser, Judith. "African American Women and Education: Marita Bonner's Response to the 'Talented Tenth.' " *Studies in Short Fiction* 34 (1997): 73–85.

Roses, Lorraine Elena, and Ruth Elizabeth Randolph. "Bonner (Occomy), Marita Odette." *Harlem Renaissance and Beyond: Literary Biographies of 100 Black Women Writers 1900–1945*. Boston: G. K. Hall, 1990. 18–23.

———. "Marita Bonner: In Search of Other Mothers' Gardens." *Black American Literature Forum* 21 (1987): 165–83.

KAY BOYLE
(1902–1992)

Sharon L. Hileman

BIOGRAPHY

Kay Boyle, the last surviving member of the "lost generation," was born on February 19, 1902, in St. Paul, Minnesota, and died after a seventy-year writing career on December 27, 1992. She was labeled the most dangerous woman in America by S. I. Hayakawa, president of San Francisco State College, who in 1967 peremptorily fired her from her faculty position during the antiwar protests and strike staged at the college. Following a successful lawsuit, Boyle was reinstated as a professor of creative writing and taught until her retirement in 1980.

The daughter, granddaughter, and niece of independent and politically active women, Boyle was well prepared to forge a unique writing career and take strong stances on the political and literary issues that appeared during each decade of her life. An expatriate woman writer in Paris during the 1920s and 1930s, Boyle was the first to sign the twelve-point writers' manifesto "The Revolution of the Word," which affirmed many tenets of modernism and damned "the plain reader." In the 1930s and 1940s, Boyle embraced political issues instead of aesthetic ones. Her novels and stories, set in war-torn Europe, portrayed the rise of Nazism, the collaboration and resistance in countries invaded by the Germans, and the aftermath of war. Blacklisted in the 1950s for supposed Communist affiliation, Boyle could no longer publish much of her work. Following the death of her third husband in 1963, she accepted a faculty position at San Francisco State College and became politically active in causes that would fuel her writing in the 1960s and 1970s.

Boyle's work was always influenced by the places she lived, and she began a nomadic existence in childhood, moving with her family to Philadelphia, Atlantic City, Washington, D.C., and Cincinnati. At the age of twenty, she went to New York, where she became an assistant to Lola Ridge, editor of *Broom* magazine. She enrolled in a fiction writing class at Columbia University and soon had her first poem published. Boyle's writing career truly began in France, however, where she moved with her husband, a French exchange student she had married in 1922. The couple lived with his family for several disastrous months and then relocated to Paris, LeHavre, and Harfleur. During these years Boyle wrote and published poems and short fiction in avant-garde literary magazines such as *This Quarter, Poetry,* and *transition*; her fellow contributors included Pound, Joyce, Hemingway, and Stein. Her first novel was lost by the publisher to whom it was sent, but in her second, *Plagued by the Nightingale,* Boyle employed autobiographical elements and gave voice to the experience of the expatriate woman artist, a topic not articulated in the works of her modern male contemporaries.

Several other novels followed, also patterned upon experiences from her life in the 1920s. *Year before Last* chronicled her relationship with Ernest Walsh, a poet and editor of the literary magazine *This Quarter,* with whom she spent the last months of his life as he painfully succumbed to tuberculosis. Boyle gave birth to Walsh's posthumous child, briefly rejoined her husband, and then returned to Paris, where she developed or renewed friendships with well-known writers and publishers: Robert McAlmon, Eugene Jolas, William Carlos Williams, and Harry and Caresse Crosby. In 1928 she moved into an artists' colony founded by Raymond Duncan (Isadora's brother), which provided experiences and insights that she fictionally depicted in the novel *My Next Bride.* It is the story of a young American woman's quest for identity in Europe, negotiated through promiscuous sexuality, unwanted pregnancy, and unsafe abortion. Again, Boyle used her own experiences to portray the female expatriate artist's conflicts and sufferings.

A period of domesticity followed, for in 1929, Boyle met Laurence Vail, whom she married several years later. The couple already had three children between them from former relationships and would eventually have three more children together. For the next ten years the family was nomadic, moving from France to Austria to England and back to France. Living in these different countries during the 1930s provided Boyle with a new focus for her fiction: international politics. *Death of a Man,* published in 1936, was one of the earliest fictional accounts of Nazism, and her short story "The White Horses of Vienna," which won the O. Henry Short Story Award in 1935, portrayed both Nazis and Jews.

In 1939 Boyle met Baron Joseph von Franckenstein, an Austrian aristocrat and scholar, who actively opposed the Nazis and would eventually become an American citizen and member of the U.S. Foreign Service. He would also become Boyle's third husband and the father of her next two children. In order to accompany him in his career in the Foreign Service, Boyle became the European correspondent for *The New Yorker* and while living in France and Germany began to incorporate the tensions of World War II into her fiction. She set her characters' relationships and conflicts against the background of death, loss, collaboration, resistance, guilt, suffering—all the painful effects of war she observed in Europe.

In the early 1950s, Franckenstein's loyalty was called into question, and both he and Boyle were accused of having Communist affiliations. Although Franckenstein was cleared of the charges, he was soon dismissed from the Foreign Service, and Boyle was fired by *New Yorker*. She was blacklisted and for the rest of the decade had difficulty publishing her writing. In 1962 Franckenstein achieved reinstatement into the Foreign Service, but he died in 1963.

At that time Boyle accepted a teaching position at San Francisco State (SFS) College and became active in civil rights and antiwar activities. Earlier in her life, the Sacco-Vanzetti case had caused Boyle to denounce the U.S. government, and her recent experience with McCarthyism had personalized her awareness of destructive practices sanctioned by the U.S. government. Consequently, she supported the student strike at SFS, hosted Amnesty International meetings in her home, and was twice arrested for blocking the Oakland Induction Center. Her essays about these events were collected in *The Long Walk at San Francisco State*; her poems from the same period appeared in *Testament for My Students*. Boyle's last novel, *The Underground Woman* (1975), incorporated her political experiences, thus combining the autobiographical elements characteristic of her early novels with the political and social concerns of her international fiction. Somewhat anticlimactically, at the age of seventy-eight, the "dangerous" woman who was the subject of a 2,000-page security file accumulated by U.S. intelligence agencies retired from San Francisco State. She remained in California until her death on December 27, 1992.

MAJOR WORKS AND THEMES

Boyle's canon, stretching over six decades, reflects her diversity and enormous productivity: In the course of her career, she published fourteen novels, ten collections of short stories and novellas, six volumes of poetry, four collections of essays, numerous translations and articles, several children's books, a unique dual memoir, and even a few ghostwritten volumes.

Like many modernists, Kay Boyle began her career by writing poetry. She proclaimed, "I have no religion except that of poetry, and in Poe, Whitman, and William Carlos Williams, I recognize the apostles of America" (Spanier, *Artist and Activist* 31). Her innovative use of language, imagery, and form has often been praised; Babette Deutsch, reviewing Boyle's first collection of poetry, commented that her "metaphors explode brilliantly" (514). Boyle published six volumes of poetry, usually one a decade, beginning with *A Glad Day* in 1938. Her early poems were often dedicated to poets or writers who were her friends ("A Valentine for Harry Crosby," "A Christmas Carol for Emanuel Carnevali"), and a number of poems written in the late 1920s were tributes to Ernest Walsh, the poet who had been her lover for several months before dying of tuberculosis.

American Citizen Naturalized in Leadville, Colorado (1944) was a long poem based on the experiences of Boyle's third husband (Joseph Franckenstein), an accomplished skier who trained for war action in Colorado. Boyle dedicated the poem to Carson McCullers, whose husband was also serving overseas when the poem was published. While the poems of the 1920s and 1930s had conflated the personal and aesthetic, with results that were sometimes impenetrable for outsiders, the *Leadville* poem combined the personal with the political. This technique would be even more apparent in Boyle's poems of the 1970s and 1980s, which condemned the racism, imperialism, and militarism that she opposed through her political actions.

Although Boyle originally defined herself as a poet, it was as a short story writer and novelist that she would achieve her greatest literary success. Early works such as *Wedding Day and Other Stories* (1930), *Plagued by the Nightingale* (1931), *Year before Last* (1932), and *My Next Bride* (1934) developed themes that the poems could not. In her fiction, Boyle was able to foreground problems in relationships and depict obstacles that prevented characters from achieving love. Bourgeois morality, the physical death of a lover, or the pain of exile and alienation were portrayed in the fiction to explain why characters could not establish close or lasting relationships.

In *Gentlemen, I Address You Privately* (1933), one of the earliest novels about homosexuality, Boyle's characters had to contend with problems created by sexual preference. Failed relationships in *Gentlemen* occurred due to the misunderstandings among and different needs of homosexuals, heterosexuals, and bisexuals. As this subject matter indicates, Boyle was unafraid of presenting sexual issues, whether in the homosexuality of *Gentlemen* or the adulterous and sexually promiscuous behavior of her female protagonists.

Boyle was interested in exploring such female protagonists' quests for identity. She specifically focused on the conflicts experienced by the young American woman living in Europe who had to learn how to reconcile her needs for independence and self-actualization with her desire for love and a fulfilling relationship. A partial resolution was postulated in *My Next Bride* where the heroine was denied a successful romantic relationship but instead entered into a rich and supportive friendship with another woman. (In this instance, Boyle denied having portrayed a lesbian relationship, which critics discerned.)

Believing it was necessary to go beyond the autobiographical female bildungsroman of her early novels, Boyle began to incorporate political concerns into works such as *Death of a Man* and *The White Horses of Vienna and Other Stories*, both published in 1936. The novel contained one of the earliest fictional portrayals of Nazism in the character of an idealistic doctor who believed the Nazis would provide solutions to social problems. Boyle was accused of harboring Nazi sympathies in *Death of a Man*, although her actual theme concerned the problem of finding causes and people worthy of commitment. Her later fiction would more clearly express the need for protagonists to engage in moral actions and develop political consciences.

Such themes inform Boyle's international novels written during the 1940s, which contain passages of journalistic reporting and are set against the backdrop of World War II. *Primer for Combat* (1942) is a novel in diary form written by an American woman protagonist living in a French village. The diary depicts the responses of the French over a 100-day period as they realize the Germans will defeat them. Boyle tries to explain the dual French responses of collaboration and resistance, realizing that these would be the alternatives for people in all countries that were defeated by the Germans. *Thirty Stories* (1946) provided Austrian, English, American, as well as French accounts of the war and included the 1941 O. Henry Award–winning story "Defeat," which portrayed the French after the armistice.

Hoping to reach a larger reading audience and also hoping for financial success, Boyle retained her wartime subject material and French settings but incorporated them into the genre of the adventure story. The resulting two novels, *Avalanche* (1944) and *A Frenchman Must Die* (1946), were both serialized by the *Saturday Evening Post*. In *Avalanche*, Boyle portrayed the French Resistance movement and hoped in this way to make Americans aware of the wartime courage and sacrifices of the French. In addition to writing one of the first books about the Resistance, Boyle made another original contribution by placing a female protagonist—an adventure heroine—at the center of action in each of her thrillers.

Her last two war novels were grim critiques rather than rollicking adventures. In *1939* (1948), she depicted the ravages of war in personal and national terms by showing its effects upon two separated lovers and upon neighboring countries that had taken opposite sides. *His Human Majesty* (1949) depicted Americans negatively, for Boyle's critique of militarism and oppression was not limited to the fascists. She realized that democracies could engage just as easily as totalitarian states in repressive practices stemming from racism, xenophobia, and a patriarchal desire for control.

Her specific condemnations of militarism appeared in *The Smoking Mountain: Stories of Postwar Germany* (1951) and *Generation without Farewell* (1960). The latter novel, like Boyle's early autobiographical fiction, presents a quest, but here the protagonist is German and male, a former prison of war (POW) who must resolve questions concerning his own and his country's guilt in order to establish a postwar identity.

Boyle's last novel, *The Underground Woman* (1975), resurrected the autobiographical female protagonist, but now she appeared as an older woman assured of her identity. Instead of being torn between art and love, she was a political activist willing to be arrested for her beliefs. Although Boyle had seemingly abandoned the personal elements characterizing her fiction of the early 1930s, preferring to emphasize political conflicts in her work of the 1940s and 1950s, she found a way to combine the two in her fiction, poetry, and essays of the 1960s and 1970s. Realizing that the personal is political is not only Boyle's insight but that of a whole generation for which she speaks in her protests against racism, war, militarism, and lack of human connection.

CRITICAL RECEPTION

Kay Boyle is considered one of the best American short story writers of the twentieth century, although her reputation has fluctuated over her long literary career. Her first publication, *Short Stories* (1929), was praised by William Carlos Williams, but he feared she might have trouble finding an audience. Critics of the 1930s agreed, believing Boyle was primarily a stylist and that her work was too difficult to read. On the other hand, Katherine Anne Porter praised Boyle's ability to tell a story and thought her use of symbolism and allegory in *Plagued by the Nightingale* was superb. Editors of the Modern Fiction series published by the Southern Illinois University Press evidently agreed with Porter, for they republished *Plagued by the Nightingale* in 1966 and *Year before Last* in 1969.

Boyle's contemporaries often disliked her themes and choices of content, which they dismissed as "trivial" (Walton 6) or "so much junk" (Rev. of *My Next Bride* 1564). This response was particularly evident in the writings of male critics assessing Boyle's portrayal of the expatriate woman artist in *My Next Bride*. Even when Boyle incorporated political issues into her fiction, critics were dissatisfied. *Death of a Man*, one of the earliest fictional treatments of Nazism, was said to lack "significant material" (Kazin 6). Misunderstanding Boyle's political position, some critics accused her of being pro-Nazi because she created a positive character with Nazi sympathies. According to Mark Van Doren, her novel tried to "hypnotize the reader" into a state of "mystical fascism" (494).

Boyle's later war fiction usually elicited more positive critical responses. Malcolm Cowley thought *Primer for Combat* was "accurate" and "honest" (614), and Raoul de Roussy de Sales said that "nothing better has been written on France since the Germans got there" (152). *Time* praised *Generation without Farewell* for its "cameralike shots of war's destruction" (Rev. of *Generation without Farewell* 94). However, when Boyle wrote her adventure novels serialized in the *Saturday Evening Post*, she unleashed a critical tirade from Edmund Wilson. Appalled at her willingness to write for commercial gain, he denounced *Avalanche* in *New Yorker* as "nothing but a piece of pure rubbish" (66).

Boyle's later political writings have been generally well received, with the *London Times Literary Supplement* praising her for upholding the American radical intellectual tradition (Chisholm 1076). Even *New Yorker* was positive in its assessment of the heroine of *Underground Woman*.

In spite of divided critical evaluations, Boyle was the recipient of numerous literary awards and honors. These include two O. Henry Awards (1935 and 1941), two Guggenheim Fellowships (1934 and 1961), election to the Henry James Chair of the American Academy of Arts and Letters (1979), a National Endowment for the Arts Senior Fellowship for Literature (1980), an endowment from the Fund for Poetry (1987), and honorary doctorates from five universities. For the past three decades Boyle has been the subject of special Modern Language Association (MLA) sessions (1979, 1987, 1991), and the 1980s heralded a resurgence of academic interest in her life and work.

Sandra Spanier published *Kay Boyle: Artist and Activist*, a critical biography, in 1986. It is a scholarly, chronological assessment of Boyle's work and contains a lengthy selected bibliography. In 1988, Spanier edited a special issue on Boyle for *Twentieth Century Literature*. Many of the articles from that volume are included in Marilyn Elkins's *Critical Essays on Kay Boyle* (1997), although the book also contains previously unpublished essays and twenty-two full-length reviews ranging from the 1920s to the 1980s. Excerpts from other reviews as well as transcripts of interviews and some of Boyle's unpublished work appear in Elizabeth Bell's *Kay Boyle: A Study of the Short Fiction* (1992). Bell's book provides a chronology and a selected bibliography that lists the contents of each collection of Boyle's stories. A major study of Boyle's fiction authored by Marilyn Elkins appeared as *Metamorphosizing the Novel: Kay Boyle's Narrative Innovations* (1993). In it, Elkins uses gender analysis to discuss Boyle's themes, her construction of modernism, and the critical reception of her fiction. Finally, a biography entitled *Kay Boyle: Author of Herself* (1994) was published by Joan Mellen, but its portrait of Boyle is extrapolated from thoughts and actions of her characters. Greater insights into Boyle may emerge from the collection of her letters that Sandra Spanier is currently preparing.

BIBLIOGRAPHY

Works by Kay Boyle

Short Stories. Paris: Black Sun, 1929.
Wedding Day and Other Stories. New York: Cape, 1930.
Plagued by the Nightingale. 1931. Carbondale: Southern Illinois University Press, 1966. (Novel)
Year before Last. 1932. Carbondale: Southern Illinois University Press, 1969. (Novel)
The First Lover and Other Stories. New York: Smith, 1933.
Gentlemen, I Address You Privately. New York: Smith, 1933. (Novel)
My Next Bride. New York: Harcourt, 1934. (Novel)
Death of a Man. New York: Harcourt, 1936. (Novel)
365 Days. Ed. Kay Boyle, Laurence Vail, and Nina Conarain. New York: Harcourt, 1936. (Short stories)
The White Horses of Vienna and Other Stories. New York: Harcourt, 1936.
A Glad Day. Norfolk, CT: New Directions, 1938. (Poems)
Monday Night. New York: Harcourt, 1938. (Novel)
The Crazy Hunter: Three Short Novels. New York: Harcourt, 1940.
Primer for Combat. New York: Simon, 1942. (Novel)
American Citizen Naturalized in Leadville, Colorado. New York: Simon, 1944. (Poem)
Avalanche. New York: Simon, 1944. (Novel)
A Frenchman Must Die. 1946. New York: New Directions, 1957. (Novel)

Thirty Stories. New York: Simon, 1946.
1939. New York: Simon, 1948. (Novel)
His Human Majesty. New York: McGraw, 1949. (Novel)
The Smoking Mountain: Stories of Postwar Germany. New York: McGraw, 1951.
The Seagull on the Step. New York: Knopf, 1955. (Novel)
Three Short Novels. 1958. New York: Penguin, 1982.
Generation without Farewell. New York: Knopf, 1960. (Novel)
Breaking the Silence: Why a Mother Tells Her Son about the Nazi Era. New York:
     Institute of Human Relations, 1962. (Essays)
Collected Poems. New York: Knopf, 1962.
Nothing Ever Breaks Except the Heart. New York: Doubleday, 1966. (Short stories)
Kay Boyle and Robert McAlmon. *Being Geniuses Together 1920–1930.* 1968. San Fran-
     cisco: North Point, 1984. (Dual autobiography)
The Long Walk at San Francisco State and Other Essays. New York: Grove, 1970.
Testament for My Students and Other Poems. New York: Doubleday, 1970.
Enough of Dying! Voices for Peace. Ed. Kay Boyle and Justine Van Gundy. New York:
     Dell, 1972. (Essays)
The Underground Woman. New York: Doubleday, 1975. (Novel)
Fifty Stories. New York: Doubleday, 1980.
This Is Not a Letter and Other Poems. Los Angeles: Sun & Moon, 1985.
Words That Must Somehow Be Said: The Selected Essays of Kay Boyle, 1927–1984. San
     Francisco: North Point, 1985.
Life Being the Best and Other Stories. New York: New Directions, 1988.
The Collected Poems of Kay Boyle. Port Townsend, WA: Copper Canyon, 1991.

Studies of Kay Boyle

Bell, Elizabeth S. "Call Forth a Good Day: The Nonfiction of Kay Boyle." *Twentieth
     Century Literature* 34 (1988): 384–91.
————. *Kay Boyle: A Study of the Short Fiction.* New York: Twayne, 1992.
Bourjaily, Vance. Rev. of *Fifty Stories,* by Kay Boyle. *New York Times Book Review* 28
     Sept. 1980: 9, 32.
Bullock, Elizabeth. Rev. of *Avalanche,* by Kay Boyle. *Book Week* 23 Jan. 1944: 2.
Burt, Struthers. "Kay Boyle's Coincidence and Melodrama." *Saturday Review of Liter-
     ature* 15 Jan. 1944: 6.
Canby, H. S. Rev. of *Gentlemen, I Address You Privately,* by Kay Boyle. *Saturday
     Review of Literature* 4 Nov. 1933: 233.
Cantwell, Robert. Rev. of *Gentlemen, I Address You Privately,* by Kay Boyle. *New
     Republic* 13 Dec. 1933: 136.
Carpenter, Richard C. "Kay Boyle." *College English* 15 (1953): 81–87.
———— "Kay Boyle: The Figure in the Carpet." *Critique* 7 (1964–1965): 65–78.
Chisholm, Anne. Rev. of *Words That Must Somehow Be Said,* by Kay Boyle. *London
     Times Literary Supplement* 27 Sept. 1985: 1076.
Clark, Suzanne. "Revolution, the Woman, and the Word: Kay Boyle." *Twentieth Century
     Literature* 34 (1988): 322–33.
Cowley, Malcolm. "Lost Worlds." *New Republic* 9 Nov. 1942: 614.
Deutsch, Babette. "An Unhabitual Way." *Nation* 12 Nov. 1938: 514.

Diamonstein, Barbaralee, ed. "Kay Boyle." *Open Secrets: Ninety-four Women in Touch with Our Time*. New York: Viking, 1972. 23–27.

Drew, Kathy. "Jails Don't Daunt Protesting Grandmother: Kay Boyle Dedicates Self to Human Dignity." *Lost Generation Journal* 4 (1976): 14–23.

Elkins, Marilyn, ed. *Critical Essays on Kay Boyle*. New York: G. K. Hall, 1997.

———. *Metamorphosizing the Novel: Kay Boyle's Narrative Innovations*. New York: Lang, 1993.

Gado, Frank. "Kay Boyle: From the Aesthetics of Exile to the Polemics of Return." Diss. Duke University, 1968.

Rev. of *Generation without Farewell*, by Kay Boyle. *Time* 25 Jan. 1960: 94.

Grumbach, Doris. Rev. of *The Underground Woman*, by Kay Boyle. *New Republic* 8 Feb. 1975: 3.

Hart, Elizabeth. Rev. of *My Next Bride*, by Kay Boyle. *Books* 11 Nov. 1934: 4.

Hatlen, Burton. "Sexual Politics in Kay Boyle's *Death of a Man*." *Twentieth Century Literature* 34 (1988): 347–62.

Hollenberg, Donna. "Abortion, Identity Formation, and the Expatriate Woman Writer: H. D. and Kay Boyle in the Twenties." *Twentieth Century Literature* 40 (1994): 499–517.

Jackson, Byron K. "The Achievement of Kay Boyle." Diss. University of Florida, 1968.

Kazin, Alfred. "Kay Boyle's New Novel." *New York Times Book Review* 11 Oct. 1936: 6–7.

Litwak, Leo. "Kay Boyle—Paris Wasn't Like That." *New York Times Book Review* 15 July 1984: 1t.

MacNiven, Ian S. "Kay Boyle's High Country: *His Human Majesty*." *Twentieth Century Literature* 34 (1988): 363–74.

Marini, Myra. Rev. of *Year before Last*, by Kay Boyle. *New Republic* 13 July 1932: 242.

Mellen, Joan. *Kay Boyle: Author of Herself*. New York: Farrar, 1994.

Meyer, Martin. "Kay Boyle's Postwar Germany." *Germany and German Thought in American Literature and Cultural Criticism*. Ed. Peter Freese. Essen: Verlag Die Blaue Eule, 1990. 205–29.

Meynell, Viola. Rev. of *Plagued by the Nightingale*, by Kay Boyle. *Nation* 1 Aug. 1931: 144.

Moore, Harry T. "Kay Boyle's Fiction." *Age of the Modern and Other Essays*. Carbondale: Southern Illinois University Press, 1971. 32–36.

Morse, Deborah Denenholz. "*My Next Bride*: Kay Boyle's Text of the Female Artist." *Twentieth Century Literature* 34 (1988): 334–46.

Porter, Katherine Anne. "Example to the Young." *New Republic* 22 Apr. 1931: 279–80.

Rev. of *My Next Bride*, by Kay Boyle. *Christian Century* 5 Dec. 1934: 1564.

"Revolution of the Word." *transition* 16–17 (1929): n. pag.

Roussy de Sales, Raoul de. Rev. of *Primer for Combat*, by Kay Boyle. *Atlantic Monthly* Dec. 1942: 152.

Sharp, Roberta. "A Bibliography of Works by and about Kay Boyle." *Bulletin of Bibliography* 35 (1978): 180–91.

Spanier, Sandra Whipple. *Kay Boyle: Artist and Activist*. Carbondale: Southern Illinois University Press, 1986.

———. "Kay Boyle: In a Woman's Voice." *Faith of a (Woman) Writer*. Ed. Alice Kessler-Harris and William McBrien. Westport, CT: Greenwood, 1988. 59–70.

———. "Kay Boyle: No Past Tense Permitted." *Twentieth Century Literature* 34 (1988): 245–57.

Strachey, Richard. Rev. *Wedding Day and Other Stories*, by Kay Boyle. *Nation* 24 Sept. 1932: 347.

Tooker, Dan, and Roger Hofheins, eds. "Kay Boyle." *Fiction! Interviews with Northern California Novelists*. New York: Harcourt, 1976. 15–35.

Trilling, Diana. Rev. of *Avalanche*, by Kay Boyle. *Nation* 22 Jan. 1944: 105.

Uehling, Edward M. "Tails You Lose: Kay Boyle's War Fiction." *Twentieth Century Literature* 34 (1988): 375–83.

Van Doren, Mark. "Under the Swastika." *Nation* 24 Oct. 1936: 494.

Walton, Edith H. Rev. of *My Next Bride*, by Kay Boyle. *New York Times Book Review* 11 Nov. 1934: 6.

Williams, William Carlos. "The Somnambulists." 1929. *Twentieth Century Literature* 34 (1988): 313–17.

Wilson, Edmund. "Kay Boyle and the *Saturday Evening Post*." *New Yorker* 15 Jan. 1944: 66–70.

PEARL S. BUCK
(1892–1973)

Ann W. Engar

BIOGRAPHY

Pearl Sydenstricker Buck was born Pearl Comfort Sydenstricker on June 26, 1892, in Hillsboro, West Virginia, to Abraham and Carie (Stulting) Sydenstricker, Presbyterian ministers on home leave from China. As an infant, Buck was taken to China, where her family eventually settled in Chinkiang. Of her six siblings, only a brother eleven years older than she and a sister seven years younger survived. Her experiences as a minority and her unhappy home life helped shape both her commitment to cultural pluralism and the large family she later created for herself.

Buck learned colloquial Chinese from her nurse, classical Chinese from a tutor, and English literature from her mother. She wandered Chinkiang's streets with her nurse, occasionally played with Chinese children, and attended the local Chinese theater. Though she felt bicultural, she also felt like a homeless outsider.

On her mother's insistence Buck from 1910 to 1914 attended Randolph-Macon Women's College in the United States, where she published short stories and poems in the undergraduate literary magazine and learned about feminist issues. Soon after her graduation, her mother became ill, and Buck returned to China. In 1917 she married J. Lossing Buck, an agricultural missionary and economist. For several years they lived in Nanhsuchou in the rural province of Anhwei and then moved to Nanking, where Lossing became a university professor. In 1920 Buck gave birth to a daughter, who suffered from phenylketonuria (PKU) and became mentally retarded; and then, on discovery of a tumor, Buck had a hysterectomy.

Buck's mother's death in 1921 inspired her to write her mother's biography, her first book (published as *The Exile* in 1936), and to aspire to become a writer. Her first professionally published work, the essay "In China, Too," appeared in the *Atlantic* in 1924. That same year she and her husband traveled to the United States and enrolled at Cornell. They adopted a child, the first of seven Buck would adopt. A year later she received a master's in English. After their return to China, she published several more short stories. She and her husband lived through tumultuous years of political revolution and an unhappy marriage.

In 1929 Buck returned to the United States to place her daughter Carol in a humane institution. She received word her first novel, *East Wind, West Wind*, would be published by the John Day Company, which over the years published almost everything she wrote. In 1931 she published *The Good Earth*, which has been one of the best-selling books of the twentieth century. John Day's president and publisher, Richard Walsh, became Buck's second husband after her 1935 divorce.

In 1934, with China in political turmoil, Buck moved to Green Hills Farm in Bucks County, Pennsylvania (now the site of the Pearl S. Buck Foundation, created in 1964). This home became her headquarters for literary and social activity. She wrote over forty novels; plays for stage, radio, television, and film; juvenile literature; biographies and autobiographies; articles; and miscellaneous works on children, gender issues, democracy, America, and other topics. She promoted cross-cultural understanding (including founding the East and West Association); was an advocate for the children, especially the disabled, mentally ill, and racially mixed (including founding Welcome House); and worked in the civil rights and women's movements.

Buck died of lung cancer on March 6, 1973, in Danby, Vermont.

MAJOR WORKS AND THEMES

Buck's masterwork, *The Good Earth*, sets the pattern for her later works. The novel portrays the life of Wang Lung, a farmer in one of the northern provinces of China who eventually prospers and becomes a wealthy landowner. It contains elements of Chinese culture to inform and fascinate American readers: the practices of slavery (including the selling of children), foot-binding, multiple wives and concubines, infanticide, and opium addiction.

Many themes of the novel, however, are not foreign to American readers. Lung's drive for success and his buying of more land whenever he gets additional money are not far from Benjamin Franklin's industry in rising to success in Philadelphia. Lung's struggles as a farmer, especially when he has to leave his land temporarily in a time of great drought, must have seemed very familiar to Americans in the midst of the Dust Bowl. His great love of the land—his refusal to sell it in even the worst of times, the strength he draws from it, his return to it at the end of his life after years of city living, and his deathbed insistence that his sons never sell the land—resembles such books as Willa Cather's *My Ántonia* with its main character who draws life from and prospers because of the soil.

Still another timeless and cross-cultural theme of the book is the differences between generations. Lung values his land, is careful with money, loves his family, and cares what others say of him. Each of his three sons, who are referred to only as "eldest son," "second son," and "youngest son," has characteristics that either exaggerate their father's weaknesses or oppose his values. The eldest son is a spendthrift and very proud; the second son cares little for reputation but is obsessed with money; the third son rejects family in favor of war. None cares anything about the land.

Buck also is interested in the abilities and the plights of women. Lung treats his wife O-lan as a servant and greatly neglects her. She is a strong, silent but ugly woman whose courage, industry, and endurance form the moral center of the novel. She despises the rich House of Hwang, where she was a slave, and is wounded when her husband takes as mistress her old master's concubine. Lung treats her as dim; but in crisis situations she is the one who speaks up and acts. She subsumes her personal self in her familial roles. At her death, Lung recognizes what she has meant to him and done for him as he says it is as though half of him were buried with her.

Similar themes occur in Buck's other works. The vulnerable life of Chinese—indeed all—women is portrayed in *The Mother*, with a main character who rejoices in birth and new life but must endure tragic relationships with a husband who deserts his family, an unfeeling daughter-in-law, an abused blind daughter, and a son beheaded by Communists. In *Dragon Seed*, Jade, who wants to be educated and fight invaders, represents the new free-thinking and clever young women of China. In *The Living Reed* the unbelievably beautiful queen of Korea, wiser and more powerful than her husband, must learn the life of common people in her country.

The Living Reed is typical of many of Buck's works. As *The Good Earth* depicted China, it contains much teaching about Korea—its geography, history, religion, literature, customs, and political turmoil. It shows generational conflict between Kim Il-han, a noble and political counselor to the queen who sees alliance with the West as inevitable, and his poet–statesman father who dreams of Korea's past glory and remains stubbornly isolationist. Il-han, like Wang Lung, recognizes the power that comes from land, but his love is for his nation, not his own property.

Buck's strength as a writer thus lies in her themes of the humanness of non-Western peoples: their love of family and the land, their struggles between generations and genders, their political strife and even cruelty, and their ultimate importance to the Western world. In addition to *The Good Earth*, her finest works are the biographies of her parents, *The Exile* and *The Fighting Angel*, which reveal missionaries' heroism but also zealous failures. Her voluminous other works explore many subjects, most important, family life, gender, colonialism and imperialism, and children.

CRITICAL RECEPTION

Buck's early works gained much critical praise, though Chinese authorities were not always pleased with her stances. *The Good Earth* was awarded the Pulitzer Prize, translated into more than thirty languages, and adapted into a play and film. In 1935 she was awarded the William Dean Howells medal for the finest work in American fiction 1930 to 1935. In 1936 she was elected to membership in the National Institute of Arts and Letters. In 1938 she became the first woman and third American to receive the Nobel Prize, awarded for her rich, generous description of Chinese peasant life and masterpieces of biography. The awarding of the prize to Buck was controversial and for years was cited as an example of the weaknesses of the judging.

Buck's later works received much criticism for their didacticism and melodrama, though they continued to be popular, especially with women. Some criticism of her work was gender or ethnically based; some was jealousy over her winning the Nobel Prize or her commercial success. Her own criteria for good writing were that it please, amuse, and entertain; but the serious subject matter of her works—foreign affairs, gender issues, child welfare, the history and culture of Asian nations—belies such criteria. In fact, Buck used her novels as political propaganda and protest and as educational tools.

From 1940 to 1990, Buck experienced a huge fall in critical approval and subsequent neglect by scholars. No full-length critical study of works was published until Paul A. Doyle's *Pearl S. Buck* in 1965; and when nothing superseded it, Doyle revised and edited it in 1980. However, in 1992, beginning with a centennial symposium at her alma mater, Randolph-Macon Women's College, she began to receive greater critical attention. Maxine Hong Kingston praised Buck for presenting Chinese characters with empathy and compassion and "translating my parents to me . . . and giving me our ancestry and our habitation" (Conn xiii). In the 1992 *Philadelphia Inquirer* article "Why Doesn't Pearl Buck Get Respect?" James Thomson claimed Buck is "the most influential Westerner to write about China since thirteenth-century Marco Polo" (A15).

In 1996 Peter Conn published Buck's biography and argued that although many of her works are considered popular fiction rather than serious literature, their wide reading audience and influence demand a more active place in American cultural history. Furthermore, he pleads for a fresh appraisal of her work, particularly her biographies. Kang Liao's 1997 *Pearl S. Buck: A Cultural Bridge across the Pacific* argues that Buck's works have far more social, historical, and cultural than literary value but praises her for progressive liberal thinking, her humanitarianism, and her multiculturalism.

BIBLIOGRAPHY

Major Works by Pearl S. Buck

East Wind, West Wind. New York: Day, 1930. (Novel)
The Good Earth. New York: Day, 1931. (Novel)
Sons. New York: Day, 1932. (Novel)
The Young Revolutionist. New York: Friendship, 1932. (Children's literature)
All Men Are Brothers. New York: Day, 1933. (Translation of *Shui Hu Chuan*)

The Mother. New York: Day, 1934. (Novel)
A House Divided. New York: Reynal, 1935. (Novel)
The Exile. New York: Reynal, 1936. (Biography)
The Fighting Angel: Portrait of a Soul. New York: Reynal, 1936. (Biography)
The Chinese Novel. Nobel lecture delivered before the Swedish Academy at Stockholm.
      12 Dec. 1938. New York: Day, 1939. (Literary criticism)
This Proud Heart. New York: Reynal, 1938. (Novel)
The Patriot. New York: Day, 1939. (Novel)
Other Gods. New York: Day, 1940. (Novel)
Of Men and Women. New York: Day, 1941. (Gender studies)
Dragon Seed. New York: Day, 1942. (Novel)
The Promise. New York: Day, 1943. (Novel)
What America Means to Me. New York: Day, 1943. (Nonfiction)
Talk about Russia with Masha Scott. New York: Day, 1945. (Nonfiction)
[Pseud. John Sedges]. *The Townsman.* New York: Day, 1945. (Novel)
Pavilion of Women. New York: Day, 1946. (Novel)
The Big Wave. New York: Day, 1948. (Children's literature)
Peony. New York: Day, 1948. (Novel)
Kinfolk. New York: Day, 1949. (Novel)
My Several Worlds: A Personal Record. New York: Day, 1954. (Autobiography)
Imperial Woman. New York: Day, 1956. (Novel)
Letter from Peking. New York: Day, 1957. (Novel)
A Bridge for Passing. New York: Day, 1962. (Biography)
The Living Reed. New York: Day, 1963. (Novel)

Studies of Pearl S. Buck

Bellman, Samuel I. "Popular Writers in the Modern Age: Constance Rourke, Pearl Buck,
    Marjorie Kinnan Rawlings, and Margaret Mitchell." *American Women Writers:*
    Bibliographical Essays. Ed. Maurice Duke, Jackson R. Bryer, and M. Thomas
    Inge. Westport, CT: Greenwood, 1983. 353–78.
Block, Irwin. *The Life of Pearl Buck.* New York: Crowell, 1973.
Conn, Peter. *Pearl S. Buck: A Cultural Biography.* Cambridge: Cambridge University
    Press, 1996.
Cwiklik, Robert. *Pearl S. Buck.* New York: Kipling, 1988.
———. *Pearl S. Buck: China's Witness.* New York: Kipling, 1989.
Doyle, Paul A. *Pearl S. Buck.* 1965. New York: Twayne, 1980.
Harris, Theodore F. *Pearl S. Buck: A Biography.* New York: Day, 1969.
———. *Pearl S. Buck, Vol. 2: Her Philosophy in Her Letters.* New York: Day, 1971.
Liao, Kang. *Pearl S. Buck: A Cultural Bridge across the Pacific.* Westport, CT: Green-
    wood, 1997.
Lipscomb, Elizabeth, Frances E. Webb, and Peter Conn, eds. *The Several Worlds of*
    Pearl S. Buck: Essays Presented at a Centennial Symposium, Randolph-Macon
    Women's College, March 26–28, 1992. Westport, CT: Greenwood, 1994.
Quach, Gianna. "Chinese Fictions and the American Alternative: Pearl Buck and Emily
    Hahn." *Tamkang Review* 24.1 (1993): 75–116.
Spencer, Cornelia. *The Exile's Daughter: A Biography of Pearl S. Buck.* New York:
    Coward, 1944.

————. *Pearl S. Buck: Revealing the Human Heart*. Chicago: Encyclopedia Britannica, 1964.

Starling, Nora. *Pearl S. Buck: A Woman in Conflict*. Piscataway, NJ: New Century, 1983.

Thompson, Dody W. "Pearl Buck." *American Winners of the Nobel Literary Prize*. Ed. Warren G. French and Walter E. Kidd. Norman: University of Oklahoma Press, 1968. 85–110.

Thomson, James C., Jr. "Why Doesn't Pearl Buck Get Respect?" *Philadelphia Inquirer* 24 July 1992: A15.

FABIOLA CABEZA DE BACA GILBERT (1894–1991)

Kate K. Davis

BIOGRAPHY

Fabiola Cabeza de Baca, a descendant of Spanish explorer Alvar Nuñez Cabeza de Baca, was born on May 16, 1894, to Graciano and Indalecia Cabeza de Baca of La Liendre, New Mexico Territory. One of four children, she was raised by her paternal grandmother, Estefana, after her mother died in 1898. Cabeza de Baca's great-grandfather, Luis Maria Cabeza de Baca, was given a land grant of 500,000 acres near Las Vegas, New Mexico (the end of the Santa Fe Trail), in 1823. Her father raised over 15,000 sheep and cattle on the high plains known as El Llano Estacado (the staked plains). Cabeza de Baca started school at age four at the Loretto Academy. In 1906, at the age of twelve, she went to Spain, where her interest in family history developed.

It was from her grandmother, the ranch *padróna*, that Cabeza de Baca learned to work hard not only for her own family but also for the extended households that comprised the ranch. She was instilled from the start with a sense of superiority conferred to her by birth within the ranch's feudal community. Young women were expected to marry and bear children. A two-year severe drought, the 1918 epidemic of Spanish influenza, and the Great Depression adversely impacted the family's livelihood. When Cabeza de Baca graduated in 1912 from the New Mexico Normal School, her family was almost bankrupt. There were few prospects for gainful employment other than as a domestic, clerk, or laundress. Teaching, however, was considered a respectable career for well-bred women.

In 1915, Cabeza de Baca taught in a one-room school house in Santa Rosa. She also taught at El Rito for four years, where she had to buy paper and pencils from her own salary of $70 a month. Cabeza de Baca earned a B.A. degree in pedagogy in 1921 from New Mexico Normal University in Las Vegas. Upon graduation, she visited Spain again. She taught for eight more years and earned a second degree in domestic sciences from New Mexico State University, Las Cruces, in 1929. Fabiola Cabeza de Baca was the first Hispanic woman hired by the New Mexico Agricultural Extension Services (NMAES). She eloped with Carlos Gilbert, an insurance broker and divorced father of two, despite her family's objections. That December, Cabeza de Baca lost her left leg to gangrene after a car crash. She became the first demonstration agent assigned to Indian Pueblos (Jensen 205).

In 1935, *Boletín de Conservar* was published, the first of many best-selling NMAES titles concerning canning and other food production methods. At that time, Cabeza de Baca worked in Chimayo, San Ildefonso, and Pojoaque Indian pueblos. *Los Alimentos y su Preparación* (1934) advocates a change from provincial methods to modern American ways. She encouraged rural Hispanic and Indian women to recycle, quilt, compete in fairs, and attend clubs as a social outlet. *Historic Cookery* (1939) stresses the importance of using basic New Mexico foods—chile, beans, and corn—daily. It sold 100,000 copies, motivating Cabeza de Baca to write. During World War II, she organized food canteens for working mothers and victory gardens. *The Good Life* (1949) integrates foods into a cultural context. Many other articles concerning Hispanic food and culture were published by nationally distributed magazines.

In 1950, the United Nations Educational, Scientific, and Cultural Organization (UNESCO) sent Cabeza de Baca to teach Latin American students in Pátzcuaro, Mexico. She introduced modern hygiene, nutrition, food preservation, and fish drying techniques to Latin American students. Cabeza de Baca was promoted to agent-at-large for Los Alamos, Sandoval, and Santa Fe Counties. In 1951, her marriage ended. She reverted back to her family name in the late 1950s.

Cabeza de Baca's interest in her family's history fostered the writing of *We Fed Them Cactus* (1954), a Hispanic folk-history classic that is still read and taught. Later, she was columnist and editorial board member for *Santa Fe Scene* (1958–1961), a short-lived magazine she helped found.

Cabeza de Baca retired in 1959 but remained an active lecturer, trainer, consultant for the Peace Corps, and volunteer for many community organizations. She won many awards, including a national Home Demonstration Agents Association Distinguished Award for Meritorious Service and a United States Department of Agriculture Superior Service Award.

Fabiola Cabeza de Baca is fondly remembered by her family as Aunt Fabulous and Aunt Faby. She was moved to a nursing home in May 1984 and died in 1991. She is buried on the Llano, at the family ranch near Newkirk, New Mexico.

MAJOR WORKS AND THEMES

Fabiola Cabeza de Baca's literary achievements can be grouped into two categories: those written before 1950 for Extension Service clients and those written afterward for Anglo audiences. Her earlier works focus on cross-cultural nutrition and stress the need for agents to be respectful of the ways of indigenous people. Often the women Cabeza de Baca tried to reach lived in remote villages and were too poor to purchase the materials and utensils necessary for modern canning processes. At first they seemed unwilling to adapt to the new methods, but they soon overcame the financial limitations by pooling together resources to set up community canneries. (Jensen 245)

From her field notes, Cabeza de Baca was able to create the first definitive collection of New Mexican recipes, *Historic Cookery*. She quantified measurements, used Spanish food names and ingredients, and wrote with an Anglo audience in mind. Critic Enrique Lamadrid considers her definition of the verb *guisar* a classic: "*Guisar* . . . the most popular word in the native homemaker's vocabulary . . . roughly translated, it means to dress up food . . . good food always deserves a finishing touch. Food must never taste flat, but it will—if it is not *guisado*" (46).

Cabeza de Baca collected oral history and folklore. *The Good Life* records the fictional Turrietta family's daily life, yearly routines, and traditions. Lamadrid calls *The Good Life* "a kind of New Mexican version of the television series *The Waltons*" because, to an outsider, the family seems poverty-stricken (46). Cabeza de Baca pays special attention to domestic activities and includes recipes in the second part of the book. *The Good Life* explains regional differences in New Mexican food (rolled versus stacked enchiladas, for example) and the variety of ingredients.

The most famous and widely read narrative by Cabeza de Baca is undoubtedly *We Fed Them Cactus*, an autobiographical accumulation of cultural knowledge told partly through the eyes of El Cuate, the camp cook. Cabeza de Baca uses him as her "informant" to corroborate oral history and establish herself as an ethnographer (McShane 190). She has a definite agenda to promote her version of the pre-Anglo Southwest to counter Anglo-American stereotyping of wealthy and corrupt landowners of the *rico* class (McShane 193).

Personal participation, oral accounts, letters, and historical research make *We Fed Them Cactus* credible. Lamadrid considers the book "an extended tribute paid to the valiant and resourceful women of the Hispanic frontier" (46). The original Spanish names of places and people reflect the family's connection to the land. Cabeza de Baca represents her family and its employees as one happy family working together. It is a romanticized portrait showing the *rico* class in a positive light that seeks to unify Hispanic cultural identity (McShane 189).

Beyond the simple recording of a young girl's life, *We Fed Them Cactus* accurately describes the hardships of ranching and the events that forced many Hispanos off the land. The Cabeza de Baca family's story reflects the social and cultural changes occurring in New Mexico in the 1920s and 1930s.

Cabeza de Baca's books are nostalgic and reflect her search for personal and cultural identity. She lived a life of amazing influence and independence despite cultural expectations of her community. Her day-to-day life dealt with the actual problems of home economics, but her literature suppresses the present and focuses on the past. Cabeza de Baca's choice of textual focus and obvious omissions are a function of her times. She witnessed the assimilation of her people into mainstream Anglo America. Readers must remember Cabeza de Baca's books were intended for Anglo readers. Her initial goal of justifying the Hispanic class system is abandoned in favor of promoting Hispanic cultural unity (McShane 194).

CRITICAL RECEPTION

Fabiola Cabeza de Baca would probably be surprised and amused at the controversy her life and works created during the Chicano movement of the 1970s and after her death. Her books received generally good reviews at the time of publication. They have since been criticized as elitist and not representative of the realistic Chicano experience.

We Fed Them Cactus was reviewed sixty-six times, six of which cited lack of structure and poor writing (Ponce 141). Most reviews favorably mention its historical significance as a book by a Hispanic woman, the author's personal achievements, her family's importance, and regional flavor. Other reviews are far less complimentary. John Rothfork writes, "The value of *We Fed Them Cactus* depends on the audience. . . . [T]hose hoping for regional history will be disappointed; those looking for an easy read will enjoy the work" (181). Undeveloped characters, poor organization, imperialist language, passionless narration, and absence of metaphor are also cited as weaknesses.

Critic Raymund A. Paredes suggests Cabeza de Baca and other early New Mexican women writers represent a "culture seemingly locked in time and barricaded against outside forces" (51). Paredes views this retreat into nostalgia and defense of the feudal system as representative of a "hacienda syndrome" (52). Francisco Lomeli credits Cabeza de Baca as the "first woman to receive some acclaim during her time for *We Fed them Cactus*" (33). He states she has had no subsequent influence on Chicano literary tradition because she "left only a mild legacy by having intrigued readers with her work's title" (34). But Ponce argues Cabeza de Baca gives voice to "colonized women" and illiterate working-class Hispanics by preserving their life stories (184). Cabeza de Baca believes she accurately represents the lives of others less educated even though she is ignorant of economic and class disparities (McShane 194).

Cabeza de Baca is also criticized for her role as a NMAES agent. Anne Goldman attacks Cabeza de Baca for acting as "mediator between the Hispanics . . . and the Anglo-American business interests promoted by the government" whose aim is "cultural obliteration" rather than good nutrition (173). Ponce counters that Cabeza de Baca had very little choice in what she taught—that the NMAES believed the government knew best—and she needed a job (105).

Fabiola Cabeza de Baca lived a productive, creative, and independent life that positively affected the lives of many rural Hispanic women. While Chicano movement critics do not regard her works as important because they condone class oppression and racism, others regard *We Fed Them Cactus* a viable contribution to women's regional writing and Chicano literature.

BIBLIOGRAPHY

Works by Fabiola Cabeza de Baca Gilbert

Los Alimentos y su Preparación. 1934. Las Cruces: New Mexico State University Extension Service (NMSUES), 1937.
Boletín de Conservar. 1935. Las Cruces: NMSUES, 1937.
Historic Cookery. Las Cruces: NMSUES, 1939.
"New Mexico Diets." *Journal of Home Economics* Nov. 1942: 668–69.
The Good Life. Santa Fe: San Vicente Foundation, 1949.
We Fed Them Cactus. 1954. Albuquerque: University of New Mexico Press, 1979.
"Foods for Easter in the Old Tradition." *New Mexico Magazine* April 1957: 23+.
"Pioneer Merchant: Don Miguel Delgado." *Santa Fe Scene* 17 May 1958: n. pag.
"Puerto de Luna." *New Mexico Magazine* Oct. 1958: 20+.
"Changing Modes of Travel." *Santa Fe Scene* 6 Dec. 1958: n. pag.
"Nineteenth Century in Santa Fe." *Santa Fe Scene* 13 Feb. 1960: n. pag.

Studies of Fabiola Cabeza de Baca Gilbert

Bullock, Alice. "A Patrona of the Old Pattern." *The New Mexican* 19 May 1968: n. pag.
Cabeza de Baca, Robert. "Doña Fabiola." *New Mexico Resources* 8 (1995): 2.
Dohme, Ralph. "SF Woman to Talk on NM Foods." *The New Mexican* 6 Feb. 1966: 2.
"Extension Service Agent to Retire after 30 Years." *Albuquerque Journal* 24 June 1959: n. pag.
Goldman, Anne. " 'I Yam What I Yam': Cooking, Culture, and Colonialism." *De/Colonizing the Subject: The Politics of Gender in Women's Autobiography*. Ed. Sidonie Smith and Julia Watson. Minneapolis: University of Minnesota Press, 1993. 169–95.
Jensen, Joan M. " 'I've Worked, I'm Not Afraid of Work': Farm Women in New Mexico, 1920–1940." *New Mexico Women, Intercultural Perspectives*. Ed. Joan M. Jensen and Darlis A. Miller. Albuquerque: University of New Mexico Press, 1986. 201–26.
Lamadrid, Enrique R. "Fabiola Cabeza de Baca Gilbert." *Chicano Writers*. Ed. Francisco A. Lomeli and Carl R. Shirley. Detroit: Gale, 1992. Vol. 122 of *Dictionary of Literary Biography*. 44–47.
Lomelì, Francisco A. "Chicana Novelists in the Process of Creating Fictive Voices." *Beyond Steréotypes: The Critical Analysis of Chicana Literature*. Binghamton, NY: Bilingual Press, 1985. 33–34.
McShane, Becky Jo Gesteland. "In Pursuit of Regional and Cultural Identity: The Autobiographies of Agnes Morely Cleaveland and Fabiola Cabeza de Baca." *Breaking Boundaries: New Perspectives on Women's Regional Writing*. Ed. Sherrie A. Inness and Diana Royer. Iowa City: University of Iowa Press, 1997. 180–96.
Parades, Raymund A. "The Evolution of Chicano Literature." *Three American Literatures: Essays in Chicano, Native American, and Asian-American Literature for Teachers of American Literature*. Ed. Houston A. Baker, Jr. New York: Modern Language Association of America, 1982. 33–79.
Pearce, T. M. "Fabiola Cabeza de Baca." *New Mexico Historical Review* Jan. 1956: 78.

Pieper, Susan. "Fabiola's Good Life." *New Mexico Resources* 8 (1995): 3–11.

Ponce, Merrihelen. "The Life and Works of Fabiola Cabeza de Baca, New Mexican Hispanic Woman Writer: A Contextual Biography." Diss. University of New Mexico, 1995.

Rebolledo, Tey Diana. "Tradition and Mythology: Signatures of Landscape in Chicana Literature." *The Desert Is No Lady: Southwestern Landscapes in Women's Writing and Art.* Ed. Vera Norwood and Janice Monk. New Haven, CT: Yale University Press, 1987. 96–124.

Rothfork, John. Rev. of *We Fed Them Cactus*, by Fabiola Cabeza de Baca. *New Mexico Historical Review* 55 (1980): 181.

Walsh, Marie T. "New Mexico's Famous Home Economist." *California Farmer* 16 Oct. 1954: 371.

WILLA CATHER
(1873–1947)

Sally E. Haldorson and Bruce A. Glasrud

BIOGRAPHY

Wilella Sibert Cather was born in a small Virginian farming community near the Blue Ridge Mountains on December 7, 1873. The eldest of seven children, Cather grew up in a busy circle of family that included her parents, six siblings, and her maternal grandparents. It was clear that even from an early age Cather was a nonconformist. Having been born "Wilella," the Cather family nicknamed her "Willie," and one assumes that the latter adoption of "Willa" was a compromise between the tomboy she was and the girl she was supposed to be. Perhaps the rebellious nature already apparent in Cather's personality was stoked by the dissension between her parents' points of view. Her father interested himself in intellectual concerns, while her mother was materialistic and placed significant value on the Victorian ideals of femininity. It is not hard to believe that these two contrasting personalities may have fired Cather's later attempts at destabilizing dichotomies and challenging tradition.

The first nine years of Cather's life in the Blue Ridge Mountains provided a sense of safeness, perhaps even of smallness. In her autobiographical works, she recalls this time in Virginia with fondness. In this context, the family's move to the Nebraska Divide when Cather was nine years old must have been unsettling. Nebraska, unlike Virginia, was immense, and Cather felt herself very small in the midst of such a land, and, it seems, her father felt the same way. For the first two years of their life in Nebraska, Cather's father made an unsuccessful attempt at farming, and eventually, in 1884, he moved his family to the small railroad town of Red Cloud. He opened a small business, but much to her mother's consternation, Cather's father never seemed to make much money.

The effect that these relocations had on Cather can be clearly seen in her fiction. While it is certainly true that fiction should never be taken as autobiography, it is also true that Cather produced her best work when populating her stories with the living soul of the land. Not only does she linger on descriptions of place, whether it be the grasses of Nebraska or the bustle of a Lincoln opera house, she portrays just how closely place is connected to the development of her characters' personalities. How did moving to Nebraska and then to Red Cloud develop Cather's personality? Whatever else, it provided her with excitement, new challenges, and sparked her imagination.

Before becoming interested in a career as a writer, Cather imagined becoming a physician. Her ambition to become a doctor may have shocked a number of people who held some lingering Victorian values, but Cather ignored her critics and further shocked them not only by pursuing male roles in theater productions but also by dressing as a boy, wearing her hair short, insisting that she be called Willie, and claiming to be her own twin brother, William. It is interesting to look at this behavior when assessing Cather's life as a whole. While there is much written about Cather's long-term lesbian relationships, and much that can be debated as to the effect her sexual orientation had on her writing, this early testing of gender boundaries and traditional sex roles can also be read as a reaction to tradition and the restrictive assumption that an ambitious woman could not be considered feminine. Cather's entire career is proof that she could indeed accomplish much as a woman and yet remain unavailable for categorization. When Cather graduated from high school in 1890, she took yet another unthinkable action: She left home, moved to Lincoln, prepped for college, and enrolled at the University of Nebraska.

During her years in college, Cather worked as drama critic for the *Lincoln Journal*. As she gained experience with writing, she began writing fiction as well as journalism. In 1892, she published the short story "Peter" in a Boston magazine. Cather graduated from the university in 1895 and returned to Red Cloud. She soon escaped Red Cloud, and in 1896, she published "On the Divide"; from this point on, Cather seemingly never stopped writing and publishing. Moving to Pittsburgh, Cather gained employment, ironically, as an editor for *Home Monthly*, a magazine for women. She also continued writing book and drama reviews for the *Pittsburgh Leader*. Her reviews were known to be quick-witted and brutally honest, especially when critiquing female writers and actors. While this seems somewhat traitorous from a twenty-first-century perspective, Cather was easily irritated by women artists who produced anything but the best-quality work.

Cather, it seems, was not satisfied with remaining merely gainfully employed. In 1902, she traveled to Europe and, in 1903, published her first book, the small volume of poems *April Twilights*. This first publication was the beginning of a long list of critically acclaimed novels, several volumes of short stories, a couple of nonfiction biographies, a book of essays, and numerous books of collected writings.

On April 24, 1947, Willa Cather died in New Hampshire at age seventy of a brain hemorrhage and was buried in New York City. On her gravestone is written a line from *My Ántonia*: "That is happiness; to be dissolved into something complete and great." Without doubt, this is a tribute to the land she loved, but perhaps it also can be read as a tribute from her readers, as Cather has truly

become an inseparable and essential representative of the American literary tradition.

MAJOR WORKS AND THEMES

It is perhaps simplest to regard Willa Cather as the last of the American
women regionalist writers who found themselves embraced by readers in the
late nineteenth and early twentieth centuries. Because of the changing culture
that came with the industrial revolution as the United States neared the turn of
the century, region-identified literature was immensely popular since it brought
the country together—brought the rural to the urban and the West to the East—
during uncertain times. Judith Fetterley and Marjorie Pryse, the editors of *American Women Regionalists*, describe a regionalist writer's dependency on place:
"[R]egional characters gain their identity from the regions they inhabit; for regional characters, living for a long time in the same place affects character. . . .
Regional writers respect and cherish the actual places that provide the environmental contexts for their characters" (xvii). In regionalist literature, place is as
key to an author's intent as character, narrator, plot, or story. For Cather, each
of her major works operates on the theme that place is central to the plot and
at times is, itself, the plot. Each character, then, is an extension of the land or
is, to some degree, an enemy of the land; for Cather, one is either an insider or
an outsider, a native or a foreigner. This is not to say that outsiders could not
become insiders or that foreigners could not carve out a place for themselves,
but in order to achieve such a position, one must confront the land.

Despite the previous publishing of *April Twilights* (a book of poetry that she
disliked so much she threw the remaining copies in a lake) and *The Troll Garden*
(a short story collection), *Alexander's Bridge* was Cather's first novel, and the
novel itself did not garner much attention. Of her earliest publications, Cather
noted that "at the time I found the new more exciting than the familiar" (Woodress, *Willa Cather* 222). Woodress himself agrees that "the themes and subjects
that she treated so luminously in her mature work all appeared in her earliest
efforts . . . but it was not until she was in her forties that she was able to utilize
effectively her own experience to weave the myth of the American past into the
magical fabric of her fiction" (*Willa Cather* xvi). It was not until *O Pioneers!*
that Cather began writing about what she knew best—Nebraska.

What is important about *O Pioneers!* is that with the creation of Alexandra
Bergson the reader is presented with a womanly ideal that is outside the traditional Victorian "angel in the house" image. Instead, Alexandra is so capable,
so strong, that her father leaves his land for her to inherit. What challenges
Alexandra more than the land itself are human relationships—with her brother,
her children, her husband, and her childhood friend, Carl. Toward the end of
the novel, while grappling with the fact that she may have no one to give her
land, she states that "we come and go, but the land is always here. And the
people who love it and understand it are the people who own it—for a little

while" (229). There is not much hope for Alexandra because she realizes that it is unlikely that there is another generation eager and energetic enough to understand the land and to work along with it.

This conflict between the old generations and the new generations appears in much of Cather's work. In many ways, this same conflict—of insider and out-sider—drives *My Ántonia* (1918). This story concerns immigrants who move west to achieve the American Dream. Starkly detailing the struggles faced by Ántonia and the Shirmerda family, Cather illustrates the realities of the inex-perienced living on untamed land. With Jim Burden as narrator, Cather creates enough distance to espouse the message that perseverance yields gain, and at the end of the novel, she presents the reader with Ántonia, the strong immigrant girl, who has become a woman who endured and produced a generation of insiders—Americans.

Cather's succeeding publications reflect these and other themes. In 1922, she published *One of Ours*, which subsequently received the Pulitzer Prize. Set in early twentieth-century Nebraska, the novel regrets the loss of an earlier pio-neering spirit of the state, and the hero escapes by fighting in World War I, then dying there. Cather's next novel, *A Lost Lady*, garnered greater praise. The novel, reflecting Cather's own views, chronicles the death of an era. Perhaps the most powerful expression of Cather's disillusionment with the modern era is her 1925 novel *The Professor's House*. This story of heroic failure is symbolic of Cather's life, her writings, and her perceptions.

In a different representation of America, Cather produced, in 1927, what she herself believed to be her greatest work, *Death Comes for the Archbishop*. As with the Nebraska of *O Pioneers!* and *My Ántonia*, it could be argued that place, the landscape and the cultural traditions of the Southwest, represents Cather's most compelling character in the novel. Readers and critics alike were impressed that Cather could create such a viable representation of the Southwest when she had, herself, spent such little time there. Despite the distinct presence of the Southwest as a realized character in *Death Comes for the Archbishop*, place stimulates rather than obscures the deeper issues of religion, faith, and cultural tradition present in the text. For Cather, place and religion are interrelated.

By the time *Death Comes for the Archbishop* was written, Cather had been experimenting with narrative structure for some time and been criticized for her lack of plot both in the above novel and in *Shadows on the Rock* (1931). *Shad-ows on the Rock* is a historical novel set in Quebec, and that province, like the Southwest of *Death Comes for the Archbishop*, is carefully realized in great detail. The rock featured in the novel represents stability in the face of change, the anchor to which a people moor themselves in a storm. For Cather, in a horrifying mutable world, she believed such a rock was necessary. As a result, *Shadows on the Rock*, while never considered a masterpiece, was one of Cather's personal favorites.

In her later novels, Cather escaped from the materialism and complexity of twentieth-century urban society by focusing on idyllic pastoral lives. She moved further away in her fiction and idealized and romanticized early societies where conflict was negligible, such as that in *Death Comes to the Archbishop*. Her penultimate novel, *Lucy Gayheart*, served to remind the reader of the virtues and values of an artist and to encourage memories of her. In her final novel, she turned to the land of her birth—the South—and penned *Sapphira and the Slave Girl*, a novel that received mixed reviews. Neither an attack on slavery nor an absolute defense of it, the novel walks a fine line in an attempt to pursue and preserve human companionship.

Cather also published poetry (with which she was not overly pleased); short stories, which she wrote during her entire career and which provide a valuable means to observe her changing approaches, interests, and themes; and essays about art and values. It was her novels, however, that laid the strongest foundation to the claim that she is one of the finest twentieth-century writers in U.S. history.

CRITICAL RECEPTION

Willa Cather's enormous influence and her overwhelmingly positive reception are evidenced by the successful publication of journals entitled *Cather Studies* and *Willa Cather Pioneer Memorial Newsletter*. Much of Cather's work has been lauded by critics and readers alike for its exquisite attention to detail and the realization of place. She has also been admired for her characterization, the ability to create living and breathing people within the pages of her novels. While some value her writing for the contribution it makes to the American West—in 1961, Cather was the first woman voted into the Nebraska Hall of Fame—others commend her for the role models she gives women when she portrays strong, autonomous female characters such as Alexandra Bergson and Ántonia Shimerda. In 1988, Cather entered the National Women's Hall of Fame in Seneca, New York.

Indeed, Cather has currently become a popular source for much feminist criticism, wherein many feminist scholars use Cather's sexual orientation to reassess Cather's work. While some scholars, such as Sharon O'Brien, assert that the lack of love relationships between Cather's male and female characters is a direct result of her sexual orientation, others, such as Joan Acocella, will go so far as to question the validity of these scholars' positioning and the resulting analysis of Cather's work. Additional scholarship focuses on Cather's feminism and techniques: Elaine Sargent Apthorp, "Speaking of Silence: Willa Cather and the 'Problem' of Feminist Biography"; Reginald Dyck, "The Feminist Critique of Willa Cather's Fiction"; and Jeane Harris, "A Code of Her Own: Attitudes toward Women in Willa Cather's Short Fiction." For a book-length study, Frances Kaye's *Isolation and Masquerade: Willa Cather's Women* is quite insightful.

Overall, scholars have been fair to Willa Cather. As guides to her works and to the scholarship, see Marilyn Arnold's *Willa Cather: A Reference Guide* and

Joan Crane's *Willa Cather: A Bibliography*. A useful compendium of earlier criticism is John Murphy's edited work *Critical Essays on Willa Cather*; see also James Schroeter's *Willa Cather and Her Critics*. Intriguing assessments of Cather can be found in Susan Rosowski, *The Voyage Perilous: Willa Cather's Romanticism*; Hermione Lee, *Willa Cather: Double Lives*; and Edward Bloom and Lillian Bloom, *Willa Cather's Gift of Sympathy*. For an evenhanded appraisal, turn to James Woodress's *Willa Cather: A Literary Life*, yet the closest to a definitive account. For a fine analysis of "Willa Cather as a Regional Writer," read the article of that title by Bernice Slote.

More recently, other critics have begun to explore additional interpretations of Cather's novels; the titles of the works are indicative of the arguments: Jamie Ambrose, *Willa Cather: Writing at the Frontier*; Sally Peltier Harvey, *Redefining the American Dream: The Novels of Willa Cather*; Jo A. Middleton, *Willa Cather's Modernism*; Patrick W. Shaw, *Willa Cather and the Art of Conflict*; and Joseph R. Urgo, *Willa Cather and the Myth of American Migration*. Interestingly, these are only a few of the topics currently being explored.

Even though one area in need of further exploration is Cather and the issue of race, Deborah Carlin's "Enslaved by History: The Burden of the Past and Cather's Last Novel" is a good starting place. Others who have delved into the topic include Marilyn Arnold, " 'Of Human Bondage': Cather's Subnarrative in *Sapphira and the Slave Girl*; Merrill Maguire Skaggs, "Willa Cather's Experimental Southern Novel"; and Guy Reynolds, *Willa Cather in Context: Progress, Race, Empire*. Too often, unfortunately, these works find ways to explain away what can only be considered racist content in Cather's works.

Much of the critical reception regarding Willa Cather centers on her novels; however, she wrote a large number of interesting and insightful short stories. These have been studied by Marilyn Arnold, *Willa Cather's Short Fiction*; Sheryl Meyering, *A Reader's Guide to the Short Stories of Willa Cather*; and Loretta Wasserman, *Willa Cather: A Study of the Short Fiction*. Over the next few years, undoubtedly more will be done with her short fiction. Apparently, most scholars agree with Cather's own assessment of her poetry; thus little scholarship has been written about it.

Regardless of what Cather may or may not have accomplished in regard to any important social concerns—whether they be ethnic, feminist, lesbian, or classist—what can and should be noted about Willa Cather, above all else, is that she was an accomplished storyteller who managed to capture the voice of a country and its people. Not only did Cather resist categorization in her own life; she defied readers and critics to categorize her work and the lives that existed within that work.

BIBLIOGRAPHY

Works by Willa Cather

April Twilights: Poems. Boston: Badger, 1903.

The Troll Garden. New York: McClure, 1905.

Alexander's Bridge. Boston: Houghton, 1912. (Novel)

O Pioneers! Boston: Houghton, 1913. (Novel)

The Song of the Lark. Boston: Houghton, 1915. (Novel)

My Ántonia. Boston: Houghton, 1918. (Novel)

Youth and the Bright Medusa. New York: Knopf, 1920.

One of Ours. New York: Knopf, 1922. (Novel)

April Twilights and Other Poems. New York: Knopf, 1923.

A Lost Lady. New York: Knopf, 1923. (Novel)

The Best Stories of Sarah Orne Jewett. Ed. Willa Cather. 2 vols. Boston: Houghton, 1925.

The Professor's House. New York: Knopf, 1925. (Novel)

My Mortal Enemy. New York: Knopf, 1926. (Novel)

Death Comes for the Archbishop. New York: Knopf, 1927. (Novel)

Shadows on the Rock. New York: Knopf, 1931. (Novel)

Obscure Destinies. New York: Knopf, 1932.

Lucy Gayheart. New York: Knopf, 1935. (Novel)

Not Under Forty. New York: Knopf, 1936.

Sapphira and the Slave Girl. New York: Knopf, 1940. (Novel)

The Old Beauty, and Others. New York: Knopf, 1948.

On Writing: Critical Studies on Writing as Art. New York: Knopf, 1949. (Nonfiction)

Writings from Willa Cather's Campus Years. Ed. James Shively. Lincoln: University of Nebraska Press, 1950. (Nonfiction)

Willa Cather in Europe: Her Own Story of the First Journey. Ed. George N. Kates. New York: Knopf, 1956. (Nonfiction)

Early Stories of Willa Cather. Ed. Mildred R. Bennett. New York: Dodd, 1957.

The Kingdom of Art: Willa Cather's First Principles and Critical Statements, 1893–1896. Ed. Bernice Slote. Lincoln: University of Nebraska Press, 1967. (Nonfiction)

Willa Cather's Collected Short Fiction, 1892–1912. Ed. Virginia Faulkner. Lincoln: University of Nebraska Press, 1970.

The World and the Parish: Willa Cather's Articles and Reviews, 1893–1902. Ed. William Curtain. 2 vols. Lincoln: University of Nebraska Press, 1970.

Uncle Valentine and Other Stories: Willa Cather's Uncollected Short Fiction, 1915–1929. Ed. Bernice Slote. Lincoln: University of Nebraska Press, 1973.

Willa Cather in Person: Interviews, Speeches, and Letters. Ed. L. Brent Bohlke. Lincoln: University of Nebraska Press, 1986.

Willa Cather: Twenty-Four Stories. Ed. Sharon O'Brien. New York: New American Library, 1987.

Studies of Willa Cather

Acocella, Joan. "Cather and the Academy." *New Yorker* 27 Nov. 1995: 56–71.

Ambrose, Jamie. *Willa Cather: Writing at the Frontier.* New York: St. Martin's, 1988.

Apthorp, Elaine Sargent. "Speaking of Silence: Willa Cather and the 'Problem' of Feminist Biography." *Women's Studies* 18 (1990): 1–11.

Arnold, Marilyn. " 'Of Human Bondage': Cather's Subnarrative in *Sapphira and the Slave Girl.*" *Mississippi Quarterly* 40 (1987): 323–38.

———. "Willa Cather." *Critical Survey of Short Fiction.* Ed. Frank N. Magill. Vol. 3. Englewood Cliffs, NJ: Salem, 1981. 1075–81.

———. *Willa Cather: A Reference Guide.* Boston: G. K. Hall, 1986.

———. *Willa Cather's Short Fiction.* Athens: Ohio University Press, 1984.

Bennett, Mildred. *The World of Willa Cather.* Lincoln: University of Nebraska Press, 1961.

Bloom, Edward, and Lillian Bloom. *Willa Cather's Gift of Sympathy.* Carbondale: Southern Illinois University Press, 1962.

Brown, E. K. *Willa Cather: A Critical Biography.* New York: Knopf, 1953.

Carlin, Deborah. "Enslaved by History: The Burden of the Past and Cather's Last Novel." *Cather, Canon, and the Politics of Reading.* Amherst: University of Massachusetts Press, 1992. 150–76, 194–96.

Crane, Joan. *Willa Cather: A Bibliography.* Lincoln: University of Nebraska Press, 1982.

Daiches, David. *Willa Cather: A Critical Introduction.* Westport, CT: Greenwood, 1971.

Dyck, Reginald. "The Feminist Critique of Willa Cather's Fiction: A Review Essay." *Women's Studies* 22 (1993): 263–80.

Fetterley, Judith, and Marjorie Pryse, eds. *American Women Regionalists, 1850–1910: A Norton Anthology.* New York: Norton, 1991.

Gerber, Philip L. *Willa Cather.* Boston: Twayne, 1975.

Harris, Jeane. "A Code of Her Own: Attitudes toward Women in Willa Cather's Short Fiction." *Modern Fiction Studies* 36 (1990): 81–89.

Harvey, Sally Peltier. *Redefining the American Dream: The Novels of Willa Cather.* Rutherford, NJ.: Fairleigh Dickinson University Press, 1995.

Hoover, Sharon. "Willa Cather: The Authority of Female." Diss. State University of New York, Buffalo, 1992.

Kaye, Frances. *Isolation and Masquerade: Willa Cather's Women.* New York: Peter Lang, 1993.

Lee, Hermione. *Willa Cather: Double Lives.* New York: Pantheon, 1990.

Lindemann, Marilee. *Willa Cather: Queering America.* New York: Columbia University Press, 1998.

McComas, Dix. "The Unrecalled Past: Nostalgia and Depression in the Middle Novels of Willa Cather." Diss. University of Massachusetts, 1997.

McDonald, Joyce. *The Stuff of Our Forebears: Willa Cather's Southern Heritage.* Tuscaloosa: University of Alabama Press, 1998.

Meyering, Sheryl. *A Reader's Guide to the Short Stories of Willa Cather.* New York: G. K. Hall, 1994.

Middleton, Jo A. *Willa Cather's Modernism: A Study of Style & Technique.* Rutherford, NJ.: Fairleigh Dickinson University Press, 1990.

Millington, Richard H. "Willa Cather and 'The Storyteller': Hostility to the Novel in *My Ántonia.*" *American Literature* 66 (1994): 689–717.

Murphy, John, ed. *Critical Essays on Willa Cather.* Boston: G. K. Hall, 1983.

O'Brien, Sharon. "Becoming Noncanonical: The Case against Willa Cather." *American Quarterly* 40 (1988): 110–26.

———. " 'The Thing Not Named': Willa Cather as a Lesbian Writer." *Signs* 9 (1984): 576–99.

———. *Willa Cather: The Emerging Voice.* New York: Oxford University Press, 1987.

Pers, Mona. *Willa Cather's Swedes: The Literary Significance of Swedish Immigrants.* Philadelphia: Coronet, 1995.

Randall, John H., III. *The Landscape and the Looking Glass: Willa Cather's Search for Value.* Boston: Houghton, 1960.

Reynolds, Guy. *Willa Cather in Context: Progress, Race, Empire.* New York: St. Martin's, 1996.

Rosowski, Susan J. "Prospects for the Study of Willa Cather." *Resources for American Literary Study* 22.2 (1996): 147–65.

———. "Recent Books on Willa Cather: An Essay Review." *Modern Fiction Studies* 36 (1990): 131–41.

———. *The Voyage Perilous: Willa Cather's Romanticism.* Ann Arbor: Books on Demand, 1986.

———. "Writing against Silences: Female Adolescent Development in the Novels of Willa Cather." *Studies in the Novel* 21 (1989): 60–77.

Rundstrom, Beth. "Harvesting Willa Cather's Literary Fields." *Geographical Review* 85 (1995): 217–29.

Schroeter, James, ed. *Willa Cather and Her Critics.* Ithaca, NY: Cornell University Press, 1967.

Seaton, James. "The Prosaic Willa Cather." *American Scholar* 67 (1998): 146–51.

Shaw, Patrick W. *Willa Cather and the Art of Conflict: Re-Visioning Her Creative Imagination.* Troy, NY: Whitson, 1992.

Skaggs, Merrill Maguire. *After the World Broke in Two: The Later Novels of Willa Cather.* Charlottesville: University Press of Virginia, 1990.

———. "Willa Cather's Experimental Southern Novel." *Mississippi Quarterly* 35 (1981–1982): 3–14.

Slote, Bernice. "Willa Cather as a Regional Writer." *Kansas Quarterly* 2.2 (1970): 7–15.

Strouck, David. *Willa Cather's Imagination.* Lincoln: University of Nebraska Press, 1975.

Tisdale, Judy Jones. "Working Women on the Frontier: Capitalism and Community in Three Willa Cather Novels." *The Image of the Frontier in Literature, the Media, and Society.* Ed. Will Wright and Steven Kaplan. Pueblo, CO: Society for the Interdisciplinary Study of Social Imagery, 1997. 177–84.

Urgo, Joseph R. *Willa Cather and the Myth of American Migration.* Urbana: University of Illinois Press, 1995.

Wagner-Martin, Linda. "Willa Cather: Reassessment and Discovery." *Contemporary Literature* 30 (1989): 444–47.

Wasserman, Loretta. *Willa Cather: A Study of the Short Fiction.* Boston: Twayne, 1991.

Woodress, James. "The Use of Biography: The Case of Willa Cather." *Great Plains Quarterly* 2 (1982): 195–203.

————. *Willa Cather: A Literary Life*. Lincoln: University of Nebraska Press, 1987.
————. "Willa Cather and History." *Arizona Quarterly* 34 (1978): 239–54.
Wussow, Helen. "Language, Gender, and Ethnicity in Three Fictions by Willa Cather."
    Women and Language 18 (1995): 52–55.

ANITA SCOTT COLEMAN
(1890–1960)

Bruce A. Glasrud and Laurie Champion

BIOGRAPHY

Black American writer Anita Scott Coleman published short stories, essays, and poems in leading magazines such as *Half-Century Magazine, Crisis, The Messenger,* and *Opportunity* during the 1920s and 1930s. Coleman's heritage is varied and unique: Born in Guaymas, Sonora, Mexico, in 1890, her mother was a slave who was bought by her Cuban father, who fought in the Civil War on the Union side. Coleman grew up in New Mexico, where she graduated from the New Mexico Teachers College. She later taught school in Los Angeles, a job that she enjoyed very much. Married, she and her husband had four children while residing in Los Angeles, where she also managed a boarding house for children and pursued her writing career. Unfortunately, little else is known about Anita Scott Coleman's life. An important early twentieth-century short-story writer and poet, more details about her life need to be uncovered.

Although Coleman published nineteen stories and several poems during the years 1919 and 1933, coinciding very closely to the New Negro movement that swept the country, she is frequently excluded from discussions of the Harlem Renaissance. But, as a Los Angeles resident, she undoubtedly participated in the exciting west coast rebirth that centered in that city. Short-lived journals were established, and nationally prominent western authors such as Langston Hughes, Wallace Thurman, and Arna Bontemps resided in or visited this "Harlem of the West." After 1933, when she published her last short story, even less is known of Coleman's life. She published collections of her poetry in 1937 and 1948 and an illustrated children's book posthumously in 1961. She died in 1960, the same year as her also forgotten contemporary Zora Neale Hurston.

MAJOR WORKS AND THEMES

The works of Anita Scott Coleman include two volumes of poetry, *Small Wisdom* (1937) and *Reason for Singing* (1948), the children's book *The Singing*

Bells (1961), and several uncollected short stories and essays. Her poetry, the majority of which consists of spiritual praises and contrasting images, has appeared in book-length publications; but her strength as a writer is in the short story genre. While a few of her poems explore issues such as the celebration of black identity, almost all of her fiction reveals social and political issues such as relationships between blacks and whites in a racist society and the plight of black women in a sexist society.

Coleman's stories do not rely heavily on plot but on thematic unity; and the points of the stories are understated or implied by use of a minimalist writing style in which few details are revealed on the surface level, which frequently makes the themes stronger than they might be if explanations were more overtly stated. For example, in "Cross Crossings Cautiously," a poor black man spends his only dollar to fulfill a young white girl's wish that he accompany her to the circus. After returning home from the circus, the girl is awakened and wonders what happened to the man who took her to the circus. Although the young girl remains unaware, readers understand that the man has been lynched for being with her. The title of the story, "Cross Crossings Cautiously," suggests that blacks should beware when mingling with whites. Coleman also shows the atrocities of segregation and the problems of black-white relations in other stories such as "Three Dogs and a Rabbit" and "The Brat." As these stories demonstrate, throughout Coleman's fiction frequently what is revealed through subtle symbols and metaphors is more important than what is stated outright.

The portrayal of relationships between blacks and whites is blended with that of religion in "White Folks's Nigger" to demonstrate that sometimes the kindness of blacks is unacknowledged by whites. Interestingly, the protagonist of "White Folks's Nigger," Amos Dickson, is dead. During his funeral it is revealed that he had lived with the white Balsam family, who had brought him to his African American community to be buried. Coleman shows segregation by pointing out that blacks and whites sit on opposing sides of the Masonic Hall, where the service is held. The only white to show grief is a white teenage girl who begins to cry because he had taken care of her. The story suggests that while the blacks are able to acknowledge Amos's good deeds, with the exception of the teenager whom he nurtured, the whites continue to damn his actions.

In addition to exploring themes concerning racism, many of Coleman's stories point out struggles of black women to gain gender equality. Because her female protagonists are African American, they are frequently discriminated against in terms of both ethnicity and gender. A series of three short stories depicting Phoebe and Peter Nettleby provide good examples of her treatment of gender issues. During the course of these stories, Phoebe matures and is able to accept people for who and what they are, rather than focusing on their economic status. By the third story, "The Nettleby's New Years," Phoebe realizes that blacks should help blacks and women help women. Coleman shows the importance of blacks uniting toward group progress rather than seeking individual status at the expense of less economically privileged blacks.

One of the strengths of Coleman's fiction is her use of innovative technical strategies. Her style is natural and poetic. In some of her stories, she uses the second person to talk directly to the reader. For example "Silk Stockings" begins "This is a plain tale of plain people" and asks readers directly to consider why stories are often about either the rich or the impoverished despite that the best stories portray ordinary people (229). The story also announces that "the moral is here" and challenges readers to "find it" (230). The story demonstrates the power of fiction to reflect truths in a way nonfiction cannot. It also blurs lines between reality and fiction and suggests through self-reflexive narrative that fiction exposes a conceptual truth not found in factual truth.

Although Coleman's artistic strengths are most strongly revealed in her fiction, she also wrote poetry. Reflective of their titles, many of the poems celebrate humanness and spirituality: "Reason for Singing" (*Reason for Singing*) celebrates the creator of the universe and praises the heavens; and "Whence Cometh Strength" (*Reason for Singing*) celebrates the peace and comfort nature offers. Coleman's strongest poetry, like her fiction, explores racial issues. In "Idle Wonder" (*Reason for Singing*), the speaker says that the whites with whom the black Agnes resides believe that she is content being their housekeeper; however, this assumption is undercut by the speaker's comparison of Agnes with her cat, who she keeps locked indoors to prevent it from associating with other cats. "On Hearing Four White Men Singing Spirituals" (*Reason for Singing*) refers to whites as "other" and points out that whites cannot express the themes of black spirituals when they sing. The speaker of "Black Baby" celebrates the African American identity of her black child by comparing his eyes with coals and diamonds. Each stanza of the poem begins with "The baby I hold in my arms is a black baby" and reinforces the celebration of African American identity (53). Other poems contrast two ideas: "Definition" (*Reason for Singing*) and "Modes" (*Reason for Singing*) contrast night against day, "Lines on Values" (*Reason for Singing*) contrasts wishes with hope, and "Life Is a See-Saw" (*Reason for Singing*) contrasts joy with sorrow.

CRITICAL RECEPTION

Although Anita Scott Coleman basically has been ignored since her death forty years ago, during her lifetime she was the recipient of prestigious awards for her writing: Her essay "Unfinished Masterpieces" won the 1926 Amy Spingarn *Crisis* second prize award; her short story "Three Dogs and a Rabbit" received the *Crisis* third prize for best short story in 1925; and although never published, her personal sketch "The Dark Horse" won second prize in the 1926 *Opportunity* literary contest. A few of her poems were anthologized by Beatrice Murphy in *Ebony Rhythm* and *Negro Voices*.

Even though Coleman's short stories reflect important concerns of women and African Americans during the early twentieth century and represent strivings of the New Negro movement, they remain uncollected in a volume. Until very recently, since the initially favorable reception of Coleman's work, she has for the most part been overlooked by critics. The resurrection of Coleman's image began with Ann Allen Shockley, who included a sketch of Coleman's life in her *Afro-American Women Writers*. Marcy Knopf's 1993 anthology *The Sleeper Wakes: Harlem Renaissance Stories by Women* includes "Cross Crossings Cautiously" and "Three Dogs and a Rabbit." Bruce A. Glasrud and Laurie Champion's *Blacks in the West: A Century of Short Stories* (2000) includes "The Little Grey House." Lorraine Elena Roses and Ruth Elizabeth Randolph's 1990 *Harlem Renaissance and Beyond: Literary Biographies of 100 Black Women Writers 1900–1945* discusses Coleman, and Mary Young's 1997 "Anita Scott Coleman: A Neglected Harlem Renaissance Writer" provides an excellent overview of themes addressed in Coleman's works.

BIBLIOGRAPHY

Works by Anita Scott Coleman

"Billie Settles the Question." *Half-Century Magazine* 7 (1919): 4.
"Love's Power." *Half-Century Magazine* 6 (1919): 6.
"Phoebe and Peter Up North." *Half-Century Magazine* 6 (1919): 4, 10.
"Phoebe Goes to a Lecture." *Half-Century Magazine* 6 (1919): 6.
"El Tisico." *Crisis* 19 (1920): 252–53.
"The Hand That Fed." *Competitor* 2 (1920): 259–61.
"Jack Arrives." *Half-Century Magazine* 8 (1920): 4, 14.
"The Nettleby's New Years." *Half-Century Magazine* 8 (1920): 4, 14–15.
"Rich Man, Poor Man." *Half-Century Magazine* 8 (1920): 6, 14.
"The Little Grey House." *Half-Century Magazine* 13 (July–Aug. 1922): 17, 19; 13 (Sept.–Oct. 1922): 4, 21.
"The Brat." *The Messenger* 8 (1926): 105–6, 126.
"Silk Stockings." *The Messenger* 8 (1926): 229–31.
"Three Dogs and a Rabbit." *Crisis* 31 (1926): 118–22.
"Unfinished Masterpieces." *Crisis* 34 (1927): 14, 24–25.
"G'Long, Old White Man's Gal." *The Messenger* 10 (1928): 81–82.
"White Folks's Nigger." *The Messenger* 10 (1928): 104+.
"Black Baby." *Opportunity* 7 (1929): 53.
"Cross Crossings Cautiously." *Opportunity* 8 (1930): 177, 189.
"The Eternal Quest." *Opportunity* 9 (1931): 242–43.
"Two Old Women A-Shopping Go!" *Crisis* 40 (1933): 109–10.
[Pseud. Elizabeth Stapleton Stokes]. *Small Wisdom*. New York: Harrison, 1937. (Poems)
Reason for Singing. Prairie City, IL: Decker, 1948. (Poems)
The Singing Bells. Illus. Claudine Nankivel. Nashville: Broadman, 1961. (Children's book)

Studies of Anita Scott Coleman

Glasrud, Bruce A., and Laurie Champion, eds. *Blacks in the West: A Century of Short Stories in the West*. Boulder: University Press of Colorado, 2000.

Kallenback, Jessamine S., comp. "Anita Scott Coleman." *Index to Black American Literary Anthologies*. Boston: G. K. Hall, 1979. 19.

Knopf, Marcy, ed. *The Sleeper Wakes: Harlem Renaissance Stories by Women*. New Brunswick, NJ: Rutgers University Press, 1993. 170–81, 268.

Roses, Lorraine Elena, and Ruth Elizabeth Randolph. "Coleman, Anita Scott." *Harlem Renaissance and Beyond: Literary Biographies of 100 Black Women Writers 1900–1945*. Boston: G. K. Hall, 1990. 59–62.

Rush, Theressa Gunnels, Carol Fairbanks Myers, and Esther Spring Arata, eds. "Anita Scott Coleman." *Black American Writers Past and Present: A Biographical and Bibliographical Dictionary*. Vol. 1. Metuchen, NJ: Scarecrow, 1975. 163.

Shockley, Ann Allen. "Coleman, Anita Scott." *Afro-American Women Writers, 1746–1933: An Anthology and Critical Guide*. Boston: G. K. Hall, 1988. 448–49.

Young, Mary E. "Anita Scott Coleman: A Neglected Harlem Renaissance Writer." *CLA Journal* 40 (1997): 271–87.

RACHEL CROTHERS
(1878–1958)

Sandra Gail Teichmann

BIOGRAPHY

Rachel Crothers was born on December 12, 1878, in Bloomington, Illinois, to Dr. Eli Kirk Crothers and Dr. Marie Depew Crothers. Crothers attended Illinois State Normal University Grammar School, and she graduated from Illinois Normal University High School in 1891 at the age of thirteen. From these early years, Crothers was drawn to the theater. She wrote and produced melodramas, she acted with the Bloomington Dramatic Club, and she gave elocution recitals. The year after graduating from high school, Crothers enrolled in the New England School of Dramatic Instruction in Boston. After only one term, she graduated in February 1892 with a certificate that confirmed her abilities to teach, recite, and read within the discipline of drama.

At the age of sixteen—against family wishes—Crothers moved to New York City. She enrolled in the Stanhope-Wheatcroft School of Acting, where after one term as a student she worked as a teacher for the next four years, coaching drama students and writing and directing plays for training. During this time, she also acted with the Lyceum Stock Company, the E. H. Southern Company, and the Christian Company. By 1903, her one-act plays began to attract notice, so she turned her full attention to writing, producing, coaching, and designing sets for her dramas.

Rachel Crothers's accomplishments at the beginning of her career are remarkable in light of her young age and a theater atmosphere hostile to the idea of women directing and staging plays. Crothers seems to have been somewhat sustained through her association with other women. She maintained family connections with her mother and sister, and she was an active member of several women's clubs within New York City's upper class.

By 1906, after extensive struggle, Rachel Crothers was a professional playwright with the successful stage production of her first professional piece, *The Three of Us*. It ran for 227 performances at the Madison Square Theater and on to London with Ethel Barrymore as the star.

Throughout her career, Rachel Crothers lived in a New York apartment on Park Avenue and, later, in a Connecticut farmhouse, where she died on July 5, 1958.

MAJOR WORKS AND THEMES

Rachel Crothers began and finished her career as a person concerned with women's issues. Her first professional success, *The Three of Us*, published in 1916 centers on the struggles of Rhy MacChesney, poor and female, in the male world of a Nevada mining town. Crothers's next play, *The Coming of Mrs. Patrick*, though focused on a woman, does not champion the feminist cause. An atmosphere of optimism and cheerfulness belies the truth of women's lives that begins to emerge in *The Three of Us*.

By the end of the decade, however, with *Myself Bettina* and *A Man's World*, Crothers returns to the social issues that continue to plague women. In these plays Crothers examines the behavior of women in response to issues of career, family, honor, moral, and intellectual freedoms. She is most interested in the motives supporting particular behaviors as her individual characters clash within the norms of their society and environment. Crothers not only lets her characters speak out in a most natural manner—contrary to the established determinism of the naturalist movement—but she also poses alternate ideologies and possibilities for a more just world for both women and men.

Myself Bettina (1908) focuses on the hostile climate—social and theological and domestic—in which contemporary women must live. Crothers's concern with issues of social justice and economic independence as well as the security of romance and marriage are complicated and complex. Crothers enlarges her focus in *A Man's World* (1915) by depicting a young woman novelist painfully aware of her struggle to juggle writing and romance with her ideal of freedom. Evidence of a double standard for women and men, indeed a barrier to woman's freedom, is the one critical issue to which Crothers continually returns.

He and She (1911) is Crothers's most intense exploration of the new woman in society. This play fully and honestly looks at the need for social and personal activism in support of feminism. Crothers contemplates feminism's ultimate impact. Continuing to be critical of society that restricts women who try to survive as artists and professionals outside the home, Crothers brings to life and light the most distant and the most intimate of barriers: society, prejudice against women, domestic role, woman's nature, family, motherhood, fear, self-doubt, and guilt.

In placing the needs of the child in conflict with the needs of the mother in *He and She*, Crothers seems to draw on her own childhood experience, a time when she needed her mother at home while her mother needed to practice medicine. Both parents were physicians, but Rachel's mother began her medical career late in life, taking her first medical course in 1877–1878 and receiving her Doctor of Medicine Degree in 1883, when Rachel was five years old. Dr.

Marie Crothers set up practice in Bloomington under great opposition from men who neither wanted nor accepted women in the profession.

Her mother's struggle may have greatly affected Rachel, the youngest of the four children. On the one hand, Crothers admired her mother for her strength, her independence, her intellect, and her accomplishments. On the other hand, she longed for love and nurture from a mother unable to provide day-to-day domestic security due to the demands of her medical career.

In *He and She*, a most important play centered on domestic and professional concerns, Crothers draws no optimistic arrows of tranquility for the future. Rather, Crothers pessimistically predicts the inevitable unrest, contention, and resistance yet to come.

In the 1920s, Crothers turns to the energy of postwar society and to irony in considering her subject. *Nice People* (1921) places the consideration of the problem facing women in the setting of a society of sophisticated rich, young, and selfish young men and women living on Park Avenue. *Mary the Third* (1923) focuses on the clash of generations resulting from the new woman's push for freedom. In *Expressing Willie* (1924), Crothers, within the setting of an opulent Long Island mansion, ridicules the popularity of Freudian fever that is sweeping the country.

By the 1930s, Crothers is again giving serious consideration to her subject of the modern woman in *Let Us Be Gay* (1929), *As Husbands Go* (1931), and *When Ladies Meet* (1932). All the plays have successful runs in New York City. In the last professionally produced play, *Susan and God*, Crothers explores modern woman's postliberation freedom in the most ironic of settings, an evangelical religious revival.

CRITICAL RECEPTION

Crothers's first professional production, *The Three of Us*, was staged in 1906 at the Madison Square Theater. Running for 227 performances, the play, starring Ethel Barrymore, was a success under Crothers's supervision. Critics praised Crother's naturalistic details both in speech and setting in the domestic melodrama. In 1907 the play went to London. To the consternation of some and the hope of others, Crothers, in this play, demonstrated her interest in women and their position within society. Some criticized the play for its parochial ideas; others—more thoughtful—predicted that her future plays would display a woman's sensitivity to the troubling domestic problems and perhaps find a means to change. By 1909, some critics were enthusiastic for Crothers's appeal—through her characters—for a single standard of morality. Many others, however, rejected the idea as ridiculous, Utopian, and predictably feminine.

Critics responding to *He and She* (mis)understand Crothers's argument to be for women remaining in the domestic sphere. The critics, however, disagreed as to favoring and opposing this notion. Though unsure of Crothers's intentions, critics continued to note her ability to convey reality through stage detail and dialogue.

In 1930, Crothers was on Ida Tarbell's list of "Fifty Foremost Women of the United States." *When Ladies Meet* was awarded the Megrue Prize and cited as one of the most outstanding plays of 1932. In 1938 Eleanor Roosevelt presented Rachel Crothers with the Chi Omega National Achievement Award. Rachel Crothers's last professionally produced play, *Susan and God* (1938), a great commercial success, ran for 288 performances.

The position of women in society is the subject of Rachel Crothers's work, and scholars such as Ann Fox, Doris Abramson, Cynthia Sutherland, and Yvonne Shafer are considering Crothers's plays in terms of her contribution to American theater and her perspective of and insight into the complexities of the male/female relationship.

BIBLIOGRAPHY

Works by Rachel Crothers

The Coming of Mrs. Patrick. Ms. Special Collections, Illinois State University Library.
Myself Bettina. Ms. The Theater Collection, New York Public Library.
He and She. 1911. *Representative American Plays 1767 to the Present Day.* Ed. Arthur Hobson Quinn. New York: Appleton, 1953. 891–928.
A Man's World. Boston: Badger, 1915.
The Three of Us. New York: French, 1916.
Nice People. 1921. *Contemporary American Plays.* Ed. Arthur Hobson Quinn. New York: Scribner's, 1923. 135–217.
Mary the Third. New York: Brentano's, 1923.
Expressing Willie. New York: Brentano's, 1924.
Let Us Be Gay. New York: French, 1929.
When Ladies Meet. New York: French, 1932.
Susan and God. New York: Random, 1938.

Studies of Rachel Crothers

Abrahamson, Irving I. "The Career of Rachel Crothers in the American Theater." Diss. University of Chicago, 1956.
Abramson, Doris. "Rachel Crothers: Broadway Feminist." *Modern American Drama: The Female Canon.* Ed. June Schlueter. Rutherford, NJ: Fairleigh Dickinson University Press, 1990. 55–65.
Conover, Susan Joy. "Social Movement in Selected Plays of Rachel Crothers." Diss. University of Nebraska, 1992.
Fox, Ann. "The 'Sweet Troubles' of a Playwright: Rachel Crothers Sets the Stage." *Text and Presentation: The Journal of the Comparative Drama Conference* 17 (1996): 20–24.
Friedman, Sharon. "Feminism as Theme in Twentieth Century American Women's Drama." *American Studies* 25.1 (1984): 69–89.

Gottlieb, Lois C. *Rachel Crothers*. Boston: Twayne, 1979.
Shafer, Yvonne. "Whose Realism? Rachel Crothers's Power Struggle in the American
    Theatre." *Realism and the American Dramatic Tradition*. Ed. William W. De-
    mastes. Tuscaloosa: University of Alabama Press, 1996. 37–52.
Sutherland, Cynthia. "American Women Playwrights as Mediators of the 'Woman Prob-
    lem.' " *Modern Drama* 21 (1978): 319–36.

H. D. (HILDA DOOLITTLE)
(1886–1961)

M. Catherine Downs

BIOGRAPHY

H. D. was born in Bethlehem, Pennsylvania, to Charles Leander Doolittle, an astronomer at Lehigh University, and Helen Eugenia Wolle Doolittle, a music teacher and painter. Through her mother, H. D. was born into the Moravian culture and faith, a faith that placed its highest trust in visionary experience. Through her maternal grandfather, her father, and later, her brother, she was surrounded by the culture of science, which demanded measurement, accuracy, discipline, and individual achievement. These twin cultures—the intense, visionary, mythic culture of the Moravians and the exact empiricism of science—helped form H. D. into the poet and novelist she later became.

In 1896 Charles was appointed Flower Professor of Astronomy at the University of Pennsylvania, and the Doolittle family moved to Philadelphia. There, a series of events began to shape H. D.'s development. Her father, whose idol was Marie Curie, became determined to teach his only daughter geometry. As H. D. was trying to learn geometry, the first modern artists were experimenting in paint to try to picture the dimension beyond the bodily eyes. The experiments of visual artists led writers, as well, to break and fragment the accepted linear sequence of prose.

H. D. entered Bryn Mawr University in 1905 but failed her mathematics exams and withdrew from the university in 1906. At Bryn Mawr, however, H. D. met fellow students William Carlos Williams and Ezra Pound (and later, she began a correspondence with Marianne Moore, who was studying biology). H. D.'s friendship with Pound led to a proposal of marriage, which horrified H. D.'s parents. Pound left for Europe, but before he did, he and his intended took walks in the nearby woods and began reading, quoting, and writing poems together. Also during her adolescence, H. D. fell in love with an art student, Frances Gregg. Ezra Pound's machinations parted the two, but again for H. D., bodily desire and artistic creation became joined in a beloved person.

H. D. left for Europe in 1911. There, Pound introduced her to his circle of

friends—William Butler Yeats and Richard Aldington, among them—and sent
H. D.'s early work to Harriet Monroe, editor of the little magazine *Poetry*, who
published "Priapus," "Hermes of the Ways," and "Epigram" in 1913. H. D.'s
career as an avant-garde writer was launched.

H. D. married Richard Aldington in 1912 (Pound had married). It seemed a
perfect match, the two writing and reading poetry together, joining passion with
artistic production. However, as World War I broke out, Aldington joined the
British forces. The stress of war caused H. D. to lose the child she was carrying.
Frightened and grieved by the loss of the baby, she refused sexual relations with
her frequently absent husband, who then began having affairs. They separated.
During the period of her breakup with Aldington, H. D. briefly lived with the
composer Cecil Gray and became pregnant with their child. Pregnant and ill
with the deadly influenza that would kill more than the war did, frightened by
her previous miscarriage, and grieving the deaths of both her brother (in the
trenches) and her father (of, apparently, grief), in 1918 H. D. found sympathy,
financial support, and deep friendship with Winifred Ellerman, the woman who
became H. D.'s beloved companion "Bryher."

H. D.'s daughter, Perdita, was born healthy and raised in a family with two
mothers (H. D. and Bryher). During the late 1920s and early 1930s the household at "Kenwin," the Bauhaus-style home in Switzerland, began editing the
film journal *Close Up* and making films. Along with Scottish director Kenneth
McPherson, they made the film *Borderline*, starring H. D. and Paul and Eslanda
Robeson, who were living in Europe during Paul's work on the English production of *Emperor Jones*. During the late 1920s as well, H. D.'s prominence
as a poet grew with the publication of a collected edition of her poems; she
tried, for the first time, to write a novel, a genre that would become a major
outlet for her ideas in the 1930s.

During the years 1933–1934 H. D. became Sigmund Freud's patient, an event
that strongly revived memories of her early years in Pennsylvania. Analysis was
important for H. D. During analysis, the recall of memory compresses remembered time with the now, and remembered places with the here. It is exactly the
idea of the presence simultaneously of all places and times that gives H. D.'s
writing its particular power.

When World War II broke out, H. D. refused to flee England for the United
States. Instead, she and Bryher stayed in the city of London during the worst
of the Blitz. During the war years, a young lecturer at Yale, Norman Holmes
Pearson, met H. D. and began a long correspondence with the poet. Pearson, a
visionary, became a liaison between H. D. (many other living poets besides),
publishers, and the academic community. Pearson set up the now-famous ar-
chive of Modernist poets in Yale's Beinecke library, where H. D.'s considerable
manuscript collection now lies. *Trilogy*, H. D.'s esteemed epic poem about war,
was urged into print by Pearson.

The 1950s were years of great productivity for H. D.; however, increasingly
they were years of isolation in hotel rooms in Switzerland until finally a broken

hip sent her to Klinik Küsnacht, a sanatorium there. Her reputation, helped by Pearson, continued to grow as she composed her last great poems: *Helen in Egypt* and *Hermetic Definition*. She died in Switzerland in 1961.

MAJOR WORKS AND THEMES

H. D. published lyric poetry, epic poetry, novels, memoirs, and histories. She was not compelled to work for her living, but perhaps she felt the need to write for her life. Possessed of a keen and searching intelligence and an intense personality, she wrote constantly and with great discipline. It is impossible to handle her enormous output here, and so a few representative works may perhaps give the flavor of her oeuvre.

H. D.'s first poems are the often-anthologized, intense, miniature verses of her first books. An example is "Oread," which refers to the Greek mythological character, Oread, nymph of the mountains. The voices of the Oreads in the tiny poem beg the sea to whip itself to a froth and throw its waves higher up on the steep, rocky shore, mingling passionately with the trees there. In another poem, H. D.'s figure of Eurydice (in "Eurydice," *Collected Poems* [1925]) lashes out against Orpheus, whose selfishness sends her back to hell. Like the Sapphic fragments, which H. D. read and appreciated (see her "Wise Sappho" essay in *Notes on Thought and Vision and the Wise Sappho*), her poems project spare, direct emotions without any additional context. That raw emotion with no explanation was different from proper, "uplifting" Victorian verse. H. D. may have begun to rely on Greek myths as the ground base to her poems because, in a changing world, they seemed ancient, rooted in truth. Much later, she would write in *The Gift*, "[Greek myth] was real. It went on happening, it did not stop" (48).

After the painful years toward the end of World War I, H. D. began writing novels that perhaps can best be described as biographies of the psyches of herself and her contemporaries. Most of the novels are romans à clef. Of these, *HERmione* and *Paint It Today* cover the actual years 1905 to 1911; *Bid Me to Live* chronicles the breakup of the H. D.–Aldington marriage and of H. D.'s friendship with D. H. and Frieda Lawrence; *Asphodel* covers the birth of Perdita; *Nights* is about bisexual love at Kenwin; *Hedylus* and *Palimpsest*, whose autobiography is more circumspect, cover the years of the late 1920s, years of comparative security and happiness. The novels are similar; they eschew conventional plotting, letting instead the plot of the psyche's thought patterns compel the reader's attention. They are written in an intense, poetic prose whose meaning is contained in images. The reader must participate in unlocking the meaning and thus recalling, reenlivening, the ancient myths and archetypes alluded to through image.

HERmione may be read to understand H. D.'s craft as a novelist. Since her novels are not conventionally plotted, the "plot" is soon told. A young woman (H. D.) seeking to create her independent, adult self, falls in love, first with a young man (Ezra Pound) and then a young woman (Frances Gregg). The love affairs are the young woman's declaration of independence from her parents as well, and so her relations with them are depicted. The plot's conventionality does not begin to explain the novel. Instead, the work's central images must be decoded.

H. D. abbreviates *HERmione*'s central character's name as "Her" or as "Herself," and in the play of H. D.'s language, it becomes clear that the names of things define selfhood and set future paths. In a central scene, Hermione, confused about her identity, notices two books, Shakespeare's *Winter's Tale* and the *Mahabharata*. "I am Her," H. D. has Hermione declare, considering the drama. "I am the AUM," she says, looking at the Hindu epic. Geometrical shapes encode additional meanings, the circle being either the magic figure of completion or a cage to entrap. The novel tells the story of "finding shape" and "finding a name." "Now," Hermione says, "I will reveal myself in words, words may now supersede a biological mathematical definition" (76). Words, especially words of mythic proportion, make sense out of the data of empirical observations made every night by H. D.'s actual father.

The late 1920s and early 1930s marked the time when H. D. began writing epic poetry, a genre for which she is most admired. In her war epic *Trilogy*, mythic persons act on timeless stages, manipulating objects—images—that carry meaning.

Trilogy's parts are "The Walls Do Not Fall," "Tribute to the Angels," and "The Flowering of the Rod." Like Ezra Pound's *Cantos* and T. S. Eliot's *Four Quartets*, it is densely allusive; its meanings are too manifold to explain here. "The Walls Do Not Fall" begins, "There, as here, ruin opens." "There" means ancient Greek temples and the tomb of Christ; "here" means in a church ruined by bombs. Throughout the poem, "There" and "here," mythic time when the gods walked, and the now of World War II are conflated. "Tribute" recalls the angels of Revelation. The angels' acts of mediation are acts of love. The poem seeks to set forth the nature of divine love; her image for that love is the circle, for which all points look toward the center ("reckless, regardless, blind to reality" [122]). "The Flowering of the Rod" describes a springtime, a rebirth, during which a sword made of applewood will flower into a plant; likewise the poem's references to the Christ story refer to birth and rebirth.

An early scene in *The Gift*, H. D.'s autobiography of her earliest years, is emblematic of her thrust as a writer and thinker. As a little girl, she writes in *The Gift*, she watched the parade of a Tom show, an abbreviated on-the-road dramatized version of *Uncle Tom's Cabin*. H. D. writes: "[T]he three children [H. D. and her brothers] . . . who stood watching, were all the children of the world; in Rome, in Athens, in Palestine, in Egypt, they had watched golden chariots, they had seen black men chained together and cruel overseers brandishing whips. It was Alexandria, it was a Roman Triumph, it was a medieval miracle play with a devil, who was Simon Legree" (18). *The Gift, The Mystery,* and *Tribute to Freud*, while "outside" of H. D.'s oeuvre as a poet and novelist, are composed of moments that H. D. herself chose to illustrate, in order, her childhood, the history of the Moravians, and her months under Freud's care. They offer interested readers keys to understand H. D.'s symbolic meaning-making project.

CRITICAL RECEPTION

H. D. was first known for her small, spare imagist poems, and that early, enthusiastic critical reception colors what happened later. *Sea Garden* received only eight reviews (according to Boughn's bibliography), but the *Collected Poems* and *Palimpsest*, published in the 1920s, received over twice that number. The first lengthy critical essays (by H. P. Collins and Glenn Hughes) were laudatory; unfortunately, Hughes's work also noted that H. D.'s poems looked backward to ancient Greece. After H. D.'s first years of recognition in the 1920s and 1930s, later critics, seeming to read H. D.'s poems through Hughes's "looked backward" idea, faulted her for living in another time and not in her own strife-torn one.

Critics and admirers helped keep H. D.'s reputation before the public during the 1930s and 1940s; Boughn lists twenty-four reviews for "The Walls Do Not Fall" and the same number for *Tribute to Freud*. At the time of her death, critics began to assess H. D.'s contribution to American letters. Norman Holmes Pearson and others (see Greenwood, Holland, and the poets Robert Duncan and Denise Levertov) praised the poet. The new psychological critics found much to admire, reading the poet (then, as now) through *Tribute to Freud*. However, the opposing camp was vocal. It had two themes, one being that H. D.'s "translations" from the Greek were not faithful (see Douglas Bush). More damning than that accusation was that H. D., like all women, wrote "emotionally" and that her work is "escapist" (see Engel). One difficulty was that the demands of new criticism could not be met by an H. D. poem. New schools of criticism had to emerge before H. D. could find her renaissance.

The emergence of feminist, biographical, and cultural criticism, plus the publication of works suppressed by H. D. during her lifetime, has moved H. D.'s works beyond the short headnote and small handful of imagist poems found in most anthologies. Critics such as Rachel Blau DuPlessis, Susan Stanford Friedman, and Susan Gubar have noted that H. D.'s novels encode the feminist dilemma of "romantic thralldom" (DuPlessis's words), in which the woman creator can see herself only through the roles of wife, daughter, or mother. A constant presence on the landscape of H. D. criticism is her biographer, Susan Stanford Friedman. In some ten to fifteen early articles beginning in the 1970s, Friedman has maintained that H. D.'s work is not driven by uncontrolled emotions, nor is it escapist. Instead, maintains Friedman, H. D. chronicled the war years in a way that was direct, engaged, and principled.

Later critics (e.g., Gelpi), working through the long poems *Helen in Egypt* and *Hermetic Definition*, have sought to place the emotional content of love poems at the center and to accord to the affective realm of human experience such importance that epic poetry may indeed be written about it and given serious thought. Biographical criticism, which connects the gestaldt of lived moments with the artifice by which they are described, is an important method of understanding the novels.

The 1970s saw the first publication or reprinting of important H. D. works; in the 1980s, that torrent of publications was followed by a flood. As a result, H. D. scholars have pursued many avenues. Beverly Lynch's work in *Lesbian Lives* asks how H. D.'s bisexuality affected her writing. Laity concerns herself with H. D.'s decadent/symbolist inheritance. Jeanne Kerblatt-Houghton, composing in French, has contributed works in the semiotic tradition, examining H. D.'s images as signs and sounds. H. D.'s work as an actress, and even as a collector of snapshots, has been considered in the work of Diepeveen, Collecott, and Friedman, the last of whom considers H. D.'s work with Paul Robeson in terms of racial tensions that had surfaced during the 1920s and 1930s in Europe. Morris's work uses deconstruction as a tool to probe the word "projection" as it exists in film and in psychology.

Contemporary Literature devoted two special issues to H. D. (autumn 1969; winter 1986). The 1969 issue is particularly important; many critics who had been or would become staples of H. D. scholarship voiced their opinions in that issue. *Sagetrieb*, a journal that began publication in 1982, published criticism about the imagist movement; a special H. D. number was published in the spring/fall number of 1995. From 1987 to 1991, Eileen Gregory published the *H. D. Newsletter* through the Dallas Institute of Humanities and Culture. That modern avatar, the Internet, indexes important H. D. sites. One site is a very useful home page (http://www.well.com/user/heddy/), which gives instructions for connecting with a listserv maintained for the H. D. Society (HDSOC-L located at listserv.uconnvm.uconn.edu).

No bibliographical essay would be complete without a note about Perdita Schaffner, who indeed grew up, married, and made H. D. a grandmother. Perdita has offered, through the years, wise, honest, and loving tributes in words to her mother and to the households that nourished her. Most of Perdita's works exist as forewords and afterwords in newly released or rereleased work, writings that constitute an important tool for the H. D. scholar. Other forewords and afterwords, such as those by Pearson and Walsh, offer firsthand biographical knowledge of the poet's life and the circumstances of composition.

A handful of full-length biographies have come out. Friedman evinces a feminist and psychological viewpoint; Guest's is an insider's understanding of the writer's life; Robinson's literary biography reads the poet's work through her Moravian background; and DuPlessis offers a feminist assessment of H. D.'s career. Volumes of letters (Bertholf; Hollenberg; Zilboorg), a bibliography (Boughn), and a slew of articles in collections offer the H. D. scholar many avenues to pursue.

BIBLIOGRAPHY

The art book school of publishing, reacting against mass publication techniques, arose about the time H. D. began publishing her first works. From the beginning of her career, launched by forty copies of *Choruses from Iphigenia in Aulus* (Cleveland: Clerk's Press [1916]), H. D. sought publication through presses that used handmade papers and set copy by hand. Although H. D. used art book presses throughout her life, their small press runs did not allow for wide dissemination of the works. I have eliminated art book publications from the list of works by H. D. (the reader may consult Boughn for a complete list).

Boughn lists 152 items written by H. D. that appeared in periodicals and some fifty theses and dissertations. These are not listed here. Also not listed are H. D.'s many volumes of lyric poetry, since the reader may consult one of the two volumes of collected poems. The few plays are omitted as well.

Some of H. D.'s works remain unpublished and are omitted from this list. Their gist may be understood through Susan Stanford Friedman's *Dictionary of Literary Biography* entry or her biography. The unpublished works, as well as H. D.'s letters and other writings, may be read in manuscript at the Collection of American Literature, Beinecke Rare Book and Manuscript Library, Yale University.

Throughout the bibliography that follows, the latest American editions were preferred. The student who wishes to consult more complete lists may begin with Boughn; next, the bibliography that appears in Michael King's edited collection *H. D.: Woman and Poet*; and then to the H. D. homepage, which maintains an up-to-the-minute list (the address is mentioned in the text).

Works by H. D.

Sea Garden. 1916. New York: St. Martin's, 1975.

Collected Poems of H. D. New York: Boni, 1925.

Palimpsest. 1926. Prof. Harry T. Moore. Afterword Robert McAlmon. Carbondale, IL: Southern Illinois University Press, 1968. (Novel)

Hedylus. Fwd. Perdita Schaffner. Afterword John Walsh. 1928. Redding Ridge, CT: Black Swan, 1980. (Novel)

"Two Americans." 1928. *New Directions* 51 (1987): 58–68. (Short story)

[Pseud. John Helforth]. *Nights.* 1935. Introd. Perdita Schaffner. New York: New Directions, 1986. (Novel)

Trilogy. 1944–1946. Introd. Norman Holmes Pearson. New York: New Directions, 1973. (Epic poem)

Tribute to Freud/Writing on the Wall/Advent. 1956. Fwd. Norman Holmes Pearson. New York: New Directions, 1974. (Nonfiction)

Bid Me to Live (A Madrigal). 1960. Fwd. Perdita Schaffner. Afterword John Walsh. Redding, CT: Black Swan, 1983. (Novel)

Helen in Egypt. 1961. Introd. Horace Gregory. New York: New Directions, 1974. (Epic poem)

The Gift, the Complete Text. 1969. Ed. Jane Augustine. Gainesville: University Press of Florida, 1998. (Autobiography)

Hermetic Definition. Fwd. Norman Holmes Pearson. New York: New Directions, 1971.
   (Poem)
The Mystery. Images of H. D. and from The Mystery. London: Enitharmon, 1976. 33–
   58. (Nonfiction)
End to Torment: A Memoir of Ezra Pound. Ed. Norman Holmes Pearson and Michael
   King. Fwd. Michael King. New York: New Directions, 1979.
HERmione. Introd. Perdita Schaffner. New York: New Directions, 1981. (Novel)
Notes on Thought and Vision and the Wise Sappho. Introd. Albert Gelpi. San Francisco:
   City Lights, 1982. (Nonfiction)
Collected Poems, 1912–1944. Ed. Louis L. Martz. New York: New Directions, 1983.
Asphodel. Ed. Robert Spoo. Durham, NC: Duke University Press, 1992. (Novel)
Paint It Today. Introd. Cassandra Laity. New York: New York University Press, 1992.
   (Novel)

Studies of H. D.

Bertholf, Robert J., ed. *A Great Admiration: H. D./Robert Duncan Correspondence,
   1950–1961*. Venice, CA: Lapis Press, 1992.
Boughn, Michael. *H. D.: A Bibliography, 1905–1990*. Charlottesville: University of Vir-
   ginia Press, 1993.
Bryher [Winifred Ellerman]. *The Heart to Artemis—A Writer's Memoirs*. New York:
   Harcourt, 1962.
Bush, Douglas. "American Poets." *Mythology and the Romantic Tradition in English
   Poetry*. Cambridge: Harvard University Press, 1937. 481–525.
Chisolm, Dianne. "H. D.'s Autoheterography." *Tulsa Studies in Women's Literature* 9.1
   (1990): 79–106.
Clark, Timothy. "Inspiration and the Romantic Body: Nietzsche and H. D." *The Theory
   of Inspiration: Composition as a Crisis of Subjectivity in Romantic and Post-
   Romantic Writing*. Manchester: Manchester University Press, 1997. 170–90.
Collecott, Diane. "Images at the Crossroads: The H. D. Scrapbook." *H. D.: Woman and
   Poet*. Ed. Michael King. Orono, ME: National Poetry Foundation, 1986. 319–67.
Collins, H. P. "H. D.'s Method" and "The Position of H. D." *Modern Poetry*. New York:
   Houghton, 1925. 154–86, 187–202.
Diepeveen, Leonard. "H. D. and the Film Arts." *Journal of Aesthetic Education* 18.4
   (1984): 57–65.
Donald, James, Anne Friedberg, and Laura Marcus. *Close-Up, 1927–1933*. Princeton,
   NJ: Princeton University Press, 1999.
Duncan, Robert. "Beginnings: Chapter 1 of the H. D. Book, Part 1." *Coyote's Journal*
   5–6 (1966): 8–31.
———. "The H. D. Book." *The Collected Writings of Robert Duncan*. Ed. Robert Bert-
   holf. Los Angeles: University of California Press. Forthcoming.
DuPlessis, Rachel Blau. *The Career of That Struggle*. Bloomington: Indiana University
   Press, 1986.
———. "Romantic Thralldom and 'Subtle Geneologies' in H. D." *Writing beyond the
   Ending; Narrative Strategies of Twentieth-Century Women Writers*. Bloomington:
   Indiana University Press, 1985. 66–83.
Edmonds, Susan. *History, Psychoanalysis, and Montage*. Stanford: Stanford University
   Press, 1994.

Engel, Bernard. "H. D.: Poems that Matter and Dilutations." *Contemporary Literature* 10 (1969): 507–22.

Friedman, Susan Stanford. "H. D." *American Poets, 1880–1945*. Ed. Peter Quartermain. Detroit: Gale, 1986. Vol. 45 of *Dictionary of Literary Biography*. 115–49.

———. "Modernism of the 'Scattered Remnant': Race and Politics in the Development of H. D.'s Modernist Vision." *H. D.: Woman and Poet*. Ed. Michael King. Orono, ME: National Poetry Foundation, 1986. 91–116.

———. *Psyche Reborn: The Emergence of H. D*. Bloomington: Indiana University Press, 1981.

———. "Who Buried H. D.? A Poet, Her Critics, and Her Place in the 'Literary Tradition.' " *College English* 36.7 (1975): 801–14.

Gelpi, Albert. "Hilda in Egypt." *Southern Review* 18.2 (1982): 233–50.

Greenwood, E. B. "H. D. and the Problem of Escapism." *Essays in Criticism* 21.4 (1971): 365–76.

Gregory, Eileen. *H. D. and Helenism: Classic Lines*. Cambridge, MA: Cambridge University Press, 1997.

Gubar, Susan. "The Echoing Spell of H. D.'s Trilogy." *Shakespeare's Sisters: Feminist Essays on Women Poets*. Ed. Sandra M. Gilbert and Susan Gubar. Bloomington: Indiana University Press, 1979. 153–64.

———. "Sapphistries." *Signs* 10.1 (1984): 43–62.

Guest, Barbara. *Herself Defined: The Poet H. D. and Her World*. New York: Doubleday, 1984.

Holland, Norman N. *Poems in Persons: An Introduction to the Psychoanalysis of Literature*. New York: Norton, 1973.

Hollenberg, Donna Krolik. *H. D. The Poetics of Childbirth and Creativity*. Boston: Northeastern University Press, 1991.

———. ed. *Between History and Poetry: The Letters of H. D. and Norman Holmes Pearson*. Iowa City: Iowa University Press, 1997.

Hughes, Glenn. "H. D.: 'The Perfect Imagist." *Imagism and the Imagists: A Study of Modern Poetry*. Stanford: Stanford University Press, 1931. 109–24.

Kerblatt-Houghton, Jeanne. "*Helen in Egypt*: Variations sur un thème sonore." *G.R.E.S.* 2 (1978): 201–13.

King, Michael, ed. *H. D.: Woman and Poet*. Orono, ME: National Poetry Foundation, 1986.

Laity, Cassandra. *H. D. and the Victorian Fin de Siècle: Gender, Modernism, Decadence*. Cambridge, MA: Cambridge University Press, 1996.

Levertov, Denise. "H. D.: An Appreciation." *Poetry* (1962): 182–86.

Lynch, Beverly. "Love, Beyond Men and Women: H. D." *Lesbian Lives: Biographies of Women from "The Ladder."* Ed. Barbara Grier and Colett Reid. Oakland: Diana Press, 1976. 259–72.

Morris, Adalaide. "The Concept of Projection: H. D.'s Visionary Powers." *Contemporary Literature* 25 (1984): 411–36.

Robinson, Janice S. *The Life and Work of an American Poet*. Boston: Houghton, 1982.

Surette, Leon, and Demetres Tryphanopoulos, eds. *Modernism and the Occult Tradition*. Orono, ME: National Poetry Foundation, 1997.

Swann, Thomas Burnett. *The Classical World of H. D*. Lincoln: University of Nebraska Press, 1962.

Wagner-Martin, Linda. *H. D.'s Fiction: Convolution to Clarity.* Princeton, NJ: Princeton University Press, 1989.
Zilboorg, Caroline, ed. *Richard Aldington and H. D.: The Early Years in Letters.* New York: Manchester University Press, 1995.
———. *Richard Aldington and H. D.: The Later Years in Letters.* New York: Manchester University Press, 1995.

ALICE MAUDE EWELL
(1860–1946)

William J. Scheick

BIOGRAPHY

Alice Maude Ewell was the granddaughter of Ellen MacGregor and Dr. Jessie Ewell, both of Episcopal Scottish descent, who in the 1830s moved from Maryland to wood-sheltered Dunblane (by Blue Run Mountain) in Prince William County, Virginia. Their eldest son, John Smith Magruder Ewell, headed a household of twelve children with his second wife, Alice Tyler, the mother of Alice Maude, born in 1860. As a child, Alice Maude, who was a cousin of the Confederate general Richard Stoddert Ewell, began reading avidly at an early age, was mostly schooled at home, and relished listening to her father and mother read books to the entire family. She became especially familiar with the works of William Shakespeare, Sir Walter Scott, Nathaniel Hawthorne, Charles Dickens, Richard Doddridge Blackmore, Robert Louis Stevenson, and James Branch Cabell. As an adult she enjoyed writing tales often set in the postbellum South for both a source of income and, in her own words, "a Way of Escape."

Late in life she expressed regret that her literary undertakings had been restricted to intervals between numerous chores inside and outside her father's house: "Now I look back, and think how that has been of all deprivations the hardest to bear. Lack of time for the best and highest work,—for deep study, fine touches, delicate finish. . . . Time for writing the best that was in me, though I had to keep on trying for the sake of the little money made. That was my greatest Deprivation." She carried another burden as well: her lifelong awareness of a "youth deprived." Ewell specifically regretted her family's postbellum economic situation, which precluded the formal education that she had always desired, particularly in "the arts and graces." When recalling this childhood deprivation and related matters at the age of seventy, she ruefully observed that "life, even at best, seems rather a tragic business" (*A Virginia Scene* 99, 106, 117). Ewell died in Richmond, Virginia, on June 25, 1946.

Ewell published a fictional historical narrative (*A White Guard to Satan*), historical juvenilia (*A Long Time Ago*), verse (*The Heart of Old Virginia*), family recollections of Prince William County (*A Virginia Scene*), and periodical writings in *Peterson's Magazine* (ten poems and twenty-seven stories), *Godey's Lady's Book* (one poem and one story), *St. Nicholas* (four poems and six stories), and *Atlantic Monthly* (nine stories).

MAJOR WORKS AND THEMES

If Ewell's achievement in verse is negligible, her historical juvenilia set in the Old South is humorously entertaining. "My Neighbor's Goose" is typical. Included in *A Long Time Ago*, this tale recounts the misadventures of Master Muffet as he tries to hide an apparent theft. Various quaint southern practices are embedded in this and the other stories in the collection. Ewell's one novel, *A White Guard to Satan*, is an enterprising exercise in southern myth-making. Published at a time when historical fiction was popular with American readers, *White Guard* presents a "secret history" of the role of women during Bacon's Rebellion, a settler uprising in 1676 that resulted in the burning of Jamestown, Virginia. Ewell excels in the genre of short fiction, where she demonstrates a talent for suspense, plotting, characterization, and especially local color. Her stories provide a rich record of southern settings, customs, speech patterns, reading interests, and postbellum changes. Ewell's periodical fiction, dating from 1883 to 1905, also reveals her evolving perspective on tradition, class, and gender as she developed a sense of herself as a writer with a social purpose.

Ewell's achievement suits recent critical interests. After "A Christmas Ghost" (1888), five years into her career, Ewell's fiction increasingly represents female selfhood as a scarcely glimpsed ghostly presence in Victorian America. "A Woman's Fancy" (1903), an adroit revision of the ghost-story genre, is Ewell's most accomplished embodiment of this theme. In this story Ewell associates the materialization, the self-fashioning, of this spectral potential female identity with the creation of a work of art.

When Ewell's women achieve an internally generated identity, they tend to be influenced by narratives; and these newly "realized" women serve, in turn, as influential narratives for other young women, including the readers of Ewell's stories. This is the central issue in the memorable "Wycham's Ordinary" (1889), an exemplary old woman's account told to two young girls about a time in 1804 when she was the housekeeper of an inn. This tale's plot may detail the strange death of a sister and brother, but its point concerns the beneficial place of storytelling in women's coming to terms with experience. This view of narrative is also the underlying message in the ingenious family story "Miss Tom and Peepsie" (1893), a recollection directed at a young female audience that concerns a dramatic change in one independent woman's self-understanding. The power of narrative to mitigate social deprivation and to inaugurate personal self-possession coalesces with Ewell's related emphasis on the narrative power of agentlike women in negotiating salutary alterations in social perspective. Often, as in "Nancy's Burin' Clo'es" (1889), Ewell's correlation of female identity and narration blurs the boundary between fact and fiction in order to suggest the potentiality of the reader to effect change in her own storylike world.

Fostering this protean sense of female agency is Ewell's keen perception of the collapse of both the class system and the economic features of the Old South. The possibility for such change commenced with the Civil War, observes a narrating witness to the enduring affection between a genteel lady and a mountain woman in "An Echo of Battle" (1892): The " 'tie of blood' . . . then drew all classes together in the beleaguered South." " 'Come Down' " (1895), another story recounted by a female witness, pertinently depicts an aristocratic woman's change of heart toward the grandson of a sexton and an innkeeper's daughter. And, relatedly, by the conclusion of "The Last of the First" (1896) a young woman, previously stigmatized by her illegitimate birth and her ignoble maternal blood, is rewarded for her filial piety in a New South where an iron mine brings communal prosperity in place of the defunct gold mine that had once enriched an elite few. Ewell's fiction depicts an ideal legacy of women abetting women, a lineage of potent female "narrative" agency that crosses generational, economic, social, and possibly, racial differences.

CRITICAL RECEPTION

To date, contemporary reviews of Ewell's books have not been located. Her latter-day critical reception is virtually nonexistent, an unsurprising fate for turn-of-the-century authors who wrote primarily for periodical markets. Ewell is accorded a brief biographical entry in *The Library of Southern Literature*, a substantial early twentieth-century effort to document the extent of the South's literary place in American letters. The entry is only partially accurate in its details, and it also insinuates that Ewell's periodical work mainly appeared in *St. Nicholas*, a well-regarded children's magazine. Since then, Ewell's work was overlooked for nearly seventy-five years, even in studies of southern writers, until her listing in Doris Robinson's *Women Novelists, 1891–1920*. Not until the editorial introductions to two collections of her short fiction and verse for *Peterson's Magazine, Godey's Lady's Book, St. Nicholas*, and *Atlantic Monthly* has Ewell received any extended critical commentary. These introductions trace Ewell's evolving awareness of female authority both in her main characters and in her narrative manner.

BIBLIOGRAPHY

Works by Alice Maude Ewell

A White Guard to Satan: Being an Account of Mine Own Adventures and Observation in That Time of the Trouble in Virginia Now Called Bacon's Rebellion, Which Same Did Take Place in the Year of Grace 1676, by Mistress Elizabeth Godstowe. Boston: Houghton, 1900. (Historical novel)

The Heart of Old Virginia. New York and Washington: Neal, 1907. (Verse)

A Long Time Ago in Virginia and Maryland with a Glimpse of Old England. New York: Neal, 1907. (Juvenilia)

A Virginia Scene, Or Life in Old Prince William. Lynchburg, VA: J. P. Bell, 1931. (Memoir)

Alice Maude Ewell's Atlantic Monthly *Fiction, 1892–1905.* Ed. William J. Scheick. Delmar, NY: Scholars' Facsimiles & Reprints, 1997. (Short stories)

Alice Maude Ewell's Peterson's Magazine *Fiction: 1883–1893.* Ed. William J. Scheick. Delmar, NY: Scholars' Facsimiles & Reprints, 1998. (Short stories and verse)

Studies of Alice Maude Ewell

Alderman, Edwin Anderson and Joel Chandler Harris, eds. *The Library of Southern Literature.* Vol. 15. Atlanta: Martin, 1910. 140.

Robinson, Doris. *Women Novelists, 1891–1920: An Index to Biographical and Autobiographical Sources.* New York: Garland, 1984. 124.

Scheick, William J. "Alice Maude Ewell: A Profile." *Ellen Glasgow Newsletter* 39 (1997): 6–7.

———. "Female Legacy, Narrative Agency and Identity in Alice Maude Ewell's Fiction." *Alice Maude Ewell's* Atlantic Monthly *Fiction, 1892–1905.* Delmar, NY: Scholars' Facsimiles, 1997. 7–25.

———. "Identity, Mediation, and Narration in Alice Maude Ewell's Early Fiction." *Alice Maude Ewell's* Peterson's Magazine *Fiction, 1883–1893.* Delmar, NY: Scholars' Facsimiles, 1998. 7–23.

JESSIE REDMON FAUSET
(1882–1961)

Rhonda Austin

BIOGRAPHY

Jessie "Redmona" Fauset was born on April 27, 1882, in Camden County, New Jersey, to Annie Redmon Fauset and Redmon Fauset, an African Methodist Episcopal minister. Upon Annie's death, Redmon Fauset married a widow with three children, and their union produced three more children.

Although several sources describe Fauset's upbringing as "prosperous," "sheltered," and "privileged," the large size of the family and her father's job as a minister, a position that required the family to relocate at the direction of his church's bishop, make it unlikely that the family was wealthy. In a letter to Fauset biographer Carolyn Sylvander, one Fauset sibling recalls that, in his memory, the family was "dreadfully poor" (qtd. in Sylvander 25).

After graduating with honors in 1900 from a Philadelphia high school where she was probably the only black student, Fauset applied to Bryn Mawr College. To avoid challenging segregated America by admitting a black student to an all-white school, an official at Bryn Mawr initiated support for Fauset to be offered a scholarship to Cornell University. She accepted and graduated Phi Beta Kappa from Cornell in 1905. Denied employment as a teacher in the segregated schools of Philadelphia, Fauset taught one year in Baltimore. Later, the multilingual Fauset taught French for fourteen years in Washington, D.C. In 1919, she earned a master's degree at the University of Pennsylvania, then moved to New York, where she began an eight-year stint as literary editor of the *Crisis*. As editor for this distinguished African American literary magazine, Fauset discovered and fostered the talents of many prominent black writers, including Jean Toomer, Countee Cullen, Langston Hughes, and Claude McKay. She also contributed significantly to black literature as editor and chief writer of the *Brownie's Book*, a magazine for black children published between 1920 and 1921. Fauset wrote the dedication for the first issue, a poem in which she stated her purpose of providing literature so black children would not have to search in vain, "For History or Song or Story/That told of Colored People's glory" (qtd. in Sylvander 115). Fauset's endeavors to promote black writers reflect her belief "in the power of art to effect change in people bound by trained prejudice and discrimination" (qtd. in Sylvander 160).

Considered a minor, though pivotal, figure of the Harlem Renaissance, Fauset authored four novels, numerous short stories, essays, poems, and articles between 1910 and 1933. Commenting on Fauset's contribution to American fiction, Hugh Gloster states, "Fauset's description of the lives and difficulties of Philadelphia's colored elite is one of the major achievements of American Negro fiction" (139). Although her novels and short fiction are significant, her primary contribution to the Harlem Renaissance may have resulted from her years as editor of *Crisis*, where she also contributed articles and reviews that concerned many aspects of the literary movements of the era.

In 1929, Fauset married Herbert Harris, and the couple lived in Harlem for several years. They later moved to New Jersey, where they lived until Harris's death in 1958. The years of Fauset's marriage were not productive writing years. She authored a few articles and reportedly worked on a fifth novel that was never published. After her husband's death she moved to Philadelphia and lived with her stepbrother Earl Huff until her death from heart disease on April 30, 1961.

MAJOR WORKS AND THEMES

Fauset's novels share several common subjects, including racism, passing, limited opportunities for African Americans and women, and miscegenation. Fauset also explores the theme of heredity versus environment as factors influencing human behavior and personality development and by delineating the effects of both on the characters in her stories and novels. One recurring message in her works is the importance of human relationships and the attainment of happiness. Her primary characters are young women who are members of the black middle class of the 1920s, a group not previously represented to any degree in American literature. In fact, the first publisher to see *There Is Confusion* rejected it on the grounds that "white readers just don't expect Negroes to be like this" (Sylvander 99). During the Harlem Renaissance when Fauset wrote most of her fiction, white-dominated publishers promoted books that depicted blacks as "primitive exotics, as free, sexually uninhibited creatures. . . . Thus Fauset's choice of subject matter was very coolly received" (McDowell 101). Like many black writers during the Harlem Renaissance, Fauset had to struggle with issues that concern a black writer forced to write for a white audience. Because Fauset portrayed characters who defy stereotypical portrayals of blacks, her works were not always well received by editors or publishers.

Without moralizing, Fauset often uses religious and fairy-tale motifs as organizing patterns for her novels. Her first novel, *There Is Confusion*, contains a plot pattern similar to traditional British bildungsroman in which characters grow and learn through a process that moves from disorder and confusion of values to a revelation of true differences (Sylvander 155). Several of Fauset's frequently depicted mulatto characters struggle with initial confusion of values and beliefs, eventually learning that life is, at best, a corrective. This is usually demonstrated in the actions of a character (usually female) who is "passing" for white in order both to gain the privileges given to whites and to avoid the pain and humiliation of discrimination in a racist society. Characters who are unable to tolerate the pain of the corrective process often suffer dire consequences in Fauset's fiction.

Plum Bun (1929) is an African American bildungsroman that contrasts the lives of Angela Murray, a light-skinned black who "passes," and her dark-skinned sister, Virginia. Angela, who becomes a successful painter, eventually reveals her true racial identity in support of a black woman who is being harassed by reporters. In an ironic twist, Angela realizes that she loves Anthony Cross, a poor black man who has himself been passing for white. Angela realizes she can be content only when she develops a new understanding of the true significance of skin color, money, and marriage.

Fauset's last two novels, *The Chinaberry Tree* (1931) and *Comedy, American Style* (1933), are both developed from previously published works of short fiction. Many of the same themes and motifs that appeared in her first two novels continue in these final two. The basic plot of *The Chinaberry Tree* concerns two black high school students who, unaware that they are brother and sister, almost marry. As a lonely child, the mulatto heroine of the novel had sat under a chinaberry tree and wondered why neither black nor white children would associate with her. Similarly, the mulatto protagonist of *Comedy, American Style* attempts to pass for white only to discover that she has sacrificed not only her son but also a sense of community and both personal and cultural pride. As in her earlier novels, in *The Chinaberry Tree* and in *Comedy, American Style*, Fauset focuses on the ironies of black life in racist America and the tragedies of black women's experience in a racist and sexist society.

CRITICAL RECEPTION

Jessie Redmon Fauset's novels initially received mixed reviews. Some of her novels received some unfavorable assessments because her portrayals of middle-class blacks defied stereotypical characterizations that white readers had come to expect and that some white reviewers appreciated and, at least to some extent, perpetuated. After her novels were praised in the 1930s by Braithwaite and others, they were soon out of print, and she became one of many neglected African American women writers.

The feminist revival that began in the 1970s helped to influence scholars to reassess works by women and minority writers. During this time, Fauset began to receive long overdue critical attention. The first book-length study of Fauset, *Jessie Redmon Fauset, Black American Writer*, by Carolyn Wedin Sylvander, provides an excellent overview of Fauset's life and insightful analyses of her novels, short stories, and poems. Wilbert Jenkins's 1986 essay "Jessie Fauset:

A Modern Apostle of Black Racial Pride" reassesses Fauset's works to demonstrate her awareness of African American cultural history and to show ways she celebrates black identity. Deborah McDowell, in her seminal essay "The Neglected Dimension of Jessie Redmon Fauset," argues that earlier critics focus on Fauset's representation of the black middle class and dismiss her portrayals of black women who struggle for equality and independence in a racist and sexist society. McDowell "plac[es] Fauset squarely among the early black feminists in Afro-American literary history" for her explorations of "female consciousness" (88). Similarly, in "Looking Back from Zora, or Talking Out Both Sides My Mouth for Those Who Have Two Ears," P. Gabrielle Foreman contends that critics of *Plum Bun* too often slight it as a romance novel that concerns passing and ignore Fauset's social message that involves the dynamics of race, class, and gender hierarchies.

Contemporary critics also praise Fauset for her "novels of manners" that reveal the black middle class in white society. Ann duCille argues against critics who assume that Nella Larsen, Fauset, and many Harlem Renaissance women poets attempt to defy stereotypical images of black women by portraying prim and proper middle-class black women. She contends that Fauset and Larsen often parody middle-class convention to present scathing critiques of middle-class values.

Critics continue to discuss Fauset as a Harlem Renaissance writer. Her works are anthologized in many anthologies of the Harlem Renaissance and in books that focus exclusively on women Harlem Renaissance writers. Fauset is frequently mentioned in critical assessments of the Harlem Renaissance and often compared with other women Harlem Renaissance writers such as Zora Neale Hurston and Dorothy West. Among Harlem Renaissance writers, Fauset is most frequently compared with Nella Larsen. As mentioned above, duCille discusses both Larsen and Fauset in terms of their feminist explorations. More recently, Jacquelyn Y. McLendon's full-length study *The Politics of Color in the Fiction of Jessie Fauset and Nella Larsen* looks at the mulatto protagonists in *Plum Bun, Comedy, American Style,* and Larsen's *Quicksand* to examine race as a social construction. Although her short stories and essays remain uncollected, Jessie Fauset, as other African American women writers, is beginning to gain the critical recognition she deserves.

BIBLIOGRAPHY

Works by Jessie Redmon Fauset

"Emmy." *Crisis* Dec. 1912: 79–87; Jan. 1913: 134–42. (Short story)
"My House and a Glimpse of My Life Therein." *Crisis* July 1914: 143–45. (Short story)
"Mary Elizabeth: A Story." *Crisis* Dec. 1919: 51–56. (Short story)
"New Literature on the Negro." *Crisis* June 1920: 78–83. (Nonfiction)
"The Sleeper Wakes." *Crisis* Aug. 1920: 168–73; Sept. 1920: 226–29; Oct. 1920: 267–74. (Short story)

"Impressions on the Second Pan-African Congress." *Crisis* Nov. 1921: 12–18. (Nonfiction)

"What Europe Thought of the Pan-African Congress." *Crisis* Dec. 1921: 60–69. (Nonfiction)

"When Christmas Comes." *Crisis* Dec. 1922: 61–63. (Short story)

"Double Trouble." *Crisis* Aug. 1923: 155–59; Sept. 1923: 205–9. (Short story)

There Is Confusion. New York: Boni, 1924.

Plum Bun: A Novel without a Moral. New York: Stokes, 1929.

The Chinaberry Tree: A Novel of American Life. New York: Stokes, 1931. New York: AMS, 1969.

Comedy, American Style. New York: Stokes, 1933. New York: AMS, 1969.

Studies of Jessie Redmon Fauset

Braithwaite, William Stanley. "The Novels of Jessie Fauset." *Opportunity* 12 (1934): 24–28.

duCille, Ann. "Blues Notes on Black Sexuality: Sex and the Texts of Jessie Fauset and Nella Larsen." *Journal of the History of Sexuality* 3 (1993): 418–44.

Feeney, Joseph J. "Greek Tragic Patterns in a Black Novel: Jessie Fauset's *The Chinaberry Tree*." *CLA Journal* 18 (1974): 211–15.

———. "A Sardonic, Unconventional Jessie Fauset: The Double Structure and Double Vision of Her Novels." *CLA Journal* 22 (1979): 365–82.

Foreman, P. Gabrielle. "Looking Back from Zora, or Talking Out Both Sides My Mouth for Those Who Have Two Ears." *Black American Literature Forum* 24 (1990): 649–66.

Gloster, Hugh. *Negro Voices in American Fiction.* New York: Russell and Russell, 1965.

Jenkins, Wilbert. "Jessie Fauset: A Modern Apostle of Black Racial Pride." *Zora Neale Hurston Forum* 1.1 (1986): 14–24.

Johnson, Abby Arthur. "Literary Midwife: Jessie Redmon Fauset and the Harlem Renaissance." *Phylon* 39 (1978): 143–53.

Jones, Sharon Lynette. "Rereading the Harlem Renaissance: The 'Folk,' 'Bourgeois,' and 'Proletarian' Aesthetics in the Fiction of Jessie Fauset, Zora Neale Hurston, and Dorothy West." Diss. University of Georgia, 1996.

Lewis, Vashti C. "Mulatto Hegemony in the Novels of Jessie Redmon Fauset." *CLA Journal* 35 (1992): 375–86.

Lupton, Mary Jane. "Bad Blood in Jersey: Jessie Fauset's *The Chinaberry Tree*." *CLA Journal* 27 (1984): 383–92.

———. "Clothes and Closure in Three Novels by Black Women." *Black American Literature Forum* 20 (1986): 409–21.

McCoy, Beth A. " 'Is This Really What You Wanted Me to Be?': The Daughter's Disintegration in Jessie Fauset's *There Is Confusion*." *Modern Fiction Studies* 40.1 (1994): 101–17.

McDowell, Deborah E. "The Neglected Dimension of Jessie Redmon Fauset." *Conjuring: Black Women, Fiction, and Literary Tradition.* Ed. Marjorie Pryse and Hortense J. Spillers. Bloomington: Indiana University Press, 1985. 86–104.

McLendon, Jacquelyn Y. *The Politics of Color in the Fiction of Jessie Fauset and Nella Larsen.* Charlottesville: University Press of Virginia, 1995.

Miller, Nina. "Femininity, Publicity, and the Class Division of Cultural Labor: Jessie Redmon Fauset's *There Is Confusion*." *African American Review* 30 (1996): 205–20.

Roses, Lorraine Elena, and Ruth Elizabeth Randolph. "Fauset, Jessie Redmon (1882–1961)." *Harlem Renaissance and Beyond: Literary Biographies of 100 Black Women Writers 1900–1945*. Boston: G. K. Hall, 1990. 102–8.

Royster, Beatrice Horn. "The Ironic Vision of Four Black Women Novelists: A Study of the Novels of Jessie Fauset, Nella Larsen, Zora Neale Hurston, and Ann Petry." Diss. Emory University, 1975.

Rueschmann, Eva. "Sister Bonds: Intersections of Family and Race in Jessie Redmon Fauset's *Plum Bun* and Dorothy West's *The Living Is Easy*." *The Significance of Sibling Relationships in Literature*. Ed. JoAnna Stephens Mink and Janet Doubler Ward. Bowling Green, OH: Bowling Green State University Popular Press, 1993. 120–32.

Sato, Hiroko. "Under the Harlem Shadow: A Study of Jessie Fauset." *The Harlem Renaissance Remembered*. Ed. Arna Bontemps. New York: Dodd-Mead, 1972. 63–89.

Shockley, Ann Allen. "Jessie Redmon Fauset, 1882–1961." *Afro-American Women Writers, 1746–1993: An Anthology and Critical Guide*. Ed. Shockley. Boston: G. K. Hall, 1988. 415–24.

Starkey, Marion. "Jessie Fauset." *Southern Workman* May 1932: 217–20.

Sylvander, Carolyn Wedin. *Jessie Redmon Fauset: Black American Writer*. Troy, NY: Whitston, 1981.

Wall, Cheryl A. "Jessie Redmon Fauset." *Women of the Harlem Renaissance*. By Wall. Bloomington: Indiana University Press, 1995. 33–84.

EDNA FERBER
(1885–1968)

Rhonda Austin

BIOGRAPHY

Edna Ferber was born on August 15, 1885, in Kalamazoo, Michigan, to Julia Neumann Ferber of Milwaukee and Jacob Charles Ferber, a Hungarian-born Jewish merchant. The younger of two daughters, Ferber spent her early years in Ottumwa, Iowa, until a blatant act of anti-Semitism precipitated her family's move to Appleton, Wisconsin, when Ferber was twelve. After high school graduation, the end of Ferber's formal education, family finances kept her from pursuing her dream of studying at Northwestern University's School of Elocution and becoming an actress. Instead, at age seventeen, she became a reporter for the *Appleton Daily Crescent*. Fired from that job because her writing style did not conform to the spare journalistic style preferred by the editor, she went on to write for the *Milwaukee Journal* until she suffered a collapse brought on by exhaustion and anemia. Recuperating at home, she wrote her first short story, "The Homely Heroine," which she sold in 1910 to *Everybody's Magazine.*

Ferber's father, an invalid for several years before his death, died during the family's tenure in Appleton, and her mother sold the family business and moved with her daughters to Chicago. Ferber's mother was a domineering woman who ruled the family for years and continued to have a great influence in the lives of her two daughters until her death. For years after Ferber achieved success as a writer, her mother lived and traveled extensively with her.

According to her biographer and great-niece Julie Goldsmith Gilbert, Ferber grew to become a "difficult" woman, a word also used to describe Ferber's mother. Although she inspired fierce loyalty among her friends and literary collaborators, who respected both her talent and dedication to her craft, few would disagree that, in later years, Ferber was also stubborn, vain, cantankerous, impatient, and demanding. "Outrage was a household word at Ferber's. She was always in a tempest about something—her publisher and her lawyers being her favorite targets" (Gilbert 116). Extremely disciplined about her writing schedule, she began each morning with a brisk walk, followed by several hours working on her latest project.

Ferber did not place much emphasis on her own sexual identity and attributed the fact that she never married to her belief that one could not be a good author and a wife-mother simultaneously. She often referred to her writing as her off-spring and used sexual imagery when speaking of her work. She equated writer's block with impotency, and when she had a productive day of writing, she would say that she felt "sated, appeased, womanly" (Gilbert 73). Though she had no children of her own, she was close to her sister's children and financially supported her sister's family.

Ferber celebrated her Jewish heritage, although she abandoned most of her formal religious rites and beliefs. Several of her works portray Jewish characters, mostly in minor roles. On being Jewish, she states, "I never have ceased to marvel at the tenacity, the courage, the high intelligence, the warm humanity, the capacity to rise above adversity, the wry humor and the spirit which, combined, have enabled us as a whole to survive in this weird world" (Gilbert 112).

Ferber gained national attention when she published her first short story, which portrayed Emma McChesney, a divorced mother who worked as a traveling underskirt salesperson. In 1911, Ferber sold the first story in the series to *American Magazine* and eventually wrote more than twenty stories featuring Emma McChesney. The McChesney stories were collected in three volumes between 1913 and 1915, and in 1915, Ferber and George V. Hobart collaborated on a play based on these stories. Ferber declined a lucrative contract to continue writing McChesney stories for *Cosmopolitan*, stating that she feared "sliding to oblivion on a path greased by Emma McChesney" (*A Peculiar Treasure* 174). Though, while writing her major novels, she continued to write short stories, she never again wrote an Emma McChesney story.

Ferber wrote eleven collections of short stories, two autobiographies, and ten plays (most in collaboration with playwright George S. Kaufman); but she is perhaps best known for her novels, nine of which have been adapted to film, including *Giant, Show Boat, Cimarron, Dinner at Eight, Come and Get It*, and the 1925 Pulitzer Prize winner *So Big*. Additionally, seven movies have been adapted from her short stories and five from her plays.

Ferber saw herself as a pioneer in terms of what she achieved as a woman in the male-dominated field of publishing. Of writing, she said, "The writer is a writer because he cannot help it. It is a compulsion. Sometimes it is called a gift, but actually it is an urge for expression that simply cannot be denied" (*A Kind of Magic* 160). During her professional life, Ferber maintained residences in Chicago and New York, but by the 1930s she considered New York her primary residence. She lived there until her death from cancer on April 16, 1968.

MAJOR WORKS AND THEMES

Ferber's dominant themes include America, its successes and failures, and women who overcome personal and cultural hardship to live up to their potential. Many of her strongest characters are working women who, like herself, are noted for their personal accomplishments rather than their relationships with men. Ferber's female characters could be described as early feminists, but not in the sense that word is used today. Ferber did not have much use for the feminist movement, although in her fiction women are always the stronger gender.

To represent these themes, Ferber uses two basic formats, often simultaneously: the generational novel and the regional novel. Her fiction is character driven and often has little plot. Her protagonists are primarily ordinary women forced to struggle against societal expectations in a male-dominated society. These women have a purpose, however, and it is usually to contrast the elements of true success with those of false success. Ferber refuses to romanticize the facts of her heroines' lives and provides no obligatory happy endings. Her intent is not to please but to show social change. Women who do not reach their potential are portrayed as either domineering, nagging, pampered social types or helpless, ultrafeminine parasites who must depend on their feminine wiles to manipulate their men (Shaughnessy 16).

Successful women in Ferber's fiction are those who, in spite of difficult circumstances and often less-than-adequate resources, survive and gain "true" success in life. In "The Homely Heroine" (1910), the heroine is a middle-aged divorcee who works as a drummer to support herself and her son. In the McChesney stories, Emma is a divorced businesswoman who makes her living selling underskirts. Ferber's unglamorous and occasionally homely heroines represent contempt for the material trappings of success: wealth, position, and possessions.

In *Fanny Herself* (1917), Ferber examines the loss of identity that is part of the price of false success. She also begins her "critique of ruthless monopolistic businesses that were destroying the competition of small independent shopkeepers" (Shaughnessy 115). *The Girls* (1921), Ferber's first generation novel, traces the decline of a once proud Chicago family through the lives of two daughters, Charlotte and Carrie Thrift. *The Girls* was perhaps Ferber's first mature novel, exploring adult subjects such as the portrayal of a character who returns from France unmarried and with a baby. Ferber illustrates with this novel the frustration and desperation that result from a woman's denial of her own need for self-expression.

Other generation novels include *Come and Get It* (1935), *Giant* (1952), and *Ice Palace* (1958). *Come and Get It* analyzes social change by contrasting America's past with America during the depression; *Giant* chronicles the "success poisoning" representative of the nation as a whole. Ferber reveals in her autobiography, *A Kind of Magic*, that she chose Texas to illustrate this theme because "[g]eographically and economically nature had thrown two hazards at the Texans; unlimited space, seemingly unlimited wealth" (247). In *Ice Palace*, set in Alaska, heroine Christine Storm is torn between the opposing ideologies of her two grandfathers: Zebedee Kennedy, a robber baron, and Thor Storm, a humanist and conservationist. The men share a love for Christine but are divided in their philosophies about what is best for her. The untenable situation Christine is placed in as a result of the two men's differences represents the larger political conflicts actually occurring in Alaska in the years shortly before it achieved statehood.

Ferber's works always represent a social message. The locales and situations feature high contrast, where characters learn from their environments; therefore, the regional format fit Ferber's purposes. One favored device is to pluck a female character from comfortable surroundings and place her in a strange and unknown land where her true character is tested. This is the case with Lesley Lynnton in *Giant* who marries Texan Bick Benedict only to discover that her proper Virginia upbringing is of little use in Texas, a place she finds not only foreign but primitive and outrageous. Other regional novels include *Cimarron*, set in Oklahoma during the late nineteenth century, and *Ice Palace*, set in Alaska; however, these are not the only Ferber works heavily identified with a particular region of the country.

CRITICAL RECEPTION

In 1925, Ferber received the Pulitzer Prize for *So Big*, written in 1924. In spite of the fact that nearly all her novels were best-sellers, Ferber's literature has been largely ignored by critics and scholars except those who reviewed the works as they appeared. Since her death in 1968, there has been a dearth of research on Ferber or her works, although her fiction has been translated into at least five foreign languages and distributed worldwide.

Initial reviews were often mixed concerning Ferber's works because she refused to ignore or tone down controversial subjects; in fact, she often overdrew characters and situations to strengthen her message. Occasionally, she could not resist the urge to imbue her characters' dialogue with a didactic message, a trait for which she has been criticized. Texans protested strenuously about stereotyping in *Giant*. *Cimarron* inspired the ire of Oklahomans who complained about what they considered unjust and unrealistic portrayals. Several reviewers commented on Ferber's tendency to be didactic. However critical the reviews, most of her works were, nevertheless, immensely popular with the public. Her body of work is significant, spanning more than half a century. Her female characters chronicle the cultural contributions women have made to the growth and development of America.

BIBLIOGRAPHY

Works by Edna Ferber

Dawn O'Hara: The Girl Who Laughed. New York: Stokes, 1911. (Novel)
Buttered Side Down. New York: Stokes, 1912. (Short stories)
Roast Beef, Medium: The Business Adventures of Emma McChesney. New York: Stokes, 1913. (Short stories)
Personality Plus: Some Experiences of Emma McChesney and Her Son, Jock. New York: Stokes, 1914.
Emma McChesney and Co. New York: Stokes, 1915. (Short stories)
Fanny Herself. New York: Stokes, 1917. (Novel)
Cheerful, by Request. Garden City, NY: Doubleday, 1918. (Short stories)
"No Apologies Needed for American Art." *Bookman* 52 (1920): 220.
The Girls. Garden City, NY: Doubleday, 1921. (Novel)
So Big. Garden City, NY: Doubleday, 1924. (Novel)
Show Boat. Garden City, NY: Doubleday, 1926. (Novel)
Mother Knows Best: A Fiction Book. Garden City, NY: Doubleday, 1927.
Edna Ferber and George S. Kaufman. *The Royal Family.* Garden City, NY: Doubleday, 1928. (Play)
Cimarron. Garden City, NY: Doubleday, 1930. (Novel)
American Beauty. Garden City, NY: Doubleday, 1931. (Novel)
Edna Ferber and George S. Kaufman. *Dinner at Eight.* Garden City, NY: Doubleday, 1932. (Play)
Come and Get It. Garden City, NY: Doubleday, 1935. (Novel)
Edna Ferber and George S. Kaufman. *Stage Door.* Garden City, NY: Doubleday, 1936. (Play)
They Brought Their Women: A Book of Short Stories. Garden City, NY: Doubleday, 1938.
A Peculiar Treasure. Garden City, NY: Doubleday, 1939. (Autobiography)
Saratoga Trunk. Garden City, NY: Doubleday, 1941. (Novel)
Edna Ferber and George S. Kaufman. *The Land Is Bright.* Garden City, NY: Doubleday, 1941. (Play)
Great Son. Garden City, NY: Doubleday, 1945. (Novel)
One Basket: Thirty-one Short Stories. Garden City, NY: Doubleday, 1947.
Giant. Garden City, NY: Doubleday, 1952. (Novel)
Ice Palace. Garden City, NY: Doubleday, 1958. (Novel)
A Kind of Magic. Garden City, NY: Doubleday, 1963. (Autobiography)

Studies of Edna Ferber

Brenni, V. J., and B. L. Spencer. "Edna Ferber: A Selected Bibliography." *Bulletin of Bibliography* 22 (1958): 152–56.
Gilbert, Julie Goldsmith. *Ferber: A Biography.* Garden City, NY: Doubleday, 1978.
Horowitz, Stephen P., and Miriam J. Landsman. "The Americanization of Edna: A Study of Ms. Ferber's Jewish American Identity." *Studies in American Jewish Litera-*

ture: From Marginality to Mainstream, a Mosaic of Jewish Writers. Vol. 2. Ed.
   Daniel Walden. Albany: SUNY, 1982. 69–80.
Shaughnessy, Mary Rose. *Women and Success in American Society in the Words of Edna
   Ferber*. New York: Gordon, 1977.
Uffen, Ellen Serlen. "Edna Ferber and the 'Theatricalization' of American Mythology."
   Midwestern Miscellany 8 (1980): 82–93.
White, William Allen. "A Friend's Story of Edna Ferber." *English Journal* 19.2 (1930):
   101–6.

DOROTHY CANFIELD FISHER
(1879–1958)

Elizabeth Wright

BIOGRAPHY

Dorothy Canfield Fisher was born on February 17, 1879, in Lawrence, Kansas, the youngest of two children born to James Hulme Canfield, then a professor of political economy and sociology at the University of Kansas, and Flavia A. Camp Canfield, an artist. During her childhood Canfield Fisher lived in college towns throughout the Midwest, including Lincoln, Nebraska, where her father served as chancellor of the University of Nebraska from 1891 to 1895. In Lincoln, Canfield Fisher established a lifelong friendship with Willa Cather, whose father also taught at the university. In 1895, the Canfields moved to Columbus, Ohio, and then to New York in 1899 so that James could accept teaching appointments at various universities.

In addition to her travels throughout the United States, Canfield Fisher also had the opportunity to make a series of trips to Europe with her mother, who kept a studio in Paris. This extensive travel inspired Canfield Fisher's interest in languages: She spoke five fluently, including French, Italian, and Spanish. After graduating from Ohio State University with her bachelor's degree in 1899. Canfield Fisher undertook graduate work in French at the Sorbonne in Paris. She later returned to the United States, where in 1904 she completed her Ph.D. in Romance Languages at Columbia University. Although Canfield Fisher was offered an assistant professorship at Case Western Reserve University, she chose instead to accept work as a secretary at Horace Mann School in New York City so she could care for her aging parents. During this time Canfield Fisher began publishing short stories in magazines such as *Everybody's* and *Harper's* and completed, with George R. Carpenter, an education textbook entitled *Elementary Composition*. In May 1907, Canfield Fisher married John Fisher, a fellow student at Columbia. Soon after their marriage the couple decided to make the Vermont farm Canfield Fisher had inherited from her great grandparents their permanent home. Although the Fishers made Arlington their primary residence for the rest of their lives, they traveled extensively, including a trip to France from 1916 to 1919 to aid the war relief effort.

In Vermont, the Fishers had planned that they would each work full-time as professional writers. Canfield Fisher was a more successful writer, however, and so John Fisher turned to aiding her career, as well as to caring for their two children, Sarah (1909) and James (1913). During the next few years, Canfield Fisher established herself as a prolific and popular writer who chose to use her maiden name for her fiction and her married name for her nonfiction works. Although her early novels *Gunhild* (1907) and *The Squirrel-Cage* (1912) did not sell well, her later novels, including *The Brimming Cup* (1921) and *The Home-Maker* (1924), became best-sellers. During this time Canfield Fisher also wrote and published several manuals on how to teach children using the method developed in Italy by Maria Montessori. In addition to her busy writing schedule, Canfield Fisher served as president of the American Association for Adult Education and in 1921 became the first woman elected to the Vermont State Board of Education.

In 1926, Canfield Fisher accepted a position on the selection committee for the newly created Book-of-the-Month Club. Until her retirement in 1951, she helped choose the books endorsed by the popular club and wrote the forwards to such Book-of-the-Month selections as *Seven Gothic Tales* by Isak Dinesen, *What Men Live By* by Leo Tolstoy, and *Black Boy* and *Native Son* by Richard Wright. In 1945, Canfield Fisher's son James was killed while serving as a medical doctor in the Philippines during World War II. Fisher was so upset by her son's death that her doctors feared her incessant crying would permanently damage her already fragile eyes.

Dorothy Canfield Fisher died in Arlington, Vermont, of a stroke on November 9, 1958.

MAJOR WORKS AND THEMES

A prolific writer, Canfield Fisher published twenty-two works of fiction, eighteen works of nonfiction, and one play, as well as several translations of Italian texts. Canfield Fisher's writing examines a variety of social concerns, including racism, anti-Semitism, the horrors of war, marriage, the restrictive nature of gender roles, and the education of children. Even as *Home Fires in France* (1918) and *The Day of Glory* (1919) reveal Canfield Fisher's abhorrence of war, many of her works focus on issues closer to home. *Hillsboro People* (1915), coauthored with the poet Sarah Cleghorn, *The Bent Twig* (1915), and *The Deepening Stream* (1930) depict Vermonters who resist allowing their unique values to be transformed by people from the "outside" world. This point is made once again in Canfield Fisher's final novel, *Seasoned Timber* (1939), as the principal of a poor Vermont academy refuses $1 million after he learns he must agree never to admit Jews in order to receive the money.

Many of Canfield Fisher's novels focus on young women who struggle to adapt to societal expectations mandating that married women should devote their lives to caring for home and family. In her first novel, *The Squirrel-Cage* (1912), Canfield Fisher rescues a woman who has married the wrong man by killing her husband. This is the only novel in which Canfield Fisher creates such a convenient solution. She forces her characters to resolve the tension caused by their unhappy marriages in *The Brimming Cup* (1921) and *Rough-Hewn* (1922). Canfield Fisher continues to focus on the issue of marriage and gender roles in the novel most well known to contemporary audiences, *The Home-Maker* (1924). Evangeline Knapp, who is ill suited to staying at home and caring for her children, is rescued when her husband, a businessman who hates his profession, is maimed in an accident. Forced to reverse roles, Evangeline thrives in the business world, while her husband succeeds in creating a stable home life in which their two children thrive.

Canfield Fisher's nonfiction writing tends to focus on her interest in education. In addition to *Elementary Composition* (1906), Canfield Fisher authored several historical narratives for young children including *Paul Revere and the Minute Men* (1950) and *Our Independence and the Constitution* (1950). *A Montessori Mother* (1912), *A Montessori Manual* (1913), and *Mothers and Children* (1914) focus on Canfield Fisher's endorsement of the Montessori method of educating children, in which schools provide students with the flexibility to direct their own education. Canfield Fisher's ideas concerning how children ought to be educated surfaces in her fiction as well: in *Understood Betsey* (1917), a novel written for young adult audiences, Canfield Fisher uses the character of Betsey to demonstrate how the Montessori method of self-discovery encourages a child to develop a sense of independence. And in "Sex-Education" (*The Bedquilt and Other Stories*) Canfield Fisher suggests that young people need objective information about sexuality, not moral platitudes, so that they make their own decisions. An ardent believer in adult education, Canfield Fisher's *Why Stop Learning?* (1927) reveals her interest in adult education.

CRITICAL RECEPTION

Although Canfield Fisher was named one of the ten most influential women in America by Eleanor Roosevelt, much of her work has slipped into obscurity since her death. Along with the publication of Ida H. Washington's *Dorothy Canfield Fisher: A Biography* in 1982, the reprint of *The Home-Maker* in 1983 has resulted in increased critical attention. In addition, Mark Madigan's 1993 edition of Canfield Fisher's letters, as well as his 1996 collection, *The Bedquilt and Other Stories*, an anthology of selected short stories by Canfield Fisher, has made both her life and her work more accessible to contemporary audiences. Finally, the creation of the Dorothy Canfield Fisher Society suggests that the author will continue to attract much deserved critical attention in the future.

Contemporary critics of Canfield Fisher's life and writing often focus on her relationship to other writers as well as her interest in the welfare of children.

Writers studied in comparison to Canfield Fisher include Sarah Orne Jewett, Mary Wilkins Freeman, Willa Cather, Edith Wharton, and Isak Dinesen. Other critics have commented on Canfield Fisher's interest in family relations. In her doctoral dissertation, Anne Downey examines how Canfield Fisher treats "everyday life" in her writing. And finally, Suzanne Rahn, author of "Empowering the Child: Rediscovering Dorothy Canfield's Made-to-Order Stories," elucidates Canfield Fisher's interest in parent-child relations.

BIBLIOGRAPHY

Works by Dorothy Canfield Fisher

Corneille and Racine in England. Diss. Coumbia University. New York: Columbia University Press, 1904.

Dorothy Canfield Fisher and George R. Carpenter. *Elementary Composition.* New York: Macmillan, 1906. (Textbook)

Gunhild. New York: Holt, 1907. (Novel)

A Montessori Mother. New York: Holt, 1912. (Nonfiction)

The Squirrel-Cage. New York: Holt, 1912. (Novel)

A Montessori Manual. New York: Richardson, 1913.

Mothers and Children. New York: Holt, 1914.

The Bent Twig. New York: Holt, 1915. (Novel)

Dorothy Canfield Fisher and Sarah N. Cleghorn. *Hillsboro People.* New York: Holt, 1915. (Short stories)

The Real Motive. New York: Holt, 1916. (Short stories)

Self-reliance. Indianapolis: Bobbs, 1916. (Nonfiction)

Dorothy Canfield Fisher and Sarah N. Cleghorn. *Fellow Captains.* New York: Holt, 1916. (Nonfiction)

Understood Betsey. New York: Holt, 1917. (Young adult novel)

Home Fires in France. New York: Holt, 1918. (Short stories)

The Day of Glory. New York: Holt, 1919. (Short stories)

The Brimming Cup. New York: Harcourt, 1921.

Rough-Hewn. New York: Harcourt, Brace, 1922. (Novel)

Raw Material. New York: Harcourt, 1923. (Short stories)

The Home-Maker. 1924. Chicago: Academy Chicago, 1983. (Novel)

Made-to-Order Stories. New York: Harcourt, 1925. (Short stories)

Her Son's Wife. New York: Harcourt, 1926. (Novel)

Life of Christ, by Giovanni Papini. Trans. Dorothy Canfield Fisher. New York: Harcourt, 1926.

Why Stop Learning? New York: Harcourt, 1927.

The Deepening Stream. New York: Harcourt, 1930. (Novel)

Basque People. New York: Harcourt, 1931. (Short stories)

Tourists Accommodated. New York: Harcourt, 1932. (Play)

Work: What It Has Meant to Men through the Ages. New York: Harcourt, 1932. (Trans. of Adriano Tilgher [Italian])

Bonfire. New York: Harcourt, 1933. (Novel)

Seasoned Timber. New York: Harcourt, 1939. (Novel)
Tell Me a Story. Lincoln: University of Nebraska Press, 1940. (Children's short stories)
Dorothy Canfield Fisher and Sarah N. Cleghorn. *Nothing Ever Happens and How It Does.* Boston: Beacon, 1940. (Children's short stories)
Our Young Folks. New York: Harcourt, 1943.
American Portraits. New York: Holt, 1946.
Four-Square. New York: Harcourt, 1949.
Our Independence and the Constitution. New York: Random, 1950. (Children's history)
Paul Revere and the Minute Men. New York: Random, 1950. (Children's history)
A Fair World for All. New York: Whittlesey, 1952. (Children's history)
Vermont Tradition. Boston: Little, 1953.
A Harvest of Stories. New York: Harcourt, 1956. (Anthology)
Memories of Arlington, Vermont. New York: Duell, 1957.
And Long Remember. New York: Whittlesey House, 1959. (Children's history)
The Bedquilt and Other Stories by Dorothy Canfield Fisher. Ed. Mark Madigan. Columbia: University of Missouri Press, 1996.

Studies of Dorothy Canfield Fisher

Apthorp, Elaine Sargent. "The Artist at the Family Reunion: Visions of the Creative Life in the Narrative Technique of Willa Cather, Sarah Orne Jewett, Mary Wilkins Freeman, and Dorothy Canfield Fisher." Diss. University of California, Berkeley, 1986.

Downey, Anne Marie. " 'The Art of Living': The Aesthetics of Everyday Life in Dorothy Canfield Fisher's Novels." Diss. University of New Hampshire, 1995.

Lovering, Joseph P. "The Friendship of Willa Cather and Dorothy Canfield." *Vermont History* 48 (1980): 144–54.

Madigan, Mark J. "A Newly Discovered Robert Frost Letter to Dorothy Canfield Fisher." *Robert Frost Review* (1994): 24–27.

———. "Profile: Dorothy Canfield Fisher, 1879–1958." *Legacy* 9 (1992): 49–58.

———. " 'This Allegation We Repudiate!': An Unpublished Poem by Dorothy Canfield Fisher." *Vermont History News* 41 (1990): 35–36.

———. "Willa Cather and Dorothy Canfield Fisher: Rift, Reconciliation, and One of Ours." *Cather Studies* 1 (1990): 115–29.

———. "Willa Cather's Commentary on Three Novels by Dorothy Canfield Fisher." *ANQ* 3.1 (1990): 13–15.

———, ed. *Keeping Fires Night and Day: Selected Letters of Dorothy Canfield Fisher.* Columbia: University of Missouri Press, 1993.

McCallister, Lois. "Dorothy Canfield Fisher: A Critical Study." Diss. Case Western Reserve University, 1970.

Price, Alan. "Writing Home from the Front: Edith Wharton and Dorothy Canfield Fisher Present Wartime France to the United States: 1917–1919." *Edith Wharton Newsletter* 5.2 (1988): 1–5.

Rahn, Suzanne. "Empowering the Child: Rediscovering Dorothy Canfield's Made-to-Order Stories." *The Lion and the Unicorn: A Critical Journal of Children's Literature* 13 (1989): 109–30.

Schroeter, Joan G. "The Canfield-Cleghorn Correspondence: Two Lives in Letters." Diss. Northern Illinois University, 1993.

————. "Crisis, Conflict, and Constituting the Self: A Lacanian Reading of *The Deepening Stream.*" *Colby Quarterly* 27 (1991): 148–60.

————. "Dorothy Canfield's *Home Fires in France* Revisited: A Revised Bibliography." *Analytical & Enumerative Bibliography* 4 (1990): 169–70.

Washington, Ida H. *Dorothy Canfield Fisher: A Biography.* Shelburne, VT: New England Press, 1982.

————. "Isak Dinesen and Dorothy Canfield: The Importance of a Helping Hand." *Continental, Latin-American and Francophone Women Writers.* Ed. Eunice Myers and Ginette Adamson. Lanham, MD: University Press of America, 1987. 89–96.

ZONA GALE
(1874–1938)

David Garrett Izzo

BIOGRAPHY

Zona Gale, born on August 26, 1874, was a novelist, short story writer, playwright, poet, and essayist. She was also a liberal democrat, suffragette, and early feminist (in professional and civic matters, if more traditional and feminine personally). Raised in Portage, Wisconsin, by Charles Franklin and Eliza Gale, Zona Gale adored her parents, and her attachment would affect her future relationships and her writing. (They would become the charming elderly couple in Gale's second book, *The Loves of Pelleas and Etarre*.) Gale received a B.A. in 1895 and an M.A. in 1899 from the University of Wisconsin and began her writing career as a local journalist before going to New York City in 1901. There, missing Portage, she started writing the short stories extolling the virtues of small-town life that marked her early fiction. In 1904, Gale returned to Portage permanently.

Her short stories about Portage (a.k.a. *Friendship Village*) made Gale a popular success. She met writer Ridgely Torrence in 1902, and her letters to him (the Torrence Papers, Princeton University) demonstrate a deeply felt spiritual love, but one she could not transcend enough to make a commitment and leave her parents. This emotional struggle would shadow her life and work and turn her writing from sentimentalism to realism to mysticism.

Gale, in 1920, achieved critical success with the novel *Miss Lulu Bett*, an example of Midwest realism that reviews compared to the work of Theodore Dreiser, Sinclair Lewis, and others. In 1921, she dramatized this novel and won a Pulitzer Prize for the play. Her realistic writing was praised throughout the 1920s.

Gale was a political and social activist in Wisconsin, where she supported the progressive Robert La Follette. She adopted two daughters as a single parent and in 1928 married William L. Breese, a childhood friend and recent widower, in a platonic union. After the deaths of Gale's mother in 1923 and her father in 1929, she became deeply interested in mystical philosophy—Vedanta, Theosophy, Madame Blavatsky,—all quite avant-garde in her time, and her work would turn to this bent, one that saw a decline in her popularity and critical regard in the 1930s. Zona Gale died of pneumonia on December 27, 1938.

MAJOR WORKS AND THEMES

Zona Gale's writing evolved through three periods: sentimentalism, realism, and mysticism. From 1907 to 1919, with her stories about Pelleas and Etarre, then Friendship Village, Gale responded to the encroaching urban industrial world by writing about the virtues of small-town life with a sharp humor and an eye for particular details that tugged at the reader's universal understanding. Her stories, before being collected in book form, appeared in national magazines that were then labeled "women's" magazines; yet her unabashed sentimentalism was grounded in the observation and depiction of real people that she knew, giving a depth of realism to the sentiment that would serve her well when she turned to her more dramatic realism. During and after World War I, the harsh realities of that conflict dictated a movement toward the recognition of tragedy, and Gale responded with a continuation of small-town life but one with a dark side.

With the novels *Birth* (1918) and *Miss Lulu Bett* (1920), "serious" critics who had not read the short stories, being suspect of their magazine origins and not knowing of the detailed realism in them, were not prepared for their praise, particularly for *Bett*, "which augmented [by Gale's] resolution to strip away the fanciful, left her with forty-five thousand words, the length of Wharton's *Ethan Frome*, and Cather's *A Lost Lady*" (Simonson 79). With *Birth* and *Bett* and the work that followed through 1928, Gale dealt with small-town "littleness" as she had done before so quaintly, but now the littleness of the small town was not such a virtue. Her characters, who once faced dilemmas that cheerful faith and fate pulled them through, were now falling through the ice: "Willy-nilly, people are buffetted, teased, wrecked, impelled. Against the gods they stand naked and terribly vulnerable. . . . Accidental circumstances, irrevocably lead to circumstances known and unknown by the helpless victim" (Simonson 74).

When, in 1921, Gale's dramatization of *Miss Lulu Bett* for the New York Stage won a Pulitzer, she entered into the top rank of 1920s realists. Gale's characterizations in this period featured men and women described sparely with emotions shown with clipped diction that was concisely forceful. Gale's Lulu was a young, unmarried woman enduring the banal in the manner of a Henry James heroine; that is, she confronted the banality, even if not overcoming it. The peak of this realistic period was the short story collection *Yellow Gentians and Blue* (1927), which relentlessly portrays life as a cycle of futility ended only by death—or so it would seem.

In 1923, after her mother died, Gale, who had mystical inclinations—see her only book of verse, *The Secret Way* (1921)—began to feel her mother's transcendental presence. Gale became even more fervent in her pursuit of mystical knowledge and in 1926 made mysticism the core of her novel *Preface to a Life*. The protagonist, Bernard Mead, is a man who has had mystical visions and sensations all of his life, but because he doesn't understand them, he thinks he's mad. In fact, most critics didn't understand them either. Moreover, in 1928, Gale published a book of essays that were imbued with her mysticism, and thereafter critics moved away from praise and toward bemused disparagement. Even when Gale returned to "realism" (mystics would dispute that the sense world is the actual reality), critics did not return to Gale.

CRITICAL RECEPTION

Prior to Gale's mystical period, she was both a popular and critical favorite. Even when her early work was reviewed as heavily sentimental, her technique, with her journalistic directness and attention to detail, was well regarded as was her colloquial sense of humor in depicting adorable, yet still recognizable, human traits and foibles: "We bask for a few hours in that human exhilarating sunshine that radiates straight from the heart of people who are real and true and big of soul" (Cooper 79). Some reviewers compared Gale to Jane Austen in that her "tea-table" banter hints of a deeper human nature. (See Rourke.)

These hints would surface clearly in Gale's period of realism, starting with *Birth*. In it, tea-table banter became bloodsport for social climbing and the domestic warfare of words between friends, families, and spouses. *Birth*'s "unromanticism" gave critics a jolt and placed Gale with Dreiser and Lewis. (See Michaud; Quinn.) *Miss Lulu Bett* proved she could sustain her realism with Constance Rourke saying that "the book stands as a signal accomplishment in American letters" (316). (See also Van Doren; Benchley.)

Beginning with her mystical novel *Preface to a Life*, critics who were unfamiliar and/or skeptical with the then-outré metaphysical movements didn't understand her themes and objectives. After World War II, many of Gale's prewar mystical influences became more mainstream—for example, the Indian writer Rabindranath Tagore, Gurdjieff, P. D. Ouspensky, Taoism, *The Bhagavad-Gita*, and *The Upanishads*. By then, other writers such as Aldous Huxley, Christopher Isherwood, and Witter Bynner were writing novels and verse successfully incorporating the mysticism that Gale had presciently tried years before.

From the 1940s through the 1960s, Gale was included in survey studies of American realism, but little new was asserted. Since the 1970s and feminist criticism, Gale has had a small resurgence of new articles and studies such as "Not in Sisterhood: Zona Gale, Willa Cather and the American Woman Writer Redefined" (Williams). What remains to be considered is a reappraisal of her mystical writing, particularly *Preface to a Life*, which would now benefit from the greater awareness of its themes that were misunderstood in 1926. As Gale herself would often write when signing her books: "Life is something other than that which we believe it to be."

BIBLIOGRAPHY

Works by Zona Gale

Romance Island. Indianapolis: Bobbs-Merrill, 1906. (Short stories)
The Loves of Pelleas and Etarre. New York: Macmillan, 1907. (Short stories)
Friendship Village. New York: Macmillan, 1908. (Short stories)
Friendship Village Love Stories. New York: Macmillan, 1909. (Short stories)
Mothers to Men. New York: Macmillan, 1911. (Novel)
Christmas. New York: Macmillan, 1912. (Novella)
Civic Improvement in the Little Towns. Washington, DC: American Civic Association, 1913. (Nonfiction)
When I Was a Little Girl. New York: Macmillan, 1913. (Short stories)
Neighborhood Stories. New York: Macmillan, 1914.
The Neighbors. Wisconsin Plays. Ed. T. H. Dickinson. New York: Huebsch, 1914. 5–63.
Heart's Kindred. New York: Macmillan, 1915. (Novel)
A Daughter of the Morning. Indianapolis: Bobbs-Merrill, 1917. (Novel)
Birth. New York: Macmillan, 1918. (Novel)
Peace in Friendship Village. New York: Macmillan, 1919. (Short stories)
Miss Lulu Bett. New York: Appleton, 1920. (Novel)
Miss Lulu Bett. New York: Appleton, 1921. (Play)
The Secret Way. New York: Macmillan, 1921. (Verse)
What Women Won in Wisconsin. Washington, DC: National Woman's Party, 1922. (Nonfiction)
Uncle Jimmy. Boston: Baker, 1922. (Play)
Faint Perfume. New York: Appleton, 1923. (Novel)
Mister Pitt. New York: Appleton, 1925. (Play)
Preface to a Life. New York: Appleton, 1926. (Novel)
Yellow Gentians and Blue. New York: Appleton, 1927. (Short stories)
Portage Wisconsin and Other Essays. New York: Knopf, 1928.
Borgia. New York: Knopf, 1929. (Novel)
Bridal Pond. New York: Knopf, 1930. (Novel)
The Clouds. New York: French, 1932. (Play)
Evening Clothes. Boston: Baker, 1932. (Play)
Old Fashioned Tales. New York: Appleton, 1933. (Short stories)
Papa La Fleur. New York: Appleton, 1933. (Novel)
Faint Perfume. New York: French, 1934. (Play)
Light Woman. New York: Appleton, 1937. (Novel)
Frank Miller of Mission Inn. New York: Appleton, 1938. (Biography)
Magna. New York: Appleton, 1939. (Novel)
Ms. Lulu Bett/Birth. Oregon, WI: Waubesha, 1994.

Studies of Zona Gale

Benchley, Robert. Foreword. *Miss Lulu Bett: An American Comedy of Manners*, by Zona Gale. New York: Appleton, 1929. iii–xvi.

Cooper, Frederick Tabor. "Friendship Village Love Stories." *The Bookman* 31 (1919): 79.

Davidson, Donald. "Worker of Ill." *Saturday Review of Literature* 6 Nov. 1929: 440.

Derleth, August. *Still Small Voice: The Biography of Zona Gale*. New York: Appleton, 1940.

Follett, Wilson. *Zona Gale*. New York: Appleton, 1923.

Forman, Henry James. "Zona Gale: A Touch of Greatness." *Wisconsin Magazine of History* 46 (1962): 32–37.

Gard, Robert. *Grassroots Theater: A Search for Regional Arts in America*. Madison: Wisconsin University Press, 1955.

Hoffman, Frederick. *The Twenties: American Writing in the Postwar Decade*. New York: Viking, 1955.

Krutch, Joseph Wood. "Zona Gale's New Manner." *Nation* 11 Dec. 1929: 725.

Maxwell, William. "Zona Gale." *Yale Review* 76.2 (1987): 221–25.

Michaud, Regis. *The American Novel Today*. Boston: Little, 1928.

Monteiro, George. "Zona Gale and Ridgely Torrence." *American Literary Realism* 3 (1970): 377–79.

Quantic, Dianne. "Anticipation of the Revolt in Nineteenth Century Middle Western Fiction: A Study of the Small Town." Diss. University of Michigan, Ann Arbor, 1972.

Quinn, Arthur Hobson. *American Fiction: An Historical and Critical Survey*. New York: Appleton, 1936.

Rideout, Walter. *The Radical Novel in the United States*. Cambridge, MA: Harvard University Press, 1956.

Rourke, Constance. "Transitions." *New Republic* 11 Aug. 1920: 316.

Simonson, Harold. *Zona Gale*. New York: Twayne, 1962.

Sutherland, Cynthia. "American Women Playwrights as Mediators of the 'Woman Problem.' " *Modern Drama* 21 (1978): 319–36.

Symanski, Karen. "Zona Gale." *American Literary Realism* 8 (1975): 260.

Van Doren, Carl. *Contemporary American Novelists*. New York: Macmillan, 1928.

Wharton, Edith. "The Great American Novel." *Yale Review* 16 (1927): 646–56.

White, Katherine. "*Miss Lulu Bett* Revived." *Turn of the Century Women* 1.2 (1984): 38–40.

Williams, Deborah. "Not in Sisterhood: Zona Gale, Willa Cather and the American Woman Writer Redefined." Diss. University of Michigan, Ann Arbor, 1996.

———. "Threats of Correspondence: Letters of Edith Wharton, Zona Gale, Willa Cather." *Studies in American Fiction* 25 (1975): 211–39.

ELLEN GLASGOW
(1873–1945)

Catherine Rainwater

BIOGRAPHY

Ellen Anderson Glasgow was born to Anne Jane Gholson and Francis Thomas Glasgow on April 21, 1873, in Richmond, Virginia, where she lived and wrote for most of the seventy-two years of her life. As the second to the youngest of ten children, she was frequently left to her own devices and developed into an imaginative child. Also an extremely sensitive, apparently somewhat willful young child, Ellen was allowed not to attend school when she refused. Though off and on she attended various private schools, she was primarily self-taught, relying heavily on her father's extensive library. Her more or less self-directed education developed a few significant gaps, which she later struggled to fill. Her elder sister Cary and Cary's husband, George Walter McCormack, assisted young Ellen and especially encouraged her writing, for which she had an obvious, early talent. Well before her fifteenth birthday, she composed poems and stories for a captive audience, her younger sister, Rebe. One of these extant childhood stories, "A Modern Joan of Arc" (ca. 1885), reveals the powerful effect that the troubled, post–Civil War South of Glasgow's youth exercised upon her burgeoning artistic sensibility. Featuring a brave, outspoken girl protagonist, the story also foreshadows the adult Glasgow's passionate commitment to women's rights.

Glasgow's paternal ancestors were Scotch-Irish pioneers who immigrated to western Virginia in the eighteenth century, whereas her maternal forebears numbered among some of the longest established of Tidewater aristocratic families. Francis Glasgow's strict Presbyterianism, combined with his stern and emotionally distant personality, doubtless took its toll on his family and shaped his daughter's creative imagination. A range of bitter and ambivalent feelings toward her father galvanized both suppressed and expressed rebellion in Glasgow throughout her life. She blamed her father for her mother's emotional collapse and eventual death in 1893 and for his insensitive treatment of her brother Frank, who eventually committed suicide in 1909. Glasgow's long unresolved conflicts with her father established a basis for her portrayal of abusive patriarchal authority throughout most of her fiction.

Following Anne Glasgow's premature demise when Ellen was only twenty, death seemed to be a regular, uninvited guest at One West Main, the Glasgow's Richmond home from the time Ellen was fourteen. In fairly quick succession, several cherished members of Ellen's family met untimely deaths, including her beloved brother-in-law Walter McCormack (who, like her brother, also committed suicide) and later her sister Cary McCormack, from cancer in 1911. These deaths were hard felt; together with rapidly worsening problems with hearing that began when Glasgow was only sixteen, such personal losses doubtless contributed to her lifelong tendency to bouts of melancholy.

Deafness made her angry and anxious. She felt that it hampered her independence and diminished her opportunities in life, though most would agree that the writer admirably resisted any apparent limitations; she traveled widely and maintained a vital network of social contacts. Nevertheless, some speculate that Glasgow's deafness might have figured in her unwillingness to marry despite two engagements, the first one in 1906 to Frank Paradise and the second one much later, during her early forties, to Henry Anderson. The most intriguing love interest in Glasgow's life, however, remains the elusive "Gerald B.," a married man with whom she apparently had an intense affair during her late twenties but whose actual identity is yet unknown.

Glasgow's first major success as a writer came with her first published novel, *The Descendant* (1897). The book initially received extensive attention for its allegedly masculine sensibility. However, after Harper's revealed Glasgow's previously concealed gender, reviewers focused ambivalently on the author's "female" intuition and sympathy while disapproving of her grim, unladylike Darwinian and Schopenhauerian views that they had earlier praised as "realistic" and "tough-minded." Undissuaded by staid critical opinions, Glasgow went on to publish nineteen novels, a book of poems, and a collection of short stories, as well as a variety of other writings including a book of criticism—all evincing relatively unorthodox women's views.

As an acclaimed Southern writer (a label that chafed, for she thought of herself as a modern American writer), Glasgow cultivated relationships with prestigious literary figures, especially publishers and reviewers who could positively affect the reception of her works. Among her significant literary associations were Walter Hines Page, Frank Doubleday, James Branch Cabell, and Allen Tate, to name only a few. She was also a great admirer of Thomas Hardy and Joseph Conrad, both of whom she eventually met. With Hardy she shared a great love for animals, particularly dogs. Indeed, her attachment to her own dogs frequently made her the focus of humor and, at times, sharp criticism for her eccentricity. Undaunted, she championed humane treatment of animals throughout her life with the same fervor that she defended the rights of women, but with even more overtly political action. Glasgow served as president of the Richmond chapter of the Society for the Prevention of Cruelty to Animals

(SPCA) for twenty years, beginning in 1924. Under her leadership, the SPCA attained substantial power and influence in the town.

One of Glasgow's chief disappointments as a writer was a perceived lack of merited recognition. Indeed, year after year, major prizes went to other writers, despite the public acclaim and critical praise that Glasgow's novels almost inevitably drew. Not until 1942 did she win a Pulitzer Prize. The award was for *In This Our Life* (1941)—ironically, a work that would not turn out to be one of her best known, despite its being made into a movie in 1941. In the long run, however, Glasgow did garner many impressive literary honors. In 1938, she became the first Virginian and the sixth woman admitted to the American Academy of Arts and Letters. By the end of her life, she had received every major award for fiction except for the Nobel Prize. Apparently, Glasgow craved recognition, but when it came, it often failed to satisfy. One reason was that her art was sometimes praised for features that she did not herself regard. Especially irksome for her was her regular consignment to the categories of regional and "older generation" writer. Glasgow considered herself a Modernist writer of universal, not merely Southern, appeal, an opinion that some of her critics have at last, in the closing years of the twentieth century, come to share.

After a career spanning almost five decades and successful by any estimation, Glasgow began to have serious heart trouble in the late 1930s that slowed the pace of her work. She suffered a series of heart attacks and increasingly poor health beginning in 1939; near the time of her death she could write for only fifteen minutes a day. She did write, however, and was at work on another novel, *Beyond Defeat* (1966), on November 21, 1945, when her weary spirit finally broke free of the constraints of human existence that had frustrated and probably inspired her as an artist. By her request, she was buried with the exhumed remains of her beloved dog Jeremy in Hollywood Cemetery in Richmond.

MAJOR WORKS AND THEMES

In the half century since Glasgow's death, her best-known and most frequently read works continue to be *Virginia* (1913), *Barren Ground* (1925), *Vein of Iron* (1935), and her much admired "Queenborough Trilogy," consisting of *The Romantic Comedians* (1926), *They Stooped to Folly* (1929), and *The Sheltered Life* (1932). Within sophisticated philosophical frames of reference implied through carefully crafted narrative strategies, the first three novels examine the hardships of life in the turn-of-the-century and early modern South, along with the particular struggles of Southern women in variously agonized relationships to stultifying social traditions. The novels comprising the Queenborough Trilogy likewise demonstrate Glasgow's increasing mastery of narrative technique; indeed, the trenchant, streamlined precision of *The Sheltered Life*, in particular, has led numerous critics to see it as her finest work. Like most of Glasgow's fiction, the works in the trilogy firmly denounce Southern traditions thwarting regional and individual development, even while they also underscore the moral and spiritual strengths of the South that were a part of the response to the Civil War and its traumatic aftermath. Though many of Glasgow's other novels, as well as her short stories and poetry, are equally deserving of attention, we may see in these six favorites the evolution of nearly all of the author's lifelong social, philosophical, and aesthetic concerns.

From the beginning of her artistic career, Glasgow challenged the views of mainstream writers of her day. She faulted some, such as William Dean Howells, for their complacent, "evasive idealism" in a period of social, political, and artistic revolution. Glasgow insisted that the times demanded skeptical tough-mindedness. She called for an American "literature of revolt"—a literature of international scope evincing a broad and disinterested, as opposed to a national or merely regional, point of view. In *Virginia*, a narrative capping the early stages of Glasgow's development as a writer when she had dealt primarily with the South in its various post–Civil War agonies, we especially observe the author's accelerated search for her own broadly modern worldview. Though this novel treats a variety of Southern issues—the decline of traditional manners and mores in an industrial town of the New South—we may also appreciate Glasgow's representation of the South as merely one part of a nation, and a world, renegotiating cherished myths and values on the threshold of a new century. *Virginia* clearly articulates Glasgow's universalist vision of the South that we see emerging throughout her earlier "social history" sequence—*The Voice of the People* (1900), *The Battle-Ground* (1902), and *The Deliverance* (1904). Her later works, including *Barren Ground* and *Vein of Iron*, continue to elaborate upon the need for American society as a whole to come to terms with difficult, complex insights into human nature and history afforded through major European thinkers of the day such as Darwin, Marx, and Freud and an array of contemporary philosophers.

Glasgow's vital interest in classical and contemporary intellectual dialogues profoundly shapes the content as well as the narrative manner of her fiction and aligns her with some of the most important turn-of-the-century and modern voices of her day. Indeed, an insufficiently appreciated aspect of Glasgow's art is its sophisticated engagement with philosophy, both Eastern and Western. Glasgow from the beginning set out to develop narrational strategies that subtly reinforce some of the overtly philosophical perspectives that her narrators and characters express. The embodiment of modern conflict in their self-reflexively tentative search for sustainable truths in an apparently chaotic universe, Glasgow's narrative strategies are designed to implicate the reader in some of the same types of agonized thought processes that her narrators and characters exhibit. *Barren Ground* and *Vein of Iron*, for instance, pose profound questions about the nature of human identity and the construction of self. In both novels, we may with some well-rewarded effort trace the influence on narrative management of a range of philosophers including Nietzsche, Schopenhauer, and William James.

Glasgow's interest in the philosophical search for something to believe in during an age of radical uncertainty reveals the characteristically dichotomous bent of her mind. Intense spiritual yearning was coupled in Glasgow with an equally powerful intellectual skepticism toward religion, an attitude doubtless fueled in part by her unhappy relationship with her inflexible, Calvinist father. Attracted to Eastern and Western mysticism and even claiming once to have had a mystically enlightening experience, Glasgow nevertheless was apparently incapable of any simple faith in an ultimate meaning beyond the inscrutable face of phenomenal existence. *The Wheel of Life* (1906), an early work and the most mystical and openly autobiographical of all of her novels, foreshadows this lifelong struggle of the author. It treats the spiritual growth of a poet, Laura Wilde, in her gradual rejection of sentimentality, love, and faith in favor of a resigned, stoical strength. Glasgow's own cynicism regarding conventional religion and the religiouslike prognostications of science in her day and her antiromantic assessment of human potential that are outlined in this and other early works eventually lead her to a Schopenhauerian view of existence. Her mature works reflect this carefully considered vision, and in *Barren Ground* and *Vein of Iron*, Glasgow's protagonists are autobiographical reflections of her own attempt to extinguish desire in a quest for a bounded, existential freedom.

This desire for as much freedom as the universe allows quite naturally led Glasgow to demand the emancipation of women. Philosophical skepticism prevented her from subscribing to any feminist utopian dream, for Glasgow was apparently not particularly convinced of males' or females' ability to create an ideal or even a tolerable reality. However, she unabashedly asserted women's intellectual equality with men and supported reforms leading to their social equality. From the beginning of her career as a writer, Glasgow created female characters who risk reputation and social position for the privilege of choosing career over marriage and motherhood, of choosing intellect and personal power over alleged women's intuition and passive compliance within a patriarchal system.

Indeed, for Glasgow, a genuine "literature of revolt" would not only revise the nation's thinking about matters political, philosophical, and spiritual, but it would eradicate destructive gender stereotypes that reinforce the quiet desperation of many, especially female, individual lives. In *The Romance of a Plain Man* (1909), a male protagonist matures emotionally and transcends socially imposed gender limitations by tending his ailing wife, whereas in *Barren Ground* and *Vein of Iron*, male characters learn to accept equal, even subordinate roles to their more capable female counterparts. Glasgow consistently debunks the myth of male supremacy in all of her works, though she always stops short of counterassertions of female supremacy. Moreover, despite her objections to the life prescribed for women of her era, not to mention her own rejection of such a life, she treats the traditionally self-sacrificing woman with respect for the hardships endured in the interests of others. Glasgow's treatment of her character Virginia in the novel of that name perhaps best exemplifies the author's compassionate attitude toward her variously suffering, fellow sojourners in the universe, whether they are male or female, orthodox or rebellious, human or nonhuman.

Another work by Glasgow, published posthumously in 1954, has received significant critical attention along with her six best-known novels. *The Woman Within*, Glasgow's autobiography, is as fascinating as her fiction for the degree to which it conceals, even as it reveals, so much about the inner life of a brilliant woman and writer. Perhaps partially influenced by H. G. Wells's ideas about telling one's life reflected in his *Experiment in Autobiography* (1934), Glasgow conceals much about her inner life but clearly delineates the artist-persona that she deliberately shaped for public consumption throughout her career. Almost infuriatingly evasive at times, *The Woman Within* withholds facts about pivotal issues in Glasgow's life, particularly facts about her father's specific abuses of her mother and the family and about the writer's apparent affair with the mysterious "Gerald B." Nevertheless, the volume speaks to us of much that we are entitled to know about a celebrated writer who valued her privacy. In particular, it reveals the vital connections that Glasgow understood to exist between an author's invention of fictions and her deliberate crafting of her own identity. What an author wants her readers to know, and the way she wants them to interpret the information, perhaps tells us as much or more about the inner mechanisms of her mind and heart than any "bare facts" could, of themselves, reveal. In short, what we value about the quality and power of Glasgow's mind that is reflected in her art is also mirrored in her final commentary on her existence that she left us in the form of her life story.

CRITICAL RECEPTION

On the one hand, Glasgow's work has been received with nearly 100 years of steady, serious attention. Critical and even popular appreciation of Glasgow's art has prevailed despite the general unavailability of most of her books over the last 40 years. On the other hand, a nagging sense that a great American writer has yet to receive her due has haunted many a noteworthy American scholar—the same feeling that vexed the author while she lived.

Glasgow's relative neglect by comparison with contemporaries such as Willa Cather, Edith Wharton, and Kate Chopin may in part be explained through understanding the place of her works within three intertwined, literary historical developments. First, her works became inextricably associated with the Southern Renascence movements of the early twentieth century; critics never ceased to categorize her as a Southern writer, despite her own voiced objections and the obviously universal themes and concerns of her narratives. Second, the New Criticism held sway during the middle years of the century when Glasgow's mature works, deserving of more extensive attention, unfortunately failed to meet the gender and aesthetic criteria implied or stated by this valuable but somewhat reductive poetics. The New Criticism could not satisfactorily recognize, much less appreciate, the profoundest features of Glasgow's art. Finally, the narrowly defined modern aesthetic that has prevailed throughout most of the twentieth century (like the New Criticism that partially created this aesthetic) has elevated to the status of high modernism a variety of paradigmatic works that blind us to the differently modern features of Glasgow's fiction. Glasgow's dialectical narrative strategies frequently amount to a search for authority and epistemological grounding; they epitomize the revolutionary, iconoclastic spirit of modernism itself rather than the reductive view of the movement that prevailed by midcentury. In short, as so much contemporary critical theory reveals, our ways of seeing literature are also ways of *not* seeing, and our insights as well as our blindness have frequently operated at Glasgow's expense.

No doubt sparked by the interest in Glasgow as Southern iconoclast, however, inklings of future, now contemporary, trends in Glasgow criticism appeared as early as 1948. With a few indisputable exceptions, however, it was not until the late 1970s that Glasgow criticism finally began to diversify, especially in the wake of the feminist movement. Since 1979, we have seen new attention to insufficiently explored or ignored aspects of Glasgow's thought and art, including such diverse subjects as Glasgow's feminism, her treatment of gender and racial issues, the ways in which her knowledge of psychology and philosophy inform her narrative strategies, and especially her notions of self and art as revealed in her autobiography *The Woman Within*. A time of recognition is at hand when we are beginning to see Glasgow as she saw herself—not behind but ahead of her time as a writer.

BIBLIOGRAPHY

Works by Ellen Glasgow

The Descendant. New York: Harper, 1897.
Phases of an Inferior Planet. New York: Harper, 1898.
The Voice of the People. New York: Doubleday, 1900.
The Battle-Ground. New York: Doubleday, 1902.
The Freeman and Other Poems. New York: Doubleday, 1902.
The Deliverance. New York: Doubleday, 1904.
The Wheel of Life. New York: Doubleday, 1906.
The Ancient Law. New York: Doubleday, 1908.
The Romance of a Plain Man. New York: Macmillan, 1909.
The Miller of Old Church. Garden City, NY: Doubleday, 1911.
Virginia. Garden City, NY: Doubleday, 1913.
Life and Gabriella. Garden City, NY: Doubleday, 1916.
The Builders. Garden City, NY: Doubleday, 1919.
One Man in His Time. Garden City, NY: Doubleday, 1922.
The Shadowy Third and Other Stories. Garden City, NY: Doubleday, 1923.
Barren Ground. Garden City, NY: Doubleday, 1925.
The Romantic Comedians. Garden City, NY: Doubleday, 1926.

The Old Dominion Edition of the Works of Ellen Glasgow. 1929. Garden City, NY:
  Doubleday. 1933.
They Stooped to Folly. Garden City, NY: Doubleday, 1929.
The Sheltered Life. Garden City, NY: Doubleday, 1932.
Vein of Iron. New York: Harcourt, 1935.
The Virginia Edition of the Works of Ellen Glasgow. New York: Scribner's, 1938.
In This Our Life. New York: Harcourt, 1941.
A Certain Measure: An Interpretation of Prose Fiction. New York: Harcourt, 1943.
The Woman Within. New York: Harcourt, 1954.
Letters of Ellen Glasgow. Ed. Blair Rouse. New York: Harcourt, 1958.
The Collected Short Stories of Ellen Glasgow. Ed. Richard K. Meeker. Baton Rouge:
  Louisiana State University Press, 1963.
Beyond Defeat: An Epilogue to an Era. Ed. Richard K. Meeker. Baton Rouge: Louisiana
  State University Press, 1966.
Ellen Glasgow's Reasonable Doubts: A Collection of Her Writings. Ed. Julius Rowan
  Raper. Baton Rouge: Louisiana State University Press, 1988.
"A Modern Joan of Arc." Ed. Pamela Matthews. *Mississippi Quarterly* 49.2 (1996):
  202–9.

Studies of Ellen Glasgow

Brantley, Will. *Feminine Sense in Southern Memoir: Smith, Glasgow, Welty, Hellman,
  Porter, and Hurston*. Jackson: University Press of Mississippi, 1991.
Bunselmeyer, J. E. "Ellen Glasgow's 'Flexible' Style." *Centennial Review* 28 (1984):
  112–28.
Godbold, E. Stanly. *Ellen Glasgow and The Woman Within*. Baton Rouge: Louisiana
  State University Press, 1972.
———, ed. *Mississippi Quarterly* 49.2 (1996). (Special Ellen Glasgow issue)
Goodman, Susan. *Ellen Glasgow, a Biography*. Baltimore: Johns Hopkins University
  Press, 1998.
Inge, M. Thomas, ed. *Ellen Glasgow: Centennial Essays*. Charlottesville: University
  Press of Virginia, 1976.
Lesser, Wayne. "The Problematics of Regionalism and the Dilemma of Glasgow's *Barren
  Ground*." *Southern Literary Journal* 11.2 (1979): 3–21.
Matthews, Pamela R. *Ellen Glasgow and a Woman's Traditions*. Charlottesville: Uni-
  versity Press of Virginia, 1994.
McDowell, Frederick P. W. *Ellen Glasgow and the Ironic Art of Fiction*. Madison:
  University of Wisconsin Press, 1963.
Rainwater, Catherine. "Ellen Glasgow's Outline of History." *The Critical Response to
  H. G. Wells*. Ed. William J. Scheick. Westport, CT: Greenwood, 1995. 125–38.
———. "Narration as Pragmatism in Ellen Glasgow's *Barren Ground*." *American Lit-
  erature* 63 (1991): 664–82.
Raper, Julius Rowan. *From the Sunken Garden: The Fiction of Ellen Glasgow, 1916–
  1945*. Baton Rouge: Louisiana State University Press, 1980.
———. "Inventing Modern Southern Fiction: A Postmodern View." *Southern Literary
  Journal* 22.2 (1990): 3–18.
———. "Invisible Things: The Short Stories of Ellen Glasgow." *Southern Literary Jour-
  nal* 9.2 (1977): 66–90.

————. "Once More to the Mirror: Glasgow's Technique in *They Stooped to Folly* and Reader-Response Criticism." *Modern American Fiction: Form and Function*. Ed. Thomas Daniel Young. Baton Rouge: Louisiana State University Press, 1989. 136–55.

————. *Without Shelter: The Early Career of Ellen Glasgow*. Baton Rouge: Louisiana State University Press, 1971.

Rouse, Blair. *Ellen Glasgow*. Boston: Twayne, 1962.

Scura, Dorothy M., ed. *Ellen Glasgow: The Contemporary Reviews*. Cambridge, MA: Cambridge University Press, 1992.

————. *Ellen Glasgow: New Perspectives*. Knoxville: University of Tennessee Press, 1995.

Tutwiler, C. C. *Ellen Glasgow's Library*. Charlottesville: Bibliographical Society of the University of Virginia, 1967.

Wagner-Martin, Linda. *Ellen Glasgow: Beyond Convention*. Austin: University of Texas Press, 1982.

SUSAN KEATING GLASPELL
(1876–1948)

Cheryl D. Bohde

BIOGRAPHY

Susan Keating Glaspell, the only daughter of Elmer and Alice Feeney Keating Glaspell, was born on July 1, 1876, to descendants of one of Davenport, Iowa's founders. Attending Central High School, she graduated in 1894. Before enrolling at Drake University in 1897, Glaspell worked for the *Davenport Morning Republican* and *The Weekly Outlook*. Demonstrating skill in oratory and writing, Glaspell graduated with a bachelor of philosophy degree in 1899. For the next two years, she reported legislative issues for the *Des Moines Daily News*. From December 1900 to April 1901, Glaspell filed twenty-six stories on a murder investigation that would serve as the basis of her one-act play *Trifles* (1915) and the short story "A Jury of Her Peers" (1917).

In 1902, Glaspell enrolled in the graduate English program at the University of Chicago; in addition, she worked as a freelance reporter for several Chicago newspapers. Returning to Davenport in 1904, she spent the next three years writing for periodicals such as *Harper's* and completing her first novel *The Glory of the Conquered* (1909). Attending Monist Society meetings in Davenport, Glaspell became friends with George Cram "Jig" Cook; they married in 1913. Prior to the marriage, Glaspell published a second novel, *The Visioning* (1911), and a collection of short stories, *Lifted Masks* (1912).

Jig Cook and Susan Glaspell became pivotal members of New York City literary and political groups. Wintering in Greenwich Village and summering in Provincetown, Massachusetts, Glaspell and Cook were friends of John Reed, Edna St. Vincent Millay, and Eugene O'Neill, all of whom belonged to the experimental theater group Provincetown Players, which produced ninety-seven plays by forty-seven authors during its eight years. While O'Neill had fifteen plays, including *The Emperor Jones*, produced, Glaspell had eleven performed, including *Trifles* (in 1916) and the radically feminist play *The Verge* (in 1921). In addition to her drama, Glaspell wrote the novel *Fidelity* (1915) and twenty short stories during her years with the theater community.

In 1922, Glaspell and Cook settled in Athens, Delphi; dying two years later, Cook was given full Greek ceremonial rites. Glaspell then returned to Provincetown, where she met writer Norman Mattson; they lived together for the next eight years, collaborating on *The Comic Artist*, which premiered at London's Strand Theatre (1928).

Returning her interests back to fiction, Glaspell published *Brook Evans* and *Fugitive's Return* within a two-year period (1928–1929). The last of her plays produced, *Alison's House*, won the 1931 Pulitzer Prize for Drama. Mattson abandoned Glaspell after publication of *Ambrose Holt and Family* in 1931. Beset by alcoholism and financial worries, she served as director of the Midwest Play Bureau of the Federal Theatre Project in Chicago (1936–1938). Returning to Provincetown in 1938, Glaspell published four novels during the next decade— *The Morning Is Near Us, Cherished and Shared of Old, Norma Ashe*, and *Judd Rankin's Daughter*—and wrote a final play, *Springs Eternal*, which remains unpublished. Susan Glaspell died on July 27, 1948, of a pulmonary embolism. Her headstone was erected in Truro's Snow Cemetery.

MAJOR WORKS AND THEMES

Before her move to Provincetown, Glaspell authored popular novels and periodical fiction. As she worked on her first novel, *The Glory of the Conquered*, Glaspell published in *Harper's Monthly Magazine, Leslie's*, and *Ladies' Home Journal*. Publishing twenty-six stories from 1904 to 1922, Glaspell set her conventional, homely characters in the midwestern city Freeport, the fictionalized Davenport, Iowa. In 1912, thirteen of the stories were collected in *Lifted Masks*. Examples of local-color fiction, her early tales, while disappointing in their lack of thematic complexity, demonstrate Glaspell's incipient preoccupation with a woman's struggle for autonomy and actualization in a patriarchal culture.

Published in 1909, *The Glory of the Conquered* was a commercial success. Subtitled "The Story of a Great Love," the work portrays the marriage of an artist and a scientist. The wife, who had denied her artistic talents during her marriage, finally embraces her art, as she perceives that the dying husband's immortality is assured in a portrait. Although an incompletely realized analysis of the restrictions of domesticity, *The Glory of the Conquered* introduced her next two novels, *The Visioning* and *Fidelity*, both of which savaged contemporary cultural conceptions of women's secondary status. Influenced by George Cram Cook's political beliefs, *The Visioning* (1911) narrates a young woman's conversion to socialism. Its realism in setting and characterization reflects Glaspell's acknowledgment of class and exploitation of the poor. *Fidelity* (1915) focuses on a woman who refuses to marry the man with whom she runs away; instead, she moves to New York to join the feminist movement. Living in Greenwich Village and Provincetown during the writing of the novel, Glaspell joined Greenwich Village's feminist Heterodoxy Club.

From 1915 to 1930, Glaspell wrote thirteen plays, each of them staged. From the first one-act play, *Suppressed Desires*, to the final three-act play, *Alison's House*, which won the 1931 Pulitzer Prize, Glaspell's writing demonstrates her increasing cognizance of the female dilemma: self-actualization versus familial and societal demands. Authoring eleven plays for the Provincetown Playhouse, formerly a fishhouse on a nineteenth-century wharf, Glaspell saw her *Suppressed Desires* open the 1915 summer season; the play reappeared on the 1916 bill, along with *Trifles* and Eugene O'Neill's *Bound East for Cardiff*. Written with Jig Cook, *Suppressed Desires* parodies the Freudian analysis enthusiastically taken up by their contemporaries.

Trifles, one of the most popular one-act plays in American theater history, is Glaspell's revision of the 1900 Hossack murder trial, which she had covered for the *Des Moines Daily News*. The story portrays two women who are bound by guilt about the absent woman suspected of murdering her husband in the marital bed. Thematically, the story displays contempt for abstract patriarchal justice: As Mrs. Hale and Mrs. Peters piece together the motive for the murder of an abusive husband by his repressed wife, the sheriff and the district attorney wander on and off stage, failing to recognize the motives embedded in the spilled sugar, the crazy quilting, the broken cage, and the dead canary. Understanding the brutality the imprisoned widow endured during her marriage, the two neighbors render their own version of justice to Minnie Foster Wright, subverting patriarchal law. In 1917, Glaspell transformed the play into the widely recognized short story "A Jury of Her Peers."

Nine other plays followed *Trifles*, including the controversial three-act play *The Verge*, appearing on the 1921 Provincetown Players' bill in New York City. Opening in a greenhouse, the play dramatizes Claire Archer's alienation from all familial and social ties. Finding sustenance only in her botanical experiments, Claire Archer rejects all of her loved ones; at the play's end, she strangles her lover before succumbing to insanity. With its unsympathetic protagonist, *The Verge*, while admired for its spare realism and its expressionistic setting, baffled audiences. The play demonstrates Glaspell's continued preoccupation with a restrictive culture: Problematically, Glaspell suggests in *The Verge* that female autonomy may annihilate reason and humanity.

Glaspell's 1930 *Alison's House*, with its forty-two performances in New York City, won a Pulitzer Prize. Loosely based on the life of Emily Dickinson, the three-act play dramatizes the reclusive poet's legacy. Set eighteen years after poet Alison Stanhope's death, the play details the family's mixed reactions to newly discovered letters revealing Alison's love for a married Harvard professor. While Alison's family debates the symbolic and financial value of the letters, members' own lives come under scrutiny. The letters are finally entrusted to the prodigal daughter who fled home with a married man; at the end of the play, she and her Victorian father are reconciled. Alison's newly disinterred poetry ameliorates the stern paternalism that had once ruined the poet's own happiness:

The next generation of women is allowed happiness despite their flouting of convention. The play was Glaspell's final drama produced, although biographers claim she authored two more plays, neither published nor produced.

As if despairing of woman's ability to achieve intellectual or social parity with men, Glaspell predicated her final novels on the theme of children, biological or spiritual, as the heirs to a distant progress. Her protagonists are women whose journeys to fulfillment are interrupted and usually forestalled; they are left with a partially comforting knowledge that the next generation will inherit the social progress denied them.

While *Ambrose Holt and Family* (1931) portrays the disillusioned protagonist Blossom who must relinquish her progressive goals to her son, the 1939 *The Morning Is Near Us* depicts Lydia Chippman's return home to recover her past. One truth uncovered is Lydia's paternity: The man she thought her biological father had been only one of her mother's lovers. The novel concludes with Lydia's reconciliation with her adopted father and her subsequent recognition that her two adopted children embody her hopes for the future. The novel was chosen as a Literary Guild selection in 1940.

Her two final novels, the 1942 *Norma Ashe* and the 1945 *Judd Rankin's Daughter*, criticize a midwestern culture for ignoring the sociopolitical changes incurred by global warfare. Like *The Morning Is Near Us, Norma Ashe* begins with nostalgia for the past: The protagonist, once an idealistic college graduate, is now a bitter, poverty-stricken woman. At Pioneer College, Norma had been mentored by an idealistic philosophy professor. Instead of pursuing her dream of graduate study, Norma married unwisely: Her husband's death leaves her impoverished. Despite her own inability to live by the idealism that had once inspired her, Norma dies with the realization that benevolence and social progress are within the reach of the next generation.

Susan Glaspell continued the theme of the woman bound by stultifying convention and gendered notions of role in *Judd Rankin's Daughter* (1945). Against the backdrop of World War II, the protagonist witnesses the unhappiness of several female family members who are trapped by convention. The novel ends unsatisfactorily with the protagonist's acceptance of her limited female roles. One wonders if Glaspell had surrendered all hope for female actualization in her final years.

CRITICAL RECEPTION

Despite winning a Pulitzer, Susan Glaspell was not included in the canon until the interest in women's writing emerged in the 1970s. While *Trifles* remains a frequently performed play and "A Jury of Her Peers" is included in literature anthologies, Glaspell's main body of work—the plays and the novels—garnered little critical attention until the 1980s.

The first major study of Glaspell was Arthur E. Waterman's 1966 *Susan Glaspell* (Twayne Series) and his "Susan Glaspell (1882?–1948)" in *American*

Literary Realism. Classifying Glaspell as a minor regionalist writer, Waterman applauds her midwestern idealism.

With an explosion of interest in "lost" writers, especially women and African Americans, Glaspell's body of work came into critical focus from three perspectives: feminism, both in her fiction and her drama; reading and gender; and theater, especially her creative relationship with Eugene O'Neill.

Glaspell's feminist themes have been explored in numerous studies. For example, Veronica Makowsky's *Susan Glaspell's Century of American Women: A Critical Interpretation of Her Work* argues Glaspell's exclusion from the canon can be attributed to the author's feminist perspective. "Forging a Woman's Identity in Susan Glaspell's Fiction" is Makowsky's analysis of Glaspell's novelistic structure as a form "more expressive of a woman's experience" (Ben-Zvi, *Essays* 317). Colette Lindroth's "Lifting the Masks of Male-Female Discourse: The Rhetorical Strategies of Susan Glaspell" discusses the feminist "subtext" of Glaspell's short fiction: Glaspell "reverses traditional notions of male competency and power and female timidity and weakness" (Ben-Zvi, *Essays* 304). In "Small Things Reconsidered: 'A Jury of Her Peers' " Elaine Hedges critiques Glaspell's evocative sense of midwestern oppression of rural women (Ben-Zvi, *Essays* 49–69).

A second critical issue centers on Glaspell as a feminist playwright. The 1981 *Plays by American Women: 1900–1930*, edited by Judith E. Barlow, includes a discussion of the Provincetown Players as an important cultural venue for women playwrights such as Djuna Barnes, Edna Ferber, and Glaspell, all of whom wrote provocative drama exploring women's roles and aspirations. Sharon Friedman's "Feminism as Theme in Twentieth-Century American Women's Drama" terms Glaspell a "dramatist of ideas," whose female protagonists "embody a statement about women's condition" (74); whereas Christine Dymkowski, in "On the Edge: The Plays of Susan Glaspell," argues that Glaspell's drama traces the feminine drive toward limitless, ungendered possibilities. Glaspell's protest of "imposed patterns of behavior that suppressed the real self" is the subject of Barbara Ozieblo's "Suppression and Society in Susan Glaspell's Theater," a study of Glaspell's interest in the theories of Sigmund Freud (Ben-Zvi, *Essays* 105–22). In "Beyond *The Verge*: Absent Heroines in the Plays of Susan Glaspell," Jackie Czerepinski analyzes Glaspell's protagonists such as Minnie Wright, Bernice, and Alison, powerful characters, yet absent from the play's action (Ben-Zvi, *Essays* 145–54). Linda Ben-Zvi, one of the primary critics of Glaspell, argues that the playwright's significance to women's dramatic art is based upon Glaspell's female perception and the poetic language required to structure it in "Susan Glaspell's Contributions to Contemporary Women Playwrights." Calling Glaspell a pioneer in twentieth-century drama, Ben-Zvi proposes Glaspell's restoration to the dramatic canon.

Glaspell's controversial *The Verge* has been the subject of extensive recent scholarship. Elin Diamond explores the play's motif of "scientific mothering" as indoctrination in " 'The Garden Is a Mess': Maternal Space in Bowles, Glaspell, Robins." Diamond argues that *The Verge* portrays a woman's refusal to adhere to the conventional tenets of maternity. In *"The Verge*: L'Ecriture Feminine at the Provincetown," Marcia Noe argues that as protagonist Clare Archer is the "antithesis of the feminine ideal," Glaspell utilizes the nonlinear female discourse characterized by Cixous, Kristeva, and Irigaray (Ben-Zvi, *Essays* 132–33). Karen Malpede's "Reflections on *The Verge*" defines Claire Archer as the tragic heroine who finds her destiny through an "act of transgression" (Ben-Zvi, *Essays* 126); thus, the revolutionary Claire Archer protests a culture that denies female potentiality. Stephen J. Bottoms's 1998 "Building on the Abyss: Susan Glaspell's *The Verge* in Production" details the difficulty of staging Claire Archer's defiance and subsequent madness for an international conference on Glaspell.

"A Jury of Her Peers" has been examined by Judith Fetterley and Annette Kolodny as illustrative of gendered reading. In "Reading about Reading: 'A Jury of Her Peers,' 'The Murders in the Rue Morgue,' and 'The Yellow Wallpaper,' " Fetterley proposes that Glaspell's short story is predicated upon female reading: The men cannot solve the mystery of John Wright's murder, for they do not comprehend the women's text—a kitchen and kitchen things—before them (148). Kolodny, in "A Map for Rereading: Or, Gender and the Interpretation of Literary Texts," argues that the male paradigm of reading ignores, at its own expense, the "gender marking" requisite to reading literary texts (460–65).

Glaspell's alliance with Eugene O'Neill and the Provincetown Players is explored in Jean Gould's *Modern American Playwrights*, which details Glaspell's and Jig Cook's contributions to native drama. Joel Pfister's 1995 *Staging Depth: Eugene O'Neill and the Politics of Psychological Discourse* compares O'Neill's themes with Glaspell's. Both, he argues, criticize their era's insistence upon gendered roles: O'Neill's *The Personal Equation* is compared to *The Verge* as explorations of the destructiveness of inequality. Glaspell and her fellow playwrights are the subject of Judith E. Barlow's "Susan's Sisters: The 'Other' Women Writers of the Provincetown Players"; as "more than a third" of Provincetown's bills consisted of plays authored by women, the importance of this regional theater to American woman's dramatic history cannot be ignored (259–60).

An example of New Historicist criticism, Ben-Zvi's " 'Murder, She Wrote': The Genesis of Susan Glaspell's *Trifles*" provides details of the December 2, 1900, murder of farmer John Hossack and the subsequent trial of his wife Margaret, purportedly asleep in the bed while her husband was struck with an axe. After covering the trial for a Des Moines newspaper, Glaspell, Ben-Zvi argues, not only contributed to the "shap[ing] of public opinion" about Margaret Hossack but also absorbed the implicit role of patriarchy in denying female self-actualization. In revisioning the trial, Glaspell "represent[s] female power not victimization" (161).

BIBLIOGRAPHY

Works by Susan Keating Glaspell

The Glory of the Conquered: The Story of a Great Love. New York: Stokes, 1909.

The Visioning: A Novel. New York: Stokes, 1911.

Lifted Masks: Stories. New York: Stokes, 1912.

Fidelity: A Novel. Boston: Small, Maynard, 1915.

Trifles. New York: Shay/Washington Square Players, 1916. (Play)

Susan Keating Glaspell and George Cram Cook. *Suppressed Desires.* New York: Shay, 1917.

The People and Close the Book: Two One Act Plays. New York: Shay, 1918.

Plays. Boston: Small, 1920.

Inheritors: A Play in Three Acts. Boston: Small, 1921.

The Verge. Boston: Small, 1921.

Bernice: A Play in Three Acts. London: Benn, 1924.

Susan Keating Glaspell and George Cram Cook. *Tickless Time: A Comedy in One Act.* Boston: Baker, 1925.

The Road to the Temple. London: Benn, 1926.

Trifles and Six Other Short Plays. London: Benn, 1926.

A Jury of Her Peers. London: Benn, 1927.

Susan Keating Glaspell and Norman Matson. *The Comic Artist: A Play in Three Acts.* New York: Stokes, 1927.

Brook Evans. New York: Stokes, 1928.

Fugitive's Return. New York: Stokes, 1929.

Alison's House: A Play in Three Acts. New York: French, 1930.

Ambrose Holt and Family. New York: Stokes, 1931.

The Morning Is Near Us: A Novel. New York: Stokes, 1939.

Cherished and Shared of Old. New York: Messner, 1940.

Norma Ashe: A Novel. Philadelphia: Lippincott, 1942.

Judd Rankin's Daughter. Philadelphia: Lippincott, 1945.

Plays by Susan Glaspell. Cambridge: Cambridge University Press, 1987.

Studies of Susan Keating Glaspell

Adler, Thomas P. *Mirror on the Stage: The Pulitzer Plays as an Approach to American Drama.* Lafayette, IN: Purdue University Press, 1987.

Alkalay-Gut, Karen. " 'Jury of Her Peers': The Importance of *Trifles*." *Studies in Short Fiction* 21 (1984): 1–9.

Atlas, Marilyn. "Creating Women's Myth: Emily Dickinson's Legacy to Susan Glaspell." *Focus: Teaching English Language Arts* 8 (1981): 55–61.

Barlow, Judith E., ed. *Plays by American Women: 1900–1930.* New York: Applause Theatre, 1985.

Barlow, Judith E. "Susan's Sisters: The 'Other' Woman Writers of the Provincetown Players." *Susan Glaspell. Essays on Her Theater and Fiction.* Ed. Linda Ben-Zvi. Ann Arbor, MI: University of Michigan Press, 1995. 259–300.

Ben-Zvi, Linda. " 'Murder, She Wrote': The Genesis of Susan Glaspell's *Trifles*." *Theatre Journal* 44 (1992): 141-62.

———. "Susan Glaspell and Eugene O'Neill." *Eugene O'Neill Newsletter* 6 (1982): 21-29.

———. "Susan Glaspell, Eugene O'Neill, and the Imagery of Gender." *Eugene O'Neill Newsletter* 10 (1986): 22-27.

———. "Susan Glaspell's Contributions to Contemporary Women Playwrights." *Feminine Focus: The New Women Playwrights*. Ed. Enoch Brater. Oxford University Press, 1989. 147-66.

———, ed. *Susan Glaspell: Essays on Her Theater and Fiction*. Ann Arbor, MI: University of Michigan Press, 1995.

Bigsby, C.W.E., ed. *Plays by Susan Glaspell*. Cambridge, NY: Cambridge University Press, 1987.

Bottoms, Stephen J. "Building on the Abyss: Susan Glaspell's *The Verge* in Production." *Theatre Topics* 8 (1998): 127-47.

Chinoy, Helen Krich, and Linda Walsh Jenkins, eds. *Women in American Theatre*. New York: Theatre Communications Group, 1987.

Diamond, Elin. " 'The Garden Is a Mess': Maternal Space in Bowles, Glaspell, Robins." *The Theatrical Gamut: Notes for a Post-Beckettian Stage*. Ed. Enoch Brater. Ann Arbor, MI: University of Michigan Press, 1995. 121-39.

Dymkowski, Christine. "On the Edge: The Plays of Susan Glaspell." *Modern Drama* 31 (1998): 91-105.

Fetterley, Judith. "Reading about Reading: 'A Jury of Her Peers,' 'The Murders in the Rue Morgue,' and 'The Yellow Wallpaper.' " *Gender and Reading: Essays on Readers, Texts, and Contexts*. Ed. Elizabeth A. Flynn and Patrocinio P. Schweickart. Baltimore, MD: John Hopkins University Press, 1986. 147-64.

Flavin, Louise. " 'A Jury of Her Peers' Needs a Jury of Its Peers." *Teaching English in the Two-Year College* 10 (1984): 259-60.

Friedman, Sharon. "Feminism as Theme in Twentieth-Century American Women's Drama." *American Studies* 24 (1994): 69-89.

Gainor, J. Ellen. "A Stage of Her Own: Susan Glaspell's *The Verge* and Women's Dramaturgy." *Journal of American Drama and Theatre* 1 (1989): 79-99.

———. "Susan Keating Glaspell." *American Playwrights, 1880-1945: A Research and Production Sourcebook*. Ed. William W. Demasters. Westport, CT: Greenwood, 1995. 109-20.

Gould, Jean. "Susan Glaspell and the Provincetown Players." *Modern American Playwrights*. New York: Dodd, 1996. 26-49.

Guber, Susan, and Anne Hedin. "A Jury of Our Peers: Teaching and Learning in the Indiana Women's Prison." *College English* 43 (1981): 779-89.

Kolodny, Annette. "A Map for Rereading: Or, Gender and the Interpretation of Literary Texts." *New Literary History* 11 (1980): 451-67.

Mael, Phyllis. "*Trifles*: The Path to Sisterhood." *Literature/Film Quarterly* 17.4 (1989): 281-84.

Makowsky, Veronica. *Susan Glaspell's Century of American Women: A Critical Interpretation of Her Work*. New York: Oxford University Press, 1993.

Malpede, Karen. *Women in Theatre: Compassion and Hope*. New York: Drama Book, 1983.

McGovern, Edythe M. "Susan Glaspell." *American Women Writers: A Critical Reference*

Guide from Colonial Times to the Present. Vol 2. Ed. Lina Mainiero and Lansdon Lynne Faust. New York: Ungar, 1980. 144–46.

Mustazza, Leonard. "Gender and Justice in Susan Glaspell's 'A Jury of Her Peers.'" *Law and Semiotics* 2 (1988): 271–76.

———. "Generic Translation and Thematic Shift in Susan Glaspell's *Trifles* and 'A Jury of Her Peers.'" *Studies in Short Fiction* 26 (1989): 489–96.

Noe, Marcia. *Susan Glaspell: Voice from the Heartland.* Macomb: Western Illinois Monograph Series, 1983.

Papke, Mary E. *Susan Glaspell: A Research and Production Sourcebook.* Westport, CT: Greenwood, 1993.

Pfister, Joel. "The Trappings of Theatre, Gender, and Desire." *Staging Depth: Eugene O'Neill and the Politics of Psychological Discourse.* Chapel Hill: University of North Carolina Press, 1995. 187–215.

Rabkin, Eric S., ed. *Lifted Masks and Other Works.* Ann Arbor, MI: University of Michigan Press, 1993.

Radel, Nicholas F. "Provincetown Plays: Women Writers and O'Neill's American Intertext." *Essays in Theatre* 9 (1990): 31–43.

Sarlos, Robert Karoly. *Jig Cook and the Provincetown Players: Theatre in Ferment.* Amherst: University of Massachusetts Press, 1982.

Schlueter, June, ed. *Modern American Drama: The Female Canon.* Rutherford, NJ: Fairleigh Dickinson University Press, 1990.

Showalter, Elaine. *Sister's Choice: Tradition and Change in American Women's Writing.* Oxford: Clarendon, 1991.

Sutherland, Cynthia. "American Women Playwrights as Mediators of the 'Woman Problem.'" *Modern Drama* 21 (1978): 319–36.

Toohey, John L. "1930–31: Alison's House." *A History of the Pulitzer Prize Plays.* New York: Citadel, 1967. 89–93.

Waterman, Arthur E. *Susan Glaspell.* New York: Twayne, 1966.

———. "Susan Glaspell (1882?–1948)." *American Literary Realism* 4 (1971): 183–91.

Weisbrod, Carol. "Images of the Woman Juror." *Harvard Women's Law Journal* 9 (1986): 59–82.

Williams, Linda. "A Jury of Their Peers: Marlene Gorris's *A Question of Silence.*" *Postmodernism and Its Discontents.* Ed. E. Ann Kaplan. London: Verso, 1988. 107–15.

JOVITA GONZÁLEZ DE MIRELES (1904–1983)

Andrea R. Purdy

BIOGRAPHY

Jovita González de Mireles was born in 1904 in Roma, Texas, to an upper-class family of Spanish/American ancestry. In 1910 she moved to San Antonio, Texas, where she and her siblings received their English-language education. She obtained her undergraduate degree in Spanish from Our Lady of the Lake College in 1927 and her master's in history under the direction of J. Frank Dobie from the University of Texas at Austin in 1930. His mentorship and their long-lasting friendship led to her first publication, "The Folklore of the Texas-Mexican Vaquero," which appeared in one of his edited journals in 1927. She also contributed the short story "Traga-Balas" ("The Bullet Swallower") to his 1935 *Puro mexicano* special issue of *Publications of the Texas Folklore Society*. In 1930 she strayed from her established voice with Dobie with a piece based on her master's thesis entitled "America Invades the Border Towns." She discussed the events between 1848 and 1930 and described them as "a racial struggle, a fight between an aggressive, conquering and materialistic people on the one hand, and a volatile but passive and easily satisfied race on the other" (472). Her second essay, "Tales and Songs of the Texas-Mexicans," included three stories portraying the devil in southern Texas, which she had presented at a reading before the Texas Folklore Society, of which she served as the first Mexican American woman president. In 1934 with the encouragement of Dobie, she applied and received a Rockefeller grant, which enabled her to write two novels, *Caballero* and *Dew on the Thorn*.

In 1935, González married E. E. Mireles. They both worked in Del Rio until 1939, when they moved to Corpus Christi to work in the school district. After her marriage, González refrained from her work on folklore, dedicating herself to her marriage and to teaching Spanish. She continued to work on her novel *Caballero* through the 1940s, collaborating with Margaret Eimer (1903–1978), who wrote under the pseudonym of Eve Raleigh. They established a partnership in Del Rio in 1937, though little about their relationship is known. While her two novels were to remain unpublished for a long time, this is not to say there was not any interest in González. Maria Cotera of the Mexican American Library Project at the University of Texas at Austin interviewed González and her husband in the 1970s, and some of her personal papers were acquired at that time. It was during this interview that unbeknownst to her husband, who declared that the novel *Caballero* had been destroyed, González signaled to Marita Cotera that this wasn't the case. González and her husband died in 1983 and 1986, respectively, leaving no heirs.

González's novels were to remain hidden until their discovery in 1992, when Isabel Cruz, who had inherited the Mireles home and belongings, mentioned to Ray J. García, a member of the Nueces County Historical Society, that she needed a place to dispose of the Mireles library. All documents obtained were subsequently archived at the Texas A & M University Corpus Christi Library. Professor José E. Limón of the University of Texas at Austin became interested in these documents when in 1993 Professor Arnoldo De León published *Mexican Americans in Texas: A Brief History* and used photos from the Mireles papers for the cover. Limón was able to identify *Caballero* as the historical novel for which he had searched. He also helped identify the second manuscript, *Dew on the Thorn*. Both novels were published in 1996 and 1997, respectively.

MAJOR WORKS AND THEMES

González's early works reflect her interest in folklore and the influence of J. Frank Dobie, specifically his ethnographic style. Her work also places her in an ethnic class distinct from that of the mestizo or the peon. The subject of her first essay "The Folklore of the Texas-Mexican Vaquero," as she told Dobie in a 1926 letter, "is not dealing with the landed proprietor who, in my part of the state, forms the better class" but with the socially alienated vaquero. Ironically, the focus of this paper is with the vaquero's racial traits instead of his alienation. The presentation is much more pastoral in theme, though it has been noted that some repression slips in when the coming of the fences is mentioned, which is associated with white ranching (Limón, "Folklore" 460). Another essay, based on her master's thesis, presented in 1930 takes up the history of south Texas between 1848 and 1930. Limón points out that "the aggressive conquering aspects of the [conquering and materialistic people] were left wholly undiscussed, while the clear implication left for the latter—the Texas Mexicans—was that, although they have suffered some injustice, (left largely unspecified), it was they who must adopt American values if racial relations were to improve" ("Folklore" 461). "Tales and Songs of the Texas-Mexicans" explores similar pastoral themes, with a couple of deviations. The first is with its presentation of three stories about the devil in southern Texas, where it also introduces the picaresque character of Pedro de Urdemañas, who convinces the devil that he should go to Texas in order to bring more people to hell. The second shows her interest in the *corrido*, which is more political in nature. She comments in particular on the "Ballad of Remigio Treviño":

This is the earliest Mexican ballad composed on Texas soil that I have found. The turbulent period following the independence of Texas was one of resistance to the Americans who came as far south as the border. I have been told that many *tragedias* (corridos) originated then, but the above is the only one I have been able to collect. ("Tales and Songs" 111)

The evolution in tone and theme in her later writings reveals a political consciousness not noticed in her earlier works. Limón sees her as a woman at "another historical moment. . . . [A]s a specific intellectual entangled between the sites of power represented by Dobie, her own race/class affiliations, and her larger community, she often repressed the better part of her political consciousness" ("Folklore" 469).

While attention has been focused thus far on González's essays, it is her novels for which she is gaining critical recognition. *Caballero: An Historical Novel* and *Dew on the Thorn* represent the beginnings of literature that concerns Mexican Americans in Texas. Both novels were published posthumously due to the concerted efforts of many people, such as José E. Limón, María Cotera, local historian Ray J. García, and of course Isabel Cruz, who donated González's work to the Texas A & M University Corpus Christi Library in 1992. *Caballero* is viewed as a Texas version of *Gone with the Wind* (Kreneck 78), but it deserves its own place as an accomplished historical romance. The novel tells the story of the Mendoza y Soría, a border family involved in the conflict between Mexico and the United States over Texas during 1848–1849. It also is intriguing because it represents the collaborative effort between Jovita González and Eve Raleigh (pseudonym for Margaret Eimer), though little information about their partnership is available.

Dew on the Thorn is a series of fictionalized accounts at the beginning of the twentieth century of a south Texas community close to the Rio Grande. It is in these two works that one sees the emergence of a woman with a critical political conscience evolving from the one who wrote folkloric articles under the mentorship of J. Frank Dobie. Looking at Jovita González personally and professionally provides a rich tapestry of life along the border and the emerging conflicts between Anglos and Hispanics, men and women, as well as social classes.

CRITICAL RECEPTION

Very little literary criticism is available about Jovita González or her works. Gradually, more critical attention focuses on González and her place in literary history. Among her early critics, James McNutt and Gloria Louise Velasquez approached her works in varying manners. McNutt offers this assessment of her in conjunction with J. Frank Dobie:

Dobie's paternalistic attitude met agreement in Miss González's own conservatism. She viewed herself as a member of the Mexican American upper class, a descendant of Spanish aristocrats. She and Dobie were sharing information about mestizo peons when they collected and discussed folklore. (252)

Ironically González devotes much of her ethnographic research in these articles to the lower classes, and it is actually her third article, "Tales and Songs of the Texas-Mexicans," where a different voice from the one in previous essays emerges, particularly in her telling of the appearance of the devil in south Texas and her discussion of Remigio Treviño, the subject of a *corrido*. Limón offers a more sympathetic yet still critical assessment of her writing about the "politically laden" *corrido*. "Even here, we clearly sense repression as she soothingly shaped her reassuring discursive flow to her audience's expectations and probably her own. Yet more than enough slipped through once again as she discussed one corrido about Remigio Treviño" ("Folklore" 465). Gloria Louise Velasquez focuses her criticisms in two ways. She examines González's work as a critic of patriarchy and as a critic of Anglo-American dominance. She finds González lacking in the first area since she

devotes little attention to the description of female experience. In her prose fiction, the female characters do not appear as protagonists and are assigned very little space within the narrative discourse. When women do appear, they are confined to traditional roles within their ethnic culture while male experience is foregrounded. (80)

The area of cultural ambivalence receives a more positive assessment because González's work displays an attitude of resistance and assimilation, which narratively shows itself in the form of ideological contradiction (Velasquez 80).

Limón acknowledges the arguments made against González's body of work, but he views González's weakness as "not ambivalence, but repression" ("Folklore" 465). He tends to view her work more paradoxically, similar to that of J. Frank Dobie. With regard to her later essays, "the articulation of this woman's critical political unconscious took her, not just to a world of men, but specifically to that of the mythic male hero, a sphere of super enhanced masculinity and a concomitant repression of women" ("Folklore" 468). Regardless of her motives, her choices provide an interesting forum for further discussion and analysis. In reading and assessing her works today, critics must constantly remember the time and place during which González wrote.

BIBLIOGRAPHY

Works by Jovita González de Mireles

"The Folklore of the Texas-Mexican Vaquero." *Publications of the Texas Folklore Society* 4 (1927): 7–22.

"America Invades the Border Towns." *Southwest Review* 15 (1930): 469–77.
"Among My People." *Publications of the Texas Folklore Society* 10 (1930): 99–108.
"Social Life in Cameron, Starr and Zapata Counties." M.A. thesis. University of Texas at Austin, 1930.
"Tales and Songs of the Texas-Mexicans." *Publications of the Texas Folklore Society* 8 (1930): 109–14.
"The Bullet Swallower." *Publications of the Texas Folklore Society* 10 (1935): 107–14.
"The Mescal-Drinking Horse." *Mustangs and Cow Horses.* (Special Issue) *Publications of the Texas Folklore Society* 16 (1940): 396–402.
Jovita González de Mireles and Eve Raleigh. *Caballero: An Historical Novel.* Ed. José E. Limón and María Cotera. College Station: Texas A & M University Press, 1996.
Dew on the Thorn. Houston: Arte Público, 1997.

Studies of Jovita González de Mireles

Cotera, María. "Deconstructing the Corrido Hero: Caballero and Its Gendered Critique of Nationalist Discourse." *Perspectives in Mexican American Studies* 5 (1995): 151–70.
Dobie, J. Frank. "González-Dobie Correspondence (1926–46)." J. Frank Dobie Collection. University of Texas at Austin.
Kreneck, Thomas H. "Recovering the 'Lost' Manuscripts of Jovita González: The Production of South Texas Mexican-American Literature." *Texas Library Journal* 74.2 (1998): 76–79.
Limón, José E. *Dancing with the Devil: Society, Gender and the Political Unconscious in Mexican-American South Texas.* Durham: Duke University Press, 1991. 221–35.
———. "Folklore, Gendered Repression, and Cultural Critique: The Case of Jovita González." *Texas Studies in Literature and Language* 35 (1993): 453–73.
———. "Mexican, Foundational Fictions, and the United States: *Caballero,* a Late Border Romance." *Modern Languages Quarterly* 57 (1996): 341–53.
McNutt, James. "Beyond Regionalism: Texas Folklorists and the Emergence of a Post-Regional Consciousness." Diss. University of Texas, 1982.
Velasquez, Gloria Louise. *Cultural Ambivalence in Early Chicana Literature.* Houston: Arte Público, 1988.

CAROLINE GORDON
(1895–1981)

Lou Halsell Rodenberger

BIOGRAPHY

Caroline Ferguson Gordon was born on October 6, 1895, in Todd County, Kentucky at Merry Mont, the home of her maternal grandmother, for whom she was named. She was the second child of three and the only daughter of James Morris Gordon and Nancy (Meriwether) Gordon. For most of her childhood, Gordon and her family lived at Merry Mont, once a tobacco plantation of more than 10,000 acres near Trenton, Kentucky, on the Tennessee border, where many of the Meriwethers still farmed. Gordon often referred to her extended family, notable for its eccentrics and individualists, as the Connection and defined the labels with which the family identified its members. The Kinky Heads took up causes and held strong opinions. The Anyhows just "did anyhow they pleased."

Gordon's father, whose passion for hunting and fishing would become the subject of her second novel, *Aleck Maury, Sportsman*, was employed at Merry Mont by Caroline's grandfather, Douglas Meriwether, to tutor his four children, including Nancy, who later became the wife of her teacher. When Caroline was school age, her father opened a classical preparatory school in Clarksville, Tennessee, where Nancy Gordon also taught and Caroline enrolled.

By 1908, James Gordon decided to change professions. He became a Church of Christ minister, moving often from church to church. Caroline spent her first two years in high school at Wilmington, Ohio, and her third enrolled at Lynchburg, Virginia, graduating in 1912 from the Princeton Collegiate Institute in Princeton, Kentucky. In 1916, she received a B.A. degree from Bethany College in Bethany, West Virginia. Her education, beginning with her first years at her father's school, emphasized Latin, Greek, and the classics, which eventually influenced both technique and theory in her concepts of what fiction should be.

Gordon lived with her family after graduation, teaching high school at Clarksville until 1920, when she took a job as a reporter with the *Chattanooga News*. In the summer of 1924, at the family home of Robert Penn Warren in Guthrie, Kentucky, where the Gordons now lived, Caroline met poet Allen Tate, already associated with the Vanderbilt University professors and graduate students known as the Agrarians. By fall, Gordon was in New York, where in 1925 she and Allen Tate were married. Their daughter Nancy was born that year.

In 1928, when Tate received a Guggenheim Fellowship, they went to Paris, where Gordon worked to finish *Penhally*, a novel in progress, encouraged by Ford Madox Ford, who had become her mentor when she worked as his secretary-typist in New York. Gordon wrote short stories as she worked on her novels and enjoyed her first success as a writer when Yvor Winters and his wife, novelist Janet Lewis, published "Summer Dust" in the fall 1929 issue of their newly established little magazine *Gyroscope*. Edward J. O'Brien included "Summer Dust" in the *Best Short Stories of 1930*. The next year, "The Long Day" appeared in *Gyroscope* and was reprinted by *Scribner's Magazine* after Scribner's publishing house editor, Maxwell Perkins, read Gordon's manuscript for *Penhally* and contracted to publish the novel. Meanwhile, the Tates moved to a country house they called Benfolly on the Cumberland River near Clarksville, where they lived until 1932, when a Guggenheim Fellowship awarded Gordon financed another year in France. While there, Gordon finished several short stories, including "Old Red," which was published in the *O. Henry Memorial Award Prize Stories of 1934*.

After two years at Benfolly, where they entertained many members of the literary establishment of the time, and the year in France, the Tates moved to Memphis in 1934, where Tate taught at Southwestern University. Gordon continued to write, often teaching as well, as the couple rarely settled for more than a year or two in one place. Frequently, they spent summers at Benfolly, living during university terms at Greensboro, Princeton, Washington, D.C., and Sewanee, where Tate edited the *Sewanee Review*. Early in 1946, the Tates, whose relationship had often been troubled, divorced, although they remarried that summer. The marriage ended with a second divorce in 1959.

By the time of her final split with Tate, Gordon had published nine novels and one collection of her short stories, *The Forest of the South*. She had coedited with Tate a short story anthology, *The House of Fiction*, for which Gordon wrote most of the concluding lengthy discussion of the techniques of fiction creation. In 1947, Gordon was baptized into the Roman Catholic Church. In 1953, she began a year's stay in Rome. For much of the remainder of her long, productive life, Gordon taught creative writing at the University of Kansas, University of Washington, Columbia University, University of California, Davis, and Purdue. Providentially, in 1966, the National Council on the Arts awarded her a grant of $10,000. She participated in numerous symposiums and conferences, finally settling for the last years of her career at the University of Dallas, a Catholic University. At age eighty-one, Gordon retired to live in Mexico near her daughter Nancy and husband Percy Wood's retirement home in San Cristóbal de las Casas in Chiapas province. On April 11, 1981, Caroline Gordon died of complications from a stroke. She is buried near her home in San Cristóbal.

MAJOR WORKS AND THEMES

Caroline Gordon learned the episodes of her colorful family history from the many front porch storytellers in the Meriwether clan. Those tales would later provide plot and action in her fiction. Because she was a traditionalist, who held that customs and beliefs handed down orally in a family should be preserved, her novels are often judged episodic. After her conversion to Catholicism, particularly, Gordon also held strong opinions about how a novel should be structured. Her often rigid theories of fiction were based on the techniques demonstrated in the works of her favorite authors, Henry James, Flaubert, and Chekhov. In her first novels, however, Gordon becomes, to her advantage, narrator of much of the Connection's family saga. Only after she began teaching creative writing and formulating more completely her ideas of what a novel should be did she seek to exemplify her theories in her own work. She also began to value even more intensely the use of Christian imagery and classical mythology as well. Consequently, her last novels were reviewed kindly by her friends but received little attention from general readers.

Gordon's first novel, *Penhally*, reshapes the history of the Meriwether family into a four-generation tale. The plot traces the family conflicts from the days of antebellum plantation life through Reconstruction to the final violent act of murder, triggered by the sale of the plantation for development into a hunt club. Although Gordon never took up the passionate defense of the southern agrarian way of life that her husband and his friends professed, she inherited the belief that materialism and industrialization threatened traditional values in the South. That belief provides a chief theme for this first work. In 1934, three years after her debut as a novelist, Gordon published what has been judged by most critics as her best novel. Based on her father's life, *Aleck Maury, Sportsman* shares much of James Morris Gordon's biography. Gordon took notes as her aging father narrated tales of his happiest times, which were those days he spent fishing and hunting, and structured a novel rich in the ritual and lore of Mr. Maury's favorite sports. The satisfactions of Maury's well-lived life make his approaching old age all the more significant as he considers the brevity of his active years, a theme implicit in several of Gordon's short stories featuring Mr. Maury.

In 1937, Gordon produced two novels. In *The Garden of Adonis*, Gordon examines the state of agriculture in the South during the 1920s and the depression days of the 1930s and explores the psychology of poor white farmers struggling to survive in those difficult days. Her second novel that year, *None Shall Look Back*, narrates the story of a young Southerner whose life is altered irreversibly by his experiences as a Confederate soldier. In this novel, Gordon implies as a major thesis that the changes effected in the young soldier's personality by battlefield experiences represent the greater tragedy of defeat and hopelessness Southerners suffered after the war.

Three years after publication of these novels, Gordon's frontier novel, *Green Centuries*, was reviewed favorably, although the novel did not produce the royalties the author had anticipated. This narrative relates the adventures of frontiersman Orion Outlaw, who leaves his home in North Carolina before the Revolution after his activities with the rebel Regulators against the King's militia are discovered. He settles with his young wife Cassy in eastern Tennessee, where he meets such real-life borderers as Daniel Boone and the Scotch trader James Adair. For this novel, Gordon's earlier research into the lives of the Cherokees provides authentic and detailed background for her descriptions of encounters between the frontiersmen and the natives. Gordon's interest in Cherokee and Shawnee history was first stimulated by an early captive narrative she casually chose from the shelves as she browsed in the Vanderbilt library. In it she learned the story of West Virginia pioneer Jennie Wiley, who was the prisoner of a Shawnee and Cherokee war party for several months. In 1932, one of Gordon's best-known short stories, "The Captive," first published in *Hound and Horn*, fictionalizes the captive's adventures. In both the novel and the short story, the author explores the toll that the hardships of frontier life imposed on family relationships as well as on other human ties.

In her next novel, *The Women on the Porch*, Gordon's narrative technique may be judged as transitional. Her plot and characterizations are reflections of her personal experience and past as previously, but Gordon experiments here with narration of the story through revelation of the thoughts of many of her characters. The plot of this work develops around the lives of a young woman, who has returned to share the lives of women relatives in her Tennessee home, and her professor husband, whom she has left in New York after learning of his unfaithfulness. Here again Gordon explores the tenuous nature of family connections.

Early in the 1950s, Gordon published two more novels, *The Strange Children* and *The Malefactors*. Neither was considered a success critically. *The Strange Children* is told from the point of view of a ten-year-old girl who relates her sometimes unreliable version of life among the puzzling house guests who come and go all summer at her rural home. Christian imagery, mythological allusions, and the strained effort to incorporate a Jamesian central intelligence into *The Malefactors* provide critics with material for analysis, not always favorable, of Gordon's aesthetics. Generally well accepted, however, was her second volume of short fiction, *Old Red and Other Stories*, which was published in 1963 and collects many of her better short stories.

Late in her life, Gordon launched plans for a two-level novel that would intertwine both family history and lore and classic mythology. She had published several of her reminiscences, which she said would be the basis for the autobiographical level, which she first planned to called *A Narrow Heart: The Portrait of a Woman* but later changed to *Behold My Trembling Heart*. Her last work, *The Glory of Hera*, which she claimed was the second level of this never completed project, retells the story of Heracles's labors. This work received little critical attention. Recently, Gordon's earlier works have been reprinted. As with many southern writers, Gordon's ability to convey sense of place and her talent for exploring the uncertainties of human interaction combined with her inherited gift for telling an engaging story have earned for her acceptance as a talented southern writer.

CRITICAL RECEPTION

Two aspects of Caroline Gordon's adult life seem to have contributed to early critical assumptions that she was a minor southern writer who did not publish her first novel until age thirty-six. Usually three or four years elapsed between the appearances of her subsequent books. First, her marriage to Allen Tate, whose reputation as a poet and biographer increased steadily during those early years of their union, presented one restraint on her pursuit of a writing career. Tate frequently suffered writer's block, and Gordon used considerable energy to encourage his finishing a project or beginning a new one. A second hindrance originated in the generous spirit of southern hospitality that compelled both Tate and Gordon to entertain house guests steadily wherever they resided. In *Close Connections: Caroline Gordon and the Southern Renaissance*, the most definitive account yet written of Gordon's life and work, author Ann Waldron portrays Gordon as chief cook and hostess to the literary friends who often numbered six or eight and who stayed several weeks at a time.

For a complete coverage of the critical reception of each of Gordon's works, Waldron's book, based on letters and interviews with those who knew Gordon, provides valuable details of both publishing history and critical appraisal. Gordon's early novels inspired critical approval, but most of the reviews were written by literary friends, including Stark Young, Ford Madox Ford, Yvor Winters, and Malcolm Cowley. *Aleck Maury, Sportsman*, her second novel and perhaps her best, received warm praise from critics. Most thought her language apt, her knowledge of nature and the art of hunting and fishing remarkable, and her craftsmanship obvious. This book remains the most popular of her novels.

One other biographical work provides insight into the reception of Gordon's work, as she perceives it, in letters she wrote to her good friend Sally Wood over a twelve-year period. As editor of *The Southern Mandarins: Letters of Caroline Gordon to Sally Wood, 1924–1937*, Wood includes explanatory biographical notes as introductions to various years covered. Valuable, too, is Andrew Lytle's foreword to this work. Lytle, who was often a guest of the Tates, provides an informative discussion of the Agrarians and Gordon's response to their ideas.

Three book-length studies, one an anthology of critical essays, present more objective critiques of Gordon's novels and short stories. In 1966, Frederick P. W. McDowell provided discussions of the author's novels as well as many short stories in a University of Minnesota Pamphlet on American Writers. In *Caroline Gordon*, McDowell is one of the first critics to note that "detachable incidents" in Gordon's novels often contribute to fragmentation of plot. Essays presented at a symposium on Gordon's short stories in 1971 at the University of Dallas appear in *The Short Fiction of Caroline Gordon*. Edited by Thomas H. Landess, the collection includes essays, by Landess, Louise Cowan, Robert S. Dupree, Jane Gibson Brown, John Alvis, and M. E. Bradford. Louise Cowan perceives in the Aleck Maury stories portrayal of an epic hero. Robert S. Dupree analyzes Gordon's short fiction as representative of her critical theories. Landess discusses the complexity of her later short fiction, and Jane Gibson Brown refutes earlier analyses of "The Captive" to proclaim that this popular story chronicles the development of the captive into a heroic figure. John Alvis praises the craftsmanship in Gordon's tales about love, and M. E. Bradford judges Gordon's Civil War stories as well made because the writer reveals "felt history." In recent years, critical appraisal of Gordon's fiction often ignores her novels and analyzes her short fiction.

In *Caroline Gordon as Novelist and Woman of Letters*, Rose Ann C. Fraistat provides a comprehensive study of the writer as novelist, teacher, and critic. Fraistat develops her theory that Caroline Gordon tells a good story in her first five novels but has not yet mastered techniques that she would later formulate in *How to Read a Novel*. More analyst of plot and technique than critic, Fraistat praises Gordon's ability to convey concrete detail and discusses at length the author's emphasis on myth and archetypal structure in her later novels, which may explain their lack of reader appeal. In *Three Catholic Writers of the Modern South*, Robert H. Brinkmeyer, Jr., includes a lengthy essay on Gordon along with those on Allen Tate and Walker Percy. In "The Key to the Puzzle: The Literary Career of Caroline Gordon," Brinkmeyer examines Gordon's fiction chronologically as revelatory of the evolution of her earlier classical vision into one that could more aptly be described as a Christian viewpoint. Perhaps one of the most cogent observations concerning Caroline Gordon's reputation comes from David Madden in his introduction to his 1971 collection of essays entitled *Rediscoveries*, which includes Brainard Cheney's reassessment of *The Malefactors*. Madden points out that Gordon "is well-known to critics but to too few readers" (2). Although long out of print, new editions of Gordon's earlier novels have recently been included in the Southern Classics Series. Ultimately, Gordon's ability as a gifted storyteller will be her lasting legacy to American letters. In his introduction to *The Collected Stories of Caroline Gordon*, published the year Gordon died, Robert Penn Warren aptly concludes that "Caroline Gordon belongs in that group of Southern women who have been enriching our literature uniquely in this century—all so different in spirit, attitude, and method, but all with the rare gift of the teller of the tale" (xiii).

BIBLIOGRAPHY

Works by Caroline Gordon

Penhally. New York: Scribner's, 1931.
Aleck Maury, Sportsman. New York: Scribner's, 1934.

The Garden of Adonis. New York: Scribner's, 1937.
None Shall Look Back. New York: Scribner's, 1937.
Green Centuries. New York: Scribner's, 1941.
The Women on the Porch. New York: Scribner's, 1944.
The Forest of the South. New York: Scribner's, 1945. (Short stories)
The House of Fiction: An Anthology of the Short Story. Ed. with Allen Tate. New York: Scribner's, 1950.
The Strange Children. New York: Scribner's, 1951.
The Malefactors. New York: Harcourt, 1956.
How to Read a Novel. New York: Viking, 1957. (Nonfiction)
Old Red and Other Stories. New York: Scribner's, 1963. (Short stories)
The Glory of Hera. Garden City, NY: Doubleday, 1972.
The Collected Stories of Caroline Gordon. New York: Farrar, 1981.

Studies of Caroline Gordon

Alvis, John. "The Miltonic Argument in Caroline Gordon's *The Glory of Hera*." *Southern Review* 16 (1980): 560–73.
Baker, Howard. "The Stratagems of Caroline Gordon; or, The Art of the Novel and the Novelty of Myth." *Southern Review* 9 (1973): 523–49.
Baum, Catherine B., and Floyd C. Watkins. "Caroline Gordon and 'The Captive': An Interview." *Southern Review* 7 (1971): 447–62.
Brinkmeyer, Robert H., Jr. "The Key to the Puzzle: The Literary Career of Caroline Gordon." *Three Catholic Writers of the Modern South*. Jackson: University Press of Mississippi, 1985. 73–117.
Brown, Ashley. "The Achievement of Caroline Gordon." *Southern Humanities Review* 2 (1968): 279–90.
———. "Caroline Gordon's Short Fiction." *Sewanee Review* 81 (1973): 365–70.
———. "*None Shall Look Back*: The Novel as History." *Southern Review* 7 (1971): 480–94.
Brown, Jane Gibson. "The Early Novels of Caroline Gordon: Myth and History as Fictional Technique." *Southern Review* 13 (1977): 289–98.
———. "The Early Novels of Caroline Gordon: The Confluence of Myth and History as Fictional Technique." Diss. University of Dallas, 1975.
Cheney, Brainard. "Brainard Cheney on Caroline Gordon's *The Malefactors*." *Rediscoveries*. Ed. David Madden. New York: Crown, 1971. 232–44.
———. "Caroline Gordon's *The Malefactors*." *Sewanee Review* 79 (1971): 360–72.
Cowan, Louise. "Nature and Grace in Caroline Gordon." *Critique* 1 (1956): 11–27.
Cowley, Malcolm. "The Meriwether Connection." *Southern Review* 1 (1965): 46–56.
Fletcher, Marie. "The Fate of Women in the Changing South: A Persistent Theme in the Fiction of Caroline Gordon." *Mississippi Quarterly* 21 (1968): 17–28.
Fraistat, Rose Ann C. *Caroline Gordon as Novelist and Woman of Letters*. Baton Rouge: Louisiana State University Press, 1984.
Landess, Thomas H., ed. *The Short Fiction of Caroline Gordon: A Critical Symposium*. Irving, TX: University of Dallas Press, 1972.
Lewis, Janet. "*The Glory of Hera*." *Sewanee Review* 81 (1973): 185–94.
Lowell, Robert. "Visiting the Tates." *Sewanee Review* 67 (1959): 557–59.

Lytle, Andrew N. "Caroline Gordon and the Historic Image." *Sewanee Review* 57 (1949): 560–86.

Madden, David, ed. *Rediscoveries*. New York: Crown, 1971.

McDowell, Frederick P. W. *Caroline Gordon*. Minneapolis: University of Minnesota Press, 1966.

Rocks, James E. "The Mind and Art of Caroline Gordon." *Mississippi Quarterly* 21 (1968): 1–16.

Rodenberger, Lou. "Caroline Gordon, Teller of Tales: The Influence of Folk Narrative on Characterization and Structure in Her Work." Diss. Texas A & M University, 1975.

———. "Folk Narrative in Caroline Gordon's Frontier Fiction." *Women, Women Writers, and the West*. Ed. L. L. Lee and Merrill Lewis. Troy, NY: Whitston, 1979. 197–208.

Squires, Radcliffe. "The Underground Stream: A Note on Caroline Gordon's Fiction." *Southern Review* 7 (1971): 467–79.

Stanford, Donald E. "Caroline Gordon." *Southern Review* 17 (1981): 459–60.

———. "Caroline Gordon: From *Penhally* to *A Narrow Heart*." *Southern Review* 7 (1971): xv–xx.

Stuckey, William J. *Caroline Gordon*. New York: Twayne, 1972.

Thorp, Willard. "The Way Back and the Way Up: The Novels of Caroline Gordon." *Bushnell Review* 6 (1956): 1–15.

Van Doren, Mark. "Fiction of the Quarter." *Southern Review* 3 (1937): 159–82.

Waldron, Ann. *Close Connections: Caroline Gordon and the Southern Renaissance*. New York: Putnam's, 1984.

Warren, Robert Penn. "The Fiction of Caroline Gordon." *Southwest Review* 20 (1935): 5–10.

Wood, Sally, ed. *The Southern Mandarins: Letters of Caroline Gordon to Sally Wood, 1924–1937*. Baton Rouge: Louisiana State University Press, 1984.

LILLIAN HELLMAN
(1905–1984)

Jennifer A. Haytock

BIOGRAPHY

Lillian Hellman was born in New Orleans, Louisiana, on June 20, 1905, the only child of Julia Newhouse and Max Hellman. When she was very young she was cared for by an African American woman, Sophronia Mason; Hellman loved Mason throughout her life and in her memoirs recalls Mason telling her, "Don't go through life making trouble for people" (*Unfinished Woman* 15). Hellman lived in New Orleans until she was six, when her family moved to New York for business reasons. For the next ten years Hellman and her mother divided their time between New York and New Orleans, where they stayed with two paternal aunts in their boarding house. Hellman attended New York University from 1922 to 1924 and Columbia University in 1926, but she did not take a degree at either institution. Her first jobs included reading manuscripts for the Horace Liveright publishing firm, reviewing books for the *New York Herald-Tribune*, reading plays, and working as a publicist. In 1925 she married press agent Arthur Kober. The couple traveled to Europe and in 1930 moved to Hollywood, where Hellman read scripts for Metro-Goldwyn-Mayer. In Hollywood she met novelist Dashiell Hammett, with whom Hellman would have a complex relationship for about thirty years. She divorced Kober in 1932.

Hellman's first play, *The Children's Hour*, appeared on Broadway in 1934. Because of its controversial inclusion of lesbianism, the play was banned in Boston, Chicago, and London. For the next few years Hellman wrote screenplays for Samuel Goldwyn (*The Dark Angel*, 1935; *These Three*, 1936; *Dead End*, 1937; *The Little Foxes*, 1941). Her next play, *Days to Come*, ran for just one week in 1936. Afterwards, Hellman traveled to France, Russia, and Spain, where she saw firsthand the fighting of the Spanish Civil War. Collaborating with Ernest Hemingway, John Dos Passos, and Archibald MacLeish, she produced *The Spanish Earth* (1937), a documentary supporting the antifascist faction in the Spanish Civil War. Her plays continued to appear on Broadway to much success; she won the New York Drama Critics' Award for *Watch on the*

Rhine (1941) and *Toys in the Attic* (1960). In 1939 she bought Hardscrabble Farm near Pleasantville, New York, where she and Hammett spent much time, although they did not actually live together.

Allegedly a pro-Communist sympathizer, Hellman was blacklisted in Hollywood in 1948. She was called to appear before the House Committee on Un-American Activities, and although she was willing to testify about herself, she refused, in a now-famous letter, to answer questions concerning anyone else: "I cannot and will not cut my conscience to fit this year's fashions, even though I long ago came to the conclusion that I was not a political person and could have no comfortable place in any political group" (*Scoundrel Time* 93). She invoked the Fifth Amendment, and although she was not charged with contempt, the blacklisting caused her to suffer financially. In 1952 she was forced to sell the farm at Pleasantville.

In the 1960s and 1970s she began once again to receive serious literary recognition. She was admitted into the American Academy of Letters in 1963, taught at Harvard University, and received honorary degrees from such institutions as Wheaton College, Brandeis University, Yale University, Smith College, New York University, and Columbia University. She won several literary awards, including the Gold Medal for Drama from the National Institute of Arts and Letters (1964), the National Institute of Arts and Letters Gold Medal (1964), the National Book Award for *An Unfinished Woman* (1970), and the Edward MacDowell Medal (1976). During these years Hellman continued to be politically active, helping to organize the Committee for Public Justice.

In Hellman's later career, many of her plays were adapted to film, including *The Children's Hour* (1962) and *Toys in the Attic* (1963), or revived on Broadway, including *The Little Foxes* (1967). Hellman's body of work also includes several important memoirs, some of them as controversial as her plays: *An Unfinished Woman* (1969), *Pentimento* (1973), *Scoundrel Time* (1976), and *Maybe* (1980). She is the subject of a film (*Julia*, 1977, starring Jane Fonda) and three plays (William Luce's *Lillian*, 1986; Richard Nelson's *Sensibility and Sense*, 1989; Peter Feibleman's *Cakewalk*, 1993). Hellman died in Vineyard Haven, Martha's Vineyard, Massachusetts, on June 30, 1984.

MAJOR WORKS AND THEMES

Hellman's plays are best known for probing social and psychological concerns, including the nature and various manifestations of evil. She also created strong female characters during a time when American theater tended to concentrate on men. Hellman's first play, *The Children's Hour* (1934), focuses on the destructive power of gossip. Based on an actual trial, the play describes two young teachers, Karen and Martha, whose lives are destroyed by a resentful student's comments about their "unnatural" relationship. Mrs. Tilford, the student's grandmother and the school's primary benefactress, believes the gossip and convinces other families to withdraw their daughters from the school. The school fails, Karen breaks off her marital engagement, and Martha confesses that in fact she has felt "that way" toward Karen. By the time Mrs. Tilford returns with apologies and a desire to make amends, Martha has killed herself, and Karen is unable to accept Mrs. Tilford's apology or money. While the play indicts careless talk and too-willing believers, the uproar surrounding Hellman's inclusion of lesbian themes on the stage initially overshadowed this point.

Hellman's plays also depict the complex relationships within families, including hostility family members feel toward and act out on each other. *The Little Foxes* (1939) follows the Hubbard siblings, a back-stabbing Southern family, as they manipulate each other for financial gain. Supposedly based on members of Hellman's mother's family, the play is set during the rise of industry in the South. Ben, Oscar, and Regina Hubbard scheme to make a deal with a Northern industrialist, but to be included Regina has to deceive her husband, Horace Giddens, into contributing money. He refuses, and in a quarrel with Regina he has a heart attack. Regina refuses to call for help, effectually killing her husband. Her daughter, disgusted by her mother and uncles, rejects Regina's plea for companionship, leaving her mother alone with her conscience and her precarious relationship with her brothers. The sequel to this play, *Another Part of the Forest* (1947), occurs a generation earlier, setting up the tensions of *The Little Foxes*. The Hubbards are known as a money-grubbing family who profited during the Civil War at the expense of their neighbors. Again, the Hubbards deceive each other and the poor, genteel Bagtry family for money. The play ends with a shift in the balance of power from father to son and a subsequent realignment of family loyalties.

World War II provided the impetus for a couple of Hellman's plays; these works emphasize personal responsibility in the face of the dangers of fascism. *Watch on the Rhine* (1941) portrays the violent confrontation between an anti-Nazi activist and a pro-Fascist mercenary in an upper-middle-class American home. Sara Farrelly has married a German, Kurt, whose work against Hitler and fascism has left him weakened and tired. Still, he knows he must return to Germany with the money he has been able to raise to support the movement. Sara's mother and brother are forced out of their self-centered world by the political realities their European visitors represent, and they become a small but active part of the resistance to fascism in Europe. *The Searching Wind* (1944) continues ideas from *Watch on the Rhine*; Alexander Hazen's failure to oppose fascism strongly enough brings upon him a degree of personal responsibility for World War II. Through flashbacks the characters discuss the significance of world events, such as Mussolini's takeover of Italy and the rise of the Nazis.

Hellman's last plays return to an emphasis on interpersonal relationships within families. *The Autumn Garden* (1951), set outside New Orleans, portrays the complex emotional and financial relationships between several characters staying at a boarding house managed by Constance Tuckerman. Nick Denery wreaks havoc on the emotional lives of several characters but is finally ruined by his drinking. The play climaxes when characters come to understand how they have lied to each other and to themselves. *Toys in the Attic* (1960), like Hellman's other plays, depends on complicated relationships between people; family members betray each other for revenge and power. This play also addresses racist attitudes and interracial relationships.

In addition to her original works, Hellman adapted four plays for Broadway. Her adaptation of Emmanuel Roblès's *Montserrat* appeared in New York in 1949; the play explores violence and individual resistance to fascism. In 1955 Hellman translated and adapted Jean Anouilh's *The Lark*, and in 1957 she wrote the libretto for the Leonard Bernstein operetta *Candide* (1956). *My Mother, My Father and Me* (1963) was adapted from Burt Blechman's novel *How Much?*

Hellman also directed three Broadway productions and reported for magazines and newspapers, including *American Spectator, Collier's, New Republic*, and *Ladies' Home Journal*. She edited the letters of Anton Chekhov (*The Selected Letters of Anton Chekhov*, 1955) and the stories of Dashiell Hammett (*The Big Knockover*, 1966).

In her later years Hellman focused on writing memoirs rather than plays, claiming that she no longer cared for the theater. *An Unfinished Woman* (1969) portrays her childhood in New Orleans, her life in New York, her visits to Europe, and her relationships with Dashiell Hammett, Dorothy Parker, and Hellman's housekeeper and friend Helen. *Pentimento* (1973) is a series of portraits of people she knew; the title is taken from the emergence of lower layers of paint on a reused canvas: "The paint is aged now and I wanted to see what was there for me once, what is there for me now" (3). In this memoir she discusses her relationship with Dashiell Hammett as well as with important women in her life, including Sophronia Mason, Helen, her New Orleans aunts, and her friend Julia, an anti-Nazi activist who was eventually tortured and killed by the Nazis. *Scoundrel Time* (1976) recalls Hellman's experiences with the House Committee on Un-American Activities, her blacklisting, and other events connected with McCarthy-era America. These memoirs were collected in *Three* (1979). Her last memoir, *Maybe* (1980), struggles with the relationship between truth and memory as Hellman tries to sort out different images of the past.

CRITICAL RECEPTION

Recent book-length studies of Hellman, such as William Wright's *Lillian Hellman: The Image, the Woman* (1986) and Carl Rollyson's *Lillian Hellman: Her Legend and Her Legacy* (1988), tend to focus on her life rather than on her work. Certainly the controversial nature of her plays, such as the lesbianism in *The Children's Hour* or the antifascism in *Watch on the Rhine*, has directed critical conversation outside the plays themselves. Mark W. Estrin, in his edited collection *Critical Essays on Lillian Hellman* (1989), however, aims to separate discussions of Hellman's life and her work.

As a woman writing plays in the midtwentieth century, Hellman has been claimed by feminist critics for providing alternatives to the weak wife and mother figures created by other dramatists. Hellman herself, however, resented the label "woman playwright." In 1941, she was targeted in an essay called "Playwrights in Petticoats" by George Jean Nathan, which claimed that although Hellman was the best of the women playwrights, "even the best of our American woman playwrights falls immeasurably short of the mark of our best masculine" (qtd. in Estrin 3). Hellman resented being categorized by her gender and rejected the idea that her memoirs defined her as a feminist. Still, as Ekaterini Georgoudaki argues in "Women in Lillian Hellman's Plays," Hellman's female characters reveal much about the roles to which American society limited women in the middle of the twentieth century and the difficulties of finding alternatives to those roles.

Critics have defined evil and its nature as a primary theme in Hellman's work. Doris V. Falk, for example, who has divided Hellman's characters into the categories of "despoilers" and "by-standers," argues that "Hellman clearly differentiates between evil as a positive, rapacious force in the first group, and evil as the negative failure of good in the second" (30). Philip M. Armato in " 'Good and Evil' in Lillian Hellman's *The Children's Hour*" explores the presence of evil beyond its simple manifestation in the child Mary Tilford; he suggests a more complex dynamic involving the various adults' treatment of each other and of Mary. Bonnie Lyons's "Lillian Hellman: 'The First Jewish Nun on Prytania Street' " shows how Hellman's plays are informed by Jewish culture and also divides the plays into two categories according to how they embody and transmit Hellman's moral vision structurally.

Critics have explored Hellman's rejection of fascism. Katherine Lederer points in particular to *Watch on the Rhine* and *The Searching Wind*; she also discusses the articles Hellman wrote about the Spanish Civil War and her experiences in Russia. Timothy J. Wiles notes further the complexities of her politics in "Lillian Hellman's American Political Theater: The Thirties and Beyond": "Her analysis of American society is essentially Marxist, since it is based on the primacy of material and economic conditions to explain social relations, and emphasizes environmental conditioning, conflict among classes, and the hope that a new person, socialist man, would be born of the conflict through the dialectical collision of opposites" (90).

Hellman's memoirs have received a complicated critical response. Critics seem to agree that the memoirs are beautifully written, if somewhat disjointed. The truth of the memoirs, however, has been a subject of controversy. Such figures as Martha Gellhorn and Mary McCarthy have attacked Hellman's version of events as false. Hellman defended herself against these charges and even brought a libel suit against McCarthy, though Hellman died before the case came to court. In "Lillian Hellman: Autobiography and Truth," Linda Wagner-Martin suggests that in her memoirs "Hellman is using the process of autobiography both to explore her memories and to challenge the notion that recollection is a means to truth" (275).

BIBLIOGRAPHY

Works by Lillian Hellman

The Children's Hour. New York: Dramatists' Play Service, 1934.

Dark Angel. Dir. Sydney A. Franklin. Adapted by Lillian Hellman and Mordaunt Sharp from the play by Guy Bolton. Goldwyn/United Artists, 1935.

Days to Come. New York: Knopf, 1936.

These Three. Dir. William Wyler. Screenplay by Lillian Hellman. Goldwyn, 1936.

Dead End. Dir. William Wyler. Screenplay by Lillian Hellman. Goldwyn, 1937.

The Spanish Earth. Dir. Joris Ivens. Screenplay by Lillian Hellman, Ernest Hemingway, John Dos Passos, and Archibald MacLeish. Discount, 1937.

The Little Foxes. New York: Random, 1939.

Little Foxes. Dir. William Wyler. Screenplay by Lillian Hellman. Goldwyn, 1941.

Watch on the Rhine. New York: Random, 1941.

The Searching Wind. New York: Viking, 1944.

Another Part of the Forest. New York: Viking, 1947.

Montserrat. New York: Dramatists' Play Service, 1950.

The Autumn Garden. Boston: Little, 1951.

Chekhov, Anton. *The Selected Letters of Anton Chekhov*. Ed. Lillian Hellman. New York: McGraw, 1955.

The Lark. New York: Random, 1956.

Candide. New York: Schirmer, 1958.

Toys in the Attic. New York: French, 1960.

My Mother, My Father and Me. New York: Random, 1963.

Hammett, Dashiell. *The Big Knockover: Selected Stories and Short Novels*. Ed. Lillian Hellman. New York: Random, 1966.

An Unfinished Woman. Boston: Little, 1969.

Lillian Hellman: The Collected Plays. Boston: Little, 1972.

Pentimento: A Book of Portraits. Boston: Little, 1973.

Scoundrel Time. Boston: Little, 1976.

Three: An Unfinished Woman, Pentimento, and Scoundrel Time. Boston: Little, 1979.

Maybe. Boston: Little, 1980.

Studies of Lillian Hellman

Armato, Philip M. " 'Good and Evil' in Lillian Hellman's *The Children's Hour*." *Educational Theatre Journal* 25 (1973): 443–47.

Bryer, Jackson. *Conversations with Lillian Hellman*. Jackson, MS: University Press of Mississippi, 1986.

Dick, Bernard F. *Hellman in Hollywood*. Teaneck, NJ: Fairleigh Dickinson University Press, 1982.

Estrin, Mark W. *Critical Essays on Lillian Hellman*. Boston: G. K. Hall, 1989.

Falk, Doris V. *Lillian Hellman*. New York: Ungar, 1978.

Feibleman, Peter. *Lilly: Reminisces of Lillian Hellman*. New York: Morrow, 1988.

Gellhorn, Martha. "On Apocryphism." *Paris Review* 79 (1981): 280–301.

Georgoudaki, Ekaterini. "Women in Lillian Hellman's Plays, 1930–1950." *Women and*

War: The Changing Status of American Women from the 1930s to the 1950s. Ed. Maria Diedrich and Dorothea Fischer-Hornung. New York: St. Martin's, 1990. 69–86.

Lederer, Katherine. *Lillian Hellman*. Boston: Twayne, 1979.

Lyons, Bonnie. "Lillian Hellman: 'The First Jewish Nun on Prytania Street.' " *From Hester Street to Hollywood: The Jewish-American Stage and Screen*. Ed. Sarah Blacher Cohen. Bloomington: Indiana University Press, 1983. 106–22.

Mellen, Joan. *Hellman and Hammett: The Legendary Passion of Lillian Hellman and Dashiell Hammett*. New York: HarperCollins, 1996.

Moody, Richard. *Lillian Hellman: Playwright*. New York: Bobbs, 1972.

Rollyson, Carl. *Lillian Hellman: Her Legend and Her Legacy*. New York: St. Martin's, 1988.

Wagner-Martin, Linda. "Lillian Hellman: Autobiography and Truth." *Southern Review* 19 (1983): 275–88.

Wiles, Timothy J. "Lillian Hellman's American Political Theater: The Thirties and Beyond." *Critical Essays on Lillian Hellman*. Ed. Mark W. Estin. Boston: G.K. Hall, 1989. 90–112.

Wright, William. *Lillian Hellman: The Image, the Woman*. New York: Simon, 1986.

ZORA NEALE HURSTON
(1891–1960)

Bruce A. Glasrud and Laurie Champion

BIOGRAPHY

Zora Neale Hurston was born on January 7, 1891, in Macon County, Alabama, the daughter of Reverend John Hurston and Lucy Potts Hurston. In 1894, she moved to Eatonville, Florida, an African American community near Orlando. Her mother died in 1904, Zora attended boarding school in Jacksonville, and for several years afterward, she performed menial jobs in various cities. After completing her high school education at Morgan Academy in Baltimore, she enrolled at Howard University, in Washington, D.C., then in 1925 attended Barnard College in New York City, where she studied anthropology under the guidance of Franz Boas and Gladys Reichard, major contributors to American anthropology.

A southern black woman, Hurston struggled to succeed as a writer amidst a publishing industry dominated by white males. In 1925, Hurston moved to New York City and became one of the most significant women of the Harlem Renaissance. Her writing career began in the mid-1920s with the publication of short stories in *Opportunity* magazine. She coedited the literary magazine *Fire!*, in which her short story "Sweat" appeared in November 1926. She collaborated with Langston Hughes to write the play *Mule Bone*, but it was neither performed nor published during her lifetime (finally printed in 1991).

In 1927, Hurston returned to Florida to conduct fieldwork and married Herbert Sheen, her first husband. In 1936, Hurston was awarded a Guggenheim Fellowship to study "Obeah" practices in the West Indies; her research eventually resulted in the publication of *Tell My Horse* (1938). In 1934, her first novel, *Jonah's Gourd Vine*, based loosely on her parents' lives, was published, followed by *Their Eyes Were Watching God* (1937) and *Moses, Man of the Mountain* (1939). Her autobiography, *Dust Tracks on a Road*, was published in 1942, for which she received the prestigious Anisfield-Wolf Book Award and appeared on the cover of *Saturday Evening Post* in 1943. Five years later (1948) her novel *Seraph on the Suwanee* appeared; the same year Hurston was indicted on a false morals charge, which was dismissed when she proved she was traveling abroad when the alleged crime occurred.

After the publication of *Seraph on the Suwanee*, Hurston resided in Florida and wrote articles for newspapers and magazines. In 1954, she wrote an infamous letter to the Orlando *Sentinel* condemning the 1954 Supreme Court's *Brown* decision that outlawed segregation in the public schools. She argued that the decision would harm the all-black schools of the South as well as the study of black culture. During the last years of her life, Hurston became reclusive and lived an obscure and impoverished life, with no meaningful employment or money to support herself. She died in a welfare home on January 28, 1960, in Fort Pierce, Florida, and is buried in a segregated cemetery. Her grave was unmarked until Alice Walker traveled to locate and rediscover Hurston. Walker placed a marker on Hurston's grave in 1973, embellished with the epitaph: "A Genius of the South."

MAJOR WORKS AND THEMES

By any reckoning, Zora Neale Hurston is a major twentieth-century author— she published four novels, an autobiography, and two works of folklore and coauthored a play. An avid writer of short stories and essays, since her death at least seven collections of her short writings have appeared. Throughout her works, Hurston portrays rural African Americans, including depictions of their cultural practices, their folklore, their social customs, their spiritual beliefs, and their dialect. In her celebration of African American folk heritage, Hurston addresses and confronts issues such as the search for a sense of community, the plight of women, romantic relationships, and the struggle for personal and cultural identity. Although in her works she shows the struggles and triumphs of African American women, her characterization of their internal, personal conflicts transcends race and gender. Her depiction of African American women is but one example of ways Hurston creates realistic portrayals of rural African Americans while simultaneously depicting universal insights and truths.

Hurston's signature writing technique is her ability to depict authentically African American folklore. Credited as the first anthology of African American folklore, *Mules and Men* presents a collection of humorous and serious essaylike works such as conversations, sermons, and jokes that reflect social customs, religious and spiritual beliefs, and local folklore of the residents of rural Florida and Louisiana. This anthropological classic considers gender roles, women on the "porch," and hoodoo. Hurston's West Indian study, *Tell My Horse*, also documents and presents folklore, especially Obeah, in those islands. Presented against the background of both African American folklore and Christian myth, *Moses, Man of the Mountain* is set in Egypt during the time of Hebrew captivity. An obvious retelling of the biblical story of Moses and the Israelites, the novel also demonstrates the plight of African Americans in the white-dominated United States. Told with a sort of tongue-in-cheek humor, the novel portrays folklore and folkways of the Hebrews, while showing how they have been enslaved. One of the strengths of *Moses, Man of the Mountain* is the humor that appears when the subtext that represents the African American slave experience is juxtaposed against the text that concerns Hebrews. Not only is the humor presented on a deeper level because Hurston allows the Hebrew experience to symbolize that of African American slaves, but the analogy created between the text and the subtext also provides a study of slave emancipation from a black viewpoint.

Although not the central subject, Hurston blends portrayals of rural African Americans and shows folk customs in *Their Eyes Were Watching God* and in *Jonah's Gourd Vine*. In *Their Eyes Were Watching God*, Hurston weaves African American culture with the idea of the need to belong to a community. Janie eventually connects with the migrant farmworkers with her ability to tell stories and experiences a spiritual kinship. This sense of belonging to a community provides her with a sense of cultural and self-identity. When she returns to Eatonville after Tea Cake dies, she has the strength and courage to retell her story to Pheoby. Because Pheoby will repeat Janie's story to others, Janie has shared with the entire community the knowledge she has gained about her heritage. Similarly, Hurston sets her novel *Jonah's Gourd Vine* in the town of Eatonville and focuses on its African American community. She portrays these people realistically, without condescending to the working-class population. Hurston celebrates the social life and religious expression of the community and shows their hoodoo beliefs, their proverbs, and their children's games.

Hurston also presents African American folk customs throughout her short stories. The title of "Uncle Monday," for example, refers to a conjure doctor who has mysteriously arisen from water and come to a small village. Among his mystical powers, Uncle Monday can shed and regrow bodily limbs; he also possesses a singing stone, the greatest charm in the world. Hurston's narrator provides many folk customs and beliefs, such as a recipe for retrieving a singing stone from a serpent. Likewise, in "Mother Catherine," Hurston describes a spiritual leader, Christ-like figure, who gives advice to people and who has borne both black and white children. Among other mystical powers, Mother Catherine is able to heal the sick. In her depiction of Mother Catherine, Hurston disrupts stereotypes by characterizing an African American woman in a role traditionally attributed to white men.

Frequently, Hurston blends the subject of cultural and personal identity with that of romantic relationships—women either discover their identities because of or in spite of their relationships with men. In *Their Eyes Were Watching God*, Janie develops from an insecure woman who depends on a man to one who celebrates her African American identity and finds emotional and economic independence. When Janie leaves Logan, she marries Joe Starks and moves to Eatonville, only to realize that her need for economic security compels her to remain his wife even though he abuses her. Long after Joe dies, Janie becomes romantically involved with the much younger Tea Cake, leaves the financial security of her store and home, and goes to southern Florida to aid migrant farm laborers. After Tea Cake's death, she returns to the security of her home to tell her story and share her experience of having fulfilled her quest for romantic love.

Troubled romantic relationships are the central subject of *Jonah's Gourd Vine*, a novel loosely based on Hurston's father. John Pearson, a minister and carpenter, develops from an illiterate sharecropper to a wealthy administrator of the Florida Baptist Convention. After leaving home and attending school, John marries Lucy Potts and has several extramarital affairs. Years later John and his family live successfully in Eatonville, an all-black community in Florida, where he is a carpenter and preacher. His philandering continues, and when Lucy dies of tuberculosis, he marries Hattie Tyson. He loses everything and leaves the ministry and Eatonville. Finally, John moves to Plant City, Florida, where he marries Sally Lovelace, regains prosperity, and becomes a pastor again. John is killed by a train after a relapse into sexual infidelity.

Unlike her other works that focus on relationships among African Americans, in *Seraph on the Suwanee*, Hurston reveals working-class whites in the small community Sawley. In this novel, the poor Arvay Henson marries Jim Meserve, and they move to Citrabelle, where Jim becomes a successful citrus grower. When Jim leaves her, she returns to Sawley, where she acknowledges her past, discovers self-identity, and comes to appreciate her heritage. After experiencing these personal growths and developing spiritual insights, she travels to the coast to find Jim and attempt to save their marriage.

Hurston's short stories also reveal wide spectrums of both healthy and unhealthy romantic relationships, as exemplified in "Sweat" and "The Gilded Six-Bits." Delia, the protagonist of "Sweat," is married to Sykes, who both mentally and physically torments her. The story begins with Sykes sliding a bullwhip across her leg to scare her because he knows she is afraid of snakes. Later, he brings a snake home, and Delia begs him to remove it from the house. At the end of the story, the snake bites Sykes. Knowing he will die before she has time to drive him to the distant hospital, Delia is relieved that poetic justice has occurred. On the other hand, "The Gilded Six-Bits" is a love story about forgiveness. The story opens with Missie May and Joe playing a game that they play regularly. A man woos Missie May with his charm and his gold, and later Joe discovers her in bed with him. Representative of his character, the gold the other man gave Missie May turns out to be fake. Joe forgives Missie May, and they return to their playful game at the end of the story. Here, Hurston portrays a compassionate man who loves his wife and who is willing to forgive her, a character who diametrically opposes Sykes.

CRITICAL RECEPTION

Initial reception of Hurston's work was not always favorable—probably because most reviewers were male. For example, Richard Wright criticized *Their*

Eyes Were Watching God because he thought it posed situations irrelevant to African American struggles. Some of her cohort writers saw her as politically conservative and were upset because she was supported by white patrons. For years after her death, Hurston became a forgotten writer. Fortunately, during the 1970s and 1980s Hurston's work was rediscovered and reassessed. Younger writers such as Alice Walker and Toni Cade Bambara acknowledged Hurston's influence, and much of her work was published for the first time or reprinted. Recently, scholars have rediscovered Hurston's work and examined it from feminist, cultural, and political perspectives.

Whether in broader topics or as the focus of their discussions, almost all critics allude to Hurston's portrayal of African American folklore. The titles of the following essays reflect their topics: Ellease Southerland's "The Influence of Voodoo on the Fiction of Zora Neale Hurston," Rachel Stein's "Remembering the Sacred Tree: Black Women, Nature, and Voodoo in Zora Neale Hurston's *Tell My Horse* and *Their Eyes Were Watching God*," and Howard J. Faulkner's "*Mules and Men*: Fiction as Folklore." Klaus Benesch, in "Oral Narrative and Literary Text: Afro-American Folklore in *Their Eyes Were Watching God*," looks at Hurston's use of black English and sees Janie's major conflict as her search for her African American cultural heritage. Mary O'Connor, in "Zora Neale Hurston and Talking between Cultures," credits Hurston with establishing for women an African American literary tradition wherein talking is a tool used to blend race and gender.

From feminist perspectives, many scholars examine Hurston's women characters and look at the social issues in Hurston's works that concern women. Alice Walker's "In Search of Zora Neale Hurston" notes that Hurston represents African American women who seek a political voice in the areas of race and gender. " 'This Infinity of Conscious Pain': Zora Neale Hurston and the Black Female Literary Tradition," by Lorraine Bethel, points out that throughout her works Hurston disrupts stereotypes of African American women portrayed by white males. Missy Dehn Kubitschek, in " 'Tuh De Horizon and Back': The Female Quest in *Their Eyes Were Watching God*," argues that Hurston's portrayal of strong and courageous black women inspired future black women writers to depict nonstereotypical black women characters. Mary Helen Washington's " 'I Love the Way Janie Crawford Left Her Husbands': Zora Neale Hurston's Emergent Female Hero" sees Janie as a leader in her community and as a developing hero.

Similarly, Gay Wilentz, in "Defeating the False God: Janie's Self-Determination in Zora Neale Hurston's *Their Eyes Were Watching God*," suggests that Janie is one of the earliest African American women characters to develop cultural and personal identity. Cheryl Wall's "*Mules and Men* and Women: Zora Neale Hurston's Strategies of Narration and Visions of Female Empowerment" views Hurston as an anthropologist and suggests ways Hurston's women are empowered. Many scholars examine Hurston as a female autobiographer: James Krasner, "The Life of Women: Zora Neale Hurston and Female Autobiography"; Elizabeth Fox-Genovese, "My Statue My Self: Autobiographical Writings of Afro-American Women"; François Lionnet, "Autoethnography: The An-Archic Style of *Dust Tracks on a Road*"; and Nellie Y. McKay, "Race, Gender, and Cultural Context in Zora Neale Hurston's *Dust Tracks on a Road*."

Hurston's contributions to literary movements such as the Harlem Renaissance and the Southern Renaissance are other areas discussed by scholars. Hurston is included in almost every discussion of the Harlem Renaissance, but essays that significantly discuss her contribution to the movement include Mary V. Dearborn's "Black Women Authors and the Harlem Renaissance," Sharon Dean and Erlene Stetson's "Flower-Dust and Springtime: Harlem Renaissance Women," John Lowe's "Hurston, Humor, and the Harlem Renaissance," and Ralph D. Story's "Gender and Ambition: Zora Neale Hurston in the Harlem Renaissance." Jan Cooper, in "Zora Neale Hurston Was Always a Southerner Too," points out that although she should be included in discussions of the Southern Renaissance, Hurston is omitted because of racial bias. Geneva Cobb-Moore's "Zora Neale Hurston as Local Colorist" establishes Hurston as a regionalist and local colorist who delineates a distinctive group of people.

Among book-length treatments of Hurston's works, several stand out. Even though published in the 1970s, Robert E. Hemenway's *Zora Neale Hurston: A Literary Biography* remains the most insightful study. Another skillful biography is Lillie P. Howard's *Zora Neale Hurston*. A valuable book on Hurston's humor is John Lowe's *Jump at the Sun: Zora Neale Hurston's Cosmic Comedy*. Neither Deborah G. Plant, *Every Tub Must Sit on Its Own Bottom: The Philosophy and Politics of Zora Neale Hurston*, nor Karla Holloway, *The Character of the Word: The Texts of Zora Neale Hurston*, can be ignored. Henry Louis Gates, Jr., and K. A. Appiah's *Zora Neale Hurston: Critical Perspectives Past and Present* is the most comprehensive collection of critical essays.

For extensive bibliographic information, three sources in particular warrant attention: Daryl Dance's fine bibliographical essay "Zora Neale Hurston" in *American Women Writers*; Rose Parkman Davis's thorough and scholarly *Zora Neale Hurston: An Annotated Bibliography and Reference Guide*; and Michele Wallace's "Who Owns Zora Neale Hurston: Critics Carve Up the Legend."

Fortunately, now that Hurston has been rediscovered, she is earning her rightful place in the American literary canon. However, as is true for any scholarly subject, and as Andrew Crosland points out in "The Text of Zora Neale Hurston: A Caution," scholars need to remember to place Hurston's works in historical and cultural context to gain broader perspectives. Her works remain visible reminders of the tribulations of being a black woman in a white and masculine-dominated society.

BIBLIOGRAPHY

Works by Zora Neale Hurston

Jonah's Gourd Vine. Philadelphia: Lippincott, 1934. (Novel)
Mules and Men. London: Kegan, 1936. (Folklore)

Their Eyes Were Watching God. Philadelphia: Lippincott, 1937. (Novel)

Tell My Horse. Philadelphia: Lippincott, 1938. (Folklore)

Moses, Man of the Mountain. Philadelphia: Lippincott, 1939. (Novel)

Dust Tracks on a Road. Philadelphia: Lippincott, 1942. (Autobiography)

Seraph on the Suwanee. New York: Scribner's, 1948. (Novel)

I Love Myself When I am Laughing . . . And Then Again When I Am Looking Mean and Impressive: A Zora Neale Hurston Reader. Ed. Alice Walker. Old Westbury, NY: Feminist Press, 1979.

The Sanctified Church: The Folklore Writings of Zora Neale Hurston. Introd. Toni Cade Bambara. Berkeley, CA: Turtle Island, 1981.

Spunk: The Selected Short Stories of Zora Neale Hurston. Berkeley, CA.: Turtle Island, 1985.

Zora Neale Hurston and Langston Hughes. *Mule Bone: A Comedy of Negro Life*. New York: HarperCollins, 1991. (Play)

The Complete Stories of Zora Neale Hurston. Ed. Henry Louis Gates, Jr., and Sieglinde Lemke. New York: Harper, 1995.

Zora Neale Hurston: Folklore, Memoirs & Other Writings. Ed. Cheryl A. Wall. New York: Library of America, 1995.

"Three by Zora Neale Hurston: Story, Essay, and Play." *Southern Quarterly* 36.3 (1998): 94–102.

Studies of Zora Neale Hurston

Awkward, Michael, ed. *New Essays on* Their Eyes Were Watching God. Cambridge: Cambridge University Press, 1990.

Beilke, Debra. " 'Yowin' and Jawin' ": Humor and the Performance of Identity in Zora Neale Hurston's *Jonah's Gourd Vine*." *Southern Quarterly* 36.3 (1998): 21–33.

Benesch, Klaus. "Oral Narrative and Literary Text: Afro-American Folklore in *Their Eyes Were Watching God*." *Callaloo* 11 (1988): 627–35.

Bethel, Lorraine. " 'This Infinity of Conscious Pain': Zora Neale Hurston and the Black Female Literary Tradition." *All the Women Are White, All the Blacks Are Men, But Some of Us Are Brave: Black Women's Studies*. Ed. Gloria T. Hull, Patricia Bell-Scott, and Barbara Scott. Old Westbury, NY: Feminist Press, 1982. 176–88.

Bloom, Harold, ed. *Zora Neale Hurston: Modern Critical Views*. New York: Chelsea, 1986.

———. *Zora Neale Hurston's* Their Eyes Were Watching God. New York: Chelsea, 1987.

Bordelon, Pam. "New Tacks on Dust Tracks: Toward a Reassessment of the Life of Zora Neale Hurston." *African American Review* 31 (1997): 5–21.

Boxwell, D. A. " 'Sis Cat' as Ethnographer: Self-presentation and Self-inscription in Zora Neale Hurston's *Mules and Men*." *African American Review* 26 (1992): 605–15.

Brigham, Cathy. "The Talking Frame of Zora Neale Hurston's Talking Book: Storytelling as Dialectic in *Their Eyes Were Watching God*." *CLA Journal* 37 (1994): 402–18.

Byrd, James W. "Zora Neale Hurston: A Novel Folklorist." *Tennessee Folklore Bulletin* 21 (1955): 37–41.

Caron, Timothy P. " 'Tell Ole Pharaoh to Let My People Go': Communal Deliverance in Zora Neale Hurston's *Moses, Man of the Mountain.*" *Southern Quarterly* 36.3 (1998): 47–60.

Cobb-Moore, Geneva. "Zora Neale Hurston as Local Colorist." *Southern Literary Journal* 26.2 (1994): 25–34.

Cooper, Jan. "Zora Neale Hurston Was Always a Southerner Too." *The Female Tradition in Southern Literature.* Ed. Carol S. Manning. Urbana: University of Illinois Press, 1993. 57–69.

Crabtree, Claire. "The Confluence of Folklore, Feminism and Black Self-Determination in Zora Neale Hurston's *Their Eyes Were Watching God.*" *Southern Literary Journal* 17.2 (1985): 54–66.

Crosland, Andrew. "The Text of Zora Neale Hurston: A Caution." *CLA Journal* 37 (1994): 420–24.

Dance, Daryl C. "Zora Neale Hurston." *American Women Writers: Bibliographical Essays.* Ed. Maurice Duke, Jackson R. Bryer, and M. Thomas Inge. Westport, CT: Greenwood, 1983. 321–51.

Daniel, Janice. " 'De Understandin' to Go 'Long Wid It': Realism and Romance in *Their Eyes Were Watching God.*" *Southern Literary Journal* 24.1 (1991): 66–76.

Davie, Sharon. "Free Mules, Talking Buzzards, and Cracked Plates: The Politics of Dislocation in *Their Eyes Were Watching God.*" *PMLA* 108 (1993): 446–59.

Davies, Kathleen. "Zora Neale Hurston's Poetics of Embalmment: Articulating the Rage of Black Women and Narrative Self-Defense." *African American Review* 26 (1992): 147–59.

Davis, Rose Parkman. *Zora Neale Hurston: An Annotated Bibliography and Reference Guide.* Westport, CT: Greenwood, 1997.

Dearborn, Mary V. "Black Women Authors and the Harlem Renaissance." *Pocahonta's Daughters: Gender and Ethnicity in America Culture.* New York: Oxford University Press, 1986. 61–70.

Dean, Sharon, and Erlene Stetson. "Flower-Dust and Springtime: Harlem Renaissance Women." *Radical Teacher* 18(1980): 1–8.

Dolby-Stahl, Sandra. "Literary Objectives: Hurston's Use of Personal Narrative in *Mules and Men.*" *Western Folklore* 51 (1992): 51–63.

Domina, Lynn. " 'Protection in My Mouf': Self, Voice, and Community in Zora Neale Hurston's *Dust Tracks on a Road* and *Mules and Men.*" *African American Review* 31 (1997): 197–209.

Donlon, Jocelyn Hazelwood. "Porches: Stories: Power: Spatial and Racial Intersections in Faulkner and Hurston." *Journal of American Culture* 19 (1996): 95–110.

Dubek, Laura. "The Social Geography of Race in Hurston's *Seraph on the Suwanee.*" *African American Review* 30 (1996): 341–51.

Faulkner, Howard J. "*Mules and Men*: Fiction as Folklore." *CLA Journal* 34 (1991): 331–39.

Fox-Genovese, Elizabeth. "My Statue, My Self: Autobiographical Writings of Afro-American Women." *Reading Black, Reading Feminist: A Critical Anthology.* Ed. Henry Louis Gates, Jr. New York: Meridian, 1990. 176–203.

Gates, Henry Louis, Jr. "Zora Neale Hurston and the Speakerly Text." *The Signifying Monkey: A Theory of Afro-American Literary Criticism.* New York: Oxford University Press, 1988: 170–216.

Gates, Henry Louis, Jr., and K. A. Appiah, eds. *Zora Neale Hurston: Critical Perspectives Past and Present.* New York: Amistad, 1993.

Glassman, Steve, and Kathryn Lee Seidel, eds. *Zora in Florida*. Orlando: University of Central Florida Press, 1991.

Harris, Trudier. "Performing Personnel in Southern Hospitality: Zora Neale Hurston in *Mules and Men*." *The Power of the Porch: The Storyteller's Craft in Zora Neale Hurston, Gloria Naylor, and Randall Kenan*. Athens: University of Georgia Press, 1996. 1–50.

Hemenway, Robert E. *Zora Neale Hurston: A Literary Biography*. Urbana: University of Illinois Press, 1978.

Hill, Lynda Marion. *Social Rituals and the Verbal Art of Zora Neale Hurston*. Washington, DC: Howard University Press, 1996.

Holloway, Karla F. C. *The Character of the Word: The Texts of Zora Neale Hurston*. Westport, CT: Greenwood, 1987.

Howard, Lillie P. *Alice Walker and Zora Neale Hurston: The Common Bond*. Westport, CT: Greenwood, 1993.

———. *Zora Neale Hurston*. Boston: Twayne, 1980.

Hubbard, Dolan. " ' . . . Ah Said Ah'd Save De Text for You': Recontextualizing the Sermon to Tell (Her)story in Zora Neale Hurston's *Their Eyes Were Watching God*." *African American Review* 27 (1993): 167–78.

Jacobs, Karen. "From 'Spy-Glass' to 'Horizon': Tracking the Anthropological Gaze in Zora Neale Hurston." *Novel* 30 (1997): 329–60.

Johnson, Barbara. "Thresholds of Difference: Structures of Address in Zora Neale Hurston." *Critical Inquiry* 12 (1985): 278–89.

Jordan, Jennifer. "Feminist Fantasies: Zora Neale Hurston's *Their Eyes Were Watching God*." *Tulsa Studies in Women's Literature* 7 (1988): 105–17.

Kalb, John D. "The Anthropological Narrator of Hurston's *Their Eyes Were Watching God*." *Studies in American Fiction* 16 (1988): 169–80.

Knudsen, Janice L. "The Tapestry of Living: A Journey of Self-Discovery in Hurston's *Their Eyes Were Watching God*." *CLA Journal* 40 (1996): 214–29.

Krasner, James N. "The Life of Women: Zora Neale Hurston and Female Autobiography." *Black American Literature Forum* 23 (1989): 113–26.

Kubitschek, Missy Dehn. " 'Tuh De Horizon and Back': The Female Quest in *Their Eyes Were Watching God*." *Black American Literature Forum* 17 (1983): 109–15.

Lionnet, Françoise. "Autoethnography: The An-Archic Style of *Dust Tracks on a Road*." *Reading Black, Reading Feminist: A Critical Anthology*. Ed. Henry Louis Gates, Jr. New York: Meridian, 1990. 382–414.

Lowe, John. "Hurston, Humor, and the Harlem Renaissance." *The Harlem Renaissance Re-Examined*. Ed. Victor A. Kramer. New York: AMS, 1987. 283–313.

———. *Jump at the Sun: Zora Neale Hurston's Cosmic Comedy*. Champaign: University of Illinois Press, 1994.

McKay, Nellie Y. "Race, Gender, and Cultural Context in Zora Neale Hurston's *Dust Tracts on a Road*." *Life/Lines: Theorizing Women's Autobiography*. Ed. Bella Brodski and Celeste M. Schenck. Ithaca, NY: Cornell University Press, 1988. 175–88.

Meisenhelder, Susan. "Conflict and Resistance in Zora Neale Hurston's *Mules and Men*." *Journal of American Folklore* 109 (1996): 267–88.

Morris, Robert J. "Zora Neale Hurston's Ambitious Enigma: *Moses, Man of the Mountain*." *CLA Journal* 40 (1997): 305–35.

Newsom, Adele S. *Zora Neale Hurston: A Reference Guide*. Boston: G. K. Hall, 1987.

O'Connor, Mary. "Zora Neale Hurston and Talking between Cultures." *Canadian Review of American Studies* (Special Issue, Part 1, 1992): 141–61.

Peters, Pearlie M. " 'Ah Got the Law in My Mouth': Black Women and Assertive Voice in Hurston's Fiction and Folklore." *CLA Journal* 37 (1994): 293–302.

Plant, Deborah G. *Every Tub Must Sit on Its Own Bottom: The Philosophy and Politics of Zora Neale Hurston.* Urbana: University of Illinois Press, 1995.

Rayson, Ann. "*Dust Tracks on a Road*: Zora Neale Hurston and the Form of Black Autobiography." *Negro American Literature Forum* 7 (1973): 39–45.

Robey, Judith. "Generic Strategies in Zora Neale Hurston's *Dust Tracks on a Road*." *Black American Literature Forum* 24 (1990): 667–82.

Sheffey, Ruthe T. "Zora Neale Hurston's *Moses, Man of the Mountain*: A Fictionalized Manifesto on the Imperatives of Black Leadership." *CLA Journal* 29 (1985): 206–20.

Sollors, Werner. "Of Mules and Mares in a Land of Difference; Or, Quadrupeds All?" *American Quarterly* 42 (1990): 167–90.

Southerland, Ellease. "The Influence of Voodoo on the Fiction of Zora Neale Hurston." *Sturdy Black Bridge: Visions of Black Women in Literature.* Ed. Roseann P. Bell, Bettye J. Parker, and Beverly Guy-Sheftall. Garden City, NJ: Anchor, 1979. 172–83.

Speisman, Barbara. "From 'Spears' to *The Great Day*: Zora Neale Hurston's Vision of a Real Negro Theater." *Southern Quarterly* 36.3 (1998): 34–46.

St. Clair, Janet. "The Courageous Undertow of Zora Neale Hurston's *Seraph on the Suwanee*." *Modern Language Quarterly* 50 (1989): 38–57.

Stein, Rachel. "Remembering the Sacred Tree: Black Women, Nature, and Voodoo in Zora Neale Hurston's *Tell My Horse* and *Their Eyes Were Watching God*." *Women's Studies* 25 (1996): 465–82.

Story, Ralph D. "Gender and Ambition: Zora Neale Hurston in the Harlem Renaissance." *Black Scholar* 20.3–4 (1989): 25–31.

Thompson, Gordon E. "Projecting Gender: Personification in the Works of Zora Neale Hurston." *American Literature* 66 (1994): 737–63.

Trefzer, Annette. " 'Let Us All Be Kissing-Friends?': Zora Neale Hurston and Race Politics in Dixie." *Journal of American Studies* 31 (1997): 69–78.

Turner, Darwin T. "Zora Neale Hurston: The Wandering Minstrel." *In a Minor Chord: Three Afro-American Writers and Their Search for Identity.* Carbondale: Southern Illinois University Press, 1971. 89–120.

Vickers, Anita M. "The Reaffirmation of African-American Dignity through the Oral Tradition in Zora Neale Hurston's *Their Eyes Were Watching God*." *CLA Journal* 37 (1994): 303–15.

Wald, Patricia. "Becoming 'Colored': The Self-Authorized Language of Difference in Zora Neale Hurston." *American Literary History* 2.1 (1990): 79–100.

Walker, Alice. "In Search of Zora Neale Hurston." *Ms. Magazine* March 1975: 74–79, 85–89.

Wall, Cheryl A. "*Mules and Men* and Women: Zora Neale Hurston's Strategies of Narration and Visions of Female Empowerment." *Black American Literature Forum* 23 (1989): 661–80.

———, ed. *"Sweat": Zora Neale Hurston.* New Brunswick, NJ: Rutgers University Press, 1997.

Wallace, Michele. "Who Owns Zora Neale Hurston: Critics Carve Up the Legend." *Invisibility Blues: From Pop to Theory*. London: Verso, 1990. 172–86.

Washington, Mary Helen. " 'I Love the Way Janie Crawford Left Her Husbands': Zora Neale Hurston's Emergent Female Hero." *Invented Lives: Narratives of Black Women, 1860–1960*. Garden City, NY, Doubleday, 1987. 237–54.

Werner, Craig. "Zora Neale Hurston." *Modern American Women Writers*. Ed. Elaine Showalter, New York: Scribner's, 1991. 221–33.

Wilentz, Gay. "Defeating the False God: Janie's Self-Determination in Zora Neale Hurston's *Their Eyes Were Watching God*." *Faith of a (Woman) Writer*. Ed. Alice Kessler-Harris and William McBrien. Westport, CT: Greenwood, 1988. 285–91.

CLEOFAS M. JARAMILLO
(1878–1956)

Kate K. Davis

BIOGRAPHY

Cleofas M. Jaramillo was born in Arroyo Hondo, just north of Taos, New Mexico, in 1878 to Miriana Lucero de Martínez and Julián Antonio Martínez, a prosperous dealer in the mercantile, mining, and livestock trades. One of seven children, Cleofas Jaramillo attended the Loretto Convent School in Taos for five years and later the Loretto Academy in Santa Fe. These schools discouraged students from speaking Spanish. She was courted by her second cousin Colonel Venceslao Jaramillo, a wealthy land and store owner from El Rito, New Mexico. They were married at a highly publicized wedding in 1898. Colonel Jaramillo was then a member of Territorial Governor Miguel A. Otero's staff and later served as state senator from Río Arriba County and delegate to the New Mexico Constitutional Convention in 1912.

The Jaramillos lived in El Rito, where their first two children died in infancy. Colonel Jaramillo's poor health necessitated a move to Denver, Colorado. Despite radium treatments at Johns Hopkins in Baltimore, he died in Denver on May 27, 1920. Cleofas Jaramillo, aged forty-two, returned with her daughter Angélica to Santa Fe. After the brutal murder of Angélica in 1931, Jaramillo, a deeply religious woman, felt a great personal and cultural loss that was to profoundly affect her writing.

The New Mexico Federal Writers Project of the 1930s encouraged a sense of value of Hispanic culture and history in Jaramillo. Authors Mary Austin and Willa Cather were important writing influences. Of Santa Fe, Jaramillo writes, "Writing and art are contagious in this old town. . . . [W]e have caught the fever. . . . [S]ome of us have the courage to try" (*Romance* 37). Jaramillo founded La Sociedad Folklórico in 1936. Members had to be of Hispanic descent, and meetings were held in Spanish.

In 1939, the lack of literature and information on the cuisine, dress, customs, and folk arts of New Mexico's Spanish-speaking peoples prompted Jaramillo to publish *Cuentos del Hogar*—a translation of twenty-five of her mother's folktales—and *The Genuine New Mexico Tasty Recipes: Potajes Sabrosos*. The latter, republished in 1981, is expanded and still in print and contains illustrations by the author. These books seek to preserve the foods and traditions of the Hispano community. As a descendant of a pioneer Spanish family, Jaramillo was intensely proud of her Spanish, not Mexican, heritage. She lived during the decades when many Hispano families, whose husbandry practices relied on communal grazing and water rights, lost their lands to Anglo ranchers. This precipitated mass migration to urban centers.

Fearing the loss of Hispano traditions and culture, Jaramillo was driven to record vanishing folklore and lifeways. She admitted to never being completely comfortable with the use of the English language but had to employ it to communicate her culture's disappearance: "I feel an appalling shortage of words, not being a writer, and writing in a language almost foreign to me" (*Romance* vii).

In 1941 Jaramillo published *Shadows of the Past (Sombras del Pasado)*, a personal narrative combined with folklore, customs, foods, education, superstition, and witchcraft of the Hispanic community. *Romance of a Small Village Girl* (1955), Jaramillo's most autobiographical work, covers her childhood, marriage, and impending sense of lost culture in an increasingly modern and urban New Mexico. She died in El Paso, Texas, on November 30, 1956.

MAJOR WORKS AND THEMES

Cleofas M. Jaramillo infuses her cookbooks and autobiographic compilations of folktales with an urgent energy—she was greatly dismayed by the silencing of the Hispanic majority by increasing Anglo power and language. *The Genuine New Mexico Tasty Recipes* (1939) is the first cookbook concerning New Mexico cuisine written by a Hispanic woman. That the thirty-three-page book is still in print more than sixty years later is tribute to its author's lifelong dream of preserving her cultural heritage.

Tey Diana Rebolledo considers *Romance of a Little Village Girl* to be Jaramillo's "most important contribution to documenting the past" (206). The work is a romantic, somewhat nostalgic rendition of Jaramillo's life as the wife of a politician. Jaramillo writes from the perceptive of a member of the *rico* class, the wealthy and privileged Hispanics, and as such it is a biased remembrance. The narrative is framed by ballad stanzas concerning the rise and fall of the Spanish people. Jaramillo begins *Romance* with a description of her home as a natural paradise, but at the end of the narrative, she returns "with nothing left but memories of our once lively, happy home, now melting in ruins" (*Romance* 187). The degradation of the land is metaphor for the loss of Hispanic culture.

Shadows of the Past, an accurate portrait of the life of a woman of the *rico* class, presents traditions normally transmitted by oral and experiential ways. It is an important documentation of upper-middle-class lifestyle written despite Anglo culture and language and Spanish patriarchal dominance.

CRITICAL RECEPTION

Shadows of the Past was considered "fascinating," "charming," and "delightfully illustrated" by reviewer Hester Jones in 1941. Recent critical responses to the works of Cleofas M. Jaramillo and other early Chicana writers are divided. Critic Raymond A. Paredes cites a "hacienda syndrome" prevalent in writing by wealthy women. He condemns their naíve and socially ignorant works as bourgeois, idealized, sentimental, nostalgic, and not focused on the reality of everyday life of the average New Mexican—the *peons* working for the *ricos*. Paredes rails against literature that glorifies the feudal systems employed by the *ricos*. Tey Diana Rebolledo argues that ignoring the middle- and upper-class experience is to ignore history and the origins of women's literature (202).

Writing by Chicano women was virtually forgotten after World War II. Since the literature was from the point of view of the privileged classes, Chicano activists and critics of the 1970s onward have disregarded these women's contributions to ethnic identity, further relegating them to the periphery. It was, in reality, extremely difficult for women, let alone Hispanic women, to break out of their rigid gender roles and into print.

Carol Jensen labels Jaramillo a "cultural and religious syncretist" who weaves together her romantic devotion to her culture's past and her personal religious experience. Jaramillo attempts to "bridge the gap between folk religion and institutional religion" (161). Rebolledo appreciates Jaramillo's works for their documentation of private lives often omitted in male narratives (208). The narratives are simplistic and still "explaining things" but also a decidedly feminine voice of a woman laughing, loving, crying, and sharing (Rebolledo 212).

Critic Ramón Sánchez believes Jaramillo attempts to preserve her cultural heritage by envisioning "a past that is morally, religiously, politically, and socially cohesive" (157). Jaramillo focuses on an idealized New Mexican culture and not reality. This framework dominates Jaramillo's work and serves to "buttress that community in reaction to perceived cultural assaults" (Sánchez 158). Sánchez grants that Jaramillo's work is an important contribution to the understanding of Hispanic culture and folklore.

BIBLIOGRAPHY

Works by Cleofas M. Jaramillo

Cuentos del Hogar (Spanish Fairy Tales). El Campo, TX: Citizen Press, 1939.
The Genuine New Mexico Tasty Recipes: Potajes Sabrosos. 1939. Rev. *The Genuine*

New Mexico Tasty Recipes: With Additional Materials on Traditional Hispano Food. Santa Fe: Ancient City, 1981.

Shadows of the Past (Sombras del Pasado). Santa Fe: Seton Village, 1941.

Romance of a Little Village Girl. San Antonio: Naylor, 1955.

Studies of Cleofas M. Jaramillo

Jensen, Carol. "Cleofas M. Jaramillo on Marriage in Territorial Northern New Mexico." *New Mexico Historical Review* Apr. 1983: 153–71.

Jones, Hester. "Two Folk-Lore Volumes." Rev. of *Shadows of the Past*, by Cleofas M. Jaramillo. *El Palacio* Nov. 1941: 237–38.

Paredes, Raymond A. "The Evolution of Chicano Literature." *Three American Literatures.* Ed. Houston A. Baker, Jr. New York: MLA, 1982. 33–79.

Rebolledo, Tey Diana. "Las Escritoras: Romances and Realities." *Pasó por Aqui: Critical Essays on the New Mexican Literary Tradition, 1542–1988.* Ed. Erlinda Gonzales-Berry. Albuquerque: New Mexico University Press, 1987. 199–214.

———. "Tradition and Mythology: Signature of Landscape in Chicana Literature." *The Desert Is No Lady: Southwestern Landscapes in Women's Writing and Art.* Ed. Vera Norwood and Janice Monk. New Haven, CT: Yale University Press, 1987. 96–124.

Sánchez, Ramón. "Cleofas M. Jaramillo." *Chicano Writers* Ed. Francisco A. Lomelí and Carl R. Shirley. Detroit: Gale, 1992. Vol. 122 of *Dictionary of Literary Biography*. 154–58.

GEORGIA DOUGLAS CAMP JOHNSON (1877–1966)

Catherine Cucinella

BIOGRAPHY

Georgia Douglas Camp Johnson, the "lady poet" of the New Negro Renaissance, wrote short fiction, plays, and poetry. Born in Atlanta, Georgia, to biracial parents, Laura Douglas (black and Native American) and George Camp (black and white), Johnson spent her early childhood in Rome, Georgia. After graduating from Atlanta University's Normal School in 1893, Johnson began a ten-year teaching career. In 1902, Johnson spent a year at the Oberlin Conservatory of Music before becoming an assistant principal in Atlanta. A year later she married Henry Lincoln Johnson, an Atlanta attorney. In 1910 the Johnsons relocated to Washington, D.C., where Henry established a law practice. His 1912 appointment as Recorder of Deeds moved the Johnsons into elite black society.

While in Washington, Johnson began writing poetry and published her first volume, *The Heart of a Woman* (1918). Between the appearance of her first poetry collection and her second one, *Bronze* (1922), Johnson initiated casual gatherings in her home. Her informal "literary salon" included writers such as Jean Toomer, Countee Cullen, Jessie Fauset, Langston Hughes, Zora Neale Hurston, W.E.B. Du Bois, Alice Dunbar-Nelson, Alain Locke, James Weldon Johnson, Angelina Grimké, and William Stanley Braithwaite.

Henry's death in 1925 left Johnson with two teenage sons to raise. Forced to work outside of the home, Johnson had little time to write, yet she did write several plays and another volume of poetry, *An Autumn Love Cycle* (1928). In 1926 her play *Blue Blood* garnered an honorable mention in the *Opportunity* play contest, and *Plumes* won first place in 1927. Only four of Johnson's many plays saw publication in her lifetime: *Blue Blood, Plumes*, and the historical plays *Frederick Douglass* and *William and Ellen Craft. A Sunday Morning in the South, Safe*, and *Blue-Eyed Black Boys* were published posthumously. She published her last volume of poetry, *Share My World*, in 1962, four years before her death on May 14, 1966.

MAJOR WORKS AND THEMES

The Heart of a Woman, Bronze, and *An Autumn Love Cycle* established Johnson's reputation as a "lady poet." Although these volumes of lyric poetry, written in traditional form, emphasize love, death, disappointment, unrealized dreams, and sadness, themes regarding spiritual triumph, poetic imagination, and strength, particularly that of women, also emerge. Braithwaite's Introduction to *Heart* points to the volume's focus on "domestic love and joy and sorrow, [and on] romantic visions" (vii). Certainly, the title of the volume and the titles of the poems ("The Heart of a Woman," "Sympathy," "Joy," "Elevation," "Peace," and "Love's Tendril") suggest such a reading.

Johnson's most anthologized poem, "The Heart of a Woman," appears to express traditional Victorian gentility and, read within the framework of Braithwaite's Introduction, may seem to reveal "the secrets of woman's nature" (ix). Johnson likens a woman's heart to "a lone bird, soft winging, so restlessly on" (1). However, a biting irony underscores the softness and gentleness of the poem. Words and phrases such as "restlessly," "falls back," "alien cage," "plight," "breaks, breaks, breaks," and "sheltering bars" disrupt traditional readings of "Heart." A careful and critical reading reveals an implicit critique of patriarchal constraints on women and their talents.

The other poems in the volume manifest the same ironic voice and tension as "Heart." For instance, "Gossamer" delineates innocence as ephemeral and "frail as cobwebs" (3); and in "Peace," peace lies in "Forgetting, and—forgot!" (9). In "Dreams of the Dreamer," dreams take the persona inward, "to the soul's hour-glass" (2). The "sheltering bars" of patriarchy not only hold a woman's heart, but they also confine her dreams. "My Little Dreams," *Heart*'s closing poem, relegates a woman's dreams (imagination, creativity, ambition) to the heart. The persona, praying to forget their existence, "folds" her dreams "within [her] heart" (62). Read through the lens of late nineteenth-century gentility, these poems express appropriate and acceptable female desires and behaviors: a quest for love, contentment with the domestic and dreams put aside. These same poems read within the framework of twentieth-century feminist or cultural sensibilities signify an ironic defiance of societal conventions.

Although returning to the same "gendered" themes in *An Autumn Love Cycle* (1928), Johnson adds race to the themes in *Bronze* (1922). The poems in *Bronze* repeat Johnson's themes of sorrow, love, and unfulfilled dreams, but they also delineate, according to Du Bois, "what it means to be a colored woman" (Introduction 7). Johnson explicitly identifies *Bronze* as racial in her author's note to the volume: "This book is the child of a bitter earth-wound. . . . I know that God's sun shall one day shine upon a perfected and unhampered people" (81). According to Tate, *Bronze* "was probably Johnson's most commercially successful book because it was packaged as a work of strong racial awareness" (liii). The poems in this volume exhibit much of the accepted racial rhetoric of the early 1920s.

The poems in *Bronze* are categorized under nine sections that include "Exhortation," "Supplication," "Shadow," "Motherhood," and "Exaltation." The titles of the individual poems make clear the racial themes in the collection: "Sonnet to the Mantled," "Prejudice," "The Passing of the Ex-Slave," "The Octoroon," "Black Woman" and "Shall I Say, 'My Son You're Branded?' " The racial tone of these poems, however, emerges as a reiteration of uplift rhetoric. Gloria T. Hull views *Bronze* as Johnson's "weakest book [which] reads like obligatory race poetry" (160). Johnson, herself, wrote to Arna Botemps "that she did not enjoy 'writing racially' " (Hull 18).

Despite this admission, Johnson's plays are decidedly racial. Tate notes that Johnson's playwriting demonstrates Johnson's "unique version of Negro folk drama" (lvii). Johnson's racial poetry and these plays about Negro life assume a social tone. For instance, both *Safe* and *A Sunday Morning in the South* dramatize an antilynching stance. Her historical plays, *Frederick Douglass* and *William and Ellen Craft*, recover a black heroic past. *Plumes*, Johnson's most celebrated play, indicts both poverty and superstition (Tate 1x). Finally, *Blue Blood* and *Blue-Eyed Black Boys* deal with miscegenation, which Hull identifies as Johnson's "lifelong preoccupation in life and art" (155).

In these overtly racial plays, Johnson does not abandon the themes that circulate within her poetry. *Plumes* further extends the poetry's acknowledgment of the inevitability of death, and it positions women's concerns at its center. This centrality of the personal also marks *Safe* and *A Sunday Morning in the South*. Regardless of the genre, Johnson remains faithful to her early themes. Commenting on Johnson's last poetry collection, *Share My World*, Hull observes that "[t]hemes rather than technique distinguish these final poems" (209). These themes distinguish and unify Johnson's oeuvre. Read with critical acumen, these themes challenge the racist and sexist system that limits female imagination, creativity, and potential.

CRITICAL RECEPTION

Claudia Tate observes that Johnson's early critics understood her "as a traditionalist and an advocate of genteel culture, who adhered to the Romantic conventions of the nineteenth-century Anglo-literary establishment" (xviii). This understanding originated from comments offered by Alain Locke, W.E.B. Du Bois, and William Stanley Braithwaite. In the Introduction to *An Autumn Love Cycle*, Locke praises Johnson for her "delicate" touch, "rhapsodic" tone, "ardent sincerity of emotion, ingenuous candor of expression," and "naïve and sophisticated style" (xvii–xviii). Braithwaite identifies *A Heart of a Woman* as "intensely feminine," using words such as "romantic," "poignant," "sympathy," "marvelous patience," and "wonderful endurance." In his less than flattering Introduction to *Bronze*, Du Bois uses references such as "simple, sometimes trite," "sincere and true."

Recent scholarship on Johnson argues for a rereading of her poetry, plays, and fiction. These critics (Hull, Tate, Harris, and Stetson) find in Johnson's work a direct challenge to the very social conventions that her early critics praised her for reinforcing. Tate asserts that "Johnson's poetic style . . . veiled her criticism of racial and gender oppressions behind the demeanor of 'the lady poet' " (xviii). In her analysis of "The Heart of a Woman," Tate points out that the alignment of a woman's heart with a soaring bird "associates the heart with . . . the poetic imagination" (1). Thus the feminine heart and the poetic imagination emerge as "synecdoches for one another" (Tate 1). This reading opens Johnson's work to other feminist inquires. Most feminist critics identify subversive and desconstructive moments in *Heart*. While Erlene Stetson argues for the "deconstructions of male fantasy" (28), Hull assets that *Heart* manifests an acknowledgment of "the oppressiveness and pain of the female lot" (157).

This awareness also underwrites Johnson's plays. Will Harris persuasively argues that Johnson, along with other black women playwrights, "formulated dramatic strategies [that] stag[ed] substantive, independent African American female presences" (205). Other critics also address Johnson's role as a dramatist within an African American tradition of women playwrights. This scholarship inscribes Johnson as a writer critically concerned with all aspects of a woman's life. Megan Sullivan points to the importance of "female-identified relationships" in *Plumes* and in *A Sunday Morning in the South*. Commenting on the latter, Sullivan writes that "[a]lthough the women in [this play] do speak out against patriarchal order, they are, nonetheless, silenced by this order" (418). Thus in her plays, Johnson refuses to separate being black from being female. This refusal occasions feminist attention as well as African American scholarship, and this scholarship adds a new dimension to Johnson's role as "lady poet" within the Harlem Renaissance.

BIBLIOGRAPHY

Works by Georgia Douglas Camp Johnson

The Heart of a Woman and Other Poems. Boston: Cornhill, 1918.

Bronze: A Book of Verse. Boston: Brimmer, 1922.

Plumes. Plays of Negro Life: A Source Book of Native American Drama. Ed. Alain Locke and Montgomery Gregory. New York: Harper, 1927. 287–99.

An Autumn Love Cycle. New York: Vinal, 1928.

Frederick Douglass. Negro History in Thirteen Plays. Ed. Willis Richardson and May Miller. Washington, DC: Associated Publishers, 1935. 145–62.

William and Ellen Craft. Negro History in Thirteen Plays. Ed. Willis Richardson and May Miller. Washington, DC: Associated Publishers, 1935. 163–86.

Share My World. Washington, DC: Halfway House, 1962.

A Sunday Morning in the South. Black Theatre, U.S.A.: Forty-five Plays by Black American Playwrights, 1847–1974. Ed. James V. Hatch and Ted Shine. New York: Free Press, 1974. 213–17.

Blue Blood. Wines in the Wilderness: Plays by African American Women from the Har-

lem Renaissance to the Present. Ed. Elizabeth Brown-Guillroy. Westport, CT: Greenwood, 1990. 17–25.

Blue-Eyed Black Boys. Wines in the Wilderness: Plays by African American Women from the Harlem Renaissance to the Present. Ed. Elizabeth Brown-Guillroy. Westport, CT: Greenwood, 1990. 33–37.

Safe. Wines in the Wilderness: Plays by African American Women from the Harlem Renaissance to the Present. Ed. Elizabeth Brown-Guillroy. Westport, CT: Greenwood, 1990. 26–32.

The Selected Works of Georgia Douglas Johnson. New York: G. K. Hall, 1997.

Studies of Georgia Douglas Camp Johnson

Harris, Will. "Early Black Women Playwrights and the Dual Liberation Movement." *African American Review* 28 (1994): 205–22.

Hull, Gloria T. *Color, Sex and Poetry: Three Women Writers from the Harlem Renaissance*. Bloomington: University of Indiana Press, 1987. 115–211.

Miller, Jeannne-Marie A. "Georgia Douglas Johnson and May Miller: Forgotten Playwrights of the New Negro Renaissance." *CLA* 33 (1990): 349–67.

Stetson, Erlene. "Rediscovering the Harlem Renaissance: Georgia Douglas Johnson, 'The New Negro Poet.' " *Obsidian* 5 (1979): 26–34.

Stewart, Jeffery C. "Alain Locke and Georgia Douglas Johnson, Washington Patrons of Afro-American Modernism." *G. W. Studies* 12 (1986): 37.

Sullivan, Megan. "Folk Plays, Home Girls, and Back Talk: Georgia Douglas Johnson and Women of the Harlem Renaissance." *CLA* 38 (1995): 404–20.

Tate, Claudia. Introduction. *The Selected Works of Georgia Douglas Johnson*. New York: G. K. Hall, 1997. xvii–lxxx.

NELLA LARSEN
(1891–1964)

C. Ann McDonald

BIOGRAPHY

An important clue to understanding Nella Larsen's early life came with the discovery by Thadious M. Davis of Larsen's birth certificate and consequently her name at birth. Born Nellie Walker on April 13, 1891, Larsen was, according to that certificate, the "colored" daughter of Mary Hanson Walker, a twenty-two-year-old Danish woman, and Peter Walker, a "colored" cook. Little else about her father's identity can be gleaned from the birth certificate, since his nationality, age, and birthplace are not recorded. One possible clue to his identity is found in the given names of Larsen's father and stepfather. What at first seems like coincidence—both men were named Peter—gives way to a more calculated possibility on further inspection: The two names may have belonged to the same man. Compounding the seeming coincidence is the fact that Peter Walker faded out of existence, with no evidence of his death beyond hearsay, around the same time that Peter Larson entered the scene. No official document records Walker's death, nor does his name appear in any public record or directory after 1891. In addition to the problems concerning Larsen's father, her relationship to her mother and sister is problematic as well; at times, both women denied knowledge of Larsen's existence. Apparently, the family found it necessary both to create a new identity for the father and to erase any evidence of the daughter. The reasons for this cover-up can be found in the issues of race and class that eventually became the thematic cornerstone of Larsen's fiction.

Mary, Anna, and Peter Larson were officially documented "white"; only Nellie Walker Larson and Peter Walker received the designation "colored." In her later years, Larsen described her father as "West Indian, but light-skinned" (qtd. in Davis 45). If Peter Walker was indeed Peter Larson, then one can assume that he was light-skinned enough to pass for white. The birth of obviously "colored" Nellie Walker, however, would have revealed his African heritage, thus warranting the designation "colored" for not only the child but also the father on Nellie Walker's birth certificate. The establishment of "white" Peter

Larson in place of "colored" Peter Walker as head of the household allowed the family to adopt the racial designation of white—excepting, of course, Nellie Walker Larson, who stood on the outside as the black stepchild. The racial designation of white was a stepping-stone in Peter Larson's upward social mobility. Being white meant that Larson could work as a railroad conductor, a position that offered prestige and financial security. Eventually, the Larsons moved from a middle-class interracial neighborhood—one where Nellie fit in— to an all-white neighborhood that represented an upward move in class position that could not include the darker child. Whether Peter Larson was Larsen's white stepfather, or whether he was "colored" Peter Walker now passing as white, the Larson's upward mobility necessitated the removal of Nella Larsen from that family. Through firsthand experience, Larsen learned both the connections between race and class and the requirements for passing into the middle class that she later explored in her novels.

Larsen enrolled in Fisk University's Normal School in 1907, at which time she became permanently estranged from her family. She studied to be a nurse from 1912 until 1915, and after her graduation she worked in the Tuskegee Institute as the head nurse of the John Andrew Memorial Hospital and Nurse Training School. Finding the Institute as stifling as Helga Crane finds Naxos in *Quicksand*, Larsen went to New York and took a nursing job there. Shortly thereafter, she met Elmer Imes, a scientist, and in 1919, they were married. Growing tired of nursing, Larsen went to work as a librarian at the Harlem branch of the New York Public Library (NYPL). During this time, Larsen became involved with the literary artists of the Harlem Renaissance. Eventually, she left the position at the NYPL and concentrated on writing fiction. In 1926, *Young's Realistic Stories Magazine* published two of her short stories under the pseudonym Allen Semi, which was her married name spelled backwards. In 1928, *Quicksand*, for which she won the Harmon Award, was published, followed by the publication of *Passing* in 1929. Her success as a writer appeared to continue with *Forum*'s publication in 1930 of her short story "Sanctuary."

Shortly after *Forum* published "Sanctuary," a scandal occurred concerning the possibility that Larsen had plagiarized a story by Sheila Kaye-Smith entitled "Mrs. Adis." Eventually, Larsen convinced the editors of *Forum* that the story was her own by producing several rough drafts, but the scandal damaged her reputation and perhaps, as some scholars speculate, her confidence in herself as a writer, since it was her last piece of published fiction. That same year, Larsen received the Guggenheim Fellowship (she was the first African American woman to do so), and she used the money to travel to Europe, where she worked on a novel, *Mirage*, which was subsequently rejected by Knopf. Though she most likely worked on at least one more novel, Larsen failed either to finish or to publish it. Other events—the failing U.S. economy and the waning interest by the public at large in African American writers—most likely contributed to the end of Larsen's literary career. Certainly the possibility exists that her later novels were not of publishable quality, though the lack of extant manuscripts prohibits scholars from making such a judgment. Whatever the cause or causes—economic depression, lack of public interest, a talent run dry, or a ruined literary reputation—the publication of "Sanctuary" effectively marks the end of Larsen's literary career.

In 1933, Larsen divorced Imes as a result of his affair with a white woman. After her marriage ended, Larsen eventually drifted out of the public eye, and she spent the last thirty years of her life as Mrs. Imes, a nurse who lived and worked in Brooklyn. On March 30, 1964, the body of Mrs. Nella Imes was discovered in her apartment. Most likely, she had been dead about a week, a testament to the solitary life she had exchanged for the hustle and bustle of literary Harlem. Larsen's literary career, however, comprised only a small portion of her life—from the publication of two articles in *Brownies' Book* in 1920 to 1930 and the publication of "Sanctuary"—and that career produced two significant novels. Furthermore, during the last thirty years of her life she conducted a successful nursing career. Though the temptation exists to see Larsen's life as a tragedy, one in which a talented woman was swallowed up by the nothingness of literary obscurity, in fact hers was a life well-lived, and the novels and short stories she produced in the late 1920s have left a legacy to the times in which she lived as well as a wealth of wisdom for generations to come.

MAJOR WORKS AND THEMES

Larsen's identity as an African American woman certainly influences her work. Both *Quicksand* and *Passing* examine what it meant to be a black woman in early twentieth-century America. However, in a time when black writers were urged to promote the political causes of the black race in their work, Larsen avoided writing purely polemical novels about race. As Cheryl A. Wall points out in *Women of the Harlem Renaissance*, "Larsen's novel [*Quicksand*] is not a polemic for any cause. She scorned purpose novels and mocked the sometimes sententious rhetoric of racial uplift" (117). Likewise, Larsen's work avoids uplifting visions of emancipated Woman and therefore does not fit a certain feminist agenda of nearly propagandistic feminine success. Her novels and short stories are a complex presentation of the crossroads between race, gender, and class that do not offer inspirational messages about these categories of identity. In fact, *Quicksand* and *Passing* each reveal the failure of both race unity and feminist sisterhood and present instead characters divided by the demands of upward class mobility. Furthermore, Larsen's writing offers a glimpse into the futility of seeking affirmation in categories of identity since, as Helga Crane finds out, identity itself is ultimately unstable. In both her short stories and novels, Larsen embarks on the modernist's examination of constructed identities and reveals in her work an early twentieth-century understanding of the subject's desire for transcendence and the ultimate frustration of that desire, using as her rubric for examination the cross sections between gender, race, and class.

Passing and the controversial "Sanctuary" both examine the complexities of race and class in relation to race loyalty. In "Sanctuary," Annie Poole must choose between familial loyalty and loyalty to the black race. Jim Hammer is a black man who inadvertently murders Annie's son, Obadiah. Clearly, Annie has a lack of respect for Jim that is based on class difference: To her, Jim is "no 'count trash" and "nuffin' . . . but a heap o' dirt" (*Intimation* 23). Nevertheless, when he comes to her for protection from the white law officers who pursue him, Annie's loyalty to her race demands that she harbor Jim, "siderin' all an' all, how Obadiah's right fon' o' you, an' how white folks is white folks" (*Intimation* 23). Both her son's apparent loyalty to the race despite class difference—for Annie, Obadiah is "too good" to his lower-class acquaintances (*Intimation* 23)—and her understanding of the nature of white people compel Annie Poole to "hide [Jim] dis one time" (*Intimation* 23). Furthermore, Annie tells Jim, "Ef de Lawd had gib you a white face 'stead o' dat dere black one, Ah shuah would turn you out" (*Intimation* 24). The race loyalty Annie expresses is relatively unproblematic, since at the time both she and Jim believe that he has killed a white man. Eventually, however, the identity of the murdered man is revealed, and at this point, the race loyalty she feels for Jim overrides her feelings of loyalty to her son. After telling the white sheriff that "Ah ain't sees nobody pass" (*Intimation* 26), Annie Poole returns to the room where Jim is hiding and tells him, "Git outer mah feather baid, Jim Hammer, an' outen mah house, an' don' nevah stop thankin' yo' Jesus he done gib you dat black face" (*Intimation* 27). Due to a sense of race loyalty, Annie *has* enabled Jim to "pass"—that is, to remain safely undetected by "white folks." This loyalty, however, comes with a price: Annie Poole must surrender her chance to avenge her son's death. Nonetheless, the short story illustrates a clear race unity that overcomes class distinction.

In *Passing*, the metaphor of "passing" again represents the idea of protecting a member of the black race from the dangers posed by "white folks," though Irene Redfield does not conquer the constraints of class that Annie Poole overcomes. In fact, Irene not only fails to place race above class but also sacrifices gender ties to the comforts of a middle-class lifestyle. This sacrifice becomes evident when Irene suspects that her husband, Brian, is having an affair with Clare Kendry, who is passing for white. Irene tries to think of a plan to end the affair between her friend and her husband, and she considers revealing Clare's secret to John Bellew, Clare's white, bigoted husband. As she contemplates betraying her friend, Irene finds herself torn between what she sees as her own self-preservation and her loyalty to the black race:

She was caught between two allegiances, different, yet the same. Herself. Her race. Race! The thing that bound and suffocated her. Whatever steps she took, or if she took none at all, something would be crushed. A person or the race. Clare, herself, or the race. It was, she cried silently, enough to suffer as a woman, an individual, on one's own account, without having to suffer for the race as well. It was a brutality, and undeserved. Surely, no other people as cursed as Ham's dark children. (*Quicksand* 225)

In this passage, Irene describes what she sees as the burden of race loyalty, a sense of obligation that is for her the curse of black people. She is unwilling to betray Clare, however, and well aware of the danger Clare would face if her husband—a white threat similar to the sheriff in "Sanctuary"—should discover Clare's secret. Nevertheless, Irene's desire for middle-class comfort is threatened by Clare's possible connection to Brian, which eventually overrides Irene's sense of loyalty to Clare's blackness.

In the novel's resolution, John Bellew discovers Clare's secret, leaving her, as Irene surmises, free to take Irene's husband. Irene's tie to Brian is not based on love or even sexual desire but on the lifestyle he can provide for her and their sons. Brian's own desire to leave the medical profession has remained a constant threat to Irene, since without the doctor husband she has acquired she would not be able to live the middle-class life to which she is accustomed. Seeing Clare, who has always wanted the life Irene leads, as a threat to her bourgeois security and comfort, Irene pushes Clare from an open window to her death. Clearly, Irene has chosen self-preservation over race loyalty; her motivation is a desire for class comforts that rely on the presence of a male figure. Earlier in their lives, Clare, the daughter of a violent alcoholic, envied the fact that Irene had a stable, caring father. Knowing that to have Irene's life means to have the man in that life, Clare apparently attempts to take that man—at least in Irene's mind. Just as Clare's ability to pass for white and therefore escape the oppressive class position of her past depended upon her husband, her entrance into the black bourgeoisie would depend on her attachment to a man. In a world where men define women's social status, Clare and Irene can afford neither gender nor race loyalty but instead become combatants in a class-based battle.

"The Wrong Man" is a "passing" story that focuses on class rather than race, yet it also touches upon the idea of unstable identities in such a way that it ties together the main concerns of Larsen's work. Julia Romley, the story's protagonist, has, through marriage, obtained an upper-class position that hides her early, lower-class position. The attendance at a party of Ralph Tyler's, a man who knows the details of her sordid past, threatens to expose her and cause her to "lose everything—love, wealth, and position" (*Intimation* 5). Clearly, this story addresses the same gender and class issues that Larsen examines more fully in *Passing*: Without a man, a woman cannot make the social climb necessary to happiness and contentment. Likewise, the story underscores the idea of the unstable, constructed identity, an idea that is obviously at the heart of the concept of passing, where one deliberately creates a public identity that is in contrast to the private self. Unstable identity becomes the ironic punchline of this story, as Julia, while pleading with a man who stands in darkness, asks that he not expose her true identity—then realizes that she has "told the wrong man" (9).

"Freedom" offers a glimpse into Larsen's modern obsession with the instability of identity and a frustrated desire for transcendence. In "Freedom," the unnamed focal character attempts to gain freedom by leaving his girlfriend. Once he does, he creates an image of her in his mind, envisioning her life without him. Eventually, he finds that she is not as all as he "visualized" (*Intimation* 15). Instead, she died in childbirth without knowing that her lover was gone. This contrast between his image of his lover and the actuality of her existence is a realization that "spoiled his life," since it reveals the instability of the identity he created for her (*Intimation* 16). Ultimately, he comes to realize that his freedom is also an illusion: "He had reached out toward freedom—to find only a mirage; for he saw quite plainly that now he would never be free. It was she who had escaped him" (*Intimation* 16). In other words, the man realizes that freedom from the constraints of the physical world comes only with death. In the end, he, like his lover, finds freedom in death, stepping through an open window in a moment that foreshadows both Clare Kendry's death and Helga Crane's descent into the quicksand of her own physical life.

Quicksand is a novel that fully explores both the search for an identity that is characterized by race, class, and gender and the inevitable failure to find that identity. Throughout the novel, Helga Crane fashions herself according to other people's ideas about race, class, and gender, only to find that none of the identities she adopts satisfy her longing to belong. In what seems to be an uncharacteristic moment for Helga, she wanders into a church ceremony where black men and especially women experience a religious frenzy and ecstasy that eventually envelops Helga. As she has done before, Helga adopts this new identity with apparent abandon, believing that the wild, spiritual elation she experiences will provide her with the sense of belonging and transcendence for which she has been searching. In the end, however, she is smothered by her life as preacher's wife, and she realizes that her sense of suffocation is not unlike the feeling of oppression that has haunted her throughout the novel:

[I]n some way she was determined to get herself out of this bog into which she had strayed. Or—she would have to die. She couldn't endure it. Her suffocation and shrinking loathing were too great. Not to be born. Again. For she had to admit that it wasn't new, this feeling of dissatisfaction, of asphyxiation. Something like it she had experienced before. In Naxos. In New York. In Copenhagen. This differed only in degree. And it was of the present and therefore seemingly more reasonable. The other revulsions were of the past, and now less explainable. (*Quicksand* 134)

Clearly, Helga's attempts to find belonging and identity have resulted in feelings of "dissatisfaction, of asphyxiation" (*Quicksand* 134). The freedom she longs for can be found—as it is found in "Freedom"—through death, an escape from the body that represents a rather morbid, hopeless transcendence. However, Helga "wanted not to leave" her children, remembering "her own childhood, lonely, unloved" (*Quicksand* 135). She tells herself that leaving her children would be different from her own abandonment as a child, since "[t]here was not an element of race, of black and white. They were all black together" (*Quick-*

sand 135). Clearly, Helga sees her children as having racial unity and therefore a sense of belonging that Helga (and perhaps Larsen) did not experience as a child. In the end, Helga is unable to escape from the life of the body, and she sinks into the oppression of birthing her fifth child. Rather than promoting racial prosperity or gender triumph, the novel—like Larsen's work in general—uses race, gender, and class as the lenses through which we view the unstable, trapped self in search of an ever-elusive transcendence.

CRITICAL RECEPTION

Like many writers of the Harlem Renaissance—women especially—Larsen's work was largely ignored until the early 1970s when feminist critics resurrected numerous literary careers, Larsen's included. Her novels, however, met with critical praise at the time of publication. A contemporary review of *Quicksand* called the book "an articulate and sympathetic first novel"; in the *World Telegram*, a reviewer claimed, "The book makes you want to read everything that Nella Larsen will ever write" (qtd. in Wall 116). W.E.B. Du Bois wrote a favorable review of *Quicksand*, stating that Larsen "has done a fine, thoughtful and courageous piece of fiction" that revealed a "subtle comprehension of the curious cross currents that swirl about the black American" (qtd. in Wall 117). *Passing* likewise garnered favorable reviews, and in general, Larsen was seen as a talented writer and literary artist. Furthermore, she received in 1928 the Harmon Award for Distinguished Achievement among Negroes (the Bronze Medal for literature) for *Quicksand* and a Guggenheim Fellowship, based on the positive reception of her first novels, to write a third. That she never lived up to the promise of the Guggenheim remains a source of wonder to critics. Indeed, the charges of plagiarism that were labeled against "Sanctuary" harmed her sterling literary reputation and cooled what had been a warm critical reception.

From the outset, however, critics have been puzzled and displeased by the endings of Larsen's novels. According to Deborah E. McDowell in the introduction to *Quicksand and Passing*, reviewers "consistently criticized the endings of her novels *Quicksand* (1928) and *Passing* (1929), which reveal her difficulty with rounding off stories convincingly" (xi). In general, such criticism has arisen from scholars who want Larsen's works to present a more uplifting, politically inspiring outcome for her African American heroines. Helga's descent, for example, into the quagmire of motherhood and wifedom provides a shocking end to a novel in which the heroine searches so convincingly for a strong identity, rejecting for the most part overtly sexist and racist offerings before she sinks into the quicksand of an oppressive married life. Likewise, Irene's murdering of her childhood friend does not provide a positive model for solidarity among either women or black people.

Contemporary critics, however, are choosing to take the novels on their own terms, recognizing in them richly woven tales that resist polemical conclusions. For example, McDowell argues that the controversial endings "if examined through the prism of black female sexuality . . . make more sense" (xii). McDowell suggests that rather than prescribing how things should be for women, Larsen's work provides a compelling critique of how things are:

[The endings of Larsen's stories] show her grappling with the conflicting demands of her racial and sexual identities and the contradictions of a black and feminine aesthetic. Moreover, while these endings appear to be concessions to the dominant ideology of romance—marriage and motherhood—viewed from a feminist perspective, they become much more radical and original efforts to acknowledge a female sexual experience, most often repressed in both literary and social realms. (xii)

From this perspective, the endings do make sense. Whereas Larsen's contemporaries argued that the endings marred her work, McDowell suggests that happier endings, though they might satisfy a political agenda, would simply provide pat answers for complicated questions. Clearly, Larsen's work goes beyond solving the political and social problems of any particular era. Instead, her stories offer an investigation into categories of identity. Finally, Larsen remains true to her modern perspective by rejecting any possibility for transcendence—political or personal—and her work ultimately rejects polemics in favor of complexity.

BIBLIOGRAPHY

Works by Nella Larsen

"Playtime: Danish Fun." *Brownies' Book* 1 (1920): 219.
"Playtime: Three Scandinavian Games." *Brownies' Book* 1 (1920): 191–92.
Rev. of *Certain People of Importance*, by Kathleen Norris. *Messenger* 5 (1923): 713.
[Pseud. Allen Semi]. "Freedom." *Young's Realistic Stories Magazine* 51 (1926): 241–43.
[Pseud. Allen Semi]. "The Wrong Man." *Young's Realistic Stories Magazine* 50 (1926): 243–46.
Quicksand. New York: Knopf, 1928.
"Moving Mosaic or N.A.A.C.P. Dance, 1929" (excerpt from *Quicksand*). All-Star Benefit Concert for the National Association of Colored People Forrest Theater, New York, program booklet, 8 Dec. 1929.
Passing. New York: Knopf, 1929.
Rev. of *Black Sadie*, by T. Bowyer Campbell. *Opportunity* 7 (1929): 24.
"The Author's Explanation." *Forum* 83 (1930): xli–xlii.
"Sanctuary." *Forum* 83 (1930): 15–18.
An Intimation of Things Distant: The Collected Fiction of Nella Larsen. Ed. Charles R. Larson. New York: Anchor, 1992.

Studies of Nella Larsen

Beemyn, Brett. "A Bibliography of Works by and about Nella Larsen." *African American Review* 26 (1992): 183–88.

Blackmore, David L. " 'That Unreasonable Restless Feeling': The Homosexual Subtexts of Nella Larsen's *Passing*." *African American Review* 26 (1992): 475–84.

Chandler, Karen M. "Nella Larsen's Fatal Polarities: Melodrama and Its Limits in *Quicksand*." *CLA Journal* 42 (1998): 24–47.

Christian, Barbara. *Black Women Novelists: The Development of a Tradition, 1892–1976*. Westport, CT: Greenwood, 1980.

Clemmen, Yves W. A. "Nella Larsen's *Quicksand*: A Narrative of Difference." *CLA Journal* 40 (1997): 458–66.

Conde, Mary. "Passing in the Fiction of Jessie Redmond Fauset and Nella Larsen." *Yearbook of English Studies* 24 (1994): 94–104.

Davis, Thadious M. *Nella Larsen, Novelist of the Harlem Renaissance: A Woman's Life Unveiled*. Baton Rouge: Louisiana State University Press, 1994.

duCille, Ann. "Blues Notes on Black Sexuality: Sex and the Texts of Jessie Fauset and Nella Larsen." *Journal of the History of Sexuality* 3 (1993): 418–44.

Esteve, Mary. "Nella Larsen's 'Moving Mosaic': Harlem, Crowds, and Anonymity." *American Literary History* 9 (1997): 268–86.

Haviland, Beverly. "Passing from Paranoia to Plagiarism: The Abject Authorship of Nella Larsen." *Modern Fiction Studies* 43 (1997): 295–319.

Hostetler, Ann E. "The Aesthetics of Race and Gender in Nella Larsen's *Quicksand*." *PMLA* 105 (1990): 35–46.

Huggins, Nathan. *Harlem Renaissance*. New York: Oxford University Press, 1971.

Hutchinson, George. "Nella Larsen and the Veil of Race." *American Literary History* 9 (1997): 329–50.

Larsen, Charles R. *Invisible Darkness: Jean Toomer and Nella Larsen*. Iowa City: University of Iowa Press, 1993.

Little, Jonathan. "Nella Larsen's *Passing*: Irony and the Critics." *African American Review* 26 (1992): 173–82.

Madigan, Mark J. "Miscegenation and 'The Dicta of Race and Class': The Rhinelander Case and Nella Larsen's *Passing*." *Modern Fiction Studies* 36 (1990): 523–29.

McDowell, Deborah E. Introduction. *Quicksand and Passing*. By Nella Larsen. Ed. Deborah McDowell. New Brunswick: Rutgers University Press, 1986. ix–xxxv.

McLendon, Jacquelyn Y. *The Politics of Color in the Fiction of Jessie Fauset and Nella Larsen*. Charlottesville: University Press of Virginia, 1995.

Monda, Kimberly. "Self Delusion and Self Sacrifice in Nella Larsen's *Quicksand*." *African American Review* 31 (1997): 23–41.

Ramsey, Priscilla. "Freeze the Day: A Feminist Reading of Nella Larsen's *Quicksand* and *Passing*." *Afro-Americans in New York Life and History* 9 (1985): 27–41.

———. "A Study of Black Identity in 'Passing' Novels of the 19th and Early 20th Century." *Studies in Black Literature* 7 (1976): 1–7.

Sato, Hiroko. "Under the Harlem Shadow: A Study of Jessie Fauset and Nella Larsen." *The Renaissance Remembered*. Ed. Arna Bontemps. New York: Dodd, 1972. 63–89.

Silverman, Debra B. "Nella Larsen's *Quicksand*: Untangling the Webs of Exoticism." *African American Review* 27 (1993): 599–614.

Sullivan, Nell. "Nella Larsen's Passing and the Fading Subject." *African American Review* 32 (1998): 373–86.

Tate, Claudia. "Nella Larsen's *Passing*: A Problem of Interpretation." *Black American Literature Forum* 14 (1980): 142–46.

Thornton, Hortense. "Sexism as Quagmire: Nella Larsen's *Quicksand.*" *CLA Journal* 16 (1973): 285–91.

Wall, Cheryl A. *Women of the Harlem Renaissance.* Bloomington: Indiana University Press, 1995.

Washington, Mary Helen. "Nella Larsen: Mystery Woman of the Harlem Renaissance." *Ms.* Dec. 1980: 44–50.

Williams, Bettye J. "Nella Larsen: Early Twentieth-Century Novelist of Afrocentric Feminist Thought." *CLA Journal* 39 (1995): 165–78.

Youman, Mary. "Nella Larsen's *Passing*: A Study in Irony." *CLA Journal* 18 (1974): 235–41.

MARGERY LATIMER
(1899–1932)

Joy Castro

BIOGRAPHY

Margery Bodine Latimer was born on February 6, 1899, in Portage, Wisconsin, the younger of the two daughters of Clark Watt Latimer, a traveling sales representative, and Laura Augusta Bodine. Genteel but not affluent, the Latimers maintained their middle-class status despite financial strain.

In 1917, Latimer published one of her short stories in the local paper, and it caught the eye of her neighbor Zona Gale, a well-known author, journalist, suffragist, and progressive political activist who would later be the first woman to win the Pulitzer Prize for Drama. Gale invited Latimer to tea and, impressed by such talent in one so young, deemed her "one of the most exquisite centres of intuitive experience imaginable" (Derleth 172). Gale, a longtime friend of Charlotte Perkins Gilman, would become Latimer's mentor and confidante for the next fourteen years.

Latimer entered Wooster College in Ohio in the fall of 1918; lonely and homesick, she returned home after a semester. In the autumn of 1919, she entered the University of Wisconsin at Madison, but her restless intellect made her impatient with the focus on sports and sororities. In 1921, Latimer moved to New York City, where she attended playwriting workshops at Columbia University, volunteered at the Henry Street Settlement House, and held a short-lived position writing fashion copy for the *Woman's Home Companion*. At Columbia, she met Blanche Matthias, the Chicago art critic and poet, with whom she developed a lasting friendship.

Conscious of her protégé's financial situation, Gale instituted the Zona Gale Scholarship at the University of Wisconsin in 1922. Its generous terms were tailor-made for Latimer, who returned to Madison as its first recipient. While there, she served on the editorial board of the university's literary magazine, to which she also contributed several striking early pieces. In 1923, she left college to focus on her writing career.

Returning to New York, Latimer continued to write while supporting herself and the dazzlingly talented leftist poet Kenneth Fearing, whom she had met at Wisconsin. She formed a close friendship with Meridel Le Sueur, the labor activist and feminist writer, who later claimed that Latimer's prose had influenced all her own writing, and eventually befriended Georgia O'Keefee, Walt Kuhn, Lewis Mumford, Carl Van Vechten, Anita Loos, and Carl and Irita Van Doren. Poet Carl Rakosi remembers Latimer's striking physical presence: "She wore no make-up, no high heels, no frills of any kind and only the most plain dresses. Her walk was unselfconscious, very straight and direct, without being masculine. What struck one immediately was her radiant presence. Blake would have described her as a cloud of gold" (qtd. in Loughridge 217).

Throughout the 1920s, Latimer published stories in a variety of journals, from mainstream publications such as *Scribner's, The Century*, and *The Bookman* to avant-garde literary reviews such as *Pagany* and *transition*, the groundbreaking Parisian journal that published Joyce, Stein, and Hemingway. She reviewed fiction for various periodicals, including the *New York Herald* and the *New York World*. Her remarkable short essay on experimental writing, "The New Freedom," which anticipates Virginia Woolf's ideas in *A Room of One's Own*, appeared in *The Reviewer* in 1924. When editor Harrison Smith formed the publishing house of Cape and Smith in 1929 to print experimental works such as Faulkner's *The Sound and the Fury*, he brought Latimer on board, publishing her novel *This Is My Body* in 1930. Smith & Haas, his subsequent publishing partnership, published Latimer's collection *Guardian Angel and Other Stories* in 1932 along with Faulkner's *Light in August*.

After her turbulent relationship with Fearing ended, Latimer was drawn by her interest in the work of Russian mystic Georgei Gurdjieff to author Jean Toomer, then the leader of the American Gurdjieff movement. In October 1931, Latimer and Toomer were married in Portage. Soon, however, they became the objects of a nationwide antimiscegenation scandal: Toomer, who claimed some African ancestry and whose book *Cane* (1923) is regarded as a harbinger of the Harlem Renaissance, was accused of trying to mongrelize America; Latimer, who could trace her Anglo-American heritage back to Puritan poet Anne Bradstreet, was seen as a traitor to white racial purity. Even *Time* magazine depicted the affair as one of racial and sexual transgression. Latimer's parents, who received threats and hate mail, left their Portage home until the scandal abated. Just ten months after her marriage, Latimer died in childbirth after delivering a healthy daughter on August 16, 1932.

MAJOR WORKS AND THEMES

Latimer was modernist to the core. Her work explores the role of art in society with the experimental language and narrative structures of the avant-garde. She interrogates the provincialism of small-town life in her novel *We Are Incredible* (1928), while illuminating the excesses of urban bohemia in such stories as

"City" and "Confession" in her collection *Nellie Bloom and Other Stories* (1929).

Her work also analyzes female experience and the changing roles of women. A critique of traditional sexual relationships informs "Mr. and Mrs. Arnold," which explores an older couple's lack of communication; "Two in Love" examines a young couple too self-conscious to continue their conventionally structured romance. The physical and emotional pleasures and pains of women's sexuality are explored throughout her work, from an overwhelming and transcendent experience of pregnancy in "The Family" (*Nellie Bloom*), to a devastating abortion in the novel *This Is My Body* (1930), to a young girl's awakening sexuality in "The Little Girls" (*Guardian Angel and Other Stories*, 1932). Stories such as "Possession" and "Guardian Angel" delineate the passionate complexities of women's relationships with each other.

Latimer's two major themes, the role of art and the role of women, merge in *This Is My Body* and stories such as "The Family" and "Guardian Angel," which explore the relation of the female artist to sexuality, domesticity, and mysticism. In rebellion against nineteenth-century prohibitive attitudes toward the body and female freedom, Latimer labored to express women's physicality, sensuality, and spirituality, while also insisting on women's intellectual capabilities and anticipating the work of later feminist writers and theorists.

CRITICAL RECEPTION

Although Louis Kampf closes his 1984 essay on Latimer with the assertion that she "richly deserves a place of honor in the history of American modernism" (246), and Daniel McCarthy argues that "a closer look at her is overdue" (475), little critical work has been done on Latimer. Her brief output, early death, and buried reputation have obscured her achievements, which rival those of her modern contemporaries.

Contemporary reviews of Latimer's fiction were extremely positive—Florence Haxton, writing for the *New York Herald Tribune*, for instance, argues that in *Nellie Bloom and Other Stories* Latimer had surpassed both Katherine Mansfield and Sherwood Anderson. Yet analysis reveals that critics rejected precisely those aspects of Latimer's work—its experimentation with language, focus on subjectivity, and disruption of traditional narrative structures—that we have come to see as defining characteristics of modernism. Gertrude Diamant in the *New York World* chides that it is "precisely because Miss Latimer can write with ruthless objectivity that it is wasteful for her to compromise her genuine power with the attempt to be modernistic" (7), and a critic for the *New York Times Book Review* censures *This Is My Body* for being "intensely subjective," arguing that "by [Latimer's] very immersion in the colors and sensations of life, she sacrifices much of the feeling of reality for which the book apparently strives" ("Hungry" 9). Another reviewer objects to the same book on the basis of its disruption of genre: "Miss Latimer's book, it seems to me, is rather to be taken as an autobiographic fragment than as a novel," a critique easily leveled against such modern classics as *A Portrait of the Artist as a Young Man* (Seaver 10). Mainstream reviewers of the period who complain that Latimer is writing "in the manner of James Joyce" or that her characters "go a little Gertrude Stein occasionally and fling fantastic chains of words about," see these resemblances as flaws ("Hungry" 9; Wakefield 10). While Joyce, Stein, and other experimental writers eventually gained admission to the canon, Latimer's work was already out of the public eye by the time this recuperation occurred.

Latimer's decision to focus on the experience of girls and women was another factor that made the critical reception of her work problematic. Latimer's novel *This Is My Body* details the coming of age of a young female writer, and reviewers in the *New York Times Book Review* and elsewhere remarked upon the book's "almost hypnotic sense of power," "standard of serious excellence," and "cultivation of an individual prose style" ("Hungry" 9; Robbins 148; *New Republic* 227). Yet they took the protagonist severely to task. "Miss Latimer's heroine," argues F. L. Robbins in the *Outlook*, "is an hysterical, egocentric girl whose talk is all of the 'realities' of life, but who has not learned the reality of her own insignificance" (148), and the novel is dismissed by the *New Republic* as the "entirely subjective story of a frenzied adolescent" (227). Reviewers felt compelled to praise the work yet derided its insistent focus on a young woman's consciousness.

Latimer's final collection of fiction, *Guardian Angel and Other Stories*, was published posthumously in 1932 to great acclaim. The title story had appeared previously in *Scribner's* as a finalist in its $5,000 story competition alongside Faulkner's "Spotted Horses," and the *New York Herald Tribune*'s reviewer compares Latimer to Katherine Mansfield and D. H. Lawrence, mourning the loss to American letters incurred by her early death. Yet the *Saturday Review* characterizes Latimer's talent as "circumscribed" due to its continued dwelling upon "so slight a theme" as "feminine adolescence: its terrors, its joys, its hesitancies" (179). Critics' preconceived notions of whose stories were important—and whose were not—had a powerful impact on Latimer's reception in the public sphere.

Critics encountering Latimer's work today have called repeatedly for recuperation. Toomer's biographers assert that her "uncharacteristic frankness" gave rise to "a phenomenal career" deserving of critical consideration (Kerman and Eldridge 192), and a recent study of Fearing calls her "immaculate, luminous, mystical, otherworldly," an "exceptionally gifted young writer" (Ryley xii). An appreciation of the unique contributions of this important modern complicates and enhances our understanding of American literary history.

BIBLIOGRAPHY

Works by Margery Latimer

"Three Sketches." *Wisconsin Literary Magazine* 20 (1921): 102–4.
"The Black Pool." *Wisconsin Literary Magazine* 22 (1922): 73–88. (Play)

"Me." *Wisconsin Literary Magazine* 23 (1923): 28.
"On the Planes." *Wisconsin Literary Magazine* 23 (1923): 7, 25.
"The New Freedom." *The Reviewer* 4 (1924): 139–40.
"Picnic Day: A Story." *New Masses* 1 (1926): n.p.
"Grotesque." *transition* 3 (1927): 51–56.
"Nellie Bloom." *Bookman* 66 (1927): 225–33.
"Penance." *The American Caravan*. Ed. Van Wyck Brooks, Lewis Mumford, Alfred
    Kreymborg, and Paul Rosenfeld. New York: Literary Guild of America–Macau-
    lay, 1927. 632–44.
We Are Incredible. New York: Sears, 1928.
"We Are Incredible." *Editor* 81 (1928): 187–89. (Nonfiction)
Nellie Bloom and Other Stories. New York: Sears, 1929.
"The Little Girls." *Pagany* 1 (1930): 66–74.
"Monday Morning." *Pagany* 1 (1930): 82–87.
This Is My Body. New York: Cape and Smith, 1930.
"Guardian Angel." *Scribner's* 89 (1931): 647–62.
Guardian Angel and Other Stories. New York: Smith & Hass, 1932. Old Westbury, NY:
    Feminist Press, 1984.
"Letters to Georgia O'Keeffe." *The New Caravan*. Ed. Alfred Kreymborg, Lewis Mum-
    ford, and Paul Rosenfeld. New York: Norton, 1936. 488–93.

Studies of Margery Latimer

Castro, Joy. " 'Splitting Open the World': Modernism, Feminism, and the Work of Mar-
    gery Latimer." Diss. Texas A & M University, 1997.
Derleth, August. *Still Small Voice: The Biography of Zona Gale*. New York: Appleton,
    1940.
Diamant, Gertrude. Rev. of *Nellie Bloom and Other Stories*, by Margery Latimer. *New
    York World* 16 June 1929: 7.
Gregory, Horace. Rev. of *Guardian Angel*, by Margery Latimer. *New York Herald Trib-
    une Books* 6 Nov. 1932: 2.
Haxton, Florence. "Irradiations in Prose." Rev. of *Nellie Bloom and Other Stories*, by
    Margery Latimer. *New York Herald Tribune Books* 12 May 1929: 3–4.
"Hungry for Life." Rev. of *This Is My Body*, by Margery Latimer. *New York Times Book
    Review* 2 Mar. 1930: 9.
Kampf, Louis. "Afterword: The Work." *Guardian Angel and Other Stories*. Old West-
    bury, NY: Feminist Press, 1984. 236–46.
Kerman, Cynthia Earl, and Richard Eldridge. *The Lives of Jean Toomer: A Hunger for
    Wholeness*. Baton Rouge: Louisiana State University Press, 1987.
Loughridge, Nancy. "Afterword: The Life." *Guardian Angel and Other Stories*. Old
    Westbury, NY: Feminist Press, 1984. 215–29.
McCarthy, Daniel. " 'Just Americans': A Note on Jean Toomer's Marriage to Margery
    Latimer." *CLA Journal* 17 (1974): 474–79.
Robbins, F. L. Rev. of *This Is My Body*, by Margery Latimer. *Outlook and Independent*
    22 Jan. 1930: 148.
Ryley, Robert M. *Kenneth Fearing: Complete Poems*. Orono, ME: National Poetry Foun-
    dation, 1994.

Seaver, Edwin. Rev. of *This Is My Body*, by Margery Latimer. *New York Evening Post*
    12 Apr. 1930: 10.
Rev. of *Guardian Angel*, by Margery Latimer. *Saturday Review of Literature* 15 Oct.
    1932: 179.
Rev. of *This Is My Body*, by Margery Latimer. *New Republic* 62 (1930): 227.
Wakefield, Eleanor. Rev. of *This Is My Body*, by Margery Latimer. *New York World* 23
    Feb. 1930: 10.

AMY LOWELL
(1874–1925)

William J. Scheick

BIOGRAPHY

Born on February 9, 1874, Amy Lowell was the last of the five children of Augustus and Katherine Bigelow Lawrence Lowell, who resided in a mansion on a ten-acre estate (Sevenels) in Brookline, Massachusetts. Raised as an Episcopalian and privately schooled in Boston until the age of seventeen, Lowell learned little of literature during her formal education. She fostered her literary interests by reading in the extensive library at home and at the Boston Athenaeum. Although Lowell dabbled in verse from an early age, it was a chance encounter with Leigh Hunt's *Imagination and Fancy* (1844) in her father's collection that inspired her serious interest in poetry. During this same interval she discovered the poetry of John Keats, whose work would profoundly influence her aesthetics. Lowell's lifelong appreciation of Keats's writings, especially their correlation of beauty and unassuageable human longing, was epitomized in her two-volume study of the poet, published in the last year of her life.

Lowell's career as a poet began with the publication of "Fixed Idea" in the *Atlantic Monthly* (1910). This poem was included in her first adult book, *A Dome of Many-Coloured Glass* (1912). Inspired by several poems by "H. D., Imagiste" in 1913, Lowell journeyed to London to meet Hilda Doolittle and Ezra Pound, both American expatriates. The encounter was energizing for Lowell. Not only was her poem "In a Garden" included in the first imagiste anthology (1914) edited by Pound, but she soon broke with Pound over the practice of Imagism. Even as Pound dismissed her version of the genre as "Amygism," Lowell served as editor of the next three anthologies entitled *Some Imagiste Poets* (1915–1917). In the United States, where Lowell became newsworthy for the light Manila cigars she smoked, she promoted the imagiste movement as the avant-guarde of American literary culture.

Several of Lowell's Imagiste works appear in *Sword Blades and Poppy Seed* (1914), but symbolic narrative in "unrhymed cadence" dominates this volume. *Sword Blades*, which was a financial success, was followed by *Men, Women and Ghosts* (1916), a collection of narrative verse that commences with "Patterns," Lowell's first and still famous poem. It was *Pictures of the Floating World* (1919), however, that primarily featured Lowell's imagiste writings, several first published in periodicals five years earlier. *Pictures* contains many of Lowell's most accomplished poetry.

In 1919, Lowell was the first woman to lecture at Harvard University. Although she was afflicted with several ailments in 1920, Lowell continued to write, lecture, give readings, entertain, and travel, including a journey to Baylor University in Waco, Texas, to receive an honorary Doctor of Literature degree. She saw *Legends* (1921), primarily a collection of symbolic narratives, sell 2,000 copies in three weeks. She was also at work on two ambitious projects: poetic versions of Florence Wheelock Ayscough's word-for-word translations of ancient Chinese verse and a biography of John Keats. Writing to Ayscough, her collaborator, about the mixed reception of their *Fir-Flower Tablets* (1921), Lowell complained of "the rings of intrigue in this poetry business." "The more successful I am, the more I am hated" by unsuccessful poets, Lowell indicated, but "the public is more and more for me" (Damon 604).

Although as yet not a word of the study of Keats had been written, its preparatory stages had been under way for some time. Lowell was also contemplating a biography of Emily Dickinson, whose work she celebrated in "The Sisters" (1922), but nothing ever came of this project. While maintaining a hectic schedule of giving lectures and writing miscellaneous works, Lowell steadily progressed with the Keats project. On the day of its publication (February 10, 1925), *John Keats* was sold out, and its second edition, not yet printed, was also sold out. By February 15, 1925, there was a fourth edition of the two-volume work.

Although she participated in various postpublication celebrations, including a well-attended dinner held in her honor, Lowell was exhausted. Her ceaseless attention to her many projects was not the main culprit, however. Her various health problems, including recurrent hernias, always taxed her stamina throughout her life. Her health was further compromised by occasional attempts at prescribed outlandish diets, such as eating nothing but tomatoes and asparagus during a trip to Egypt in 1898, designed to treat a lifelong weight problem that was apparently the result of an undiagnosed thyroid condition. On May 12, 1925, with Ada Dwyer Russell at her bedside, Lowell died shortly after a stroke. Within the two weeks following her cremation, a rumor spread in England that Lowell, in imitation of Keats, died as a result of the hostile British reaction to her biography.

Lowell had been preparing two manuscripts for publication when she died. Both *What's O'Clock* (1925), with examples of outstanding Imagiste verse, and *East Wind* (1926) were guided through the press by Russell, who also compiled *Ballads for Sale* (1927). *What's O'Clock* was awarded the Pulitzer Prize in 1926 and outsold any other volume of verse by Lowell. Many of Lowell's best poems appear in these volumes, some previously printed but left uncollected since

1919. "Phantasms of War," consisting of eleven poems completed by 1918, remains in manuscript.

MAJOR WORKS AND THEMES

Amy Lowell excelled in three types of writing: criticism, imagiste poetry, and dramatic narratives. Her study of John Keats, an acknowledged accomplishment in its day and still a reliable resource in our time, was the crowning achievement in an intellectual endeavor that included *Six French Poets: Studies in Contemporary Literature* (1915) and *Tendencies in Modern American Poetry* (1917). These collections of critical essays are highly opinionated, such as when Lowell expressly correlates race and art. *Tendencies*, nevertheless, also represents a dramatic moment in the recognition of emergent American voices. Lowell designates Edwin Arlington Robinson and Robert Frost, whose new manner begins the revision of older verse patterns, as representatives of the first stage toward a true American poetry. Edgar Lee Masters and Carl Sandberg, whose work explores provocative subjects, express the second stage. And John Gould Fletcher and H. D. (Hilda Doolittle), whose imagiste verse establishes new attitudes and techniques, are identified by Lowell with the third stage.

Lowell's pronouncements on behalf of imagiste poetry, in lectures and prefaces, were especially significant in her time. For Lowell, the heritage of the imagiste verse included the poetry of William Blake, Samuel Taylor Coleridge, Edgar Allan Poe, and Stéphane Mallarmé and other French symbolists. Lowell's art-for-art's sake theory of imagism emphasized the use of striking image, conciseness of focus, direct speech, subtle rhythms, freedom of subject matter, and exemption from moral. Imagiste verse invokes rather than describes, intimates rather than preaches, so that the reader must actively engage the sensory impressions of the poem in pursuit of its meaning.

Although Lowell's narrative poems were more popular with her contemporary readers, her imagiste poetry comprises her greatest accomplishment. In the best of this verse Lowell offers glimpses into a mystery that fascinated her throughout her life: the human experience of the ambiguous antithetical binaries of existence that apparently emerge when the mind contemplates the nature of existence. This glimpse—a fugitive coalescence of thought and feeling—is the epiphanic outcome of an emphasis on perspective in her poems. In "A Year Passes" (in *Pictures of the Floating World*), for example, perspective is determined by consciousness. Such self-awareness detects contradictory impressions resulting from a gap between an observing mind and what it observes. Art is presented in "A Year Passes" as an unsatisfying human response to the problem of perspective, specifically the tendency of human consciousness to sense an exiling "distance" between itself (here) and nature (there).

The human mind, as represented in Lowell's poetry, is especially stirred by its awareness of the transience of human life. In response to this awareness, as the celebration of stained glass (art) in "Fragment" (in *A Dome of Many-*

Coloured Glass) suggests, the mind transforms ordinary pieces of life into a rainbowlike aesthetics. Art is like the rainbow, at once a beautiful promise of life and a memorial to human mortality. For Lowell, the rainbowlike aesthetics of art is beauty wrought from the pain of consciousness. Her poems, accordingly, convey a sense of human exclusion from any apparent intimations of eternal beauty. Although the mind is attracted to the beautiful regenerative cycles of nature, it cannot take romantic comfort from them and, instead, becomes keenly aware of its own eventual extinction as a conscious (observing) faculty. The mind is drawn to nature yet peculiarly feels alienated from it, *as if* it were exiled from nature's indifferent beauty.

The first verse of Lowell's "Twenty-Four Hokku on a Modern Theme" (in *What's O'Clock*, 1925), an imagiste jewel, reveals the mind's paradoxical attraction to and alienation from nature. At first, the narrator in this poem, like the spectator in "A Year Passes," seems uplifted in a romantic way. In the hokku the speaker appears to be thrilled by the reappearance of a stately perennial flower. The larkspur's "heavenly blue" refers not only to its remarkable skylike color but also to its *apparent* transcendental beauty, which (like the very perenniality of the plant) gives an impression of another order of being other than the mere mortal one of the observer in the verse.

The last line of the hokku, like of the ending of "A Year Passes," takes an unexpected turn, as the reader's attention shifts from the romantic scene (nature) to the observer (mind). The observer now seems afflicted, rather than uplifted, as she dejectedly intuits a contrast between human temporality and natural duration. The "at least" suggests a consolation *halfheartedly* received by the narrator. The observer's mind in the hokku simultaneously registers an attraction toward and an alienation from beautiful nature. And this ambivalence of consciousness at the end of the poem in turn potentially vexes the reader's memory of the opening word of the verse. Upon rereading, the word "again" is now uncertainly nuanced, leaving the reader (like the narrator) divided between two options. "Again" can express joy or exasperation depending on the emphasis, the intonation, placed on the word by the speaker or the reader, now mutual observers indeed.

"The Fisherman's Wife" (in *Pictures of the Floating World*) also highlights this strange amalgam of loss and gain. The husband is away at sea, and the wife is alone on the land. But her deprivation fosters an unusual sensitivity in her as she detects a kinship between the wind and the waves, and between the trees on the shore and the wood of the husband's boat. This sensibility of relation is paradoxically based on separation (division) and distance. In absence she discovers a heightened sense of presence. Does the fisherman's wife feel this intensely about her husband when they are physically close, or does absence always make her heart grow fonder? The poem is about a painful consciousness, dependent on painful absence (loss by separation or death), that *enables* the perception of beautiful closeness (presence).

Another version of this theme occurs in "A Lady to Her Lover" (in *Pictures of the Floating World*). Here the observer contemplates the mortality of affection. The speaker anticipates the winterlike death of springlike love, now that the autumnal stage has become evident to her. (The falling leaves likely allude to the sexual divestiture of clothing or, less specifically, the abandonment of decorum for intimacy.) The narrator prizes the relationship precisely from this perspective of inevitable privation. She commissions the memoriallike artification of the beloved while the relationship is still extant. Afflicted by a consciousness of time and by an awareness of being outside nature's recuperative features, the narrator has felt exiled from the Edenic relationship even at its springlike onset. On the other hand, the narrator's sense of inevitable temporal alienation from the beloved accounts for her keen awareness and appreciation of the beauty of their relationship. The extent to which her sensibility has been cut in two is registered in the word "therefore," which is as ambiguous in tone as is the opening word "again" in the hokku.

So, well before the "winter" stage of their relationship, the narrator arranges for an "at least" compensation, the memorializing of their affection in art. The "snow-white jade" of the artwork in this poem expresses humanity's consciousness-driven, forlorn desire to suspend and idealize time by freezing quotidian change into some permanent perfect form. But this "frozen" ideal form of the "snow-white jade" also inherently displays the ambiguous binaries it is designed to counter: It is at once reflective of and divergent from the beautiful source of its inspiration even as the painful consciousness of its owner is simultaneously attracted to and disaffected from its natural subject (her lover). The word "cut" in both "A Lady to Her Lover" and "A Year Passes" suggests the pain (loss) associated with the perception of beauty (gain) expressed in art. Art, for Lowell, necessarily depends on the afflictive ("at least") beauty that the mind is enabled to perceive and value as a result of its awareness of the passage of time. Since art derives in response to the "cutting" (hurtful and artistic) perspective of estrangement, it is always bound by and intrinsically reflects the inexplicable division between the mind's being "here" and at the same time longing for some inaccessible "there" beyond the mind.

This ambiguous binary of mutually reinforcing oppositions, including the human mind's simultaneous attraction to and feeling of exclusion from natural beauty, is also often the subject of Lowell's narrative verse. "Off the Turnpike" (in *Men, Women and Ghosts* and recently reprinted in *Alfred Hitchcock Mystery Magazine* [January 1997]) is a dramatic monologue in which a widow explains why she is leaving town. Six months after the death of her husband, she uncovered a severed hand beneath her beautiful lilac bushes. She hastily reburied the hand, but over time she never escaped its impact on her mind. Much later she looked again for the hand, but no amount of digging located it. She obsessively searched for it until, worried over being committed to an asylum, she sold the farm and is now leaving town. Like many of Lowell's other narrative poems, "Off the Turnpike" is a symbolic tale. It concerns the mind's compromised, ambivalent appreciation of beauty (nature) that results from the mind's consciousness of human mortality.

The female speaker in "Patterns" (in *Men, Women and Ghosts*) protests the mental constructions of society that prevent her from being as free as the flowers she observes. She imagines an Edenic garden where she would join her lover. But he has been slain in a war, and his death, representing human mortality in general, has at once sensitized her to and separated her from the splendor of existence (nature). Before his death she was not able to appreciate natural beauty with an intensity equal to her present perception; but this newfound appreciation is of a bitter sort because natural beauty, while heightened by her loss, seems remote and "other" to her divided consciousness. The narrator of "Patterns" is afflicted by a beauty that seems to exclude her even while, paradoxically, it seems to imprison her.

Lowell's dramatic monologues capture the rhythms of speech in a way that suits her goal of dissolving the boundaries between verse and prose. Iambic pentameter, the standard English meter, struck Lowell as too heavy for her experiments in polyphonic ("many-voiced") writing. She preferred "the long, flowing cadence of oratorical prose" managed like rhythms and motifs in a symphonic composition. Such an approach abetted Lowell's claim that her poems were designed to be read aloud.

CRITICAL RECEPTION

A Dome of Many-Coloured Glass, Lowell's first adult book, sold very poorly in its initial edition. Although *Sword Blades and Poppy Seed* received a mixed critical response, it was widely reviewed and generally applauded. This launching of Lowell's career as a poet was reinforced by the three editions of *Men, Women and Ghosts*. There is "nothing [else] exactly like the art" in *Men, Women and Ghosts*, reported a reviewer in the *Boston Evening Transcript* (B., 9). In his *Boston Evening Transcript* commentary on *Pictures of the Floating World*, which also saw three editions, John Livingston Lowes observed that the 173 poems in this volume "enhance our sense of the fresh and vivid beauty of a thousand familiar things" (11). *Legends* also sold very well. It is, according to William Rose Benét, a "weirdly beautiful work that could never . . . be mistaken for the work of anyone else" (176). *John Keats*, however, marketed better than any other Lowell book produced during her lifetime. The sales of the posthumous *What's O'Clock*, which was awarded the Pulitzer Prize, surpassed any other volume of Lowell's verse. During her lifetime, Lowell's work generally tended to be reviewed more favorably in America than in England, and this bias was especially true concerning her biography of Keats.

The number of Lowell's poems included in anthologies of American literature has declined during the last fifty years. "Patterns" (1915), at once controversial and popular in its day, is currently the most often reprinted of Lowell's verse.

This dramatic monologue received close analytical attention during the 1930s in S. Foster Damon's *Amy Lowell* (1935) and Cleanth Brooks, Jr., and Robert Penn Warren's *Understanding Poetry* (1938). Such regard for savoring the intricacies of Lowell's vers libre, combined with explicit praise for her technical achievement in John Livingston Lowes's *Essays in Appreciation* (1936) and John Gould Fletcher's *Life Is My Song* (1937), encountered head winds of opposition from other critics who claimed that Lowell was more memorable for her energy than for her poetry.

The opposition voices prevailed, and Lowell's verse never received the New Critical explication urged by Brooks and Warren. Instead, her life and times became the texts of choice for Lowell scholars for the next forty years. These biographical studies featured Lowell's flamboyant personal characteristics and her interactions with other writers of her day. These works were often ambivalent about their biographical subject, and some inclined toward disparagement, as is evident in Clement Wood's hostile *Amy Lowell* (1926) and Horace Gregory's dismissive *Amy Lowell* (1958). Gregory concluded that Lowell's verse amounted to "a lifeless monument to ten years of industry." Overlooked by such critics is the likelihood that Lowell's recurrent theme of the human mind's simultaneous attraction to and feeling of exclusion from natural beauty amounts to a confession of deep personal feeling that empowered her to produce scintillating Imagiste verse, lost treasure awaiting discovery.

At the end of the 1970s and during the 1980s Lowell's poetry received better attention, notably in Glenn Richard Ruihley's *The Thorn of a Rose* (1975), which focuses on Lowell's search of transcendence. Especially noteworthy is Richard Benvenuto's *Amy Lowell* (1985), a meticulous review and thoughtful reconsideration of the poet's writings. Benvenuto pertinently concludes "that so few of her good poems are generally known at all is almost certainly due to the fact that too many of her readers have been content to make generalizations about her poetry instead of engaging it critically." Nevertheless, the life-and-times approach to Lowell's career continues—but with a difference. Commencing with Jean Gould's *Amy* (1975), several critics have focused on Lowell's transgression of the gender boundaries of her day. They emphasize her masculine mannerisms, her love poetry addressed to other women, her erotic female imagery, and particularly her eleven-year shared-home relationship with Ada Dwyer Russell as evidence of Lowell's lesbian sensibility.

BIBLIOGRAPHY

Works by Amy Lowell

Amy Lowell and Katherine Bigelow Lawrence Lowell. *Dream Drops, or Stories from Fairy Land, by a Dreamer.* Boston: Cupples, 1887. (Children's short stories)

A Dome of Many-Coloured Glass. Boston: Houghton, 1912. (Verse)

Sword Blades and Poppy Seed. New York: Macmillan, 1914. (Verse)
Six French Poets: Studies in Contemporary Literature. New York: Macmillan, 1915.
    (Criticism)
Some Imagiste Poets. 3 vols. Boston: Houghton, 1915–1917. (Anthologies)
Men, Women and Ghosts. New York: Macmillan, 1916. (Verse)
Tendencies in Modern American Poetry. New York: Macmillan, 1917. (Criticism)
A Miscellany of American Poetry. 2 vols. New York: Harcourt, 1917–1918. (Anthologies)
Can Grande's Castle. New York: Macmillan, 1918. (Verse)
Pictures of the Floating World. New York: Macmillan, 1919. (Verse)
Legends. Boston: Houghton, 1921. (Verse)
Amy Lowell and Florence Ayscough. *Fir-Flower Tablets.* Boston: Houghton, 1921.
    (Verse translations)
A Critical Fable. New York: Houghton, 1922. (Verse)
John Keats. 2 vols. Boston: Houghton, 1925. (Criticism)
What's O'Clock. Ed. Ada Dwyer Russell. Boston: Houghton, 1925. (Verse)
East Wind. Ed. Ada Dwyer Russell. Boston: Houghton, 1926. (Verse)
Ballads for Sale. Ed. Ada Dwyer Russell. Boston: Houghton, 1927. (Verse)
The Madonna of Carthagena. N.p.: Privately printed, 1927. (Verse)
Selected Poems of Amy Lowell. Ed. John Livingston Lowes. Boston: Houghton, 1928.
    (Verse)
Poetry and Poets: Essays. Ed. Ferris Greenslet. Boston: Houghton, 1930. (Criticism)
The Complete Poetical Works of Amy Lowell. Boston: Houghton, 1955. (Verse)

Studies of Amy Lowell

B., W. S. Rev. of *Men, Women and Ghosts*, by Amy Lowell. *Boston Evening Transcript*
    21 Oct. 1916: 9.
Benét, William Rose. "Amy Lowell and Other Poets." *Yale Review* 11 (1921): 175–80.
Benvenuto, Richard. *Amy Lowell.* Boston: Twayne, 1985.
Brown, Tom. "The 'Little Controversy' over *Magenta*: Amy Lowell and the South Car-
    olinians." *English Language Notes* 22 (1984): 62–88.
Bryher, Winifred. *Amy Lowell: A Critical Appreciation.* London: Eyre, 1918.
Damon, S. Foster. *Amy Lowell: A Chronicle.* Boston: Houghton, 1935.
Flint, F. Cudworth. *Amy Lowell.* Minneapolis: University of Minnesota Press, 1969.
Francis, Lesley Lee. "A Decade of 'Stirring Times': Robert Frost and Amy Lowell."
    New England Quarterly 59 (1986): 508–22.
Gage, John T. *In the Arresting Eye: The Rhetoric of Imagism.* Baton Rouge: Louisiana
    State University Press, 1981.
Gould, Jean. *Amy: The World of Amy Lowell and the Imagist Movement.* New York:
    Dodd, 1975.
Gregory, Horace. *Amy Lowell: Portrait of the Poet in Her Time.* New York: Nelson,
    1958.
Lauter, Paul. "Amy Lowell and Cultural Borders." *Speaking the Other Self: American
    Women Writers.* Ed. Jeanne Campbell Reesman. Athens: University of Georgia
    Press, 1997. 288–96.
Lowes, John Livingston. Review of *Pictures of the Floating World*, by Amy Lowell.
    Boston Evening Transcript 4 Oct. 1919: 11.

Ruihley, Glenn Richard. *The Thorn of a Rose: Amy Lowell Reconsidered.* Hamden, CT:
     Archon, 1975.
Scheick, William J. "Art of Estrangement: Four Imagiste Poems by Amy Lowell." *Journal of Imagism* 3 (1998): 29–40.
Wood, Clement. *Amy Lowell.* New York: Vinal, 1926.

MINA LOY
(1882–1966)

Rhonda Pettit

BIOGRAPHY

Although she died as an American citizen, Mina Loy entered the world in London, England, on December 27, 1882, as Mina Gertrude Lowy. Early portraits show her dressed in Victorian garb. By 1917, she would be the *New York Evening Sun*'s prototype of the "modern woman."

Loy's mother, Julia Bryan, a British Protestant steeped in Victorian values, believed her daughter's primary goal in life should be to marry well. Her father, a Hungarian Jewish tailor named Sigmund Lowy whose artistic sensibilities were subsumed by the desire for financial and social success, appreciated Loy's early talents but often conceded to Julia's religious and domestic tyranny. Loy and her two sisters, Dora born in 1884, and Hilda born in 1890, were raised by a series of nurses who held their jobs until Julia judged them to be too lenient. Loy's Victorian childhood was thus characterized by ongoing conflicts: between parents, between mother and daughter, and within Loy as she turned to a world of imagination and art. These unresolved conflicts would translate into bouts of depression and self-doubt throughout Loy's life.

When Loy was old enough, Sigmund sent her to a progressive school in Hampstead. Conflicts with her mother, now over the content of her paintings, intensified. Yet following graduation, Loy convinced her parents to send her to art school in London, where she came under the influence of pre-Raphaelite and decadent painters. Later she attended another art school in Munich, where she experienced, for the first time, independence and the avant-garde. Sitting in a London parlor until the proper husband came along would be impossible now. Chaperoned by a friend of the family, Loy attended an art academy in Paris in 1903.

By New Year's Eve, 1903, Loy was married to British-born artist Stephen Haweis and four months pregnant with Oda Janet, who would die shortly after her first birthday. Loy's first marriage was an unhappy one, marked by infidelities and held together by income provided by Loy's father. (She changed her name to Loy during this period.) Her second child, Joella, was fathered by Loy's lover in 1907 but adopted by Stephen. By then they had moved to Florence, Italy, and two years later she and Stephen had a son, Giles.

During her Florence years, Loy was exposed to ideas and people that were defining the modern struggle against Victorian convention. She read Freud and Bergson and befriended Isadora Duncan, Gertrude Stein, and Mabel Dodge. Two purveyors of futurism, F. T. Marinetti and Giovanni Papini, became her lovers. Although she objected to the misogyny it embodied, futurism's focus on artistic experimentation energized Loy. She continued to paint between episodes of depression, exhibiting in London and Paris, but would eventually turn to experimental forms of poetry and prose as her primary mode of self-expression. Both Mabel Dodge and Carl Van Vechten placed Loy's poems in American magazines such as *Camera Work* and *Others*, generating for her a reputation as a free verse poet and a futurist. But by 1916, Florence and futurism had lost its hold on Loy. With Europe embroiled in war, Stephen pursuing a new life overseas, and the children in the care of servants, Loy left for New York.

The avant-garde of New York City welcomed Loy; she was beautiful, multilingual, and a touchstone for futurist and other European avant-garde thinking. She developed friendships with painter Marcel Duchamp, with photographer Man Ray, and with William Carlos Williams, Djuna Barnes, and other writers associated with the Provincetown Players. She wrote, performed, and created a number of lampshade designs that were very popular. Eventually she secured a divorce from Stephen and met the love of her life—Arthur Cravan, a boxer, poet, and relative of Oscar Wilde. As part of Cravan's scheme to avoid military service, they moved to Mexico in 1917, where they married and conceived a child, Fabienne. Cravan disappeared at sea shortly before they were to leave for South America; it is unknown what happened to him. Loy never recovered from the loss.

From 1918 to 1923, Loy lived briefly in South America, New York, Florence, and Berlin before settling herself and her two daughters within the expatriate community in Paris. (Giles, with whom she refused contact because he was with his father, would die during this period from a rare form of cancer.) Here she became a regular at Sylvia Beach's Shakespeare & Co. bookshop without losing the friendship of Gertrude Stein, who was jealous of Beach's support for James Joyce. She befriended the women in Natalie Barnes's lesbian salon, although she remained heterosexual; Djuna Barnes captures her as Patience Scalpel in *Ladies Almanack*, her affectionate satire on Barnes's salon. Loy's first book of poems, *Lunar Baedecker* (*sic*), was published by Robert McAlmon's Contact Press. With financial backing from Peggy Guggenheim, she managed a shop that featured some of her designs and continued to write. But as Hitler threatened Europe, most of the expatriate community began to dissolve. Her daughter Joella, married to art enthusiast Julian Levy, had already left for New York City. Loy and Fabienne would join her in 1937, eking out an existence in the Bowery section until after the war. Perceiving herself as an outsider, Loy identified with the bums she saw in the street and used garbage—paper cups, tin cans, egg shells, rags, metal scraps, wire, and string—to create a series of montages about their lives; she also wrote poems about them. She became an American citizen in 1946.

Fabienne married, divorced, and remarried, as had Joella; both sisters and their second husbands moved to Aspen, Colorado, after the war. Loy eventually followed them in 1953. She continued to work on montages but no longer wrote poetry. In 1958, Jonathan Williams published an expanded collection of her poems, *Lunar Baedeker & Time-Tables*; and in 1959, an exhibit of her Bowery montages appeared in the Bodley Gallery, New York. She died on September 29, 1966, in Aspen, Colorado, of pneumonia.

MAJOR WORKS AND THEMES

Loy began her creative life as a visual artist, but her reputation as a modernist rests on her poetry and manifestos. Her work is interwoven with strands of autobiography, modern aesthetic, and feminist critique. Loy writes in free verse, using short lines, spaces within the lines, indentations, dashes, alliteration, plosives, slant rhyme at the end and within lines, polysyllabic diction, scientific terminology, satire, irony, apostrophe, anagrams, and abstraction. Her images, ranging from the starkly modern to the fin de siècle decadent, use Dickensian compression, yet her lines move slowly. The overall effect is a sharply chiseled, long and narrow poem that resists simplistic reading. As with the writing of Gertrude Stein and James Joyce, we cannot analyze the subject matter of Loy's poems without first immersing ourselves in the language that constructs it.

Loy playfully masks identities in her most overtly autobiographical poems. "The Effectual Marriage" features Gina and Miovanni, a transposition of the first letters of Mina and Giovanni Papini, one of her futurist lovers. The transposition serves a comic effect as well, for the poem describes the self-centered, me-first behavior of Miovanni. In other poems, Loy resists naming; "Partuition" describes the birth of Oda Janet, and "Sketch of a Man on a Platform" concerns F. T. Marinetti. Loy's sexually explicit "Songs to Joannes" (also published, in a shorter version, in 1923 as "Love Songs") offers a composite of her lovers with perhaps Papini foremost in mind. Her longest and most complex autobiographical poem, "Anglo-Mongrels and the Rose," is a modern sequence chronicling the life and identity of a female artist.

Loy's feminism arises in part from her experience with her Futurist lovers and life in Florence. Although she had no interest in reform feminism, insisting in "Feminist Manifesto" that it was "inadequate," she offered satiric commentary on marriage and romance. House imagery, typically used to mock the expectations associated with domesticity, recurs in many of these poems. Deceit, rather than love, is to be found in "At the Door of the House." Sexual desire without fulfillment occurs in "Virgin Plus Curtains Minus Dots," a satire on the dowry ("dots") system of marriage. Loy also de-romanticizes romance while at

the same time mourning a lack of true feeling. Incorporating the machine imagery of futurist aesthetics, "Human Cylinders" pictures love as void of any
human or spiritual significance.

In her sequence "Three Moments in Paris," Loy examines love within a frame
of colliding literary and social values: Victorian masculine prerogative and feminine passivity in a decadent setting of modern free love. The first "moment,"
"One O'Clock at Night," is influenced by Futurist concepts the speaker claims
she doesn't understand. This type of irony permeates the entire sequence and
much of Loy's poetry overall. Lovers meet in a café characterized by decay in
"Café du Neant," while female virgins remain as blind and cheap as the museum
dolls in "Magasins du Louvre." The poems in Loy's "Three Moments in Paris"
sequence are indeed captured moments of observation; their detailed, relative
brevity reveals the complexity of human interaction. Whether granted, forced,
or bought, love is the object Loy's poetic subjects desire but fail to comprehend
or achieve on any substantive level. And like their subject matter, the form of
Loy's poem sequence (and of most of her poems) is difficult to embrace due to
its prickly verbal play. Her poems rise like cacti in the desert of modern romance.

Although Loy is particularly adept at writing the unlovable love poem, her
thematic range includes other topics. Some of her poems not only use other
modern artists as their subject; they articulate the modern aesthetic she and
others were shaping. "Lunar Baedeker," the title poem to her only book (which
has been revised, expanded, and reprinted three times so far), satirically guides
us through fin de siècle decadence. The collection of poems by this title takes
us into a more modern landscape. In "Brancusi's Golden Bird," Loy describes
the famous sculpture in abstract terms that suggest and implicity defend the
methods of abstract art. The form used in "Gertrude Stein"—one of Loy's short-
est, most condensed poems—parallels Stein's efforts to distill essential meanings
from language. This poem is usefully read beside Loy's essay "Gertrude Stein,"
originally published in *Transatlantic Review* in 1924. Other poems that portray
avant-garde artists and art include "Joyce's Ulysses," " 'The Starry Sky' of
Wyndam Lewis," "Nancy Cunard," and "Jules Pascin." Loy offers a bold assertion of the modern artist as genius in "Apology of Genius." Using the form
of the manifesto, Loy celebrates futurism in "Aphorisms on Futurism" and implicitly critiques its misogyny in "Feminist Manifesto."

When Loy returned to New York City prior to World War II, she wrote poems
influenced by aging, the war, and the Bowery neighborhood in which she lived.
Of these, one of the most striking is "Hot Cross Bum," a poem infusing the
hellish life of street bums with dignity and beauty without resorting to sentimentality. Remarkably, the poems written during this period remain consistent
in form and technique with her earlier work. Loy was not a poet who went
through phases of technical development. She authenticated her unique poetic
voice through its repetition over the course of a lifetime.

CRITICAL RECEPTION

Loy's literary reputation can be likened to that of many women writers from the first half of the twentieth century. She was initially successful, subsequently forgotten, and is currently being restored to her place in the canon. Her restoration thus far falls into two distinct phases: an initial effort that lost momentum and a second wave that is still rising.

Editors took an interest in Loy's poems prior to U.S. involvement in World War I. Although Amy Lowell detested the sexual explicitness in Loy's "Love Songs," Alfred Kreymborg, editor of *Others*, admired her work even though he found it difficult to understand. During the 1920s, her poetry was praised and compared with that of Marianne Moore by T. S. Eliot in *The Egoist*, Ezra Pound in *The Little Review*, and William Carlos Williams in *Kora in Hell*. Eliot preferred Moore's work, whereas Pound and Williams gave Loy the edge. Yvor Winters also admired her work, comparing it to the poems of Emily Dickinson. Edwin Muir applauded the mystical nature of Loy's poetry in a review of *Lunar Baedecker* (*sic*) published in *The New Age*, while Harriet Monroe rejected that element in her review, published in *Poetry*. Loy's poetry helped fuel the debate among editors and poets concerning the appropriate form and content of modern verse.

By midcentury, with *Lunar Baedecker* (*sic*) long out of print and Loy all but forgotten, a small cadre of poets and publishers—Kenneth Rexroth, Jonathan Williams, and James Laughlin—began the arduous process of promoting her work. Jonathan Williams edited and published a second edition of her book, titled *Lunar Baedeker & Time-Tables*, in 1958; no one but Rexroth would review it. Nevertheless, she became an important influence on the Black Mountain School of poets—in particular, Paul Blackburn, Robert Creeley, and Denise Levertov—and was admired by writers as diverse as Louis Zukofsky, Henry Miller, and Thomas Merton.

The second wave of Loy's regeneration has coincided to some extent with the second wave of feminism. Her role as a shaper of modernism emerged when feminist scholars began to challenge and reconstruct the male-dominated canon established largely by the New Critics. Virginia M. Kouidis published the first in-depth, book-length study of Loy's work in 1980. Through its careful analysis of Loy's poems and manifestos, *Mina Loy: American Modernist Poet* demonstrates how Loy's work belongs in the modern canon and serves as an important precursor, along with Gertrude Stein and James Joyce, to postmodern writing. Yet she maintains that Loy lacked the discipline to move her poetry beyond its initial experimentation. Kouidis also establishes Loy as an American, rather than a British, poet, in part because her language and forms represent a rejection of British tradition.

Limited editions of some of Loy's poems began to appear in the 1980s, as well as a third edition of her book, this one titled *The Last Lunar Baedeker*, edited by Roger L. Conover in 1982. This time the book was reviewed by modern scholar Hugh Kenner in the *New York Times Book Review*, who applauded her desire "to be the Brancusi of poetry." Meanwhile, feminist scholars such as Shari Benstock and Carolyn Burke were examining Loy's work in the context of other modern women writers. Burke's interest would culminate in a valuable biography, *Becoming Modern: The Life of Mina Loy*; its publication in 1996 coincided with a fourth edition of Loy's book, also edited by Roger Conover, *The Lost Lunar Baedeker*. The latter editions of *Lunar Baedeker* by Conover contain helpful introductions and detailed notes to the poems, laying much of the groundwork for future scholarship.

Although Helen Vendler has questioned Loy's importance, scholars continue to examine her poetry and prose. In the late 1980s and early 1990s, scholars such as Burke, Rachel Blau DuPlessis, and Elizabeth Arnold began to discuss the nature of Loy's debt to futurism and her role in developing an experimental poetics, suggesting a critical move beyond simple recovery. Another example of this kind of scholarship can be found in Sascha Feinstein's book *Jazz Poetry from the 1920s to the Present*, in which he discusses "Crab Angel," "Lady Laura in Bohemia," "Mexican Desert," and "The Widow's Jazz." Feinstein places these poems in a tradition of jazz-influenced poetry not only because they refer to jazz but because their abstraction and jagged meter simulate the sounds of jazz. Loy's use of Christianity and Freudianism, as well as her appropriation of fin de siècle decadent imagery, has been discussed by Keith Tuma and Marisa Januzzi, respectively. "Anglo-Mongrels and the Rose," thought by Burke and others to be an important modern epic comparable to Eliot's "The Waste Land," has received thoughtful scrutiny by Marjorie Perloff. Some of these articles appear in the first collection of critical essays devoted to Loy's work, *Mina Loy: Essays on the Poetry*, edited by Keith Tuma and Maeera Schreiber in 1998. Discussions of Loy's work and life also can be found on the Internet through the Web sites of the Academy of American Poets and an online literary magazine, *Jacket*, edited by Australian poet John Tranter.

Loy wrote a number of autobiographical narratives that were never published. Elizabeth Arnold edited and published one of these, *Insel*, in 1991. More may be forthcoming, promising to further expand Loy scholarship.

BIBLIOGRAPHY

Works by Mina Loy

Lunar Baedecker. Paris: Contact, 1923.
Lunar Baedeker & Time-Tables. Highlands, NC: Williams, 1958.
At the Door of the House. North Hampton, MA: Aphra, 1980.
Love Songs. North Hampton, MA: Aphra, 1981.
Virgins Plus Curtains. Rochester, NY: Good Mountain, 1981.
The Last Lunar Baedeker. Ed. Roger L. Conover. Highlands, NC: Jargon Society, 1982.

Insel. Ed. Elizabeth Arnold. Santa Rosa, CA: Black Sparrow, 1991.
The Lost Lunar Baedeker. Ed. Roger L. Conover. New York: Noonday, 1996.

Studies of Mina Loy

Arnold, Elizabeth. Afterword. *Insel.* By Mina Loy. Ed. Elizabeth Arnold. Santa Rosa,
    CA: Black Sparrow, 1991. 179–87.
———. "Mina Loy and the Futurists." *Sagetrieb* 8 (1989): 83–117.
Augustine, Jane. "Mina Loy: A Feminist Modernist Americanizes the Languages of Fu-
    turism." *Mid-Hudson Language Studies* 12 (1989): 89–101.
Benstock, Shari. *Women of the Left Bank: Paris, 1900–1940.* Austin: University of Texas
    Press, 1986.
Burke, Carolyn. "Accidental Aloofness: Barnes, Loy and Modernism." *Silence and
    Power: A Re-Evaluation of Djuna Barnes.* Ed. Mary Lynn Broe. Carbondale:
    Southern Illinois University Press, 1991. 67–79.
———. *Becoming Modern: The Life of Mina Loy.* New York: Farrar, 1996.
———. "Getting Spliced: Modernism and Sexual Difference." *American Quarterly* 39
    (1987): 98–121.
———. "Mina Loy." *The Gender of Modernism.* Ed. Bonnie Kime Scott. Bloomington:
    Indiana University Press, 1990. 230–37.
———. "The New Poetry and the New Woman: Mina Loy." *Coming to Light: American
    Women Poets in the Twentieth Century.* Ed. Diane Wood Middlebrook and Mar-
    ilyn Yalom. Ann Arbor: University of Michigan Press, 1985. 37–57.
———. "Without Commas: Gertrude Stein and Mina Loy." *Poetics Journal* 4 (1984):
    43–52.
Conover, Roger L. Introduction. *The Last Lunar Baedeker.* By Mina Loy. Highlands,
    NC: Jargon Society, 1982. xv–lxi.
———. Introduction. *The Lost Lunar Baedeker.* By Mina Loy. New York: Farrar, 1996.
DuPlessis, Rachel Blau. " 'Seismic Orgasm': Sexual Intercourse, Gender Narratives, and
    Lyric Ideology in Mina Loy." *Studies in Historical Change.* Ed. Ralph Cohen.
    Charlottesville: University of Virginia Press, 1992. 264–91.
Eliot, T. S. [T. S. Apteryx]. Rev. of *Lunar Baedecker* [*sic*], by Mina Loy. *The Egoist* 5
    (1918): 70.
Feinstein, Sascha. *Jazz Poetry: From the 1920s to the Present.* Westport, CT: Praeger,
    1997.
Januzzi, Marisa. "Mongrel Rose: The 'Unerring Esperanto' of Loy's Poetry." *Mina Loy:
    Essays on the Poetry.* Ed. Keith Tuma and Maeera Schreiber. Orono, ME: Na-
    tional Poetry Foundation, 1998.
Kenner, Hugh. "To Be the Brancusi of Poetry." Rev. of *The Last Lunar Baedeker*, ed.
    Roger L. Conover. *New York Times Book Review* 16 May 1982: 7, 30.
Kinnehan, Linda A. *Poetics of the Feminine: Authority and Literary Tradition in William
    Carlos Williams, Mina Loy, Denise Levertov, and Kathleen Fraser.* Cambridge:
    Cambridge University Press, 1994.
Kouidis, Virginia M. *Mina Loy: American Modernist Poet.* Baton Rouge: Louisiana State
    University Press, 1980.
Kreymborg, Alfred. *Our Singing Strength: An Outline of American Poetry, 1620–1930.*
    New York: Coward, 1929. 488–89.

Monroe, Harriet. "Guide to the Moon." *Poetry: A Magazine of Verse* October-March
    1923–1924: 100–03.
Morse, Samuel French. "The Rediscovery of Mina Loy and the Avant Garde." *Winscon-
    sin Studies in Contemporary Literature* 2 (1961): 12–19.
Muir, Edwin, "Recent Verse." *New Age* 6 March 1924: 223.
Perloff, Marjorie. "English as a Second Language: Mina Loy's 'Anglo-Mongrels and the
    Rose.' " *Mina Loy: Essays on the Poetry*. Ed. Keith Tuma and Maeera Schreiber.
    Orono, ME: National Poetry Foundation, 1998.
———. "The Mina Loy Mysteries: Legend and Language." Rev. of *Becoming Modern:
    A Life of Mina Loy*, by Carolyn Burke, and *The Lost Lunar Baedeker*, ed. Roger
    L. Conover. *American Book Review* 18.1 (1996): 16–17, 26.
Pettit, Rhonda. " 'Three Moments in Paris.' " *Masterplots II: Poetry—Supplement*. Ed.
    John Wilson and Philip K. Jason. Pasadena, CA: Salem, 1998. 3576–79.
Pound, Ezra. "Marianne Moore and Mina Loy." *Selected Prose 1909–1965*. New York:
    New Directions, 1973. 424–25.
———. "Others." *Little Review* March 1918: 56–58.
Rexroth, Kenneth. "Les Lauriers Sont Coupes." *Circle* 1 (1944): 69–72.
Tranter, John, ed. "Mina Loy Feature." *Jacket* 5 (Oct. 1998). Online. Internet. Available:
    http//www.jacket.zip.com.au/jacket05/index05.html
Tuma, Keith. " 'Anglo-Mongrels and the Rose.' " *Sagetrieb* 11 (1992): 207–8.
———. "Loy at Last." Rev. of *The Lost Lunar Baedeker*, by Mina Loy. Ed. Roger L.
    Conover. *Jacket* 5 (Oct. 1998). Online. Internet. Available: http//www.jacket.
    zip.com.au/jacket05/index05.html
Tuma, Keith, and Maeera Schreiber. *Mina Loy: Essays on the Poetry*. Orono, ME: Na-
    tional Poetry Foundation, 1998.
Vendler, Helen. "The Truth Teller." Rev. of *Becoming Modern*, by Carolyn Burke, and
    The Lost Lunar Baedeker, ed. Roger L. Conover. *New York Review of Books* 19
    Sept. 1996: 60.
Weiss, Andrea. *Paris Was a Woman: Portraits from the Left Bank*. San Francisco:
    Harper-Collins, 1995.
Williams, William Carlos. *Prologue to Kora in Hell: Improvisations*. Boston: Four Sea-
    sons, 1920.
Winters, Ivor. "Mina Loy." *Dial* 80 (1926): 496–99.

CLARE BOOTHE LUCE
(1903–1987)

Laura Shea

BIOGRAPHY

Clare Boothe Luce was born in New York City on March 10, 1903, the daughter of Anna Clare Snyder Boothe, a former showgirl, and William Boothe, an itinerant violinist, who abandoned the family after the birth of their daughter and one son. Anna Boothe's ambitions for her beautiful daughter included a stage career and marriage to a wealthy husband, both of which were accomplished by the time Clare reached the age of twenty. In 1913, the same year that Anna divorced her husband on the grounds of desertion, her daughter understudied Mary Pickford in two plays and later appeared in walk-on roles in two Biograph silent pictures. Luce's self-education through an intensive reading program, focusing on the works of George Bernard Shaw, her intellectual hero, in addition to training in etiquette received as a scholarship student at exclusive boarding schools, did little to prepare her for marriage in 1923 to George Brokaw, an alcoholic millionaire more than twice her age. The marriage produced one child, a daughter named Ann, and ended in 1929.

Freed by her alimony settlement from financial struggle for the rest of her life, Luce began to focus on her writing career, first as a self-appointed caption writer at *Vogue*. There, she adopted both a breezy writing style and the habit of choosing well-connected lovers, including Frank Crowninshield, the associate editor who hired her and shared her interest in society and the arts, and Donald Freeman, from whom she learned how to polish her writing while she polished her image. Freeman's death in a car crash in 1933 led to Luce's appointment a week later to the position previously held by Freeman as managing editor of *Vanity Fair*.

Marriage in 1935 to Henry Luce, cofounder of *Time* and founder of *Fortune*, achieved for Luce not only a match with a millionaire who was the very model of the self-made man but also access to a magazine empire and to public life. A power couple for the midtwentieth century, the Luces developed the idea for *Life* on their honeymoon, although Luce had no role in editing the magazine.

Her greatest literary success came with the play *The Women*, a biting satire of Manhattan socialites, filmed in 1939 with an all-star cast.

With the outbreak of war, Luce traveled to Europe as a war correspondent for *Life*, where she reported on conditions for servicemen at the front. Election to Congress as the representative from Connecticut in 1942 expanded her public life, and she was mentioned as a possible vice-presidential candidate in 1944. The death of her much-neglected daughter Ann in an automobile accident in 1944 led to a period of severe depression followed by her conversion to Catholicism in 1945, the same year she was reelected to Congress. She left Congress but remained active in Republican politics, campaigning for the election of Eisenhower to the White House in 1952. In 1953, Luce was nominated and confirmed as U.S. Ambassador to Italy, a post she resigned in 1956. Her nomination as Ambassador to Brazil in 1959 survived severe political attacks, but she resigned the appointment that same year. She also made the seconding speech for Barry Goldwater's presidential bid at the 1964 Republican Convention.

The death of Henry Luce in 1967 of acute coronary thrombosis prompted Luce to move to a house in Hawaii. In 1970, *Slam the Door Softly*, her last published play, offered a comic reworking of Ibsen's *A Doll's House*, indicating her newfound interest in feminism. Appointed to the Foreign Intelligence Advisory Board by President Ronald Reagan in 1981, Luce received the Presidential Medal of Freedom in 1986. She died of a brain tumor in Washington, D.C., on October 9, 1987.

MAJOR WORKS AND THEMES

The writing life of Clare Boothe Luce can be thematically organized according to the developments in her personal life. As a teenager, she wrote five short plays in which she experimented with different dramatic forms. After stints at various fashion magazines, her knowledge of the celebrity set led to her first book, *Stuffed Shirts* (1931), a satiric collection of short stories about America's monied class, a group that both fascinated and repelled her. In November 1935, Luce's first professional production opened on Broadway. *Abide with Me* is a thinly disguised attack on her first husband and his old-money crowd. Critics panned the melodramatic exercise, suggesting that it was too personal a work to attract a wide audience.

The next Broadway outing would be hugely successful. *The Women* follows its heroine, Mary, from the loss of her husband to a designing woman to her use of an intelligent ruse to regain him. With an all-female cast, the play satirizes "a malicious pack of leisure-class urban guerillas who spend their days having their nails done and their nights dreaming of sinking them into one another's flesh" (Marks E1). The mixed critical reaction did little to discourage the play's popular success, beginning with a 657-performance Broadway run, followed by revivals that continue to this day, including a 1992 postmodern deconstruction by director Anne Bogart and a 1999 revival directed by Kyle Donnelly, who treats the play as a cousin to the screwball comedy. Luce wrote two more clever and commercial Broadway successes: *Kiss the Boys Good-Bye* (1938) and *Margin for Error* (1940).

After her conversion to Catholicism, Luce attempted to invest her dramatic writing with her newly acquired faith. This attempt at moral writing resulted in a number of shelved screen projects and only one completed film, *Come to the Stable*, and a stage hagiography, *Child of the Morning*, which closed out of town. Her years as a war correspondent, culminating in *Europe in the Spring*, a chronicle of life at the front, signaled her entry into the world of politics, which ended, for the most part, her life as a creative writer. A brush with feminism in the early 1970s is reflected in *Slam the Door Softly*; true to form, it is a comic treatment of Ibsen's *A Doll's House*.

CRITICAL RECEPTION

The life and career of Clare Boothe Luce have been critiqued far more extensively than her work. Indispensable to students of Luce is Mark Fearnow's *Clare Boothe Luce*, a research and production sourcebook including a scholarly appraisal of primary and secondary sources. Luce's literary reputation rests primarily on *The Women*. Though audiences enjoyed the play, some reviewers were troubled by the fact that so acidic a comedy had been written by a woman, not only an unladylike activity but also faintly immoral in its presentation of a cast of "unregenerate worldlings" (Atkinson 13).

Academic critics have discussed *The Women* in relation to issues of gender. Susan Carlson, in "Comic Textures and Female Communities 1937 and 1977," compares *The Women* to Wendy Wasserstein's *Uncommon Women and Others*, finding that "the two plays disclose the kind of female characters and communities comedy encourages and discourages" (564). In *The American Drama since 1930*, Joseph Mersand, the first scholar to devote an entire chapter to Luce's work, identifies the ability of women writers to discover in the ordinary details of life an extraordinary meaning. Joan T. Hamilton's "Visible Power and Invisible Men in Clare Boothe's *The Women*" finds in the play "a fragmentation of female desire, its diffusion and misdirection. In effect, the play demonstrates the inadequacy of the social structure (or, for that matter, the traditional comedic frame) to accommodate women and their desire(s)" (32–33). In "Social Darwinism in the Powder Room: Clare Boothe's *The Women*," Mary Maddock argues that "these women sublimate their gender frustration by turning their attack on each other rather than confronting the real causes of their pain: men and the expectations of a society caught in economic and social crisis" (81). With subsequent revivals of the play, Luce defended *The Women* against its critics, insisting that it was a product of its time and that "the closed upper-class society in which women saw marriage as a commercial enterprise" no longer existed (qtd. in Lester 44).

BIBLIOGRAPHY

Works by Clare Boothe Luce

The Women. New York: Random, 1937. (Play)
Kiss the Boys Good-Bye. New York: Random, 1938. (Play)
Europe in the Spring. New York: Knopf, 1940. (Nonfiction)
Margin for Error. New York: Random, 1940. (Play)
"The Valor of Homer Lea [Introduction]." *The Day of the Saxon*. By Homer Lea. New York: Harpers, 1942. 1–31.
Introduction. *Saints for Now*. New York: Sheed, 1952.
Slam the Door Softly. New York: Dramatists Play Service, 1970.
Clare Boothe Luce and Rodelle Weintraub. "The Gift of Imagination: An Interview with Clare Boothe Luce." *Fabian Feminist: Bernard Shaw and Woman*. Ed. Rodelle Weintraub. University Park: Pennsylvania State University Press, 1977. 53–59.

Studies of Clare Boothe Luce

Atkinson, Brooks. "*The Women*: A Comedy in Three Acts by Clare Boothe." *New York Times* 28 Dec. 1936: 13.
Carlson, Susan L. "Comic Textures and Female Communities 1937 and 1977: Clare Boothe and Wendy Wasserstein." *Modern Drama* 26 (1984): 564–73.
Fearnow, Mark. *Clare Boothe Luce*. Westport, CT: Greenwood, 1995.
Hamilton, Joan T. "Visible Power and Invisible Men in Clare Boothe's *The Women*." *American Drama* 3 (1993): 31–53.
Lester, Elenore. "*The Women*: Older But Not Wiser." *Ms*. Aug. 1973: 42–45.
Lyons, Joseph. *Clare Boothe Luce: Author and Diplomat*. New York: Chelsea, 1989.
Maddock, Mary. "Social Darwinism in the Powder Room: Clare Boothe's *The Women*." *Journal of American Drama and Theatre* 2.2 (1990): 81–97.
Marks, Peter. "Pit Vipers of the 30's, and Echoes of Today." *New York Times* 28 Jan. 1999: E1+.
Mersand, Joseph. *The American Drama since 1930*. New York: Modern Chapbooks, 1949.
O'Hara, Frank Hurburt. *Today in American Drama*. Chicago: University of Chicago Press, 1939. 202–4.
Shadegg, Stephen. *Clare Boothe Luce: A Biography*. New York: Simon, 1970.
Sheed, Wilfrid. *Clare Boothe Luce*. New York: Dutton, 1982.
Smiley, Sam. *The Drama of Attack: Didactic Plays of the Great Depression*. Columbia: University of Missouri Press, 1972. 188–92.
Willis, Ronald Gary. "The Persuasion of Clare Boothe Luce." Diss. Indiana University, 1993.

MABEL DODGE LUHAN
(1879–1962)

Lisa Abney

BIOGRAPHY

Mabel Dodge Luhan was born on February 26, 1879 in Buffalo, New York, to wealthy parents, Charles and Sara Cook Ganson. Raised in affluence, she grew up in a home filled with physical comforts but short on love or affection. Nannies raised Luhan for the most part, and although she saw her parents daily, no real bond between them developed. Her mother was strong-willed and decisive, whereas her father lacked determination and was prone to fits of temper. Thus, her relationship with her family remained tense throughout her life. Luhan, as a youth, attended private schools in Buffalo and roamed her safe, wealthy neighborhood playing with her schoolmates and friends.

When she reached the age of twenty-two, Luhan impulsively married Karl Evans, a young, handsome, irresponsible man. This marriage marked the first of many failed relationships and marriages for Luhan. With Evans, she had her only son, John. Luhan reported that only during pregnancy had she gained a sense of purpose. However, once John was born, this emotion faded, and she again began to pass her time searching for her role in the world. Shortly after John's birth, Karl died from an accidental shooting related to a hunting accident. After his death, Luhan felt slightly liberated, but again, a feeling of dissatisfaction overcame her since she no longer had the role of wife. To combat Luhan's depression, angst, and the scandal arising from an affair with her married gynecologist, her family sent her to Europe where she met the wealthy Edwin Dodge, who pursued her with relentless ardor. They married and settled in Italy, and in Florence, the pair built an opulent Renaissance-style mansion, the Villa Curonia. During this time in Florence, Luhan met Gertrude and Leo Stein, who shaped and added new dimensions to her views about life, art, and aesthetics. Gertrude and Luhan became friends and exchanged a series of letters for a number of years, yet from time to time, their relationship underwent several serious fractures.

Before her marriage to Dodge dissolved, Luhan returned to New York, which she was loathe to do. To cheer her and help her to adjust, her sculptor friend, Jo Davidson, introduced Luhan to many prominent artists and social reformers of the day such as Walter Lippman, Hutchins Hapgood, Margaret Sanger, and John Reed. Her apartment became a salon of great importance to aspiring writers, artists, and social reformers. Unfortunately, the relationship between Dodge and Luhan proved to be an unhappy one, and they officially divorced after several difficult years of marriage. During this time, she began a series of failed romances with men who frequented her salon. Her relationships puzzled her friends, and the depth of her need to find purposefulness and sense of self reemerged during every new relationship. This quest resulted in her third marriage to Maurice Sterne, an artist that Luhan followed to the West.

Luhan met her fourth husband while still married to Sterne. Antonio (Tony) Luhan, a Native American of the Tiwa tribe, became her lover, spiritual guide, soul mate, and companion. The pair married on April 23, 1923. Their union drew much criticism from both tribal members and Anglo acquaintances of Luhan. Their marriage was not always happy, yet for the first time, Luhan had found a person who loved, cared for, and helped her understand her own self-worth. During their marriage, Luhan met D. H. and Frieda Lawrence and many other important artists. She developed a strong relationship with Lawrence, and indeed, this relationship caused problems with Frieda, who was jealous of Lawrence's relationship with Luhan. Nonetheless, Tony and Luhan lived together until Luhan died on August 18, 1962. Their relationship and their residence, El Gallo, reflected their eclectic and varied cultural backgrounds, which seemed to blend and enabled them to overcome the obstacles that they faced in the wake of their mixed relationship.

MAJOR WORKS AND THEMES

Mabel Dodge Luhan wrote several journal articles and a series of autobiographical works that were published from 1933 to 1937. Additionally, she penned *Lorenzo in Taos* (1932) and *Winter in Taos* (1935). Luhan's themes, unlike those of other writers of the modern period, demonstrate both the need and the manner in which people can attain higher levels of spirituality and a more fully developed sense of self by living in harmony with their environment. Luhan's writing illustrates that Taos and the west, in general, are major energy centers for the natural world. Luhan's acclaim derived more from her circle of literary and artistic associates than from her writing.

Lorenzo in Taos (1932) remains one of Luhan's most interesting and simultaneously shocking works. The piece profiles her turbulent relationship with D. H. Lawrence and his wife Frieda. Lawrence captured Luhan's interest and desire, and she longed to become his muse, whereas he, on the other hand, felt the need to attempt to re-create Luhan. He viewed her as the Jungian archetype, the Great Mother. Unfortunately, her relationship with the Lawrences remained complex and difficult and finally suffered a nasty fracture. Luhan's *Lorenzo in Taos* details their relationship while revealing the potent, vibrant, natural world of Taos and illustrating its role as a center for creative energy. Since Lawrence had died already when she began her work on *Lorenzo*, Luhan focused upon Robinson Jeffers as her male muse for the work. Without a man to need her, Luhan felt she could not create or exist at a level of self-fulfillment. Jeffers served her purpose for this work.

In 1924, Luhan began work on her autobiography, and she worked solidly on it for some ten years. The four volumes contain detailed accounts of her life and her contacts with other artists and writers during the three major periods of her life. This daunting challenge of depicting her life became Luhan's driving passion. Her first volume, *Intimate Memories: Background*, is considered the strongest because of its evocative descriptions of Victorian child-rearing practices. The work profiles her early life and experiences as a youth in an upper-class family.

As successful as the first volume was, her second and third books were significantly less so. The second volume focuses on Luhan's experiences in Europe. However, it lacks a contiguous narrative at times, and the piece tends to be weakly structured. The third book of the series, *Movers and Shakers*, describes her life as a leader of the American avant-garde in Greenwich Village. The work chronicles modern writers and artists and their endeavors during this turbulent time before the prewar era. Her fourth work of the series was more successful than the previous two books. *Edge of Taos Desert* illustrates Luhan's view of the West as a new world. This work describes her life in Taos, her experiences with the Lawrences, and her marriage to Antonio Luhan.

Luhan's 1935 work *Winter in Taos* provides a depiction of the West in relation to the tides of the natural world and the relationship of humans to the natural. This piece focuses upon the connection between the organic world and Western cultural traditions. *Winter in Taos* illustrates a balance between the elements and the humans who live in them.

CRITICAL RECEPTION

Major literary critics initially lacked interest in Luhan's work. However, many among her literary circle and others who knew of Luhan and her work regarded some of the writing as interesting, whereas others viewed it with less fervor. None of her works was widely reviewed; in fact, she received only spotty attention, at best, from the important literati of the East once she moved to Taos. Few literary critics enjoyed "her subject matter, her hyperbolic style or her romantic sensibility" (Rudnick 256).

Luhan's *Winter in Taos* became her most popular piece of writing. Both Thornton Wilder and Willa Cather heartily lauded the work for its vivid depiction of the American West and its people, whereas critics in the East largely disregarded it. The work maintains its reputation as an innovative and detailed presentation of the area and the involvement between the human and environmental life cycles.

The first work of her *Intimate Memories* series gained the highest critical acclaim; the volume drew high praise from critics and Luhan's friends. For example, a reviewer for the *New Republic* said, "Here is the beginning of a life work as significant in its own right as any one of a chosen number of French eighteenth century memoirs written before the revolution" (qtd. in Rudnick 257). Several other favorable reviews accompanied this one; the radical Left, however, possessed a different set of opinions. They argued that the upper-class radicals of Luhan's era had done little to aid the cause and called Luhan and her colleagues "foolish bohemians" (Rudnick 271).

The second volume, *European Experiences*, lacks the form and content of the others, and reviewers showed little enthusiasm for the work and called it narcissistic and shallow. In the third volume, *Movers and Shakers*, which profiles Luhan's life in Greenwich Village, Luhan again failed to draw much critical attention. The Marxists panned the work—asserting that all prewar liberals were essentially powerless hedonists. Other reviewers simply noted that the book, as her previous work, was too self-involved. Granville Hicks advocated the book to social historians who might be intrigued by the account that Hicks termed "destruction that can be wrought by money when it is in the hands of intelligence and determination" (qtd. in Rudnick 258). While these three books maintained similar writing styles and foci, the last work of the series, *Edge of Taos Desert*, broke from her usual style and subject matter.

In *Edge of Taos Desert* (1937), Luhan attempted to focus upon the nurturing nature of the desert. Either critics took the position that she had written a brilliant work, or they hated the piece. Eastern critics found that the spiritual element of the text was phony and overdone, whereas those of the southwestern and western region of the United States maintained the view that her work was serious and profound. Generally, her friends, such as Ansel Adams, praised the work, and this work above all others gained the most acclaim from those who knew Luhan.

The value of Luhan's work lies largely in its vivid depiction of her world in its various stages. Indeed, she is best known for her circle of important literary figures and for her patronage of these artists. Her work as mentor is that for which she is noted, yet her literary works deserve greater examination and research.

BIBLIOGRAPHY

Works by Mabel Dodge Luhan

Lorenzo in Taos. New York: Knopf, 1932.
Intimate Memories: Background. New York: Harcourt, 1933.
European Experiences: Volume Two of Intimate Memories. New York: Harcourt, 1935.

Movers and Shakers: Volume Three of Intimate Memories. New York: Harcourt, 1935.
Winter in Taos. New York: Harcourt, 1935.
Edge of Taos Desert: An Escape to Reality. New York: Harcourt, 1937.
Taos and Its Artists. New York: Duell, 1947.
Una and Robin. Ed. Mark Schorer. Berkeley: Friends of the Bancroft Library, University
    of California, 1976.

Studies of Mabel Dodge Luhan

Gallup, Donald, ed. *Flowers of Friendship: Letters Written to Gertrude Stein*. New York:
    Knopf, 1953.
Hahn, Emily. *Mabel: A Biography of Mabel Dodge Luhan*. Boston: Houghton, 1977.
Lasch, Christopher. *The New Radicalism in America (1889–1963): The Intellectual as a
    Social Type*. New York: Vintage, 1965.
Nelson, Jane. *Mabel Dodge Luhan*. Boise: Boise State University Press, 1982.
Rudnick, Lois Palken. *Mabel Dodge Luhan: New Woman, New Worlds*. Albuquerque:
    University of New Mexico Press, 1984.

CARSON McCULLERS
(1917–1967)

Julie Buckner Armstrong

BIOGRAPHY

Carson McCullers—born Lula Carson Smith on February 19, 1917—was destined for fame from the womb. Her mother, Marguerite Waters Smith, believed that prenatal omens had decreed her child a prodigy, and to some extent, those omens proved true. McCullers achieved immediate success at twenty-three with *The Heart Is a Lonely Hunter*, enjoyed status as a wunderkind in the 1940s, then spent the next twenty years of her life in literary decline after a series of strokes left her a semiinvalid.

McCullers spent her childhood years in Columbus, Georgia, in a comfortable and loving middle-class home that included her mother, her father Lamar Smith (a watch repairman and jeweler), and two younger siblings, Lamar, Jr, and Margarita. Her earliest talents pointing toward a career as a concert pianist, she abandoned those plans during her senior year of high school, when recuperation from a case of rheumatic fever left her questioning both her stamina and genius as a musician. Soon after, she moved to New York City, where she studied creative writing at Columbia and New York Universities. On a visit home, she met her future husband, James Reeves McCullers, Jr., a young soldier stationed at Ft. Benning, Georgia, who also dreamed of a writing career.

Revealing a pattern that would manifest itself for the rest of her life, McCullers passed her late teens and early twenties through periods of slow, meticulous writing, alternating with bouts of debilitating sickness and a very active social life balanced by intense loneliness and depression. A series of illnesses during her courtship with Reeves prevented her from finishing her university courses; she ultimately had three strokes before she was thirty, leaving her partially paralyzed on the left side. Carson's marriage to Reeves on September 20, 1937, occasioned brief happiness and a move to Charlotte, North Carolina, where she began work on her first novel. By the time the couple moved to Greenwich Village in New York City, she had finished her second novel and conceived of a third. Her increasing success as a writer, however, led to personal conflict. As Reeves failed to realize his own literary aspirations, he began to drink heavily, and his temper often became violent, while Carson contributed to the couple's problems with affairs, frequent illnesses, and a demanding work ethic. The couple split and reconciled several times, with a final separation occurring just prior to Reeves's suicide in 1953.

Despite illness and marital trouble, McCullers's twenties and early thirties were socially and professionally rewarding. Supported by various literary awards, she produced her best work—four novels, one adapted into a play, and several short stories—at the Yaddo artists' colony in Saratoga Springs, New York. McCullers counted among her friends the literary elite of both America and Europe, and she had a reputation as a prolific drinker and smoker who moved frequently from one intensive personal relationship to another. Her romantic involvements included both men and women, a lifestyle about which McCullers was very open. She also cultivated an androgynous persona, wearing closely cropped hair and men's clothes. Her active social life and open sexual exploration, however, masked deep loneliness and insecurity. Yet these emotions found an expression in her work that contributed to its popular and critical acclaim.

In McCullers's late thirties, paralyzing strokes and other health problems began to impede her writing. She began to spend more time in the Nyack, New York, home purchased by her mother in 1945, at first under Marguerite's care and later under Dr. Mary Mercer's, a psychiatrist and friend whom McCullers credited for helping her overcome a deep depression. Because of decreased mobility, McCullers began writing less original, successful, or extended work, although she did produce short pieces for magazines and collaborated on dramatizations of earlier novels. She labored for nearly ten years on a final novel, which was a personal and popular success more than a critical one.

McCullers's first novel, *The Heart Is a Lonely Hunter*, defines her life. Its publication ensured her immediate fame and a lasting place in American literature, and its meditation on human isolation and desire speaks to the woman behind the author. In 1967, shortly before shooting was to begin on a film adaptation of this novel, McCullers had a massive brain hemorrhage that left her comatose for over six weeks. She died on September 29 and was buried in Oak Hill Cemetery, near the Hudson River in Nyack.

MAJOR WORKS AND THEMES

Known primarily as a fiction writer, Carson McCullers also wrote plays, essays, and poetry. Her novels and short stories are thematically consistent—exploring isolation, loneliness, and unfulfilled desire. The fiction is also noted for its frequent use of adolescent, grotesque, and socially marginalized characters to convey these themes. Music makes a frequent appearance, too, as allusion, symbol, and structuring device. Despite such consistency, McCullers is a remarkably difficult writer to classify. Her work has been regarded as both highly symbolic and socially realistic, as both typically southern and a decided rejection of the southern fictional milieu.

The Heart Is a Lonely Hunter (1940) establishes McCullers's basic themes and reveals how such difficulties in classification emerge. Set in a southern mill town but illustrating broadly human emotions, the novel provides a symbolic comment upon loneliness and desire, while at the same time looking at very real socioeconomic issues. The central character is John Singer, an intelligent and sympathetic deaf mute who listens to and seems to understand the innermost feelings of others: Biff Brannon, an androgynous cafe owner; Jake Blount, an alcoholic and itinerant Marxist; Benedict Mady Copeland, a black doctor with dreams of racial uplift; and Mick Kelley, a poor, adolescent girl passionately devoted to classical music. The irony does not lie in Singer's inability to hear— he can read lips—but in his inability to care deeply enough; his real concern is Spiros Antonapoulos, his former roommate and a current resident of a mental hospital, who barely notices Singer's visits and gifts. Antonapoulos's death leads to the distraught Singer's suicide, leaving other characters to their directionless lives.

McCullers published her second novel, *Reflections in a Golden Eye*, just one year after *The Heart Is a Lonely Hunter*, continuing her look at individuals whose lives intersect but never truly connect. This time, however, her characters are more symbolically stylized and her situations more grotesque. The stern Captain Penderton detests his voluptuous, simple-minded wife Lenora and secretly desires her lover, Major Langdon. The Major's wife, Alison, finds more in common with her effeminate houseboy than she does her very masculine husband. Their loneliness and frustrated desire manifests itself in several shocking scenes: Alison's self-mutilation with garden shears, Captain Penderton's sadistic beating of Lenora's horse, and his subsequent murder of another character. If *Heart*'s style is contrapuntal with its five intersecting themes, *Reflections*'s is dissonant, with notes that clash and never achieve harmony.

A bizarre love triangle and musical allusion also form the crux of McCullers's next major work, *The Ballad of the Sad Cafe* (published in *Harper's Bazaar* in 1943 and in book form in 1951). Here the triangle consists of the Amazonian Amelia Evans who loves her dwarfed and hunchbacked cousin, Lymon Willis, who in turn loves Marvin Macy, Amelia's sinister ex-husband. The novella is notable for its use of elements from the ballad: mixing the common and the supernatural, relating tales of love and physical strength, and even ending with a coda. This final comment, which turns to a chain gang harmonizing on the outskirts of town, speculates that the only possible union is one achieved in bondage. *Ballad* also contains McCullers's famous meditation upon the nature of love, in which her narrator outlines the divergent, and mostly negative, situations of both lover and beloved. As McCullers notes in other works, desire can rarely be quenched and loneliness only temporarily ameliorated.

The same themes culminate in *The Member of the Wedding*, published in 1946 and later developed into a Broadway play of the same title. Its main character is Frankie Adams, spiritual sister to Mick Kelley and Amelia Evans. Twelve-year-old Frankie (later calling herself F. Jasmine and Frances) wears boys' clothes, feels like a circus freak because she has grown so tall so quickly, and laments her status as a member of nothing. She spends long, uneventful summer days in the kitchen with John Henry, her six-year-old cousin, and Berenice, the family cook, playing cards and discussing the upcoming wedding of her brother. When Frankie seizes upon a plan of escape from monotony—running away with the couple for their honeymoon—she is happy to find herself part of something: She has found what she calls her "we of me." Her dreams are thwarted when she is dragged screaming from the car, but she later emerges, through several difficult trials, as a typical teenager with a new friend her own age.

McCullers's stories often rely on themes and techniques found in the major novels. "Wunderkind" (1936), her first published story, is a semiautobiographical sketch that concerns initiation into adulthood, with its main character realizing that her dreams of being a concert pianist will not materialize. "A Tree. A Rock. A Cloud" (1942) contains a familiar philosophical description of individuals' difficulties with love. Both can be found in *The Collected Stories*, edited by Virginia Spencer Carr. *The Mortgaged Heart* (1971), a posthumous collection edited by McCullers's sister Margarita G. Smith, contains stories, essays, and most notably "The Mute," an early sketch for *The Heart Is a Lonely Hunter*.

Other writings by the author include the 1961 novel *Clock without Hands*; a play, *The Square Root of Wonderful* (1958); and a collection of children's verse, *Sweet as a Pickle and Clean as a Pig* (1964).

CRITICAL RECEPTION

If McCullers is a difficult writer to classify, she is also difficult to judge. Critics have debated her status and abilities, and they have also changed their focus over time: Earlier examinations outline themes, strategies, and symbols, and later studies concentrate on her fiction's social and political aspects, particularly its portrayal of gender. Examples of criticism on McCullers can be found in two essay collections, one edited by Harold Bloom and another by Beverly Lyon Clark and Melvin J. Friedman. Judith Giblin James's *Wunderkind: The Reputation of Carson McCullers, 1940–1990* offers an extended survey of the criticism as well as an extensive bibliography. Another valuable resource is the most recent annotated bibliography of primary and secondary works, edited by Adrian M. Shapiro, Jackson R. Bryer, and Kathleen Field. The best general overviews of McCullers are Virginia Spencer Carr's *Understanding Carson McCullers* and Margaret McDowell's *Carson McCullers*. Two studies of McCullers's life are instrumental for understanding her reception. The first critical biography was Oliver Evans's *The Ballad of Carson McCullers*, but Carr's *The Lonely Hunter* is the most indispensable. The latter changed the face of

McCullers studies with its revelations about the author's sexuality and her tortured relationship with her husband.

Many studies of McCullers focus on identifying themes and structures in her work. Dayton Kohler, one of the first to provide an in-depth look at the writer, examines thematic and stylistic patterns, focusing on loneliness and longing as unifying ideas, and Sue B. Walker discusses McCullers's exploration of love. Ihab Hassan's "The Alchemy of Love and Aesthetics of Pain" describes her use of grotesque and southern Gothic elements, and another stylistic examination, by Barbara Nauer Folk, provides a look at music as symbol and narrative framework. Most criticism of McCullers focuses on her novels, but Robert S. Phillips covers alienation and the grotesque in her short stories, while Mary McBride is one of the few to write extensively about the author's forays into the theater.

Although discussions of McCullers unite around themes of loneliness, grotesque characters, and musical structures, many critics disagree when assessing the writer. Ihab Hassan, Louise Westling, and many others take for granted McCullers's place in the canon of southern literature. However, Delma Eugene Presley and Louis D. Rubin, Jr., argue that McCullers does not fit the profile of the typical southern author. Both also agree that her art breaks down when she literally and metaphorically strays from her regional roots. A near-consensus minimizes her status as an important writer, judging the later work inferior to her earlier successes. In "The Lonely Heart of Carson McCullers," for instance, Robert Drake demonstrates how the author loses control of her art. On the other hand, Lubbers's "The Necessary Order: A Study of Theme and Structure in Carson McCullers' Klaus Fiction" demonstrates how her work evolves. Early biographer Oliver Evans comments on such evaluations, arguing persuasively in two articles that McCullers, a decidedly major author, is frequently misunderstood.

The most recent criticism takes a second look at McCullers, in particular the previously neglected sociopolitical elements of her work. Gayatri Spivak leads the way in 1979, arguing that issues of race, class, and gender offer a fruitful line of investigation for McCullers studies. Louise Westling's discussion of the writer's female characters in *Sacred Groves and Ravaged Gardens* provides the most extended, and perhaps one of the best, treatments of gender identity construction. In "Homoerotics and Human Connections," Lori J. Kenschaft examines the reasons for and difficulties of reading McCullers as a lesbian writer. Some critics have also begun to write about race in specific texts: An article by Thadious M. Davis shows how McCullers revises African American characters when she adapts *The Member of the Wedding* from novel to play, and one by Laurie Champion profiles racial differences in *The Heart Is a Lonely Hunter*. Extended examinations of issues surrounding race and class in McCullers's fiction remain to be done.

BIBLIOGRAPHY

Works by Carson McCullers

The Heart Is a Lonely Hunter. Boston: Houghton, 1940.
Reflections in a Golden Eye. Boston: Houghton, 1941.
The Member of the Wedding. Boston: Houghton, 1946.
The Ballad of the Sad Cafe: The Novels and Stories of Carson McCullers. Boston: Houghton, 1951.
The Member of the Wedding: A Play. New York: New Directions, 1951.
The Square Root of Wonderful: A Play. Boston: Houghton, 1958.
Clock without Hands. Boston: Houghton, 1961.
Sweet as a Pickle and Clean as a Pig. Illus. Rolf Gérard. Boston: Houghton, 1964. (Children's verse)
The Mortgaged Heart. Ed. Margarita G. Smith. Boston: Houghton, 1971. (Short stories, essays, and poems)
The Collected Stories. Introd. Virginia Spencer Carr. Boston: Houghton, 1987.

Studies of Carson McCullers

Bloom, Harold, ed. *Carson McCullers: Modern Critical Views.* New York: Chelsea House, 1986.
Carr, Virginia Spencer. *The Lonely Hunter: A Biography of Carson McCullers.* Garden City, NY: Doubleday, 1975.
———. *Understanding Carson McCullers.* Columbia: University of South Carolina Press, 1990.
Champion, Laurie. "Black and White Christs in Carson McCullers' *The Heart Is a Lonely Hunter.*" *Southern Literary Journal* 24.1 (1991): 47–52.
Clark, Beverly Lyon, and Melvin J. Friedman, eds. *Critical Essays on Carson McCullers.* New York: Hall, 1996.
Davis, Thadious M. "Erasing the 'We of Me' and Rewriting the Racial Script: Carson McCullers' Two *Member(s) of the Wedding.*" *Critical Essays on Carson McCullers.* Ed. Beverly Lyon Clark and Melvin J. Friedman. New York: Hall, 1996. 206–19.
Drake, Robert. "The Lonely Heart of Carson McCullers." *Christian Century* 10 Jan. 1968: 50–51.
Evans, Oliver. "The Achievement of Carson McCullers." *English Journal* 51 (1962): 301–8.
———. *The Ballad of Carson McCullers: A Biography.* New York: Coward, 1966. Rpt. of *Carson McCullers: Her Life and Work.* London: Owen, 1965.
———. "The Case of Carson McCullers." *Georgia Review* 19 (1965): 188–203.
Folk, Barbara Nauer. "The Sad Sweet Music of Carson McCullers." *Georgia Review* 16 (1962): 202–9.
Hassan, Ihab. "The Alchemy of Love and Aesthetics of Pain." *Modern Fiction Studies* 5 (1959–1960): 311–26.
James, Judith Giblin. *Wunderkind: The Reputation of Carson McCullers, 1940–1990.* Columbia, SC: Camden, 1995.

Kenschaft, Lori J. "Homoerotics and Human Connections: Reading Carson McCullers 'As a Lesbian.' " *Critical Essays on Carson McCullers*. Ed. Beverly Lyon Clark and Melvin J. Friedman. New York: Hall, 1996. 220–33.

Kiernan, Robert F. *Katherine Anne Porter and Carson McCullers: A Reference Guide*. Boston: Hall, 1976.

Kohler, Dayton. "Carson McCullers: Variations on a Theme." *College English* 13 (1951): 1–8. Pub. simultaneously in *English Journal* 40 (1951): 415–22.

Lubbers, Klaus. "The Necessary Order: A Study of Theme and Structure in Carson McCullers' Fiction." *Jarbuch für Amerikastudien* 8 (1963): 187–204.

McBride, Mary. "Loneliness and Longing in Selected Plays of Carson McCullers and Tennessee Williams." *Modern American Drama: The Female Canon*. Ed. June Schlueter. Rutherford, NJ: Fairleigh Dickinson University Press, 1990. 143–50.

McDowell, Margaret. *Carson McCullers*. Boston: Twayne, 1980.

Phillips, Robert S. "Freaking Out: The Short Stories of Carson McCullers." *Southwest Review* 63 (1978): 65–73.

Presley, Delma Eugene. "Carson McCullers and the South." *Georgia Review* 28 (1974): 19–32.

Rubin, Louis D., Jr. "Carson McCullers: The Aesthetics of Pain." *Virginia Quarterly Review* 53 (1977): 265–83.

Shapiro, Adrian M., Jackson R. Bryer, and Kathleen Field. *Carson McCullers: A Descriptive Listing and Annotated Bibliography of Criticism*. New York: Garland, 1980.

Spivak, Gayatri Chakravorty. "Three Feminist Readings: McCullers, Drabble, Habermas." *Union Seminary Quarterly* 35 (1979–1980): 15–34.

Walker, Sue B. "The Link in the Chain Called Love: A New Look at Carson McCullers' Novels." *Mark Twain Journal* 18 (1976): 8–12.

Westling, Louise. *Sacred Groves and Ravaged Gardens: The Fiction of Eudora Welty, Carson McCullers, and Flannery O'Connor*. Athens: University of Georgia Press, 1985.

EDNA ST. VINCENT MILLAY
(1892–1950)

Robert Johnson

BIOGRAPHY

Born February 22, 1892, Edna St. Vincent Millay was eight years old when her mother took the rare step for her day of divorcing her husband and then remaining a single parent. Consequently, Millay grew up in a nontraditional, female, domestic world. Unwashed dishes might have accumulated, but Millay and her sisters never lacked for spunk, or intellectual and artistic stimulation. Once, after broken pipes puddled their house with frozen water, they simply ice-skated (Gould 20).

Millay, her unusual middle name taken from a hospital where her uncle had received care, was called "Vincent" by her family. She developed early interests in music, literature, and languages, and in 1906—in a children's magazine— she published her first poem. However, the event that probably most directly shaped her creative life was being published in a 1912 national anthology, *The Lyric Year*. Millay's poem "Renascence" received critical acclaim, and readers were stunned to find that its author, "E. Vincent Millay," was young and a woman (Gould 4, 14; Brittin 2, 4).

After high school, Millay was aided by a wealthy patron in moving to New York, then to enter Vassar College in 1913. Millay chafed at college rules. She smoked, kept odd hours—poems, she testified, arrived when they chose—she skipped classes. A "thread of rebellion" characterized her time on campus. Yet she so dazzled as a student that although she finished her senior year under suspension, the college president bent rules to allow her being graduated with classmates (Dash 131–36).

Millay spent the years 1917 through 1920 in New York. She mingled with Greenwich Village writers, thespians, radicals, hangers-on—people redefining what it meant to be talented and young. Millay's liberated style of life, her success with poems and in the local theater world—her circle of ardent male admirers—exemplified freedom for which many bright-minded women yearned. Indeed, her collection *A Few Figs from Thistles* (1920), with its famous admission "My candle burns at both ends" (*Collected Poems* 127), provided a rallying point for readers who imagined in Millay a new kind of woman who dared to be brilliant, take lovers, and subvert gender expectations.

In the Village Millay began, as well, to earn a small income from magazine writing. During the winter 1920–1921, Millay sailed for France, sponsored by *Vanity Fair* magazine. In Europe, she penned humorous sketches and began work on a novel. She journeyed as far as Albania, then quite off the beaten track (Brittin 15). Meanwhile, her book *Second April* (1921) confirmed for readers the strength of Millay's talent by delving into more philosophical issues than had previous work. In 1923, health failing from exhaustion and assorted medical difficulties, Millay returned to the United States and strode into history: She became the first woman to be awarded the Pulitzer Prize for Poetry.

Having spurned a string of suitors, in 1923, Millay became the wife of Eugen Boissevain, a Dutch-born importer. Big, robust, Boissevain loved to surround himself with artistic people. Judging Millay's talents more important than his own interests, he took over financial and household duties. Eugen would rush to the phone to avoid Millay's having to respond. His wife, he told a reporter, "must not be dulled by routine acts." For their permanent home, in 1925 the couple purchased a farm near Austerlitz, New York, and called the place Steepletop (Dash 169).

In the mid-1920s, Millay and her husband traveled to Europe and the Far East; she made a series of tours speaking across the United States. Millay's consciously theatrical readings, performed in lustrous long evening gowns, established her as an American artistic icon.

The 1920s, though, eventually ushered in more difficult times for the poet. In 1927 Millay joined the thousands of Americans drawn to protest the planned execution of alleged anarchists Sacco and Vanzetti. When she was arrested in Boston with a crowd angered by the action, her political involvement changed the public's image of her as flapper sensualist. By the early 1930s her writing began to reflect a concern for the mysterious and darker side of human behavior.

Moreover, even as she continued to polish her art, ill health and mischance darkened her personal life. In 1936, she was thrown from the door of a car and suffered injuries inducing chronic pain. That same year the manuscript of a poetic drama for voices upon which she was working burned in a hotel fire, forcing her to rewrite from memory. Continuing medical difficulties left her increasingly dependent on alcohol and medication (Brittin 26). Joan Dash records that the 1930s were trying years for Millay: "Her popularity was not what it once was—the fantastic adulation of the early 1920s was quite gone," and critics were now taking her to task for not having grown with the times (203).

The war years brought further change. Millay entered the era with pacifist leanings, but after steady news of Nazi brutalities, Millay "deliberately turned her poetic lines into propagandistic ploughshares" (Thesing 4). As she admitted later, pushing herself to meet deadlines and her need to compose topical verse in support of Allied war efforts much reduced the quality of her labors. In addition, the wartime loss of her husband's business holdings overseas affected her economic status. By the mid-1940s the pressure had taken its toll: She collapsed with a "nervous breakdown" and for a while could not write. What is more, a group of close persons had died, and Millay was separated from many former acquaintances (Brittin 26).

Following the war, Millay rekindled her poetic efforts, yet seemed to some friends reduced in stature, a woman marked by life. Eugen worked to create a protective atmosphere around her—he was heard to refer to his charge as "my child." The couple withdrew into their private world at Steepletop. In 1949, Eugen died after what appeared to have been a successful operation. Millay returned home and, after deep grieving, pushed herself back to health and productivity. She passed away but a year later. Millay was found dead sitting on the stairs in the house at Steepletop, a glass of wine at her side, on October 19, 1950 (Dash 220, 224).

MAJOR WORKS AND THEMES

The publication of "Renascence" in 1912, critics argue, established themes that will be found in the body of Millay's work. The poem captures the ruminations of a young person caught between twin recognitions: of the immensity of the cosmos and of the sure limits suggested by standing on earth. Boundaries and desire, yearnings and confinement—polarities anchor the speaker and join her with humankind. *Renascence and Other Poems* (1917) accompanies the piece with other early work and establishes twin primary formats for Millay's verse: "the short lyric and the sonnet" (Fried, "Edna" 291).

Millay's *A Few Figs from Thistles* (1920), with its impulsive Jazz Age energy, catapults the poet's fame. *Figs* collects a "compendium of wayward female voices" (Fried, "Edna" 292). One poem asserts a woman's telling her lover, "I shall forget you presently, my dear" (*Collected Poems* 571), effusing the impudence her fans associated with Millay's verse. Yet commentators have noted that beneath this flippant surface attitude Millay's poems were redefining the limits of female speech simply by assuming that she, in fact, could write in such a bold fashion.

With *Second April* (1921) Millay moved into more "contemplative" poems (Dash 151). Included, for example, is an elegy for a Vassar classmate. The new love sonnets, Fried advises, match the earlier "cynical voice of the worldly-wise new woman" with formally poetic observations of an artist whose need for love roots itself back into classical times ("Edna" 293). This volume presents a maturing woman, not "the astonishing girl" (Dash 152). Millay can attest that "Life is a quest and love a quarrel," but among the world's "bastard" flowers, away from the glare and out in the weeds, moments of "blessèd" quiet might be found (*Collected Poems* 74). Iconoclasts, that is, can garner something other than headlines. The book, too, offers Millay's first work in free verse, "Spring," in which April is said to arrive "like an idiot, babbling and strewing flowers" (*Collected Poems* 53), its beauty insufficient in itself, though, to offer human life meaning.

The Harp-Weaver and Other Poems (1923) builds around "The Ballad of the Harp-Weaver," a narrative describing a poor woman's sacrifices for her son and a tribute to Millay's mother Cora. Included in the collection, as well, is Millay's famous sonnet "What lips my lips have kissed" (*Collected Poems* 602), with its evocation of a woman's memories of uncountable lovers, and a series of "Sonnets from an Ungrafted Tree," documenting a farm woman's returning to minister to her estranged husband's death.

In *The Buck in the Snow* (1928) Millay broaches yet wider concerns, including directly political commentary. As did her era, writes Brittin, "Millay embraced the idea of an indifferent universe" (81). The title poem recounts the narrator's watching a deer and doe dash through an orchard, then discover the buck shot dead, its "wild blood scalding the snow" (*Collected Poems* 228). Limning parallel brutality, "Justice Denied in Massachusetts" images the tilling of "blighted earth" to speak of dire lessons learned from the Sacco and Vanzetti case (*Collected Poems* 231).

One of Millay's most powerful contributions to American poetry arrives with *Fatal Interview*, fifty-two sonnets published in 1931. The group narrates the history of a dangerous love affair, and critics suggest that the series may document a relationship between Millay and writer George Dillon. Its poems equaling in number the weeks in the year, the collection captures such an affair almost as a natural progression. Historically, sequences of the sort have watched the rise and fall of love through male eyes—and complained of female mutability—but *Fatal Interview* plants the reader within the mind of a suffering woman. As an artist, Millay was taking a chance publishing such sentiments. Patricia Klemans affirms that "Millay was writing perfect love sonnets at a time when love seemed trite and the sonnet was 'out' " (11).

Wine from These Grapes (1934) speaks in an angry tone. Rising from the terrors of the Great Depression, the book marks a shift in voices for Millay that poet Louise Bogan likens to the movement from youthful to more mature work in the canon of Yeats (Thesing 7). Emblematic of the anthology is the sonnet series "Epitaph for the Race of Man." Brittin remarks that Millay "evidently did not intend the sequence to be regarded as . . . gloomy" but to sound a "challenge" for mankind to rise above its potential for self-destruction (93). However, the poems often have been taken to reflect a brooding over human greed and lack of self-awareness. Millay evidently spoke to her times: She was reading to packed houses; the book sold remarkably well and went through multiple printings (Gould 230–32).

Hunstman, What Quarry? (1939) offers poems old and new, some dating back to the 1920s (Brittin 105). The title poem refers to the choice a hunter makes between pursuing a night with a woman or chasing a fox. He takes after the fox—Millay's lament, perhaps, for the state of the world on the eve of war.

The book contains, as well, six poems dedicated to poet Elinor Wylie and po-litical statements like "Stay That We Saw Spain Die," a mournful reflection on the torments of the Spanish Civil War.

Millay's World War II efforts focus on patriotic writing. Millay documents her anger at the Nazis and demonstrates her sense of duty to speak for democ-racy. *Make Bright the Arrows* (1940) evokes Joan, "the Maid of Orleans," and memories of England before German bombs had fallen. Millay's ballad *The Murder of Lidice* (1942) was broadcast nationally on radio and describes the horrors of the Nazis destroying a town in Czechoslovakia.

Mine the Harvest (1954), presenting work from the last decade of Millay's life, and *Collected Poems* (1956) appear after Millay's death. Brittin notes that *Harvest* delivers poems "simple and controlled, not artificial or contrived," al-lowing a sense of closure. The collection resonates a kind of "Humanistic Sto-icism," he argues, evoking the strength of "enduring pain and loss" (119). In addition, Millay echoes a search for unity, purity, and integration of spirit, the desire to "speak aloud in honest speech" (*Collected Poems* 508), concerns for which date back to her early writing. "Ragged Island," for example—a poem named for an actual island she and Eugen purchased off the coast of Maine—hungers for peace available under "silent spruces," surrounded by an ocean "with death acquainted, yet forever chaste" (*Collected Poems* 444).

Millay successfully published in genres other than poetry. Her play *Aria da Capo* (1920) received enthusiastic reaction. *The King's Henchman* (1927), fea-turing Millay's libretto, was produced by the Metropolitan Opera. *Distressing Dialogues* gathers witty satirical prose Millay placed under the name Nancy Boyd. In addition, collaborating with George Dillon, in 1936 Millay published a translation of Baudelaire's *Flowers of Evil* (Thesing 11–12).

CRITICAL RECEPTION

Passionately championed by young women who were maturing in the 1920s, Millay nonetheless suffered heavily at the hands of critics who later proposed that her work had not developed along sufficiently modern lines. Since about the 1960s, though, more and more scholarly readers have demanded that Millay be reconsidered and have found in her work the voice of a powerful, emerging female consciousness grappling with issues central for late twentieth-century writers.

Commentaries Millay garnered from her initial trio of volumes, William Thes-ing notes, "were the most favorable that she received during the three decades of her writing career." As an instance, critic Louis Untermeyer thought that *Renascence* demonstrated an "untutored sincerity, a direct and often dramatic power that few of our most expert craftsmen can equal" (5). By the time that *Figs* had reached the public, Brittin sums, Millay was "regarded as a leading American lyric poet." "A Wunderkind of 1912," she grew with fame to be considered a spokesperson for her generation (128).

By the late 1920s and into the following decades, especially after publication of *The Buck in the Snow*, Millay's critical reputation faltered. Millay's growing social consciousness and her work on behalf of the war effort distanced many readers. Every bit as influential in the changing climate of opinion that greeted her work was the growing prominence of formalist "New Criticism." Privileging complexity and subtlety, multiple elusive meanings, distanced ironic narration, the New Critics and their followers honored symbolically laden works. In contrast, Millay appeared to say what she meant, showed her narrator's feelings directly; and, often as not, readers equated the narrative voice *with* the poet herself. As a result, while she might well display Modernist attitudes (about sexuality, the universe, time), Millay was judged to be harkening after older eras.

For a sense of the evaluations Millay received during this swing period in her career, one might well read Cleanth Brooks's review "Edna Millay's Maturity" or John Crowe Ransom's "The Poet as Woman," both from the mid-1930s. Brooks laments, "Miss Millay has not grown up" (2). Millay, he believes, lacks a "tragic" attitude. Millay is "content with a supple and full-voiced utterance, and the imagery is—in the best sense of the word—decorative merely. . . . There are no subtle insights" (3–4). Ransom, in a more detailed meditation, admits that Millay is "an artist" and that her "career has been one of dignity and poetic sincerity." Yet she does not rank with first-rate poets, he believes, because she "is also a woman" and speaks as one. "A woman lives," he proposes, "for love," whereas men grow beyond the affections to become thinkers, too. Millay, he judges, "is rarely and barely intellectual, and I think everybody knows it" (783–84).

In more recent years, critics have resurrected Millay's status. As an example, in a late-1970s essay " 'Being Born a Woman': A New Look at Edna St. Vincent Millay," Patricia Klemans asserts that Millay "proclaims a feminist philosophy" (7). Klemans reports that when Millay's reputation dimmed, the poet fell victim of the "tastes of the time" (11). Though shoved "to the back shelves for so many years," Klemans writes, "Millay's books deserve a new reading" (18). In another later 1970s commentary, Jane Stanbrough argues that close reading of Millay's language indicates that below the surface of bright rebellion lies a troubling and profound understanding of the limits of female freedom.

Further refining this call for rereading Millay, in the following decade Debra Fried states that all poetic "forms and genres are not natural but ideological." She judges that Millay restructures the sonnet genre "with the revisionary force of a woman poet who, however rearguard in the phalanx of modernism, recognizes that she has inherited a genre laden with figurations exclusive to a male poetic authority," and who, in effect, thwarts male power by making the genre speak for her ("Andromeda" 17).

Suzanne Clark adds in "The Unwarranted Discourse: Sentimental Community, Modernist Women, and the Case of Millay" that in veering from knowledge born of sentiment "Modernist poetics excluded female poets at the level of theory" (133). "When a woman poet like Edna St. Vincent Millay defied the laws of modesty, obscurity, and constraint to reach out for her woman readers," Clark judges, "she earned the contempt of critics" (138–39). Women who wrote to establish a sense of community were "disenfranchised" by modernism's "academic priesthood." Millay's "poetic style is founded on commonality": While she may "shock her audience . . . she does not separate herself from them" (141). Millay "lets us see our readerly dilemma. We can be cold and lonesome critics, or we can join the circle" of fulfilled life (147). Jan Montefiore claims that much of Millay's work, ultimately, must be viewed as Romantic in tone. Millay demonstrates "the value of the experience of loving, whatever pain it may bring" (122). Entering the 1990s, Cheryl Walker notes that Millay is a poet whose work "thrives on physical experience." A central value of Millay's work, Walker feels, is that it "makes the female body more than a set of implied gestures," more than simply something that is seen (*Masks* 136–37).

Summing the tone of recent Millay scholarship, Fried comments: "The point is not to costume Millay as a radical thinker ahead of her time" but "to hold Millay's work up to the light of our time and see what has been heretofore hidden in shadow" ("Edna" 299).

Several volumes are inescapably valuable to anyone pursuing the reshaping of Millay's critical history. First published in the 1960s, Norman A. Brittin's *Edna St. Vincent Millay* functions as a watershed document, presenting a powerful overview of Millay's career, as well as parsing major poems. Judith Nierman's *Edna St. Vincent Millay: A Reference Guide* (1977) provides a thorough overview of criticism available by the 1970s. William B. Thesing's *Critical Essays on Edna St. Vincent Millay* (1993) opens with a concise history of Millay's life, career, and scholarly reputation, then compiles critical reactions from throughout her career. Celebrating the one hundredth anniversary of the poet's birth, Skidmore College hosted a 1992 national conference to reappraise the poet's accomplishments. Diane P. Freedman has collected papers from the conference in *Millay at 100: A Critical Reappraisal* (1995). In addition, at the date of this writing, at least two major projects are afoot attempting to provide a new, definitive Millay biography.

Edna St. Vincent Millay, Colin Falck sums, "has been buried twice over": once by modernism; once by academic critics. Yet in her technical skill and remarkable conversational clarity of voice, "this intense, thoughtful, and magnificently literate poet" deserves a central place in the modern literary landscape (xxix–xxx).

BIBLIOGRAPHY

Works by Edna St. Vincent Millay

Renascence and Other Poems. New York: Kennerley, 1917.
A Few Figs from Thistles. New York: Shay, 1920.

Aria da Capo. New York: Kennerley, 1921. (Play)

Second April. New York: Kennerley, 1921.

The Harp-Weaver and Other Poems. New York: Harper, 1923.

[Pseud. Nancy Boyd]. *Distressing Dialogues*. New York: Harper, 1924. (Mixed genres)

The King's Henchman. New York: Harper, 1927. (Opera)

The Buck in the Snow and Other Poems. New York: Harper, 1928.

Fatal Interview. New York: Harper, 1931.

Wine from These Grapes. New York: Harper, 1934.

Edna St. Vincent Millay and George Dillon. *Flowers of Evil*. New York: Harper, 1936. (Translation of Baudelaire)

Conversation at Midnight. New York: Harper, 1937. (Drama for voices)

Hunstman, What Quarry? New York: Harper, 1939.

Make Bright the Arrows: 1940 Notebook. New York: Harper, 1940.

Collected Sonnets. New York: Harper, 1941.

The Murder of Lidice. New York: Harper, 1942.

Collected Lyrics. New York: Harper, 1943.

Letters of Edna St. Vincent Millay. Ed. Allan Ross Macdougall. New York: Harper, 1952.

Mine the Harvest. New York: Harper, 1954.

Collected Poems. New York: Harper, 1956.

Studies of Edna St. Vincent Millay

Atkins, Elizabeth. *Edna St. Vincent Millay and Her Times*. Chicago: University of Chicago Press, 1936.

Brittin, Norman A. *Edna St. Vincent Millay*. Rev. ed. Boston: Twayne, 1982.

Brooks, Cleanth. "Edna Millay's Maturity." *Southwest Review* 20.2 (1935): 1–5.

Cheney, Anne. *Millay in Greenwich Village*. University, AL: University of Alabama Press, 1975.

Clark, Suzanne. "Jouissance and the Sentimental Daughter: Edna St. Vincent Millay." *Sentimental Modernism: Women Writers and the Revolution of the Word*. Bloomington: Indiana University Press, 1991. 67–96.

———. "The Unwarranted Discourse: Sentimental Community, Modernist Women, and the Case of Millay." *Genre* 20 (1987): 133–52.

Dash, Joan. "Edna St. Vincent Millay." *A Life of One's Own: Three Gifted Women and the Men They Married*. New York: Harper, 1973. 117–227, 352–58.

Falck, Colin. Introduction. *Edna St. Vincent Millay: Selected Poems*. Centenary Edition. New York: HarperPerennial, 1992. xv–xxx.

Farr, Judith. "Elinor Wylie, Edna St. Vincent Millay, and the Elizabethan Sonnet Tradition." *Poetic Traditions of the English Renaissance*. Ed. Maynard Mack and George de Forest Lord. New Haven: Yale University Press, 1982. 287–305.

Freedman, Diane P., ed. *Millay at 100: A Critical Reappraisal*. Carbondale: Southern Illinois University Press, 1995.

Fried, Debra. "Andromeda Unbound: Gender and Genre in Millay's Sonnets." *Twentieth Century Literature* 32.1 (1986): 1–22.

———. "Edna St. Vincent Millay: 1892–1950." *Modern American Women Writers*. Ed. Elaine Showalter. New York: Scribner's, 1991. 287–302.

Gould, Jean. *The Poet and Her Book: A Biography of Edna St. Vincent Millay*. New York: Dodd, 1969.

Gray, James. *Edna St. Vincent Millay*. St. Paul: University of Minnesota Press, 1967.

Gurko, Miriam. *Restless Sprit: The Life of Edna St. Vincent Millay*. New York: Crowell, 1962.

Jones, Phyllis M. "Amatory Sonnet Sequences and the Female Perspective of Elinor Wylie and Edna St. Vincent Millay." *Women's Studies* 10 (1983): 41–61.

Klemans, Patricia A. " 'Being Born a Woman': A New Look at Edna St. Vincent Millay." *Colby College Quarterly* 15 (1979): 7–18.

Montefiore, Jan. "Romantic Transcendence: Edna St Vincent Millay." *Feminism and Poetry: Language, Experience, Identity in Women's Writing*. London: Pandora, 1987. 115–25, 193.

Nierman, Judith. *Edna St. Vincent Millay: A Reference Guide*. Boston: Hall, 1977.

Ransom, John Crowe. "The Poet as Woman." *Southern Review* 2 (1936–1937): 783–806.

Stanbrough, Jane. "Edna St. Vincent Millay and the Language of Vulnerability." *Shakespeare's Sisters: Feminist Essays on Women Poets*. Ed. Sandra M. Gilbert and Susan Gubar. Bloomington: Indiana University Press, 1979. 183–99, 327–28.

Thesing, William B., ed. *Critical Essays on Edna St. Vincent Millay*. New York: Hall, 1993.

Walker, Cheryl. "Antimodern, Modern, and Postmodern Millay: Contexts of Revaluation." *Gendered Modernisms: American Women Poets and Their Readers*. Ed. Margaret Dickie and Thomas Travisano. Philadelphia: University of Pennsylvania Press, 1996. 170–88.

———. "Women on the Market: Edna St. Vincent Millay's Body Language." *Masks Outrageous and Austere: Culture, Psyche, and Persona in Modern Women Poets*. Bloomington: Indiana University Press, 1991. 135–64.

MARGARET MITCHELL
(1900–1949)

Rhonda Austin

BIOGRAPHY

Margaret Munnerlyn Mitchell was born on November 8, 1900, in Atlanta, Georgia, to Mary Isabelle (Stephens) Mitchell and Eugene Muse Mitchell, an attorney. Her only sibling was an older brother, Stephens. Growing up, she spent many childhood afternoons visiting the Cyclorama building, which housed a huge painting that depicts the 1864 battle for Atlanta.

A precocious child and avid reader, Mitchell read Shakespeare, Scott, and Dickens when she was a child. From 1914 to 1918 she attended Washington Seminary, a leading private school for young writers. After graduation, she became engaged to Clifford Henry, a young soldier and friend of her brother's. When Henry was sent overseas during World War I, Mitchell enrolled in Smith College, but she did not excel at anything and wrote to her brother, "If I can't be first, I'd rather be nothing" (Farr 46).

Henry was killed in France in October 1918, and Mitchell's mother died of pneumonia the following January. Mitchell completed her freshman year at Smith, then returned to Atlanta to assume responsibilities as mistress of her father's mansion on Peachtree Street. Trained early in ballroom dancing, horsemanship, and etiquette, as a debutante she would run afoul of local society matrons by performing in public the infamous Apache Dance from a popular movie of the day, *The Sheik of Araby*. The scandalous performance cost Margaret an invitation to join the prestigious Junior League, a slight she felt for years to come.

In September 1922, Mitchell married Berrien K. "Red" Upshaw, her longtime suitor. She chose the flamboyant, adventurous Upshaw over her other serious suitor, John Marsh, who would later become her second husband. A good friend of Upshaw's, Marsh served as best man at the Mitchell-Upshaw nuptials. Upshaw's genial manner masked a dark side, however, and after only a few months, the marriage dissolved amid accusations that Upshaw's alcoholism and violent temper resulted in Mitchell's physical and emotional abuse. Reportedly, Marsh gave Upshaw a loan, after which Upshaw agreed to an uncontested divorce. In exchange, Mitchell agreed not to press assault charges against him (Edwards 103).

With her marriage over and her reputation in shreds, Margaret took a job with the *Atlanta Journal Sunday Magazine*. Initially assigned to write fashion and society articles, she soon progressed to serious journalistic writing. Her newspaper work raised her consciousness of human misery and made her more aware of her privileged position. Some of her assignments exposed her to jails, hospital emergency rooms, and parts of Atlanta devastated by the Civil War. She commented to a friend, "Nowadays girls do get out more, people do know more, but even so, one good whiff of the police station on a hot July day would do a lot for a lot of people" (Farr 69).

In 1924, Mitchell and Marsh resumed their courtship and were married on July 4, 1925. The Atlanta newspapers treated the union like a first marriage, making no mention of her previous union to Upshaw. Eventually, her association with the literary community helped her regain her reputation. Her marriage to Marsh would prove enduring, and the couple was devoted to each other until her death.

In 1926, Mitchell left her job at the *Atlanta Journal* to become a full-time wife to John, stating that John's career would be the only public achievement in the Marsh family (Farr 77). When she reinjured an ankle hurt previously in 1911 and 1920 riding accidents, she was forced to remain in bed for several weeks. John brought home stacks of books for her to read from the public library and is reported to have said, "It looks to me Peggy, [his nickname for her] as though you'll have to write a book yourself if you're to have anything to read" (Farr 78). Whether this oft-reported quote is fact or myth, it appears that those weeks in bed were a contributing factor in Mitchell's decision to write her own book.

The last chapter of *Gone with the Wind* was the first to be written. Mitchell did copious amounts of research and worked on the chapters nonconsecutively. With the exception of the first chapter, the book was substantially complete by 1929. For years, the stacks of envelopes, each containing a chapter, all but disappeared into a closet where they remained for several years.

In 1935, Mitchell was introduced to Harold Latham, a Macmillan Publishing representative who was in Atlanta scouting new material. Encouraged by Medora Perkerson, a friend from her *Atlanta Journal* days, Mitchell agreed to let Latham read her not-quite-completed manuscript. The stack of envelopes she delivered to his hotel reached to her shoulders. Latham read the manuscript on the train to New Orleans and recognized its merit immediately (Farr 94). In the version Latham read, the heroine was dubbed Pansy O'Hara. Only later was her name changed to Scarlett.

Gone with the Wind was published and released on June 30, 1936, and became an instant sensation, selling over 330,000 copies in its first two months. By December of that year, over 1 million copies had been sold (Farr 132). Fame had a negative effect on Mitchell. She was overwhelmed by the book's popularity and, although gratified by its success, found herself unprepared for the changes it wrought in her life. She was besieged by reporters, requests for donations, fans, and telegrams. In a letter to fellow southerner Herschel Brickell, she states, "If I had known being an author was like this, I'd have thought several times before I let Harold [Latham] go off with my dog-eared manuscript. . . . being antisocial by nature and accustomed to a very quiet life, it has all been too much for me" (Farr 143).

When her husband's health began to deteriorate, she assumed many of the responsibilities of his business and his care. She never again wrote for publication, fearing the consequences of doing so. In a new will penned after the success of the book, she dictated that all manuscripts and notes should be destroyed after her death and that no license would ever be granted for comic strips, abridgments, or sequels to *Gone with the Wind*. However, one sequel appeared in 1991, and reportedly discussions are currently ongoing with the Mitchell estate for a second.

Mitchell died on August 16, 1949, five days after being struck by a speeding car while crossing a street near her home to attend a movie with her husband. Subsequently, the great majority of her writings and notes were destroyed according to her instructions. However, John Marsh deposited one large sealed envelope in Citizens and Southern National Bank in Atlanta with instructions that the envelope never be unsealed unless the need arose to prove authorship of *Gone with the Wind*.

MAJOR WORKS AND THEMES

Written during the depression, *Gone with the Wind* chronicles the disintegration of Southern society in the antebellum period of the Civil War. The reader views the story through the eyes of a single observer, Scarlett O'Hara. Though an imperfect heroine, Scarlett's experiences are representative of a broad spectrum of emotions and complications and are intensified by her interactions with a core group of Southern families portrayed in the novel. Other female characters provide contrast to and perspective for Scarlett's limited viewpoint.

The book addresses many social ills of the period, including poverty, carpetbaggers, racism, and the emergence of the Ku Klux Klan, elements of which were glossed over in the 1939 film adaptation. Although sometimes criticized for perpetuating stereotypes, the novel portrays the entire spectrum of political, racial, and sexual debate in the antebellum Southern experience.

The triumph of the human spirit over adversity and tragedy is an enduring theme of the novel, although Mitchell doesn't provide her reader with a typical "happily ever after" ending, a fact that has sparked much debate from initial publication. The long-suffering, angelic Melanie sacrifices her life trying to have a child, and Scarlett, after all she endures, does not succeed in convincing Rhett to remain with her at the end of the novel. Still, Scarlett does not despair but resolves to find a way to work things out, as documented in the now-classic last line of the novel, "After all, tomorrow is another day."

CRITICAL RECEPTION

In 1937, *Gone with the Wind* was awarded a Pulitzer Prize for American Literature from 1936 and the annual award of the American Booksellers Association. Immediately successful with the public, the novel initially received mixed reviews from the critics. Most early critics praised it for its dramatic structure and architectural quality, but few could agree on its lasting value. John Peale Bishop in *New Republic* referred to the novel as "one more of those 1000 page novels, competent but neither very good nor very sound" (qtd. in Pyron, *Recasting* 7). A spate of gender-related criticism focused on the romance or the "femaleness" of the novel, panning it for its romantic elements. At the other end of the spectrum, the reviewer for the *New York Sun* suggested that "in spaciousness, emotional power (and no American writer has approached Miss Mitchell in this respect) and in its picturing of a vast and complex social system in time of war, *Gone with the Wind* is most closely allied to Tolstoy's *War and Peace*" (qtd. in Pyron, *Recasting* 5). Some critics have compared Mitchell's book favorably with Faulkner's *Absalom, Absalom!* and Welty's *Delta Wedding*, both of which portray strong southern female characters. However, the overall consensus of the initial reviews was that *Gone with the Wind* was not only good; as Pyron notes, it could be favorably compared with the "monumental novels of the nineteenth century by Tolstoy, Dickens, and Thackeray; that its dramatic or architectural structure was compelling; that its characters lived; that its spirit and enthusiasm were contagious; and that its author was a gifted storyteller" (*Recasting* 207).

After the 1939 release of the film, critics often confused the novel with the film adaptation or left the novel unexamined altogether, preferring to focus on the popular film. Until about 1970, the association between the novel and the film version was so deeply rooted that criticism of the novel virtually disappeared. Cultural changes such as the civil rights and women's movements may be partially responsible for a recent reevaluation of *Gone with the Wind*. Biographies of Mitchell in the intervening years may also have contributed to a renewed academic interest that reflects the biases of earlier studies. A comprehensive overview of more recent criticism can be found in Pyron's bibliographical essay included in his 1983 essay collection *Recasting*: Gone with the Wind *in American Culture*. The long-term literary value of Mitchell's only novel has yet to be determined, although no one now disputes its popularity. *Gone with the Wind* ranks second only to the Holy Bible in all-time sales.

BIBLIOGRAPHY

Works by Margaret Mitchell

Gone with the Wind. New York: Macmillan, 1936.

Studies of Margaret Mitchell

Beye, Charles R. *"Gone with the Wind* and Good Riddance." *Southwest Review* 78 (1993): 366–80.

Edwards, Anne. *Road to Tara: The Life of Margaret Mitchell.* New Haven, CT: Ticknor & Fields, 1983.

Farr, Finis. *Margaret Mitchell of Atlanta: The Author of* Gone with the Wind. New York: William Morrow, 1965.

Gaillard, Dawson. *"Gone with the Wind* as Bildungsroman or Why Did Rhett Butler Really Leave Scarlett O'Hara?" *Georgia Review* 28 (1974): 9–18.

Gelfant, Blanche H. *"Gone with the Wind* and the Impossibilities of Fiction." *Southern Literary Journal* 13.1 (1981): 3–31.

Goodwyn, Frank. "The Ingenious Gentleman and the Exasperating Lady: Don Quixote de la Mancha and Scarlett O'Hara." *Journal of Popular Culture* 16.1 (1982): 55–71.

Hanson, Elizabeth I. *Margaret Mitchell.* Boston: Twayne, 1991.

Harwell, Richard, ed. *Margaret Mitchell's* Gone with the Wind *Letters, 1936–1949.* New York: Macmillan, 1976.

May, Robert E. *"Gone with the Wind* as Southern History: A Reappraisal." *Southern Quarterly* 17.1 (1979): 51–64.

Meindl, Dieter. "A Reappraisal of Margaret Mitchell's *Gone with the Wind." Mississippi Quarterly* 34.4 (1981): 414–34.

Morton, Marian J. " 'My Dear, I Don't Give a Damn': Scarlett O'Hara and the Great Depression." *Frontiers* 5.3 (1980): 52–56.

Pyron, Darden Asbury, ed. *Recasting*: Gone with the Wind *in American Culture.* Miami: University Press of Florida, 1983.

———. *Southern Daughter: The Life of Margaret Mitchell.* New York: Oxford University Press, 1991.

Schefski, Harold K. "Margaret Mitchell: *Gone with the Wind* and *War and Peace." Southern Studies* 19 (1980): 243–60.

Spadoni, Carl. "The Dutch Piracy of *Gone with the Wind." Papers of the Bibliographical Society of America* 84.2 (1990) 131–50.

Stern, Jerome. *"Gone with the Wind*: The South as America." *Southern Humanities Review* 6 (1972): 5–12.

Sutherland, Daniel E. "Southern Carpetbaggers in the North; or, Ashley Wilkes, Where Are You Now?" *McNeese Review* 24 (1977–1978): 9–17.

Watkins, Floyd C. *"Gone with the Wind* as Vulgar Literature." *Southern Literary Journal* 2.2 (1970): 86–103.

MARIANNE MOORE
(1887–1972)

Ernest J. Smith

BIOGRAPHY

Marianne Moore was born in the home of her maternal grandfather (the Reverend John Riddle Warner) in Kirkwood, Missouri, on November 15, 1887, and it was here that she lived until the age of seven. She never met her father, John Milton Moore, who, a few months prior to her birth, suffered a nervous breakdown from which he never recovered. Following the breakdown, at least partially the result of a business failure, the family had moved from Massachusetts back to the father's native Ohio. Marianne's mother, Mary Warner, took her young son John Warner (called Warner) to Kirkwood where her father, a widower for over twenty years, was pastor of the First Presbyterian Church. Marianne Moore grew up in an atmosphere of religious belief, and her devotion to family, particularly her mother and brother, was lifelong. She never married, and aside from her time away at college, Moore would live with her mother until Mary Warner's death in 1947.

After John Riddle Warner died in 1894, the family moved near Pittsburgh to live with relatives, before settling in nearby Carlisle, Pennsylvania, in 1896. Moore was enrolled at the Metzger Institute, a private school for girls, where her mother was teaching. She entered Bryn Mawr College in 1905, earning her A.B. in 1909, focusing in history, biology, and law after being advised not to major in English. Her writing, she was told, lacked clarity. Nevertheless, Moore published poems in the college's literary magazine between 1907 and 1909, enjoyed the study of both painting and prose, particularly class exercises in imitating various prose styles, and submitted both poems and a story to the *Atlantic* during her senior year.

Following her graduation from Bryn Mawr, Moore spent a year taking clerical courses at Carlisle Commercial College, then began teaching typing, stenography, bookkeeping, commercial law, and other subjects at Carlisle Indian School. She also traveled to Europe with her mother in 1911. By 1914, the department where she taught had been discontinued, and Moore was subsequently without regular employment until 1918. Her writing was ongoing, however. The Bryn Mawr alumnae magazine received several of her poems between 1910 and 1915, and in 1915, Moore published a total of sixteen poems in *The Egoist* (London), *Others* (New York), and *Poetry* (Chicago). Her intellectual life was flourishing even before she and her mother moved to New York in 1918. She was reading Pound and Eliot before 1915, exchanging books and journals with well-educated neighbors in her Carlisle community, making trips into New York to visit art exhibitions and galleries, and becoming interested in the women's suffrage movement. As a result of her published poems in 1915, she began a lifelong correspondence with H. D. and met William Carlos Williams.

The 1918 move to Greenwich Village in New York City was crucial for Moore, especially in the acceleration of her literary career. She began working at a branch of the New York Public Library, and around 1920, she met Scofield Thayer and James Sibley Watson, who became co-owners of the influential literary magazine *The Dial*. In 1920 Moore also met Bryher (Winifred Ellerman), H. D.'s lover and later lifelong companion. Moore and Bryher struck a friendship that would result in an enduring correspondence. It was Bryher, H. D., and Robert McAlmon who arranged the publication of Moore's *Poems* (1921) in England. Moore received copies in July 1921, and while she did not have a hand in the selection or arrangement of the twenty-four poems, her correspondence reveals that she had been contemplating a book of poems previously. Her second volume, *Observations* (1924), contained fifty-three poems chosen by Moore, including her major long poems "Marriage" and "An Octopus," inspired by her trips of 1922 and 1923 to visit Warner in Bremerton, Washington, and their hike on Mt. Rainier. By 1924, when she received the prestigious Dial Award, she had also published important reviews of major works by Eliot, Pound, Williams, H. D., and Stevens. Her career was well under way, and in 1925, she ascended to the position of editor at *Dial*.

Moore's four-year stint as editor was so demanding that she ceased publishing poems for nearly seven years, yet her work at *Dial* is nearly as important as her early poetry in the shaping of modernism. The magazine was truly international in scope, publishing important work by poets, essayists, and prose fiction writers, as well as visual artists, both American and European. Among the contributors between 1925 and 1929, the period of Moore's editorship, were Eliot, Pound, Williams, Wallace Stevens, E. E. Cummings, Hart Crane, D. H. Lawrence, W. B. Yeats, Thomas Mann, and visual artists such as Picasso, Cocteau, Georgia O'Keefe, Wyndam Lewis, and Charles Sheeler. As the 1920s drew to a close, *Dial* lacked the financial resources necessary to continue publication, so the July 1929 issue was the final number. Later that fall, Moore and her mother moved from Manhattan to Brooklyn. Soon thereafter, Moore commenced publishing poems, and in the early 1930s, some of her better-known animal poems appeared: "The Jerboa" (1932), "The Plumet Basilisk" (1932), and "The Frigate Pelican" (1934). Moore met the young poet Elizabeth Bishop in 1934, and the two developed a lifelong friendship.

At T. S. Eliot's urging, Moore published her *Selected Poems* in 1935, to favorable reviews. A year later *The Pangolin and Other Verse* appeared, followed by *What Are Years* (1941). Moore was by now a well-established and highly regarded poet, particularly among her literary peers, and she continued a lively interaction, largely through written correspondence, with both her contemporaries and younger writers. The political unrest of the 1930s disturbed Moore, and some of her letters reveal a struggle with the relationship of art to politics. In her verse, rather than address political events directly, her typical approach is to treat broad subjects that have moral and political implications, subjects such as freedom, heroism, and imprisonment.

During the 1940s Moore became more of a public literary figure, giving lectures and readings and holding short-term teaching assignments. *Nevertheless* (1944) won the Harriet Monroe Poetry Award, and later in the decade she won a Guggenheim and a grant from the American Academy of Arts and Letters. Although her mother's death in 1947 was a devastating loss, her many friendships, including a new one with W. H. Auden, helped to see her through. After her *Collected Poems* appeared in 1951, she was awarded the Bollingen Prize, the National Book Award, and the Pulitzer Prize within the space of three years. Her translation of *The Fables of La Fontaine* followed in 1954, and she published two additional volumes of poetry, as well as an essay collection, during the 1950s. Even as she became the grandam of American poetry in the 1960s, appearing on television and popular magazine covers, she continued to write and publish. Her career culminated with *The Complete Poems* in 1967, but she continued writing until a major stroke disabled her in 1969. She died on February 5, 1972.

MAJOR WORKS AND THEMES

Moore's significance in shaping modern poetry is almost incalculable. As editor of *The Dial* for four years, her interaction with major literary figures, not just American but international, is a testimony to her dedication to the enduring value of art. What is all the more striking is that amidst all these varied and powerful possibilities of influence, she remains as startlingly original as any poet America has produced. The extensive use of quotation in her poetry may seem to parallel the allusiveness of Pound and Eliot, but she pulls from a more varied array of sources than either of these contemporaries. Drawing on her background and interests in science and history, her wide reading in both literary and popular sources such as newspapers and magazines, as well as the contemporary media of radio and television, Moore broadened the material available for poetry. Her notion of what constitutes textuality, along with the attention to language's role as mediator, continues to influence recent developments in schools of postmodern American writing such as language poetry.

While clearly an avant-garde, experimental modernist, Moore is also important for the precision and accuracy she insisted on in poetic language. David

Perkins suggests that her "effort for exact presentation of the object and the use of prose rhythms" links her with the imagists (555). Moore's descriptiveness is the hallmark of her style, but her wit exceeds that of any other modernist, and her flexible stanza forms and line lengths make her work immediately identifiable on the page. Bonnie Costello notes how Moore's poems are often "daringly asymmetrical," the lines continually readjusting and testing the limits of the margin as well as language itself (4). She is the only American modernist to experiment with syllabic verse and, along with Stevens and Williams, one of the first Americans to consider ways in which modern, post-impressionist European painting might suggest techniques for modern poetry. Like Stevens and Virginia Woolf, her work engages the modern theme of perception and representation, the question of how we order and present observation and experience in language.

While some critics would argue that Moore's essential work is contained in her earliest volumes, her *Complete Poems* demonstrates that she was still writing innovative poems at least through the 1950s. Her best-known early poem is "Poetry," with its famous opening line "I, too, dislike it." The poem exists in both a longer and much-distilled shorter version, which make for a delightful comparison, but both conclude with an emphasis on the "genuine" as the true test of poetry. Two longer poems from *Observations* (1924) are major achievements: "Marriage" and "An Octopus." In the 1930s and 1940s Moore began writing more poems using animals as subjects, with "The Plumet Basilisk," "The Jerboa," "The Frigate Pelican," and "The Pangolin" among her strongest. *What Are Years* (1941) included her important landscape poem "Virginia Britannia"; and as Moore became an increasingly public figure, her later volumes contained many fine shorter poems, some of them occasional or commissioned works, including several poems on baseball. In addition to translating the *Fables* of La Fontaine, the 1950s saw the appearance of a collection of essays, *Predilections*, and the brief essay "Humility, Concentration, and Gusto" offers a useful statement on her artistic values.

CRITICAL RECEPTION

Moore's work was favorably received and reviewed throughout her lifetime. Ezra Pound was one of the first to take note, praising her work as early as 1918. The fact that H. D., Bryher, and Robert McAlmon published Moore's *Poems* (1921) without her knowledge confirms that her reputation was an international one as early as 1915, when her poetry appeared in *The Egoist*. While some reviewers had problems understanding her work, finding the diction arcane or esoteric, major contemporaries such as Eliot, Williams, and Stevens wrote favorably of her work in the 1920s and 1930s. Later in her career, the important poet-critic Randall Jarrell characterized her as one of modern poetry's great innovators, in terms of both content and style.

During her lifetime, Moore was awarded nearly every major American literary prize given for poetry, and in addition to her appearances in several forms of popular media, a profile-article in the February 16, 1957, *New Yorker* presented her to an even wider audience. Beginning with Jean Garrigue's overall assessment of Moore's work in 1965, a wide variety of critical studies have appeared, confirming her position as one of the most important modern American poets. Moore's influence is evident in critical studies from the two generations of poets succeeding her, including Donald Hall's *Marianne Moore: The Cage and the Animal* (1970) and Grace Schulman's *Marianne Moore: The Poetry of Engagement* (1986).

Charles Molesworth, Moore's biographer, has noted how the selections in the *A Marianne Moore Reader* (1961), including her humorous correspondence with the Ford Motor Company, present Moore as "a grandmotherly figure" who appears almost "genderless." Given major early poems like "Marriage," it is indeed astonishing that modern critical views on Moore seem to assume that her work does not engage the issues of a woman's life, an assumption corrected by significant essays of the 1980s and 1990s such as Alicia Ostriker's "What Do Women (Poets) Want? H. D. and Marianne Moore as Poetic Ancestresses" (1986), Marilyn L. Brownstein's "The Archaic Mother and Mother and Mother: The Postmodern Poetry of Marianne Moore" (1989), and Kirstin Hotelling's " 'The I of Each Is to the I of Each, a Kind of Fretful Speech Which Sets a Limit on Itself:' Marianne Moore's Strategic Selfhood" (1998).

In addition, recent studies of Moore have taken an interdisciplinary approach, exploring her interest in science, technology, and the visual arts. Significant work in this area includes book-length studies by Elisabeth W. Joyce, Linda Leavell, and Lisa M. Steinman. The publication of a generous selection of Moore's letters in 1997, edited by Bonnie Costello, was a major event for her readers and scholars. The bulk of Marianne Moore's papers are held by the Rosenbach Museum and Library in Philadelphia.

BIBLIOGRAPHY

Works by Marianne Moore

Poems. London: Egoist, 1921.
Observations. New York: Dial, 1924.
Selected Poems. New York: Macmillan, 1935; London: Faber, 1935.
The Pagolin and Other Verse. London: Brendin, 1936.
What Are Years. New York: Macmillan, 1941.
Nevertheless. New York: Macmillan, 1944.
Collected Poems. New York: Macmillan, 1951; London: Faber, 1951.
The Fables of La Fontaine. New York: Viking, 1954. (Translations)
Predilections. New York: Viking, 1955; London: Faber, 1955. (Nonfiction)
Like a Bulwark. New York: Viking, 1956.
Idiosyncrasy and Technique. Berkeley: University of California Press, 1958. (Nonfiction)
O to Be a Dragon. New York: Viking, 1959.

A Marianne Moore Reader. New York: Viking, 1961.

The Absentee: A Comedy in Four Acts. New York: House of Books, 1962. (Dramatic adaptation of Maria Edgeworth's novel)

The Arctic Ox. London: Faber, 1964.

Tell Me, Tell Me. New York: Viking, 1966.

The Complete Poems of Marianne Moore. New York: Macmillan, 1967.

The Complete Prose of Marianne Moore. Ed. Patricia C. Willis. New York: Viking, 1986.

The Selected Letters of Marianne Moore. Ed. Bonnie Costello. New York: Knopf, 1997.

Studies of Marianne Moore

Borroff, Marie. *Language and the Poet: Verbal Artistry in Frost, Stevens, and Moore.* Chicago: Chicago University Press, 1979.

Brownstein, Marilyn L. "The Archaic Mother and Mother and Mother and Mother: The Postmodern Poetry of Marianne Moore." *Contemporary Literature* 30 (1989): 13–32.

Costello, Bonnie. *Marianne Moore: Imaginary Possessions.* Cambridge: Harvard University Press, 1981.

Garrigue, Jean. *Marianne Moore.* Minneapolis: University of Minnesota Press, 1965.

Goodridge, Celeste. *Hints and Disguises: Marianne Moore and Her Contemporaries.* Iowa City: University of Iowa Press, 1989.

———. *Marianne Moore.* (Special issue) *Sagetrieb* 6 (1987).

Hadas, Pamela White. *Marianne Moore: Poet of Affection.* Syracuse: Syracuse University Press, 1977.

Hall, Donald. *Marianne Moore: The Cage and the Animal.* New York: Pegasus, 1970.

Hotelling, Kirstin. " 'The I of Each Is to the I of Each, a Kind of Fretful Speech Which Sets a Limit on Itself: Marianne Moore's Strategic Selfhood." *Modernism/Modernity* 5 (1998): 75–96.

Joyce, Elisabeth W. *Cultural Critique and Abstraction: Marianne Moore and the Avant-Garde.* Lewisburg: Bucknell University Press, 1998.

Kappel, Andrew J., ed. *Marianne Moore.* (Special issue) *Twentieth Century Literature* 30 (1984).

Leavell, Linda. *Marianne Moore and the Visual Arts: Prismatic Color.* Baton Rouge: Louisiana State University Press, 1995.

Miller, Cristanne. *Marianne Moore: Questions of Authority.* Cambridge: Harvard University Press, 1995.

Molesworth, Charles. *Marianne Moore: A Literary Life.* New York: Atheneum, 1990.

Ostriker, Alicia. "What Do Women (Poets) Want? H. D. and Marianne Moore as Poetic Ancestresses." *Contemporary Literature* 27 (1986): 475–92.

Parisi, Joseph, ed. *Marianne Moore: The Art of a Modernist.* Ann Arbor: UMI Research Press, 1990.

Perkins, David. *A History of Modern Poetry: From the 1890s to the High Modernist Mode.* Cambridge: Harvard University Press, 1976.

Schulman, Grace. *Marianne Moore: The Poetry of Engagement.* Urbana: University of Illinois Press, 1986.

Sielke, Sabine. *Fashioning the Female Subject: The Intertextual Networking of Dickinson, Moore, and Rich.* Ann Arbor: University of Michigan Press, 1997.

Stapleton, Laurence. *Marianne Moore: The Poet's Advance*. Princeton, NJ: Princeton University Press, 1978.

Steinman, Lisa M. *Made in America: Science, Technology, and American Modernist Poets*. New Haven, CT: Yale University Press, 1987.

―――. " 'So As to Be One Having Some Way of Being One Having Some Way of Working': Marianne Moore and Literary Tradition." *Gendered Modernisms: American Women Poets and Their Readers*. Ed. Margaret Dickie and Thomas Travisano. Philadelphia: University of Pennsylvania Press, 1996. 97–116.

Tomlinson, Charles, ed. *Marianne Moore: A Collection of Critical Essays*. Englewood Cliffs, NJ: Prentice, 1969.

Willis, Patricia C. *Marianne Moore: Vision into Verse*. Philadelphia: Rosenbach Museum and Library, 1987.

―――, ed. *Marianne Moore: Woman and Poet*. Orono, ME: National Poetry Foundation, 1990.

MOURNING DOVE (HUM-ISHU-MA) [CHRISTINE QUINTASKET] (1882?–1936)

Beverly G. Six

BIOGRAPHY

Assumed to be a member of the Colvile tribe, Mourning Dove (Christine Quintasket) was born between 1882 and 1888 to Lucy Stukin and Joseph Quintasket. Many details about her life remain undocumented or controversial, and her own fictionalized autobiographical accounts add to discrepancies. She wrote under the name Morning Dove (translated from Hum-ishu-ma), corrected to Mourning Dove in 1921 to symbolize the hardships of her life. Taught Native customs and both Native and Catholic religion by her mother, she entered Goodwin Mission School in 1895. She was alienated and unhappy, remained briefly, became ill, and was sent home. There she learned English from pulp novels belonging to Jimmy Ryan, her family's adopted Anglo son, and Native folklore from an adopted grandmother. In 1898 she returned to Goodwin Mission School and adjusted well. She returned to the reservation in either 1899 (to care for an expanding family) or 1902 (when her mother died). After her father remarried in 1904, she attended Fort Shaw Indian School, in Great Falls, Montana. She married Hector McLeod in 1909; they soon separated. In 1912 she began and abandoned *Cogewea*, and from 1912 or 1914–1921 she collected Okanogan tales. She studied typing and basic writing at a Calgary business school from 1913 to 1915 and taught at Inkameep Okanogan reserve in British Columbia, in 1917 or 1918. In 1914 she met Lucullus McWhorter, who encouraged her and edited her work until his death. In 1919 she married Fred Galler and wrote, despite chronic illnesses, after long days of work, primarily as a migrant laborer. *Cogewea*, edited by McWhorter, was published in 1927; *Coyote Stories*, edited by Heister Guie, was published in 1933. Mourning Dove was the first Native American woman to be made an honorary member of the Eastern Washington Historical Society (1927) and to be elected to the Colville Council (1935); she was active in reservation politics, speaking publicly for Native rights. She died on August 8, 1936, and was buried in Okanogan, Washington, under the marker "Mrs. Fred Galler." The words "MOURNING DOVE, Colville Author, 1884–1936" were added to her tombstone later. Her autobiography, edited by Jay Miller, was published in 1990.

MAJOR WORKS AND THEMES

Until the recent discovery of Alice Callahan's 1891 *Wynema*, Mourning Dove was thought to be the first Native American woman to publish a novel; she is still the first Native American woman to publish a novel that conveyed Native history, cultural practices, and religion through the blending of fictional narrative and folktales. Her intent in writing was to preserve and explain Native culture. As a folklorist, she preserved the stories of a diminishing oral tradition and demonstrated their importance as literature and their meaning for Native culture; major fictional themes include prejudice against the "half-breed," the struggle to preserve Native cultures amid social change, and social conflicts between Anglos and Native Americans. After *Cogewea*, Paula Gunn Allen's *Woman Who Owned the Shadows* was the next novel by an Indian woman with a mixed-blood, female protagonist.

Cogewea, the Half-Blood (1927) has three weaknesses: formulaic "romance-novel" structure, distracting, labored "western" dialogue, and problems resulting from McWhorter's heavy-handed editing. Cogewea, the half-breed heir to a ranch, is nearly compromised and then deserted by an Anglo-American, Densmore; she then marries a half-breed, Jim LaGrinder. McWhorter's editorial intrusions are most obvious in erudite diatribes, explanatory notes, and, possibly, abrupt shifts in Cogewea's diction. In one example, Cogewea shifts immediately from "I guess he savied it was time that I possessed some glad rags! Maybe he tumbled that I had about earned them" to "If the malady is deep seated, an abatement must not be expected in so short a time. An absorption remedy of any nature is usually slow of results and a persistent and potent application is ofttimes necessary" (82–83). A major strength is the author's use of Cogewea's grandmother and spiritual mentor, the Stemteemä, to advance the plot. Cogewea's assertion that "[i]t is practically impossible for an alien to get at our correct legendary lore" (94) illustrates Mourning Dove's intent to preserve the integrity of Native culture.

In *Coyote Stories* (1933), Mourning Dove strove to preserve the tales and provide an accurate account of Okanogan beliefs for "the children of another race to read" (Preface 12). The twenty-seven tales, collectively a characterization of the trickster Coyote, are both etiological and didactic and contain multicultural motifs. "The Spirit Chief Names the Animal People" explains the origins of animal names, the Indian people, and the sweat-lodge ritual; Coyote receives his powers and the title "Spirit Chief." Etiological titles include "How Turtle Got His Tail," "Why Badger Is So Humble," and "Why Mosquitoes Bite People." "Coyote Juggles His Eyes," with variants of "Red Riding Hood" motifs, explains bluebird's tiny eyes, and Coyote learns not to imitate the gifts of others.

The footnotes and the sophisticated spelling and syntax are assumed to be Guie's editorial mark, but the tales retain the conventional structures of oral traditions.

Tales of the Okanogans (1976), edited by Donald M. Hines, contains thirty-eight tales, some included in *Coyote*, some unpublished elsewhere. These etiological and didactic tales follow oral conventions and contain editorial incursions in explanatory notes and grammatical corrections.

Mourning Dove: A Salishan Autobiography (1990) is important for autobiographical and ethnographic information in the author's personal narrative and descriptions of Okanogan cultural practices. Jay Miller believed she "intended her efforts to be edited" (Introduction xxxiii); given unfinished manuscripts, he selected and arranged entries, corrected spelling and grammar, noted authorial fabrications, and added explanatory notes. Mourning Dove intended for her life story to help Okanogans "record their traditions and gain all the rights they . . . [were] entitled to" (32). A didactic tone is evident. "My Life" ends with "Whatever I dreamed . . . I always bore in mind the teachings of my parents that truthfulness and honesty must be the objective in future life" (33). "The Big Snow and Flood Rampage" ends with: "[T]he important lesson . . . was that we could best survive by working together" (166). There is an unacknowledged feminist theme; Section I is "A Woman's World" (one-third of the chapters), and much of the tribal history (III. Okanogan History) is told from the women's viewpoint. Section II ("Seasonal Activities") describes origins of tribal rituals and religion. Despite three editors, the entire Mourning Dove canon irreplaceably preserves the cultural beliefs, history, and literature of the Okanogans and establishes her as an early feminist and talented American author.

CRITICAL RECEPTION

The majority of criticism about Mourning Dove's works concerns *Cogewea* and centers on three perceived problems—the degree to which McWhorter altered the text, the multiple shifts in Cogewea's diction, and the formula-western format—and on the work as a Native American text. When *Cogewea* was published, reviewers, citing two title-page authors and the scholarly intrusions, questioned whether a Native American woman wrote it.

Midcentury critics flawed *Cogewea* for its editorial intrusions and noted that the formula-western genre overshadowed the Native voice (see Brown's summary in *Dictionary of Native American Literature*); later critics see the novel as a significant Native text, although most acknowledge Mourning Dove's complaint to McWhorter after publication that she was unhappy and "surprised at the changes . . . [he] made" (Karell 451; Halverson 109).

Bernardin, questioning the premise of "authentic" Native voice, argues that Cogewea's mixed diction illustrates the "cultural and linguistic dislocations" (495) of American Indians, especially mixed bloods, and concludes that the mixed authorship and combination of romance genre and Okanogan folklore support the mixed blood–dilemma theme. Halverson sees the novel's editorial problems as a conflict between "lived" and mythical perceptions of the West. She asserts that it is "an ironic reworking of the [western] genre" (106), with the white man's betrayal of the Native maiden as a major theme.

Karell argues that readers cannot assume Mourning Dove wrote the "simple" passages and McWhorter the scholarly ones; she concludes that the multiple voices illustrate Cogewea's refusal to be solely Anglo *or* Native and develop the mixed blood–dilemma theme. She labels *Cogewea* "a compelling series of collaborations crossing gender, race, religious, and interpersonal boundaries" (464). Viehmann agrees that Cogewea's shifts in diction illustrate "her inability to choose between two different ways of life" (236); examining parallels between Okanogan stories and the plot, she insists that the folklore makes the text "a narrative of mixed descent" (242). Wilson agrees that the folklore is essential, making "[t]he novel . . . an extension of the Okanogan oral tradition, creating a thematic bridge between the oral word and the written text" (28).

Coyote Stories (1933) receives less critical attention, although initially it was so favorably received that it was reprinted immediately in 1934. Modern criticism is mixed. Brown points out that the book preserves Native culture and makes that culture "comprehensible" to an Anglo audience ("Mourning Dove" 261) and praises its doing so without sacrificing the "dynamic" of that literature ("Mourning Dove's Canadian" 119). Fisher examines Native authors' problems in preserving the communal, oral traditions when forced to publish in singular voice and written form.

Coyote criticism primarily examines the effects of editing. Schneider feels that Guie's editing "compromised authenticity" (470) but argues also that the stories transcend that to represent the Native American "spirit." His labeling the tales "ancient explanations" (471), however, ignores their folkloric significance. Despite folklore scholars' acceptance that each storyteller amends stories, Miller decries Mourning Dove's bowdlerization of the stories for an Anglo audience and asserts they "are not true to Salishan recitations" ("Bison Book Edition" ix). Concluding that "[h]er treatment of Coyote is particularly cursory" (x), he devotes the remainder of his introduction to his own description of Coyote. In "A Voice from the Past" Brown praises the strong, feminist voice and laments Miller's misogynistic editing in both *Coyote Stories* and Mourning Dove's *Autobiography*.

Critical commentary on the *Autobiography* (1990) centers on editorial voice and autobiographical value. Schneider believes Miller controlled "content and presentation" but asserts Mourning Dove controlled voice and "thematic development" (470). He believes "it is an account of tribal life written by a tribal member" and concludes that Miller's editing gives the work "its academic and long-term value" (470–71). Bowering argues that the book is open-ended and representative of the contemporary viability of Salishan culture and people.

Critical evaluation of the *Autobiography* is difficult because the text existed only in rough, manuscript form during the author's lifetime and was published after heavy editing. Mourning Dove's editors pose critical problems for all her works. *Coyote Stories* also has not been adequately evaluated as folklore; it is an excellent example of the traditional purposes and conventional forms of oral literature. As the most recent criticism on *Cogewea* shows, however, Mourning Dove is now beginning to receive the attention she deserves as a major author in the Native American canon.

BIBLIOGRAPHY

Works by Mourning Dove

Cogewea, the Half-Blood. Ed. Lucullus V. McWhorter. 1927. Lincoln: University of Nebraska Press, 1981.
Coyote Stories. Ed. Heister Dean Guie. 1993. Lincoln: University of Nebraska Press, 1990.
Tales of the Okanogans. Ed. Donald Hines. Fairfax, WA: Ye Galleon, 1976.
Mourning Dove: A Salishan Autobiography. Ed. Jay Miller. Lincoln: University of Nebraska Press, 1990.

Studies of Mourning Dove

Beidler, Peter G. "Literary Criticism in *Cogewea*: Mourning Dove's Protagonist Reads *The Brand.*" *American Indian Culture and Research Journal* 19.2 (1995): 45–65.
Bernardin, Susan K. "Mixed Messages: Authority and Authorship in Mourning Dove's *Cogewea, the Half-Blood*: A Depiction of the Great Montana Cattle Range." *American Literature* 67 (1995): 487–509.
Bowering, George. "The Autobiographings of Mourning Dove." *Canadian Literature* 144 (1995): 29–40.
Brown, Alanna K. "Mourning Dove." *Dictionary of Native American Literature.* Ed. Andrew Wiget. New York: Garland, 1994. 259–64.
———. "Mourning Dove's Canadian Recovery Years, 1917–1919." *Canadian Literature* 124–125 (1990): 113–22.
———. "Mourning Dove's Voice in *Cogewea.*" *Wicazo Sa Review* 4.2 (1988): 2–15.
———. "A Voice from the Past." *Woman's Review of Books* 8.2 (1990): 19–20.
Fisher, Alice Poindexter. "The Transportation of Tradition: A Study of Zitkala-Sa and Mourning Dove, Two Transitional American Indian Writers." Diss. City University of New York, 1979.
Halverson, Cathryn. "Redefining the Frontier: Mourning Dove's *Cogewea, the Half-Blood*: A Depiction of the Great Montana Cattle Range." *American Indian Culture and Research Journal* 21.4 (1997): 105–24.
Karell, Linda K. " 'This Story I Am Telling You Is True': Collaboration and Literary Authority in Mourning Dove's *Cogewea.*" *American Indian Quarterly* 19 (1995): 451–65.
Miller, Jay. Introduction. *Mourning Dove: A Salishan Autobiography.* By Mourning Dove. Ed. Jay Miller. Lincoln: University of Nebraska Press, 1990. xi–xxxix.
———. "Introduction to the Bison Book Edition." *Coyote Stories.* By Mourning Dove. Ed. Heister Dean Guie. Lincoln: University of Nebraska Press, 1990. v–xvii.

Schneider, William. Rev. of *Mourning Dove: A Salishan Autobiography* and *Coyote Stories* (Bison Books edition), by Mourning Dove. *Ethnohistory* 38 (1991): 469–71.

Viehmann, Martha L. " 'My People . . . My Kind': Mourning Dove's *Cogewea, the Halfblood* as a Narrative of Mixed Descent." *Native American Writers*. Ed. Harold Bloom. Philadelphia: Chelsea House, 1988. 227–42.

Wilson, Michael. "Writing a Friendship Dance: Orality in Mourning Dove's *Cogewea*." *American Indian Culture and Research Journal* 20.1 (1996): 27–41.

JOSEPHINA NIGGLI
(1910–1983)

Catherine Cucinella

BIOGRAPHY

Josephina Niggli, playwright, poet, short story writer, and novelist born in Monterrey, Nuevo León, Mexico, on July 13, 1910, lived most of her life in the United States. Her father, Frederick Ferdinand, a Texan, managed a cement factory in Mexico, and the family lived in the northern Mexican town of Hidalgo. Niggli, home-schooled by her mother, Goldie Morgan Niggli, until entering Main Avenue High School in San Antonio, Texas, received her B.A. from the Incarnate Word College. During her college years, Niggli published articles in *Mexican Life* and *Ladies' Home Journal*. Her early creative efforts earned her prizes both in fiction writing (*Ladies' Home Journal*) and poetry (the National Catholic Poetry Contest). In her undergraduate years, Niggli's father published the first collection of her poems, *Mexican Silhouettes* (1928, revised 1931).

After her graduation from Incarnate Word College, Niggli spent four years studying with the San Antonio Little Theater, where she worked on her playwriting skills before enrolling in the Carolina Playmakers program at the University of North Carolina. She received her M.A. from the University of North Carolina in 1937. In addition to producing her master's thesis *Singing Valley* in 1936, the Carolina Playmakers produced *Tooth or Shave* (1935, 1936), *The Cry of Dolores, Soldadera, The Red Velvet Goat, Azteca, Sunday Costs Five Pesos* (1936), and *The Fair-God* (1937).

In the years 1935–1936 and 1937–1938 Rockerfellow Fellowships allowed Niggli the opportunity to work in the theater in Mexico. During this time Margaret Mayorga published Niggli's play *This Is Villa* in *The Best One-Act Plays of 1938*; Niggli's historical play *Soldadera* was published in Mayorga's *The Best One-Act Plays of 1937*. After receiving the 1938 Fellowship of the Bureau of New Plays, Niggli moved to New York. In 1939 Niggli began teaching English and drama at the University of North Carolina, Chapel Hill. Niggli also worked in Hollywood (1948) and studied at the Abbey Theater in Dublin (1950) and at the Old Vic School in Bristol (1955). From 1956 to 1975, Niggli taught English and drama at Western Carolina University.

Niggli also published three novels, *Mexican Village* (1945), *Step Down, Elder Brother* (1947), and *A Miracle for Mexico* (1964) as well as a book on play-writing, *Pointers on Playwriting* (1945).

MAJOR WORKS AND THEMES

In the introduction to the 1994 edition of *Mexican Village*, María Herrera-Sobek writes that Niggli, born in Mexico of Scandinavian American parents, "grew up bilingual and bicultural," thus presenting "a unique case vis-à-vis questions of ethnic identity and nationality" (xvii). As an inhabitant of a border town, Niggli understood the struggles involved in negotiating a mixed cultural identity. Identity construction within a national and ethnic context emerges as a major theme in Niggli's body of work. In addition, Niggli complicates accepted gender roles, problematizes racial boundaries, and challenges hierarchies and class systems within Mexico. Along with these issues, Mexican history and folklore delineate the major thematic aspects of Niggli's work.

In *Mexican Village* Bob Webster, who enters the town of Hidalgo as an outlander, an outsider, embodies Niggli's concern with cultural identity. Clearly an American by mannerism and name, Webster's "straight black hair" and "brown face" shatter the villagers' understanding of *yangui*. In one sense, Webster, the son of an Anglo father and a Mexican American mother, belongs to the northern village of Hidalgo, yet in another sense, he also belongs to white America. Raymund A. Paredes elucidates the difficulties of constructing an identity that straddles two or more cultures: "In creating Webster, Niggli was pointing to the Mexican-American as a distinctive type, as someone apart from both the *mexicano* and the *yanqui* who could build his own identity on the foundation of two cultures" (89).

Although locating the motivation for Webster's journey to Mexico in the demands of his blood, Niggli also suggests the importance of cultural memory in the form of stories and legends in Webster's quest. Throughout *Mexican Village*, Niggli carefully intermingles the folktales, legends, and songs of Mexico. Tía Magdalena, a *bruja* (eagle witch), brings to the novel all the folklore and legend of the *bruja*; and her position as witch intervenes in many of the narratives. Thematically, Niggli presents a novel that takes seriously the place of folklore in the cultural consciousness of Mexico.

Although Niggli's plays display the same thematic concerns as *Mexican Village*, her historical drama *Soldadera* offers a striking example of Niggli's challenge to the traditional representation of the woman-soldier as merely a camp follower and by implication a prostitute. These women-soldiers, all of whom hold on to the memories of "those horror-ridden years before 1910," emerge as crucial participants in the Agrarian Revolution (Niggli, *Folk Plays* x). *Soldadera* clearly gives voice to these often misrepresented women.

CRITICAL RECEPTION

The scholarship on Josephina Niggli recognizes her as an early Chicano/a writer. Raymund A. Paredes, in his essay "The Evolution of Chicano Literature," marks Niggli's *Mexican Village* as "a landmark in Mexican-American history" (88). María Herrera-Sobek views Niggli as a border writer and precursor of Chicano/a literature who deals with the themes, legends and history of Mexico (Introduction). Frederick H. Koch, founder and director of the Carolina Play-makers, saw Niggli as a Mexican writer whose plays "speak for her people with authentic realism and poetic feelings" (xiii). In the Foreword to *Mexican Folk Plays*, Rodolfo Usigli, of the Theatre of the National University of Mexico, addresses the authenticity and lyricism of Niggli's plays and places her within a tradition of Mexican playwrights (xvii). While acknowledging Niggli's selection of material as "accurate and definitely Mexican" (xix), Usigli laments the fact that Niggli writes in English, and he sees her as capable of helping to shape a poetic theater in Mexico.

These early comments point to Niggli as a Mexican writer attempting to represent Mexican culture for Americans. Koch states that *Mexican Folk Plays* represent Niggli's hope that her works "serve somewhat toward a better understanding of our Mexican neighbors" (xiii). The idea of intended audience and the problems of writing in English for an American audience engender comment in Niggli scholarship. In his discussion on Niggli's play *Soldadera*, Usigli questions her treatment of "essentially" Mexican material. As a play for a "foreign public," Usigli finds *Soldadera* satisfying; however, he goes on to say that "it is [his] feeling that if presented to a Mexican public, the treatment of *Soldadera* would have to be somewhat different to be altogether satisfactory" (xix). Although Usigli does not specify what changes would accommodate a Mexican public, his remarks imply the difficulty of presenting a work that would please both Mexican and American audiences. Clearly Niggli's work demonstrates the anxiety and difficulty of reconciling or negotiating bicultural impulses.

Paredes views Niggli's articulation of these impulses as evidence of early Chicano/a writing. Herrera-Sobek also considers Niggli a Chicana writer. As Herrera-Sobek argues, Niggli's work does clearly represent a border literature. Like Paredes, Herrera-Sobek points to Bob Webster in *Mexican Village* as a marker of Niggli's attempt "to cross the cultural boundaries between Mexico and Anglo American culture" (xxvii). While acknowledging the difference between Niggli's character and the majority of Chicanos'/as' experiences, Herrera-Sobek views Niggli as a border writer because of her concerns with questions of nationality and ethnic origins (xxviii).

In her attempt to question the notions of nationality and ethnicity, Niggli often draws on both Mexican and gender stereotypes. While Usigli suggests that Niggli's folk subjects are free from the "picturesque and the vulgar," he also recognizes her portrayals of stereotypes. Usigli identifies Niggli's stereotypes as representative of the folk in the northern provinces of Mexico: "Miss Niggli's elements are not universally Mexican . . . but her characters contain the essentials of any Mexican small-town folk attitude towards life" (xviii). Herrera-Sobek more directly addresses Niggli's use of stereotypes and her need to appeal to the American public: "Through the insertion of familiar models (i.e. stereotypes), Niggli sought to render acceptable to the American public that which to them was exotic and different" (xxix). Niggli enacts a compromise in her work through the juxtaposition of some stereotypes with carefully crafted and fully developed characters. Paredes explains, "To be sure, some of [Niggli's] characters verge close to stereotypes: the swaggering *macho*, the haughty Spaniard, the long-suffering Mexican women. But Niggli also presents strong men who are nonetheless sensitive and vulnerable, *gachupines* who treat the Indians decently, and women . . . who truckle before no man" (90). These critics do not ignore Niggli's use of stereotypes, but they seem to agree that Niggli's work more often than not exposes stereotypes as creative devices. They further acknowledge that Niggli's characterization emerges as one of the very strong elements in her body of work.

The critical response to Niggli's work also focuses on her use of folklore, legend, and history in her plays and novels. This use of folklore places Niggli in a tradition of Latin American writers dating to the colonial period in Mexico. Herrera-Sobek identifies elements in Niggli's writing that manifest in the writings of Gabriel García Márquez such as the appearance and reappearance of characters in her stories and her use of folklore both to structure and to develop plot (xxv). The inclusion of folklore and popular songs does not function as mere decoration; rather, according to both Herrera-Sobek and Paredes, it adds to the cultural ambience of Niggli's work.

As she draws on the legends, myths, songs, and history of Mexico, Niggli also relies on the sounds of the Mexican language in her representation of Mexico and Mexicans. Although written in English, her work reproduces the syntactical and idiomatic qualities of the Spanish language through literal translations such as "the family Castillo" or "the father of Servero" (Paredes 90; Herrera-Sobek xxv). Paredes offers a strong assessment of Josephina Niggli's influence, contribution, and place in a Chicano/a literary tradition: "Niggli's greatest achievement was to delineate an important aspect of Mexican-American experience and to create a distinctive ambience for its presentation" (91).

BIBLIOGRAPHY

Works by Josephina Niggli

Mexican Folk Plays. Chapel Hill: University of North Carolina Press, 1938.
Pointers on Playwriting. Boston: Writer, 1945.
Miracle at Blasise, a Play in One Act. London: French, 1946.
Pointers on Radio Writing. Boston: Writer, 1946.
Mexican Village. 1945. Albuquerque: University of New Mexico Press, 1994.

Step Down, Elder Brother. New York: Rinehart, 1947.
A Miracle for Mexico. Greenwich, CT: New York Graphic Society, 1964.
New Pointers on Playwriting. Boston, Writer, 1967.

Studies of Josephina Niggli

Herrera-Sobek, María. Introduction. *Mexican Village.* By Josephina Niggli. Albuquerque: University of New Mexico Press, 1994. xvii–xxix.
———, ed. *Beyond Stereotypes: The Critical Analysis of Chicana Literature.* Binghamton, New York: Bilingual Review, 1985.
Hicks, Emily D. *Border Writing: The Multidimensional Text.* Minneapolis: University of Minnesota Press, 1991.
Koch, Frederick H. Introduction. *Mexican Folk Plays.* Chapel Hill: University of North Carolina Press, 1938. vii–xiii.
Paredes, Raymund "The Evolution of Chicano Literature." *Melus* 5 (1978): 71–110.
Parr, Carmen Salazar, and G. M. Ramirez. "The Female Hero in Chicano Literature." *Beyond Stereotypes. The Critical Analysis of Chicana Literature.* Ed. María Herrera-Sobek. Binghamton, New York: Bilingual Review, 1985. 47–60.
Usigli, Roldolfo. Foreword. *Mexican Folk Plays.* By Josephina Niggli. Ed. Frederick H. Koch. Chapel Hill: University of North Carolina Press, 1938. xv–xx.

FLANNERY O'CONNOR
(1925–1964)

Leslie Winfield Williams

BIOGRAPHY

Mary Flannery O'Connor was born in Savannah, Georgia, on March 25, 1925, the only daughter of Edward and Regina Cline O'Connor. As a young girl, she was educated in Roman Catholic schools, and her Catholicism in the heart of the Bible Belt provided her with a unique and powerful perspective in her work. Though she retained an orthodox faith throughout her life, her stories were not traditionally pious.

In 1941, O'Connor's father died of disseminated lupus, and she and her mother moved first to Atlanta, then to her mother's hometown of Milledgeville, Georgia, where O'Connor graduated from high school in 1942. She attended the local Georgia Woman's College, where she edited the literary quarterly the *Corinthian* and drew cartoons for the college paper. From 1945 to 1948, she attended the Iowa Writers Workshop, where she received a master's degree. She then left for New York for a brief stay at Yaddo writer's colony. In 1950, she moved to a farm in Connecticut with Robert and Sally Fitzgerald for approximately a year and a half. The Fitzgeralds provided her with encouragement and introduced her to other writers.

In 1950, on the train home to Georgia for Christmas, O'Connor became ill with the disseminated lupus that had earlier killed her father. She moved with her mother to the family farm, Andalusia, on the outskirts of Milledgeville. There, her health was stabilized, although her life was restricted by a meticulous daily regimen and the steroid drugs that exhausted her energies. She was able to write for only two or three hours in the morning, pouring her energies into her work. She enjoyed the company of friends and other visitors who came to Andalusia. Travel and speaking engagements drained her strength, but she was an avid correspondent, answering the many people who wrote to her. She died of lupus in Milledgeville, Georgia, on August 3, 1964, at age thirty-nine.

MAJOR WORKS AND THEMES

Flannery O'Connor's corpus is small. Besides six stories written for her master's thesis at Iowa and early portions of *Wise Blood*, all her work was written in the fourteen years between the onset of her illness and her death. The body of her work consists of two short novels, *Wise Blood* and *The Violent Bear It Away*, and two collections of short stories, *A Good Man Is Hard to Find* and *Everything That Rises Must Converge*. Her occasional prose and speeches are collected in *Mystery and Manners* and her letters in *The Habit of Being*.

With such a small, concentrated output, she is generally considered to have mastered the short story and not the novel. She says, "For those of us who want to get the agony over in a hurry, the novel is a burden and a pain" (*Mystery and Manners* 77). She was attracted to brevity, concentration, and dark humor.

One of the most mentioned themes in Flannery O'Connor's work is her portrayal of the South. Though holding a place in the Southern Gothic tradition of the Southern Renaissance, O'Connor's sense of place is not the essential element in her work. She uses the South's geography, fundamentalism, manners, and people (especially country people) to convey a deeper message that becomes accessible through these particulars. Generally speaking, the South is a vehicle for her, not an end.

Many complaints are leveled against O'Connor for failing miserably as a Southern writer. People pointed out to her that Georgia was not at all how she illustrated it, "with escaped convicts roaming the roads exterminating families or Bible salesmen prowling around looking for girls with wooden legs" (*Mystery and Manners* 38). Despite criticism, for O'Connor the South is the perfect grounding for her stories. Religious conviction can still be made believable in the South; in fact, religious enthusiasm is accepted as one of the South's prevalent features. In the heart of the South, ordinary people know and read the Bible; thus, writer, readers, and characters all share a common religious influence.

O'Connor's goal is to explore deeper kinds of realism than mere regionalism requires. The South provides fertile ground for probing faith: "I think it is safe to say that while the South is hardly Christ-centered, it is most certainly Christ-haunted. The Southerner, who isn't convinced of it, is very much afraid that he may have been formed in the image and likeness of God" (*Mystery and Manners* 44–45). O'Connor writes about what she knows. The concrete details of the experience of life, including place, are important. Just as important, though, is to probe the mystery beneath the particular locale, which often creates "bizarre" characters and events not considered "realistic" by those who are looking for superficial mimetic fidelity.

Other themes in O'Connor's work include her reaction to certain aspects of the culture in general, especially the denial of mystery and the loss of faith. America had become a "materialistic" culture, which did not trust or recognize realities other than those our senses verify or our minds contain. Rationalism had created a sharp gulf between the reality accessible to intellect and that which the intellect cannot comprehend. Kathleen Feeley quotes *Democracy in America* by Alexis de Tocqueville, who calls our reliance on reason and thought alone a "national malaise," stating that Americans deny what we cannot comprehend, leaving us little faith for the extraordinary and a distaste for the supernatural (54).

O'Connor concurs with this as the predominant view of the culture: "For nearly two centuries the popular spirit of each succeeding generation has tended more and more to the view that the mysteries of life will eventually fall before the mind of man" (*Mystery and Manners* 158). She is consumed with finding a way to combat this notion. Her stories are unrelenting attempts to reveal, point to, suggest, describe the mystery beyond the natural world. She is determined to portray humanity as more than corporeal, our existence as higher, deeper than the concrete alone; yet she knows it is through the concrete that the spiritual is reached and revealed.

The pattern in most of her stories is that the protagonist is filled with personal pride—pride in self-reliance, in class status, or in ability. The central character is led, often through a series of bizarre and shocking events, to a moment of epiphany in which the self is annihilated. In "Everything That Rises Must Converge," the moment is traumatic humiliation for Julian's mother. In "The Artificial Nigger," the moment of insight leads to grace and repentance, when Mr. Head is remorseful after realizing his own pridefulness and sin for leaving his grandson Nelson. In other stories, the moment of epiphany occurs at the moment of death. For both Mrs. May in "Greenleaf" and the grandmother in "A Good Man Is Hard to Find," death is the price paid to recognize their pride and self-righteousness.

O'Connor's work is also a reaction against the cultural loss of faith. Two major characters in her novels represent two types of Americans she is reacting to. At the beginning of *Wise Blood*, Hazel Motes is an empiricist who believes that truth consists only of what one can prove through the senses. George Rayber, the rationalist in *The Violent Bear It Away*, believes that the real is rational, and vice versa; the universe has an order that humans are capable of understanding and controlling. Both these attitudes, empiricism and rationalism, lead to despair, damnation, and spiritual death (Keller).

O'Connor speaks to Americans living in the post-Christian era, those for whom God is dead. In her nonfiction prose and speeches, she is acutely conscious of being a believer in a nonbelieving age. Critics seize on this dilemma, especially when confronted with her powerful but hardly traditionally religious style. This paradox is at the center of the critical disputes over interpretation: How can stories containing such violence, horror, and freakish people also contain an affirmation of faith? How can such emotionally inaccessible characters be explained at all, much less in terms of religion? After all, the religious hints in her work are so enigmatic that most of the early critics missed them entirely. Given that her stated audience is "unsaved," and that she wants to reach them with a spiritual message, she certainly picks an odd way to go about it.

One explanation for her style is that because the base of American cultural assumptions and a shared understanding of the Christian faith had disappeared, O'Connor is forced to develop a way to get people's attention. In her struggle between rhetoric and style, apology and art, art wins out over faith (speaking in terms of the execution of her work, not in her personal life).

Because she is writing from a minority stance as a rhetorician, she has to find the best tools for making the best case. She cannot assume that readers outside the South understand the fundamentals of the Christian experience; therefore, she has to get across both the events of the story as well as the religious significance of the events. As rhetorician, O'Connor first reaches the reader on a level common to all humanity, the sensual and the concrete. Then she objectifies the characters' experiences and shocks the reader. Finally, she uses language sacramentally as the definitive rhetorical to help readers unlock the meaning.

As she emphasizes over and over in her speeches, O'Connor uses the concrete as a means to break through the natural world to the mystery beyond. Like magical realism, the concrete is a toehold into our own palpable reality, so that once we have accepted the physical world described in familiar detail, we are able to accept a thrust beyond into a realm of the spiritual, or nonmaterial. Any person, with or without theological background, can relate to the details of her text. The reader is hooked by emotional association. Examples of powerful metaphor and description occur throughout her corpus. The criminal's car in "A Good Man Is Hard to Find" is a "big black battered hearse-like automobile"; the mother's face is "as broad and innocent as a cabbage." Hazel Motes's car in *Wise Blood* is repeatedly referred to as a "rat-colored car." Clothes, faces, possessions, and scenery are specific and unforgettable. The concrete gives a terra firma from which to behold the glimpses of grace that she then shows us unexpectedly. The reader is more likely to believe the glimpses if surrounded by familiar, concrete detail.

Many critics complain that her characters are inaccessible: We are rarely shown what goes through their heads or hearts. As a rhetorical tool, this method allows her to keep the vision from being too particular. If the experience of a character is too far out of the reader's range, he or she may be able to follow the thinking but cannot claim it personally. The objectification of experience is a tool that allows O'Connor to transfer her vision as nearly whole as possible to the reader.

Another rhetorical device she uses is to shock the reader by heightening both events and people, through violent situations. She does not use violence gratuitously. Never an end in itself, violence "is the extreme situation that best reveals what we are essentially" (*Mystery and Manners* 3). Faith, she writes elsewhere, is not a cozy electric blanket but a cross. Because death is the ultimate manifestation of grace, the ultimate triumph of Christ, then the moment of death is also the supreme moment of grace. To make this point unmistakably clear to nonbelievers, she portrays the ultimate in violence to alert her spiritually sleepy readers to this central paradoxical truth.

Another means of shocking the reader is O'Connor's use of the grotesque. If we dismiss her freaks as having nothing to do with us, we miss the point. As she points out, "When an artist uses a freak for a hero, he is not simply showing us what we are, but what we have been and what we could become" (*Mystery and Manners* 118). The freaks are us; we are her grotesqueries, driven to the edge. She uses exaggerated figures, such as Hazel Motes, who atones for his sins by wrapping barbed wire around his chest and walking with glass shards in his shoes, or Parker in "Parker's Back," who tattoos every available inch of his body. As a result of depicting such extremes, O'Connor not only gets the reader's attention, but she fights the hazy compassion associated with religious sentimentality. She does not want to elicit a "nice" emotion, a sweet, pleasant, vaguely religious feeling; rather, she wants the reader to see how far sin carries human beings.

The final tool in addressing a post-Christian audience is her symbolic, imagistic language. If a sacrament is defined as "the outward and visible sign of an inward and spiritual grace," then her language is sacramental, both in a literary and theological sense. Though her words create strong, metaphorical word pictures, even her most literal language is infused with suggestion of a different, more mysterious, connotative order. In short, it is poetic, bearing more weight than the denotative meanings of the individual linguistic units. "Fiction," she says, "is an incarnational art" (*Mystery and Manners* 68).

O'Connor's use of the language and her refusal to lower standards raise her work above the level of didacticism and apology to art; and it is because she does not succumb—at least in the texts themselves—to the temptation to explain their meaning that a variety of interpretations, both religious and secular, are legitimate.

CRITICAL RECEPTION

A history of O'Connor criticism reveals 1957 as a watershed year, when she published "The Fiction Writer and His Country," her first Christian essay. Before 1957, critics generally did not pick up on the religious cues in the texts, and the spiritual dimension in her work was largely ignored. Critics focused on her language, characterization, and technical skill. Richard Stern commented on her "unusual portraits of unusual characters"; a Kansas City paper wrote, "These stories are technically excellent, spiritually empty" (Schloss 13–14). R.W.B. Lewis remarked that though Hazel Motes was not a sympathetic character, O'Connor's language was "clear and vivid," her prose "remarkably pure and luminous," concluding that *Wise Blood* was an aimless attack on Southern Fundamentalism (Stephens 50).

Letters reveal that O'Connor's response to these remarks was dismay. John

Hawkes suggested that her intent might be anagogical. Then, in 1957, she revealed herself as a Christian writer, and this admission presented a critical dilemma still under debate today: Does the reader have to share or be schooled in the Christian perspective to understand her work? Those with a New Critical bent would say that her stated intent should have no bearing on the interpretation of the texts themselves; other critics such as Ted Spivey in 1987, in an article on New Criticism versus Deconstruction, argued for an "intertextual approach," considering her comments on her work an essential ingredient in the correct interpretation. O'Connor states her own position: "The intentions of the writer have to be found in the work itself and not in his life" (Schloss 15). At any rate, since 1957, critics have been divided over the religious elements in her work.

On the religious side, critics are varied in their conclusions about O'Connor's work. Robert Drake suggests that Jesus Christ is the main character in all of O'Connor's fiction and that the one story she tells over and over is her hero's confrontation with Him. Stanley Edgar Hyman suggests that her work is about the search for redemption in Christ and the hero's recognition of vocation. Critics write of the effect of redemptive grace, some reducing the action of her stories to a common sequence: an initial rebellion against belief, a crisis of faith, and a resolution in a moment of grace.

Critics arguing for a secular interpretation are led by Josephine Hendin, who examines O'Connor's psychology, suggesting that religion could have been an effective way to express and contain an irreligious kind of fury. She suggests that the process of writing, not the texts themselves, was probably redemptive for O'Connor, considering her life situation. She concludes that O'Connor's essay "The Fiction Writer" probably did more to mislead readers than to inform them because critics became willing to accept her statements of intention as accurate descriptions of her art (18). This, she says, is a mistake.

Critics in the middle include John Hawkes, who suggests that her Catholicism and moral bias disappear in the creative process. Many others claim that her orthodoxy is only one aspect of her work. David Eggenschwiler argues for a Christian humanistic approach, combining psychological, social, and religious elements, but concluding that some form of anagogical reading is necessary: "The reader who respond[s] to a single level of meaning would be responding not only partially, but wrongly; would be denying her central assumptions about existence" (13).

On the one hand, O'Connor has given us clues as to her intentions as writer. However, because many of her stories give only an occasional phrase to clue the reader that the story is supposed to be taken in a specifically religious sense, one is free to interpret the stories in other ways as well. In the end, they stand on their own as examinations of the human experience and thus remain open for psychological, social, textual, and other venues of literary or personal interpretation.

BIBLIOGRAPHY

Works by Flannery O'Connor

Wise Blood. New York: Harcourt, 1952.
A Good Man Is Hard to Find. New York: Harcourt, 1955.
The Violent Bear It Away. New York: Farrar, 1960.
Everything That Rises Must Converge. New York: Farrar, 1965.

Studies of Flannery O'Connor

Asals, Frederick. *Flannery O'Connor: The Imagination of Extremity*. Athens: University of Georgia Press, 1982.

Balee, Susan. *Flannery O'Connor: Literary Prophet of the South*. New York: Chelsea, 1994.

Baumgaertner, Jill P. *Flannery O'Connor: A Proper Scaring*. Wheaton, IL: Shaw, 1988.

Bloom, Harold, ed. *Modern Critical Views: Flannery O'Connor*. New York: Chelsea, 1986.

Brinkmeyer, Robert H. *The Art and Vision of Flannery O'Connor*. Baton Rouge: Louisiana State University Press, 1989.

Browning, Preston M., Jr. *Flannery O'Connor*. Carbondale: Southern Illinois University Press, 1974.

Coles, Robert. *Flannery O'Connor's South*. Baton Rouge: Louisiana State University Press, 1980.

Desmond, John. *Risen Sons: Flannery O'Connor's Vision of History*. Athens: University of Georgia Press, 1987.

Di Renzo, Anthony. *American Gargoyles: Flannery O'Connor and the Medieval Grotesque*. Carbondale: Southern Illinois University Press, 1993.

Drake, Robert. *Flannery O'Connor: A Critical Essay*. Grand Rapids, MI: Eerdmans, 1966.

Driskell, Leon V., and Hoan T. Brittain. *The Eternal Crossroads: The Art of Flannery O'Connor*. Lexington: University Press of Kentucky, 1971.

Eggenschwiler, David. *The Christian Humanism of Flannery O'Connor*. Detroit, MI: Wayne State University Press, 1972.

Farmer, David. *Flannery O'Connor: A Descriptive Bibliography*. New York: Garland, 1981.

Feeley, Kathleen. *Flannery O'Connor: Voice of the Peacock*. New Brunswick, NY: Rutgers University Press, 1972.

Fickett, Harold, and Douglas R. Gilbert. *Flannery O'Connor: Images of Grace*. Grand Rapids, MI: Eerdmans, 1986.

Fitzgerald, Robert and Sally Fitzgerald. Eds. *Mystery and Manners: Occasional Prose*. New York: Farrar, 1969.

The Habit of Being. Ed. Sally Fitzgerald. New York: Farrar, 1979.

Friedman, Melvin J., and Beverly Lyon Clark. *Critical Essays on Flannery O'Connor*. Boston: G. K. Hall, 1985.

Friedman, Melvin J., and Lewis A. Lawson, eds. *The Added Dimension: The Art and Mind of Flannery O'Connor*. New York: Fordham University Press, 1977.

Gentry, Marshall Bruce. *Flannery O'Connor's Religion of the Grotesque*. Jackson: University Press of Mississippi, 1986.

Getz, Lorine M. *Nature and Grace in Flannery O'Connor's Fiction*. New York: Mellen, 1982.

Giannone, Richard. *Flannery O'Connor and the Mystery of Love*. Urbana: University of Illinois Press, 1989.

Grimshaw, James A., Jr. *The Flannery O'Connor Companion*. Westport, CT: Greenwood, 1981.

Hawkes, John. "Flannery O'Connor's Devil." *Sewanee Review* 70 (1962): 395–407.

Hendin, Josephine. *The World of Flannery O'Connor*. Bloomington: Indiana University Press, 1970.

Hyman, Stanley Edgar. *Flannery O'Connor*. Minneapolis: University of Minnesota Press, 1966.

Keller, Jane Carter. "The Figures of the Empiricist and the Rationalist in the Fiction of Flannery O'Connor." *Arizona Quarterly* (1972): 263–73.

Kessler, Edward. *Flannery O'Connor and the Language of Apocalypse*. Princeton, NJ: Princeton University Press, 1986.

Magee, Rosemary. *Conversations with Flannery O'Connor*. Jackson: University Press of Mississippi, 1987.

Martin, Carter W. *The True Country: Themes in the Fiction of Flannery O'Connor*. Nashville: Vanderbilt University Press, 1968.

May, John R. *The Pruning Word: The Parables of Flannery O'Connor*. Notre Dame: University of Notre Dame Press, 1976.

McFarland, Dorothy Tuck. *Flannery O'Connor*. New York: Ungar, 1976.

McMullen, Joanne Halleran. *Writing against God: Language as Message in the Literature of Flannery O'Connor*. Macon, GA: Mercer University Press, 1996.

Muller, Gilbert H. *Nightmares and Visions: Flannery O'Connor and the Catholic Grotesque*. Athens: University of Georgia Press, 1972.

Orvell, Miles. *Flannery O'Connor: An Introduction*. Jackson: University Press of Mississippi, 1991.

———. *Invisible Parade: The Fiction of Flannery O'Connor*. Philadelphia, PA: Temple University Press, 1972.

Paulson, Suzanne Morrow. *Flannery O'Connor: A Study of the Short Fiction*. Boston: Twayne, 1988.

Schloss, Carol. *Flannery O'Connor's Dark Comedies: The Limits of Inference*. Baton Rouge: Louisiana State University Press, 1980.

Spivey, Ted R. "Flannery O'Connor, the New Criticism, and Deconstructionism." *Southern Review* 23.2 (1987): 271–80.

Stephens, Martha. *The Question of Flannery O'Connor*. Baton Rouge: Louisiana State University Press, 1973.

Whitt, Margaret Earley. *Understanding Flannery O'Connor*. Columbia: University of South Carolina Press, 1995.

DOROTHY PARKER
(1893–1967)

James Ward Lee

BIOGRAPHY

Late in life, if Dorothy Parker's phone rang or her doorbell chimed, she was likely to snap, "What fresh hell is this?" She had come to see her life as a series of hells, but this was not new; for decades, her poems and stories—even her journalism—spoke her distrust of life and her disappointment at her place in the great scheme of things—if indeed there was a scheme at all. One of her most famous verses is "Resume," which lists all the possible ways to kill yourself. After enumerating knives, guns, and poison, and considering hanging, drowning, and drugging, the speaker concludes, "you might as well live." Not exactly a celebration of life, but what was there to celebrate when one went from fresh hell to fresh hell? Her dark view of life made her writing sharp and bitter and funny and right on the mark for the between-the-wars decades. This sharp and bitter and dark little woman with the viper tongue ran rampant in American literary circles from just after World War I until about the time of World War II. She lived until 1967, but her heyday was during the Roaring Twenties and the Depression Thirties.

Born Dorothy Rothschild in West End, New Jersey, on August 22, 1893, Parker grew up in New York City, which was always her artistic milieu. Born of a Jewish father and a Scottish mother who died early, Dorothy attended private schools in New York and New Jersey and hit the Gotham literary scene with a burst of wit and irony while still in her early twenties. As a teenager, she published verses in *Vogue* and was soon hired by publisher Frank Crowningshield to write cutlines and cartoon captions. By 1917, she was reviewing plays for *Vanity Fair*, and in 1919, she founded the famous "Round Table" of the Algonquin Hotel on West Forty Fourth Street in New York City. The Algonquin Round Table became the most famous "literary salon" in America, though, unlike the celebrated European salons, it was merely a luncheon club with a floating membership of journalists, editors, and writers. During the glory years of what some have called "The Vicious Circle," lunch at the Algonquin might include playwrights George S. Kaufman, Mark Connolly, Laurence Stallings, and Robert Sherwood; *New Yorker* founding editor Harold Ross; humorists Franklin P. Adams, Heywood Broun, Alexander Woollcott, and Robert Benchley. It might also include actors Harpo Marx and Tallulah Bankhead, novelist Edna Ferber, and sports and fiction writer Ring Lardner. But at the center of this circle of writers—many now barely remembered except in histories of New York literati—was always Dorothy Parker, the funniest and sharpest of the group.

In the early 1920s, Parker wrote articles for *Life, Saturday Evening Post*, and *Ladies' Home Journal*. Her first short story, "Such a Pretty Little Picture," was published in *Smart Set* in 1922; her second story, the still widely anthologized "Too Bad," appeared in the same magazine a year later. "Too Bad" is a typical Parker story of a marriage—and a pair of lives—gone bad from apathy. The refrain line, spoken by two women who are rehashing the breakup of the Weldons, is "too bad." Of course the couple have nothing in common but boredom, and the separation is anything but "too bad." Throughout the 1920s, Parker wrote stories for some of the leading magazines of the times—*American Mercury, New Yorker, Cosmopolitan, Harper's Bazaar*. But it was her relationship with *New Yorker* that helps define the work of Dorothy Parker. It can also be argued that Parker helped to set the fictional and poetic course of Harold Ross's *New Yorker*, which began in 1925—and published the first of many Parker stories in February of that year. "Slick," "sophisticated," "cynical," and "modern" define *New Yorker*, and they are almost perfect descriptions of Parker's work as well. Her heroes and heroines are members of what was once called the Café Society or the Smart Set or the Flapper Generation. Parker and *New Yorker* got their start during the time that Frederick Lewis Allen in *Only Yesterday* called an era of "blue skies and bathtub gin." Representative of a decade of Prohibition, the Jazz Age, F. Scott and Zelda Fitzgerald, Jay Gatsby and Daisy, boom and bust, the people of the 1920s were wild and whirling, disillusioned by the horrors of a war just over and one soon to come, "a lost generation," as Gertrude Stein was to call them. World War I had destroyed certainty, and the men and women of the Roaring Twenties were left in what many saw as a godless universe.

Twice in the 1920s Parker attempted suicide and had at least one abortion. She married Edwin Parker the same year America entered World War I; she divorced him in 1928, and despite another marriage—two, actually, but to the same man (Alan Campbell)—she remained "Mrs. Parker" for the rest of her life. She spent some of the 1930s in Hollywood as a screenwriter, but her volumes of verse and her stories brought her the recognition that she enjoys today. She published forty-eight stories, hundreds of sketches, reviews, articles, and four volumes of poetry. She wrote, alone or with a collaborator, half a dozen plays and revues and wrote, rewrote, or participated in some thirty screenplays. Among the movies she worked on are *Paris in the Spring* (1935), *The Big Broadcast of 1936, A Star Is Born* (1937), *The Little Foxes* (1941), Alfred

Hitchcock's *Saboteur* (1942), and the Bette Davis vehicle *Mr. Skeffington* (1944). She worked on many others for which she did not receive screen credit but for which she was making what amounted to a fortune in those days— $5,200 a week. Her days as a screenwriter ended with her being blacklisted in 1949 during the "Red Scare" that ended so many Hollywood careers. She was branded "the queen of the Communists" by anonymous right wingers and denounced to J. Edgar Hoover by Walter Winchell.

Dorothy Parker returned to New York, wrote for *Esquire* for a time, and ended her days in more or less obscurity in a small hotel in New York. In 1954, she wrote a play with Arnaud D'Usseau that ran forty-five performances. The play, *The Ladies of the Corridor*, did not receive a good critical reception, though Parker said, "It was the only thing I ever did that I was proud of." After her death on June 7, 1967, in New York City, her ashes were stored in a file drawer in a New York law office until 1988 when they were transferred to the office of the National Association for the Advancement of Colored People (NAACP) in Baltimore. They now occupy a place of honor at a memorial garden of the NAACP, the organization that was named as a legatee in her will. Her proposed epitaph was "Excuse my Dust."

MAJOR WORKS AND THEMES

Dorothy Parker's major works are to be found in four volumes of verse and three volumes of stories published during the 1920s and 1930s; several collected editions published both during her lifetime and after her death; two collections of criticism published after her death; and the wonderful *Portable Dorothy Parker* in the Viking Portable Library series. Parker's *Portable* was published in 1944 and was among the first ten in the Viking series. It is interesting—and important—to note that of the first ten of the Viking Portables, only three have never gone out of print—*Shakespeare, The World Bible*, and *The Portable Dorothy Parker*. The first *Portable Dorothy Portable* (1944) was introduced by Somerset Maugham, and the revised edition (1973) by Brendan Gill, a staff writer for *New Yorker*. Various editions of Parker's collected works appeared from time to time, but the *Complete Stories* appeared from Penguin in 1995, and a selection of fugitive poems appeared under the title *Not Much Fun: The Lost Poems of Dorothy Parker* in 1996. Finally, *Dorothy Parker: The Complete Poems* was published by Penguin in 1999.

The poems and stories of Dorothy Parker owe a great debt to A. E. Housman, the almost perfect cynic, whose poems say very much the same thing that Parker's poems do: Life is pointless, youth is fleeting, old age is worse than death. Housman celebrates those young men who have the nerve to kill themselves in preference to growing old—"If the sickness is in your soul,/Stand up and end it like a man." The only two ages bearable for both Parker and Housman are youth and death. Parker and Housman find themselves in a godless universe where one is, as Housman says, "A stranger and afraid/In a world I never made."

Of course since Parker's narrators are women and Housman's all young men, there is a dimension in Parker's poems not found in the verses of the author of *A Shropshire Lad*. Parker's women have to contend with love in a different way from the lads in Housman's England. Her ladies are expected to change each time they meet a new man, but as readers of Parker have come to know, her women refuse to conform. Nor did Dorothy Parker: she vows to stay the way she is because "she does not give a damn." It is interesting to note that Parker and Housman are not only alike in themes but also in style. Each wrote the carefully crafted, epigrammatic poem. Usually short, always rhymed, and always with a snap at the end. Housman's observation that "There's this to say for blood and breath/They give a man a taste for death" or Parker's "You might as well live" are quick and summary endings.

Parker's short fiction resembles her poetry in that it concerns feckless people, boredom, sickness with life, and the hollowness of the modern world. In "Big Blond," probably her most anthologized story, we see most of Parker's themes— fictional and poetic—developed. Hazel Morse is "of the type that incites some men when they use the word 'blond' to click their tongues and wag their heads roguishly" (*Complete Stories* 105). She is also described as "a woman given to recollections. At her middle thirties, her old days were a blurred and flickering sequence, and imperfect film, dealing with the actions of strangers" (*Complete Stories* 105). She drifts aimlessly from man to man and from drink to drink. When insomnia—the emblem for existential angst in modern fiction—over-comes her, she buys some veronal and begins the slide that will almost certainly lead to her death. The story, which won the 1929 O. Henry Short Fiction Award, is typical of Parker's work in that we see the vapidity of "Uptown New York" in those years of total disillusionment that Fitzgerald and Hemingway depict with such clarity.

Many of her stories were published in *New Yorker* and are archetypes of the story that has come to be called *New Yorker*-style—short, glittering, sophisti-cated reflectors of the hollowness of modern urban life. One of the most mem-orable of her *New Yorker*-style stories is "From the Diary of a New York Lady during Days of Horror, Despair, and World Change" (1933). The narrator of this short monologue speaks to her diary from Monday through Friday of a typical week. The woman has no inner life and flits from party to party and shop to shop. In a typical passage, she tells of her manicurist's arrival at her fashionable apartment:

Miss Rose came about noon to do my nails, simply *covered* with *the* most divine gossip. The Morrises are going to separate *any* minute, and Freddy Warren definitely has ulcers, and Gertie Leonard simply *won't* let Bill Crawford out of her sight even with Jack Leonard *right there in the room*, and it's all true about Sheila Phillips and Babs Deering. It *couldn't* have been more thrilling. Miss Rose is *too* marvelous; I really think that a lot of times people like that are a lot more intelligent than a lot of people. Didn't notice until after she was gone that the damn fool had put that *revolting* tangerine-colored polish on my nails; *couldn't* have been more furious. Started to read a book but too nervous. (*Complete Stories* 191)

Such a passage needs no comment.

CRITICAL RECEPTION

The final critical word is not in on Dorothy Parker. During her lifetime, she, along with Thurber, Robert Benchley, Franklin P. Adams, Alexander Woollcott, and Heywood Broun, was all the rage among the smart set and graced the pages of periodicals like *New Yorker, Smart Set, Vogue*, and *Cosmopolitan*. Time has not dealt kindly with most of those New York wits, though Parker has never completely fallen from favor. However, she does not appear in critical articles alongside the big names of her time—Fitzgerald, Faulkner, Hemingway, Cather, Frost, Millay, Steinbeck, O'Neill, or Wharton. But Dorothy Parker won't go away. *The Portable Dorothy Parker* is a case in point. There is also the fact of her presence on the Internet: There must be fifty or sixty web sites devoted to Parker, though most of them are merely collections of her aphorisms. But one webmeister has gone to the trouble to produce an extensive bibliography of her works and works about her. Some of her works are on audiotape, and PBS produced a documentary on the Algonquin Round Table. The television production was not to celebrate great writers but to call attention to the "great American salon." The film *Dorothy Parker and the Vicious Circle*, starring popular actor Jennifer Jason-Leigh, was not a great success, but it brought Parker to the attention of a new and younger audience.

One of the most balanced assessments of Dorothy Parker's work is to be found in Brendan Gill's 1973 introduction to *The Portable Dorothy Parker*. He says, "Readers coming to Mrs. Parker for the first time may find it as hard to understand the high place she held in the literary world of forty or fifty [now sixty or seventy] years ago as to understand the critical disregard into which she subsequently fell" (xv). Gill does not overpraise Parker, but he does recognize that there was more to her works than can be found in those by such writers as Benchley and Woollcott and others of the Round Table. Gill says, "If it is easier to visit the world of the twenties and thirties through Mrs. Parker's short stories and soliloquies than through her verse, it is also more rewarding; to a startling degree, they have a substance, a solidity, that the poems do not prepare us for" (xix). It is easy to call her poems a series of clever wisecracks, but her use of language is still sharp and oftentimes startling. As she herself said in a *Paris Review* interview in 1956, "Wit has truth in it; wise-cracking is simply callisthenics with words" (Capron 81). To dismiss her verse as a series of wisecracks is to miss a point about poetry, about literary style.

It is true that Dorothy Parker is not Faulkner, but as Regina Barreca points out in the introduction to *Dorothy Parker: The Complete Stories*, there were a "gang of critics who sought to punish her for the authenticity and lack of pretense in her writing," but "Parker hold[s] a glass up to life, lightly. She wins, finally, because her success affords her the last laugh" (xix). Dorothy Parker is, admittedly, a minor writer, but at her best, her stories and poems hold a mirror up to life—and, as Hamlet says, that is "the purpose of playing."

BIBLIOGRAPHY

Works by Dorothy Parker

Enought Rope. New York: Boni, 1926.
Sunset Gun. New York: Boni, 1928.
Dorothy Parker and Elmer Rice. *Close Harmony, or The Lady Next Door: A Play in Three Acts*. New York: French, 1929.
Laments for the Living. New York: Viking, 1930.
Death and Taxes. New York: Viking, 1931.
After Such Pleasures. New York: Viking, 1933.
Not So Deep as a Well. New York: Viking, 1936. (Poems)
Soldiers of the Republic. New York: Woollcott, 1938.
Here Lies: Collected Stories. New York: Viking, 1939.
The Portable Dorothy Parker. Introd. Somerset Maugham. New York: Viking, 1944. Rev. ed. Introd. Brendan Gill. New York: Viking, 1973.
Dorothy Parker and Armand D'Usserau. *The Ladies of the Corridor*. New York: Viking, 1954. (Play) *Constant Reader: A Month of Saturdays*. Introd. Lillian Hellman. New York: Macmillan, 1971. (Criticism)
Dorothy Parker and Ross Evans. *The Coast of Illyria*. Iowa City: University of Iowa Press, 1990. (Play)
Dorothy Parker: Complete Stories. Ed. Colleen Breese. New York: Penguin, 1995.
Not Much Fun: The Lost Poems of Dorothy Parker. Ed. Stuart Y. Silverstein. New York: Scribner's, 1996.
Dorothy Parker: The Complete Poems. Ed. Colleen Breese. New York: Penguin, 1999.

Studies of Dorothy Parker

Barreca, Regina. Introduction. *Dorothy Parker: Complete Stories*. Ed. Colleen Breese. New York: Penguin, 1995. vii–xix.
Bunkers, Suzanne L. " 'I Am Outraged Womanhood': Dorothy Parker as Feminist and Social Critic." *Regionalism and the Female Imagination* 4 (1978): 25–34.
Calhoun, Randall. *Dorothy Parker: A Bio-Bibliography*. Westport, CT: Greenwood, 1992.
Capron, Marion. "Dorothy Parker." *Paris Review* 13.4 (1956): 73–87.
Cooper, Wyatt. "Whatever You Think Dorothy Parker Was, She Wasn't." *Esquire* July 1968: 56+.
Craig, Andrea Ivanov. "Being and Dying as a Woman in the Short Fiction of Dorothy Parker." *Performing Gender and Comedy: Theories, Texts and Contexts*. Ed. Shannon Hengen and Nancy A. Walker. Amsterdam: Gordon and Breach, 1998. 95–110.

Freibert, Lucy M. "Dorothy Parker." *American Short-Story Writers, 1910–1945*. Ed. Bobby Ellen Kimbel. Detroit: Gale, 1989. Vol. 86 of *Dictionary of Literary Biography*. 223–33.

Frewin, Leslie. *The Late Mrs. Dorothy Parker*. New York: Macmillan, 1986.

Gill, Brendan. Introduction. *The Portable Dorothy Parker*. New York: Viking, 1973. vii–xxii.

Horder, Mervyn. "Dorothy Parker: An American Centenary." *Contemporary Review* 26 (1993): 320–21.

Keats, John. *You Might as Well Live*. New York: Simon, 1970.

Kinney, Arthur. *Dorothy Parker*. Boston: Twayne, 1978.

———. "Dorothy Parker's Letters to Alexander Woollcott." *Massachusetts Review* 30 (1989): 487–515.

Labrie, Ross. "Dorothy Parker Revisited." *Canadian Review of American Studies* 7 (1976): 48–56.

Meade, Marion. *Dorothy Parker: What Fresh Hell Is This?* New York: Penguin, 1989.

Melzer, Sondra. *The Rhetoric of Rage: Women in Dorothy Parker*. New York: Lang, 1997.

Miller, Nina. "Making Love Modern: Dorothy Parker and Her Public." *American Literature* 64 (1992): 763–84.

Shanahan, William. "Robert Benchley and Dorothy Parker: Punch and Judy in Formal Dress." *Rendezvous: Journal of Arts & Letters* 3.1 (1968): 23–34.

Simpson, Amelia. "Black on Blonde: The Africanist Presence in Dorothy Parker's 'Big Blonde.' " *College Literature* 23 (1996): 105–16.

Toth, Emily. "Dorothy Parker, Erica Jong, and New Feminist Humor." *Regionalism and the Female Imagination* 3 (1977): 70–85.

Treichler, Paula A. "Verbal Subversions in Dorothy Parker: 'Trapped Like a Trap in a Trap.' " *Language & Style: An International Journal* 13.4 (1980): 46–61.

Walker, Nancy A. "The Remarkably Constant Reader: Dorothy Parker as Book Reviewer." *Studies in American Humor* 3.4 (1997): 1–14.

KATHERINE ANNE PORTER
(1890–1980)

Lou Halsell Rodenberger

BIOGRAPHY

Katherine Anne Porter was born on May 15, 1890, in Indian Creek, a frontier settlement near Brownwood, Texas. Originally named Callie Russell, she was the fourth of five children born to Harrison Boone Porter and Mary Alice Jones Porter. Katherine Anne's mother died of complications after the birth of a daughter when the impressionable Callie was two years old. Soon after, her father moved to the home of his mother, Catherine Anne Skaggs Porter (known as Aunt Cat) in Kyle, Texas, south of Austin, and left the rearing of his children to the indomitable woman who later was recreated as the grandmother in Porter's fiction. For years, Porter romanticized her childhood, leaving the impression in interviews that her grandmother owned both a plantation and a substantial house in town. In truth, Porter's father contributed little to the upbringing of his children, financially or emotionally. It was left up to his mother, who as a widow had been forced to sell most of her holdings, to struggle to support her son's four surviving children. Porter's childhood home was a small four-room house, hardly adequate as shelter, much less as model for the comfortable, book-filled dwelling emerging from Porter's lively imagination later.

After her grandmother's sudden death when Porter was eleven, the peripatetic lifestyle she experienced the remainder of her long life began. The family moved first to San Antonio, where Katherine Anne and her older sister Gay had the opportunity to attend a good school for one year. At the Thomas School, a private school for girls, Porter studied elocution, drama, art, and dancing. Later, in her early teens, she helped support the family as a teacher of dance and dramatic arts in Victoria, Texas. At age sixteen, she married John Henry Koontz, a rancher's son from nearby Inez. Too young and flighty for marriage, Porter remained with Koontz until 1913, converting to Roman Catholicism during that time. An avid reader, Porter, always restless, was already writing, although not yet published. She left Koontz in Corpus Christi and went to Chicago, where she planned to become an actress. Unsuccessful, she returned to Texas in 1915 and filed for divorce. By 1916, she was a patient at a sanitarium in Carlsbad, Texas, where, as she recovered from tuberculosis, she became friends with the journalist Kitty Barry Crawford. Returning to Fort Worth with Crawford, Porter began her early career as a newspaperwoman.

By 1918, Porter was working for the *Rocky Mountain News* in Denver, where she almost died from influenza. Soon after her recovery, she left for New York and for the next decade made four extended visits to Mexico. Writing publicity for a film company, periodical articles, and critical reviews supported Porter until she began publishing her short fiction. Although she published three children's stories in 1920, her first acknowledged short story, "María Concépción," appeared in *Century* in 1922. The publication in 1930 of a collection of her fiction, *Flowering Judas and Other Stories*, focused critics' attention on her talents as a gifted storyteller. Critical praise led to her first Guggenheim Fellowship, which took her to Europe between 1933 and 1935, where she lived in Berlin, Basle, and Paris. An expanded edition of *Flowering Judas and Other Stories* in 1935 received a Book of the Month Club award in 1937.

Two other collections, *Pale Horse, Pale Rider: Three Short Novels* and *The Leaning Tower and Other Stories*, published in 1939 and 1944, were received well by critics. National recognition of Porter as a writer of note came when *The Collected Stories of Katherine Anne Porter*, published in 1965, earned the Pulitzer Prize, the National Book Award, and the Gold Medal for Fiction awarded by the National Institute of Arts and Letters.

Three years before, critics had not been so kind when she published her only novel, *Ship of Fools*, which had been in progress for twenty-five years. The novel was popular with readers, however, which assured Porter's financial security.

In her lifetime, Katherine Anne Porter moved often, searching for a compatible mate and an ideal home. She was married three more times, only briefly each time, lived in Maryland, Connecticut, Washington, Pennsylvania, Baton Rouge, Houston and New York, and taught at several universities, including Stanford and the University of Michigan. She rarely returned to her native state. In 1936, she visited her family and her mother's grave at Indian Creek. She came to the University of Texas campus in 1958 as an invited speaker. An unfortunate misunderstanding developed because university officials had given her the impression that a library there would be named for her. Such an honor was not forthcoming. Subsequently, she withdrew her offer to donate her papers to the university and presented them to the University of Maryland. Although *Pale Horse, Pale Rider* was considered for the first book award the Texas Institute of Letters (TIL) offered in 1939, regionalist J. Frank Dobie received the honor. In 1962, Porter's national standing belatedly was recognized by TIL members, who named *Ship of Fools* best book of fiction and awarded her the Jesse H. Jones Book Prize.

Her final visit to Texas, however, was a success. In 1976, Howard Payne University, a small church-supported university in Brownwood near her birthplace, invited Porter to campus to receive an honorary doctorate and to lecture as the centerpiece of a symposium on her work. Her visit to her mother's grave and the ardent attention her hosts paid to her comfort and entertainment gave Porter the best reception she had received in her home state since her departure almost sixty years earlier. She left for her home in Maryland resolved to be buried at Indian Creek, next to her mother's grave.

After several debilitating strokes, Porter died on September 18, 1980, in a nursing home near Washington. Her simple but elegant gravestone in Indian Creek Cemetery is inscribed: "In my end is my beginning."

MAJOR WORKS AND THEMES

Two traits of Katherine Anne Porter seem to have contributed to her production of a relatively small canon in her ninety years. Her first diversion was her need to move restlessly from place to place for most of her life. Even when briefly settled, she was never able to sustain the discipline required to write for many days at a time. Nevertheless, her short stories, particularly, were never submitted for publication until the writer was satisfied she had produced polished pieces of fiction. Her stories generally fall into categories as far as subject matter is concerned. Her first fiction is set in Mexico, where Porter witnessed and participated in a peripheral way in the cultural revolution that troubled that country during the decade in which she spent so much time there. "María Concépción" and "The Flowering Judas" are the most often anthologized of the six short stories based on her experiences in Mexico. She also published four other stories, "Hacienda," "The Martyr," "That Tree," and "Virgin Violetta," distilled from her observations and personal interaction with both the natives and revolutionary leaders. Thematically, Porter's Mexico stories develop the painful consequences of betrayal and the resulting disillusionment, which would become the leitmotif of much of Porter's fiction.

In her most celebrated stories, Porter creates the autobiographical Miranda, whom she follows through her childhood, adolescence, and final independent young adulthood. Many of the stories are obviously set in Porter's native state. Six of the Miranda stories are collected under the title "The Old Order" in *The Old Order: Stories of the South*, published in 1955. The 1955 volume also includes "Old Mortality," a three-part story, in which Part I introduces the child Miranda's family, an extended household, given to romanticizing the past. Part II narrates Miranda's experiences in a convent school in New Orleans, where she and her sister learn some truths about past family heroes. The final section chronicles her return home to attend an uncle's funeral. It is in the last episode that Miranda, who has eloped sometime before, decides to leave her husband and make her own history, unburdened by family myths and legends. "Old Mortality," more than any of the Miranda stories, probes the sense of betrayal and the shattering of illusion Porter so often associates with family connections.

The stories designated under the title "The Old Order" include "The Source" and "The Journey," which reveal the strengths of the grandmother, her history, her opinions, and her habits as Miranda observes them, both at home in town and on annual family stays at the grandmother Sophia Jane's farm. "The Witness" and "The Last Leaf" develop the personalities of Uncle Jimbilly and Nannie, former slaves who have remained with the family. Still loyal, both, however, demonstrate independent minds as they go about their daily lives. "The Circus" and "The Fig Tree" (included in "The Old Order" after publication in *Harper's* magazine in 1960) explore the childhood terrors an imaginative Miranda suffers. The story in this group most often subject for critical appraisal is "The Grave." This narrative focuses on an adventure in a former family graveyard where Miranda and her older brother Paul find, significantly, a gold ring and a dove-shaped screw head in an empty grave. Before the adventure ends with Paul's skinning of a pregnant rabbit, Miranda has been initiated into what it means to be female, a concept she has never considered before. Most of the "old order" stories were originally published in 1944 in *The Leaning Tower and Other Stories*, but it was Porter's later organization of the stories more or less chronologically for publication in the 1955 edition of *The Old Order* that gave the episodes coherence in terms of Miranda's development. A decade later, *The Collected Stories of Katherine Anne Porter* won the Pulitzer Prize and the National Book Award.

Other short stories of note in Porter's canon include "The Jilting of Granny Weatherall," which narrates the last bitter thoughts of an old woman on her deathbed, who can remember only that she was jilted on her wedding day and that she has had her revenge by prevailing as the hardworking wife of another man. Another story, "He," recounts events in the life of a family given to hypocritical rationalization of their mistreatment of a mentally deficient son. Development of a similar theme informs the story "Holiday," in which a boarder in the home of a German family discovers that the crippled servant girl is daughter of the host couple and learns some truths when she tries to determine what the inarticulate misfit wants. Yet another neglected child's life is explored in "The Downward Path to Wisdom."

Before collections of her short stories were published, Porter established her reputation as an accomplished writer with the publication of *Pale Horse, Pale Rider: Three Short Novels* by Harcourt Brace in 1939. Included are the title story, "Noon Wine," and "Old Mortality." Actually long short stories, "Pale Horse, Pale Rider" and "Noon Wine" are as carefully crafted as "Old Mortality." "Pale Horse" is yet another Miranda story. Here, Miranda is an adult journalist in Denver who comes close to death when she contracts the killer influenza so prevalent during World War I. Graphically and dramatically, Porter describes the near-death encounter she herself experienced when she contracted the disease in 1918. To this narrative, she attaches a love story in which the soldier lover, who at first ministers to Miranda, loses his own life to the disease. Developed as a series of delirious dreams, this tale advances still further the quest through which Miranda seeks her true identity.

Porter's third short novel, "Noon Wine," filmed as a movie at least twice, tells the strange story of the indefensible murder of the stranger who comes seeking Helton, the hired man, who has turned the Thompsons' hard scrabble farm in Texas into a prosperous operation. Thompson, the incompetent farmer who hired Helton, commits the murder and then claims defense of Helton as his motive. Successful legally in his defense, he becomes instead a pariah in the community. His inability to convince his neighbors of his innocence leads finally to his suicide. The cynicism apparent here in Porter's condemnation of rural Texas values in the early twentieth century reveals more dramatically her rejection of her early upbringing and native state than perhaps any other of her works.

By the 1940s, Porter had published numerous essays and speeches. In 1952, *The Days Before* collected many of these prose works. Her subjects reveal her eclectic reading and wide circle of literary acquaintances. Essay discussions include such writers as Gertrude Stein, Katherine Mansfield, Thomas Hardy, Ford Madox Ford, and Virginia Woolf. Several essays recount her Mexico experiences. Among the better of her essays on writing is "Noon Wine: The Sources," later much quoted. Porter has strong opinions about writers she likes as well as those for whom she has little regard. (She particularly denigrates the talents of Stein.) *The Collected Essays and Occasional Writings of Katherine Anne Porter* appeared in 1970. Collected also have been her letters, published in 1990.

Although Porter often mentioned having in progress several novels and a biography of Cotton Mather, which she actually worked on for many years, her only long work of note is the novel *Ship of Fools*. Upon its long-awaited publication both in Boston and in London in 1962, the novel received mixed reviews. Set in the 1930s, this work narrates events that occur on a long ocean voyage on board the *Vera*, which is sailing from Veracruz to Bremerhaven. Porter weaves several themes into the narration of multiple stories involving the actions of individual passengers as well as the interaction of groups of these unfortunate personalities. The chief theme of the novel's episodic plot illuminates human capacity for evil action excused by illusions masking the truth. Porter's cynicism and unrelenting negative view of humankind in this work earned her much unfavorable criticism, but the novel was popular with readers. She soon sold film rights and enjoyed the financial relief the profits from this work afforded her.

CRITICAL RECEPTION

Katherine Anne Porter often made clear that she thought of herself as the "first serious writer from Texas." Her personal assessment seems to be substantiated by the numerous times her short stories have been included in American literature anthologies and by the increasing volume of critical essays and biographical studies her relatively small canon has inspired. Almost all critics note that her narrative style, although complex in its subtleties, is both classic and direct. Porter's use of both irony and symbolism is also often noted.

Even though Porter essentially completed her writing career in the early 1960s, critics often made erroneous connections between her fiction and her early life until Joan Givner published the first authentic biography of Porter in 1982. Porter romanticized her upbringing as one that provided a sedate childhood in a genteel southern home. With access to the writer's papers and diligent pursuit of facts, Givner furnishes the background for a more thorough understanding of Porter's fiction in *Katherine Anne Porter: A Life*.

Contributing further to an understanding of Porter's personality and intellect is Janis Stout's *Katherine Anne Porter: A Sense of the Times*. Stout bases this intellectual biography on a careful reading of Porter's letters as well as those of her correspondents. For an understanding of Porter's shift from liberal sympathy with Communist causes to conservative criticism of both Communists and Fascists in her later years, Stout's study both analyzes and enlightens. Stout has also written extensively on Porter's style in *Strategies of Reticence: Silence and Meaning in the Works of Jane Austen, Willa Cather, Katherine Anne Porter, and Joan Didion*.

Darlene Harbour Unrue has published two volumes of criticism including *Truth and Vision in Katherine Anne Porter's Fiction*, in which she establishes the connections between Porter's chaotic life and her fiction and makes clear that Porter's fiction should be considered as a unified whole in order to understand her themes and mission as an artist. In *Understanding Katherine Anne Porter*, Unrue discusses each of Porter's works and adds to an understanding of how Porter's aesthetic and political theories were formed during her years in Mexico and Europe in the 1920s and 1930s. Thomas Walsh argues in his study *Katherine Anne Porter and Mexico: The Illusion of Eden* that Porter's prevalent theme of search for a lost paradise began with her fiction based on her Mexico experiences. In *Katherine Anne Porter: The Regional Stories*, Winifred J. Emmons discusses Porter's stories set in the Southwest. Jane Krause DeMouy develops the theory in *Katherine Anne Porter's Women: The Eye of Her Fiction* that the women in Porter's work demonstrate that the writer herself is torn between her need for love and approval in her traditional role as woman and her conflicting determination to live and write as an independent unhampered by inherent cultural expectations.

Countless critical essays assessing Porter's fiction have been published in literary journals. The earlier pieces generally were written by the author's literary friends, which included Robert Penn Warren, Allen Tate, Caroline Gordon, Andrew Lytle, Edmund Wilson, and Cleanth Brooks. Rarely negative in their appraisals, the writers generally discuss style, Porter's use of irony and symbolism, and her sources. Several collections of these essays as well as of articles and interviews have been published in recent years. Joan Givner edited a gathering of the many interviews and journalistic pieces relating to Porter in *Kath-*

erine Anne Porter: Conversations. In 1988, a symposium at Texas A & M University on the author, her life, and her work attracted Porter scholars. In *Katherine Anne Porter and Texas: An Uneasy Relationship*, Clinton Machann and William Bedford Clark collected and edited these symposium papers, which include Sylvia Ann Grider's "A Folklorist Looks at Katherine Anne Porter," Cleanth Brooks's "The Woman and Artist I Knew," Janis P. Stout's "Estranging Texas: Porter and the Distance from Home," Darlene Unrue's "Porter's Sources and Influences," and Sally Dee Wade's "A Texas Bibliography of Katherine Anne Porter." The volume also features essays by Don Graham, Joan Givner, Thomas Walsh, and Paul Porter. Ten years later, in May 1998, another symposium at Southwest Texas State University attracted numerous scholars, whose essays are collected in the fall 1998 issue of the journal *Southwestern American Literature*. These essay collections have served to draw attention to Porter's work and to introduce new perspectives on the value of her canon.

BIBLIOGRAPHY

Works by Katherine Anne Porter

Flowering Judas and Other Stories. New York: Harcourt, 1930.
Katherine Anne Porter's French Song Book. Paris: Harrison, 1933. (Translation)
Hacienda. New York: Harrison, 1934.
Noon Wine. Detroit: Schuman's, 1937.
Pale Horse, Pale Rider: Three Short Novels. New York: Harcourt, 1939.
The Leaning Tower and Other Stories. New York: Harcourt, 1944.
The Days Before. New York: Harcourt, 1952. (Nonfiction)
The Old Order: Stories of the South. New York: Harcourt, 1955.
Ship of Fools. Boston: Little, 1962. (Novel)
The Collected Stories of Katherine Anne Porter. New York: Harcourt, 1965.
The Collected Essays and Occasional Writings of Katherine Anne Porter. New York: Delacorte, 1970.
The Never-Ending Wrong. Boston: Little, 1977. (Nonfiction)
Letters of Katherine Anne Porter. Ed. Isabel Bayley. New York: Atlantic Monthly, 1990.
This Strange Old World *and Other Book Reviews*. Ed. Darlene Harbour Unrue. Athens: U of Georgia P, 1991.
Uncollected Early Prose of Katherine Anne Porter. Ed. Thomas F. Walsh and Ruth M. Alvarez. Austin: U of Texas P, 1993.

Studies of Katherine Anne Porter

Austenfeld, Thomas. "Katherine Anne Porter Abroad: The Politics of Emotions." *Literatur in Wissenschaft und Unterricht* 27 (1994): 27–33.
Baldeshwiler, Eileen. "Structural Patterns in Katherine Anne Porter's Fiction." *South Dakota Review* 2 (1973): 45–53.
Barnes, Daniel R., and Madeline T. Barnes. "The Secret Sin of Granny Weatherall." *Renascence* 39 (1987): 396–405.

Busby, Mark, and Dick Heaberlin, eds. *Katherine Anne Porter*. (Special issue) *Southwestern American Literature* 24 (1998).

DeMouy, Jane Krause. *Katherine Anne Porter's Women: The Eye of Her Fiction*. Austin: University of Texas Press, 1983.

Emmons, Winfred J. *Katherine Anne Porter: The Regional Stories*. Austin: Steck, 1967.

Featherstone, Joseph. "Katherine Anne Porter's Stories." *New Republic* 4 Sept. 1965: 23–26.

Gaston, Edwin W., Jr. "The Mythic South of Katherine Anne Porter." *Southwestern American Literature* 3 (1973): 81–85.

Givner, Joan. *Katherine Anne Porter: A Life*. New York: Simon and Schuster, 1982.

———, ed. *Katherine Anne Porter: Conversations*. Jackson: University Press of Mississippi, 1987.

Hardy, John E. *Katherine Anne Porter*. New York: Frederick Ungar, 1973.

Hartley, Lodwick, and George Core, eds. *Katherine Anne Porter: A Critical Symposium*. Athens: University of Georgia Press, 1969.

Hendrick, George. *Katherine Anne Porter*. New York: Twayne, 1965.

Hilt, Kathryn, and Ruth M. Alvarez. *Katherine Anne Porter: An Annotated Bibliography*. New York: Garland, 1990.

Jones, Suzanne W. "Reading the Endings in Katherine Anne Porter's 'Old Mortality.' " *Southern Quarterly* 31 (1993): 29–44.

Kiernan, Robert F. *Katherine Anne Porter and Carson McCullers: A Reference Guide*. Boston: G. K. Hall, 1976.

Liberman, M. M. *Katherine Anne Porter's Fiction*. Detroit: Wayne State University Press, 1971.

Lopez, Enrique Hank. *Conversations with Katherine Anne Porter: Refugee from Indian Creek*. New York: Little, 1981.

Machann, Clinton and William Bedford Clark, eds. *Katherine Anne Porter and Texas: An Uneasy Relationship*. College Station: Texas A & M University Press, 1990.

Mooney, Harry John, Jr. *The Fiction and Criticism of Katherine Anne Porter*. Pittsburgh: University of Pittsburgh Press, 1957.

Nance, William L. *Katherine Anne Porter and the Art of Rejection*. Chapel Hill: University of North Carolina Press, 1964.

Prater, William. " 'The Grave': Form and Symbol." *Studies in Short Fiction* 6 (1969): 336–38.

Schwartz, Edward Greenfield. "The Fictions of Memory." *Southwest Review* 45 (1960): 204–15.

Stout, Janis P. "Katherine Anne Porter." *Texas Women Writers: A Tradition of Their Own*. Ed. Sylvia Ann Grider and Lou Halsell Rodenberger. College Station: Texas A & M University Press, 1997. 124–33.

———. *Katherine Anne Porter: A Sense of the Times*. Charlottesville: University Press of Virginia, 1995.

———. *Strategies of Reticence: Silence and Meaning in the Works of Jane Austen, Willa Cather, Katherine Anne Porter, and Joan Didion*. Charlottesville: University Press of Virginia, 1990.

Tanner, James T. F. *The Texas Legacy of Katherine Anne Porter*. Denton: University of North Texas Press, 1991.

Thomas, M. Wynn. "Strangers in a Strange Land: A Reading of 'Noon Wine.' " *American Literature* 47 (1975): 230–46.

Unrue, Darlene Harbour. "Katherine Anne Porter and Henry James: A Study in Influence." *Southern Quarterly* 31 (1993): 17–28.
———. "Katherine Anne Porter, Politics, and Another Reading of 'Theft.' " *Studies in Short Fiction* 30 (1993): 119–26.
———. *Katherine Anne Porter's Poetry.* Columbia: University of South Carolina Press, 1996.
———. *Truth and Vision in Katherine Anne Porter's Fiction.* Athens: University of Georgia Press, 1985.
———. *Understanding Katherine Anne Porter.* Columbia: University of South Carolina Press, 1988.
Walsh, Thomas F. *Katherine Anne Porter and Mexico: The Illusion of Eden.* Austin: University of Texas Press, 1992.
Warren, Robert Penn, ed. *Katherine Anne Porter: A Collection of Critical Essays.* Englewood Cliffs, NJ: Prentice, 1979.
West, Ray B. *Katherine Anne Porter.* Minneapolis: University of Minnesota Press, 1963.

MARJORIE KINNAN RAWLINGS
(1896–1953)

Janet K. Turk

BIOGRAPHY

Marjorie Kinnan Rawlings was born on August 8, 1896, in Washington, D.C. Her father, Arthur Frank Kinnan, was an examiner for the U.S. Patent Office, and her mother, Ida May Traphagen Kinnan, was a homemaker. Four years later, Rawlings's brother, Arthur Houston, was born. While the family's home was in the Brookland suburb of Washington, they also had a dairy farm only ten miles away in the Rock Creek area of Maryland. The family spent as much time as possible at the farm. Many of Rawlings's fondest memories were of the times she spent with her father simply enjoying the land. Clearly, this early and lifelong affinity to the land and its inhabitants helped mold Rawlings's perspectives about life and presented itself in her most popular writing.

In 1913, Arthur Kinnan died from a kidney infection, but his plan to send his children to the University of Wisconsin did not die with him. As soon as Rawlings completed her senior year of high school, the family moved to Madison. In September of 1914, Rawlings began her college career as an English major at the University of Wisconsin. She immediately immersed herself in campus life, and in her junior and senior years, Rawlings held several staff positions for the school yearbook and worked as an associate editor of the Wisconsin *Literary Magazine*. In her position of associate editor, she met Charles Rawlings, her future husband.

One year after graduating, Marjorie Kinnan married Charles Rawlings, and the couple moved to Rochester. Because of the scarcity of jobs, Charles abandoned his attempts at finding work as a writer and became a traveling shoe salesman. Meanwhile, Rawlings continued to seek employment with various newspapers. In 1920, she landed a position with the Louisville *Courier-Journal* and the Rochester *Journal-American*. She wrote a daily syndicated column titled "Songs of the Housewife" from May 1926 through February 1928. This column applauded housewives and the duties associated with home, husband, and children. Since Rawlings had no children, hated housework, and had a frequently absent husband, the fact that she was able to write upbeat features about and for housewives exemplifies her writing skills. However, Rawlings was not content and continued to send out manuscripts of her fiction, all of which were rejected. When asked years later about "Songs," Rawlings replied that she had avoided one kind of prostitution but had succumbed to another. Nonetheless, she did acknowledge that her time spent as a journalist afforded her the opportunity to study people and the emotions she perceived that they felt. This ability to tap into the people she was writing about is one of the characteristics that made her later fiction so lifelike and enjoyable.

March 1928 brought about change for Rawlings. She and Charles visited Florida, and later in the summer they bought the Cross Creek property. The couple moved to Florida in November, and Rawlings immediately began to record her impressions of the land and the people. In March 1930, she sold her first story, "Cracker Chidlings," to *Scribner's*. "Chidlings" offers vignettes of her Cracker neighbors and their real-life experiences. Nine months later she sold the story "Jacob's Ladder" to the magazine. With this story of a young Cracker couple buffeted by life, Rawlings caught the attention of Maxwell Perkins, the editor of *Scribner's*. He became Rawlings's personal friend, and she became his protégée. One year later, *South Moon Under* was published, and it met with immediate critical and popular success.

While her writing career swiftly was becoming all that she had dreamed, Rawlings's personal life was not. Charles decided he could not tolerate Cross Creek or his wife's success, so he filed for divorce and left Rawlings to fend for herself at the orange grove. After a period of emotional depression, Rawlings focused her attention once more on her Cracker neighbors. In July 1933, she went to live with the family of Cal Long in the Big Scrub. It was here that she gathered the material for what would become her most popular book—*The Yearling*.

Before settling down to work on *The Yearling*, Rawlings had to face the inadequacies she experienced after her divorce. Because of her fragile emotional state, even the land no longer offered the peace she once gathered from it, so her friend Dessie Vinson devised a solution. Dessie and Rawlings ventured on a trip down a hundred miles of the upper St. Johns River. With the exception of some money for gas and basic food supplies, the women only had the bare necessities with them: a row boat powered by an old outboard motor, even older maps that no longer were accurate, an old cast iron pot, a shotgun, and sleeping bags. Rawlings later gave an account of this adventure in "Hyacinth Drift." In this writing, the winding, unpredictable river and the irritating hyacinths become metaphors for the problems and self doubt Rawlings experienced in her life after the divorce. Upon return to Cross Creek after the trip, she once again felt a connection to the land and began work on *The Yearling*.

Other adventures for Rawlings included alligator, bear, and rattlesnake hunting and meeting Ernest Hemingway, F. Scott Fitzgerald, and Thomas Wolfe. However, these are eclipsed by the success she experienced with the publication of *The Yearling* in February 1938. The book became an immediate best-seller, and Rawlings was viewed as a national celebrity. MGM bought the film rights, and in May 1939, she received the Pulitzer Prize for fiction.

In October 1942, after the completion of *Cross Creek*, her autobiographical account of her life there, Rawlings married Norton Sanford Baskin, the manager of Castle Warden Hotel in St. Augustine. From that point on, Rawlings divided her time between St. Augustine and Cross Creek. Rawlings desired quiet times with her husband and freedom to write; however, a real character from *Cross Creek* sued her for defamation of character. In the book, Rawlings characterizes Zelma Cason as "an ageless spinster resembling an angry and efficient canary" and further states that she cannot decide if Zelma should have been born a man or a monster (48–49). Zelma became enraged and sued Rawlings for $100,000.

The trial lasted until May 1947 and went all the way to the Florida Supreme Court. Rawlings lost the case and was directed to pay Zelma damages of $1 plus costs. While the trial illustrated Rawlings's tenacious spirit, it also brought to light her seriously declining health. She suffered from glaucoma, underwent five major surgeries, and developed heart problems. Five years later, in February 1952, Rawlings suffered a heart attack; she recovered but never fully. After pushing herself to complete yet another novel despite doctors' orders that she must slow down, in 1953 Rawlings began researching information for a biography of Ellen Glasgow. On December 14 of the same year, Rawlings, age fifty-seven, died from a massive cerebral hemorrhage. She is buried in Antioch Cemetery near Island Grove, Florida.

MAJOR WORKS AND THEMES

"Regionalist" and "regional literature" were labels Rawlings considered less than meaningful, and she always sought to dispel them; however, the fact remains that her early published works are clearly regional writing. "Cracker Chidlings," "Plumb Clare Conscience," and "Alligators" were all published in the early 1930s, and all strongly rely on realistic and accurate depictions of the Florida landscape and Rawlings's Cracker neighbors. In these anecdotal tales, she explores the attitudes and foibles of the people, while accurately capturing their speech patterns and dialect. The stories obviously contain local color, yet they also represent people who are not overwhelmed by their dire circumstances and know how to enjoy life.

"Jacob's Ladder" was also published in the early 1930s, but to categorize it as regional writing is to neglect the substance of this story. "Jacob's Ladder," *South Moon Under* (1933), parts of *Cross Creek* (1942), and *The Yearling* (1938) offer characters who struggle against great odds presented by the reality of their living conditions.

Alienation is a main theme in many of Rawling's works. Often the alienation pertains to a lack of community. In *Cross Creek* Rawlings presents several chapters illustrating this issue. In "Antses in Tim's Breakfast," Rawlings struggles with being an outsider and not understanding how the community functions. She offers a job to an impoverished man's wife, and the man, Tim, is offended because white women do not ask other white women to do their laundry. The offense is so great that Tim's wife is no longer able to talk to Rawlings, and the couple soon moves away from her grove. In "Jacob's Ladder" the young Cracker woman Florry is also distanced from people. When Florry meets Mart and runs away with him, she faces more alienation, the worst of which becomes her lost affinity with the land. This same type of loss occurs in "Hyacinth Drift" (1933) when Rawlings tells of having to leave Cross Creek because she no longer feels a connection to the land.

Cosmic consciousness or cosmic awareness is another theme that emerges in much of Rawlings's work. In *The Sojourner* (1953) the main character, Ase Linden, is an Everyman figure who develops a complex and mature understanding of human life and destiny. Ase learns to accept the pattern of life and not pass judgment on that over which he has no control. The notion of cosmic awareness also appears in Rawlings's use of nature's cycles in *The Yearling*, a novel that encompasses one year of both a boy's life and that of a yearling deer. Likewise, almost all of the Florida tales mention lunar cycles, the rise and fall of tides, and the timing of various seasons and how these cosmic patterns affect the characters and animals in the fiction.

Perhaps one of Rawlings's most effective themes is self-reliance, particularly for women. "Gal Young Un," the best-known story in *When the Whippoorwill* (1940), opens with Mattie living alone, supporting herself, and being content. However, a bootlegger enters the scene, dates Mattie, and eventually marries her. The marriage between Mattie and Trax creates disastrous effects for the previously independent woman. Mattie's problems predominantly are caused by her return to a patriarchal system from which she has been long absent; only when she realizes that she does not need a man's protection and throws out Trax does she become whole again. The story ends with Mattie's awareness that she is strong enough to survive on her own. The central theme of self-reliance is supported by the minor theme of love's betrayal.

"The Pelican's Shadow," anthologized in *The Marjorie Rawlings Reader* (1956), presents a theme similar to that of "Gal Young Un." Elsa, fresh from college, lands a job at a women's magazine. She meets Howard Tifton after corresponding with him about his articles, and shortly after, the two are married. Elsa gives up her job to be the kind of wife Howard expects her to be. However, this action is not enough to satisfy him. He finds her gift for critical analysis "unfortunate" and tells her that she must develop her "latent femininity." His pet name for her is Mouse, and it is not long before the mouse feels as if her "fur were being worn off in patches" (361). One day while waiting for Howard to return from work, Elsa spots a pelican. The bird flies over her head, creating a shadow. Elsa thinks of the pelican's greedy habits of devouring everything it sees; she then describes its appearance. The irony of this description is that she uses almost the same terms by which she had earlier described her husband.

Clearly, this story illustrates the idea that women must be self-reliant, not male reliant, in order to live fulfilling lives.

Rawlings's most popular work of all time is *The Yearling*. The central theme is the struggle of a boy's coming of age. Jody finds a fawn and raises it, but soon Flag becomes too big to keep penned and eats the family's sparse but very needed garden. Ma Baxter tells Jody that he must kill the yearling. Jody runs away and begins an adventure similar to those found in *Huckleberry Finn*. In this novel, Ma Baxter is the strong figure, whereas Penny Baxter, the father, is a quiet, introspective man who finds solace in the scrub. However, nature is not always gentle to the Baxters, and the parallel symbolism of the fawn and Jody enhances the yearling status of the boy and creates a deeper poignancy about his passage into manhood.

Cross Creek is second only to *The Yearling* in popularity and success. Readers and scholars alike find value in this semiautobiographical account of Rawlings's years spent in and around the Cross Creek area. Rawlings finds a connection with nature at the Creek, but a similar correlation with the community of people there is much harder for her to achieve. The first several chapters present Rawlings as outsider, but slowly she becomes an accepted member of the community. The chapter titled "Hyacinth Drift" is the best known of the book. It presents the same type of circular pattern and growth experienced by several of her fictional characters, but the chapter is specifically about Rawlings and her boat trip with Dessie. Her archetypal river trip is one in which she journeys through her personal heart of darkness. The chapter presents an account of the healing power of the river without specifically identifying the cause of Rawlings's mental anguish.

CRITICAL RECEPTION

Although Rawlings was a prolific and popular writer, her works have been largely neglected by critics and scholars, partially because she has been labeled both a regionalist and a children's writer. Even though she won the Pulitzer Prize for fiction in January 1939, the first extensive study of her work did not appear until 1966 when Gordon E. Bigelow published *Frontier Eden: The Literary Career of Marjorie Kinnan Rawlings*, a critical biography. Bigelow was the first person to note the lack of attention Rawlings's writings have received, and he contends, "Although America's literature in the present century is unusually rich, it is not so rich that writings as good as her best should suffer this kind of neglect indefinitely" (xiv). Samuel Bellman, whose Twayne series book *Marjorie Kinnan Rawlings* (1974) is an attempt to enlighten readers about the merits of Rawlings's writing, supports Bigelow's position by observing that Rawlings "is generally ignored by the critics and official arbiters of literary fashion" (preface). Bigelow's book offers more detail about the author than her works, but his overall observation is that Rawlings was a regionalist, specifically a "Southern regionalist" (68). Bellman concurs with Bigelow but moves beyond the regionalist idea to note circular patterns, cosmic awareness, and ideas about nature reminiscent of Thoreau's *Walden* in *The Yearling* and *Cross Creek* as well as in the shorter works of fiction. Elizabeth Silverthorne offers an interesting view of Rawlings's life in *Marjorie Kinnan Rawlings: Sojourner at Cross Creek* (1988), but analysis is limited to reprinted excerpts from reviews of her fiction. These are enhanced by a close look at the writer and how her work frequently paralleled her life and philosophy of life.

Several brief scholarly articles have been published that offer analysis of Rawlings's work. Most of the articles pertain to dialect, use of landscape, or Rawlings's personal life as an influence on her fiction. One article that stands apart is Janet Boyd's " 'Cinderella' in the Swamp: Marjorie Kinnan Rawlings's Fractured Fairy Tale." Boyd carefully analyzes "Gal Young Un" from a feminist perspective and notes that other people's inability to thoroughly critique or categorize Rawlings's fiction stems not from Rawlings's lack of skill but from not applying feminist theories to her work.

BIBLIOGRAPHY

Works by Marjorie Kinnan Rawlings

"Cracker Chidlings." *Scribner's* Feb. 1931: 127–34.

"Jacob's Ladder." *Scribner's* Apr. 1931: 351–66, 446–64.

"Plum Clare Conscience." *Scribner's* Dec. 1931: 622–26.

Marjorie Kinnan Rawlings and Fred Tompkins. "Alligators." *Saturday Evening Post* 23 Sept. 1933: 16–17, 36–38.

"Hyacinth Drift." *Scribner's* Sept. 1933: 169–73.

South Moon Under. New York: Scribner's 1933.

Golden Apples. New York: Scribner's, 1935.

"Having Left Cities Behind Me." *Scribner's* Oct. 1935: 246.

"Mountain Rain." *Scribner's* July 1938: 63.

The Yearling. New York: Scribner's, 1938.

"In the Heart." *Collier's* Feb. 1940: 19.

"Regional Literature of the South." *College English* 1 (1940): 381–89.

When the Whippoorwill. New York: Scribner's, 1940.

"Provider." *Woman's Home Companion* June 1941: 20.

Cross Creek. New York: Scribner's, 1942.

"Cross Creek Breakfasts." *Woman's Home Companion* Nov. 1942: 72.

Cross Creek Cookery. New York: Scribner's, 1942.

"Fanny—You Fool!" *Vogue* July 1942: 42.

"Here Is Home." *Atlantic* Mar. 1942: 277–85.

"Sweet Talk Honey!" *Vogue* Dec. 1942: 77.

"Trees for Tomorrow." *Collier's* 8 May 1943: 14.

"Florida: A Land of Contrasts." *Transatlantic* 14 (1944): 12–17.

"Black Secret." *The New Yorker* 8 Sept. 1945: 20.

"Miriam's Houses." *The New Yorker* 25 Nov. 1945: 24.

"Mountain Prelude." *Saturday Evening Post* 26 Apr. 1947: 10ff; 3 May 1947: 36ff; 10

May 1947: 38ff; 17 May 1947: 40ff; 24 May 1947: 36ff; 31 May 1947: 40ff. (Serial novel)

"Friendship." *Saturday Evening Post* 1 Jan. 1949: 14.

"Portrait of a Magnificent Editor as Seen in His Letters." *Publishers' Weekly* 1 Apr. 1950: 1573.

The Sojourner. New York: Scribner's, 1953.

Secret River. New York: Scribner's, 1955.

The Marjorie Rawlings Reader. Ed. Julia Scribner Bigham. New York: Scribner's, 1956.

Studies of Marjorie Kinnan Rawlings

Acton, Patricia Nassif. "The Author in the Courtroom: The *Cross Creek* Trial of Marjorie Kinnan Rawlings." *Rawlings Journal* 1 (1988): 29–40.

Bellman, Samuel I. " 'Love's Labors Lost': Marjorie Kinnan Rawlings on Marriage." *Marjorie Kinnan Rawlings Journal of Florida Literature* 4 (1992): 33–39.

————. *Marjorie Kinnan Rawlings.* New York: Twayne, 1974.

————. "Marjorie Kinnan Rawlings: A Solitary Sojourner in the Florida Backwoods." *Kansas Quarterly* 2 (1970): 78–87.

Bigelow, Gordon E. *Frontier Eden: The Literary Career of Marjorie Kinnan Rawlings.* Gainesville: University of Florida Press, 1966.

————. "Marjorie Kinnan Rawlings' Wilderness." *Sewanee Review* 73 (1965): 299–310.

Bigelow, Gordon E., and Laura V. Monti, eds. *Selected Letters of Marjorie Kinnan Rawlings.* Gainesville: University of Florida Press, 1983.

Boyd, Janet L. " 'Cinderella' in the Swamp: Marjorie Kinnan Rawlings's Fractured Fairy Tale." *Marjorie Kinnan Rawlings Journal of Florida Literature* 2 (1988–1990): 1–22.

Dukes, Thomas. "*Cross Creek* as the Autobiography of an Alienated Woman." *Marjorie Kinnan Rawlings Journal of Florida Literature* 2 (1988–1990): 89–108.

Figh, Margaret Gillis. "Folklore and Folk Speech in the Works of Marjorie Kinnan Rawlings." *Southern Folklore Quarterly* 2 (1947): 201–9.

McLaughlin, Robert. "The 'On-Natural' Narratives of Quincy Dover." *Marjorie Kinnan Rawlings Journal of Florida Literature* 4 (1992): 41–49.

————. "Symbolic Divergence: Communication and Alienation in Marjorie Kinnan Rawlings's 'The Pelican's Shadow.' " *Marjorie Kinnan Rawlings Journal of Florida Literature* 3 (1991): 49–58.

Nordloh, David. "Circular Journeys in *The Yearling.*" *Marjorie Kinnan Rawlings Journal of Florida Literature* 4 (1992): 25–31.

Parry, Sally E. " 'Make the Message Clear': The Failure of Language in Marjorie Kinnan Rawlings's *New Yorker* Stories." *Marjorie Kinnan Rawlings Journal of Florida Literature* 5 (1993): 39–49.

Prenshaw, Peggy Whitman. "Marjorie Kinnan Rawlings: Woman, Writer, and Resident of Cross Creek." *Rawlings Journal* 1 (1988): 1–17.

————. "The Otherness of *Cross Creek.*" *Marjorie Kinnan Rawlings Journal of Florida Literature* 4 (1992): 17–24.

Richie, Rebecca. "The St. John's River in the Work of Marjorie Kinnan Rawlings." *Marjorie Kinnan Rawlings Journal of Florida Literature* 5 (1993): 61–66.

Rowe, Anne. "Rawlings on Florida." *Marjorie Kinnan Rawlings Journal of Florida Literature* 5 (1993): 67–71.

Saffy, Edna. "Marjorie Kinnan Rawlings's Theory of Composition." *Marjorie Kinnan Rawlings Journal of Florida Literature* 2 (1988–1990): 109–29.

Schmidt, Susan. "Finding a Home: Rawlings's *Cross Creek*." *Southern Literary Journal* 26 (1994): 48–57.

Silverthorne, Elizabeth. *Marjorie Kinnan Rawlings: Sojourner at Cross Creek*. Woodstock, NY: Overlook, 1988.

Snyder, Robert. "*Cross Creek*: In Print, On the Screen, and in the Critics' Minds." *Marjorie Kinnan Rawlings Journal of Florida Literature* 2 (1988–1990): 73–88.

Tarr, Roger. "Observations on the Bibliographic and the Textual World of Marjorie Kinnan Rawlings." *Rawlings Journal* 1 (1988): 41–49.

LOLA RIDGE
(1873–1941)

Nancy Berke

BIOGRAPHY

Lola Ridge was born on December 12, 1873, in Dublin, Ireland. Christened Rose Emily Ridge, she was the only surviving child of Joseph Henry and Emma Reilly Ridge. Ridge spent her childhood and adolescence in Australia and New Zealand, where she developed interests in art, music, and poetry. In 1895, after a brief, unhappy marriage to a New Zealand gold mine manager, she went to Sydney, Australia, and studied painting with Julian Ashton at the Academie Julienne. Although Ridge intended to become a painter, she had also begun writing poetry. Yet before immigrating to the United States, upon her mother's death in 1907, she destroyed most of this early verse—something that she later regretted.

Ridge moved to New York City in 1908 and initially supported herself by drawing illustrations, doing factory work, being an artist's model, and writing ad copy and popular fiction. She also worked as an education organizer for the anarchist Ferrer Association's Modern School. She founded its magazine, *Modern School*, as well as edited its first issue. Ridge also held editorials stints with the modern journals *Others* and *Broom*. Through her involvement with the Ferrer Association, Ridge met and later married David Lawson, a Glasgow-born anarchist engineer. Her period with the Ferrer Association also introduced her to the preeminent anarchist figures Emma Goldman and Alexander Berkman. Ridge contributed poems to Goldman and Berkman's important journal *Mother Earth*. She also read her poems at labor rallies in New York's Union Square and at radical dinners such as the one held for Alexander Berkman on the eve of his deportation.

Ridge lived a largely hand-to-mouth existence in a series of lofts and cold-water flats in and around New York's Greenwich Village. She steadfastly refused financial help from friends while at the same time was generous to those in need. In 1928 Ridge spent the summer at the prestigious artist's colony Yaddo, where she wrote *Firehead*, a book-length verse poem about the Crucifixion, which was also an allegory of the trial and execution of the Italian anarchists Nicola Sacco and Bartolomeo Vanzetti. Ridge took part in the massive Sacco and Vanzetti defense campaign, spearheaded by a number of prominent artists and intellectuals. She was knocked down by a police horse for refusing to vacate the protest site on the eve of the two mens' execution, August 22, 1927, and was later arrested for her action. In 1929, Ridge, who was continually in ill health, was diagnosed with pulmonary tuberculosis. In 1931–1932 she traveled to the Middle East, and in 1935–1937 a Guggenheim Fellowship allowed her to travel in Mexico. In 1934 and 1935 she was also awarded the Shelley Memorial Prize. In her foreign travels, Ridge researched a project that she hoped would become a five-book cycle that included *Firehead*. She titled the project "Lightwheel," which would explore ancient Babylon, Renaissance Italy, Mexico at the time of the conquistadors, Revolutionary France, and postwar Manhattan. Lola Ridge died in her home in Brooklyn on May 19, 1941, leaving this epic work unfinished. In all, she published five collections of poetry.

MAJOR WORKS AND THEMES

Lola Ridge was first and foremost a political poet, and her desire to represent social injustice is one of the defining aspects of her poetics. Ridge was also influenced by the imagist poetry movement, and her first book *The Ghetto and Other Poems* (1918) contains a variety of poems written in this image-centered, free verse style. This book is also significant because of its lyric discussions of urban life. Its title poem, "The Ghetto," a long poem in nine sections of imagist snapshots, depicts Jewish immigrant working-class life on New York City's Lower East Side. Throughout *The Ghetto and Other Poems*, Ridge explores the ordinary lived experiences of women and men, as well as her belief in the promises and possibilities of her adopted land, America. Yet a recurring subject for Ridge is always class struggle. The poems "Lullaby" and "Frank Little at Calvary," while highly visual, focus their attention on two significant, albeit forgotten, events in American labor history. "Lullaby," a ballad written in dialect, describes the murder of a black infant by white women during a race riot in East St. Louis, Illinois. "Frank Little at Calvary" comments upon the lynching of an Industrial Workers of the World (IWW) organizer at Anaconda, Montana.

Ridge's second book, *Sun-Up* (1920), is also indebted to the imagist movement but is a more personal collection than *The Ghetto and Other Poems*. The title poem "Sun-Up," a three-part long poem, is written from a child's perspective and reflects upon the poet's own childhood. The poems "In Harness" and "Reveille" continue Ridge's interest in representing labor exploitation and unrest. As in all her poetry collections, Ridge divides her poems into groups, and in a section entitled "Windows," she explores the contradictory magic of the metropolis.

Red Flag (1927) indicates by its title Ridge's interest in revolutionary politics, and there are a number of poems in this collection about the Russian Revolution. Yet the majority of poems deal with spiritual questions, in addition to a series of imagist portraits of the poet's friends and contemporaries. There are also two notable and unusual exceptions. "Electrocution" and "Morning Ride" are political poems that also question poetic form. "Electrocution" is a sonnet, which graphically and gruesomely describes a man's death in the electric chair, thus subverting the sonnet tradition's emphasis on themes of love and/or honor. "Morning Ride" evokes modernist and futurist collage, experiments with typeface, and borrows from advertising and vernacular expression. Yet the poem's subject is hardly as playful as its form suggests. It reminds readers of the lynching of a young Jewish factory manager, Leo Frank, who was falsely convicted of raping and murdering a fourteen-year-old female employee.

Ridge's last two books, *Firehead* and *Dance of Fire*, reveal a shift in style and subject. In both books Ridge reverts to more formal language and structure and shows a greater interest in mysticism. In *Firehead* (1929), Ridge provides not a narrative but rather a nine-part meditation on the Crucifixion, each part from the point of view of individuals such as Mary Magdalene, Judas, John, and Peter. *Dance of Fire* (1935), Ridge's last book, explores both social and mystical themes, yet the two most powerful works in this collection—"Three Men Die," about the execution of Sacco and Vanzetti (along with the gangster Maderios), and "Via Ignis," an obscure sonnet sequence and exploration of history—are more meditations on social and historical themes than actual narratives of events.

Ridge also published some nonfiction—mostly book reviews—in important magazines such as *Poetry, Dial, New Republic*, and *Saturday Evening Post*. A small but significant example of her nonfiction prose was published posthumously as "Woman and the Creative Will" in a women's studies journal in 1981. This piece, edited by Elaine Sproat, was originally a lecture that Ridge gave in 1919 on the subject of women and art. She had planned to write a book entitled *Woman and the Creative Will* and received a grant to work on it. However, due to lack of interest from Viking Press, her then publisher, and a series of illnesses, she never completed the project. In this lecture Ridge presciently examines the social construction of gender. Her discussion predates by ten years the classic text on feminism and art, Virginia Woolf's *A Room of One's Own*.

CRITICAL RECEPTION

When Lola Ridge died in 1941 her *New York Times* obituary noted that she was one of America's leading contemporary poets; however, she is almost completely forgotten today. As a result of the serious neglect of this important anarchist-feminist poet, there exists very little scholarly work on her. There is, however, access to Lola Ridge's life and work through her papers, which are housed in the Sophia Smith Collection, Smith College Library, Northampton,

Massachusetts. Elaine Sproat is writing a biography of Ridge and is also completing an edition of Ridge's collected poems to be published by the National Poetry Foundation at the University of Maine at Orono.

What critical assessment there is of Ridge's work falls into two categories: the assessment done by her contemporaries and the assessment that has come about due to the effort of second-wave feminist and New Left–influenced scholars. Generally favorable reviews of Ridge's poetry appeared in *Poetry, Nation, New York Times, Chicago Tribune, Saturday Review of Literature*, and *Commonweal*. Most of these assessments are of their time, especially those by her male contemporaries, who apparently judge poetic performance through distinct gender divisions. Whether praising or criticizing her work, male reviewers seem to find it somewhat masculine. Alfred Kreymborg finds her to be "a prototype of the artist rebels of Russia, Germany and Austro-Hungary . . . men like Dostoyevsky, Gorky . . . Heine, Hauptmann, Schnitzler" ("A Poet in Arms" 336). Conrad Aiken characterizes Ridge's writing in *The Ghetto* as "strident," a quality he equates with being unfeminine. As he remarks about Ridge, "She arranges her figures for us with a muscular force which seems masculine; it is singular to come upon a book written by a woman in which vigor is so clearly a more natural quality than grace" (83). Yet Emanuel Carnevali, while finding her work "strong and virile," and casting it above the poetics of "women artists" like Emily Dickinson, Adelaide Crapsey, and Amy Lowell, deems it necessary to characterize Ridge as "a poet, that's all" (332). What most reviews of Ridge's books have in common in their emphasis on the social aspects of her work. They agree that her interpretations of the external world are far superior to her technique. As Hart Crane maintains in his review of *The Ghetto*, "I have felt the interpretive aspects of her work to be its most brilliant facet. When work is so widely and minutely reflective of its time, then, certainly, other than questions of pure *aesthetique* must be considered" (202).

Two important critical books of the modern period also make mention of Ridge's poetic contributions. Kreymborg in his *A History of American Poetry: Our Singing Strength* finds Ridge's poetic achievements in her use of the visual and claims her weaknesses lie in the technical and aural aspects of prosody. Horace Gregory's *A History of Modern Poetry: 1900–1940* locates Ridge within the context of 1930s social poetry and not primarily with the Imagist teens and twenties, which is part of Kreymborg's assessment. Critical appraisals of Ridge's work begin to dwindle after her death. The simultaneous rise of the apolitical New Criticism and the Cold War's antiradical fervor created an inhospitable environment for poets such as Lola Ridge. One important critical exception, however, is Edmund Morgan and Louis Joughin's *The Legacy of Sacco and Vanzetti*, which combines legal and literary scholarship to discuss the effects of the Sacco and Vanzetti case on American society and culture in the decades that followed. Louis Joughin's chapters on the literary culture surrounding the Sacco and Vanzetti case point to Lola Ridge as one of the chief poets.

Descriptions of Ridge and aspects of her career are scattered throughout literary memoirs and histories by Robert McAlmon and Kay Boyle, Emanuel Carnevali, Matthew Josephson, Alfred Kreymborg, Harold Loeb, Gorham Munson, Katherine Anne Porter, and William Carlos Williams. More recent scholarship looks at her influence more selectively. Joan Mellon's biography of Kay Boyle, *Kay Boyle: Author of Herself*, has several chapters outlining Lola Ridge's mentoring and influence on the young Boyle. Paul Avrich's study of the anarchist Ferrer Association, *The Modern School Movement*, discusses Ridge's early career as an organizer. Perhaps the most comprehensive of these more recent texts is William Drake's *The First Wave: Women Poets in America, 1915–1945*. Drake cites Lola Ridge as a central figure in his effort to recover the multifaceted, often interwoven, cultural and political milieu in which American women poets worked and lived.

Before Drake published his book as part of the recovery work being done on neglected women poets, Louise Bernikow's groundbreaking 1974 anthology, *The World Split Open: Four Centuries of Women Poets in England and America, 1552–1950*, reconsidered Ridge's work as part of "the buried history within the buried history," (45) as Bernikow refers to American women writers on the Left. Feminist scholarship in the 1990s, partly indebted to Cary Nelson's important theoretical work on modern poetry, *Repression and Recovery: Modern American Poetry and the Politics of Cultural Memory, 1910–1945*, reconsiders the challenges to modernism created by American women social poets such as Lola Ridge. Donna Allego's 1997 dissertation "The Construction and Role of Community in Political Long Poems by Twentieth-Century American Women Poets" and Nancy Berke's 1998 dissertation "Not Sappho: Sacco': Radicalism and Resistance in American Women's Poetry, 1915–1945" both devote chapters to Ridge. Martha A. Wilson and Gwendolyn Sell offer some brief commentary on Lola Ridge's and Genevieve Taggard's radical and feminist poetics in their *Arkansas Quarterly* essay "Lola Ridge and Genevieve Taggard: Voices of Resistance." Finally Nancy Berke's forthcoming essay "Ethnicity, Class, and Gender in Lola Ridge's 'The Ghetto' " in *Legacy: A Journal of American Women Writers* is the first scholarly article in which Ridge is the exclusive subject. It examines Ridge's importance to the interdisciplinary fields of ethnic, gender, and working-class studies.

BIBLIOGRAPHY

Works by Lola Ridge

The Ghetto and Other Poems. New York: Huebsch, 1918.
"Woman and the Creative Will." 1919. *Occasional Papers in Women's Studies*. Ed. Elaine Sproat. Ann Arbor: University of Michigan Press, 1981. (Lecture)
Sun-Up and Other Poems. New York: Huebsch, 1920.
Red Flag. New York: Viking, 1927.
Firehead. New York: Payson, 1929.
Dance of Fire. New York: Smith, 1935.

Studies of Lola Ridge

Aiken, Conrad. "The Literary Abbozzo." Rev. of *The Ghetto and Other Poems*, by Lola Ridge. *Dial* Jan. 1919: 83–84.

Allego, Donna. "The Construction and Role of Community in Political Long Poems by Twentieth-Century American Women Poets." Diss. University of Southern Illinois, Carbondale, 1997.

Avrich, Paul. *The Modern School Movement*. Princeton, NJ: Princeton University Press, 1980.

Benet, William Rose. Rev. of *Red Flag*, by Lola Ridge. *Saturday Review of Literature* 31 Dec. 1927: 483.

Berke, Nancy. "Ethnicity, Class, and Gender in Lola Ridge's 'The Ghetto.' " *Legacy: A Journal of American Women Writers*. Forthcoming.

———. " 'Not Sappho, Sacco': Radicalism and Resistance in American Women's Poetry, 1915–1945." Diss. City University of New York Graduate School, 1998.

Bernikow, Louise. *The World Split Open: Four Centuries of Women Poets in England and America, 1552–1950*. New York: Vintage, 1974.

Carnevali, Emanuel. "Crucible." Rev. of *Sun-Up and Other Poems*, by Lola Ridge. *Poetry* Mar. 1921: 332–34.

Crane, Hart. "Review of *The Ghetto and Other Poems*." *The Complete Poems and Selected Letters and Prose of Hart Crane*. Ed. Brom Weber. New York: Anchor, 1966. 201–2.

Drake, William. *First Wave: Women Poets in America, 1915–1945*. New York: Macmillan, 1987.

Flanner, Hildegarde. "Miss Ridge's Quest." Rev. of *Dance of Fire*, by Lola Ridge. *Poetry* Oct. 1935: 40–42.

Gregory, Horace. *A History of American Poetry, 1900–1940*. New York: Harcourt, 1946.

———. Rev. of *Dance of Fire*, by Lola Ridge. *Saturday Review of Literature* 8 June 1935: 17.

Kreymborg, Alfred. *A History of American Poetry: Our Singing Strength*. New York: Tudor, 1929.

———. "A Poet of Arms." Rev. of *The Ghetto and Other Poems*, by Lola Ridge. *Poetry* Mar. 1919: 335–40.

McAlmon, Robert, and Kay Boyle. *Being Geniuses Together 1920–1930*. Garden City, NY: Doubleday, 1968.

Mellon, Joan. *Kay Boyle: Author of Herself*. New York: Farrar, 1994.

Monroe, Harriet. "A Symphony of the Cross." Rev. of *Firehead*, by Lola Ridge. *Poetry* Apr. 1930: 36–41.

Morgan, Edmund, and Louis Joughin. *The Legacy of Sacco and Vanzetti*. New York: Harcourt, 1948.

Munson, Gorham. *The Awakening Twenties: A Memoir-History of a Literary Period*. Baton Rouge: Louisiana State University Press, 1985.

Nelson, Cary. *Repression and Recovery: Modern American Poetry and the Politics of Cultural Memory, 1910–1945*. Madison: University of Wisconsin Press, 1989.

Porter, Katherine Anne. *The Never Ending Wrong*. Boston: Little, 1977.

Quartermain, Peter. "Lola Ridge." *American Poets, 1880–1945*. Ed. Quartermain. Detroit: Gale, 1993. Vol. 54 of *Dictionary of Literary Biography*. 353–61.

Wilson, Martha A., and Gwendolyn Sell. "Lola Ridge and Genevieve Taggard: Voices of Resistance." *Arkansas Quarterly* (1993): 124–33.

ELIZABETH MADOX ROBERTS (1881–1941)

Suzanne Disheroon Green

BIOGRAPHY

Elizabeth Madox Roberts is best known for her poetry and her first novel, *The Time of Man*. Roberts was born on October 30, 1881, in Perryville, Kentucky, near the site of a pivotal Civil War battle. Her father, Simpson Roberts, was a descendant of the pioneer Abram Roberts who entered Kentucky from the Southern Piedmont area through Boone's Trace during the eighteenth century. Her mother's family also came from pioneer stock, tracing their roots to David Garvin, a six-month bond-slave who served time to repay his passage as a stowaway.

Simpson Roberts was intermittently a scholar, schoolmaster, surveyor, farmer, and civil engineer, who also served as a Confederate soldier under General Bragg beginning in 1863. On December 26, 1878, he wed Mary Elizabeth Brent. Brent was the granddaughter of a Union officer who defected to the Southern cause after being wounded at Shiloh and discharged from the Northern army.

Elizabeth Madox Roberts, the second of eight children, was raised in a family of somewhat divided loyalties in a state with similar identity issues: She was "closely identified . . . with the two most colorful aspects of Kentucky history" (McDowell 21)—the Civil War and the Westward Expansion. She spent most of her life in Springfield, Kentucky, and the region provided the basis for much of her fiction.

Roberts enrolled at the State College of Kentucky (now University of Kentucky) in 1900, but the ill health that she battled for much of her life forced her to withdraw. For the next decade, she taught in both public and private schools. Teaching also taxed her fragile health, and as a result, in 1910, she moved to Colorado to live with her sister so that she might recover from her respiratory illness. During this period, she wrote her first published work, a volume of poetry titled *In the Great Steep's Garden* (1915) (Goeller 310–11).

In 1917, Roberts enrolled at the University of Chicago and began to study writing seriously. She became a member, and later president of, the University

Poetry Club, where she became acquainted with Harriet Monroe, the editor of *Poetry Magazine*, and this acquaintance led to the publication of several of Roberts's poems. She also met other poets whose work was featured in *Poetry*, including Vachel Lindsay, Edgar Lee Masters, and Carl Sandburg.

After completing her degree in 1921, Roberts returned to Springfield and began writing. She produced seven novels, two collections of short fiction, and three volumes of poetry. In 1931, Roberts began suffering from a skin disease that slowed her productivity as a writer but that led her to take up weaving, an "activity that she often likened to writing, seeing parallels between the colors of yarn and the words of a story" (Groeller 312). She continued to write until the time of her death. Roberts succumbed to Hodgkin's disease in 1941 at the age of fifty-nine.

MAJOR WORKS AND THEMES

Although Roberts concentrated much of her attention on the novel form, she has largely been remembered as a poet. Her first volume of poetry, *In the Great Steep's Garden*, was intended to attract the attention of tourists, as it described the foliage of Colorado in majestic detail. Two additional volumes of poetry, *Under the Tree* and *Songs in the Meadow*, are intended for a youthful audience, and these volumes have been compared with works such as Robert Louis Stevenson's *A Child's Garden of Verses*. *Songs in the Meadow* is composed of ballads, sonnets, and free verse inspired by Walt Whitman and Gerard Manley Hopkins (Groeller 312).

Despite the popularity of her poetry, Roberts was simultaneously identified with the emerging southern and western regional literatures, in large part because of the focus of her novels. Roberts's first novel, *The Time of Man*, was also her most successful with both critical and popular audiences. In this work, the protagonist, Ellen Chesser, embarks on an introspective journey in which she seeks a sense of her self and her sexuality—a journey that critics have often compared to that of Odysseus. Unlike many of her contemporary literary counterparts, she becomes aware of and accepts her sexuality because she grows up "in harmony with the natural world." However, the harshness of the subsistence farming that provides her family's meager living "thwarts any desire to develop autonomy" (Harrison 29).

In *The Great Meadow*, her other critical and popular success, Roberts creates a female western hero in the context of a historical romance. The story of Diony Hall, the novel follows her progress as she immigrates to Kentucky from her home in tidewater Virginia. Her movement "parallels the westward march of the American colonists. At once an archetype of the American pioneer who longs for adventure, and yet needs beauty and order in her life, Diony sees herself constantly on the edge of civilization, embodying the tension between her mother's mountain spirit and her father's aristocratic sensibility" (Groeller

312). *The Great Meadow* demonstrates Roberts's tendency to find mythic patterns in the pioneer experience.

Roberts's other novels include *Jingling in the Wind*, a satiric piece; *A Buried Treasure*, based on a true story; *He Sent Forth a Raven*, an "ambitious but uneven novel" about an aristocratic Southern "misanthrope"; and *Black Is My True Love's Hair*, which shows Roberts's "continuing interest in both rural Kentucky and the life of the mind" (Groeller 312). Her interest in Kentucky is further reflected in her short fiction collections, *Not By Strange Gods* and *The Haunted Mirror*.

Roberts's fiction is best described as representing a cultural shift from iconoclasm to the question of old messages and old ways—a questioning that led to an appreciation of the writers of the Southern Renaissance.

CRITICAL RECEPTION

Roberts's first work to receive critical acclaim is her novel *The Time of Man*. Chosen as a Book-of-the-Month Club main selection in 1926, *The Time of Man* was one of three novels by southern writers to achieve such a level of success. Of all the novels appearing during this year, only a total of nine received this popular recognition.

The Time of Man and *The Great Meadow* were Roberts's most successful works, as they coincided with "the waves of fashion" in the literary community (Bryant 5). Her novels are unique for their time, making use of realism, lyrical prose, and literary allusion to explore her greatest subject, the Kentucky pioneer. She has been linked with William Faulkner and Thomas Wolfe as part of a "new generation of authors [who] rose to take their places in the Southern literary landscape" (Bryant 5). For example, *My Heart and My Flesh* has been called a precursor to Faulkner's *Absalom! Absalom!* Roberts, along with Faulkner, Wolfe, and the Agrarian "men's club" (Donaldson 507) have been credited with the rise of the Southern Renaissance.

BIBLIOGRAPHY

The bulk of Roberts's papers are housed at the Library of Congress (LOC). The LOC Collection holds manuscripts, galleys and page proofs, correspondence, notes and drafts from works in progress, and a variety of marginalia. Other papers and portions of Roberts's library are held by the Filson Club (Louisville, Kentucky) and St. Catharine College (St. Catharine, Kentucky). The remainder of extant correspondence—"virtually all with literary friends and associates" including Harriet Monroe and Allen Tate—is housed in private collections. Despite the substantial extant papers, however, a full-length biographical study has not appeared. This is due in part to Roberts's own reluctance to publicize her personal life. Accordingly, many of her letters to family members and other literary friends were destroyed, presumably at the author's request. She considered her workshop and its (results) her "private domain" and warned potential intruders accordingly: "My Relation to my Notebook is that of a Guinea-hen to her nest. If you put your Hand into the Guinea-hen's nest She will never return to it. Eggs must be taken, if at all, with a long-handled spoon" (Slavick 754).

Works by Elizabeth Madox Roberts

In the Great Steep's Garden. Colorado Springs: Gowdy, 1915. (Poems)
Under the Tree. New York: Huebsch, 1922. (Children's poems)
The Time of Man. New York: Viking, 1926. (Novel)
My Heart and My Flesh. New York: Viking, 1927. (Novel)
Jingling in the Wind. New York: Viking, 1928. (Novel)
The Great Meadow. New York: Viking, 1930. (Novel)
A Buried Treasure. New York: Viking, 1931. (Novel)
The Haunted Mirror. New York: Viking, 1932. (Short stories)
He Sent Forth a Raven. New York: Viking, 1935. (Novel)
Black Is My True Love's Hair. New York: Viking, 1938. (Novel)
Songs in the Meadow. New York: Viking, 1940. (Children's poems)
Not By Strange Gods. New York: Viking, 1941. (Short stories)

Studies of Elizabeth Madox Roberts

Bernstein, Stephen. "Comprehension, Composition, and Closure in Elizabeth Madox Roberts' *The Time of Man*." *Kentucky Review* 10.1 (1990): 21–37.
Bryant, J. A. Jr. *Twentieth-Century Southern Literature*. Lexington: University Press of Kentucky, 1997.
Campbell, Gladys. "Remembering Elizabeth." *Southern Review* 20 (1984): 821–28.
Campbell, Harry Modean, and Ruel E. Foster. *Elizabeth Madox Roberts: American Novelist*. Norman: University of Oklahoma Press, 1956.
Donaldson, Susan V. "Gender, Race, and Allen Tate's Profession of Letters in the South." *Haunted Bodies: Gender and Southern Texts*. Ed. Anne Goodwyn Jones and Susan V. Donaldson. Charlottesville: University Press of Virginia, 1997. 492–518.
Foster, Ruel E. "An Undiscovered Source for Elizabeth Madox Roberts' 'On the Mountainside.' " *West Virginia University Philological Papers* 15 (1966): 57–61.
Goeller, Allison D. "Elizabeth Madox Roberts." *American Novelists 1910–1945. Part 2: Fitzgerald-Rölvaag*. Ed. James J. Martine. Detroit: Gale, 1981. Vol. 9 of *Dictionary of Literary Biography*. 310–13.
Hall, Wade. "Place in the Short Fiction of Elizabeth Madox Roberts." *Kentucky Review* 6.3 (1986): 3–16.
Harrison, Elizabeth Jane. *Female Pastoral: Women Writers Re-Visioning the American South*. Knoxville: University of Tennessee Press, 1991.
Joyner, Nancy Carol. "The Poetics of the House in Appalachian Fiction." *The Poetics of Appalachian Space*. Ed. Parks Lanier, Jr. Knoxville: University of Tennessee Press, 1991. 10–27.
Kramer, Victor A. "Through Language to Self: Ellen's Journey in *The Time of Man*." *Southern Review* 20 (1984): 774–84.
Lesemann, Maurice. "Elizabeth Madox Roberts: A Reminiscence." *Southern Review* 20 (1984): 817–20.

Lewis, Janet. "Elizabeth Madox Roberts, A Memoir." *Southern Review* 20 (1984): 803–16.

———. "Letters from the Little Country: The Summers of 1919 and 1920." *Southern Review* 20 (1984): 829–35.

McBride, Anne K. "The Poetry of Space in Elizabeth Madox Roberts' *The Time of Man.*" *Southern Literary Journal* 18.1 (1985): 61–72.

McDowell, Frederick P. W. *Elizabeth Madox Roberts.* New York: Twayne Press, 1963.

Mellard, James. "The Fiction of Social Commitment." *The History of Southern Literature.* Ed. Louis D. Rubin, Blydlen Jackson, Rayburn S. Moore, Lewis P. Simpson, and Thomas Daniel Young. Baton Rouge: Louisiana State University Press, 1985. 351–62.

Murphy, John J. "Coming of Age and Domesticating Space in the Wilderness: Roberts's *The Great Meadow* and Cather's *Shadows on the Rock.*" *Willa Cather Pioneer Memorial Newsletter* 33.3 (1989): 26–31.

Niles, Mary. "Social Development in the Poetry of Elizabeth Madox Roberts." *Markham Review* 2.1 (1969): 16–20.

Seltzer, Sandra. "Some Similarities between Three Heroines: Tess d'Urberville, Ellen Chesser, and Kristin Lavransdatter." *Kentucky Folklore Record* 24 (1978): 84–102.

Sherry, Pearl Andelson. "Symbolism in the Letters of Elizabeth Madox Roberts." *Southern Review* 20 (1984): 824–28.

Simpson, Lewis P. "Introduction: Recovering Elizabeth Madox Roberts." *Southern Review* 20 (1984): 749–51.

———. "The Sexuality of History." *Southern Review* 20 (1984): 758–802.

Slavick, William H. "Taken with a Long-Handled Spoon: The Roberts Papers and Letters." *Southern Review* 20 (1984): 752–73.

Smith, Jo R. "New Troy in the Bluegrass: Vergilian Metaphor and *The Great Meadow.*" *Mississippi Quarterly* 22 (1969): 39–46.

Spivey, Herman E. "The Mind and Creative Habits of Elizabeth Madox Roberts." *All These to Teach: Essays in Honor of C. A. Robertson.* Ed. Robert A. Bryan, Alton C. Morris, A. A. Murphree, and Aubrey L. Williams. Gainesville: University of Florida Press, 1965. 237–48.

Tate, Linda. "Against the Chaos of the World: Language and Consciousness in Elizabeth Madox Roberts's *The Time of Man.*" *Mississippi Quarterly* 41 (1987): 95–111.

———. "Elizabeth Madox Roberts: A Bibliographical Essay." *Resources for American Literary Study* 18 (1992): 22–43.

Tyree, Wade. "Time's Own River: The Three Major Novels of Elizabeth Madox Roberts." *Michigan Quarterly Review* 16 (1977): 33–46.

Warren, Robert Penn. "Elizabeth Madox Roberts: Life Is from Within." *Saturday Review* 9 Mar. 1963: 20–21, 38.

DOROTHY SCARBOROUGH
(1878–1935)

Sylvia Ann Grider

BIOGRAPHY

Emily Dorothy Scarborough, born near Tyler, Texas, on January 27, 1878, was the youngest child of John Scarborough and Mary Ellison, both of whom were loyal Confederates. Throughout her life, Dorothy regarded herself as both a southerner and a Texan. The Scarboroughs had two other children while they lived in Smith County, a son, George, and another daughter, Douglass. In the mid-1880s, the family moved to the western frontier settlement of Sweetwater, hoping that the dry air would help Mrs. Scarborough's weak lungs. Unfortunately, the climate did little to alleviate Mrs. Scarborough's poor health; in fact, it may have made her worse.

In 1887, the family moved again, this time so that the children could be decently educated. Baylor University had just moved from Independence to Waco, so the decision to move to Waco was a natural one for this devout Southern Baptist family.

Upon moving to Waco, John Scarborough set up a law practice and dealt in real estate. He was also immediately elected to the Board of Trustees of Baylor University. The Scarboroughs had an elegant Victorian-styled home built adjacent to the college campus, and the family lived there until Dorothy finally left.

Scarborough, or Dottie, as she was fondly called, grew up literally on the Baylor campus. Students and faculty alike were accustomed to the child sitting in the trees deeply engrossed in a book. George and Douglass preceded her as students at Baylor. She completed her B.A. in English at Baylor in 1896 and her M.A. in 1899.

As a Baylor co-ed, Scarborough's social and intellectual life was focused on her love of literature. She contributed poems, essays, sketches, and short stories to various Baylor student publications. As her writing matured, she began to win campus literary prizes. She also was an eager participant in the activities of the Calliopean Literary Society, and one of her major duties was to write to famous authors and request greetings and copies of their works to be read aloud at club meetings.

After completing her M.A., Scarborough was hired to teach English grammar and literature to Baylor undergraduates. Although she was immensely popular with her students, she quickly bored of the drudgery of reading student compositions and yearned for more time to devote to her own writing. To further her literary interests, she began attending summer sessions at the University of Chicago and pondered whether to quit her job at Baylor and enroll at the University of Chicago full-time as a doctoral student in literature. During this period, she began sending manuscripts to various publications, but there is no record of any of these early works being published. Other than the items in campus literary magazines, her first published work was her collection of poetry *Fugitive Verses* (1912). In 1910 Scarborough and three other Baylor faculty women toured Europe, and Scarborough stayed on to study at Oxford, although at that time the university did not formally admit women to classes. When she returned to Waco, she was more restless than ever, especially after both her brother and her sister married and left home.

When her mother died in 1915, Scarborough, who had fulfilled her filial responsibility as the unmarried daughter, leased the house and moved to New York City, where her brother was already a successful playwright, to study literature at Columbia University. She never again lived in Texas. Upon the successful completion of her Ph.D. and publication of her dissertation, *The Supernatural in Modern English Fiction* (1917), she was hired to teach creative writing at Columbia, a position she held until her death in 1935.

Although she was highly regarded as a teacher, Scarborough's ambition was to be a professional writer. In 1919 she published a whimsical essay-memoir, *From a Southern Porch*, in which she began to develop character sketches and techniques that she used later in her fiction. In 1923 she published her first novel, *In the Land of Cotton*, in recognition of which Baylor awarded her an honorary doctorate.

Before leaving Baylor, she served as president of the Texas Folklore Society (TFS). To prepare for her TFS presidential address, she undertook considerable fieldwork and collecting of the folksongs of the local black people in and around Waco. As soon as she was settled into the routine of teaching at Columbia, she resumed this research by distributing a circular requesting more song texts. With the assistance of the distinguished folklorist George Lyman Kittredge of Harvard, she crafted this material into her first serious folklore collection, *On the Trail of Negro Folk-Songs* (1925), and was immediately recognized throughout the academic community as an authority on the genre.

The year of 1925 was the highpoint of her life. Not only was *On the Trail of Negro Folk-Songs* published that year but also her dramatic and controversial novel *The Wind* and a putative autobiographical novel, *The Unfair Sex*, which was serialized in the Texas magazine *The Woman's Viewpoint*.

She was much sought after as a speaker and was also a frequent guest on radio talk shows. She wrote book reviews for New York newspapers and edited two collections of ghost stories. Although her primary interest was in her own writing, she never neglected her creative writing students. She founded the Writers' Club, the programs of which featured writers and other literary figures in New York City. She also hosted regular at-homes for Texans and other southerners passing through town. Although her most popular course was in short-story writing, she herself found time to publish few stories. After *In the Land of Cotton* and *The Wind*, she continued to write novels and in rapid succession published *Impatient Griselda* (1927), *Can't Get a Redbird* (1929), and *The Stretch-Berry Smile* (1932). She wrote a nonfiction book for children, *The Story of Cotton* (1933), and edited a collection of short stories for classroom use, *Selected Short Stories for Today* (1935).

During the depths of the depression, she returned to folklore for creative inspiration and undertook the research and fieldwork for what turned out to be her last book, *A Song-Catcher in Southern Mountains: American Folksongs of British Ancestry*, which was published postumously in 1937. She was reading the proofs for this book when she died of a heart attack on November 7, 1935.

MAJOR WORKS AND THEMES

Scarborough's early works included an assortment of essays, reviews, poems, short stories, and scholarly articles. Since her lifelong ambition was to be a successful novelist, she concentrated her creative energies on that genre. Almost all of her work is set in Texas. When she published her first novel, *In the Land of Cotton*, she envisioned it as the opening volume in a trilogy about the cotton industry, but this dream never materialized. All of her novels exhibit Scarborough's distinctive literary style of including tidbits of folk wisdom and local color, including folksong stanzas, in order to further the action of the plot. *Impatient Griselda*, her creative retelling of the Lilith legend, is perhaps her most realistic novel and was a Book of the Month alternate. But her Baptist friends and family were critical of the character flaws and sexual appetites of some of the characters. *Can't Get a Redbird*, a thinly disguised biography of a well-known planter and labor organizer, was unsuccessful, primarily because of an unfortunate business agreement with the American Cotton Growers Association that a committee of cotton executives would exercise editorial control over the content of the novel. *The Stretch-Berry Smile*, a bittersweet tale of an unhappy love triangle, written during the depths of the depression, did not sell well either.

CRITICAL RECEPTION

Dorothy Scarborough today is remembered primarily as the author of *The Wind*, which was first published anonymously as a marketing gimmick. The novel, probably influenced by her early years in Sweetwater, is a scathing study of the effects of the incessant wind and other environmental and psychological hardships endured by settlers during the drought of the 1880s in Texas. In the dramatic conclusion, The Wind, a terrifying western Demon Lover, drives the heroine to murder and madness. With its unremittingly harsh and realistic descriptions of the people and landscape, Scarborough's novel invoked the wrath of Texans who preferred a more positive depiction of their beloved state. There were rumors of book burnings until Scarborough's authorship was revealed, and she returned to the state for a speaking engagement.

Although her two major folksong collections are both regarded as classics of the genre for their time, they are both marred by what modern readers and scholars recognize as the condescending and stereotyped portrayals of both southern blacks and mountain whites.

In spite of these criticisms of her other works, *The Wind* still stands today as a dramatic literary tour de force; none of her other novels approaches it in creative power. Because of this novel, Dorothy Scarborough's position is secure as a notable early twentieth-century woman writer. In fact, one might even say that she wrote her own epitaph in the opening line: "The wind was the cause of it all."

BIBLIOGRAPHY

Works by Dorothy Scarborough

Fugitive Verses. Waco: Baylor University Press, 1912.
"Traditions of the Waco Indians." *Publications of the Texas Folklore Society* 1 (1916): 50–54.
The Supernatural in Modern English Fiction. New York: Putnam's, 1917.
"The Engagement Ring." *Harper's* 137 (1918): 57–64.
Famous Modern Ghost Stories. Ed. Dorothy Scarborough. New York: Putnam's, 1919.
From a Southern Porch. New York: Putnam's, 1919.
"The Drought." *Century Magazine* 100 (1920): 12–22.
Humorous Ghost Stories. Ed. Dorothy Scarborough. New York: Putnam's, 1921.
"The 'Blues' as Folksongs." *Publications of the Texas Folklore Society* 2 (1923): 52–66.
In the Land of Cotton. New York: Macmillan, 1923.
On the Trail of Negro Folk-Songs. Cambridge: Harvard University Press, 1925.
The Unfair Sex. The Woman's Viewpoint 3.7 (Nov. 1925): 11–13, 77–80; 3.8–9 (Dec. 1925–Jan. 1926): 30–34, 87, 91, 94–95; 3.10 (Feb. 1926): 21–22, 50–51, 68; 3.11–12 (Mar.–Apr. 1926): 41–44; 4.1 (May): n.p.; 4.2 (June 1926): 42–44; 4.3 (July 1926): 53–58; 4.4 (Aug. 1926): n.p.; 4.5 (Sept. 1926): 45–49; 4.6–7 (Oct.–Nov. 1926): 54–61; 4.8 (Dec. 1926): 55–62. (Serial novel)
The Wind. New York: Harper, 1925.
Impatient Griselda. New York: Harper, 1927.
Can't Get a Redbird. New York: Harper, 1929.
The Stretch-Berry Smile. Indianapolis: Bobbs, 1932.
The Story of Cotton. New York: Harper, 1933.

Selected Short Stories for Today. Ed. Dorothy Scarborough. New York: Farrar, 1935.

"Negro Folklore." *Encyclopaedia Britannica.* Vol. 16. Chicago: Encyclopedia, Inc., 1937. 200.

A Song Catcher in Southern Mountains: American Folksongs of British Ancestry. New York: Columbia University Press, 1937.

Studies of Dorothy Scarborough

Beard, Joyce Juanita. "Dorothy Scarborough: Texas Regionalist." M.A. Texas Christian University, 1965.

Cranfill, Mabel. "Dorothy Scarborough." *Texas Monthly* 4 (1929): 212–27.

Dixon, Arline Harris. "The Development of the Novel: Lectures of Dorothy Scarborough." M.A. Baylor University, 1943.

Grider, Sylvia Ann. "The Folksong Scholarship of Dorothy Scarborough." *Publications of the Texas Folklore Society* 49 (1990): 97–103.

———. "Mythic Elements in *The Wind.*" *Texas Women: The Myth, the Reality.* Ed. Joyce Thompson. Denton: Texas Woman's University Press, 1987. 29–34.

———. "The Showdown between Dorothy Scarborough and Judge R. C. Crane." *West Texas Historical Association Yearbook* 62 (1986): 5–13.

Heavens, Jean Earl. "Dorothy Scarborough: Fictional Historian." M.A. University of Texas at El Paso, 1968.

Johnson, Ellen L. "The Unpublished Mountain Folk-Songs Collected by Dorothy Scarborough." M.A. Baylor University, 1941.

Leake, Grace Hillary. "Dorothy Scarborough: A Splendid Southerner." *Hollands: The Magazine of the South* 47 (1928): 5, 63, 65.

Maxwell, Mary Rebecca. "Short Story Lectures of Dorothy Scarborough." M.A. Baylor University, 1942.

Middlebrook, Anne. "Dorothy Scarborough's Lectures on the Technique of the Novel." M.A. Baylor University, 1943.

Muncy, Elizabeth Roberta. "Dorothy Scarborough: A Literary Pioneer." M.A. Baylor University, 1940.

Neatherlin, James. "Dorothy Scarborough: Form and Milieu in the Works of a Texas Writer." Diss. University of Iowa, 1973.

Quissell, Barbara. "Dorothy Scarborough's Critique of the Frontier Experience in *The Wind.*" *Women, Women Writers, and the West.* Ed. L. L. Lee and Merrill Lewis. Troy, NY: Whitson Publishing, 1979. 173–95.

Scarborough, Sheree. "Feminism in the Life and Work of Emily Dorothy Scarborough." M.A. University of Texas at Austin, 1984.

Slade, Carole. "Authorship and Authority in Dorothy Scarborough's *The Wind.*" *Studies in American Fiction* 14 (1986): 85–91.

Trantham, Carrie P. "An Investigation of the Unpublished Negro Folk-Songs of Dorothy Scarborough." M.A. Baylor University, 1941.

Truett, Luther J. "The Negro Element in the Life and Work of Dorothy Scarborough." M.A. Baylor University, 1967.

Whitcomb, Virginia Roland. "Dorothy Scarborough: Bibliography and Criticism." M.A. Baylor University, 1945.

ANNE SPENCER
(1882–1975)

Sara Andrews Johnston

BIOGRAPHY

Anne Spencer, poet, political activist, host, and friend and confidante to writers and activists associated with the Harlem Renaissance, was born on a plantation in Henry County, Virginia, the only child of recently freed slaves Joel Cephus and Sarah Louise Bannister. Her mother was the daughter of a well-established former slaveholder and a slave, while her father had a mixed black, white, and Native American ancestry. After clashing over how she should be raised, her mother left her father and settled in Bramwell, West Virginia, a resort town where she worked as the head cook in a hotel, placing her daughter in the foster home of a prosperous barber. Since her mother found the available black school for miners' children unacceptable for her daughter, whom she wished to raise with the sense of an aristocratic heritage, Spencer did not learn to read well until sent to Virginia Theological Seminary in Lynchburg at age eleven. However, she took quickly to reading and the humanities and gave the valedictory address when she graduated at seventeen, having developed by then a lifelong taste for reading, research, and reflection.

After marrying fellow student Edward Spencer in 1901, she settled in Lynchburg, ultimately in a home that became a stopping place for traveling African American writers, intellectuals, professionals, entertainers, and activists, particularly in the 1920s and 1930s, notable among them James Weldon Johnson, W.E.B. Du Bois, and Langston Hughes. James Weldon Johnson, whom she first met in 1919 when he was traveling as field secretary of the National Association for the Advancement of Colored People (NAACP) and she was helping to establish a local chapter in Lynchburg, became her literary mentor when he discovered her poetry and arranged for its publication in the *Crisis*, which he edited, as well as in the anthology that he compiled, *The Book of American Negro Poetry* (1922), also enabling her to establish other contacts through which her work was published. Her home and well-cultivated garden became an oasis for Johnson and other literary figures who also sought Spencer's advice and encouragement in their writing.

MAJOR WORKS AND THEMES

In the 1920s Anne Spencer's poems were published frequently in anthologies of African American poetry, though she never published a book of poems. Apparently much of her unpublished work has not survived; Lee Greene has created the only collection of her work to date, including forty-two of her fifty surviving poems, in the appendix of his critical biography *Time's Unfading Garden*. Page references for quotations from her poetry are to that collection. Spencer draws much imagery from the natural world, especially from her garden, and occasionally from a religious or mythic tradition. She writes of love, friendship, self-actualization, and the injustices of oppression that block it. Some of her poetry is directly inspired by personal relationships, but much forms a controlled, metaphorical, and seldom overtly angry statement of the value of those who have been oppressed.

With "Before the Feast at Shushan" Anne Spencer inaugurated her publishing career in the *Crisis* in February 1920. Written without rhyme and with a varying meter, it conveys the undulation of passionate desire in alteration with a harsh, patriarchal rule and presents Oriental sensuality. The defiance of King Ahasuerus by the beautiful Queen Vashti, who refuses to display herself before him and his drunken counselors, as recounted in Chapter 1 of the Book of Esther, is foreshadowed in the first stanza of this dramatic monologue by the king, who imagines his arms reaching out "to be mocked by the softly kissing body of the wind" (195). Ahasuerus ultimately refuses to be instructed by Vashti, who has presented herself as a prophet who has come to teach that love is sacred and that women are to be treated with respect; instead, Persia's lord reminds her that he teaches her and leaves her as he desires; she is simply an object of, and essentially slave to, his passion. With startling sexual imagery to have been composed well before 1920, Anne Spencer announces her protest against subjugation based on sex.

"Letter to My Sister" (first published in 1927 as "Sibyl Warns Her Sister") echoes this protest against the subjugation of women in highly ironic language. On one level, it is simply a protest against inevitable and often overwhelming problems (as Anne Spencer said to Lee Greene of this poem, "You don't ever get clear of problems") (*Time's Unfading Garden* 107); on another level, it suggests male gods who are "Juggernaut," with a dominion over women like that of King Ahasuerus. The "Letter" begins, "It is dangerous for a woman to defy" such gods, which Vashti has done (194). The only solution for a woman seems to be to hide her actual thoughts and feelings, locking her heart. Spencer had no sister but was writing to express her kinship with her "spiritual sisters," as Lee Greene has stated (*Time's Unfading Garden* 107).

In "White Things" Spencer expresses a similar sympathy for African American men as well as women, whose power she represents as having been blanched. The incident that sparked this poem was actually the 1918 lynching of a pregnant black woman whose child was ripped from her womb and crushed under the heels of a white man, as she was consumed by the flames from gasoline applied to her clothing (*Time's Unfading Garden* 130). Considering its provocation, the rage expressed is highly controlled, though apparently unacceptable to editors of the time, who never reprinted the poem or included it in anthologies after its initial publication in *Crisis* in 1923.

"White Things" creates a forceful statement; it approaches iambic pentameter and is entirely in couplets except for the last three lines of each of its two stanzas, the penultimate line of which, as the only unrhymed line, creates a break in intensity before the closure of the final rhyme and startling image: In the first stanza, power blanches a rose's blood into a white poppy-flower; in the second stanza, a black's skull is swung by a white ghoul. A Similar, though less violent, blanching has occurred to the hands of the persona in "Lady, Lady." Here, work for others has crumpled like unbleached roots.

However, just as Spencer finds both beauty and power in the heart of this Lady who has endured a yoke of subservience, she likewise finds beauty and power at a raucous carnival in the form of a cheery young girl in "At the Carnival." First published in 1922 in *The Book of American Negro Poetry*, "At the Carnival" portrays its speaker in a "gray" mood happening upon the "unholy incense" of carnival food, with dancing and gambling, where nothing is what it seems (177). In contrast, the gaze of a young female diver is uninhibited and pure. The speaker identifies herself with other carnival performers as those who need heaven-sent leaven. The search for beauty in ordinary, and even sordid, experiences, as well as in ordinary and oppressed individuals, is the most powerfully animating feature of Anne Spencer's poetry, as it was also in her lifetime cultivation of a garden. As her speaker says in "Questing," she must learn to recognize beauty in order to avoid wandering aimlessly with no direction in life.

There is also often a mystical, elusive, inexplicable element to her narratives that haunt the reader, as in "Substitution," which celebrates the power of thought as it emanates from a divine idea. The thought of the speaker in a crowded room lifts her and her companion from bondage to paradise so that the two can walk close together in a sacred garden that the divine bids them to tend. The garden is then a fit metaphor for her work. As Lee Greene's title indicates, it represents the beauty that ordinary materials can contribute to under loving and respectful cultivation.

CRITICAL RECEPTION

Lee Greene has surveyed reviews contemporaneous with the publication of Anne Spencer's poetry, primarily in the 1920s (*Time's Unfading Garden* 54–55, 63), to which this discussion is indebted. Johnson's inclusion of five poems of Anne Spencer's in *The Book of American Negro Poetry* (1922) elicited favorable comments in the *Liberator* (April 1922) and the *Nation* (June 7 1922), where she is classed with those who are the hope of a developing Negro poetry and hailed as a poet whose work deserves much greater attention than it has received (Greene 54). Robert Littell in the *New Republic* (12 July 1922) concludes that Anne Spencer has "great mastery over dreamy, half-mystical melodies" (qtd. in Greene, 54). Lee Greene notes that "Before the Feast at Shushan" received favorable attention from many associated with the Harlem Renaissance, prompting numerous requests from magazines and anthologies through the 1920s for more of her work. Countee Cullen's inclusion of ten of her poems in his anthology *Caroling Dusk* prompted Amey Smyth of the *Detroit Free Press* (27 Nov. 1927) to assert that she wielded "the cold pen of a Negro Amy Lowell" (qtd. in Greene 63).

Greene has acknowledged Anne Spencer's slender output, citing her devotion to family and community activities and her view of her own writing as primarily a personal activity for which she did not seek publication, though she was encouraged and shepherded by Johnson in that endeavor. He admits that she is not "a major or even a grossly neglected minor" poet but that she is still "an important American poet," not only for "her infrequent publications of some fine specimens of early twentieth-century poetry" but also for the sheer fact that she became such an "accomplished poet" "given her background and environment and the American cultural situation of the time" (150); specifically, he points to her living in a small southern, racially unsettled town with few cultural advantages for blacks, not even a library (though she worked to rectify that situation in opening the first black public library at Dunbar High School). Gloria Hull established much of the later tone and approach to Spencer's poetry, calling her "a more arresting poet" than her friend Georgia Douglas Johnson, noting, "Her forms are an eccentric mixture of free verse and rhymed, iambic-based lines. The result works, but it defies precise categorization" (171).

Although Erlene Stetson sees the work of Spencer as hardly ever rebellious, she notes that she defies the label of "lady poet" rather well, with her "subjective and otherworldly poetry" (409). In contrast, Maureen Honey, who includes fourteen of Spencer's poems in an anthology of the Harlem Renaissance, takes special note of "White Things" as "a sophisticated analysis of power lust," portraying the "connection between male domination, white supremacy, and the destruction of nature" (8). Greene calls it one of "the best poems of racial protest published in twentieth-century America" ("Anne Spencer" 255). In *The First Wave: Women Poets in America, 1915–1945*, William Drake perceptively observes, "Many of her poems touch on the theme of a higher spiritual revelation hidden within what is dark, undervalued, or disregarded" (215). He also notes her affinity for Robert Browning and Gerard Manley Hopkins as poets "who had a love of gnarled language similar to her own" (217). Drake astutely assesses her technical predilection for "clusters of irregular and asymmetrical lines" (though she "occasionally resorted to conventional rhymed stanzas") "in a diction that ranged from the traditionally poetic to the contemporary conversational, emphatic with condensed restlessness" (217).

Charita M. Ford's appreciative essay in *Sage* (1988), a scholarly journal on black women, demonstrates that Anne Spencer's work is being rediscovered by black feminists who are looking to her as an early ancestress. Represented in the first edition of *The Norton Anthology of Modern Poetry* but omitted in the second, Spencer's work has more recently appeared in several other Norton anthologies. In *The Norton Anthology of Literature by Women* (1996), she is credited with producing "a number of the finest poems published during the Harlem Renaissance" (1366). In *The Norton Anthology of African American Literature* (1997), her verse, though acknowledged to be often about nature, is seen as modern in its irony, complexity, "enigmatic, allusive quality" and "emphasis on privacy of vision" (946). *The Literature of the American South* (1998) represents her poetry as more about "nature, love, beauty, friendship, and death" than about racial protest, with a searching for "spiritual beauty" that could classify her as "a sort of twentieth-century African American Emily Dickinson," though acknowledging that she definitely observed and "spoke with her own voice" (386).

BIBLIOGRAPHY

Works by Anne Spencer

"The Poems." *Time's Unfading Garden: Anne Spencer's Life and Poetry*. Ed. J. Lee Greene. Baton Rouge: Louisiana State University Press, 1977. 175–97.

Studies of Anne Spencer

Andrews, William L., ed. *The Literature of the American South: A Norton Anthology*. New York: Norton, 1998.
The Anne Spencer Memorial Foundation. *Echoes from the Garden: The Anne Spencer Story*. Washington, DC: Byron Studios, 1980. (Documentary film)
Clark, Keith. "Anne Spencer: Poet, Librarian." *Notable Black American Women*. Ed. Jessie Carney Smith. Detroit: Gale, 1992. 1061–64.
Dean, Sharon G. "Anne Spencer." *American Poets, 1880–1945*. Ed. Peter Quartermain. Detroit: Gale, 1987. Vol. 54 of *Dictionary of Literary Biography*. 420–27.
Drake, William. *The First Wave: Women Poets in America, 1915–1945*. New York: Macmillan, 1987. 211–21, 227–28, 231–32, 235–38.
Ford, Charita M. "Flowering a Feminist Garden: The Writings and Poetry of Anne Spencer." *Sage* 5.1 (1988): 7–12.
Forsell, Mary. "Stanzas from a Southern Garden." *Victoria Magazine* 10.4 (1996): 74–78.
Gates, Henry Louis, Jr., and Nellie Y. McKay, eds. *The Norton Anthology of African American Literature*. New York: Norton, 1997.
Gilbert, Sandra M. and, Susan Gubar, eds. *The Norton Anthology of Literature by Women: The Traditions in English*. New York: Norton, 1996.
Greene, J. Lee. "Anne Spencer." *Afro-American Writers from the Harlem Renaissance to 1940*. Ed. Trudier Harris and Thadious M. Davis. Detroit: Gale, 1987. Vol. 51 of *Dictionary of Literary Biography*. 252–59.
———. "Anne Spencer of Lynchburg." *Virginia Cavalcade* 27 (1978): 178–85.

————. *Time's Unfading Garden: Anne Spencer's Life and Poetry*. Baton Rouge: Louisiana State University Press, 1977.

Honey, Maureen, ed. *Shadowed Dreams: Women's Poetry of the Harlem Renaissance*. New Brunswick, NJ: Rutgers University Press, 1989.

Hull, Gloria T. "Afro-American Women Poets: A Bio-Critical Survey." *Shakespeare's Sisters*. Ed. Sandra M. Gilbert and Susan Gubar. Bloomington: Indiana University Press, 1979. 171–72.

McCormick, Kathleen. "Spencer's Gifts." *Historic Preservation* Jan.–Feb. 1994: 66–69, 92–94.

Roses, Lorraine Elena, and Ruth Elizabeth Randolph. "Anne Bethel Bannister Scales Spencer." *Harlem Renaissance and Beyond: Literary Biographies of 100 Women Black Writers 1900–1945*. Boston: G. K. Hall, 1990. 298–303.

Stetson, Erlene. "Anne Spencer." *CLA Journal* 21 (1978): 400–409.

GERTRUDE STEIN
(1874–1946)

Lisa Abney

BIOGRAPHY

The life of Gertrude Stein began on February 3, 1874, in Allegheny, Pennsylvania. Stein was born to Amelia Keyser Stein and Daniel Stein, German Jewish immigrants who had relocated to the United States. The couple earned a stable income from their clothing business and lived quite comfortably. Shortly after Gertrude's birth, the family moved to Austria, where they remained until 1879. The Steins then moved back to America; they settled in Oakland, California. Soon after this move, Gertrude's mother developed cancer and died when Gertrude was still young. Her father then died unexpectedly when Gertrude was only seventeen years of age. Orphaned, she and Leo, her younger brother, stayed with an older brother, Michael, and his wife Sarah. The older Stein sibling and his wife took the youths into their home for a time, but when Michael and Sarah moved elsewhere, Gertrude and Leo moved to Baltimore to live with an aunt.

Upon arrival to the East, Gertrude enrolled at Radcliffe University, and Leo attended Harvard University. Gertrude developed a strong interest in the work of psychologist William James, and she became quite a scholar in psychology. After graduation from Radcliffe, she returned to Baltimore, where she enrolled in medical school at Johns Hopkins. Her work there, however, left her unfulfilled, and she ceased her medical studies. In 1903, she moved to Paris, where Leo had relocated earlier. He attempted to begin a career as an artist there, and Gertrude began writing at night after her famous salon parties would end. She dedicated a good portion of the period between 1903 and 1914 to the cultivation of various artists, particularly, Picasso, Matisse, and Braque. Gertrude developed close relationships with artists such as Picasso and Matisse, and her influence upon their work and the marketing of those works is remarkable. Her home became a gallery. With the help of Leo, she developed a vast following of artists who longed to be included in her circle.

Gertrude's writing efforts resulted in her first novella, *Q.E.D.*, which was not published until 1950 after her death in the collection *Things as They Are*. Stein's first published work, *Three Lives*, appeared in 1909; this collection was influenced by her reading of Flaubert. In 1910, Gertrude invited Alice B. Toklas to live with her in Paris as her social companion, secretary, and loyal friend. Toklas aided Stein's writing by helping to prepare drafts and editing for her. Indeed, Toklas served Gertrude in an invaluable manner as hostess for various visitors' wives whose husbands had come for an audience with Gertrude.

Just before World War I, she published *Tender Buttons*, a collection of prose poems. Stein and Toklas had gone to England in 1914 to publicize her writings and to find a publisher for her works. The pair stayed in England for eleven weeks due to the war. They returned to Paris in mid-October, only to be exposed to rationing and raids by the Germans. They moved temporarily to the Mediterranean, spending a year in Majorca where Stein continued her poetic works. By 1916, the pair began to feel hemmed in by their life in the Mediterranean, and they returned to France. Stein, upon her removal back to France, volunteered for the war effort by buying a truck that Stein called "Auntie" and learning to drive it for relief efforts. Stein enjoyed her work at the war hospitals, and her contact with the soldiers became the first subjects of her works that later became the 1922 *Geography and Plays*, which was published at her own expense in America.

In 1925, Gertrude published *The Making of Americans*, which brought her acclaim as a literary experimentalist and helped to develop her reputation as a member of the literati and established her as a literary expatriate. During this period, she wrote various word portraits, composing one for Mabel Dodge Luhan and several in honor of Picasso and other artists. Her works appeared in magazines such as *Vanity Fair* and *Rogue*. During the time between the wars, many of Stein's short pieces were consigned by magazines that offered her publications but no money. Her friends during this period came more from literary circles and less from the groups of artists with whom she had fostered relations in the earlier part of the century. Stein's decreased funds due to the war limited her ability to purchase the cubist works that she had admired and had collected for the past few years. She remained on good terms with the artists despite her lack of funds for art. Picasso and Juan Gris were two of her favorite friends, and Matisse maintained his friendship with her also. Stein never embraced the work of the surrealists, who were burgeoning while she was in Paris, yet she did value the relationships with surrealist Rene Crevel and other writers of her era such as Apollinaire and Cocteau. In spite of these relationships, she lacked close meaningful interchanges, as she was egotistical and, at times, insular.

While the French writers and her circle of artists occupied a portion of her time, a burgeoning group of American and English expatriates began to enter her life. She spent time with these young writers, mostly young men, at teas and dinners that she and Alice B. Toklas hosted at their home. They eschewed the cafe night life and decadent existence of these youthful writers. Instead, Stein entertained at home and spent the majority of her time with social calls and appointments relating to her writing. She guided the majority of the expatriate writers of the 1920s and 1930s, and borrowing a term from a local auto mechanic, she coined the term "lost generation." These writers such as Hemingway, Fitzgerald, Sherwood Anderson, and T. S. Eliot came to Stein for advice and guidance as they commenced their careers. Her influence came in a less intrusive manner than did that of Ezra Pound, who often boldly corrected and edited the young writers with whom he associated. Favoring the notion of less intrusive advice, Stein made suggestions and gave general information about publishing their works.

Hemingway valued her suggestions though found her to be difficult and intimidating sometimes. Later, after a good deal of time had passed, he penned a scandalous profile of Stein and Toklas in *A Moveable Feast*. Certainly, the works of Fitzgerald and Hemingway would have both been different, had they not made contact with Stein. Ultimately, Stein's influence upon Hemingway was greater than her influence on Fitzgerald, who she found to be undisciplined and insecure. For all Fitzgerald's faults, Stein maintained an unwavering loyalty to his work, particularly *The Great Gatsby* and *This Side of Paradise*.

During the 1920s and 1930s, Stein entertained some of the most influential literati of her time: Ford Madox Ford, William Carlos Williams, Thornton Wilder, Edith Sitwell, Robert Coates, Louis Bromfield, and briefly, T. S. Eliot. The salon culture that she propagated directed and molded the writers of her era.

Stein's life was filled with writing and touring during the 1930s, and upon her return to France after an American tour, she endured major difficulties as World War II broke out. She and Toklas moved to the border of France and Switzerland. She gained the protection of Bernard Fay, a Vichy official and director of the Bibliotheque nationale. The decision to stay in unoccupied France was still dangerous as Jewish inhabitants of France were often bundled off to concentration camps. In 1943, the pair moved to Culoz to endure the end of the war, and Stein and Toklas endured many tense moments when a German officer occupied their house. Through these difficulties, Stein grew to understand the importance of politics and freedom. Stein and Toklas moved back to Paris after the liberation and tried to resume their lives as before the war.

During this period, Stein gained the admiration of many Americans because of her writings of the period such as *Wars I Have Seen*, and American soldiers often gathered at her apartment at the rue Christine. In this time, Stein covered postwar activities in Germany for *Life* magazine. Gradually, Stein became increasingly tired, and while on vacation in Luceau, she saw a specialist who sent her to the American Hospital in Neuilly. There she underwent an unsuccessful operation for cancer, and she lapsed into a coma and died on July 27, 1946.

MAJOR WORKS AND THEMES

Gertrude Stein's works can be classified as being on the leading edge of avant-garde writing during her life. Stein's work in general can be characterized as innovative, puzzling, and at times, entertaining. She explored new styles of writing that espoused the expected modern themes such as isolation, loss of community, alienation, man's inhumanity to man, the quest for individuality in a world of conformity, and of course, the skewed vision of love of modern humans. Her works often lacked standard English punctuation, and she prided herself upon her ability to be an innovator in written form.

Stein's work can be divided into three periods of writings. Her first period of writing that ended around the beginning of World War I includes narrative works such as *Three Lives* and *Q.E.D. Four Saints in Three Acts*, though published in 1934, represents more appropriately Stein's first period of writing. During her second period of writing, Stein produced many largely unattended works, which delve into the psychological aspects of humanity. Stein's third major period of writing includes her autobiographical pieces and her better-known fiction. This period lasted until her death in 1946.

Stein became most well known for her fiction works and her autobiographical writing, although she wrote opera librettos and some drama. Stein wrote her earliest work, *Q.E.D.*, in 1903; however, the work did not see publication until 1950, after her death. The novella, unlike her other pieces, relates a linear narrative about three women in a love triangle. These women, Mabel Neathe, Helen Thompson, and Adele (whose last name is not revealed in the text) illustrate the influence that Henry James's writing had upon Stein; they are independent women who have monetary resources and travel to Europe in the fashion of many of James's characters. The underlying structure of the work is that of a triangle. Three books comprise the novella, and each is named for a side of a triangle. There are many related scenes involving threes in this work. Ultimately, the novella is a psychological novel that addresses personality types. Stein's belief that people are essentially born with particular personality characteristics becomes the focus of the work. In typical modern tradition, the work ends as it begins, with little motion toward change and with stagnancy.

Stein's second important work, *Three Lives*, profiles three women in short vignettes. This series of three short stories gained acclaim for its innovative narrative style and for Stein's depiction of three female servants, Lena, Melanctha, and Anna. "The Gentle Lena" and "The Good Anna" are shorter works, while "Melanctha" runs the length of a novella. Stein's objective in the work is to illustrate the characters' personality traits and to develop a narrative strategy reflective of an innovative narrative technique that goes beyond chronological narration. Additionally, Stein's depiction of Melanctha provides one of the first examples of a white writer assuming the voice of an African American character. The work was hailed and supported by Richard Wright for its depiction of Melanctha; other critics praised the work for its illustration of Melanctha's sexual awakening. In *Three Lives*, Stein's protagonists understand their places in society and illustrate innovations in characterizations because they are explored in snapshot fashion. Unlike mainstream fiction of the time, this work depicts these women in a kind of frozen space; they become static characters who illustrate little movement toward different or new lives. These vignettes and episodic pieces again allow Stein to experiment with new narrative styles and structures that would be used extensively in Stein's next work, *The Making of Americans*.

The Making of Americans remains one of Stein's most difficult and elusive works. In this piece, she experiments with grammatical and narrative structures for some 925 pages of small type. An abridged version exists for the text, yet this version runs some 400 pages and draws few readers into the story because of its fragmented style and difficult language. Leon Katz transformed the work into a significantly more accessible dramatized version, yet it has not attracted overwhelming audiences. Stein began writing this piece in 1903, but she did not begin to work on the final draft until 1908. In this novel, she focuses upon the relationships between two immigrant families. Her interest in the work lies in the temperaments of the characters as individuals and with the external and internal natures of the characters. Stein worked to deliver the abstract nature of these characters rather than to depict these characters in their actual states. Stein, as she does in many of her works, emphasizes characterization rather than plot in the novel. While the work focuses upon the lives of two families, the Herslands and the Dehnings, Stein creates confusion by naming several characters the same names. Through this naming cycle, Stein attempts to show the inherent similarities of all immigrant families. The work, while distinctive in its innovative structure, illustrates the modern tradition of static characters and the breakdown of community. For most readers, the effort required to read the work detracts from any enjoyment that can be gleaned from the piece.

While *The Making of Americans* remains illusive for most readers, Stein's next work, *A Long Gay Book* (also titled *Matisse, Picasso and Gertrude Stein, with Two Shorter Stories*) breaks with traditional form, theme, and plot more dramatically than does *The Making of Americans*. *A Long Gay Book* derives from Stein's experiences with people with whom she was acquainted and with their psychological types. Since the published text exists as an unrevised draft, it remains less fictionalized than does *The Making of Americans*. Here, Stein experiments with language more than in her earlier texts, decreasing paragraph lengths as the text concludes and minimalizing plot, characterization, and meaning. The book becomes an exercise in linguistic play, not representative of what she asserts, "a history of every possible kind of human being" (*Long* 3).

Stein's next book, *Two: Gertrude Stein and Her Brother* (1951), diverges from *The Making of Americans* and *A Long Gay Book* in narrative style. This largely autobiographical work focuses upon Stein's relationship with her brother Leo and with the entrance of Alice B. Toklas into Stein's life. The work relates a linear narrative that is unusual for Stein's writing, and it enumerates the difficulty that Stein and Leo underwent after Toklas came to live with them. Stein's life with her domineering brother became quite difficult during this time, and by 1913, Leo had moved from the apartment, and their relationship faltered.

They never spoke again. After her split with her brother, Stein dived into her writing, and her next major work was a series of world portraits of artists such as Matisse and Picasso. She continued her experimentation with language and forms, and in 1914, Claire Marie Press published *Tender Buttons*.

Tender Buttons is a difficult work to categorize. This modern piece develops into a series of brief descriptions. Many critics consider *Tender Buttons* a celebration of the ordinary, whereas others view it with less admiration. Stein divides the piece into three sections—"Objects," "Food," and "Rooms"—and within each, she composes a series of prose poems that doubtless do not always address the entitled subjects. Again, with this work, like others, Stein tests the connections between meaning and word representation. Another of Stein's experiments occurred when she decided to write an opera. Her *Four Saints in Three Acts* and *The Mother of Us All* are two of her operatic endeavors.

Four Saints in Three Acts focuses upon the lives of St. Theresa of Avila and St. Ignatius Loyola. There are four saints mentioned in the play, but these two become the principal saints of the work. This opera was coauthored by Virgil Thomson. The work debuted in 1934 in Hartford, Connecticut, and was performed by an African American cast. The piece derives from Stein's interest in the ritual of religion. *Four Saints* occupies an important work of Stein's middle period, yet the piece is largely neglected due to its genre.

From around the late 1930s to her death in 1946, Stein's work became the publication of experimental pieces such as *Lucy Church Amiably, Mrs. Reynolds*, and *Ida*. Though Stein wrote novels, she never truly grasped the novel as a form. Her inability to present standard narrative form, plot, and character made her a less-successful novelist than others of her time, yet *The Making of Americans, Mrs. Reynolds*, and "Melanctha" garner some acclaim for their originality; however, unlike traditional novels, they lack conventional fictional development.

One of Stein's most important works is *The Autobiography of Alice B. Toklas*, which illustrates maturity and comprehensibility that her other works lack. This piece profiles Stein's life at 27 Rue de Fleurus with Toklas and the pair's circle of friends. *The Autobiography* illustrates an interesting and innovative narrative strategy—Stein appropriates Toklas's persona while telling her own story rather than that of Toklas. The narrative voice of the piece, while labeled as Toklas's, remains distinctively Stein's. The work is filled with vivid depictions of Stein and Toklas's social group, and this work is the one that solidified her place among significant modern artists. The work contains a high level of narrative sophistication. The piece indeed receives the most popular attention of all of Stein's works.

Stein's final work, *Wars I Have Seen*, reveals the journal that Stein kept for fifteen months during the German occupation. The topic of the work is daily life in occupied France. The piece offers a moving depiction of the difficulties of war and occupation. Within the text, however, Stein shows both the best and worst of humanity through many examples of hardship and generosity.

CRITICAL RECEPTION

Gertrude Stein is well known and respected for her role as mentor and commentator of expatriate culture and writing, yet her work, particularly the more obscure works from the middle period of her writing, has remained largely neglected. Her literary endeavors that provided contiguous narratives such as *Three Lives* display many modern themes and typify the work of the period. Her later works, such as *The Autobiography of Alice B. Toklas* and *Wars I Have Seen*, drew greater critical attention for their journalistic/observational styles.

Most critical pieces regarding Stein's work focus primarily upon *Three Lives, The Making of Americans*, and *The Autobiography of Alice B. Toklas*. Donald Sutherland's 1951 work *Gertrude Stein: A Biography of Her Work* remains the authoritative piece regarding Stein's work; however, some other newer critical works have also emerged. Allegra Stewart's 1967 work *Gertrude Stein and the Present* and Michael J. Hoffman's 1976 *Gertrude Stein* have proven to be important texts regarding Stein's body of work. Rather than examining Stein's often difficult work, critics frequently focus on her impact on more highly acclaimed writers of the time such as Hemingway, Fitzgerald, and Anderson. Shari Benstock's *Women of the Left Bank: Paris, 1900–1940* remains one of the few contemporary book-length studies that includes and addresses the work of Stein. In 1986, Harold Bloom edited a critical volume of collected essays regarding Stein's work as part of the Chelsea House Series. Aside from the works mentioned, few major biographical or critical pieces regarding Stein have been published within the past ten years. Several dissertations and numerous articles have addressed some of Stein's work, but there is still much research to be done.

Essays from the later part of this century focus upon Stein's use of language and her intent. Marjorie Perloff's " 'Grammar in Use': Wittgenstein, Gertrude Stein, and Marinetti" deals with her language structure and development, whereas Kirk Curnutt's "Parody and Pedagogy: Teaching Style, Voice, and Authorial Intent in the Works of Gertrude Stein" illustrates an approach to Stein's work that some critics have taken in examining Stein's variant grammar and innovative techniques in narrative voice. Georgia Johnston in her article "Narratologies of Pleasure: Gertrude Stein's *The Autobiography of Alice B. Toklas*" examines Stein's work in light of new narrative theories. Many other new articles adopt approaches from psychoanalytical and cultural criticism.

Of all Stein's literary fiction works, *Three Lives* generally draws the most critical attention. Upon publication, Richard Wright endorsed her effort and lauded her ability to portray an African American protagonist. Others read "The Gentle Lena" and "The Good Anna" with equal approval and interest. The text has become a standard piece in many American literature anthologies. Many of Stein's peers such as Sherwood Anderson praised Stein's skill and innovation in her use of language. Anderson writes:

She is making new, strange, and to my ears sweet combinations of words. As an American writer I admire her because, she, in her person, represents something sweet and healthy in our American life, and because I have a kind of undying faith that what she is up to in her word kitchen in Paris is of more importance to writers of English than the work of many of our more easily understood and more widely accepted word artists. (8)

Anderson was not alone in his praise of Stein's works. William Carlos Williams and Katherine Anne Porter also addressed her works with favorable review.

The Making of Americans, Stein's most difficult work, drew fire from some critics and readers for its length and obscurity. Edmond Wilson asserts, "I have not read this book all through, and I do not know whether it is possible to do so" (14). Other critics call the book masterful in its creation of characters, although most do attest to the difficulty of the work's language. Katherine Anne Porter favorably discusses the work in her essay "Everybody Is a Real One." In this work, she asserts that the plot comes in waves. Porter states, "It is astounding, you read on out of chagrin" (11). *The Making of Americans* remains one of Stein's most daunting works, yet at the same time, elements of the piece such as characterization endure and confirm its importance in the chain of literary history.

Stein's work, though at times troubling, maintains an important place in literary history because of its innovative styles to which postmodern writing techniques can be traced. Stein's interest in psychology and human nature defines the limits of her characters and the actions that they perform in texts, and this perhaps influences the plot development and structure of her work. While Stein's importance as an influence upon twentieth-century art and writing cannot be ignored, her work itself has been overlooked and is ripe for reexamination and analysis.

BIBLIOGRAPHY

Works by Gertrude Stein

Three Lives. New York: Grafton, 1909.
Portrait of Mabel Dodge at the Villa Curonia. Florence, Italy: Privately printed, 1912.
Tender Buttons. New York: Claire Marie, 1914.
Geography and Plays. Boston: Four Seas, 1922.
The Making of Americans. Paris: Contact Editions, 1925.
A Book Concluding with As a Wife Has a Cow: A Love Story. Illus. Juan Gris. Paris: Editions de la Galerie Simon, 1926.
Composition as Explanation. London: Hogarth, 1926.
A Village Are You Ready Yet Not Yet A Play in Four Acts. Paris: Editions de la Galerie Simon, 1928.
Useful Knowledge. New York: Payson, 1928.

Dix Portraits. Paris: Libraire Gallimard, 1930.

Lucy Church Amiably. Paris: Plain Edition, 1930.

Before the Flowers of Friendship Faded Friendship Faded. Paris: Plain Edition, 1931.

How to Write. Paris: Plain Edition, 1931.

Operas and Plays. Paris: Plain Edition, 1932.

The Autobiography of Alice B. Toklas. New York: Harcourt, 1933.

Matisse Picasso and Gertrude Stein with Two Shorter Stories. Paris: Plain Edition, 1933.

Four Saints in Three Acts, an Opera to Be Sung. New York: Random, 1934.

Portraits and Prayers. New York: Random, 1934.

Lectures in America. New York: Random, 1935.

Narration. Chicago: University of Chicago Press, 1935.

The Geographical History of America. New York: Random, 1936.

Everybody's Autobiography. New York: Random, 1937.

Picasso. Paris: Libraire Floury, 1938.

The World Is Round. New York: Scott, 1939.

Paris France. London: Batsford, 1940.

What Are Masterpieces. Los Angeles, CA: Conference, 1940.

Ida. New York: Random, 1941.

Petits Poemes Pour in Livre de Lecture. Charlot, France: Collection Fontaine, 1944.

Wars I Have Seen. New York: Random, 1945.

Brewsie and Willie. New York: Random, 1946.

Selected Writings of Gertrude Stein. Ed. Carl Van Vechten. New York: Random, 1946.

Four in America. New Haven, CT: Yale University Press, 1947.

The Mother of Us All. New York: Music, 1947.

Blood on the Dining Room Floor. Pawlet, VT: Banyan, 1948.

Last Operas and Plays. Ed. Carl Van Vechten. New York: Rinehart, 1949.

Things as They Are. Pawlet, VT: Banyan, 1950.

Two: Gertrude Stein and Her Brother and Other Early Portraits 1908–1912. New Haven, CT: Yale University Press, 1952.

Mrs. Reynolds and Five Earlier Novelettes. New Haven, CT: Yale University Press, 1952.

Bee Time Vine and Other Pieces 1913–1927. New Haven, CT: Yale University Press, 1953.

As Fine as Melanctha. New Haven, CT: Yale University Press, 1954.

Painted Lace and Other Pieces. New Haven, CT: Yale University Press, 1956.

Stanzas in Meditation and Other Poems. New Haven, CT: Yale University Press, 1956.

Alphabets and Birthdays. New Haven, CT: Yale University Press, 1957.

A Novel of Thank You. New Haven, CT: Yale University Press, 1958.

Gertrude Stein on Picasso. Ed. Edward Burns. New York: Liveright, 1970.

Fernhurst, Q.E.D., and Other Early Writings. New York: Liveright, 1971.

Money. Los Angeles: Black Sparrow, 1973.

Reflections on the Atomic Bomb. Los Angeles: Black Sparrow, 1973.

How Writing Is Written. Los Angeles: Black Sparrow, 1974.

Studies of Gertrude Stein

Anderson, Sherwood. "An American Impression." *The Portable Sherwood Anderson.* Ed. Horace Gregory. New York: Viking, 1977.

Benstock, Shari. *Women of the Left Bank: Paris, 1900–1940*. Austin: University of Texas Press, 1986.

Bloom, Harold, ed. *Gertrude Stein*. New York: Chelsea, 1986.

Bridgman, Richard. *Gertrude Stein in Pieces*. New York: Oxford University Press, 1970.

Curnutt, Kirk. "Parody and Pedagogy: Teaching Style, Voice, and Authorial Intent in the Works of Gertrude Stein." *College Literature* 23.2 (1996): 1–24.

Haas, Robert Bartlett, and Donald Clifford Gallup. *A Catalogue of the Published and Unpublished Writings of Gertrude Stein*. New Haven, CT: Yale University Press, 1941.

Hoffman, Fredrick. *Gertrude Stein*. Minneapolis: University of Minnesota Press, 1961.

Hoffman, Michael J. *Gertrude Stein*. Boston: Twayne, 1976.

Johnston, Georgia. "Narratologies of Pleasure: Gertrude Stein's *The Autobiography of Alice B. Toklas*." *Modern Fiction Studies* 42 (1996): 590–606.

Mellow, James R. *Charmed Circle: Gertrude Stein and Company*. New York: Praeger, 1974.

———. "Gertrude Stein." *American Writers in Paris, 1929–1930*. Vol. 4 of *Dictionary of Literary Biography*. Ed. Karen Lane Rood. Detroit: Gale, 1980. 361–73.

Miller, Rosalind. *Gertrude Stein: Form and Intelligibility*. New York: Exposition Press, 1949.

Perloff, Marjorie. " 'Grammar in Use': Wittgenstein, Gertrude Stein, and Marinetti." *South Central Review* 13.2–3 (1996): 35–62.

Porter, Katherine Anne. "Everybody Is a Real One." *The Days Before*. New York: Harcourt, 1952.

Reid, Benjamin L. *Art by Subtraction: A Dissenting Opinion of Gertrude Stein*. Norman: University of Oklahoma Press, 1958.

Sprigge, Elizabeth. *Gertrude Stein: Her Life and Work*. New York: Harper, 1957.

Steiner, Wendy. *Exact Resemblance to Exact Resemblance: The Literary Portraiture of Gertrude Stein*. New Haven, CT: Yale University Press, 1978.

Stewart, Allegra. *Gertrude Stein and the Present*. Cambridge: Harvard University Press, 1967.

Sutherland, Donald. *Gertrude Stein: A Biography of Her Work*. New Haven, CT: Yale University Press, 1951.

Toklas, Alice B. *What Is Remembered*. New York: Holt, 1963.

Wilson, Edmond. *Axel's Castle: A Study in the Imaginative Literature of 1890–1930*. New York: Scribner's, 1931.

Wilson, Robert A. *Gertrude Stein: A Bibliography*. New York: Phoenix Bookshop, 1974.

GENE STRATTON-PORTER
(1863–1924)

Barbara Ryan

BIOGRAPHY

Born in 1863 on a farm near Wabash, Indiana, Geneva Grace Stratton was the youngest of twelve children born to Mark Stratton and Mary (Schallenberger) Stratton. When her mother became ill in 1874, she went to live in Wabash and completed several years of high school. She married Charles Darwin Porter, the owner of two drugstores, in 1886. Their married life began in Geneva, Indiana. Two years later, she gave birth to her only child, Jeannette.

Bored with the rounds of tea-drinking that were considered ladylike, the newly nicknamed "Gene" took up nature photography in a large wetlands near her home. The Limberlost Swamp teemed with bird and insect life but was known as a hideout for tramps and scofflaws. Armed with a pistol and carrying a heavy camera tripod over one shoulder, the self-taught naturalist spent years trudging through this dangerous area, looking for birds and moths to photograph. After selling bird studies to national magazines like *Recreation* and *Outing*, Stratton-Porter wrote a lightly autobiographical story called "Laddie, the Princess, and the Pie." Encouraged by its publication in 1901, she blended her photographic and literary gifts in a brief first novel, *The Song of the Cardinal*. This story of a crabbed farmer and his silent wife renewing their love as they care for a wounded bird won critical praise and achieved surprising sales. By 1925, Stratton-Porter saw five novels reach the year-end best-seller list.

Most cherished for novels set in the Limberlost like *Freckles, At the Foot of the Rainbow*, and *The Harvester*, Stratton-Porter has been credited with selling 50 million books. Several were nature studies, but the nonfiction never sold as well as the stories about young adults, like *A Girl of the Limberlost*, who face challenges and danger as they learn to appreciate Nature in an exotic wetlands. Fans of the Limberlost novels responded with special intensity to a character called "the Birdwoman," a nature photographer with the wisdom and wit to counsel youth. Identified with Stratton-Porter, this character led many to regard the Indiana author as a friend. Soon, her work was translated into Arabic, Finnish, Dutch, German, Czech, Japanese, French, Norwegian, Spanish, Swedish, Korean, Danish, and Afrikaans. Several of her books were also published in Braille.

Midcareer novels like *Laddie* and *A Daughter of the Land* were set in scenes reminiscent of Stratton-Porter's girlhood days; the exception, *Michael O'Halloran*, begins in Chicago but moves its child protagonists to farmland. Two children's stories, *After the Flood* and *Morning Face*, also appeared at this time. Though always known as the "Lady of the Limberlost," Stratton-Porter's appeal was secure enough to survive the move to an elegant woodland retreat near Kendallville, Indiana. Both this residence and the one in Geneva are now State Historic Sites. Stratton-Porter said she left Geneva because the Limberlost was drained; however, the move allowed an informal separation from Charles Porter, who did not share her naturalist pursuits. When Stratton-Porter moved again in 1920, this time to California, she left her husband behind but took along a young niece, Leah Stratton. She also adapted her novels' plots and settings to the new terrain. *Her Father's Daughter* describes the California desert and its native plants, while *The Keeper of the Bees* is set on the Pacific Coast. Living in Los Angeles, Stratton-Porter was joined by Jeannette, who was divorced, and two granddaughters.

Best-selling novels were the mainstay of a reputation so gigantic that Stratton-Porter was truly a household name. Her fame grew still more, though, when she began to make films based on her most popular novels. Never daunted by a challenge, Stratton-Porter opened her own film studio so that she could retain control of her stories and found time to write a column for *Good Housekeeping* magazine. There, she advised in the tone of a cheerful grandmother who might have been a tomboy in her youth. Most of Stratton-Porter's work for this periodical was collected in a posthumous publication, *Let Us Now Highly Resolve*. As the title indicates, patriotism was a leading concern at the end of Stratton-Porter's long career. She also wrote verse during her later years, like "Euphorbia" and *The Firebird*. However, readers preferred her optimistic novels about the moral education available to those who studied Nature's ways.

Enormous fame carried a price tag; for instance, while still in Indiana, Stratton-Porter complained about gawkers' encroachment on her wildflower garden. More often, though, she defied those who disparaged her work by pointing to the vast quantities of fan mail she received. Using these letters as evidence of her appeal to ordinary people's hopes and dreams, Stratton-Porter asked "city critics" to show greater understanding of readers' taste for stories about "true blue" protagonists who act according to a traditional moral code. When accused of purveying "molasses fiction," she agreed with a smile. "What a wonderful compliment!" Stratton-Porter preened. "Molasses is more necessary to the happiness of human and beast than vinegar, and overindulgence in it not nearly so harmful to the system" (Porter Meehan 136). This was the confidence of a writer making regular appearances on the best-seller list.

Busy and active to the last, the "Lady of the Limberlost" died in a car accident at the age of sixty-one. Her last novel, *The Magic Garden*, was published post-humously. Information about Nature's wilder side is at a minimum in this book because Stratton-Porter had little time for fieldwork in her later years. Yet its heroine is devoted to the flower garden she prepares for the man she loves. In 1928, Jeannette Porter Meehan wrote a loving memoir of her mother. A year later, she published *Freckles Comes Home*, which was probably elaborated from Stratton-Porter's notes.

MAJOR WORKS AND THEMES

Stratton-Porter's most popular works were and are the linked nature-novels situated in an Indiana swamp: *Freckles, A Girl of the Limberlost,* and *The Harvester.* All three teach that trustworthiness and courage grow "naturally" out of an appetite for nature and are filled with the kind of nature study that teenagers can teach themselves to do. Stratton-Porter characters are routinely healed, for instance, of physical and psychic wounds by long walks along woodland trails and by attention to wild and semiwild creatures, especially insect life. Significantly, several Limberlost characters mature by learning to respect and love uncultivated land of which they are initially afraid.

Preeminent among the qualities of a Stratton-Porter protagonist is an attribute that might be called "self-trust," for one of her favorite sayings was, "Know you're right, then go ahead." Starting with the hero of *Freckles*, Stratton-Porter's admirable characters learn to do for themselves, expecting no favors or handouts. The best example of this kind of protagonist is the Harvester, an herbalist-hero who resembles Henry Thoreau. The novel that told his story was received enthusiastically and remains Stratton-Porter's single most popular book. This character is certain that life in the woods teaches everything worth knowing. "You not only discover miracles and marvels," he tells a town-dwelling friend, "but you get the greatest lessons taught in all the world ground into you early and alone—courage, caution, and patience" (*Harvester* 30–31).

With the exception of the strange *The White Flag*, a novel that betrays Stratton-Porter's desire to win critical acclaim, novels by this writer offer paeans to self-reliance, dignity, and happy homes. Most of the homes in question are achieved through hard work because Stratton-Porter's typical protagonist is an orphan or a young adult who has been ineptly parented. Leading characters win with help from older characters who share their "can do" attitude, but along the way, each demonstrates the benefits of learning to forgive, persevere, practice thrift, and uphold the Golden Rule. Self-denial, an important but muted theme, is rewarded; similarly, sustained attention to moral and civic responsibilities plays a larger part than luck in Stratton-Porter's philosophy.

CRITICAL RECEPTION

After winning reviewers' praise for *The Song of the Cardinal*, Stratton-Porter could not please the tastemakers of her day. Literary arbiters had so little patience with the fact that millions cherished Stratton-Porter's novels that she and her work came to epitomize the popular but pernicious effects of sentimentality in professional readers' eyes. Recent interest in conservation and regionalism has brought her fiction back into discussion.

Stratton-Porter's nonfiction garnered little attention except insofar as leading naturalists dismissed her field studies as amateurish. Her photography attracted admirers; the poems were and are ignored.

BIBLIOGRAPHY

Works by Gene Stratton-Porter

The Song of the Cardinal. Indianapolis: Bobbs, 1903. (Novel)
Freckles. New York: Doubleday, 1904. (Novel)
At the Foot of the Rainbow. New York: Outing, 1907. (Novel)
What I Have Done with Birds: Character Studies of Native American Birds Which Through Friendly Advance I Induced to Pose for Me, or Succeeded in Photographing by Good Fortune, with the Story of My Experiences in Obtaining Their Pictures. Indianapolis: Bobbs, 1907. (Nature study; revised and enlarged as *Friends in Feathers* [1917])
Birds of the Bible. Cincinnati: Jennings; New York: Eaton, 1909. (Nature study)
A Girl of the Limberlost. New York: Doubleday, 1909. (Novel)
Music of the Wild: With Reproductions of the Performers, Their Instruments and Festival Halls. Cincinnati: Jennings, 1910. (Nature study)
After the Flood. Indianapolis: Bobbs, 1911. (Children's book)
The Harvester. Garden City, NY: Doubleday, 1911. (Novel)
Moths of the Limberlost. Garden City, NY: Doubleday, 1912. (Nature study)
Laddie. Garden City, NY: Doubleday, 1913. (Novel)
Michael O'Halloran. Garden City, NY: Doubleday, 1915. (Novel)
Morning Face. Garden City, NY: Doubleday, 1916. (Children's book)
Homing with the Birds: The History of a Lifetime of Personal Experience with the Birds. Garden City, NY: Doubleday, 1917. (Nature study)
A Daughter of the Land. Garden City, NY: Doubleday, 1918. (Novel)
Her Father's Daughter. Garden City, NY: Doubleday, 1921. (Novel)
The Keeper of the Bees. Garden City, NY: Doubleday, 1921. (Novel)
The Firebird. Garden City, NY: Doubleday, 1922. (Poems)
Jesus of the Emerald. Garden City, NY: Doubleday, 1923. (Poems)
The White Flag. Garden City, NY: Doubleday, 1923. (Novel)
Wings. Garden City, NY: Doubleday, 1923. (Nature study)
Tales You Won't Believe. Garden City, NY: Doubleday, 1925. (Nature study)
Let Us Highly Resolve. Garden City, NY: Doubleday, 1927. (Nonfiction)
The Magic Garden. Garden City, NY: Doubleday, 1927. (Novel)

Studies of Gene Stratton-Porter

Cooper, Frederic Taber. "Popularity of Gene Stratton-Porter." *Bookman* 41 (1915): 670–71.

"C. W." "An Appreciation." *Bookman* 49 (1916): 145–46.

Long, Judith Reick. *Gene Stratton-Porter: Novelist and Naturalist*. Indianapolis: Indiana Historical Society, 1990.

Porter Meehan, Jeannette. *The Lady of the Limberlost: The Life & Letters of Gene Stratton-Porter*. Garden City, NY: Doubleday, 1928.

Richards, Bertrand F. *Gene Stratton-Porter*. Boston: Twayne, 1980.

Ryan, Barbara. " 'Wherever I Am Living': The 'Lady of the Limberlost' Re-Situates." *Breaking Boundaries: New Perspectives on Regional Fiction*. Ed. Diana Royer and Sherri Inness. Iowa City: University of Iowa Press, 1997. 162–79.

SUI SIN FAR (EDITH MAUDE EATON) (1865–1914)

Carman C. Curton

BIOGRAPHY

The writer known as Sui Sin Far was born Edith Maude Eaton on March 15, 1865, in Macclesfield, England. She was the second of fourteen children and the oldest daughter of Edward Eaton, an English silk merchant, and Grace A. Trefusis Eaton, a Chinese woman educated in England. Although Sui Sin Far did not look like a child of "mixed" races, she was singled out because of her parentage and closely examined as a curiosity by the adults around her, and she was alternately tormented and snubbed by Caucasian children in her schools and neighborhoods.

Sui Sin Far's family moved often when she was young, traveling between England, the United States, and Canada during the first eight years of her life. The family, which grew by one child approximately every year, settled in Montreal, Canada, in 1873, where Sui Sin Far lived for the next twenty-five years and to which she returned often between residencies in Jamaica, San Francisco, Los Angeles, Seattle, and Boston.

Between 1898 and 1912 Sui Sin Far worked as a stenographer and typist to support herself as she moved from city to city. In addition, she bartered her skills as a writer, trading articles for train fare across the United States and Canada.

Although she supported herself through her secretarial work, Sui Sin Far began publishing short stories and nonfiction essays in U.S. newspapers in the 1880s. During her travels across the United States and Canada, she continued to write and publish short stories and worked as a journalist, reporting on the Chinese communities in the cities where she lived and worked.

Sui Sin Far's life encompassed the same contradictions that her fiction and nonfiction addressed. She wrote clever and sympathetic portrayals of the Chinese who lived in North America at a time when racist violence and oppressive "head" taxes imposed on Chinese people who lived and traveled in Canada and the United States were common. In addition, although she traveled under her

legal name, Edith Maude Eaton, she often signed her writings and her correspondence with her Chinese pseudonym and publicly admitted her "Eurasian"
heritage at a time when miscegenation was illegal in much of the United States.

Sui Sin Far published her only collection of short stories, *Mrs. Spring Fragrance*, in 1912. She died in Montreal on April 7, 1914, of a heart ailment.

MAJOR WORKS AND THEMES

As one of the first Eurasian women in North America, Sui Sin Far was aware
of the many categories into which she did not fit neatly as she struggled to form
her own identity in the face of nineteenth-century definitions of race. Throughout
her work, she utilized her own knowledge of the value of specific racial identities
and of various strategies for subverting them to demonstrate the fragility of such
definitions. In the process, she worked to reverse her readers' own ideas of racial
stereotypes.

Sui Sin Far's stories and essays demonstrate a broad range of cultural boundaries at their most fluid. In stories such as "Tian Shan's Kindred Spirit," "The
Sing Song Woman," and "A Chinese Boy-Girl," characters slip in and out of
constraining identities with ease, good humor, and generally positive consequences. She presents similar stories of people who switch identities in her
nonfiction sketches "Like the American" and "The Story of Forty-Niner."

As a Chinese North American who officially "passed" as Caucasian when she
traveled, Sui Sin Far was keenly aware of the difficulties for Chinese travelers
of crossing U.S. and Canadian borders. Her stories realistically portray the hardships of Asian North Americans who crossed international borders. In "Mrs.
Spring Fragrance" the title character's husband ironically "consoles" a white
acquaintance for his regret that Mr. Spring Fragrance's brother is held in deten-
tion by immigration authorities even though it is against the principles of "real
Americans." The pain caused by such detentions is also portrayed in "In the
Land of the Free," which movingly describes a Chinese American woman's
agony at being separated from her two-year-old son for nearly a year while an
immigration lawyer extorts money from the family.

Through her fiction and nonfiction stories, Sui Sin Far remains a staunch
defender of the Chinese in North America. In the essay "Chinese Workmen in
America" she highlights the status and wealth Chinese travelers achieve, but she
also reminds her readers of the benefits that Chinese workers have provided for
the North American industrial expansion, emphasizing their contributions to
trade, as well as their work in the railroad and mining industries.

In both her short stories and her newspaper accounts of life in various Chi-
natowns, when her subjects become so assimilated into the dominant culture
that they nearly cease to identify themselves as Chinese, the outcomes are usually negative. When her stories portray characters who force others to assimilate,
as well, the results are always devastating. Stories with such themes include

"The Wisdom of the New," "Pat and Pan," "The Americanizing of Pau Tsu," and " 'Its Wavering Image.' "

In her memoir "Leaves from the Mental Portfolio of an Eurasian," Sui Sin Far addresses the difficulties of being both Caucasian and Chinese in North America. She recounts the difficulty of revealing her heritage after hearing her neighbors and coworkers make racist remarks. She addresses similar Chinese prejudices when she relates that Chinese women say Chinese men may not want to marry her because of her mixed heritage. In this essay she tells of a young woman, presumed to be herself, who breaks off an engagement partly because her fiancé wishes her to say she is Japanese rather than Chinese. In "Leaves," Sui Sin Far describes herself both as torn between the heritages of her mother and her father and as being a "connecting link" joining East and West.

CRITICAL RECEPTION

Key to the rediscovery of Sui Sin Far's work is the new recognition of the contributions of women and minorities to American literature. Her short stories are valuable to readers today because they often feature the points of view of Chinese American and Canadian women and children, counterbalancing earlier notions that only Chinese men lived and worked in North American "bachelor societies." In addition, she makes sharp use of the racial classifications that she, herself, bridged to create characters who challenge stereotypical portrayals and demonstrate the mutability of such systems of identification.

Recent recovery of her work and attempts to construct a biography begin with S. E. Solberg's "Sui Sin Far/Edith Eaton," published in 1981, which credits her for attempting to write effective prose that, nonetheless, does not escape stereotypical portrayals of the Chinese as mysterious or inscrutable. In 1983, Amy Ling continues the recovery effort with "Edith Eaton," which outlines the economic motivations behind the anti-Chinese sentiment of the time and credits Sui Sin Far for being the first American writer, of any race, to present fully rounded portrayals of Chinese people.

The first book-length assessment of Sui Sin Far's work is Annette White-Parks's *Sui Sin Far/Edith Maude Eaton: A Literary Biography*. This text offers a comprehensive bibliography of seventy-five essays and short stories by Sui Sin Far, as well as a detailed reconstruction of her biography and an assessment of the quality of her work in the context of the circumstances of her life and of acceptable literary forms in her time. "Between the East and West," by Xiao-Huang Yin, also offers a thorough overview of the writer's available works and credits her as the first fiction writer to establish "a unique Chinese-American sensibility" (80).

Recent critics counter Solberg's earlier assessment of Sui Sin Far's characters as mere stereotypes. In *Conflicting Stories* Elizabeth Ammons argues that the stories collected in *Mrs. Spring Fragrance* use wittily ironic commentary to undermine racist portrayals of Chinese Americans. Ning Yu also asserts, in "Fanny Fern and Sui Sin Far," that the title character in *Mrs. Spring Fragrance* utilizes a double-voiced irony to challenge the racism and sexism of North American culture.

Other assessments of Sui Sin Far's stories focus on her characters' use of disguise to hide their gender or ethnicity. Annette White-Parks's " 'We Wear the Mask' " contends that the motif of concealed identities is part of a "trickster" strategy that allows each story to subvert readers' assumptions about racist stereotypes and restrictive gender roles. Similarly, Carol Roh-Spaulding says in " 'Wavering' Images" that Sui Sin Far uses her characters' adept evasions and disguises to model new possibilities of self-definition as well as to reject the necessity of claiming a definite, singular racial identity.

Since Sui Sin Far spent many years in the United States and traveled frequently between the United States and Canada, James Doyle addresses whether she should be labeled a Chinese American or a Chinese Canadian writer. In "Sui Sin Far and Onoto Watanna" he says that Sui Sin Far's work has been ignored by Canadian scholars and that American assessments of her writing have privileged her attention to Chinese American communities in the United States over her Canadian experiences.

BIBLIOGRAPHY

Works by Sui Sin Far

Mrs. Spring Fragrance. Chicago: McClurg, 1912.
Mrs. Spring Fragrance and Other Writings. Ed. Amy Ling and Annette White-Parks. Urbana: University of Illinois Press, 1995. (Fiction and nonfiction)

Studies of Sui Sin Far

Ammons, Elizabeth. *Conflicting Stories: American Women Writers at the Turn into the Twentieth Century*. New York: Oxford University Press, 1991.
Doyle, James. "Sui Sin Far and Onoto Watanna: Two Early Chinese-Canadian Authors." *Canadian Literature* 140 (1994): 50–58.
Lee, Rachel C. "Journalistic Representations of Asian Americans and Literary Responses, 1910–20." *An Interethnic Companion to Asian American Literature*. Ed. King-Kok Cheung. New York: Cambridge University Press, 1997. 249–73.
Ling, Amy. "Edith Eaton: Pioneer Chinamerican Writer and Feminist." *American Literary Realism* 16 (1983): 287–98.
———. "Pioneers and Paradigms: The Eaton Sisters." *Between Worlds: Women Writers of Chinese Ancestry*. New York: Pergamon, 1990. 21–55.
Prather, William N. "Sui Sin Far's Railroad Baron: A Chinese of the Future." *American Literary Realism* 29.1 (1996): 54–61.
Roh-Spaulding, Carol. " 'Wavering' Images: Mixed-Race Identity in the Stories of Edith

Eaton/Sui Sin Far." *Ethnicity and the American Short Story*. Ed. Julie Brown. New York: Garland, 1997. 155–76.

Solberg, S. E. "Sui Sin Far/Edith Eaton: First Chinese-American Fictionist." *MELUS* 8.1 (1981): 27–39.

White-Parks, Annette. *Sui Sin Far/Edith Maude Eaton: A Literary Biography*. Urbana University of Illinois Press, 1995.

———. " 'We Wear the Mask': Sui Sin Far as One Example of Trickster Authorship." *Tricksterism in Turn-of-the-Century American Literature: A Multicultural Perspective*. Ed. Elizabeth Ammons and Annette White-Parks. Hanover: University Press of New England, 1994. 1–20.

Yin, Xiao-Huang. "Between East and West: Sui Sin Far—the First Chinese-American Woman Writer." *Arizona Quarterly* 47.4 (1991): 49–84.

Yu, Ning. "Fanny Fern and Sui Sin Far: The Beginning of an Asian American Voice." *Women and Language* 19.2 (1996): 44–47.

GENEVIEVE TAGGARD
(1894–1948)

David Garrett Izzo

BIOGRAPHY

Poet Genevieve Taggard was born in Waitsburg, Washington, on November 28, 1894, the first of three children to James Nelson Taggard and Alta Gale Arnold. Both lay Christian missionaries, Taggard's parents moved to Hawaii to open a school for native children when she was two. Taggard played with the island children, and her Hawaiian idyll featured a contradiction that would shape her future: Although her parents encouraged her to accept the diversity of people of color, and she would be a social liberal thereafter, their rigid fundamentalism—in their home no book other than the Bible was permitted—seemed in conflict with a less formal attitude toward their daughter's playmates. Inevitably, Taggard, her imagination enlivened by the island beauty and the diversity of the natives, would read other books secretly. The danger involved in the act of reading heightened her love of literature, particularly lyric poetry, which was the medium that best matched the beautiful environs. It was mystical, and Taggard began there an introspection that would lead her to metaphysical poetry and Emily Dickinson.

In 1914, Taggard's family left Hawaii for San Francisco. Friends of the family helped Taggard attend the University of California at Berkeley. (Her parents, struggling to make ends meet, had become less rigid as concerned their earlier restrictions.) Taggard said, "I earned what I could while going to college. Finally, I became editor of the *Occident*, the college literary magazine, which paid a small salary" ("Taggard" 1380). Two of her English instructors were the poets Witter Bynner and Leonard Bacon. From Bynner came a predilection for the metaphysical; from Bacon there was a classical emphasis.

In 1920, Taggard traveled to New York City, and *Harper's* magazine published her poem "An Hour on a Hill." She worked for publisher B. W. Huebsch and also continued to contribute poems and reviews to the many "small" literary magazines that proliferated in the 1920s after the success of Harriet Monroe's *Poetry*, a decade earlier. With friends, Taggard started one of these little magazines, *The Measure*. In 1921, she married Robert Wolf and had a daughter, Marcia. Taggard's first book of poems, *For Eager Lovers* (1923), celebrated her first year of marriage.

Taggard published more verse during the 1920s while studying the metaphysical poets. This pursuit culminated with her 1929 anthology *Circumference: Varieties of Metaphysical Verse 1456–1928*. In 1931, with a Guggenheim Fellowship, Taggard wrote *The Life and Mind of Emily Dickinson*. In 1932, she began to teach. Her first position was at Bennington College in Vermont. Taggard, in 1934, divorced Wolf. A year later, she married Kenneth Durant, who worked for *Tass*, the Soviet news agency. Her socialism became more radical, as did her poetry. In 1935, she went to teach at Sarah Lawrence College in Bronxville, New York, where she would remain until 1946. That year, Taggard would have to retire from teaching due to health problems caused by progressive hypertension. She died in 1948.

MAJOR WORKS AND THEMES

Taggard's Hawaiian childhood would remain a dominant influence in her work. The natural beauty there inspired an early passion for Keats and she said, "His luxury suited the island radiance" ("Taggard" 1380). Her lyricism was the result. Conversely, Hawaii also inspired her radical socialism, as she had hated how the American tourists treated the natives who were her only friends.

Taggard, from her very first published poem—a tribute to her Berkeley teacher, the poet Witter Bynner, written in 1919—considered the duality of public and private selves. In that poem, she wrote: "You have a gallant way with you my friend" ("XXVII" 58). Yet it mattered less to her that he was a famous poet, as the heart behind his pen mattered more. Contemplation of inner/ outer, public/private, the real and the surreal, would move her verse toward Dickinson and the metaphysicists. Still, her first volume, *For Eager Lovers* (1923), was more concerned with a happy first year of marriage and her lyricism included the poem "With Child," which critic Edmund Wilson praised for its visceral yet not painful account of childbearing.

The peak of her lyric verse came with the 1928 volume *Traveling Standing Still*, in which critic William Rose Benet said "her best poems are to be found" (*Fifty* 127). These poems expressed a joy in solitude engendered by Taggard's island youth where being the "different one" among the natives imbued her with a sense of independence but also with the outsider's guarded wisdom. Benet asked her to choose a poem for his anthology *Fifty Poets* and to explain why. Taggard said, "One Summer evening in 1928 in a special key of loneliness and intensity and certainty, the whole thing came as if dictated" (128). The poem, "Try Tropic," is about how one tries to escape from one's own self but never can, no matter what one does or where one goes: "Nothing will help, and nothing do much harm" (129). Moreover, she said, "When I wrote it . . . I had myself and you, reader, in mind . . . and many others . . . all of us, and there are many now—who run through books and landscapes looking for something, with worn faces. I choose this poem because it is about our life and our way of behaving" (*Fifty* 127–28).

In 1928, Taggard was thinking in transcendent terms as she was about to publish her anthology of metaphysical poets with an introduction ruminating on what "metaphysical" means. Her view explains her own work and themes therein. Taggard believed Donne and Dickinson were the "only genuinely metaphysical poets of the first order of clarity," although she allowed for many runners-up (*Circumference* 4). She wrote that they were the metaphysical exemplars for not being constrained by technique and seeking subtlety through "the form of an idea. Ideas are . . . beautiful in their entire uniqueness as pure form when simply revealed as idea. To give an idea no form but itself, to show it as organic by an inner music, as if the bones of a skeleton were singing in their own rhythm—that is the technical obsession of the metaphysical poet" (10). With her musical analogy, one sees why Taggard later derived satisfaction that some of her verse's "inner music" was set to actual music by Aaron Copland, among others.

In 1931, Taggard wrote her study of Dickinson, adding to the then early Dickinson scholarship. In fact, her championing of metaphysical verse at a time when current events were demanding stark realism was another example of Taggard's rebelliousness (although she would shortly turn to realism herself). This work influenced others who were willing to still make room for "pure form simply reveled as idea" as a contrast to the "poetry-as-news" then prevalent.

CRITICAL RECEPTION

Genevieve Taggard's poetry was well regarded upon publication; however, as with many poets who wrote Left-leaning verse in the 1930s, this political work obscured her critical reputation as concerned what was written before and after it. From her first volume, *For Eager Lovers* (1923), Taggard was recognized as a new force with Louis Untermeyer saying of her verse: "It is a woman speaking . . . instead of rhetoric, we have revelation" (600). Throughout the 1920s, the word that repeated in the reviews of her work was "lyrical," which reflected her youth in Hawaii and her early admiration of Keats.

Her work was appreciated by her peers, who also admired her intellectual scholarship in the genre of poetry. In 1930, Taggard's study of Emily Dickinson and her anthology of metaphysical poets with its astute introduction solidified her reputation as a poetic theorist. Of the former, Louis Untermeyer wrote that it was a "beautifully written study, keen and sensitive" (1179), and of the latter, "[H]er preface is excellent, achieving a pointed and delicate critical analysis" (qtd. in Gregory 6).

In the 1930s, Taggard's verse turned to sociopolitical themes for which her earlier lyrical technique was not suited, and she turned more to "proselike" verse, as did many of her activist contemporaries. Critics were not as receptive to this change in style and subject: "For all her vitality, [she] seems at the moment to be in some confusion as to just what her poetic direction should be" (Lechlitner 7). In the 1940s, with the publication of *Long View* and *Slow Music*, Taggard returned to her earlier method. Of *Slow Music*, her last book of verse, it was said: "In this book of poems, Miss Taggard appears gallant, various, and warm. I know of no poet to whom the lyric gift appears more native" (Caldwell 31).

After her death in 1948, Taggard went into critical eclipse. In the 1990s, however, there was some new interest in her work from both the feminist (Miller, Wilson) and political perspectives (Allegro).

BIBLIOGRAPHY

Works by Genevieve Taggard

"XXVII." *W. B. in California*. Berkeley, CA: Privately printed, 1919.

For Eager Lovers. New York: Selzer, 1923. (Poems)

Hawaiian Hilltop. San Francisco: Wyckoff & Gelber, 1923. (Poems)

May Days: An Anthology of Verse from the Masses and Liberator. Ed. Taggard. New York: Boni, 1925.

Words for The Chisel. New York: Knopf, 1926. (Poems)

"Preface and Two Chapters from the Book of Merryall." *American Caravan*. Ed. Alfred Kreymborg, Lewis Mumford, and Paul Rosenfeld. New York: Macauley, 1928. 369–78. (Poems)

Traveling Standing Still. New York: Knopf, 1928. (Poems)

Circumference: Varieties of Metaphysical Verse 1456–1928. Ed. Taggard. New York: Covici-Friede, 1929. (Anthology)

Monologue for Mothers. New York: Random, 1929. (Poems)

The Life and Mind of Emily Dickinson. New York: Knopf, 1931. (Biography)

Remembering Vaughn in New England. New York: Arrow, 1933. (Nonfiction)

"Try Tropic." *Fifty Poets*. Ed. William Rose Benet. New York: Duffield, 1933. 127.

Not Mine to Finish. New York: Harper, 1934. (Poems)

Ten Introductions: A Collection of Modern Verse. Ed. Taggard, and Dudley Fitts. New York: Arrow, 1934.

Calling Western Union. New York: Harper, 1936. (Poems)

Collected Poems. New York: Harper, 1938.

Long View. New York: Harper, 1942. (Poems)

"Taggard, Genevieve." *Twentieth Century American Authors*. Ed. Stanley Kunitz and Howard Haycraft. New York: Wilson, 1942. 1380–81.

A Part of Vermont. East Jamaica, VT: River Press, 1945. (Poems)

Slow Music. New York: Harper, 1946. (Poems)

Origin: Hawaii. Ed. Donald Angus. Honolulu: Angus, 1947. (Poems)

Studies of Genevieve Taggard

Allegro, Donna M. "The Construction and Role of Community in Political Long Poems by Twentieth Century Women Poets." Diss. Southern Illinois University, 1997.

Arvin, Newton. Rev. of *Traveling Standing Still*, by Genevieve Taggard. *New York Herald Tribune Books* 9 May 1926: 6.

Benet, William Rose. Rev. of *Calling Western Union*, by Genevieve Taggard. *Saturday Review of Literature* 7 Nov. 1936: 24.

Caldwell, J. R. Rev. of *Slow Music*, by Genevieve Taggard. *Saturday Review of Literature* 11 Jan. 1947: 31.

Gregory, Horace. Rev. of *Circumference: Varieties of Metaphysical Verse 1456–1928*, by Genevieve Taggard. *Books* 23 Feb. 1930: 6.

Kunitz, Stanley J., and Howard Haycraft, eds. "Taggard, Genevieve." *Twentieth Century American Authors*. New York: Wilson, 1942. 1380–81.

Lechlitner, Ruth. Rev. of *Collected Poems*, by Genevieve Taggard. *Books* 4 Dec. 1937: 12.

———. Rev. of *Not Mine to Finish*, by Genevieve Taggard. *Books* 28 Oct. 1934: 7.

Lins, Kathryn Lucille. "An Interpretive Study of Selected Poetry of Genevieve Taggard." M.A. University of Hawaii, 1956.

Miller, Nina. "The Bonds of Free Love: Constructing the Bohemian Self." *New York Genders* 11 (1993): 37–57.

———. "Love Poetry and the New Woman: Literary Negotiations." Diss. Northwestern University, 1992.

Stauffer, Donald A. "Genesis, or the Poet as Maker." *Poets at Work*. New York: Harcourt, 1948. 61–67.

Untermeyer, Louis. Rev. of *For Eager Lovers*, by Genevieve Taggard. *Saturday Review of Literature* 23 Apr. 1923: 600.

———. Rev. of *The Life and Mind of Emily Dickinson*, by Genevieve Taggard. *Saturday Review of Literature* 5 July 1930: 1179.

Wilson, Martha, and Gwendolyn Sell. "Lola Ridge and Genevieve Taggard: Voices of Resistance." *Arkansas Journal* 2 (1993): 124–33.

Rev. of *Words for the Chisel*, by Genevieve Taggard. *New York Times* 9 May 1926: 6.

SARA TEASDALE
(1884–1933)

David Garrett Izzo

BIOGRAPHY

Sara Teasdale was born on August 4, 1884, to St. Louis bluebloods John Warren Teasdale and Mary Elizabeth Willard (forty-five and forty, respectively). As the last sibling of two brothers and a sister who were twenty, fifteen, and seventeen years older, Sara was doted on by "five" parents. This attention in childhood was both nurturing *and* sheltering. Her adult years were spent in the frustration of never being able to recreate her youth. As a teen, she wrote poetry with her close-knit cocoon of friends, and her principal poetic influences were Christina Rosetti and the Greeks. The affluent Teasdale traveled widely in the United States and abroad. In 1907, she self-published her first volume of verse, *Sonnets to Duse* (referring to actress Eleonora Duse). In 1912, America's poetry renaissance began with Harriet Monroe's *Poetry: A Magazine of Verse*, based in Chicago. *Poetry* became a powerfully influential venue for the discovery of new voices who were able to showcase not just a poem or two but six or seven. In addition to featuring Teasdale, who would spend more and more time in Chicago, other area poets published in *Poetry* were Carl Sandburg, Edgar Lee Masters, and Vachel Lindsay.

Teasdale met Lindsay, a poet and performance artist—his dramatized recitals were legendary—in 1912 and began a futile courtship. He dedicated his books to her, and she is the "Princess" in his "The Chinese Nightingale." Lindsay was eccentric, flamboyant, and sometimes overwhelmingly enthusiastic—all of which were outward symptoms of his great insecurity. Teasdale admired him and did care for him, but his demeanor and more rustic background did not match Teasdale's own status as represented by her parents, who did not approve of him. Lindsay persisted, and Teasdale, in 1914, as some personal recollections have recounted (Untermeyer, Rittenhouse, Tietjens, Monroe), married businessman Ernst Filsinger to finally dissuade Lindsay. Nonetheless, Lindsay and Teasdale remained friends. Her marriage was safe and kept her in the affluence in which she grew up. Still, Filsinger was not a fellow artist, and as Teasdale's fame as a poet grew, her safe choice conflicted with her new world of artists and intellectuals.

In 1915, Teasdale's *Rivers to the Sea* received great critical praise. Her tall, willowy, and fragile presence encouraged many admirers, and fellow poets wrote poems to and about her (Witter Bynner, John Hall Wheelock, etc.). Teasdale's verse thrived, as did Lindsay's, who remained devoted to her. In 1917, her *Love Songs* was a great success for a book of verse, appearing in five editions and winning the Columbia Poetry Prize. Teasdale's frail health (much of which may actually have been symptoms of depression) became a greater factor in her life. In 1929, despite no outward hints of dissatisfaction, she divorced Filsinger. Her biographer wrote: "There were two conflicting desires within the poet's nature that had been battling for supremacy since childhood. One was . . . to love and be loved . . . the other was the old wish for solitude where her spirit found its greatest renewal" (Carpenter 289). Teasdale may have also regretted not having allowed herself to love an artist.

When the depression era came in, lyrical poetry went out. In October 1931, Vachel Lindsay killed himself. On January 29, 1933, so did Sara Teasdale.

MAJOR WORKS AND THEMES

Sara Teasdale's first book, *Sonnets to Duse* (1907), "was testimony to the poet's overwhelming attraction to beauty, and in it are to be seen the three chief influences of her early period: the musical quality that she had absorbed from [Heinrich] Heine's poetry, her admiration for Eleonora Duse, and her identification with Sappho and her deep love for ancient Greece" (Carpenter 335). *Helen of Troy* (1911) begins with monologues concerning love as "spoken" by Helen, Beatrice, Sappho, Marianna Alcoforando, the Portugese nun, Guenevere, and Sappho's student Erinna. Each monologue dramatizes different phases of a woman's love with an intensity that recognized Teasdale as a new romanticist. Also included were poems detailing her travels of the preceding years.

Rivers to the Sea (1915) no longer uses surrogates but speaks in Teasdale's own voice. Intensely personal, she depicts her lifelong struggle with "the desire for beauty and the ability to enjoy it in solitude, and the conflicting desire for love and the presence of a lover" (Carpenter 337). Poems much anthologized from this volume were "The Look," and "I Shall Not Care." Herein, Teasdale also tried free verse for the first time. Now recognized as the leading romantic poet of her time, Teasdale's 1917 volume was titled *Love Songs*, and she continued her praise of beauty. In "Barter" she writes: "Spend all you have for loveliness" (*Collected* 97).

Flame and Shadow (1920) continues her love themes, but now thirty-six, Teasdale tempers her effusive declarations with hints of her more tangible conflict with the differences between the mind's purity and life's mundane realities. There are poems about death, grief, loss, and inexorable time that will become the dominant strains in her last two volumes, *Dark of the Moon* (1926) and

Strange Victory (1933). "These poems are enriched with an austerity, a noble-ness, a resignation with no self-pity and no bitterness; they are stripped down to the very essence of wisdom born out of suffering" (Carpenter 344). *Strange Victory* includes her elegy for Vachel Lindsay, written just before she took her own life.

Teasdale also edited two anthologies: *The Answering Voice* (1917), which featured poems only by women, and *Stars To-night* (1930), which contained poems for children.

CRITICAL RECEPTION

Sara Teasdale was a critical as well as popular favorite in the 1910s, 1920s, and early 1930s. Her success opened doors for more women such as Edna St. Vincent Millay, Margaret Widdemar, and Elinor Wylie, among others. She was very generous in her support of female peers and used her popularity to publish an anthology of their verse.

From her first book, *Sonnets to Duse and Other Poems* (1907), Teasdale was noticed, with British writer/critic Arthur Symons admiring Teasdale's musical cadences. *Helen of Troy* (1911) was transitional. Its dramatic monologues were not rhymed and fared not as well with readers and critics who preferred the author's magazine verses, which were lyrically sonorous. Teasdale's 1920 re-vision attempted to smooth the rough edges, and today the original edition is seen as one to be studied for the hints of what she would achieve with her breakthrough volume *Rivers to the Sea* (1915).

Teasdale was pleased that the verse in *Rivers to the Sea* was compared to Christina Rosetti, Blake, and Houseman. Influential poets and critics such as William Stanley Braithwaite, Edwin Markham, Harriet Monroe, Jessie Ritten-house, and Arthur Symons praised without reservations the delicate simplicity that managed to convey both joy and wistfulness. The combined American and British appreciation warranted a German translation at the end of World War I.

Teasdale's *Love Songs* (1917) was chosen by Columbia University as the best book of poetry for the year. This was the nation's highest honor and the fore-runner of the Pulitzer Prize in this genre before Pulitzers were given in verse. Critics agreed with the honor, and Teasdale became synonymous with a new Romanticism. Her esteem rose so quickly that the next year she became a judge deciding on the 1918 winner (a tie: Carl Sandburg and Margaret Widdemar).

In her next book, *Flame and Shadow* (1920), Teasdale, having been affected by her country's entry into World War I, now tempered her Romanticism with fear. Critics noted her new direction, with Marguerite Wilkinson declaring that Teasdale "has found a new philosophy of life and death" (10). Among others, Babette Deutsch also praised the mature wisdom that was equal to a postwar audience that required it.

Teasdale's frail health began to cast a pall over her life and work. She did not publish *Dark of the Moon* until 1926, and the critics observed that the title indicated there was less contrast of light and dark, as in her previous book, and more of a somber shade throughout. Again the critics were uniformly in admiration of her continuing depth of feeling contained within the sonorous lyricism that still remained in her work. Many believed it was her best work. Few realized that its foreboding reflected her being increasingly drawn to death. Another seven years would pass before her last book, *Strange Victory* (1933), would appear posthumously. The book was another critical and popular success and, as such, a tribute to her memory. Her biographer wrote that her last three books were her best, saying: "These later poems increasingly reveal her courageous outlook upon the mysteries of life and death; in them, she asserts her faith in the inviolateness of the human soul amid perishable things and fugitive emotions" (Carpenter 328).

After her death, poetry in general moved away from Teasdale's type of delicate lyricism, which mirrored more of the era directly before hers than her own era or the years to follow. Until recently, her work has been largely ignored, even having been left out of *The Norton Anthology of Modern Poets*, which otherwise includes poets preceding her. This is regrettable. Without the enormous critical and popular success of Teasdale in her own time, there would have been fewer opportunities for other women during and after her own achievements.

BIBLIOGRAPHY

Works by Sara Teasdale

Sonnets to Duse and Other Poems. Boston: Poet Lore, 1907.
Helen of Troy and Other Poems. New York: Putnam's, 1911.
Rivers to the Sea. New York: Macmillan, 1915.
The Answering Voice: One Hundred Love Lyrics by Women. Ed. Teasdale. Boston: Houghton, 1917.
Love Songs. New York: Macmillan, 1917.
Flame and Shadow. New York: Macmillan, 1920.
Dark of the Moon. New York: Macmillan, 1926.
Stars To-night, Verses Old and New for Boys and Girls. Ed. Teasdale. New York: Macmillan, 1930. (Anthology of children's poetry)
Strange Victory. New York: Macmillan, 1933.
The Collected Poems of Sara Teasdale. New York: Macmillan, 1937.
Mirror of the Heart, Poems of Sara Teasdale. Ed. William Drake. New York: Macmillan, 1984.

Studies of Sara Teasdale

Carpenter, Margaret Haley. *Sara Teasdale: A Biography*. New York: Schulte, 1960.
Cohen, Edward. "The Letters of Sara Teasdale to Jessie B. Rittenhouse." *Resources for American Literary Study* 4 (1974): 225–27.

D'Amico, Diane. "Saintly Singer or Tanagara Figure? Christina Rosetti through the Eyes of Katherine Tynan and Sara Teasdale." *Victorian Poetry* 32 (1994): 387–407.

Deutsch, Babette. Rev. of *Dark of the Moon*, by Sara Teasdale. *New Republic* 1 Dec. 1926: 26.

Drake, William. *Sara Teasdale: Woman and Poet*. Knoxville: Tennessee University Press, 1979.

Kilmer, Joyce. Rev. of *Riders to the Sea*, by Sara Teasdale. *Bookman* 42 (1915): 457.

Mannino, Maryann. "Sara Teasdale: Fitting Tunes to Everything." *Turn of the Century Women* 5 (1990): 37–41.

Masters, Edgar Lee. *Vachel Lindsay*. New York: Scribner's, 1935.

Monroe, Harriet. "Sara Teasdale." *Poets & Their Art*. New York: Macmillan, 1932. 72–77.

Perry, Ruth, and Maurice Sagoff. "Sara Teasdale: Friendships." *New Letters* 46.1 (1979): 101–7.

Rittenhouse, Jessie. *My House of Life*. Boston: Houghton, 1934.

Ruggles, Eleanor. *The West-Going Heart*. New York: Norton, 1959. (Biography of Lindsay)

Russell-Swafford, Anne. "Influence of Sara Teasdale on Louise Bogan." *CEA Critic* 41 (1979): 47–52.

Saul, George Brandon. "A Delicate Fabric of Birdsong: The Verse of Sara Teasdale." *ARQ* 13 (1957): 62–66.

Schoen, Carol. *Sara Teasdale*. New York: Twayne, 1986.

Sprague, Rosemary. *Imaginary Gardens: A Study of Five American Poets*. Philadelphia: Chilton, 1969.

Tietjens, Eunice. *The World at My Shoulder*. New York: Macmillan, 1938.

Untermeyer, Louis. *From Another World*. New York: Harcourt, 1939.

Wilkinson, Marguerite. Rev. of *Flame and Shadow*, by Sara Teasdale. *New York Times* 31 Oct. 1920: 10.

Woodward, Deborah. "The More Fragile Boundary: The Female Subject and the Romance Plot in the Texts of Edna St. Vincent Millay, Elinor Wylie, Sara Teasdale, Louise Bogan." Diss. University of Michigan, Ann Arbor, 1990.

EUDORA ALICE WELTY
(1909–)

Beverly Forsyth

BIOGRAPHY

Eudora Alice Welty was born on April 13, 1909, in Jackson, Mississippi, the oldest of three children. Her father, Christian Webb Welty, from Ohio, met her mother, Mary Chestina Andrews, a schoolteacher in the mountains of West Virginia, when he went to work in an office for a lumber construction company. When the young couple married, they moved to Jackson, Mississippi, where he worked as an executive with the Lamar Life Insurance Company.

Her parents loved literature and impressed upon their daughter a deep love of books at a very young age. One of Welty's fondest memories is of her parents reading aloud to each other. Welty's love of the spoken word and the themes she was exposed to as a child surfaced years later in her own work. Fairy tales, myths, and legends, which became a familiar literary staple to young Welty, are subtly interwoven in her own writing.

Except for short periods, Welty has spent her whole life in Jackson, Mississippi, where she still lives. She graduated from Central High School in 1925 and attended her first two years of college at Mississippi State College for Women (MSCW), from 1925 to 1927. While at MSCW, Welty worked as a freshman reporter for the college newspaper, *Spectator*. In her junior year, she transferred to the University of Wisconsin in Madison, where she completed her last two years, earning a Bachelor of Arts degree in 1929. Welty's mother emotionally supported Welty's budding desire to become a writer. Although Welty's father did not oppose her, he was concerned that she wouldn't be able to support herself. Although Welty desperately wanted to pursue writing, she knew that she did not want to be a teacher. To prepare for future employment, Welty took some graduate courses in advertising at Columbia University Graduate School of Business in New York City from 1930 to 1931. When Welty's father died in 1931 at the age of fifty-two, she returned home to Jackson to live.

Over the next few years, Welty worked for different newspapers and for the Jackson radio station WJDX. During the depression in the 1930s, Welty worked as a junior publicity agent for the Works Progress Administration (WPA) in Mississippi. Although Welty only worked for the WPA three years (1933–1936), this position marked a turning point in Welty's career and solidified her desire to write. As Welty traveled all over the state of Mississippi, she interviewed people, wrote stories for county papers, and took pictures. She got the opportunity to see her state up close in a way that she had never seen it before. Welty described the experience as the germ of her desire to become a writer. In her travels, she saw the different sides to her home state during the depression. As she traveled on different assignments, Welty gathered material for her own stories.

Welty's literary rise seems almost fairy-tale. In the May–June 1936 issue, her short story "Death of a Traveling Salesman" was published by *Manuscript*, a small bimonthly magazine, and her short story "Magic" was published in the September–October 1936 issue. Although the editors Mary Lawhead and John Rood could not afford to pay the new author, Rood assured Welty that important publishers watched the small magazine for emerging literary talent. In 1940, Diarmuid Russell, the son of the poet George William Russell, had read the short story and immediately contacted Welty upon opening his own agency and asked Welty if he could represent her as an agent.

In 1941, *Atlantic Monthly* published "A Worn Path" and "Why I Live at the P.O."; her collection of short stories *A Curtain of Green* was published the same year. Welty received immediate acclaim. She won second prize for the O. Henry Memorial Contest Award for "A Worn Path." Editors took notice of Welty's stories, and some wrote to the young writer, encouraging her to write a novel. Following *A Curtain of Green* (1941) came Welty's short novel *The Robber Bridegroom* in 1942.

In 1943, Welty signed with Harcourt Brace and published her second collection of short stories, *The Wide Net and Other Stories*. Her short story "Livvie Is Back" won first prize in the O. Henry Memorial Contest Award. In 1944, she served as a staff reviewer for the *New York Times Book Review*.

Welty produced her most significant works within a twenty-year time frame. In 1955, *The Ponder Heart* (1954), which was well received, was awarded the William Dean Howells Medal of the Academy of Arts and Letters. Fifteen years passed between her fourth short story collection, *The Bride of the Innisfallen and Other Stories* (1955) and her novel *Losing Battles* (1970). Written during the time that Welty cared for her sick mother, *Losing Battles* is Welty's longest piece of fiction. At sixty-three, Welty won the Pulitzer Prize for her novel *The Optimist's Daughter* (1972), which solidified her place in the American literary canon. *The Optimist's Daughter* is the story of a woman coming to grips with her father's death.

Welty's short stories, reviews, and essays have appeared in *Southern Review, American Prefaces, Decision, Harper's, The Hudson Review, New Directions, Sewanee Review, Southern Review, Tomorrow, Yale Review, Prairie Schooner,*

Accent, Atlantic Monthly, Harper's Bazaar, Saturday Review, and *The New Yorker*.

Welty has received widespread international acclaim and won numerous honors. Her work has been translated into Danish, Swedish, Japanese, Chinese, French, Dutch, Italian, Burmese, German, Greek, Czech, Polish, Argentinian, Rumanian, and Russian. She has received the Guggenheim Fellowship, served as an Honorary Consultant in American Letters for the Library of Congress, and was elected to the American Academy of Arts and Letters and the National Institute of Arts and Letters. Awards she has received include: the William Dean Howells Medal from the American Academy of Arts and Letters, the Ingram Memorial Foundation Award in Literature, the Gold Medal for the Novel from the National Institute of Arts and Letters, the Frankel Humanities Prize of the National Endowment for the Humanities, the Pulitzer Prize, the National Medal of Literature, the Medal of Freedom Award, the first Cleanth Brooks Medal, and the PEN-Malamud Award. In 1987, she was named a Chevalier de l'Ordre des Arts et Lettres by the French government, and she received France's Légion d'Honneur in 1996.

MAJOR WORKS AND THEMES

Welty's literary career has spanned more than fifty years. Although Welty is often described as a southern writer, she holds a prominent place among American writers. Welty is well known for a few frequently anthologized stories, primarily, "Petrified Man," "Powerhouse," "Why I Live at the P.O.," "Death of a Traveling Salesman," and "A Worn Path"; however, she has written and published four short-story collections, five novels, and her childhood memoirs. She has also published reviews, literary essays on the craft of writing, and photography collections.

Welty's fiction extends beyond simple labels. Although her writing is best noted for her historical works about southern families, critics are taking a fresh look at her fiction. Among the traditional themes of family, perseverance, love, loyalty, and redemption, critics are noticing a complex weave of themes that deal with isolation, entrapment, perversion, violence, and sexuality.

Although small towns or rural Mississippi serve as the settings for most of her fiction, Welty delves beyond the southern genteel facade to reveal characters who live on the fringes of society. Many of her characters have been described as monstrous, grotesque, demented, bizarre, and deformed. Welty also uses many themes from Greek and Roman mythology, fairy tales, and legends. With paradoxical irony, Welty's work is simultaneously viewed as historical and realistic in its depictions of regional dialect, tradition, ritual, and social, racial, and economic class divisions.

Welty's fiction often concerns themes of alienation and isolation. "A Worn Path" and "Why I Live at the P.O." are two prominent stories in Welty's first collection, *A Curtain of Green and Other Stories* (1941); both stories feature isolated characters who feel alienated from mainstream society. In "A Worn Path" Phoenix Jackson, an old Negro woman, makes a long trek into Natchez, where she must obtain medicine for her grandson. As she strives forward despite her own frail health and failing memory, she forgets the reason why she must go to Natchez. In the end she remembers the medicine and decides to buy her ill grandson a small Christmas present with her last two nickels. In "Why I Live at the P.O.," the narrator, Sister, recounts the story of Stella-Rondo's rivaling vindictiveness and her own estrangement from the family.

Fairy tales and mythology frequently play a central theme in Welty's fiction. Welty titled her first novel, *The Robber Bridegroom* (1942), after Grimm's *Robber Bridegroom*. In *Eudora Welty*, J. A. Bryant, Jr., observes that traces and suggestions of other fairy tales can also be found, including "The Little Goose Girl," "Rumpelstiltskin," "Little Snow White," "The Fisherman and His Wife," "Beauty and the Beast," "Cinderella," and the myth of Cupid and Psyche (17): *The Golden Apples* (1949), a collection of short stories, is set in the Mississippi Delta town of Morgana. The stories draw heavily from Greek mythology. *The Bride of the Innisfallen and Other Stories* (1955), Welty's fourth collection of short stories, lacked the commercial and critical interest of her other works; however, critics are beginning to focus their critical attention on this collection. Among these seven stories, which center around the journey motif, Welty used the contemporary Deep South, a Civil War setting, and her own European travels. In "Circe," the sorceress gives her version of Odysseus's visit to her mythical island.

Welty's lighthearted works have earned her high praise. *The Ponder Heart* (1954), which received numerous positive reviews, was awarded the William Dean Howells Medal of the Academy of Arts and Letters. Miss Edna Earle Ponder manages the Beulah Hotel. She tells a traveling salesman the comical history of her family and the townfolks.

Many of Welty's other short stories depict strong regional characters set against a historical backdrop. Welty's second collection of stories, *The Wide Net and Other Stories* (1943), deals with marriage, birth, rebirth, tradition, and isolation. In "The Wide Net," William Wallace's wife Hazel has disappeared and is presumed drowned in a nearby river. Aided by the country folks, William Wallace drags the river in search of Hazel's body.

Welty is also acclaimed for her portrayal of southern realism. *Delta Wedding* (1946) concerns a nine-year-old girl who has lost her mother and is taken into the Fairchild family by her Aunt Ellen. In *The Heart of the Story*, Peter Schmidt says that *Delta Wedding* is an important departure in the way Welty has portrayed female characters; Schmidt says, "The most positively portrayed maternal presence in Welty's fiction up until that time, Ellen Fairchild best represents Welty's shift of focus in the early and mid-1940s from repressive relations among women to nurturing and empowering ones" (198). *Losing Battles* (1970), which deals with a family reunion, is Welty's longest work. Set in the 1930s, three generations of Granny Vaughn's descendants gather at her matriarchal home to celebrate her ninetieth birthday. As the family is gathered, they receive news of the death of Miss Julia Mortimer, the local schoolteacher. In Peggy Whitman Prenshow's *Eudora Welty: Critical Essays*, Robert B. Heilman's *"Losing Battles* and Winning the War" explores the layering of family dramas; he states that *Losing Battles* "explores some unclear but serious history that has an impact on the present . . . and though it in no way minimizes rifts and tensions, the novel perceives reunion as a symbol of residual unity among country kinfolk rather than as an ironic recorder of disunity in a country family" (274–75). In 1973 *The Optimist's Daughter* (1972) won the Pulitzer Prize. The story, which parallels events in Welty's own life, explores the parent-child bond. Laurel, a young woman who has left the South, returns to New Orleans to be with her dying father. After his death, she and Fay, her young stepmother, return to the small Mississippi town where she grew up. In *Eudora Welty*, Elizabeth Evans states, *"The Optimist's Daughter* shares with other of Miss Welty's works a thematic interest in family, community, social mores, marriage, loneliness, and the continuity of life that love provides" (123).

A chronological reading of Welty's short fiction reveals her literary development. *The Collected Stories of Eudora Welty* (1980) gathers together for the first time the four volumes *A Curtain of Green and Other Stories* (1941), *The Wide Net and Other Stories* (1943), *The Golden Apples* (1949), *The Bride of the Innisfallen and Other Stories* (1955), plus two uncollected stories, "Where Is the Voice Coming From" (1963) and "The Demonstrators" (1966). These forty-one stories, which range from the early 1940s to the mid-1960s, appear in the order of their publication and reflect Welty's growth as a short-story writer.

Welty's keen interest in photography complements her literary vision. *One Time, One Place* (1971), a collection of photographs that Welty took during the Great Depression, includes a foreword written by the author. She took the pictures while she traveled her home state working for the WPA. Welty's interest in photography paralleled her writing career. Much of Welty's nonfiction has been published as essays and reviews. *The Eye of the Story* (1978), *One Writer's Beginnings* (1984), and *A Writer's Eye: Collected Book Reviews* (1994) as well as Welty's essays prefacing her photography collections provide a revealing glimpse into the writer's mind. In *One Writer's Beginnings*, which consists of three essays, "Listening," "Learning to See," and "Finding a Voice," Welty describes her childhood and her views on the writing process; she states, "My temperament and my instinct had told me alike that the author, who writes at his own emergency, remains and needs to remain at his private remove. I wished to be, not effaced, but invisible—actually a powerful position" (87).

CRITICAL RECEPTION

Reviewers often have conflicting interpretations regarding Welty's fiction. Because she mixes mythology and fairy-tale motifs with realistic depictions of southern life, her short stories and novels are difficult to categorize. Ruth M.

Vande Kieft's *Eudora Welty*, published in 1962 and revised in 1987, was the first important critical study of Welty's work. She traces consistent patterns in Welty's fiction and devotes chapters in both editions to Welty's use of mythic motifs in *The Golden Apples* (1949).

In *Eudora Welty's Achievement of Order*, Michael Kreyling focuses on Welty's techniques as the unifying force in her fiction, and Albert J. Devlin, in *Eudora Welty's Chronicle*, traces the historical aesthetics of place, particularly Welty's home state of Mississippi, as an important element in Welty's cultural vision.

"Gothic" is a word frequently used when discussing Welty's fiction. Critics see strong Gothic elements in Welty's use of plot, setting, character, imagery, and vocabulary. However, for Welty to be strictly labeled as a Gothic writer would seriously limit both Welty and her work. Ruth D. Weston, author of *Gothic Traditions and Narrative Techniques in the Fiction of Eudora Welty*, states that the Gothic landscapes are to be expected from a writer who came to maturity in a land haunted by ghosts, religion, and the Confederate dead (3–4).

Essay collections often explore Welty's thematic spectrum. In *A Still Moment: Essays on the Art of Eudora Welty*, John F. Desmond says that the contemporary reader cannot appreciate Welty's work because her work is based on a metaphysical sense of human emotions and human existence that the reader has lost. Desmond states, "[B]eneath the many shapes her fictional world has given us lies a constant and unchanging core, a metaphysical sense which informs every mode of being she examines: personality, time, eternity, memory, dream, love, beauty, aloneness—all of those motions of the spirit which are incapable of exhaustion" (viii). Because, Desmond argues, the reader has lost this metaphysical sense of mystery, the reader experiences a "gap" between Welty's vision and society's loss of wonder. In *Modern Critical Views: Eudora Welty*, editor Harold Bloom assembles a range of critical essays arranged in chronological order of publication date. Authors include Katherine Anne Porter, Robert Penn Warren, Ruth M. Vande Kieft, Joyce Carol Oates, Reynolds Price, and Cleanth Brooks. John Edward Hardy explores regional symbolism in *Delta Wedding* (1946), Daniele Pitavy-Souques compares structural similarities in *The Golden Apples* (1949) to the myth of Perseus, Cleanth Brooks analyzes Welty's use of southern dialect, and Oates compares Welty to Kafka. Joyce Carol Oates states, "Eudora Welty baffles our expectations. Like Kafka, with whom she shares a number of traits, she presents the distortions of life in the context of ordinary, even chatty life; she frightens us" (71).

Both Welty and her fiction are the subject of new and bold interpretations. Peter Schmidt's *The Heart of the Story: Eudora Welty's Short Fiction*, which focuses primarily on Welty's short stories, draws heavily from contemporary American feminist criticism. He offers bold interpretations to Welty's tragic and comic stories as well as Welty's use of female fright figures. Schmidt says, "Sibylline and Medusan images are buried deeply within Welty's stories, appearing only briefly within figures of speech before disappearing again, because of how powerful and dangerous she finds them" (265). In *Eudora Welty: Two Pictures at Once in Her Frame*, Barbara Harrell Carson suggests Welty's work embodies an Eastern philosophical holism where the writer sought to balance the contraries evident in her work. Carson states, "In Welty's writings, life is not a matter of warring, irreconcilable opposites: subject-object, mind-matter, life-death, good-evil, past-present. Instead, hers is a vision of reality in which the traditional opposites exist in polar unity" (x). According to Carson, one pole does not cancel out its opposite. Each pole is necessary for the existence of the other. The dynamic interplay of the two poles is closely associated with the Eastern principles of yin and yang.

Diana R. Pingatore's *A Reader's Guide to the Short Stories of Eudora Welty* is a comprehensive guide to the forty-one stories that appear in *The Collected Stories of Eudora Welty* (1980). Each chapter of the book, which is divided into five separate sections, deals with the story's publication history, circumstances surrounding Welty at the time she wrote or revised the story, the relationship of the story to Welty's other works, a section on interpretations and criticism over fifty years arranged in chronological order, and a works cited section for each story that also serves as a bibliographical reference (Pingatore xi–xii).

Ann Waldron, author of *Eudora: A Writer's Life*, has written the first biography of Welty. The biography traces the author's childhood, family, friendships, education, employment, literary relationships, significant publications, and any aspect that influenced Welty's work. Waldron has made a significant contribution in chronicling the life and achievements of an elusive literary icon.

BIBLIOGRAPHY

Works by Eudora Alice Welty

A Curtain of Green and Other Stories. Garden City, NY: Doubleday, 1941.
The Robber Bridegroom. Garden City, NY: Doubleday, 1942. (Novel)
The Wide Net and Other Stories. New York: Harcourt, 1943.
Delta Wedding. New York: Harcourt, 1946. (Novel)
Music from Spain. Greenville, MS: Levee, 1948.
The Golden Apples. New York: Harcourt, 1949. (Short stories)
The Ponder Heart. New York: Harcourt, 1954. (Novel)
The Bride of the Innisfallen and Other Stories. New York: Harcourt, 1955.
Place in Fiction. New York: House of Books, 1957.
Three Papers on Fiction. Northampton, MA: Smith College, 1962.
The Shoe Bird. New York: Harcourt, 1964. (Children's book)
Thirteen Stories. Ed. Ruth M. Vande Kieft. New York: Harcourt, 1965.
A Sweet Devouring. New York: Albondocani, 1969. (Nonfiction)
Losing Battles. New York: Random, 1970. (Novel)
One Time, One Place: Mississippi in the Depression: A Snapshot Album. New York: Random House, 1971. (Photographs)
The Optimist's Daughter. New York: Random, 1972. (Novel)

A Pageant of Birds. New York: Albondocani, 1974. (Photographs)

Fairy Tale of the Natchez Trace. Jackson: Mississippi Historical Society, 1975.

The Eye of the Story: Selected Essays and Reviews. New York: Random, 1978.

Ida M'Toy. Urbana: University of Illinois Press, 1979. (Nonfiction)

Women!! Make Turban in Own Home! Winston-Salem, NC: Palaemon, 1979.

Acrobats in a Park. Northridge, CA: Lord John, 1980.

The Collected Stories of Eudora Welty. New York: Harcourt, 1980.

Moon Lake and Other Stories. Franklin Center, PA: Franklin, 1980.

One Writer's Beginnings. Cambridge: Harvard University Press, 1984. (Autobiography)

In Black and White. Introd. Anne Tyler. Northridge, CA: Lord John, 1985.

The Little Store. Newton, IA: Tamazunchale, 1985.

Eudora Welty: Photographs. Foreword Reynolds Price. Jackson: University Press of Mississippi, 1989.

A Writer's Eye: Collected Book Reviews. Jackson: University Press of Mississippi, 1994.

Studies of Eudora Alice Welty

Appel, Alfred, Jr. *A Season of Dreams: The Fiction of Eudora Welty.* Baton Rouge: Louisiana State University Press, 1965.

Arnold, Marilyn, "Eudora Welty's Parody." *Notes on Mississippi Writers* 11 (1978): 15–22.

Bloom, Harold, ed. *Modern Critical Views: Eudora Welty.* Introd. Harold Bloom. New York: Chelsea, 1986.

Brinkmeyer, Robert H., Jr. "An Openness to Others: The Imaginative Vision of Eudora Welty." *Southern Literary Journal* 20.2 (1988): 69–80.

Bryant, J. A., Jr. *Eudora Welty.* Minneapolis: University of Minnesota Press, 1968.

Carson, Barbara Harrell. *Eudora Welty: Two Pictures at Once in Her Frame.* Troy, NY: Whitston, 1992.

Champion, Laurie, ed. *The Critical Response to Eudora Welty's Fiction.* Westport, CT: Greenwood, 1994.

Devlin, Albert J. *Eudora Welty's Chronicle.* Jackson: University Press of Mississippi, 1983.

———, ed. *Welty: A Life in Literature.* Jackson: University Press of Mississippi, 1987.

Davis, Charles E. "Eudora Welty's Blacks: Name and Cultural Identity." *Notes on Mississippi Writers* 17 (1985): 1–8.

Desmond, John F. *A Still Moment: Essays on the Art of Eudora Welty.* Metuchen, NJ: Scarecrow, 1978.

Evans, Elizabeth. *Eudora Welty.* New York: Ungar, 1981.

Gretlund, Jan Nordby. *Eudora Welty's Aesthetics of Place.* Columbia: University of South Carolina Press, 1997.

Gygax, Franziska. *Serious Daring from Within: Female Narrative Strategies in Eudora Welty's Novels.* Westport, CT: Greenwood, 1990.

Hardy, John Edward. "*Delta Wedding* as Region and Symbol." *Sewanee Review* 60 (1952): 397–417.

Keys, Marilynn. " 'A Worn Path': The Way of Dispossession." *Studies in Short Fiction* 16 (1979): 354–56.

Kreyling, Michael. *Author and Agent: Eudora Welty and Diarmuid Russell.* New York: Farrar, 1991.

————. *Eudora Welty's Achievement of Order*. Baton Rouge: Louisiana State University Press, 1979.

Lindberg, Stanley W. *Eudora Welty's Achievement of Order*. Baton Rouge: Louisiana State University Press, 1980.

————."Learning from Miss Welty." *Georgia Review* 53.1 (1999): 7–14.

Manning, Carol S. *With Ears Opening Like Morning Glories: Eudora Welty and the Love of Storytelling*. Westport, CT: Greenwood, 1985.

Marrs, Suzanne. *The Welty Collection: A Guide to the Eudora Welty Manuscripts and Documents at the Mississippi Department of Archives and History*. Jackson: University Press of Mississippi, 1988.

May, Charles E. "Why Sister Lives at the P.O." *Southern Humanities Review* 12 (1978): 243–49.

Pingatore, Diana R. *A Reader's Guide to the Short Stories of Eudora Welty*. New York: G. K. Hall, 1996.

Polk, Noel. *Eudora Welty: A Bibliography of Her Work*. Jackson: University Press of Mississippi, 1994.

Porter, Katherine Anne. Introduction. *A Curtain of Green*. By Eudora Welty. Garden City, NY: Doubleday, 1941.

Prenshaw, Peggy Whitman, ed. *Conversations with Eudora Welty*. Jackson: University Press of Mississippi, 1984.

————. ed. *Eudora Welty: Critical Essays*. Jackson: University Press of Mississippi, 1979.

————. *More Conversations with Eudora Welty*. Jackson: University Press of Mississippi, 1996.

Price, Reynolds. "Finding Eudora." *Georgia Review* 53.1 (1999): 17–18.

————. "The Onlooker, Smiling: An Early Reading of *The Optimist's Daughter*." *Shenandoah* 20 (1969): 58–73.

Schmidt, Peter. *The Heart of the Story: Eudora Welty's Short Fiction*. Jackson: University Press of Mississippi, 1991.

Trouard, Dawn, ed. *Eudora Welty: Eye of the Storyteller*. Kent, OH: Kent State University Press, 1990.

Turner, W. Craig, and Lee Emling Harding, eds. *Critical Essays on Eudora Welty*. Boston: G. K. Hall, 1989.

Vande Kieft, Ruth M. *Eudora Welty*. New York: Twayne, 1962.

Waldron, Ann. *Eudora: A Writer's Life*. New York: Doubleday, 1998.

Warren, Robert Penn. "The Love and Separateness in Miss Welty." *Kenyon Review* 6 (1944): 246–59.

Weston, Ruth D. *Gothic Traditions and Narrative Techniques in the Fiction of Eudora Welty*. Baton Rouge: Louisiana State University Press, 1994.

Yeager, Patricia. " 'Because a Fire Was in My Head': Eudora Welty and the Dialogic Imagination." *PMLA* 99 (1984): 955–73.

————. "The Case of the Dangling Signifier: Phallic Imagery in Eudora Welty's 'Moon Lake.' " *Twentieth Century Literature* 28 (1982): 431–52.

DOROTHY WEST
(1907–1998)

Laurie Champion

BIOGRAPHY

Dorothy West was born the only child to Rachel Pease Benson and Isaac Christopher West on June 2, 1907, in Boston, Massachusetts. Her father, freed from slavery at age seven, later settled in Boston, where he profited from a wholesale fruit company and was known as the "Black Banana King" of Boston. Her mother, who came from a large family, was born in South Carolina and later moved to Springfield, Massachusetts, where she met West's father. The Wests were among the first black bourgeoisie to reside in the Oak Bluffs section of Martha's Vineyard. West was given private tutoring when she was a toddler, entered public school at age four, transferred when she was ten to a private girl's school, and later studied at Columbia University.

West's first publication, the short story "Promise and Fulfillment," appeared in the *Boston Post* when she was only fourteen. In 1926, shortly before she turned eighteen, West's story "The Typewriter" shared *Opportunity* magazine's second prize with Zora Neale Hurston's story "Muttsy." After her initial visit to New York to receive her award, West returned to Boston, where she attended Boston University for a short time before returning to New York to participate in the Harlem Renaissance. She became friends with prominent intellectuals and writers such as Zora Neale Hurston, Countee Cullen, Wallace Thurman, Arna Bontemps, Langston Hughes, and Nella Larsen.

During this time, West wrote mostly short stories, which appeared in magazines such as *Saturday Evening Quill*. In 1927, she performed in the original stage production of *Porgy* and also traveled to London in the summer of 1929 to perform in the play. In 1932, West went to Russia with Langston Hughes and twenty other African Americans to film *Black and White*, a documentary about American racism. The film was never produced because of political controversy, but West remained in Russia with Langston Hughes for a year. West proposed marriage to Hughes, but his exact response is not known. In her many generous interviews, West remained reluctant to discuss her relationship with Hughes.

In 1933, when West returned to the United States from Russia, most of the major members of the Harlem Renaissance were no longer living in New York. Attempting to recognize prominent African American writers, in 1934, West funded and edited the literary magazine *Challenge*, which folded in 1937 for lack of funding. Soon afterward, West launched the literary magazine *New Challenge*, which she edited with Marian Minus and Richard Wright. Appearing in the only issue of *New Challenge* was Wright's famous essay "Blueprint for Negro Writing" and works by notable authors such as Margaret Walker and Ralph Ellison.

After *New Challenge* folded, West worked for eighteen months as a welfare investigator, then joined the Federal Writers' Project. In 1943, West left New York to return to Oak Bluffs. She contributed regularly to the *New York Daily News* and completed her novel *The Living Is Easy*, which was published in 1948. West soon began another novel, tentatively entitled *Where the Wild Grape Grows*. She sent samples of this work in progress to potential publishers, but it was not well received because it concerned the black middle class. She incorporated most of *Where the Wild Grape Grows* into a new novel, *The Wedding* (1995). During the 1960s and 1970s, West held various jobs such as a clerk for the *Vineyard Gazette* and as a cashier for a restaurant, while continuing to write *The Wedding*. She also wrote columns for *Vineyard Gazette* such as "The Cottager's Corner," about blacks on the island.

Like *The Living Is Easy, The Wedding* portrayed elite African Americans; but with the rise of the Black Arts movement, West feared that *The Wedding* would be rejected by African Americans for its portrayal of elitist blacks, who were considered Uncle Toms during the time. She was also aware that the novel would not be accepted by white readers because it defied stereotypes of African Americans, so rather than risk rejection from both black and white audiences, West ceased to work on the novel.

After many years of obscurity as a writer, in 1982, when the Feminist Press reprinted *The Living Is Easy*, West received renewed critical acclaim. She engaged in public speeches, performed book signings, generously granted interviews, and was noted as the only living participant of the Harlem Renaissance. After Doubleday editor Jacqueline Kennedy Onassis encouraged West to finish *The Wedding*, it appeared in 1995, forty years since West began writing it. That same year, shortly after the publication of *The Wedding, The Richer, the Poorer* was published by Doubleday. It consists of seventeen short stories and thirteen reminiscent personal essays, most of which originally appeared in publications between the 1920s and 1940s. Recently, the much celebrated *The Wedding* was adapted into an Oprah Winfrey miniseries, and *As I Remember It: A Portrait of Dorothy West* appeared as a PBS film. After many years of remaining unrecognized for her skills as a writer, West has finally begun to gain long overdue acclaim. In Boston, on August 16, 1998, West's death marked the end of the last living member of the Harlem Renaissance.

MAJOR WORKS AND THEMES

Dorothy West's novels, *The Living Is Easy* and *The Wedding*, are part of a long tradition of novels by black women that began in the late nineteenth century with Frances Harper's *Iola Leroy*, continued through the Harlem Renaissance with novels such as Nella Larsen's *Quicksand* and Jessie Fauset's *The Chinaberry Tree* and *There Is Confusion*, and is represented more recently in works such as Andrea Lee's *Sarah Phillips* and Gloria Naylor's *Linden Hill*. Like these authors who illustrate upper-middle-class African Americans, West shows pretentiousness of the socially elite, such as the Bostonians in *The Living Is Easy* who avoid association with members of the lower classes and obsess over "which parties and churches to attend and which to avoid" (Cromwell 358).

The Living Is Easy and *The Wedding* concern important gender, race, and class issues. *The Living Is Easy* portrays light-skinned protagonist Cleo Jerico, who marries an older businessman, Bart Judson, in order to secure status among prestigious black elites of Boston. She invites her three sisters to live with her. Through portrayals of Cleo's childhood and her three sisters' attitudes, West explores gender roles and demonstrates that superficial middle-class values do not lead to self-fulfillment. Similarly, *The Wedding* satirizes middle-class values. The novel, set on Martha's Vineyard, depicts young Shelby Coles, who plans to marry a white jazz musician. With the exception of her grandmother, her family disapproves of her plans. Another central conflict in *The Wedding* involves Lute McNeil, a black man who tries to persuade Shelby to marry him instead of her white fiancé. The novel traces five generations and shows both personal and historical background for the context of the lives of the Coles. In both *The Wedding* and *The Living Is Easy*, West portrays blacks and women who defy stereotypes and challenges readers to consider complex dilemmas that deal with power and economics.

West's novels are important contributions to African American literature, but she excels in the short-story genre. As she says, "I think of myself first as a short story writer" (McDowell 281). Although most of West's short stories and essays originally appeared in journals and magazines between the 1920s and the 1940s, they remained uncollected until the 1995 publication of *The Richer, the Poorer: Stories, Sketches, and Reminiscences*. Unlike her novels, West's short stories show the despair of the lower class, such as the degraded janitor in "Jack in the Pot" who cannot afford a funeral for his daughter. Throughout the collection, the plight of the economically disadvantaged is frequently revealed through West's use of dualisms, which are most blatantly revealed in the title story "The Richer, the Poorer" and in "The Happiest Year, the Saddest Year." In "The Richer, the Poorer," Bess marries a musician immediately after high school, while her sister, Lottie, works and saves money. Later in life Lottie realizes she has experienced a shallow life and vows to adopt a lifestyle similar to Bess's. West supports Bess's philosophy, one that advocates that life's joys are found not in material wealth but in strong personal relationships. Also representative of economic matters, two stories in the collection express denominations of money as titles: "The Five-Dollar Bill" and "The Penny." In general, these stories show ironic results of economic concerns. For example, personal triumphs are reduced in the lives of the middle class because they focus on social status and material gain at the expense of cultural, personal, and internal rewards.

West's stories also explore gender and race issues. For example, "Hannah Byde" exposes ways that striving for social prestige relates to women. Hannah is an unfulfilled, frustrated housewife, expected to be a model wife to her financially secure husband. Unlike some of the wives of socially prominent men in *The Living Is Easy* and *The Wedding*, who seem oblivious that they encourage the very values that demean them as women, Hannah understands her predicament. Striving for social status at the expense of racial and cultural concerns is the prevalent theme in "An Unimportant Man." The story concerns Zeb, who dreams of becoming "a Darrow for his race, eloquently pleading a black man's cause" (139). Because his wife is concerned with social prestige, Zeb eventually encourages his daughter to forfeit her dreams of becoming a dancer because he presumes that he is helping his race by seeking middle-class values like those expressed by his friend Parker, who does not celebrate his African American identity. Unfortunately, like the professionals in *The Living Is Easy*, Parker has become part of an insular, segregated subsociety striving for social status but never gaining acceptance from the larger society.

Although West's writings do not represent the degree of race consciousness found in many works by black writers who during the first half of the century expressed anger toward racial oppression that included rejecting whites, her writings reveal the need for social change based on race, class, and gender equality. A powerful writer, Dorothy West represents well the Harlem Renaissance.

CRITICAL RECEPTION

When it originally appeared, West's *The Living Is Easy* was reviewed widely and received mixed reviews. While critics pointed out West's strong characterization of Cleo, some also noted its flawed ending. Since *The Living Is Easy* was West's only full-length publication for over forty years, until very recently it has received the most critical attention. One recent essay, Lawrence R. Rodgers's "Dorothy West's *The Living Is Easy* and the Ideal of Southern Folk Community," focuses exclusively on *The Living Is Easy* and suggests that the novel "uses satire to revise the (male) Great Migration novel" (161).

Reviewers in general celebrated the 1995 publication of *The Wedding*, although some noted the flawed ending; however, apparently some reviewers received preview copies of the novel in which Doubleday's ghostwriters had tacked on an ending unapproved by West. Eventually, with the help of noted black scholar Henry Louis Gates, Jr., West was given the opportunity to complete her novel, and other reviewers were able to read the definitive text. Praise for *The Wedding* is exemplified in Susan Kenney's review for *New York Times Book Review*: "It's as though we've been invited not so much to a wedding as to a full-scale opera, only to find that one great artist is belting out all the parts. She brings down the house" (12). *The Richer, the Poorer* was published the same year as *The Wedding* and received overwhelmingly favorable reviews. Jack Moore, writing for *Studies in Short Fiction*, praised West's ability to depict honestly the feelings and thoughts of children and says the book represents West's artistic gifts to her readers. Since the publication of *The Wedding* and *The Richer, the Poorer* West has received renewed critical attention. Currently in press is guest editor Sharon Jones's issue of *Langston Hughes Review*, which will focus on Dorothy West.

BIBLIOGRAPHY

Works by Dorothy West

"Hannah Byde." *Messenger* July 1926: 197–99.
"Prologue to a Life." *Saturday Evening Quill* Apr. 1929: 5–10.
"The Black Dress." *Opportunity* 12 (1934): 140, 158.
"Dear Reader [from *Challenge*]." 1934. *Voices from the Harlem Renaissance*. Ed. Nathan Irvin Huggins. New York: Oxford University Press, 1976. 391–93.
"Editorial [from *New Challenge*]." 1937. *Voices from the Harlem Renaissance*. Ed. Nathan Irvin Huggins. New York: Oxford University Press, 1976. 393–94.
The Living Is Easy. Boston: Houghton, 1948.
The Richer, the Poorer: Stories, Sketches, and Reminiscences. New York: Doubleday, 1995.
The Wedding. New York: Doubleday, 1995.

Studies of Dorothy West

Bontemps, Arna. "In Boston." Rev. of *The Living Is Easy*, by Dorothy West. *New York Herald Tribune Weekly Book Review* 13 June 1948: 16.
Champion, Laurie. "Social Class Distinctions in Dorothy West's *The Richer, the Poorer*." *Langston Hughes Review*. Forthcoming.
Clark, Dorothy A. "Rediscovering Dorothy West." *American Visions* 8 (1993): 46–47.
Clark, Edie. "Dorothy West, Novelist: Weaver of Possibilities." Rev. of *The Wedding*, by Dorothy West. *Yankee* 59 (1995): 83–85.
Cromwell, Adelaide M. Afterword. *The Living Is Easy*. 1948. Old Westbury, NY: Feminist Press, 1982. 349–64.
Dalsgard, Katrine. "Alive and Well and Living on the Island of Martha's Vineyard: An

Interview with Dorothy West, October 29, 1988." *Langston Hughes Review* 12.2 (1993): 28–44.

Daniel, Walter C. "*Challenge Magazine*: An Experiment That Failed." *CLA Journal* 19 (1976): 494–503.

Ferguson, Sally Ann H. "Dorothy West." *Afro-American Writers, 1940–1955*. Ed. Trudier Harris and Thadious M. Davis. Detroit: Gale, 1988. Vol. 76 of *Dictionary of Literary Biography*. 187–95.

———. "Dorothy West and Helene Johnson in *Infants of the Spring*." *Langston Hughes Review* 2.2 (1983): 22–24.

Gates, Henry Louis, Jr. "Beyond the Color Line." *New Yorker* 7 Sept. 1998: 82–83.

Jimoh, A. Yemisi. "Dorothy West." *Contemporary African American Novelists*. Ed. Emmanuel S. Nelson. Westport, CT: Greenwood, 1999. 475–81.

Kenney, Susan. "Shades of Difference." Rev. of *The Wedding*, by Dorothy West. *New York Times Book Review* 12 Feb. 1995: 11–12.

Krim, Seymour. "Boston Black Belt." Rev. of *The Living Is Easy*, by Dorothy West. *New York Times Book Review* 16 May 1948: 5.

McDowell, Deborah E. "Conversations with Dorothy West." *The Harlem Renaissance Re-Examined*. Georgia State Literary Studies Ser. 2. Ed. Victor A. Kramer. New York: AMS Press, 1987. 265–82.

Moore, Jack B. Rev. of *The Richer, the Poorer: Stories, Sketches and Reminiscences*, by Dorothy West. *Studies in Short Fiction* 33 (1996): 593–95.

Newson, Adele S. "An Interview with Dorothy West." *Zora Neale Hurston Forum* 2 (1987): 19–24.

Parker, Gwendolyn M. "Echoes from the Harlem Renaissance." Rev. of *The Richer, the Poorer*, by Dorothy West. *New York Times Book Review* 6 Aug. 1995: 12.

Rodgers, Lawrence R. "Dorothy West's *The Living Is Easy* and the Ideal of Southern Folk Community." *African American Review* 26 (1992): 161–72.

Rueschmann, Eva. "Sister Bonds: Intersections of Family and Race in Jessie Redmon Fauset's *Plum Bun* and Dorothy West's *The Living Is Easy*." *The Significance of Sibling Relationships in Literature*. Ed. JoAnna Stephens Mink and Janet Doubler Ward. Bowling Green, OH: Bowling Green State University Popular Press, 1993. 120–32.

Skow, John. "The Second Time Around." Rev. of *The Wedding*, by Dorothy West. *Time* 24 July 1995: 67.

Steinberg, Sybil. "Dorothy West: Her Own Renaissance." *Publishers Weekly* 3 July 1995: 34–35.

Washington, Mary Helen. "I Sign My Mother's Name: Alice Walker, Dorothy West, Paule Marshall." *Mothering the Mind: Twelve Studies of Writers and Their Silent Partners*. Ed. Ruth Perry and Martine Watson Brownley. New York: Holmes, 1984. 142–63.

"West, Dorothy." *Current Biography Yearbook*. Vol. 58. Ed. Elizabeth A. Schick. New York: Wilson, 1997. 604–8.

EDITH WHARTON
(1862–1937)

David J. Caudle

BIOGRAPHY

Best known for her novels and short fiction, Edith Wharton's prodigious body of work concerns a wide variety of topics. Born Edith Newbold Jones on January 24, 1862, in New York City, she spent her formative years touring Europe with her family and returned in 1872 to live in New York and in Newport. Wharton loved the culture, art, and architecture of Europe, and she felt like an exile upon her return to America.

As an adult, she resided in Europe and believed French culture to be superior to all others. As a child and adolescent, Wharton spent most of her time in her father's library, and in her autobiography she referred to literature as her "secret garden." Neither her family nor her society encouraged her literary aspirations, since both viewed such an avocation with the same disdain with which they viewed manual labor. Her formal education was consigned mainly to governesses and focused on the skills necessary for her to assume her place in society properly: how to dress fashionably, entertain formally, and converse in French. In later life, Wharton described herself as a "self made man" in terms of her intellectual development.

Wharton's parents, Lucretia Stevens Rhinelander and George Frederick Jones, came from families of such wealth and social prominence as to assure the family's inclusion in the "four hundred." This elite group comprised the highest level of New York society and was limited to a select group of long-established families. This insular society cultivated leisure and valued appearances above all else and provided Wharton with ideas for her fiction. Because Wharton's intellectual and literary interests disturbed her parents, they advanced her social debut by a year in the hope that social activity or romance would lead her into more socially acceptable pastimes. Six years later, at the age of twenty-three and nearing her circle's definition of spinsterhood, she married Edward "Teddy" Wharton and settled in Newport. Teddy, from a socially prominent but no longer wealthy Boston family, epitomized the anti-intellectual aristocracy that Wharton was later to satirize in much of her fiction. He was a poor match for the ambitious Wharton, and her mental and physical health, which declined precipitously early in her marriage, greatly improved after she embarked on her literary career. Teddy's health, on the other hand, steadily declined as Edith began to experience success and recognition as a writer and intellectual. They divorced in 1913, after Edith discovered that he had embezzled large sums of money from her trust fund to support a long-term mistress and a number of short-term affairs. Although she could at times be cold, and was a social and intellectual elitist, Wharton was also a witty and engaging conversationalist whose numerous lifelong friends included Henry James. Wharton's most intense romance, which lasted from 1908 to 1911, was with W. Morton Fullerton, who at one time was romantically involved with Oscar Wilde and several other prominent people of both genders.

Wharton's high level of energy and prodigious organizational skills led to many political and social achievements. During World War I, she campaigned tirelessly for U.S. entry on the side of France, and her fund-raising and other charitable work on behalf of Belgian and French refugees led to her appointment as Chevalier of the Legion of Honor. She became an internationally recognized expert in both interior design and landscape architecture, and in 1921, she became the first woman to be awarded a Pulitzer Prize, which she received for *The Age of Innocence*. In 1923, she returned to America for the last time, becoming the first woman to receive an honorary degree from Yale University. In 1935 she suffered a mild stroke and temporarily lost sight in one eye but recovered and returned to work. In 1937 she suffered another, more crippling stroke and died on August 11 at the age of seventy-five.

MAJOR WORKS AND THEMES

Wharton's fiction exemplifies the realist tradition, and most of Wharton's novels and short stories are set at the turn of the century, focusing on the lives of the Old New York aristocracy. Many of her works reveal the suffocating conformity imposed by this society and the emotional sacrifices demanded of those who desired respectability. The plots of Wharton's fictional works unfold in the minds of her characters, often as they lose their innocence or experience self-realization. Her characters find themselves trapped in untenable situations because of demands placed on them by their social positions or their aspirations.

The widely acclaimed *The Age of Innocence* is set in 1870s New York society, which Newland Archer and Ellen Olenska find much more complicated and demanding than they at first imagine. Their social obligations prove insurmountable as they search for happiness and freedom. Archer's wife is the perfectly finished product of this society, and her husband quickly realizes that she is thus utterly predictable. Like many of Wharton's female characters, she is uninterested in intellectual pursuits and is so emotionally detached as to appear cold.

Yet she is also a tragic figure because although she does not wish to defy social conventions, she suffers as much on account of these social constraints as her husband and his would-be lover. Archer possesses many of the characteristics that typify Wharton's male characters, and since he lacks the courage to defy social conventions, he destroys any opportunity to find happiness. Unlike the other female characters in the story, Ellen Olenska frees herself from the constraints of society by traveling in Europe and divorcing her husband. Her independence contrasts with the conformity that oppresses her counterparts and illustrates both the costs and benefits of defying accepted social roles. The novel combines bittersweet nostalgia with incisive social critique. *The Age of Innocence* focuses on a subculture that lies outside the experience of most readers, but its themes of suffering, denial, and resignation have universal appeal.

Although its setting makes it unrepresentative of Wharton's other work, *Ethan Frome* is perhaps her most popular novel. Its simple but compelling plot portrays the triumph of petty social conventions over the ambitious individual. Ethan Frome is a young farmer who is unable to fulfill his dream of becoming either an engineer or a chemist. He is obligated to manage a farm, to care for his mother during her long terminal illness, and later to remain in a loveless marriage with a nagging hypochondriac, Zeena. Ethan finds love and inspiration when Zeena's cousin, Mattie Silver, comes to live with the Fromes, and for the first time he is able to imagine the possibility of a fulfilling life. Zeena becomes jealous of Mattie and orders her to leave. On the way to the rail station, Ethan fulfills his promise of a sleigh ride during which Mattie declares that she would rather die than leave him. She asks Ethan to crash the sleigh into a large elm tree. Ethan, equally distraught, complies but loses courage and flinches at the last moment. The belatedly aborted crash leaves Mattie paralyzed and Ethan incurably lame, and both in the care of his cruel wife. Yet Zeena is also a victim of her impoverished environment, and her animosity toward Mattie is understandable in light of the threat to her meager life. Set in the bleak world of western Massachusetts, far from Wharton's personal experience, it presents a vision of thwarted emotions and unfulfilled passions that are a recurrent theme in her work. Wharton masterfully uses the climate and geography of the novel's setting to symbolize the cold and harsh emotional world inhabited by her characters.

The setting of her novel *The House of Mirth* more closely resembles the world in which Wharton lived, and in it she critiques high society by focusing on the aspects of their character that its members must repress in order to be accepted. This work also centers on characters who are marginalized by society because of their nonconformity, unconventional lifestyles, or poverty. Lily Bart, the poor relation of a wealthy and socially prominent family, seeks to advance herself by finding a wealthy husband. In the process, she is blackmailed, accused of adultery, and forced to become a milliner to support herself, an act that seals her rejection by upper-class society. She dies of a drug overdose just as the man she loves arrives with a proposal of marriage. Lily's fate illustrates the rigid boundaries and limited options established by aristocratic society and the toll that they take on those both within and outside of the group.

Wharton's collection of four novellas, *Old New York*, reflects themes similar to those of *The House of Mirth*. In "False Dawn," Lewis Raycie is disinherited by his father and rejected by society because he chooses to become an artist. After his death, Raycie's descendants sell his work to finance houses, cars, and jewelry, illustrating Old New York's lack of appreciation for art. The other three stories in *Old New York* treat the consequences of living as an insider or as a marginalized member of society. In "The Spark," Hayley Delane distinguishes himself from the other young men of his class by volunteering for service in the Civil War rather than using his money and influence to avoid it. He returns to his comfortable position in society, which outwardly suits him as he accommodates himself to the group's expectations. Soon he seems no different from the other young aristocrats except in his kindness toward other people and animals and his habit of quoting poetry. Delane recalls Walt Whitman, whom he met in the war, with great personal affection, but due to his parents' insistence on the use of only "proper" English, he is unable to appreciate the "uneducated" poet's work. His response to Whitman's poetry illustrates the pernicious effect of rigid class hierarchies and arbitrary social distinctions.

In contrast to the rejected Lewis Raycie of "False Dawn" and the insider's perspective of Hayley Delane in "The Spark," the other two works in *Old New York* present characters who live on the margins of society. In "The Old Maid," Charlotte Lovell transgresses the bounds of society by secretly bearing an illegitimate child. In order to remain an accepted member of society and to provide a satisfactory life for her daughter, she is forced to conform to the stereotype of the cold, unlovable old maid. Charlotte gives up her child and accepts her marginal but respectable role in society rather than facing the rejection and poverty that openly raising her child would bring.

In "New Year's Day," Lizzie Haldane also crosses the bounds of social acceptability, as a discretely unfaithful wife and not-quite-proper widow. She is forced to become the mistress of a man who in return provides the funds to allow her unsuspecting husband to think that he is supporting her in a manner commensurate with their social position. She must maintain this arrangement even after her husband's death because her society allows no place for an independent woman and provided no opportunity for a woman to support herself honorably. Both Charlotte and Lizzie are forced to sacrifice their integrity in order to provide for the people they love while maintaining a veneer of respectability. They are also both impoverished emotionally and intellectually, since, like Lily Bart, they have internalized the strictures of their society.

Wharton also produced a substantial body of short fiction, in which she deals with many of the same themes as her longer works. "Roman Fever" combines the traditional elements of the genre with a narrative technique that blurs the line between the voice of the narrator and that of the story's two main characters.

Most of the plot unfolds within the minds of the characters, and she ingeniously presents within the course of one afternoon's fragmented conversation a lifetime of psychological development. The surprise ending both subverts the readers' expectations and allows them to infer a great deal of what goes unspoken in the story itself.

"The Other Two" also exemplifies elements present in much of Wharton's other work. Alice Waythorn's third husband enters married life naively, feeling in complete control of his wife. He blames her two former husbands for ending their relationships with her and imagines her as a victim and himself as a savior. Like many of Wharton's male characters, he lacks courage, allowing him to lose control of his destiny and to become trapped by social conventions. Mrs. Waythorn illustrates the cold and emotionally constrained woman combined with the newly wealthy social climber, character types that appear frequently in Wharton's fiction. The story unfolds largely in Mr. Waythorn's mind, and as the tale ends, he is coming to the uncomfortable realization that his wife is more victimizer than victim and that he has unknowingly surrendered control of the circumstances of his life.

CRITICAL RECEPTION

Wharton's work was immensely popular during her life and remains so today. Her works on interior design and landscape architecture have become classics in their fields. As her career as a writer of fiction peaked in the 1920s, she was considered by many critics to be America's premier writer of fiction and a legitimate candidate for the Nobel Prize. Both *The House of Mirth* and *The Age of Innocence* were best-sellers, and many of her literary works were serialized in popular magazines and have been adapted for the stage and film.

Scholars divide the critical reception of Wharton's work during her lifetime into three phases: 1899–1905, 1906–1920, and 1920–1938. From 1899 to 1905, she was sometimes praised, but often criticized, as a lesser derivative of Henry James. The comparison is ironic, since Wharton did not care for the work of James's "Major Phase" and told her editor that she found these novels "unreadable" (Tuttleton xi). Wharton's work from 1906 to 1920 laid to rest any questions of her being nothing more than a lesser James. During this period Wharton produced much of her best work, and she distinguished herself as a technical master as she developed and explored the themes that would come to characterize her work. Both the reading public and literary critics embraced Wharton's writing, although some were disturbed by what they perceived as class bias and an overly cultivated style. The third phase of Wharton criticism marked a decline in Wharton's critical and popular standing that lasted into the 1970s. Many critics came to view her work as old-fashioned and Wharton herself as both bitter toward and out of touch with modern society.

The rise of feminist criticism not only shed new light on many of Wharton's themes and characterizations but also served as a vehicle to introduce her work to a new generation of readers. This development roughly coincided with the opening of her personal papers, in 1968. The universal appeal of her themes and her mastery of literary technique is exemplified by the many new editions of her work that appear each year and the scholarly interest that her unpublished papers continue to generate.

Yale University holds much of Wharton's surviving correspondence, three unpublished articles on landscape architecture, and numerous other fragments. The University of Indiana holds her diaries and notes for her autobiographical writings. Wharton's remaining papers are scattered in numerous university and private archives, along with the Library of Congress and the New York Public Library.

BIBLIOGRAPHY

Works by Edith Wharton

Edith Wharton and Ogden Codman, Jr. *The Decoration of Houses*. New York: Scribner's, 1879. (Interior design)

The Greater Inclination. New York: Scribner's, 1899. (Short stories)

The Touchstone. New York: Scribner's, 1900. (Novel)

Crucial Instances. New York: Scribner's, 1901. (Short stories)

The Valley of Decision. 2 vols. New York: Scribner's, 1902. (Novel)

The Descent of Man. New York: Macmillan, 1904. (Short fiction)

Italian Villas and Their Garden's. New York: Century, 1904. (Landscape design)

The House of Mirth. New York: Scribner's, 1905. (Novel)

Italian Backgrounds. New York: Scribner's, 1905. (Travel literature)

The Fruit of the Tree. New York: Scribner's, 1907. (Novel)

Madame de Treymes. New York: Scribner's, 1907. (Novel)

The Hermit and the Wild Woman. New York: Scribner's, 1908. (Short stories)

A Motor-Flight through France. New York: Scribner's, 1908. (Travel literature)

Artemis to Actaeon and Other Verse. New York: Scribner's, 1909. (Poems)

Tales of Men and Ghosts. New York: Scribner's, 1910. (Short stories)

Ethan Frome. New York: Appleton, 1912. (Novel)

The Reef. New York: Appleton, 1912. (Novel)

The Custom of the Country. New York: Scribner's, 1913. (Novel)

Fighting France, from Dunkerque to Belfort. New York: Scribner's, 1915. (War report)

The Book of the Homeless. Ed. Edith Wharton. New York: Scribner's, 1916.

Xingu and Other Stories. New York: Scribner's, 1916. (Short stories)

Summer. New York: Appleton, 1917. (Novel)

The Marne. New York: Appleton, 1918. (War novel)

French Ways and Their Meaning. New York: Appleton, 1919. (Social criticism)

The Age of Innocence. New York: Appleton, 1920. (Novel)

In Morocco. New York: Scribner's, 1920. (Travel literature)

The Glimpses of the Moon. New York: Appleton, 1922. (Novel)

A Son at the Front. New York: Scribner's, 1923. (War novel)

Old New York. New York: Appleton, 1924. (Four novellas)

The Mother's Recompense. New York: Appleton, 1925. (Novel)
The Writing of Fiction. New York: Scribner's, 1925. (Literary criticism)
Here and Beyond. New York: Appleton, 1926. (Short stories)
Twelve Poems. London: Medici Society, 1926. (Poems)
Twilight Sleep. New York: Appleton, 1927. (Novel)
The Children. New York: Appleton, 1928. (Novel)
Hudson River Bracketed. New York: Appleton, 1929. (Novel)
Certain People. New York: Appleton, 1930. (Short stories)
Human Nature. New York: Appleton, 1930. (Short stories)
The Gods Arrive. New York: Appleton, 1932. (Novel)
A Backward Glance. New York: Appleton, 1934. (Autobiography)
The World Over. New York: Appleton, 1936. (Short stories)
Ghosts. New York: Appleton, 1937. (Short stories)
The Buccaneers. New York: Appleton, 1938. (Novel)
The Collected Short Stories of Edith Wharton. Ed. R.W.B. Lewis. New York: Scribner's,
    1968. (Short stories)
The Letters of Edith Wharton. Ed. R.W.B. Lewis and Nancy Lewis. New York: Mac-
    millan, 1988. (Correspondence)

Studies of Edith Wharton

Bauer, Dale M. *Edith Wharton's Brave New Politics.* Madison: University of Wisconsin
    Press, 1994.
Bell, Millicent, ed. *The Cambridge Companion to Edith Wharton.* New York: Cambridge
    University Press, 1995.
Bendixen, Alfred, and Annette Zilversmit. *Edith Wharton: New Critical Essays.* New
    York: Garland, 1992.
Clubbe, John. "Interiors and the Interior Life in Edith Wharton's *The House of Mirth*."
    Studies in the Novel 28 (1996): 543–64.
Colquitt, Clare. "Contradictory Possibilities: Wharton Scholarship 1992–1994: A Bibli-
    ographic Essay." *Edith Wharton Review* 12 (1995): 37–44.
Dwight, Eleanor. *Edith Wharton: An Extraordinary Life.* New York: Abrams, 1994.
Dyman, Jenni. *Lurking Feminism: The Ghost Stories of Edith Wharton.* New York: Lang,
    1996.
Erlich, Gloria. *The Sexual Education of Edith Wharton.* Berkeley: University of Califor-
    nia Press, 1992.
Fedorko, Kathy A. *Gender and the Gothic in the Fiction of Edith Wharton.* Tuscaloosa:
    University of Alabama Press, 1995.
Fracasso, Evelyn E. *Edith Wharton's Prisoner's of Consciousness: A Study of Theme
    and Technique in the Tales.* Westport, CT: Greenwood, 1994.
Fryer, Judith. *Felicitous Space: The Imaginative Structures of Edith Wharton and Willa
    Cather.* Chapel Hill: University of North Carolina Press, 1986.
Gimbel, Wendy. *Edith Wharton: Orphancy and Survival.* New York: Praeger, 1984.
Goodman, Susan. *Edith Wharton's Inner Circle.* Austin: University of Texas Press, 1994.
Joslin, Katherine. *Edith Wharton.* New York: St. Martin's, 1991.
Joslin, Katherine, and Alan Price. *Wretched Exotic: Essays on Edith Wharton in Europe.*
    2nd ed. New York: Lang, 1996.

Kennedy, Fraser. *Ornament and Silence: Essays on Women's Lives*. New York: Knopf, 1996.

Kiloran, Helen. *Edith Wharton, Art and Illusion*. Tuscaloosa: University of Alabama Press, 1996.

Lewis, R.W.B. *Edith Wharton: A Biography*. 2 vols. New York: Harper, 1975.

Lindbergh, Gary H. *Edith Wharton and the Novel of Manners*. Charlottesville: University Press of Virginia, 1975.

MacComb, Debra Ann. "New Wives for Old: Divorce and the Leisure-Class Marriage Market in Edith Wharton's *The Custom of the Country*." *American Literature* 68 (1996): 765–97.

Macnaughton, William R. "Edith Wharton, *The Reef*, and Henry James." *American Literary Realism* 26 (1994): 43–59.

Price, Alan. *The End of the Age of Innocence: Edith Wharton and the First World War*. 2nd ed. New York: St. Martin's, 1996.

Quay, Sara Elisabeth. "Edith Wharton's Narrative of Inheritance." *American Literary Realism* 29 (1997): 26–48.

Saunders, Catherine E. *Writing in the Margins: Edith Wharton, Ellen Glasgow, and the Literary Tradition of the Ruined Woman*. Cambridge: Harvard University Press, 1987.

Showalter, Elaine, ed. *Modern American Women Writers*. New York: Scribner's, 1991.

Singley, Carol J. *Edith Wharton: Matters of Mind and Spirit*. New York: Cambridge University Press, 1995.

Tinter, Adeline R. *Edith Wharton in Context: Essays on Intertextuality*. Tuscaloosa: University of Alabama Press, 1999.

Tuttleton, James W., Kristin O. Lauer, and Margaret P. Murray, eds. *Edith Wharton: The Contemporary Reviews*. New York: Cambridge University Press, 1992.

Waid, Candace. *Edith Wharton's Letters from the Underworld: Fictions of Women and Writing*. Chapel Hill: University of North Carolina Press, 1991.

White, Barbara Anne. *Edith Wharton: A Study of the Short Fiction*. New York: Twayne, 1991.

Wolff, Cynthia Griffin. *A Feast of Words: The Triumph of Edith Wharton*. New York: Oxford University Press, 1977.

Wright, Sarah Bird. *Edith Wharton's Travel Writing: The Making of a Connoisseur*. New York: St. Martin's, 1997.

ELINOR WYLIE
(1885–1928)

Margaret Barbour Gilbert

BIOGRAPHY

Elinor Morton Hoyt was born on September 7, 1885, into a socially prominent Philadelphia family and educated at private schools. Her elopement in 1911 with a much older married man, Horace Wylie, created a scandal, which was published in newspapers throughout the country. The couple fled to England to live, leaving behind Wylie's first husband, an admiral's son, whom she married in 1905 and who later committed suicide, and their tiny son to be cared for by others for the rest of his life. Following in the footsteps of his father, Wylie's son committed suicide in 1936.

In England she and Horace Wylie lived together unmarried until 1916, when they returned to the United States because of the war, and were married. Their return coincided with the publication of Elinor Wylie's first book of poems, *Nets to Catch the Wind*, in 1921, a compilation she had worked on for ten years. In the United States they lived in the capital, where Horace Wylie found a minor government position. Elinor's brother, the painter Henry Martin Hoyt, introduced her to Yale friends Sinclair Lewis and William Rose Benet, and through their influence, her poems began to appear in important American magazines of the day: *Century, Nation, Poetry, New Republic*, and *Vanity Fair*.

The critical acclaim that greeted *Nets to Catch the Wind* led her to move to New York City, where she lived for the rest of her life. She would periodically travel to Connecticut, to England, or to the MacDowell Colony for artists and writers in New Hampshire, where she wrote many of her poems.

In 1923 she divorced Wylie and married William Rose Benet. She then worked for a time as poetry editor at *Vanity Fair*. In 1923, that same year, her second book of poetry, *Black Armour*, received even better reviews than her first, *Nets to Catch the Wind*. She had turned to novel writing to supplement her income, and in 1923, *Jennifer Lorn*, the novel she had written at Benet's suggestion, became a best-seller. Three more novels were to provide a steady income. *Jennifer Lorn* was followed by *The Venetian Glass Nephew* in 1925.

The Orphan Angel was Wylie's most popular novel and a Book of the Month Club selection in 1926. When *Trivial Breath*, her third books of poems, appeared in 1928, Wylie had already had one heart attack and suffered increasingly from frail health. Still she was able to complete her last novel, *Mr. Hodge and Mr. Hazard*, in 1928 and a final book of poems, *Angels and Earthly Creatures*, published in 1929.

Though she had been in poor health since 1914, she spent her last years collecting books and Shelley letters, buying Paris clothes, and enjoying a celebrity that the writer Carl Van Doren likened to that of a "white queen."

Elinor Wylie died suddenly of Bright's disease on December 16, 1928, on the very day she finished her last volume of poems, *Angels and Earthly Creatures*. Her novels and many of her poems dramatize the sexual conflict in fiction and poetry that Wylie felt throughout her life in her three marriages.

MAJOR WORKS AND THEMES

Within a span of ten years Wylie published four books of verse and four novels. *Incidental Numbers*, a small collection of poems composed between 1902 and 1911, was Elinor Wylie's first book of poems and contains distinct aesthetic patterns of vision and technique that characterized Wylie's art throughout her career. Its theme of escape prefigures later Wylie poems in which the speaker sets herself apart from the human world. The volume was privately printed in England in an edition of sixty copies while she was living there with Horace Wylie. Her mother paid the publication costs.

Nets to Catch the Wind, published almost ten years later, is Wylie's first professional book and won the Julia Ellsworth Ford Prize for the best collection of poems published in 1921, the year Edna St. Vincent Millay published *Second April*, Marianne Moore *Poems*, and H. D. *Hymen*. It is the work of a writer with a more complex and developed imagination.

Three basic themes of pain and escapism are presented in this volume: the pain suffered by the poet/speaker at the hands of a callous world, the need to escape the world, and the attractions of a private universe. The latter theme assumes importance in Wylie's later volumes of verse. She becomes increasingly concerned with the relationship between art and life.

Nets to Catch the Wind contains many of Wylie's best poems and the poems that made her famous: "Wild Peaches," "August," and "Velvet Shoes." "August" (a single sonnet), like "Wild Peaches" (a sequence of four sonnets), dramatizes a distinct kind of sensibility. By showing the diversity of the poet/speaker's reactions to contrasting kinds of stimuli, "August" depicts a nature that responds only to the most subdued and subtlest sensations. In the sonnet's octave, the poet compares an African American with a barrow "tawnier than wheat" and filled with smoldering daisies to a great brazier borne along the street by captive leopards. The daisies become like leopards. In the sestet the poet longs for the coolness of water lilies.

In contrast, "Wild Peaches" suggests a sensibility that craves austereness. "There is something," says the lyric speaker in the fourth and climactic poem of the sequence, "in this richness that I hate." Against the oppressive lushness of the rich Maryland tidewater country, the fourth sonnet sets a stark New England landscape. Nothing but starkness and simplicity satisfy a sensibility that is wearied by surfeit and satiety. Technical virtuosity of the kind displayed in "August" and "Wild Peaches" won Elinor Wylie a reputation for faultless technique.

Published in 1923, *Black Armour* heightened Wylie's reputation for technical brilliance. The motif of *Black Armour* is courage. The book is Wylie's "armour" against a malicious world. Many of the poems use nostalgic scenery and knightly figures to conjure a romance superior to any the present could offer. "Now That Your Eyes Are Shut" and the famous sonnet "Let No Charitable Hope" establish themes of the poet's despair of achieving her desire to be a true poet like the Romantics and an ambivalent response to her own womanhood, wherein she laments the beauty and weakness that enslave her. "Parting Gift," one of Wylie's best poems, is a sixteen-line poem achieved through careful arrangement of lines of varying lengths and skillful off-rhymes. It is unusual because it is one of Wylie's few poems in free verse.

Black Armour discloses Wylie's ambivalence about her personal nature, but it also addresses the problem of her art. In *Black Armour* it begins to assume importance as she attempts to formulate an aesthetic. Some of the poems describe the sort of art Wylie herself produced. Others consider its virtues or limitations.

Trivial Breath, published in June 1928, is concerned with the nature of art. But this time it is related to a governing theme, the greatness of Shelley. *Trivial Breath* marks the serious beginning of Elinor Wylie's poetic recourse to a private Shelleyesque symbolism and iconography, which interfered with her development as a poet and led her to lose contact with the original voice of her early poems. It is significant that *Trivial Breath* is the least distinguished of her books of verse. "Speed the Parting" is her most famous poem in this collection. It is a twenty-eight-line poem in A/B rhyme scheme directly addressed to someone the poet loves and whose death she fears.

Trivial Breath, whose chief themes are art and human imperfection, begins and ends with poems addressed to Wylie's idol, Shelley. Four sonnets, entitled "A Red Carpet for Shelley," articulate what remained a major anxiety of her career—that despite industry and skill, she lacked the voice needed to become a significant poet.

Angels and Earthly Creatures, her last book, appeared in the spring following her death in 1928. Many of the poems of *Angels and Earthly Creatures* attempt the complex juxtapositions of the sacred and profane battle between body and soul that are associated with Elizabethan and Jacobean poetry. *Angels and Earthly Creatures* is a strong narrative of unrequited love, whose title is taken from a sermon by John Donne. Whereas Shelley had been the subject and focus of *Trivial Breath, Angels and Earthly Creatures* contained a sequence of nineteen sonnets to Wylie's lovelorn romantic interest Clifford Woodhouse, an English aristocrat, who was also married.

The attractions of aesthetic art and its dangers and limitations, when it approaches decadence, are major themes of Wylie's poems and two of her novels, *Jennifer Lorn* (1923) and *The Venetian Glass Nephew* (1925). *Jennifer Lorn* is a humorous Gothic romance set in India with an English heroine, against the excesses of sensibility. *The Venetian Glass Nephew* concerns a vision of sexual conflict rendered in the language of fantasy and allegory. It reveals a beautiful and lively girl in Italy who agrees to become a porcelain figure so that she can please a husband made of glass.

The Orphan Angel (1926) is Wylie's account of Shelley's adventures in America, a historical romance that treats the greatness of Shelley as a person and poet as he travels from Boston to San Diego. *The Orphan Angel* enlarges on Wylie's earlier themes of the influence of art on imagination and its power over the real.

In *Mr. Hodge and Mr. Hazard* (1928), set in England with an American hero, the distinctions between Romanticism and late nineteenth-century art are made in fictional terms. Wylie makes a further contrast between what she considered great art (Romantic art) and the narrower self-conscious art of aestheticism. She failed to complete another novel to Shelley (*April, April*) set in Greenwich Village.

Wylie's poems are often brilliant with short lines and clean, compact small stanzas. They are precipitated by some commonplace experience with a sudden revelation or insight into the essential meaning of the metaphor of the poem. All of the poems are carefully crafted and studded with fanciful and exotic images. There is nothing left to the casualness of free verse. Many of the best poems are sonnets, and most of the poems employ a traditional rhyme scheme, usually AB/AB. Her metrical facility, apt rhymes, and use of the traditional forms of sonnet and ballad were remarkable. But it is the individual quality of voice and form that makes her poet's voice distinct, her particular use of metaphor and language that gives her verse its distinction.

Elinor Wylie's first book *Nets to Catch the Wind* was possibly her best. Poems such as "Beauty," "Wild Peaches," "August," "Bronze Trumpets and Sea Water," "The Eagle and the Mole," "Velvet Shoes," "Atavism," "Escape," and "The Tortoise in Eternity" are impressive demonstrations of Wylie's talent. "The vigor, precision, compression, concreteness, freshness, and completely functional quality of the language suggest that the author is reporting authentic, flesh and blood responses to her experiences—not merely affecting poetic poses. These qualities had they been consistently attained, would have put her poetry squarely in the tradition of her great contemporaries" (Gray 22–23). These early poems also became hallmarks of her poetic style, however much she later tried to change. These are the poems that people remember her by.

CRITICAL RECEPTION

Elinor Wylie's brief publishing career spanned just eight years, from her first volume *Nets to Catch the Wind* (1921) to the collection completed at the time of her death, *Angels and Earthly Creatures* (1929). However, in this brief period, she was able to build a reputation for herself as a significant poet.

The *Collected Poems of Elinor Wylie*, edited by William Rose Benet, appeared in 1932, and her *Collected Prose* appeared the following year. *Last Poems* (1943) brought together previously uncollected poems, as well as some early poems from *Incidental Numbers* and transcriptions from manuscripts.

During her lifetime she achieved fame easily and won not merely popularity but the respect of important artists such as William Butler Yeats, William Faulkner, and Aldous Huxley. Since that time she has been in many ways neglected. There has been little adequate criticism of her work.

Two comprehensive critical studies of Elinor Wylie have appeared: Thomas Gray's (unsympathetic) *Elinor Wylie* (1969) and *The Life and Art of Elinor Wylie* (1983), by Judith Farr. Farr treats Wylie's works as an expression of a special form of Romantic sensibility, which is preoccupied with the problem of the relationship between art and nature. She places her poems in context with the English and European tradition, particularly that of the eighteenth and nineteenth centuries, and therefore outside modernism.

The number of articles dealing with Elinor Wylie is not large, and few of them are current. Among the more important criticism of her work is Cleanth Brooks's essay "Poets and Laurcates" that points out Wylie's kinship with a "coterie" of female poetasters (391–98). It is important because it illustrates a trend of criticism that has attempted to devalue Wylie as a poet. Malcolm Cowley has concluded in "The Owl and the Nightingale" that Elinor Wylie's only achievement was to write magazine verse that was not offensive to the intelligence (624–26), and Alfred Kazin in "The Exquisites" has condemned Elinor Wylie's extravagance in prose in his book *On Native Grounds*: "In her novels she was obsessed by the need to make ornate pictures. Everywhere in them human beings are wrought into marble and ironwork, draped luxuriously like silk dolls, sculptured into a frieze, and given a language so overwhelmingly rapturous as to become meaningless" (242). The most elaborate effort to make Elinor Wylie into a neo-metaphysical poet, along with T. S. Eliot, the Fugitives, MacLeish, and Hart Crane, is discussed in *The Metaphysical Passion*, by Sona Raiziss (228–29). The claim in Allen Tate's essay "Elinor Wylie's Poetry" that none of Wylie's poems have genuine style is extreme and untrue (107). Tate also explores what some critics feel to be a weakness of the bulk of her lyric poems and of her novels, the lack of voice grounded in a personal vision. "The Pattern of Atmosphere" approaches Tate's conclusion that Wylie lacked the convictions upon which a true style is nourished (273–82). On the other hand, Edmund Wilson's eulogy "In Memory of Elinor Wylie" praises Wylie and her work, noting that is important for its definition of Wylie's symbolic significance for her admirers and for its appraisal of the worth of her poetry and prose. In her early brilliant poems her voice is fresh and unique and connects to her emotions and her life. It becomes somewhat displaced and distorted as her Shelley obsession grows. Julia Cluck examines Wylie's preoccupation with Shelley and the Shelley allusions abundant in Wylie's work in "Elinor Wylie's Shelley Obsession."

There is one full-length biography of Wylie: Stanley Olson's *Elinor Wylie: A Life Apart* (1979). Personal memoirs and appreciations include Carl Van Doren's *Three Worlds* (1936), William Rose Benet's *The Poetry and Prose of Elinor Wylie* (1934), Wilson's reviews and eulogy in *Shores of Light* (1952), Mary Colum's *Life and the Dream* (1947), Elizabeth Sergeant's *Fire under The Andes, a Group of North American Portraits* (1927), and Nancy Hoyt's portrait of her sister, *Elinor Wylie: Portrait of an Unknown Lady*.

It is hard to imagine that Elinor Wylie was the exact contemporary of Ezra Pound, T. S. Eliot, Robert Frost, Vachel Lindsay, and Virginia Woolf, whom she knew socially, or H. D., Marianne Moore, and Edna St. Vincent Millay, who copied Wylie's *One Person* sequence of nineteen sonnets to a lover in her own book *Fatal Interview*. She has been so neglected as almost to belong to another age.

The poetry of Elinor Wylie has been treated by different critics as traditionalist, lyricist, metaphysical, and romantic, yet none of these labels defines the quintessential element of her work. Anger, sexual passion, and grief are expressed in Wylie's work, carrying an emotional content that cannot be denied because of the careful form she imposed upon it.

BIBLIOGRAPHY

Works by Elinor Wylie

Incidental Numbers. London: Privately printed, 1912.
Nets to Catch the Wind. New York: Harcourt, 1921.
Black Armour. New York: Doran, 1923.
Jennifer Lorn. New York: Doran, 1923.
The Venetian Glass Nephew. New York: Doran, 1925.
The Orphan Angel. New York: Knopf, 1926.
Mr. Hodge and Mr. Hazard. New York: Knopf, 1928.
Trivial Breath. New York: Knopf, 1928.
Angels and Earthly Creatures. New York: Knopf, 1929.
Collected Poems of Elinor Wylie. Ed. William Rose Benet. New York: Knopf, 1932.
Collected Prose of Elinor Wylie. Ed. William Rose Benet. New York: Knopf, 1933.
Last Poems of Elinor Wylie. New York: Knopf, 1943.

Studies of Elinor Wylie

Brooks, Cleanth. "Poets and Laureates." *Southern Review* 2 (1936): 391–98.

Cluck, Julia. "Elinor Wylie's Shelley Obsession." *PMLA* 56 (1941): 841–60.

Cowley, Malcolm. "The Owl and the Nightingale." *Dial* 74 (1923): 624–26.

Farr, Judith. *The Life and Art of Elinor Wylie*. Baton Rouge: Louisiana State University Press, 1983.

Gray, Thomas A. *Elinor Wylie*. New York: Twayne, 1969.

Kazin, Alfred. "The Exquisites." *On Native Grounds*. New York: Reynal and Hitchcock, 1942. 227–46.

Olson, Stanley. *Elinor Wylie: A Life Apart*. New York: Dial, 1979.

Raiziss, Sona. *The Metaphysical Passion: Seven Modern American Poets and the Seventeenth Century Tradition*. Philadelphia: University of Pennsylvania Press, 1952.

Tate, Allen. "Elinor Wylie's Poetry." *New Republic* 7 Sept. 1932: 107.

Wilson, Edmund. "In Memory of Elinor Wylie." *New Republic* 6 Feb. 1929: 316.

———. "The Pattern of Atmosphere." *Poetry* 15 (1932): 273–82.

ANZIA YEZIERSKA
(1883?–1970)

Aleta Cane

BIOGRAPHY

Born on the Russian-Polish border in about 1883, Anzia Yezierska, one of ten children of a rabbi, emigrated to New York's Lower East Side in 1892. Family life was chaotic and unhappy as Rabbi Yezierska studied Torah while his daughters worked in sweatshops and his wife took in boarders. Outspoken and demanding from childhood, Yezierska quarreled with her father, whom she saw as an impediment to her success as an individual. In 1899 she rented a room at the Clara de Hirsch Home for Working Girls to escape her family. A wealthy benefactor paid her tuition at Columbia University so that she could become a cooking teacher. In order to defray her school expenses, Yezierska worked in a laundry. She felt humiliated in the presence of her native-born classmates and teachers who seemed uncaring of her struggle to survive and to study. Graduating from Teacher's College in 1904, she began teaching cooking in the public schools but hated the work and soon left it.

Yezierska was attracted to and pursued Arnold Levitas for several months but then inexplicably married Jacob Gordon, Levitas's friend. Since she refused to consummate the marriage, it was annulled after six months, and Yezierska married Levitas. Yezierska chafed at household duties and went to live with a sister in California while she was pregnant with her daughter Louise. In 1915 she separated from Levitas, moving with her daughter to California. There she published her first story, "The Free Vacation House." Yezierska began to see herself as a writer and spokesperson for the Jewish immigrant community. She sent Louise to live with Levitas when they returned to New York.

Back in New York, unable to garner any teaching positions, she marched into the Columbia University office of John Dewey and demanded his assistance. The two were attracted to one another: she, the passionate, vital, demanding Jewish immigrant; he, the rational, subdued Protestant American. Dewey encouraged Yezierska's writing and allowed her to attend his graduate seminar. He hired her to work as a translator on a research project on Philadelphia's

Polish community. They shared an intense relationship, but when he pursued physical intimacy, she refused him. He left on a lengthy trip, and Yezierska tried but failed to rekindle the spark between them by writing to him.

In spite of his absence, Dewey continued as a powerful influence in Yezierska's work. He is the model for all the well-born, Protestant American men— the love objects of most immigrant Jewish women in Yezierska's fiction. Dewey represents both the lure and the danger of assimilation to Yezierska.

Yezierska's "Fat of the Land" was selected as best short story of 1919, and in 1920 Houghton Mifflin and Company published her first anthology of stories, *Hungry Hearts*. She inscribed a copy to Dewey, "See I have done the impossible for you. . . . I've plucked out the chaos of my soul" (Henriksen 144). After the success of *Hungry Hearts*, Yezierska was given a three-year contract to adapt her story into a screenplay by Samuel Goldwyn. However, the original film was too stark, and the studio tacked on an impossibly sunny ending that she disliked. Living in real comfort for the first time of her life, Yezierska felt cut off from her ghetto inspiration.

Returning to New York, she published *Salome of the Tenements* (1923), based on the true story of her friend Rose Pastor, who married the philanthropist Graham Stokes. Like many of her stories, this novel depicts the immigrant achieving her heart's desire only to perceive the goal as empty, separating her from the source of her vitality, her traditions. Yezierska's semiautobiographical novel *Bread Givers* (1925) concludes with a reconciliation with the protagonist's difficult father, but such a rapprochement with her own father proved impossible. *Arrogant Beggar* (1927) again explores the theme of the immigrant woman and her desire to succeed in America.

Yezierska was a difficult individual. She befriended, presumed upon, and discarded many people. She was estranged from her religious brothers and criticized the conventional lives chosen by her sisters. She demanded financial aid from her siblings when she needed it but withheld money from family when she had it.

A fellowship at the University of Wisconsin took her to Madison in 1929. She moved to Vermont for eighteen months to live cheaply during the depression. Unhappy there, she moved back to New York. In 1950, her final autobiographical novel, *Red Ribbon on a White Horse*, was published, and she became a book reviewer for the *New York Times*. Yezierska died in Ontario, California, on November 22, 1970.

MAJOR WORKS AND THEMES

Yezierska explores two major themes throughout her oeuvre. The first is the immigrant's ambivalence about the American Dream and the spiritual goals of her traditional past. For Yezierska, the immigrant's difficult position represents one of America's great failures. A second theme explores the achievement of the Dream only to find that without beauty and love the victory is hollow. This is the theme of "The Fat of the Land" and of her novel *Salome of the Tenements* (1923), in which the protagonist goes to great lengths to marry a millionaire philanthropist. She gains the man, only to discover that she has lost her soul. The novel also explores the theme of the "inhuman activities of philanthropy" (138). The social worker's goal of instant assimilation is portrayed as more of a shameful burden than a blessing to the recipients. Yezierska's story collection, *Children of Loneliness* (1923), extends the themes of *Hungry Hearts* but demonstrate a greater mastery on the part of the author in separating particular issues into discrete stories.

In Yezierska's 1925 semiautobiographical novel *Bread Givers*, she depicts her struggle to become a writer and a member of the larger world outside the ghetto. The theme of the Jewish immigrant woman, thirsty for beauty and hungry for a better life, is reprised in the 1927 novel *Arrogant Beggar*. Yezierska's female protagonists usually realize that they cannot achieve fulfillment in the arms of a well-born American. The protagonist of *Arrogant Beggar* achieves salvation in the arms of a fellow immigrant artist after giving up her affection for a wealthy American man. Her 1932 novel *All I Could Never Be* fictionally examines Yezierska's love for John Dewey, which she believed moved her from self-doubt to self-assurance as a writer.

Red Ribbon on a White Horse (1950), her final autobiographical novel, sufficiently revived her career so that the *New York Times* hired her as a book reviewer.

CRITICAL RECEPTION

The critical reception of Yezierska's work is mixed, at best. About *Hungry Hearts* a *New York Times* reviewer wrote: "Many realistic tales of New York's ghetto have been written, but in point of literary workmanship and in laying bare the very souls of her characters, the superior of Miss Yezierska has not yet appeared" (qtd. in Henriksen 145). The commentary in *Dial* suggested a lack of restraint and that the writing was "thin and sentimental" (qtd. in Schoen 33). But it is exactly her passion and rough style that beguiled the *Bookman* and the *Nation*, who agreed that the book was sentimental, but "she has struck one or two notes that our literature can never again be without" (qtd. in Schoen 34).

Salome also elicited a variety of responses. *New York Tribune* said it was "sentimental, illogical, hysterical, and naive, but still a work of art," and the *New York Herald* declared that although the book had many faults, it represented "the burning of elemental passion" (qtd. in Henriksen 180). The *Literary Digest International Book Review*'s James Harvey Robinson praised Yezierska's "vivid and colorful style and a varied honesty rarely equaled" (qtd. in Henrisken 181).

The Jewish press's reception of *Children of Loneliness* was distinctly unfavorable. In her use of dialect, Jewish critics argued that she was mocking the broken speech of the ghetto. *Bread Givers* was similarly received by Jewish critics, and *New York Tribune* reported its boredom with the repetition of her themes. Her later book *All I Could Never Be* was universally panned. *New York Times* dismissed it as "no more a new book than a new edition of a previous publication" (qtd. in Henriksen 246). *Arrogant Beggar* was also negatively reviewed.

Red Ribbon on a White Horse, however, received more favorable critical reception. Robert Langbaum, in *Commentary*, wrote that it dealt honestly with the Jewish immigrant who "having rejected his old culture finds in America no new culture to take its place" (qtd. in Schoen 113). Feminist and Jewish scholarship took a renewed interest in Yezierska's work starting in the 1970s, prompting her daughter to write Yezierka's biography. Yerzierka's autobiographical fiction is, today, anthologized in college texts and taught as an example of the voice of the Jewish immigrant at the turn of the century.

BIBLIOGRAPHY

Works by Anzia Yezierska

Hungry Hearts and Other Stories. 1920. New York: Persea, 1985.
Children of Loneliness. 1923. New York: Funk and Wagnalls, 1923.
Salome of the Tenements. 1923. Urbana: University of Illinois Press, 1995.
Bread Givers. 1925. New York: Persea, 1975.
Arrogant Beggar. New York: Doubleday, 1927.
All I Could Never Be. New York: Brewer, Warren and Putnam, 1932.
Red Ribbon on a White Horse. 1950. New York: Persea, 1987.
The Open Cage: An Anzia Yezierska Collection. New York: Persea, 1979.
How I Found America. Ed. Louise Levitas Henriksen. New York: Persea, 1991.

Studies of Anzia Yezierska

Avery, Evelyn. "Oh My *Mishpocha!* Some Jewish Women Writers from Antin to Kaplan View the Family." *Studies in American Jewish Literature* 5 (1986): 44–53.
Dearborn, Mary. *Love in the Promised Land: The Story of Anzia Yezierska and John Dewey*. New York: Free Press, 1988.
Drucker, Sally-Ann. "Yiddish, Yidgin, and Yezierska: Dialect in Jewish-American Writing." *Yiddish* 6. 4 (1987): 99–113.
Ferraro, Thomas, J. " 'Working Ourselves Up' in America: Anzia Yezierska's *Bread Givers*." *South Atlantic Quarterly* 89. 3 (1990): 547–81.
Golub, Ellen. "Eat Your Heart Out: The Fiction of Anzia Yezierska." *Studies in American Jewish Literature* 3 (1983): 51–61.
Henriksen, Louise. *Anzia Yezierska: A Writer's Life*. New Brunswick, NJ: Rutgers University Press, 1988.
Kamel, Rose. " 'Anzia Yezierska, Get Out of Your Own Way': Selfhood and Otherness in the Autobiographical Fiction of Anzia Yerzierska." *Studies in American Jewish Literature* 3 (1983): 40–50.

Levenburg, Diane. "Three Jewish Writers and the Spirit of the Thirties." *Book Forum* 6 (1982): 233–44.

Levin, Tobe. "How to Eat Without Eating: Anzia Yezierska's Hunger." *Cooking by the Book*. Ed. Mary-Anne Schofield. Bowling Green, OH: Popular Press, 1989. 220–29.

Levinson, Melanie. " 'To Make Myself for a Person': 'Passing' Narratives and the Divided Self in the Work of Anzia Yezierska." *Studies in American Jewish Literature* 13 (1994): 2–9.

Regenbaum, Shelly. "Art, Gender and the Jewish Tradition in Yezierska's *Red Ribbon on a White Horse* and Potok's *My Name Is Asher Lev*." *Studies in American Jewish Literature* 7.1 (1998): 55–66.

Sachs, Susan Hersch. "Anzia Yezierska: 'Her Words Dance with a Thousand Colors.' " *Studies in American Jewish Literature* 3 (1983): 62–67.

Schoen, Carol B. *Anzia Yezierska*. Boston: G. K. Hall, 1982.

Shapiro, Ann. "The Ultimate *Shaygets* and the Fiction of Anzia Yezierska." *MELUS* 21.2 (1996): 79–88.

Weinthal, Edith. "The Image of the City in Yezierska's *Bread Givers*." *Studies in American Jewish Literature* 13 (1994): 10–13.

Wexler, Laura. "Looking at Yezierska." *Women of the Word: Jewish Women and Jewish Writing*. Ed. Judith Baskin. Detroit, MI: Wayne State University Press, 1994. 153–81.

Wilentz, Gay. "Cultural Mediation and Immigrant's Daughter: Anzia Yezierska's *Bread Givers*." *MELUS* 17.3 (1991–1992): 33–41.

ZITKALA-ŠA (GERTRUDE SIMMONS BONNIN) (1876–1938)

Beverly G. Six

BIOGRAPHY

Zitkala-Ša was born Gertrude Simmons on February 22, 1876, on the Yankton (Sioux) Reservation, South Dakota, to Ellen Simmons, a Yankton-Nakota. Her Anglo father, named Felker, deserted them; Simmons was her stepfather's name. She had christened herself Zitkala-Ša (Red Bird) and published her major literary works under that name.

In 1884, Zitkala-Ša left the reservation for White's Manual Institute in Wabash, Indiana. "Americanized" there, she suffered continual humiliation and confusion about identity. She was back home in 1887, but, no longer suited to reservation life, returned to school, Santee Normal Training School in 1888–1889 and White's in 1891.

From 1895 to 1897 Zitkala-Ša attended Earlham College in Richmond, Indiana, where she published essays and poetry in the school newspaper and won second place in an 1896 state oratorical contest, despite facing a banner bearing an Indian caricature labeled "Squaw." She taught at Carlisle Indian School from 1897 to 1899 when, disillusioned with assimilationist policies, she resigned.

During 1900–1902, she studied violin at New England Conservatory of Music, toured Europe with the Carlisle Band, and soloed at the 1900 Paris Exposition. She became a notable public performer and began to publish in popular magazines.

In 1901 Zitkala-Ša published *Old Indian Legends* in order to preserve Nakota oral traditions; the book was a landmark as the first of its kind written by a Native American woman.

In 1902 Zitkala-Ša worked at the Standing Rock Agency (North Dakota) and married fellow worker Raymond Talesfase Bonnin on May 10. Their son, Ohiya (Raymond O. Bonnin), was born in 1903. From 1902 to 1916 the Bonnins worked for the Uintah and Ouray Agency Utah, and Zitkala-Ša collaborated with William Hanson on the opera *Sun Dance*, which premiered in Utah in 1913 and was performed by the New York Opera Guild in 1935.

In 1916, she became the secretary for the Society of American Indians in Washington, D.C., editing their journal *American Indian Magazine* from 1918 to 1919. Her editorials began to reflect her political agenda. In 1921 she published *American Indian Stories* and established the Indian Welfare Committee to continue her fight for Indian rights and citizenship through the General Federation of Women's Clubs.

In 1923 Zitkala-Ša was part of an Indian Rights Association committee that investigated government policies in Oklahoma. Their 1924 report effected major changes in Native representation in governmental policymaking. In 1926 she founded the National Council of American Indians, remaining sole president until 1938.

Zitkala-Ša died in Washington, D.C., on January 26, 1938. Services for this self-avowed pagan and Native activist were held in the Church of Latter Day Saints, with burial in Arlington Cemetery.

MAJOR WORKS AND THEMES

Zitkala-Ša is notable as one of the first Native American women to publish in popular periodicals in an Anglo-dominated industry without the extensive revision and influence of a male editor. Writing in non-Native literary forms, she used her "assimilationist" education to preserve her Native heritage and to examine themes that are major concerns for contemporary Native American writers: cultural and political conflicts between Native and colonizer societies, reaffirmation of individual and tribal identity, the centrality of oral traditions, and the destructiveness of assimilation.

She produced only two major literary works. The tales in *Old Indian Legends* center upon an immortal trickster figure, Iktomi. Folkloric literary devices include shape-changing animal/humans, no delineation between physical and spiritual worlds, and didactic or etiological themes. The didactic tales teach Dakota values and practical wisdom. In "Iktomi and the Fawn," Iktomi learns to be himself; in "Iktomi and the Coyote," he learns to "[m]ake sure the enemy is stone dead before you make a fire" (42); and in "Iktomi and the Muskrat," he learns hospitality. The aeteological tales explain the origins of humankind ("The Badger and the Bear") and evil ("Ilya the Camp-Eater"). As examples of the purpose and oral conventions of storytelling, they are major contributions to the Native American canon.

In *American Indian Stories* Zitkala-Ša reprinted early autobiographical essays and fiction published in popular magazines from 1900 to 1902 and added additional stories and essays that reflect her later political concerns, thus illustrating her literary versatility and political evolution. Themes include Native American identity, landownership and self-determination, and disenfranchisement.

"Indian Childhood" is the story of Zitkala-Ša's lessons in Dakota customs and values, with her mother's moral instructions woven throughout beadwork instruction and family stories about relatives killed by the "heartless paleface"

(11). Poetic descriptions and humorous anecdotes describe an idyllic life that contrasts strongly with the later misery in "School Days" and "Indian Teacher." Images of brutal "Americanization" permeate the schooldays essays, including the red apples that lured Zitkala-Ša from the reservation and traumatic humiliations: hair cutting, Anglo clothing, and English acquisition. In "Indian Teacher" she counts the cost; in exchange for "the white man's papers," she has lost "mother, nature, and God" (97).

The remaining stories and essays are more defiant. In "The Great Spirit" Zitkala-Ša repudiates Christianity and asserts her paganism; in "Blue-Star Woman" and "Indian Problem" she rails against the theft of Native lands, allotments, and legal rights. "A Warrior's Daughter," a surprisingly feminist text, proclaims the strength of Dakota womanhood, and in "A Dream" a Native woman reconnects with her dead grandfather and is filled with "new hope for her people" (158). In their themes and rhetoric, these essays and stories prefigure contemporary Native American literature.

CRITICAL RECEPTION

Zitkala-Ša wrote essays, short fiction, folklore, drama, political treatises, and autobiography, pioneering in women's and Native American publishing in her English proficiency, use of multiple genres, and expression of Native bicultural dilemmas. Critics ascribe to her three writing purposes: preservation of traditions, mediation between cultures, and governmental manipulation.

Early criticism is favorable but reflects turn-of-the-century biases. One 1900 reviewer, noting she was, before assimilation, "a veritable little savage," condescendingly acknowledged the "rare command of English and much artistic feeling" in her essays ("Persons" 330).

The majority of contemporary criticism concerns Zitkala-Ša's role as autobiographer and political activist; thus, *American Indian Stories* receives more attention than *Old Indian Legends*. The autobiographical essays are most often assessed in comparison with other early Native autobiographies or as political statements. Stout sees them as political and autobiographical ("Literature") and judges them superior to other Native autobiographies, "which tend to be more apologetic with regard to traditional upbringing and do not reveal the authors' feelings about the world at large" ("Zitkala-Ša" 304). Picotte feels they "were meant to inform white people about the American Indians and their unique condition" (xv).

The criticism on *Stories* lacks adequate attention to literary composition, although different sections of *The Oxford Companion to Women's Writing in the United States* (Davidson and Wagner-Martin) note briefly her use of multiple genres. In the section "Native American Writing: Nonfiction," Catherine Taylor labels the autobiographical essays "political autobiography" and the *Oklahoma* report a major "work of investigative journalism" (619). In "Motherhood," Blythe Forcey and Elaine Orr feel the autobiographical essays represent "both the

Native American mother's central role in storytelling and the systematic erasure of her cultural and linguistic power by Anglo culture" (581). In *American Indian Quarterly*, Johnson and Wilson examine ways her political writings effected reform.

A notable exception is Cutter's assessment that Zitkala-Ša "subverts traditional modes of autobiographical and linguistic self-authentication" (31). She concludes that Zitkala-Ša "initiates a reconsideration of the oppressive nature of Euro-American discursive and cultural practices, and . . . [transforms] language itself" (41).

The opera *Sun Dance* lacks critical assessment and recognition of Zitkala-Ša's contribution despite Hanson's acknowledgment that she was "co-author and collaborator" and its value as an example of the bicultural dilemma of Native Americans caused by the loss of their cultural heritage (3).

Old Indian Legends also deserves more critical attention as a literary genre. Fisher focuses on elements of Zitkala-Ša's life that affected her effort to bridge between oral and written forms ("Transportation"). Stout insists the collection pioneers "the legitimacy of joining a personal voice to traditional themes" ("Zitkala-Ša" 305).

Although critics agree on Zitkala-Ša's place in Native American and women's literary history, analysis has focused on her life, preservation of Native traditions, and political aims, with less criticism of her works as literature. With her inclusion in a list of titles "now regarded as among the most important in United States literary history" (Ammons 707), however, Zitkala-Ša is beginning to receive the scholarly recognition she deserves.

BIBLIOGRAPHY

Works by Zitkala-Ša

Old Indian Legends. 1901. Lincoln: University of Nebraska Press, 1985.
American Indian Stories. 1921. Lincoln: University of Nebraska Press, 1985.

Studies of Zitkala-Ša

Ammons, Elizabeth. "Progressive Era Writing." *The Oxford Companion to Women's Writing in the United States*. Ed. Cathy N. Davidson and Linda Wagner-Martin. New York: Oxford, 1995. 707–8.
Cutter, Martha J. "Zitkala-Sä's Autobiographical Writings: The Problems of a Canonical Search for Language and Identity." *MELUS* 19.1 (1994): 31–44.
Davidson, Cathy N., and Linda Wagner-Martin, eds. *The Oxford Companion to Women's Writing in the United States*. New York: Oxford, 1995.
Fisher, Alice Poindexter. Foreword. *American Indian Stories*. Lincoln: University of Nebraska Press, 1985. v–xx.
———. "The Transportation of Tradition: A Study of Zitkala-Sa and Mourning Dove,

Two Transitional American Indian Writers." Diss. City University of New York, 1979.

Hanson, William F. *Sun Dance Land*. Provo, UT: J. Grant Stevenson, 1967.

Johnson, David L., and Raymond Wilson. "Gertrude Simmons Bonnin, 1876–1938: 'Americanize the First Americans.' " *American Indian Quarterly* 12 (1988): 27–40.

"Persons Who Interest Us." *Harper's Bazaar* 14 Apr. 1900: 330.

Picotte, Agnes M. Foreword. *Old Indian Legends*. Lincoln: University of Nebraska Press, 1985. xi–xviii.

Stout, Mary A. "Zitkala Sa." *Dictionary of Native American Literature*. Ed. Andrew Wiget. New York: Garland, 1994. 303–7.

———. "Zitkala-Sa: The Literature of Politics." *Coyote Was Here: Essays on Contemporary Native American Literary and Political Mobilization*. Ed. Bo Schöler. Aarhus, Denmark: University of Aarhus, 1984. 70–78.

SELECTED BIBLIOGRAPHY

Allen, Paula Gunn. *The Sacred Hoop: Recovering the Feminine in American Indian Tradition*. Boston: Beacon, 1986.

Ammons, Elizabeth. *Conflicting Stories: American Women Writers at the Turn into the Twentieth Century*. New York: Oxford University Press, 1991.

————, ed. *Short Fiction by Black Women, 1900–1920*. New York: Oxford University Press, 1991.

Asian Women United of California, eds. *Making Waves: An Anthology of Writing by and about Asian American Women*. Boston: Beacon, 1989.

Awkward, Michael. *Inspiriting Influences: Tradition, Revision, and Afro-American Women's Novels*. New York: Columbia University Press, 1989.

Baker, Houston A., Jr., ed. *Workings of the Spirit: The Poetics of Afro-American Women's Writing*. Chicago: University of Chicago Press, 1991.

Barlow, Judith E., ed. *Plays by American Women: 1900–1930*. New York: Applause Theatre, 1985.

Barolini, Helen, ed. *The Dream Book: An Anthology of Writings by Italian-American Women*. New York: Schocken, 1985.

Barrett, Eileen, and Mary Cullinan, eds. *American Women Writers: Diverse Voices in Prose since 1845*. New York: St. Martin's, 1992.

Bataille, Gretchen M., ed. *Native American Women: A Biographical Dictionary*. New York: Garland, 1993.

Bataille, Gretchen M., and Kathleen Mullen Sands. *American Indian Women, Telling Their Lives*. Lincoln: University of Nebraska Press, 1984.

Bell-Scott, Patricia, and Juanita Johnson-Bailey, eds. *Flat-Footed Truths: Telling Black Women's Lives*. New York: Holt, 1998.

Benstock, Shari. *Women of the Left Bank: Paris, 1900–1940*. Austin: University of Texas Press, 1986.

Bloom, Harold, ed. *Asian-American Women Writers*. Philadelphia: Chelsea, 1997.

————. *Black American Women Fiction Writers*. New York: Chelsea, 1995.

Brazon, Joanne M. *Black Women Writing Autobiography: A Tradition within a Tradition*. Philadelphia: Temple University Press, 1989.

Brown, Anita, ed. *The 100 Best Books by American Women, 1833–1933*. Chicago: Associated Authors Service, 1933.

Brown-Guillory, Elizabeth. *Their Place on the Stage: Black Women Playwrights in America.* Westport, CT: Greenwood, 1988.

———, ed. *Women of Color: Mother-Daughter Relationships in 20th-Century Literature.* Austin: University of Texas Press, 1996.

Buhle, Maril J. *Women and the American Left: A Guide to Sources.* Boston: G. K. Hall, 1983.

Cade, Toni (Bambara), ed. *The Black Woman: An Anthology.* New York: New American Library, 1970.

Cahill, Susan. *Writing Women's Lives: An Anthology of Autobiographical Narratives by Twentieth Century American Women Writers.* New York: Harper Perennial, 1994.

Carby, Hazel V. *Reconstructing Womanhood: The Emergence of the Afro-American Woman Novelist.* New York: Oxford University Press, 1987.

Carroll, Rebecca, ed. *I Know What the Red Clay Looks Like: The Voice and Vision of Black Women Writers.* New York: Crown, 1994.

Chapman, Dorothy Hilton, comp. *Index to Poetry by Black American Women.* Westport, CT: Greenwood, 1986.

Chin, Frank, Jeffery Chan, Lawson Inada, and Shawn Wang, eds. *Aiiieeee! An Anthology of Asian-American Writers.* Washington, DC: Howard University Press, 1974.

Chinoy, Helen Krich, and Linda Walsh Jenkins, eds. *Women in American Theatre.* New York: Theatre Communications Group, 1987.

Christian, Barbara. *Black Women Novelists: The Development of a Tradition, 1892–1976.* Westport, CT: Greenwood, 1980.

Clark, Suzanne. *Sentimental Modernism: Women Writers and the Revolution of the Word.* Bloomington: Indiana University Press, 1991.

Cooper, Helen M., Adrienne Auslander Munich, and Susan Merrill Squier. *Arms and the Woman: War, Gender, and Literary Representation.* Chapel Hill: University of North Carolina Press, 1989.

Coven, Brenda. *American Women Dramatists of the Twentieth Century: A Bibliography.* Metuchen, NJ: Scarecrow, 1985.

Cutter, Martha. *Unruly Tongue: Identity and Voice in American Women's Writing, 1850–1940.* Jackson: University Press of Mississippi, 1999.

Dance, Daryl Cumber, ed. *Honey, Hush! An Anthology of African American Women's Humor.* New York: Norton, 1998.

Dandridge, Rita B., ed. *Black Women's Blues: A Literary Anthology, 1934–1988.* New York: G. K. Hall, 1992.

Dodd, Elizabeth. *The Veiled Mirror and the Woman Poet: H. D., Louise Bogan, Elizabeth Bishop, and Louise Glück.* Columbia: University of Missouri Press, 1992.

Drake, William. *The First Wave: Women Poets in America. 1915–1945.* New York: Macmillan, 1987.

DuBois, Ellen Carol, and Vicki L. Ruiz. *Unequal Sister: A Multicultural Reader in U.S. Women's History.* New York: Routledge, 1990.

Duke, Maurice, Jackson R. Bryer, and M. Thomas Inge, eds. *American Women Writers: Bibliographical Essays.* Westport, CT: Greenwood, 1983.

DuPlessis, Rachel Blau. *Writing beyond the Ending: Narrative Strategies of Twentieth-Century Women Writers.* Bloomington: Indiana University Press, 1985.

Evans, Mari, ed. *Black Women Writers (1950–1980): A Critical Evaluation.* Garden City, NY: Anchor-Doubleday, 1984.

Fetterley, Judith, and Marjorie Pryse, eds. *American Women Regionalists: 1850–1910.* New York: Norton, 1992.

Ghymn, Esther Mikyung. *Images of Asian American Women by Asian American Women Writers.* New York: Lang, 1995.

Gilbert, Sandra M., and Susan Gubar. *No Man's Land: The Place of the Woman Writer in the Twentieth Century.* 2 vols. New Haven, CT: Yale University Press, 1988.

Gould, Jean. *Modern American Women Poets.* New York: Dodd, 1984.

Green, Rayna. *Native American Women: A Contextual Bibliography.* Bloomington: Indiana University Press, 1983.

Hamer, Judith A., and Martin J. Hamer, eds. *Centers of the Self: Short Stories by Black American Women from the Nineteenth Century to the Present.* New York: Hill and Wang, 1994.

Herrera-Sobek, María, ed. *Beyond Stereotypes: The Critical Analysis of Chicana Literature.* Binghamton, NY: Bilingual Review, 1985.

Howard, Sharon M. *African American Women Fiction Writers, 1859–1986: An Annotated Bibliography.* New York: Garland, 1989.

Hull, Gloria T. *Color, Sex and Poetry: Three Women Writers of the Harlem Renaissance.* Bloomington: Indiana University Press, 1987.

Jehenson, Myriam Yvonne. *Latin-American Women Writers: Class, Race, and Gender.* New York: State University of New York Press, 1995.

Jones, Anne Goodwyn. *Tomorrow Is Another Day: The Woman Writer in the South, 1859–1936.* Baton Rouge: Louisiana State University Press, 1981.

Knopf, Marcy, ed. *The Sleeper Wakes: Harlem Renaissance Stories by Women.* New Brunswick, NJ: Rutgers University Press, 1993.

Koppelman, Susan, ed. *Women in the Trees: U.S. Women's Short Stories about Battering and Resistance, 1839–1994.* Boston: Beacon, 1996.

Levy, Helen Fiddyment. *Fiction of the Home Place: Jewett, Cather, Glasgow, Porter, Welty, and Naylor.* Jackson: University Press of Mississippi, 1992.

Ling, Amy. *Between Worlds: Women Writers of Chinese Ancestry.* New York: Pergamon, 1990.

Mainiero, Lina, and Langdon Lynne Faust, eds. *American Women Writers: A Critical Reference Guide from Colonial Times to the Present.* 4 vols. New York: Ungar, 1979–1982.

Mannin, Beverly. *Index to American Women Speakers, 1828–1978.* Metuchen, NJ: Scarecrow, 1980.

Manning, Carol, ed. *The Female Tradition in Southern Literature.* Urbana: University of Illinois Press, 1993.

Middlebrook, Diane Wood, and Marilyn Yalom, eds. *Coming to Light: American Women Poets in the Twentieth Century.* Ann Arbor: University of Michigan Press, 1985.

Miner, Madonne M. *Insatiable Appetites: Twentieth-Century American Women's Bestsellers.* Westport, CT: Greenwood, 1984.

Moore, Lisa C., ed. *Does Your Mama Know? An Anthology of Black Lesbian Coming Out Stories.* Decatur, GA: RedBone, 1997.

Mullen, Bill, ed. *Revolutionary Tales: African American Women's Short Stories, from the First Story to the Present.* New York: Dell, 1995.

Norwood, Vera, and Janice Monk, eds. *The Desert Is No Lady: Southwestern Landscapes in Women's Writing and Art.* New Haven, CT: Yale University Press, 1987.

Rabinowitx, Paula. *Labor and Desire: Women's Revolutionary Fiction in Depression America*. Chapel Hill: University of North Carolina Press, 1991.

Reardon, Joan, and Kristine A. Thorsen. *Poetry by American Women, 1900–1975: A Bibliography*. Metuchen, NJ: Scarecrow, 1979.

Redfern, Bernice. *Women of Color in the United States: A Guide to the Literature*. New York: Garland, 1989.

Reesman, Jeanne Campbell, ed. *Speaking the Other Self: American Women Writers*. Athens, University of Georgia Press, 1997.

Robinson, Doris. *Women Novelists, 1891–1920: An Index to Biographical and Autobiographical Sources*. New York: Garland, 1984.

Roses, Lorraine Elena, and Ruth Elizabeth Randolph. *Harlem Renaissance and Beyond: Literary Biographies of 100 Black Women Writers 1900–1945*. Boston: G. K. Hall, 1990.

———, eds. *Harlem's Glory: Black Women Writing, 1900–1950*. Cambridge, MA: Harvard University Press, 1996.

Saxton, Marsha, and Florence Howe, eds. *With Wings: An Anthology of Literature by and about Women with Disabilities*. New York: Feminist Press, 1987.

Schlueter, June, ed. *Modern American Drama: The Female Canon*. Rutherford, NJ: Fairleigh Dickinson University Press, 1990.

Schweik, Susan. *A Gulf So Deeply Cut: American Women Poets and the Second World War*. Madison: University of Wisconsin Press, 1991.

Shockley, Ann Allen, ed. *Afro-American Women Writers, 1746–1933: An Anthology and Critical Guide*. Boston: G. K. Hall, 1988.

Showalter, Elaine. *Sister's Choice: Tradition and Change in American Women's Writing*. Oxford: Clarendon, 1991.

———, ed. *Modern American Women Writers*. New York: Scribner's, 1991.

Sicherman, Barbara, and Carol Hurd Green, eds. *Notable American Women: The Modern Period*. Cambridge, MA: Belknap Press of Harvard University Press, 1980.

Smith, Barbara, ed. *Home Girls: A Black Feminist Anthology*. New York: Kitchen Table/ Women of Color Press, 1983.

Stauffer, Helen Winter, and Susan J. Rosowski, comps. *Women and Western American Literature*. Troy, NY: Whitston, 1982.

Stein, Rachel. *Shifting the Ground: American Women Writers' Revisions of Nature, Gender, and Race*. Charlottesville: University Press of Virginia, 1997.

Stetson, Erlene, ed. *Black Sister: Poetry by Black American Women, 1746–1980*. Bloomington: Indiana University Press, 1981.

Tate, Claudia. *Domestic Allegories of Political Desire: The Black Heroine's Text at the Turn of the Century*. New York: Oxford University Press, 1992.

Wagner, Lilya. *Women War Correspondents in World War II*. Westport, CT: Greenwood, 1989.

Walden, Daniel, ed. *Twentieth-Century American-Jewish Fiction Writers*. Vol. 28 of *Dictionary of Literary Biography*. Detroit: Gale, 1984.

Wall, Cheryl A. *Women of the Harlem Renaissance*. Bloomington: Indiana University Press, 1995.

Warhol, Robyn R., and Diane Price Herndl, eds. *Feminisms: An Anthology of Literary Theory and Criticism*. New Brunswick, NJ: Rutgers University Press, 1997.

Washington, Mary Helen, ed. *Invented Lives: Narratives of Black Women, 1860–1960*. Garden City, NY: Doubleday, 1987.

Waugh, Patricia. *Feminine Fictions: Revisiting the Modern*. New York: Routledge, 1989.

Westling, Louise. *Sacred Groves and Ravaged Gardens: The Fiction of Eudora Welty, Carson McCullers, and Flannery O'Connor*. Athens: University of Georgia Press, 1985.

White, Barbara A. *American Women Writers: An Annotated Bibliography of Criticism*. New York: Garland, 1977.

———. *Growing Up Female: Adolescent Girlhood in American Fiction*. Westport, CT: Greenwood, 1985.

Willis, Susan, ed. *Specifying: Black Women Writing the American Experience*. Madison: University of Wisconsin Press, 1987.

INDEX

Boldface page numbers indicate main entries.

ABOUT THE EDITOR AND CONTRIBUTORS

LISA ABNEY earned her Ph.D. from the University of Houston in 1997 after obtaining a B.A. and an M.A. from Texas A & M University. She currently serves as Director of the Louisiana Folklife Center at Northwestern State University of Louisiana. She is an Assistant Professor of English in the Department of Language and Communication. Her research interests lie in linguistics, folklore, modern American literature and British literature. She has obtained funding to conduct the "Linguistic Survey of North Louisiana," and she is in the process of collecting fieldwork for the project.

JULIE BUCKNER ARMSTRONG holds a Ph.D. from New York University and teaches English and Women's Studies at Valdosta State University. Her creative and academic writing has appeared in the *Southern Quarterly* and *The Distillery*, and she is currently editing a collection of essays on teaching the civil rights movement.

RHONDA AUSTIN is a Texas writer, editor, and teacher. Currently, she is a Lecturer at Sul Ross State University in Alpine, Texas. She has published several short stories and done journalistic writing. She is past editor of *SAGE*, the Sul Ross literary magazine, and is currently creating an online writing lab to be used by university students.

ALLISON BERG is Assistant Professor of Writing and American Culture at James Madison College, Michigan State University. She has published numerous articles on early twentieth-century American writers, including Pauline Hopkins, William Faulkner, and Marita Bonner.

NANCY BERKE teaches English and Women's Studies at Hunter College, City University of New York. She is working on a book on American women's social poetry of the Modern period. Her article on the same topic, "Anything That Burns You: The Social Poetry of Lola Ridge, Genevieve Taggard, and Margaret

Walker," was recently published in the Spanish bilingual journal *Revista Canaria de Estudios Ingleses.*

CHERYL D. BOHDE, a tenured Instructor of English at McLennan Community College, earned a Ph.D. in American literature in 1992 from Texas A & M University. After completing a dissertation on Poe, Hawthorne, Fuller, and Melville and mid-nineteenth-century magazines, she publishes and presents studies on the significance of the nineteenth- and twentieth-century press to cultural studies. She is currently working on a book about David Koresh and the media.

ALETA CANE completed her doctoral dissertation "The *Forerunner* of Charlotte Perkins Gilman: Text and Context" and recently received her Ph.D, with distinction, from Northeastern University, where she is currently a Continuing Lecturer of Composition and American Literature. She is currently coediting, with Susan Alves, *"The Only Efficient Instrument": 19th Century Women Writers and the Periodical, 1860–1916.*

JOY CASTRO is Assistant Professor of English at Wabash College in Indiana, where she teaches twentieth-century American literature, British modernism, and creative writing. Her fiction has appeared in such journals as *Quarterly West, Chelsea,* and *Mid-American Review,* and she is currently working on a critical study of Margery Latimer.

DAVID J. CAUDLE is a Ph.D. candidate at the University of North Texas. His Forthcoming dissertation is titled *Dispatches from the Confederate Front: The Life and Correspondence of John Kennedy Toole.* He is co-author, with Suzanne Disheroon Green, of *Kate Chopin: An Annotated Bibliography of Secondary Works* (Greenwood, 1999) and *Kate Chopin's At Fault* (2001). He has also published a number of essays and book chapters dealing with American literature and linguistic approaches to literature.

LAURIE CHAMPION is Assistant Professor of English at San Diego State University, Imperial Valley. She specializes in American women writers, African American writers, and short-story theory. She has edited several books and published essays in journals such as *Southern Quarterly, Journal of the Short Story in English, Studies in Short Fiction,* and *Langston Hughes Review.*

CATHERINE CUCINELLA recently received her Ph.D. from the University of California at Riverside, where she is a Faculty Fellow. She specializes in American literature, feminist studies, and critical theory. Currently, she is working on a study of Bradstreet, Dickinson, Bishop, and Moore.

CARMAN C. CURTON has degrees from Michigan State University and the University of North Texas. She teaches literature and composition in Denver and is currently writing about portrayals of Asian American women writers in literature textbooks.

KATE K. DAVIS is a graduate student in English at Sul Ross State University in Alpine, Texas. She has published fiction and nonfiction. Her work has most recently appeared in *Texas Short Stories II* (2000).

M. CATHERINE DOWNS teaches literature and composition at Texas A & M University at Kingsville. Her scholarly interests concern writers of the early modern period, art, and science. *Becoming Modern: Willa Cather's Journalism,* a study of Willa Cather's literary responses to her work as a journalist, appeared in 1999. Downs is also working on a study of H. D. and turn-of-the-century theories about hypergeometry and the fourth dimension.

ANN W. ENGAR is a Presidential Teaching Scholar at the University of Utah. She has published numerous biographical articles as well as essays on women's literature, teaching, theater, and Utah history. Her essay "Johnson in a Western Civilization Course" recently appeared in *Approaches to Teaching the Works of Samuel Johnson* (1993). She is also a senior bibliographer for the Modern Language Association.

CARMINE ESPOSITO is a doctoral student at the University of Connecticut, where he is currently studying American and British modern literature.

BEVERLY FORSYTH, an English Instructor at Odessa College, has written for both scholarly and commercial publications including *Studies in the Novel, New Texas, English in Texas, Research and Reflections,* the *South Carolina Review, Cosmopolitan, USA Today, Dallas Morning News, Texas Business,* and the *Christian Science Monitor.* She is currently pursuing her doctoral studies in American literature with a subfield in Women's Studies.

MARGARET BARBOUR GILBERT is the new third place winner for the Mudfish Poetry Prize as well as Grand Prize Winner of the North American Open Poetry competition. She has a Master's in Creative Writing from City College of New York, and her poems have appeared in *Crazyhorse, Callaloo, Mudfish, Exquisite Corpse,* and other periodicals. She teaches at Bergen Community College.

BRUCE A. GLASRUD is Dean of Arts and Sciences and Professor of History at Sul Ross State University in Alpine, Texas. He has recently compiled a bibliography of African Americans in the West and coedited *Blacks in the West: A Century of Short Stories.*

SUZANNE DISHEROON GREEN serves as Assistant Professor of American Literature at Northwestern State University in Natchitoches, Louisiana. She received her Ph.D. in English from the University of North Texas in 1997. She is the coauthor, with David J. Caudle, of *Kate Chopin: An Annotated Bibliography of Critical Works* (1999). She is presently at work on a volume of essays on contemporary Louisiana writers, entitled *Songs of the New South*, and is editing Kate Chopin's *At Fault* with David J. Caudle. She has published and presented numerous articles on Kate Chopin and Southern writers, most recently including "How Edna Escaped: THE LIFE IS A JOURNEY Conceptual Metaphor in *The Awakening*," forthcoming in *The Poetics of Cognition*.

SYLVIA ANN GRIDER is Associate Professor of Anthropology at Texas A & M University, where she teaches courses in folklore and Texas culture. She is past president of both the Texas Folklore Society and the American Folklore Society. She has published widely on topics ranging from children's ghost stories to graffiti. With Lou Rodenberger, she coedited *Texas Women Writers: A Tradition of Their Own* (1997).

SALLY E. HALDORSON received her B.A. from St. Olaf College in Northfield, Minnesota, and her M.A. in Creative Writing and English Literature from the University of Wisconsin at Milwaukee. Currently living in Milwaukee, she is an Adjunct Instructor of Composition and Literature for Upper Iowa University and is also employed as a client services associate for a book fulfillment service and reseller.

JENNIFER A. HAYTOCK is a doctoral candidate at the University of North Carolina at Chapel Hill. She has published essays on Ernest Hemingway and Thornton Wilder. Recently, "Women, Philosophy, and Culture: Wilder's Andrian Legacy" appeared in *Thorton Wilder: New Essays* (1999). Her dissertation addresses the relationship of domestic writing in America to writing about World War I.

SHARON L. HILEMAN is Professor of English, Co-Coordinator of Women's Studies, and Chair of the Department of Languages and Literature at Sul Ross State University in Alpine, Texas. She has taught courses on women's multicultural writing and regional fiction and has published articles on women's lifewriting in the genres of autobiographical fiction, letters and journals, and prison narratives. With grants from the National Endowment for the Humanities, she has worked on projects concerning women's letters, postcolonial fiction from Africa and the Caribbean, and new media technology. Her current work focuses on postcolonial women's texts and strategies for reading and teaching them.

DAVID GARRETT IZZO is a former journalist from New York City who more recently has published books and articles on the authors and the literature of the 1910s, 1920s, and 1930s in the United States and United Kingdom that include Aldous Huxley, W. H. Auden, Christopher Isherwood, Thornton Wilder, Stephen Vincent Benet, Archibald MacLeish, Vachel Lindsay, and many others. He recently co-edited *Thorton Wilder: New Essays* (1999). He has also written and performed a one-man play, *The American World of Stephen Vincent Benet*.

ROBERT JOHNSON lives and writes in Wichita Falls, Texas, where he teaches at Midwestern State University. His recent short stories have appeared in *Crab Creek Review, Hodgepodge, Loonfeather, Palo Alto Review, Panhandler, Phoenix, Pleiades, Seattle Review, Story Short*, and *Thema*.

SARA ANDREWS JOHNSTON is a Lecturer in the English Department at North Carolina State University. She received her Ph.D. in Twentieth Century British and American Literature, with a minor in Romantic and Victorian Literature, from the University of North Carolina at Chapel Hill, where she has also taught composition and film criticism. She has published an essay on the African American poet Julia Fields in *Contemporary Poets, Dramatists, Essayists, and Novelists of the South*, edited by Robert Bain and Joseph M. Flora, and has coauthored, with William Harmon, an article about T. S. Eliot forthcoming in *Yeats-Eliot Review*.

DENISE D. KNIGHT is Professor of English at the State University of New York College at Cortland, where she specializes in nineteenth-century American literature. She is author of *Charlotte Perkins Gilman: A Study of the Short Fiction* (1997) and editor of *The Diaries of Charlotte Perkins Gilman* (1994), *The Yellow Wall-Paper and Selected Stories of Charlotte Perkins Gilman* (1994), *The Later Poetry of Charlotte Perkins Gilman* (1996), and *Nineteenth-Century American Women Writers: A Bio-Bibliographical Critical Sourcebook* (1997).

JAMES WARD LEE, Emeritus Professor of English at the University of North Texas, now serves as Acquisitions Consultant for Texas Christian University Press. He is author of many books, articles, reviews, and short stories. A well-known scholar of Texas literature, he has edited several volumes of works about and by Texas writers, including *The Texas Tradition: Fiction, Folklore, History* (co-edited with Don Graham and William T. Pilkington (1983). He lives in Forth Worth, Texas.

C. ANN MCDONALD received her doctorate from Vanderbilt, where she studied British and American modernism. Her dissertation, for which she received a travel fellowship to conduct research in Ireland, examines the relationship between W. B. Yeats and Maud Gonne. She is currently a full-time faculty member at Trident Technical College in Charleston, South Carolina.

RHONDA PETTIT is Assistant Professor of English at the University of Cincinnati's Raymond Walters College in Blue Ash, Ohio. Her study of Dorothy Parker, *A Gendered Collision: Sentimentalism and Modernism in Dorothy Par-*

ker's Poetry and Fiction, was published in 2000. She also has published an introduction to the life and work of Native American poet Joy Harjo in Boise State University's Western Writers Series; articles on Parker, James Joyce, and Seamus Heaney; interviews with poets David Lehman and Phil Paradis; and her own poetry.

ANDREA R. PURDY is an Adjunct Professor of Spanish at Colorado State University in Fort Collins, Colorado. Her professional interests include Spanish American literature with an emphasis on marginalized writers.

CATHERINE RAINWATER, Associate Professor of English, teaches literature and writing at St. Edward's University in Austin, Texas. She is the author and/or coeditor of numerous publications including books as well as articles and reviews in journals. In 1990, she was awarded the Norman Foerster Prize by the Modern Language Association for her work in American Indian literature. Currently, she is president of the Ellen Glasgow Society and editor of *The Ellen Glasgow Newsletter*. Her most recent work is *Dreams of Fiery Stars: The Transformations of Native American Fiction* (1999).

LOU HALSELL RODENBERGER, Professor Emeritus in the Department of English at McMurry University, is coeditor with Sylvia Grider of *Texas Women Writers: A Tradition of Their Own* (1997). Her other works include an anthology, *Her Work: Stories by Texas Women* (1982), a critical study of novelist Jane Gilmore Rushing (Boise State University Western Writers Series, # 118), and essays on women writers and southwestern life and literature. A past president of the Texas Folklore Society and West Texas Historical Association, she has also served on the board of directors of the Western Literature Association. She is coauthor and editor with Sylvia Grider of *21 Texas Short Stories by Texas Women: Then and Now*, soon to be released.

BARBARA RYAN is Assistant Professor at the University of Missouri at Kansas City. She is working on a book about Gene Stratton-Porter that will take into account this neglected writer's shrewd manipulation of the high/low culture division that was still new in U.S. letters.

WILLIAM J. SCHEICK is J. R. Millikan Centennial Professor at the University of Texas at Austin. He has published a number of books, including *Contemporary American Women Writers: Narrative Strategies* (1985), *Fictional Structure and Ethics: The Turn-of-the-Century English Novel* (1990), and *The Ethos of Romance at the Turn of the Century* (1994).

LAURA SHEA is Assistant Professor of English at Iona College in New Rochelle, New York. Her essays and reviews on topics in drama and theater have appeared in *Theatre Journal, Theatre Annual*, and *The Comparatist*.

BEVERLY G. SIX is Assistant Professor of English at Sul Ross State University, Alpine, Texas, where she teaches composition and literature. Her areas of specialization include medieval literature, folklore and multicultural literature, and Native American literature, with a particular interest in literary portrayals of Native American spirituality.

ERNEST J. SMITH is Associate Professor of English at the University of Central Florida, where he teaches courses in modern American poetry. He is the author of *The Imaged Word: The Infrastructure of Hart Crane's White Buildings* (1990) and has published essays on John Berryman, Edna St. Vincent Millay, Adrienne Rich, and other twentieth-century poets. His current work involves the meeting of poetry and history in contemporary American poetry.

SANDRA GAIL TEICHMANN writes poetry, fiction, literary nonfiction, drama, essays, and articles. Many of her works have been published in literary journals. A book of her collected poetry, *Slow Mud*, was published in 1998. She has two books forthcoming: *Women on Trains* and *Woman of the Plains*.

JANET K. TURK is an English Lecturer at Lamar University in Beaumont, Texas. She received her Bachelor of Arts in English in 1994 and her Master's in 1996.

LESLIE WINFIELD WILLIAMS received her Ph.D. from the University of Houston in 1994. She serves as Division Chair of Fine Arts/Communications and teaches English and creative writing at Midland College in Midland, Texas. Her book-length publications include *Night Wrestling* (1997) and *Seduction of the Lesser Gods* (1997). She has also published poetry in journals such as *RiverSedge, Christianity and Literature, Radix*, and *Christian Century*.

RICHARD J. WILLIAMSON is Assistant Professor of English at Muskingum College in New Concord, Ohio. His area of specialization is nineteenth-century American literature.

ELIZABETH WRIGHT is a graduate student in English at the University of New Mexico, where she is writing a dissertation on twentieth-century American women writers and the politics of literacy.

KIRSTIN R. HOTELLING ZONA is Assistant Professor of Modern Poetry and Poetics at Illinois State University. She has published articles on Marianne Moore, Elizabeth Bishop, and May Swenson and is currently finishing a book entitled *After Autonomy: The Feminist Poetics of Marianne Moore, Elizabeth Bishop, and May Swenson.*